Media Ethics and Global Justice in the Digital Age

Today's digital revolution is a worldwide phenomenon, with profound and often differential implications for communities around the world and their relationships to one another. This book presents a new, explicitly international theory of media ethics, incorporating non-Western perspectives and drawing deeply on both moral philosophy and the philosophy of technology. Clifford Christians develops an ethics grounded in three principles – truth, human dignity, and nonviolence – and shows how these principles can be applied across a wide range of cases and domains. The book is a guide for media professionals, scholars, and educators who are concerned with the global ramifications of new technologies and with creating a more just world.

CLIFFORD G. CHRISTIANS is Research Professor of Communications, Professor of Journalism, and Professor of Media Studies Emeritus at the University of Illinois, Urbana-Champaign. His coauthored books include *Normative Theories of the Media* (2009), *Ethics for Public Communication* (2011), *Communication Theories in a Multicultural World* (2014), *The Ethics of Intercultural Communication* (2015), and *Media Ethics: Cases and Moral Reasoning* (2017).

D0911529

Communication, Society and Politics

Editors

W. Lance Bennett, University of Washington
Robert M. Entman, The George Washington University
Politics and relations among individuals in societies across the world are being transformed by new technologies for targeting individuals and sophisticated methods for shaping personalized messages. The new technologies challenge boundaries of many kinds – between news, information, entertainment, and advertising; between media, with the arrival of the World Wide Web; and even between nations. Communication, Society and Politics probes the political and social impacts of these new communication systems in national, comparative, and global perspective.

Other Books in the Series

(*continued after the Index*)

Media Ethics and Global Justice in the Digital Age

CLIFFORD G. CHRISTIANS

University of Illinois, Urbana-Champaign

CAMBRIDGE
UNIVERSITY PRESS

CAMBRIDGE
UNIVERSITY PRESS

Shaftesbury Road, Cambridge CB2 8EA, United Kingdom

One Liberty Plaza, 20th Floor, New York, NY 10006, USA

477 Williamstown Road, Port Melbourne, VIC 3207, Australia

314–321, 3rd Floor, Plot 3, Splendor Forum, Jasola District Centre, New Delhi – 110025, India

103 Penang Road, #05–06/07, Visioncrest Commercial, Singapore 238467

Cambridge University Press is part of Cambridge University Press & Assessment,
a department of the University of Cambridge.

We share the University's mission to contribute to society through the pursuit of
education, learning and research at the highest international levels of excellence.

www.cambridge.org
Information on this title: www.cambridge.org/9781316606391

DOI: 10.1017/9781316585382

© Clifford G. Christians 2019

First published 2019

A catalogue record for this publication is available from the British Library

ISBN   978-1-107-15214-4   Hardback
ISBN   978-1-316-60639-1   Paperback

Cambridge University Press & Assessment has no responsibility for the persistence
or accuracy of URLs for external or third-party internet websites referred to in this
publication and does not guarantee that any content on such websites is, or will
remain, accurate or appropriate.

This book is dedicated

to

Priscilla Jean Christians an *imago Dei*

and to

my family *summum bonum*

who teach me the morality of virtue with their exemplary lives and

duty ethics with their perspicacious minds.

Contents

Contents ix

Foreword

The rapid development and spread of digital media technologies are often referred to in revolutionary terms. Indeed, the impact of these technologies on the media industry and journalistic practices has been rapid and varied. The migration of audiences to the online sphere caused the collapse of established business models in legacy media, while rejuvenating ways of reporting, storytelling, and connecting with publics. Digital media have been praised for democratizing the production of news by increasing citizen participation, at the same time as the appetite of tech giants to devour smaller and independent outlets has been bemoaned. The social and political impacts of these technologies have been equally far-reaching. While the digital media's global reach has created new networks for solidarity around causes from climate change to war resistance, it has also managed to reach into the most intimate spheres of individuals by mining their data and invading their privacy. Digital media have been credited with facilitating the fall of repressive regimes (refer to the exaggerated claims around the role of social media in the "Arab Spring") as well as providing platforms to those who spread terror (for instance, the online display of beheadings). The connections made on mobile phones, via email or the World Wide Web, have given us a sense of being drawn into an interconnected global community where we bear witness to and express our outrage at injustices. Yet, these connections can also remain limited to the solipsistic "filter bubbles" where people's worst biases are confirmed, and they are emboldened to spew racist diatribes, hate speech, and character assassinations online that threaten to tear up the social fabric.

It is clear, therefore, that although digital media represent major technological advances, they are not neutral or value free. Therefore, while digital media technologies are in many ways radically new, the ethical questions they raise have for centuries been at the core of our being human: What is truth and how do we know it? How do I live together with others? How do I respect the dignity of those who are different from me? How can I contribute to a world that is fair and just?

The ethics of being in a world shaped by digital media extends beyond technocratic regulatory aspects. It demands of us difficult choices in all areas of our lives: what images we choose to consume, what information we decide to share, what global struggles for justice we engage in. In the contemporary world, we do not merely appropriate media as tools; we are immersed in them as an environment. Because these media shape our way of being in the world and how we relate to others, the ethical choices they demand of us are of an ontological category – going to the core of our very being.

Clifford G. Christians has a keen eye for the complicated and contra-dictory ethical challenges we face in a world shaped by digital media. To deal with these difficult questions, he takes us back to the fundamental questions of ethics and justice in moral theory. His dazzling mastery of the wide literature in moral philosophy as well as in media, technology, and society makes him a trusted guide through the moral maze of life in a digital era. Not only does he masterfully draw on theoretical insights to meet problems of practice and policy, but he also advances the frontiers of media ethics significantly on a theoretical level, by engaging in con-versations with traditions that developed outside Western orthodoxy, for instance, African philosophy, Latin American liberation theology, Confucianism, and Islamic traditions. But Christians's engagement with traditions outside the West should not be mistaken for the mere curiosity of a traveling collector. He is deeply invested in diversifying epistemology as a matter of justice. He is not only intent on redressing the historical imbalances and imperialisms in knowledge production. His urgency to de-Westernize media ethics is also born out of the realization that there will be no solving the intricate and serious issues facing humans in an inter-connected and interrelational world if this is attempted in isolation. Christians is correct in understanding the task of global media ethics as going beyond merely the token inclusion of a broader diversity of per-spectives, but also as working toward a more just and equitable global communications environment.

The need for a global perspective is all the more important given the amplification of communication beyond borders made possible by digital technologies. The limitations of thinking about the world in terms of the Westphalian nation-state have become clear from these flows and contra-flows of information. As we have seen in the way that many states in the Global North have grappled to find an appropriate policy response to the influx of refugees, the values of hospitality and cosmopolitanism are again high on the global agenda. As we know from ongoing political economy critiques of the internet, the digital media landscape in many ways mirrors wider global socioeconomic inequalities. The ethical implications of these asymmetries often remain implicit in these critiques. What this book does to draw on the principles of distributive justice, to reflect more clearly and explicitly on the moral dimensions of the digital divide, is therefore very important.

Thinking about media ethics in the global digital environment raises questions too profound to consider within the confines of the frameworks of professionalism and codification. These questions demand a reexamination of the very foundations upon which ethical theory should rest in a rapidly globalized yet stubbornly unequal world. This book rises to the challenge in a lucid and path-breaking way. In following the three principles of truth, human dignity, and nonviolence, Christians develops a theoretical foundation of universal protonorms that is at once a humanocentric rather than an instrumentalist or technologically deterministic approach and is sufficiently open ended to form the basis for moral engagement across borders. Technology may offer us new tools to work toward the good, but it cannot by itself generate a value system; we need to develop this out of core beliefs and commitments. Christians roots this value system in the primacy of life itself, in which communication is the connective tissue across cultures, and relationship is at the core of our being. Linked to the sacredness of life is a respect for human dignity and a commitment to peace as interlinked protonorms that underpin our thinking about being in the digital world.

The emphasis on relationship is not only vital for developing an ethics that responds to the interconnections made possible by digital media technologies but also for an ethics that strives to overcome the Western parochialism that has hitherto characterized much of the field. If we strive to reach the aim of understanding media ethics in global, non-imperialistic terms, "relationship" and "community" should be understood in their broadest possible sense. Relationship does not have much ethical depth if it only applies to those closest to us, those with whom we agree, or those we identify with. Nor does community retain its revolutionary power if it merely entails tolerance of the other, instead of being rooted in the much more difficult and transformative imperative of love. Relationship and community in a global sense dare us to care for those distant others who are caught in the web of poverty and conflict, to intervene in the plight of those who cannot contribute anything to our own welfare, to engage with suffering instead of merely being spectators. This is what the sacredness of life looks like in a digital era: to use technology not as an end in itself, nor as a means to strengthen the economic position or political prowess of the media, but to transform digital media from a technocratic tool to a meeting place where we can look into the face of the Other as we struggle to learn what it means to live a life that is truthful, sacred, and dignified.

We can only meet this Other if we approach the engagement truthfully. Honesty, fairness, and truth are more than quaint slogans for media outlets. These values are prerequisites for our very being as creatures-in-relation. If the lie could travel halfway around the world while the truth was still putting its boots on in Mark Twain's day, then lies today can circumnavigate the globe several times due to the increased speed and reach of digital technologies. But if truth is a foundational value for human beings, as this book argues, it should be defined more broadly than mere facticity in the disinterested, "objective" mode. Truth is that which resonates with our deepest experiences, hopes, and fears. We know from the panic around "fake news" that digital media afford opportunities for lies and half-truths to spread quickly, but we recognize with consternation that their appeal is possible from the loss of trust in mainstream or legacy news media. An ethical media in the digital age is one that does not exploit hopes and fears with the cynical intent of stoking fires, but one that listens to audiences with the honest intent of interpreting their expressions – whether these be joy, fear, or outrage – and tries to imagine what it must be like to stand in their shoes. Such a moral imagination, channeled through honest storytelling, can create the deeper understanding of the world and of each other that humans inherently crave. If journalism will not attempt to reconnect with emotions, identities, and cultural locations in the deeply truthful way that Christians describes, demagogues and populists will usurp the connection, with disastrous effect.

The media we need, therefore, is one that distills truthful meaning out of the bewildering array of facts now available to us through the wide and seemingly omnipresent digital media. But we also require media to help us transform truth into empathy. This is where we need the second proto-norm, human dignity, to be restored to the center of media ethics in a digital world. Where superficial debate, voyeurism, mining of data, and extreme speech threaten to overshadow the potential of these new platforms to make connections, foster community, and provide alternative perspectives, the monitorial, detached stance is not an adequate ethical response. While there have been many examples of how digital media can help monitor the excesses of corporate and political power and mobilize citizens to rise up, monitoring cannot be the only way to ensure the flourishing of human beings in all dimensions. An ethics of care and community on a global scale is required to foster a media that can contribute to the alleviation of poverty and redress of historical injustices and work toward a world where human rights and equality are paramount. This is a task of literally global proportions. The universal, however, is also reflected in the particular – in the everyday practices of representation and narrative. How journalists depict people, how they talk about them, who they talk about, and about whom they remain silent matter deeply. The struggle for truth, dignity, and nonviolence in a digital age is not one to be waged in isolation. In this, Christians leads the way in drawing from a variety of articulations of ethical theory around the world, while remaining conscious of the importance of anchoring such cultural diversity in shared ethical protonorms.

The ultimate challenge of this book, therefore, is one that oscillates between the local and the global, the specific and the universal. Final closure is not achieved; the dialectic ensures that ethical reflection remains dynamic and productive. On one side of the local-global coin is the need to be attuned to the specificity of lived experience, expressions of affect, and cultural identity. This is where the absolutist ethics of Enlightenment rationality is undone as we reach down to the grassroots and listen carefully to hear voices we may have missed before. These might be voices of rage, anguish, or anger, but they need to be listened to even if they sound different from the sounds of "rational deliberation" we are familiar with in the elite public sphere. These are the voices of the poor, of women and children, of victims of racism and homophobia, of the Southern subaltern. If we listen closely to these voices in localities, we will hear how the protonorms of truth, dignity, and nonviolence are given concrete meaning through the practical wisdom of everyday, lived culture. In this attempt to move away from the Western-centric history of media ethics it is important that this ethnographic thickening of protonorms should not be done in a patronizing fashion considered merely as local color to illustrate or

provide evidence for theories developed elsewhere. The knowledge gen-
erated in localities, especially those in the Global South that have for so
long been relegated to the margins of media ethical theory building, needs
to be treated seriously on the level of theory and not merely application.
This is the ongoing and pressing project of "decolonizing" media ethics
scholarship. Seeing the local and the global as two sides of the same coin,
however, means that this local knowledge will then be used to inform our
understanding of what is universal, what is shared, what has global
relevance for being human in this digital age.

   Clifford Christians's scholarship is deeply reflective, theoretically solid,
international in its outlook, and inspiring in its commitment to the public
good. Despite pointing to the many atrocities, conflicts, and moral failures
around the globe that have militated against the sacredness-of-life protonorms – truth telling, human dignity, nonviolence – the book's overarching tone is optimistic. It displays a belief in the innate goodness of human
beings and considers technology to be determined by human actions – not
the other way around. This emphasis on agency is hopeful and inspiring.
This landmark book is a vital companion as we explore the ethics of living
with and within digital media in a global world – to help us understand
who we are in this new digital world, and who we may yet become.

Herman Wasserman

Professor of Media Studies, Director of the Center for Film and
Media Studies, University of Capetown; Editor-in-Chief,
African Journalism Studies

Acknowledgments

W. Lance Bennett and Robert M. Entman, editors of the exceptional series "Communication, Society and Politics," are *sine qua non*. They thought the idea of this book was worth recommending to the editorial rigors of Cambridge University Press. Working days at the O'Hare Hilton with colleagues were formative in getting the thesis straight and the early chapters reviewed: Stephanie Bennett, Geri Forsberg, Patrick Plaisance, and Calvin Troup. I am deeply indebted to the additional astute colleagues who have read and critiqued chapters and major sections: Harris Breslow, Thomas Cooper, Robert Fortner, Steve Jones, Qingli Li, Robert Mejia, and Ned O'Gorman, and to other colleagues for reading the book in its entirety: Changfeng (Sophia) Chen, David E. Carrillo Fuchs, Theodore Glasser, Ran Ju, Christian Sandvig, Stephen J. A. Ward, Edward Wasserman, and Herman Wasserman. Robert Z. Cortes for his PhD dissertation has studied all the chapters and traced their intellectual trajectories over the course of my scholarship.

Team members of the Qatar National Research project (Leon Barkho, Hala Guta, Haydar Sadig) facilitated my application of the truth and human dignity principles to the Arab states of the Persian Gulf. In our collaboration on *Ethics for Public Communication,* Mark Fackler and John Ferré taught me how to integrate ethical theory with case studies; the summaries of "Al Jazeera English" included in Chapter 3 and "Russell Means: Oglala Sioux Activist" in Chapter 4 are based on that collaboration. Bushra Hameedur Rahman of the University of the Punjab is a source of constant inspiration on media responsibility and the ethics of nonviolence under conditions of oppression. Raluca-Nicoleta Radu of the University of Bucharest has been instructive on the nature of moral argument in global justice. I first published on universals in Thomas W. Cooper's *Communication Ethics and Global Change* in 1988, and he has been a key intellectual colleague on universalism ever since. Arnold De Beer, with his expertise bridging the North-South divide, enabled publications and conference venues over the decades. The winners of the Clifford G. Christians Ethics Research Award (administered by Shing-Ling Sarina Chen) have enlightened me on media ethics theory, with the astute Award committee members my academic heroes: Ronald Arnett, Deni Elliott, Robert Fortner, and Lee Wilkins. Visiting research scholars at Illinois from around the world in their working with me on media ethics have added scope and depth to my scholarship.

PhD students at the University of Illinois who read these and similar materials, and developed commentary and papers based on them in seminars on International Media Ethics and Philosophy of Technology, have been invaluable. Ran Ju, doctoral student at Illinois, reformatted the entire book and stimulated endless ideas in our discussions and tutorials. Yayu Feng, PhD candidate at Illinois, completed the research on data mining. Min Wang, while a Visiting Scholar from Wuhan University, assisted with empirical research on media violence.

Work at the Center for Advanced Study, University of Stellenbosch, with Shakuntala Rao, Stephen Ward, and Herman Wasserman, was essential for establishing the ontological foundation of theory that this book represents. The International Ethics Roundtables with those educators and Lee Wilkins, in Capetown (University of Stellenbosch), Dubai (Zayed University), Delhi (Jawaharlal Nehru University), and Beijing (Tsinghua University), brought together regional and national experts on the definition and character of universals in ethics; this book benefits throughout in both theory and practice from the Roundtable participants. Editing *The Ellul Studies Forum* for nearly two decades broadened my perspective on the philosophy of technology by scholars around the world. Fulbright Fellowships in Finland, Ukraine, and Tanzania helped refine my approach to cosmopolitanism, and I thank my host universities and professors, Kaarle Nordenstreng, Mariya Tytarenko, and Ayub Rioba. Professor Shan Bo's International Conference on Multicultural Communication at Wuhan University in its biannual meetings has expanded my understanding of human dignity in intercultural settings. Abderrahmane Azzi organized multiple meetings and seminars at the University of Sharjah that advanced my thinking on the absolutes-universals distinction. Colleagues in communications and philosophy in South Korea have been indispensable on substantive issues of theory, with the meetings of the Korean Society for Journalism and Communication Studies, and the workshops sponsored by the Korean National Commission for UNESCO that included the South Pacific agenda, of special importance. The working papers at the Euricom Colloquium (Piran, Slovenia) hosted by Slavko Splichal formalized my approach to the ethics of nonviolence. Venicio de Lima of the University of Brasilia taught me Paulo Freire's cultural theory. Timothy Scanlon, my host professor at Princeton University, aided in developing a critique of professional ethics. Oliver O'Donovan, then of Oxford University, clarified for me the systematic structure of natural reality crucial to Chapter 2. Nicholas Wolterstorff of Yale University Emeritus and Shakuntala Rao of the State University of New York were especially influential on the concept of justice.

These acknowledgments illustrate my indebtedness to able educators around the world. They are representative of my gratitude to faculty colleagues and students and media professionals on more than one hundred occasions in forty countries working from nine native languages who have responded analytically over the years at conferences, lectures, workshops, and seminars to major ideas in this book; they have helped develop such concepts as protonorms, universals, relativism, communication theory, instrumentalism, and human-centered technology. Changfeng Chen, member of the Academic Committee of the State Council – China, and Herman Wasserman, author of the recent *Media, Geopolitics, and Power: A View from the Global South*, represent educators with a global mind that this book has attempted to emulate.

Acknowledgment is in order for permission granted from *The New Yorker* for the extended quotation in Chapter 4 from "*Rolling Stone* and the Temptations of Narrative Journalism." Oxford University Press has given permission for references to Chapter 2 and Chapter 12 in *Ethics for Public Communication. Rethinking Media, Religion and Culture* is the home of my original work on Heidegger's philosophy of technology ("Technology and Triadic Theories of Mediation"), and Sage Publications granted permission to revisit some of its basic ideas in Chapter 1. As with the *Proslogion* of Anselm, *fides quaerens intellectum*.

The book's dedication to my family is an elfin tribute to my three sons and their spouses and four grandchildren, whose lives of authentic dwelling and loving orality make Heidegger's and Ong's versions elementary. I'm grateful they join me in working and praying for a communications world of truth, human dignity, and nonviolence, *Deo volente*.

Introduction

A new information age is taking shape, with upheavals across the globe. "The information revolution has been changing the world profoundly and irreversibly for some time now, at a breath-taking pace, and with unprecedented scope. It has made the creation, processing, management, and utilization of information vital issues" (Floridi, 2013, p. xii). According to Leah Lievrouw (2011, p. 1), "The proliferation and convergence of networked media and information technologies have helped generate a renaissance of new genres and modes of communication, and have redefined people's engagement with media … Media audiences and consumers are now also media users and participants immersed in complex ecologies of divides, diversities, networks, communities and literacies." In W. Lance Bennett's (2016, p. ix) reflections on the news, "the media system has fragmented into broadcast and cable channels, online platforms and social media … an expanding mediaverse that resembles a big bang of proliferating online competitors that are stealing audiences and ad revenues and challenging the very definition of news itself." In a special issue of *African Journalism Studies*, the new digital technologies on the African continent "have radically altered virtually every aspect of news gathering, writing and reporting" (Mabweazara, 2015, p. 2; cf. Wasserman, 2018, pp. 154–162).

The revolution in communication technologies is a worldwide phenomenon. High-tech electronic firms are re-mapping the planet into digital form. More than four thousand science parks around the world are a paradise for computer entrepreneurs. China's Alibaba e-commerce Group is larger than Facebook, Amazon, and IBM combined. In the United States, more than five thousand communications and cyber companies are clustered in Silicon

Valley, California, and Silicon Alley, New York. Bangalore, India, is an information technology megacity, and Tel Aviv a global attraction for hi-tech start-ups and venture capital investments. South Korea has the greatest broadband penetration and is a world leader in the online-gaming phenomenon (Jin, 2010). Singapore is called "Intelligent Island," given its aim to link every office, home, and school to a multimedia network. The AI Bridging Cloud Infrastructure (ABCI) in Japan became operational in 2018 as the world's fastest supercomputer. Geography has been organized by political coordinates – Eastern Bloc, Global South, Cold War superpowers, nonaligned movement, European colonialism. But now the globe is being ordered by the Web 2.0 phenomenon.

The new media congeries of optical fiber, cloud data storage, wireless communication, and satellite technology, although inescapably global, are local and personal as well. DirecTV, MP3 music, pocket computers, online databases, digital imaging, Open Source Software, video games – cyberspace is becoming the everyday communication world in societies everywhere. Five billion mobile phones worldwide are the new technology leader, accounting for 10 percent of all internet usage on the planet (International Telecommunications Union, 2017). China leads the world with more mobile phones than citizens, and this technology is similarly a phenomenon in Africa: "The unprecedented diffusion and pervasiveness of the mobile phone across social classes in Africa remain one of the most significant exemplars of the impact of digital technologies on the continent. It has proved critical in shaping everyday life" (Mabweazara, 2015, p. 2). Grant Kien's book-length study of mobile phones in North America, China, Korea, and Japan describes a "seismic shift" in the global citizens' media to fluidity – what Zygmunt Bauman (2005) calls "liquid modernity." Smart phones have "re-invented" electronic space as "mobile territory" and "transit itself is a new normal" (Kien, 2009, p. 2).

The new technologies are giving us communication abundance but with complications and contradictions. Schools teach computer literacy, while terrorists on four continents use online networks to coordinate planning. Finance and banking are the most advanced information systems in history; they led the world into an economic depression.[1] The growth of sectarianism and fundamentalism is making democracy nearly impossible. The Westphalian model of state sovereignty is in crisis, with globalization drawing the "administrative-material functions of the state into increasingly

---

[1] For Hoogvelt (2001), "The global financial network is the mother of all networks; it strides atop the entire edifice of global economic activities" (p. 128).

volatile contexts that far exceed any one state's capacities" (Benhabib, 2004, p. 4). The new technological landscape has created unprecedented opportunities for expression and interaction, while the elementary distinction between fact and fiction erodes. The inequalities of ethnicity, gender, and immigration are devastating; education is underfunded even as consumerism prospers (Commers et al., 2008). Data mining is a formidable challenge for media credibility. The unlimited amount of electronic data is a golden resource of information for reporting and persuasion, but no logical categories exist that are standardized. Big data lead to technological imperatives without transparency, with data-management techniques tending to determine what is newsworthy and cinematic.

The revolution in technology is engaging media studies across the curriculum (Curran, 2012; McChesney, 2013). Political communication gives it priority, particularly its meaning for the participation of citizens in democratic life. Communication research is probing what it entails for both quantitative and interpretive methodologies. International communication searches for the most appropriate concepts to summarize it – "digital age," "neoliberalism," "the era of interconnection," for example. History is rewriting its typologies to understand media technology's continuities and discontinuities in comparative terms. The Oxford philosopher Luciano Floridi (2013) calls on his discipline to provide "a foundational treatment of the phenomenon and the ideas underlying the information revolution" (p. xii), a challenge he emulates himself (cf. Floridi, 2011).[2]

Media ethics has begun to engage the technological revolution also; but in theory and application it ought to foreground the philosophy-of-technology tradition to do so competently. In presenting a new perspective on international media ethics, this book demonstrates why and how our theorizing gives the philosophy of technology intellectual priority. Engaging moral philosophy as it does for the *ethics* side of the equation, the philosophy of technology anchors the *media* dimension.

PRINT AND BROADCAST JOURNALISM

Historically, mass communication ethics developed in parallel with print technology; in that founding period, the predilection was news. The harms

---

[2] Floridi's understanding of intellectual history leads to the provocative and illuminating conclusion that today's information revolution is as pathbreaking as those led by Copernicus, Darwin, and Freud (*The Fourth Revolution: How the Infosphere Is Reshaping Human Reality*, 2014).

an unregulated press could do to society were first connected to ethical principles in North America and Europe in the 1890s, when scholars began assessing journalism academically. These initial explorations inspired the first systematic work in media ethics during the 1920s in the United States. In Europe also, several ethical issues with a journalism orientation emerged in the early twentieth century. Sensationalism was considered contrary to the public service role of the newspaper. Junkets and freebies, criticized already in the nineteenth century, were treated more formally in the context of increasing business competition.

The intellectual roots of the democratic press were formed when print technology was the exclusive option, so most of the research in media ethics centered on newspaper reporting – the gathering, publication, and dissemination of news. Many of the perpetual issues in journalism ethics – invasion of privacy, conflict of interest, sensationalism, confidentiality of sources, and stereotyping – received their sharpest focus in a print context.

Edmund Lambeth's *Committed Journalism: An Ethic for the Profession* (1992) outlines a framework for ethical journalism from the codes, values, and best practices in the field. Nicholas Russells's *Morals and the Media: Ethics in Canadian Journalism* (1994) analyzes reporters' ethical responsibility for the issues journalism faces as a profession. Philip Seib and KathyFitzpatrick's *Journalism Ethics* (1997) uses case studies to explore the journalist's duties. John Merrill's *Journalism Ethics: Philosophical Foundations for the News Media* (1997) explores such concepts as individualism and responsibility to understand everyday journalism practice. In Steven Knowlton's *Moral Reasoning for Journalists: Cases and Commentary* (1997), real-life cases are combined with ethical principles to teach journalists how to balance competing interests. Francis Kasoma's *Journalism Ethics in Africa* (1994) applies ethical theory to photojournalism and news reporting. Charles Frost in his *Media Ethics and Self-Regulation* (2000) concentrates on the everyday problems of working journalists in Britain. Pedro Gomes's *Direto de Ser: An Ètica da communicao na Amèrica Latina* (1990) applies the principles of liberation theology to journalism in the Latin American context. In their *Ethics and the Australian News Media* (1994), John Hurst and Sally White compare the moral standards of the Australian press with those of journalists in Western society generally.

The technology of news systems changed in the late twentieth century. With the decade of the 1990s, television became the primary source of news, and information radio, such as National Public Radio (NPR), was vital. Even as television established itself as the principal arbiter of news, the norm of truthfulness from print set the standard for broadcast. Research emphasizing the news function examined cases and problems from broadcasting, the wire service agencies, and documentaries, in addition to everyday reporting. James Ettema and Theodore Glasser's *Custodians of Conscience* (1998) on investigative journalism was based on extensive interviews with award-winning newspaper and television reporters. The authors concluded that investigative journalists trained in either technology are the custodians of the public conscience.

Thomas Cooper's comprehensive bibliography, *Television and Ethics* (1988b), called for a shift to television and film ethics in their own right. And some book-length treatments began to emerge that took seriously the technological properties of the visual media. *Image Ethics* did not construct a full-scale theory of visual ethics but began articulating a coherent ethics of representation (Gross et al., 1988). Val Limburg's *Electronic Media Ethics* (1984) applied the classical principles of ethics to the broadcast era – news, advertising, and business management. Julianne Newton's *The Burden of Visual Truth* (2001) on the news media combined visual communication theory with research on photojournalism and media imagery. Despite sporadic efforts to make the new broadcast technologies a distinct variable, the content of the news profession remained the preoccupation of media ethics.

In the earliest attempts to internationalize communication ethics, journalism was the core idea also: (1) the MacBride Report and (2) comparative research on journalism's codes of ethics. For these two defining episodes in the history of media ethics, print technology was the dominant context. Broadcast news was included only when it was deemed relevant.

One significant historical event for internationalizing media ethics was the publication in 1980 of the MacBride Report, *Many Voices, One World: Towards a New More Just and More Efficient World Information and Communication Order.* As president of the International Commission for the Study of Communication Problems and Irish diplomat, Sean MacBride supervised a review for the United Nations Educational, Scientific and Cultural Organization (UNESCO) of international media policies and practices, communication and human rights, cultural diversity and professional journalism. The recommendations of *Many Voices, One World* established the debates ever since over the economic concentrations of media industries, journalism education in the developing world, the possibilities for democratic politics through the convergence of digital information systems, and the consolidation of free trade in communications products and services under the aegis of the World Trade Organization.

With the MacBride Report as background, the International Organization of Journalists produced a document called "International Principles of Professional Ethics in Journalism" at meetings in Prague and Paris in 1983. It emphasized the people's right to germane information from the news media: "Mass communication ethics in terms of issues, participation, and setting – both professional and academic – had passed the international watershed" and had done so largely in categories established for newspaper reporting (Christians, 2000, pp. 29–32).

Codes of ethics were a second impetus to international media ethics. Codes of ethics for professional and academic associations had appeal in the 1990s and were seen as the conventional format for moral principles. For the most part, the journalism profession in various countries shared that understanding. The first comprehensive treatment by an international network of scholars, *Communication and Global Change,* appeared in 1989 edited by Thomas Cooper. Surveys of the codes of journalism ethics from thirteen countries were included. In the European context, Kaarle Nordenstreng's *Reports on Media Ethics in Europe* (1995) included empirical studies on the way self-regulation was done in the European region. It advanced the earlier work of Pauli Juusela (1991) on ethics codes in twenty-four journalism organizations, and it included surveys of European media councils, examination of journalism codes of ethics in general, and research on the Finnish journalists' adoption of their own code of ethics. Kai Hafez's (2002) comparison of codes includes the Middle East and Muslim Asia; the detailed Bahrani "Journalism Code of Ethics" is one illustration, orienting its content to news under the traditional rubric, "free and responsible journalism" (www.bahranijournalistics.org/Referen ces_and_documents/Meethaq). Calling itself a "globally oriented media service," Al Jazeera internationalized its 2006 and 2008 code of ethics in 2014 with "journalism values" its central axis (http://www.aljazeera.com/aboutus/2006/11/20085251857336927771.html). Ita Himelboim and Yehiel Limor (2011) represent sophisticated research in this area, comparing more than two hundred media codes of ethics, while continuing the traditional emphasis on journalism.

As academic media ethics was systematized and internationalized during the eras of print and broadcasting, the essence of their technologies did not appear on the ethics agenda. The preoccupation with news content in print journalism carried over into broadcast technology. The list of ethical issues that emerged in radio and television news was not fundamentally different from those in print. Professional ethics monopolized by print became media criticism, in effect, when applied to broadcasting.

Broadcast journalism, rather than understood as electronic communication in its own right, was seen as entertaining and lacking in substance compared to print. Instead of reconceiving truth for audio and visual technologies, linearity peculiar to print was the critical standard for judging radio and television news. Only intermittently did the scholars of media ethics scrutinize the transformation in technological form.

THE DIGITAL ETHICS AGENDA

For communication technologies, the early twenty-first century is a period of spectacular growth and substantial change, with few intellectual resources from the ethics of print and broadcast to address them. In the current digital era of networking, search engines, computer databases, online and cyberspace, media ethics is challenged to develop an agenda that reflects the distinctive properties of the new global system.

Ethical Issues from Media Studies

An early version of agenda setting was Thomas Cooper's "New Technology Effects Inventory: Forty Leading Ethical Issues" in a special issue of the *Journal of Mass Media Ethics* devoted to new media technologies (1988a). Cooper's typology has established itself in the literature: (a) some issues continue ethical concerns of the past, (b) a few issues are new, and (c) others create levels of complexity heretofore unknown (1988a, pp. 71–82). A content analysis of academic textbooks, journal articles that survey the state of the art in media ethics, and the assessments of professionals identify eight issues, three from Cooper's first category, one in the second, and four in category three.

Ongoing Issues

(1) In today's digital world, the ethical problem of distributive justice continues as before. Justice is the defining norm for all social institutions, including the policies and practices of media organizations. Regarding the principle that products and services ought to be distributed equitably, media access should be available to everyone as an essential need, regardless of income or geographical location. An ethics of justice in which distribution is based on need defines human necessities as those related to survival or subsistence – food, housing, clothing, safety, education, and medical care; none of these is frivolous or an individual whim. Everyone is entitled, without regard for personal achievement, to that which makes

human existence possible.[3] The new technologies cannot be envisioned except as a necessity, so the issue of just allocation remains on the agenda.

Global media networks make the world economy run, they give access to agricultural and health care information, they organize world trade, and they are the channels through which the United Nations and political discussion flow; through them, we monitor both war and peace. Therefore, as a necessity of life in a global order, information and communication technology (ICT) systems ought to be distributed impartially, regardless of income, race, geography, or merit (Christians, 2011b, p. 7).

However, the offline inequities of print and broadcast technologies continue to exist in the digital era. Information technology compounds the injustice of the digital divide – understood in a narrow sense as between rich and poor (Norris, 2001), and on a deeper level in terms of social divides (Bugeja, 2017). "Unless we manage to solve it," Floridi argues, "the digital divide may become a chasm, generating new forms of discrimination between those who can be denizens of the infosphere, and those who cannot" (2014, pp. 48–49). Technological societies have high levels of computer concentration with the opposite true of nonindustrial societies. In the United Nations data on internet penetration rates in 2017, developed societies score 81 percent, compared with 40 percent in developing countries and 15 percent in the least developed countries (International Telecommunications Union, 2017). There is a correlation between per capita gross national product and internet distribution, with 2017 data indicating that 84 percent of households in Europe are connected, compared with 18 percent in Africa (International Telecommunications Union, 2017). The world's nearly one billion people in urban slums are largely disenfranchised: "The internet media do not just perpetuate social inequalities, but often multiply them. In reality, the global village is a gated community" (Debatin, 2008, p. 260).

Lev Manovich (2012) raises the justice issue for big data in somewhat different terms. He argues that big data create a new class hierarchy in which its people and organizations can be categorized into three groups: "those who create data, those who have the means to collect it, and those who have the expertise to analyze it" (p. 470). This elite stratification in the era of big data represents a new social domain that may reinforce

---

[3] This argument for distributive justice is based on the standard account of basic human needs. The capabilities approach of Amartya Sen and Martha Nussbaum is another formulation, accounted for in Chapters 2 and 4.

digital inequality. It raises ethical questions such as privacy intrusion and business manipulation without informed consent from consumers.

(2) Harold Innis's *Empire and Communication* (1952) identified political empire as an issue with print technology, and it continues for digital ethics today. Printed documents enabled the control of geographical space; for Innis, strengthening the power of the political elite by print technologies was a profound moral issue. Print enabled governments to standardize, administer, and hold accountable their political regimes.

With digital technology, the empire problem means state surveillance in unprecedented terms (Ess, 2012, p. 54).[4] Six weeks after the September 11, 2001, attacks on New York's World Trade Center, President George W. Bush signed the USA Patriot (Uniting and Strengthening America by Providing Appropriate Tools Required to Intercept and Obstruct Terrorism) Act into law. The act shifted the Department of Justice's goal from prosecuting terrorists to preventing terrorism, and that historic change in U.S. policy continues with only minor modifications. Within U.S. borders, it initiated the relentless campaign to tighten security. Protection against terrorism has allowed a secret information-gathering process, not for probable cause, but for any alleged reason to investigate insurgency. Upon its frequent renewal, the technicalities of the USA Patriot Act have been refined, but its expansive powers remain intact. In the revelations of Eric Snowden and their aftermath, the U.S. National Security Agency is abusively intrusive into private affairs at home and into government affairs internationally. Historical archives, ethnographic research, and media content analysis verify that terrorism, anti-democratic state secrecy, and speculative technological practices are organizing U.S. security policy with negative consequences long term.

Expanded judicial authority to detain and profile also appeared after 9/11 in Canada's Anti-Terrorism Act; in the United Kingdom's counterterrorism laws (tightened even further after the July 7, 2005, attacks in London); and in France, Sweden, Germany, Denmark, Singapore, and Austria. India's Home Ministry now has the right to monitor and decrypt digital messages whenever it judges eavesdropping to be vital to national security (Bajaj & Austen, 2010, pp. Bl, B8). In 2005, Australia passed a stringent Anti-Terrorism Act, adding counterterrorism amendments in 2015 that its critics consider a breach of human rights and politically divisive. These are international illustrations that the pressure toward allowing abusive

---

[4] Carlson & Ebel (2012) focus the empire issue on the power that military technology gives to the state (for summary, see p. 225).

police and military force has taken the foreground; searching for alternative approaches and fresh thinking on surveillance is rarely on the agenda. In international counter-terrorism, new media technologies and networks are making high-technology surveillance intractable.

Harris Breslow argues for "flow and mobility" as two "emergent properties" of globalization, and this networked apparatus redefines the scope and character of surveillance in "supermodernity" (Breslow & Ziethen, 2015, pp. 6–7):

People, materiel, finances, information, and cultural objects circulate among hubs within a network of delimited routes whose smooth functioning requires the continuous surveillance of everything that is moving therein. The surveillance of these circulatory networks enables the establishment of behavioral norms based upon the protocols of movement and behavior across a network and within any of the hubs found within a network. (Breslow & Ziethen, 2015, p. 10; cf. pp. vii–xx, 3–23; cf. Breslow & Mousoutzanis, 2012)

In the globalized era of network space, in Breslow's terms, "Subjects . . . move through at least two types of nodes: Nodes of surveillance and control, where they are observed and disciplined, and ideological nodes where subjectivity is inculcated and informed" (Breslow & Ziethen, 2015, p. 15). Given the "flow and mobility" understanding of surveillance in supermodernity, democratic societies everywhere face a conundrum – aggressive data gathering is judged to be essential even though the process erodes the very democratic values that warrant protection.

(3) The issues of political economy are salient for today's digital media as they were for print and broadcast. With the new electronic technologies radically rupturing media systems worldwide, institutional structures are of special importance to global media ethics. A long-term study of thirty countries indicates that the concentration of media ownership continues to escalate, with the internet amplifying cross-national condensation (Noam, 2016). With the new "distribution technologies and deregulated markets . . . a handful of conglomerates dominate the media landscape . . . and produce a synergy that maximizes profits and decreases risk" (Wasko, 2014, pp. 67–68). Christian Fuchs (2014) makes the ongoing importance of political economy a scholarly imperative: "The information economy is not new, postmodern or radically discontinuous. It is rather a highly complex formation in which various contemporary and historical forms of labour, exploitation, different forms of organization of the productive forces, and different modes of production are articulated with each other and form a dialectic of exploitation" (p. 296).

Nick Couldry and James Curran (2003) bring the new media environment into focus. In their view, "media power is an increasingly important emergent form of social power in complex societies whose basic infrastructure depends increasingly on the fast circulation of information and images" (p. 4). They are particularly concerned for news and public information where diversification is vital for an informed society (cf. Curran & Seaton, 2009). In addition, "Far from media simply being there to guard us against the overweening influence of other forms of power (especially government), media power is itself part of what power watchers need to watch" (Couldry & Curran, 2003, p. 4; cf. Curran, 2002). Couldry and Curran (2003) examine the question of whether the internet, with its potential to reach a global audience, can challenge the oligarchy of large media concentrations. Their *Contesting Media Power* (2003) uses case studies and theoretical essays (from Taiwan, Chile, Indonesia, Malaysia, Russia, North America, and Europe) to examine the ways in which new technologies can provide an alternative to and contradict the dominant media brokers.

Working with a critical-institutional perspective, Judy Wajcman of the London School of Economics shifts the mechanical focus on technological products and tools to the organizational issues of the workplace and in corporate management. In her feminist theory of technology, the fundamental problem of the technological revolution is gender identity and equality. In Wajcman's perspective, the ICT revolution exacerbates the gendered character of technology rather than resolves it (1991, 2004, 2008, 2010, 2015). Her analyses of the gendering of technology are grounded in a larger historical model commensurate with post-Marxist understandings of social transformation.

For Nick Dyer-Witheford of the University of Western Ontario, the information age constitutes an episode in the historic conflict over global capitalism. His critical theory of technology exposes the contradictions and crises of information technology serving world capitalism. Grounded in Antonio Negri and the Italian autonomist tradition, his philosophy of technology lays the groundwork for a radically alternative vision of community and communication beyond the control of markets. His four books, *Cyber Marx: Cycles and Circuits of Struggle in High Capitalism* (1999), *Digital Play: Technology, Markets and Culture* (with Stephen Kline, 2003), *Games of Empire: Global Capitalism and Video Games* (with Greig de Peuter, 2009), and *Cyber-Proletariat: Global Labour in the Digital Vortex* (2015), ensure that a critical perspective on technology will exist alongside philosophies of technology in Aristotle and Heidegger. He understands capitalism as cycles of struggle now being played out in global information structures.

Christian Fuchs is likewise theoretically sophisticated. To get beyond the user experience and to evaluate functional approaches to the social media, Fuchs systematically reworks critical theory. His *Digital Labour and Karl Marx* (2014) is an illustration. Chapters 2 to 5 review theoretical approaches that "take seriously how the economic interacts with culture and the media" (p. 73). He develops his own theory within that context, essentially a "reconstruction of Marx's labour theory of value" (pp. 46–58). Fuchs's perspective demonstrates that "the global collective ICT worker consists of many different workers: unpaid digital labourers, a highly paid and highly stressed knowledge worker aristocracy, knowledge workers in developing countries, Taylorist hardware assemblers and manufacturers, slave mine workers, and others" (2014, p. 296). As with Coudry and Curran, Fuchs (2014) applies his theorizing to issues of digital structure and corporate platforms worldwide, such as unpaid mineral extraction in the Democratic Republic of Congo (chap. 6), software production in India (chap. 8), and workers in the Foxconn ICT factories in China (chap. 7). His *Social Media: A Critical Introduction* (2017) includes the Arab Spring, China's Wiebo, and the worldwide network brokers Airbnb and Uber Technologies, Inc.

New Issue

(4) Inscribed in the new technologies themselves is global citizenship. The character and process of citizenship have always been a concern for democratic publics (Damsholt, 2009; Overholser & Jamieson, 2005, chaps. 20–24; Entman, 1989). But the global citizen mandate for the digital age is fundamentally new. As Kwame Anthony Appiah (2006) observes, the idea of a "citizen of the cosmos" has existed in the West since the fourth century B.C., but the concept could not be meaningfully implemented across the centuries until today's worldwide network of information. Its typical designation "cosmopolitanism" must be understood as signifying a new era in history. As Charles Ess (2012a) describes it, "because our communications can quickly and easily reach very large numbers of people around the globe, our use of digital communication technologies makes us citizens of the world in striking new ways" (p. 18).

News media practitioners and media scholars concerned with ethics need to engage "citizenship" with a world mind. Their ways of knowing in the era of digital media must be redirected from immediate and national circles to a respect for humanity's moral capacity as a species. As Stephen

Ward's *Global Journalism Ethics* (2010) puts it, media professionals need "a cosmopolitan commitment to humanity" (p. 213); they ought to "pursue the good within the bounds of global justice" (p. 5). Nigel Dower uses cosmopolitanism as the framework in his *World Ethics: The New Agenda* (2007), defining it as "a set of values to be accepted everywhere" (chap. 5). For media ethics to frame itself in cosmopolitan terms, the definition of "citizens' obligations to others" will be a difficult and ongoing issue on the agenda (cf. MacKinnon, 2013).[5]

In her Seeley Lectures at Cambridge University, Seyla Benhabib (2004) made political membership a premier issue in understanding global justice. Her philosophical perspective rooted in Kant's "cosmopolitan right" and Arendt's "the right to have rights" discusses citizenship struggles from the perspective of international justice rather than that of nation-state policies: "Transnational migrations, and the constitutional as well as policy issues suggested by the movement of people across state borders, are central to interstate relations and therefore to a normative theory of global justice" (Benhabib, 2004, pp. 2–3). Consistent with the argument of *Media Ethics and Global Justice in the Digital Age* regarding this fourth agenda item, exclusionary citizenship and practices of immigration and border control are a moral project, and "nowhere are the tensions between the demands of postnational universalistic solidarity and the practices of exclusive membership more apparent than at the site of territorial borders and boundaries" (Benhabib, 2004, pp. 2–3, 17).[6]

In cosmopolitan media ethics, it is the world that draws, not the individual who extrapolates. As developed in Chapter 6, the reality of purposive human existence is the context within which the world mind resolves issues of citizenship. W. Lance Bennett's "Changing Citizenship in the Digital Age" studies the "differing views of what constitutes civic engagement and citizenship for young people both on and off line" (2008, p. 2). Comparative and strategic research such as this is necessary for

---

[5] Such new thinking involves for Foucault (1984), for example, emancipation from the political regime in which we are situated. Developing world-mindedness entails a struggle against the ideological violence of states that oppress their subjects. The Canadian theory of social communications is presented in Chapter 1. For a history of this tradition, describing affinities of its founder Harold Innis with Michel Foucault, see Heyer (1988, chap. 10; cf. Crowley & Heyer, 2010).

[6] Benhabib and Resnik's *Migrations and Mobilities: Citizenship, Borders, and Gender* (2009) argues for the central role of gender in understanding the nature of citizenship in today's mobile world.

global media ethics to analyze properly the digital–politics relationship for the twenty-first century (cf. Reysen & Katzarska-Miller, 2013).

Issues More Complex

Charles Ess (2012b) emphasizes Cooper's third category: issues made much more complicated by the media revolution so that standard ethics, the classic approaches, are no longer appropriate. For those who take technology seriously, this posture makes sense. As Ess (2012b) remarked, "Ongoing technological development and diffusion of digital devices will continue to drive a parallel expansion in the range, scope, and complexity of the ethics challenges evoked by these devices" (p. xv). Ess considers the new social media as technologies appropriate first of all for society as a whole, that is, for "the rest of us" outside the political-economic elite. From this perspective, he concludes that three core people-issues are newly multifaceted by the digital media: violence, privacy, and pornography.

(5) The ethics of violence in television and cinema is compounded by interactive violence in video games and made nearly unmanageable by web-based hate sites thriving around the globe. Violence in television and film has been a major ethical issue for decades. From the horrific shootings in the United States at Columbine (Colorado) High School in 1999 to similar tragedies in other states and countries before and since, teenagers who slaughter their classmates and teachers, and then kill themselves, are linked by debate and research to the culture of violence in which they live. While the United States leads the world in the amount of violence on television, television programming in all parts of the globe contains excessive violence, including a high percentage of guns as weapons, with the brutal consequences not depicted adequately. For media ethics, there is special concern about the sexual violence in video games and in music video, and about the sadistic torture of slasher films delivered online to home media centers.

A new dimension of violence has emerged with hate speech on the internet. "Stormfront" was the first white supremacist website begun in 1995. As website technology mushroomed, the number of active hate sites has grown to an estimated fifty thousand worldwide. Neo-Nazi websites are viciously anti-Semitic, some of them disavowing the Holocaust. Other religious groups are targeted also, such as websites that are anti-Muslim, anti-Hindu, and anti-Catholic. Racist contempt includes comparisons with animals and excrement, and the pro-violence websites advocate race war. In the United States, arrests for hate crimes continue to accelerate, with growing evidence that hate speech and hate crimes are consociated. As elaborated in Chapter 5, internet racial propaganda operates by the moral exclusion that turns human beings into subhuman entities without claims or rights. It is a fundamental dismissal of the ethics of being and requires a moral rebuttal beyond the demands for legal restrictions.

Media ethics promotes the common good, but violent cinema illuminates evil. Violent video games teach skills for annihilating others. Hate sites are sectarian and media ethics is challenged to capacity (Beam & Spratt, 2009). Ess (2012a) is correct about the complexities that weave their way through this research and scholarship: "How to determine causal linkages between consumption and the use of such materials, and just what harms and/or liberations they may foster (if any)" (p. 180). Miguel Sicart's *The Ethics of Computer Games* (2011) is a sophisticated example of the new thinking that is required of media ethics in the digital era. Sicart argues correctly that gaming is an intricate network involving moral obligations, though its design is oriented to technological mechanisms and gaming technique. In a follow-up volume, *Beyond Choices: The Design of Ethical Gameplay* (2013), he calls for video and computer games that engage the players' moral imagination. Sicart (2013) contends correctly that high-resolution games can be created that are both entertaining and "vehicles for ethical reflection."

(6) Louis Hodges's (1983) essay on media ethics and privacy establishes the moral issues for print and broadcasting. Privacy enters the US agenda through the Warren and Brandeis essay, "The Right of Privacy," in the *Harvard Law Review* (December 15, 1890). Privacy is defined as the legal right of humans to control the time, place, and circumstances of information about themselves. Democracies as a system of governance are distinctive in these terms. Legally, it means that citizens have freedom from government control over what they themselves control. Totalitarian societies, on the other hand, use the near absence of privacy to regiment a servile populace. Thus, here is the formal criterion of public policy following Hodges's logic: the intimate life space of individuals cannot be invaded without permission unless the revelation averts a public crisis and all other means to deal with the issues have been exhausted.

But the appeal in this definition of privacy to a sacred sequestered self is not credible in the digital era of abundant social networking sites. Micromedia imaging, podcasts, instant messaging platforms, and smart phones are increasingly used to publicize personal and intimate information within the so-called anonymity of the digital environment. Bernhard Debatin gives this overview:

ICTS have greatly facilitated data collection, privacy invasion and surveillance. Abuse of personal data by third parties, as well as harassment and identity theft are oft-criticized side effects of data networks and new communication technology. Popular Web 2.0 applications such as social networking sites, provide a convenient socializing tool for its users who often carelessly reveal detailed personal information in their profiles. This makes social networking sites gigantic data collection agencies that allow highly individualized forms of marketing and advertising through the coordination of user profiles and user behaviors. (2008, p. 261)

Big data companies like Amazon.com, Tencent Holdings, Google, Alibaba, and Yahoo accumulate personal information that threatens privacy: "Facebook is often at the center of a data privacy controversy, whether it's defending its own enigmatic privacy policies or responding to reports that it gave private user data to the USA's National Security Agency" (Waxer, 2013, p. 2). Mark Zuckerberg's testimony before the US House and Senate on April 10–11, 2018 indicates that the privacy issue for the social media continues unresolved. Triggered by the unlawful sale of Facebook data to Cambridge Analytica during the US 2016 presidential campaign, Zuckerberg evaded the complexities of privacy protection despite tough questioning; and Congress was unwilling to consider the regulation of Facebook's tracking practices. The hearing made it obvious that Facebook's problematic business policies are not facing legal censure in the United States as they are in the European Union (http://abc7news .com/technology/Zuckerberg-faces-tougher-questions-at-house-hearing/ 33328948/).

Cecilia Friend and Jane Singer's *Online Journalism Ethics* (2007) reconstructs the invasion of privacy issues for journalism in terms that account for the technological revolution. In *Online Ethics*, the traditional legal context for understanding privacy has become controversial with internet technology: the digital is not geographically limited and laws are nation-state oriented (pp. 95–97); the definition of "journalist" is disputed and therefore it is also contested what "legal or ethical precepts related to information gathering and dissemination" are applicable to whom (p. 81, cf. pp. 104–109). In addition, the source of electronic data is often unknown and impossible to verify, making "compelling public need" an inapplicable standard. For Friend and Singer, the "core concepts of human dignity and the common good" continue to be relevant for the privacy question, but online journalists, bloggers, media organizations, and academic specialists face a major challenge to clarify the issues in the internet era and to identify the relevant policies and procedures.

Luciano Floridi's "Ontological Interpretation of Informational Privacy" (2013, pp. 228–260) is a radical perspective (*radix*, root) and most compatible with the ethics of being of this book. Floridi defends an "informational interpretation of the self"; therefore, "anything that affects the informational life of the self affects its very essence" (p. 228). Regarding the issue at hand, "a breach of one's informational privacy is a form of aggression against one's personal identity" (p. 228). Privacy is not a "pressing issue" because of the "dramatic increase in ICTs' data processing capacities" and "the quantity and quality of data that they can collect, record, and manage" (p. 230). Such an approach does not account for the fundamental change in the nature of privacy in the information age: "ICTs are more redrawing rather than erasing the boundaries of informational privacy" (p. 230). "The new challenges posed by ICTs" have their roots in an "unprecedented transformation in the ontology of the informational environment, of the information agents embedded in it, and of their interactions" (p. 231). In his *Fourth Revolution* (2014), Floridi calls informational privacy "one of the defining issues of our age" (p. 100; cf. chap. 5).

For social media networks, policy makers, and media professionals, the question is not, first of all, how to deal with the legal aspects of privacy case by case. Their commitment to the integration of privacy with human dignity is the most pressing concern in this revolutionary era in media technologies. To the extent that privacy as a moral good is known and appreciated in public life, the details of privacy protection in law, and in professional practice and user interaction, will be interpreted correctly.

(7) While definitions of sexuality differ widely across cultures, erotica among consenting adults is generally distinguished from pornography. Legitimate erotica is typically considered a personal choice as long as those choices do not infringe on the rights of another. The moral issues regarding its illegitimate opposite, pornography, were not resolved during the eras when print and broadcast technologies were dominant, and the abundance of pornography online complicates any resolution now. Wendy Wyatt and Kris Bunton's (2009) review of the literature on pornography identifies two polarized camps over four decades, neither suitable for today's titanic shift in pornography's distribution (pp. 149–161). Anti-pornography activists call for legal remedies and public condemnation; anti-censorship civil libertarians ignore the harms of pornographic images and texts. In the context of this contorted public discourse, the US Supreme Court in 1996 established a three-part definition of obscenity: "of prurient interest," "patently offensive," and "utterly without

redeeming value." Only with respect to children has the law been minimally effective in the United States through the Children's Internet Protection Act first issued in 2000.

The meager vocabulary for intelligent discussion and the ambiguous legalisms of pre-digital mediation are marginalized by the "technological blurring of the once clear lines between the actual or the real (as primarily material) and the virtual (as grounded in diverse computational technologies)" (Ess, 2012b, p. xiii). The idea of mutual consent is apropos online, as it is offline; mediated sex can be bizarre and oppressive. But virtual technology does not create children; it does not spread AIDS; it does not draw women into the agonizing decision to abort. The proliferating exchange of sexual images via smart phones has required a new term "sexting," but whether it needs more laws and a redesigned ethics is debatable. Adults caught sexting racy messages or risqué photos at or away from work are embarrassed and sometimes fired. Sexting nude photos among teenagers is typically considered harmless fun but not immoral. The question for ethics is being able to distinguish what is consensual, and therefore acceptable, from cyberbullying and sexting of no redeeming value (Oravec, 2012). Amy Hasinoff's (2015) book-length treatment, *Sexting Panic*, argues against criminalization and for recognizing the participants' capacity to distinguish the consensual from the malicious.

Ess's "technological blurring" is a major challenge for media ethics. It shifts the arguments about pornography versus censorship to a different debate: must online pornography presume real persons to be meaningful or are screen entities radically other and, if so, of no moral concern? For example, in this controversy over the virtual–real relationship, what ethical judgments are valid regarding virtual child pornography? If online entities are being distributed, there is no harm to actual children. Yet, generally speaking, our moral instincts resist approval. Digital ethics has the complicated dualism of the actual human and the technological to overcome. Waytt and Bunton (2009) recommend an alternative to the strident polarization through an ethics of pornography "that works within rather than against eroticism" (p. 157). Global media ethics needs that alternative pathway as it redefines pornography with the virtual–personal relation not fully understood.

(8) The ethics of representation faces the demand to specify how gender, ethnicity, and class are symbolized in global electronic technologies. Multiculturalism in the era of broadcast media was a key sociopolitical issue. This issue continues with digitalization, complicated by

the contradictory trends of cultural homogeneity and resistance in the age of ICTs and the social media: "Reflecting a social dynamic we have hardly begun to comprehend, global integration is proceeding alongside socio-cultural disintegration, the resurgence of various separatisms, and international terrorism" (Benhabib, 2002, p. 8). The extraordinary challenge is to take seriously both globalization and multiculturalism, though the news media's penchant for specificity in everyday affairs makes the one-many integration difficult.[7]

For media ethics, in theory and research, contrary to an ethnocentrism of judging other groups against a dominant Western model, other cultures are not considered inferior, only different (cf. Audi, 2007). Global media ethics requires an escape from cultural imperialism by immersion in native languages to understand them in their own terms and from the inside out. Rather than superficial attention to courtesies, social quirks, and habits, a deep understanding of culture is necessary for transnational ethics. Cultures are complex and multilayered; they express our worldviews and make life meaningful. Misrepresenting them is an obvious contravention of the ethics of being.[8]

---

[7] Entman & Rojecki's (2000) research on the race dimension of cultural pluralism has become a classic in media studies. As developed in Chapter 4, this sophisticated research of the broadcast era sets the standard for the study of multiculturalism in mobile phone networks, and in Facebook, Reddit, Weibo, Renren, and Twitter communities.

[8] The cultural studies approach is pertinent in clarifying this eighth agenda topic. Scholarship in cultural studies is essential background for the ethics of human dignity in Chapter 4. However, only those trajectories in cultural studies that engage and produce theory are compatible with the philosophy-of-technology and moral-philosophy integration of this book; these trajectories are chosen in awareness of Morris's banality concern. Meaghan Morris's *Banality in Cultural Studies* (1988/1990) rebukes her field for pursuing the trivial instead of the substantial. Its founding as British Cultural Studies was a complex historical, intellectual, and political event. She is concerned with the ways in which cultural studies' research into the dynamics of everyday life and the drama of popular culture can become routinized and perfunctory: "In Baudrillard's words, we tend to study what is banal and leave aside what is fatal. That is to say, cultural studies is being directed toward unimportant issues that constitute an endless loop that eventually lead to the same results" (Bziker, 2013, p. 1). The current vogue becomes the pathway to publication rather than intellectual achievement: "Cultural studies tends to become banal when economic and institutional forces militate against the production of new, innovative, and contextually defined theory and research, favoring instead the reproduction of already proven (that is, salable) scholarship" (Striphas, 2000, p. 2).
  While Morris speaks to a hollowed-out approach to cultural studies with a fifty-year history, and digital ethics is new, her argument about theory is *a propos* as the field of media ethics takes shape in digital terms. For Morris, attention to theory pushes academia to new challenges and problematics. Making theory transparent pays off in substance; theories are provocateurs of intellectual productivity.

Universal ethical principles in the past have proved to be oppressive. They typically have been designed from a certain perspective – Western, male, modernist, for example – and then imposed on others in a patronizing manner. The foundational work *Cultural Pluralism and Moral Knowledge* (Paul et al., 1994) indicates how dangerous all normative theories are whether classical or contemporary. Sometimes they are imperialistic, and often they provide an ethical veneer above cultural difference rather than promote ethical dialogue across cultures (cf. Fleischacker, 1994). Herman Wasserman (2018), citing Pankaj Ghemwat and Stephen Marshall, warns of "the 'world is flat' trap in which globalization is celebrated for the connections it creates but less attention is paid to its attendant inequalities and power relations" (p. 118). For multiculturalism, the global media ethics that is legitimate cannot be abstract and absolutist, but humanistic in respecting the diversity of the human race while seeking commonness among peoples everywhere (Christians, 2014).

Seyla Benhabib demonstrates in *The Claims of Culture* that a "vision of cultures as essentially contested and internally riven narratives is compatible with a commitment to discourse ethics" (2002, p. xi). This demonstration that a "normative universalism and a pluralist view of culture can be reconciled" (2002, p. xi) serves as a theoretical model for dealing with this agenda item on multiculturalism. *Media Ethics and Global Justice in the Digital Age* likewise weaves "empirical and normative considerations" together to show that "sensitivity to the politics of culture and a strong universalist position are not incompatible" (2002, p. x; cf. chap. 2).[9]

Critique

Specialized research on specific media tools, such as Facebook, Renren, and weblogs, is typical in communication studies. But for scholars who work on the new interactive media system as a whole, identifying the core issues has priority. And many agenda lists include the eight items

---

The quality of theory likewise determines the future of media ethics in the digital age. Theories of technology as illustrated earlier by Floridi, Wajcman, Dyer-Witheford, and Fuchs interrogate the media ethics agenda and prevent its banality. They add important problems for digital ethics to address. However, theoretical work in cultural studies does not in itself finally resolve the agenda debates. For the agenda-setting task, the philosophy of technology is indispensable.

[9] In her double recognition of a complex interactive universalism and the "radical hybridity and polyvocality of all cultures," Benhabib's engagement with multiculturalism represents an alternative to Samuel Huntington's (1996) confusion of constructivist premises with essentialist conclusions (Benhabib, 2003, pp. 25, 187–188).

summarized earlier: distributive justice, empire, institutional structures, global citizenship, violence, privacy, pornography, and multiculturalism. But a definitive agenda that marshals resources and advances agreement on the major issues will not take place if technology itself is treated in mechanical terms. Contrary to the ethics of print and broadcasting where technological form was treated minimally, the technological features of digital ethics must be highlighted.

In the important work of agenda setting, the theory of technology customarily assumed has been its neutrality. In the commonplaces of agenda formation, technology is treated functionally, tracking the number of products and the patterns of distribution and concentrating on the demographics of age, education, income, and geography. Technology per se is not seen as a crucial variable; only the uses to which we put it matter. However, in the perspective of this book, technologies are not neutral but value laden; philosophical work, such as Floridi's (2011) on the nature of technology as a whole, is necessary before there can be productive agreement on the digital ethics agenda.

The Causality Problem

In working on an ethics agenda for the digital era, if the philosophy of technology is ignored, the problem of causality is typically unattended. The eight issues that constitute the mainstream agenda for communication studies beg the question of causality. If agenda setting is determined in functional terms by research on technological products, causality is not addressed because it has no conceptual bearing on whether surveillance, pornography, privacy, and violence, for example, merit the ethicist's attention.

In the philosophy-of-technology literature, there are appeals to structure, organizational culture, and institutional policies; agendas are driven by the complexities of history. Long-term problematics emerge that demand our best scholarship on the agenda-setting task. Heidegger's *The Question Concerning Technology* (1977b), for example, is grounded in the causality problem. Aristotle's four causes are said to have commanded philosophers' attention since the fourth century BC (pp. 6–12). Instead of ignoring causality, our philosophical task is to reconstruct it and reapply it. As an analytic tool, Aristotle's efficient cause characterizes the mainstream view and his formal causality the theorists' view. But both causes are critiqued by and transformed through Heidegger's occasioning. In his terms, the presumption of human agency in handcraft or in artistic production is too raw and uncomplicated to account for our existence in the world (*Dasein*) (Heidegger, 1962). The ancient understanding of cause as effecting, starting, and imposing presumes a subject-object dualism. Occasioning denies that dichotomy and defines agency in contextual terms – nurturing, inducing something to come forth but always in the "letting/letting-it-happen" mode (Heidegger, 1977b, pp. 6–12; cf. Rojcewicz, 2006, pp. 29–40).

Heidegger is referenced here to signal a new direction in agenda setting. As the humanocentric philosophy of technology is developed in this book, critically interpretive knowledge takes hold, to replace the thinness of neutrality and functionalism. Various versions of technological determinism are critiqued as theoretically unsophisticated. *Media Ethics and Global Justice in the Digital Age* aims to show that combining serious work in the philosophy of technology with moral philosophy yields an agenda of three major principles that are explicitly transnational and make media ethics intellectually sustainable. These three issues for media ethics in the digital era – truth, human dignity, nonviolence – encompass the whole technological range from the social media to ICT organizations. The philosophy of technology produces a human-centered theory of media technology that is integrated into research and case studies. An agenda emerges for a new theory of communication ethics that is international, multicultural, and gender inclusive.

A CONCEPTUAL DILEMMA

While developing an ethics agenda for the digital era, a complicated issue needs to be addressed; without the resources of the philosophy of technology, this conceptual dilemma will persist unchanged. I speak of the pessimism-optimism debate. While often a feature of other technologies – medical and agricultural, for example – pessimism-optimism has particular salience in media technologies. In Robin Mansell's (2012) analysis, the internet literature falls into two broad camps, the celebrants and the skeptics. In Floridi's politics of the new digital technologies, the two extremes are optimistic support for their creating personal fulfillment and lamenting their delocalization as a global mistake (2014, p. 39). The philosophy of technology demonstrates that this trajectory is fruitless intellectually. It calls for a new approach to global media ethics that steps outside this unproductive dualism.

Optimism and pessimism represent two opposing worldviews. Pessimism is a state of mind that anticipates undesirable outcomes, with optimists believing that the possibilities at hand will be fulfilled.[10] But optimism and pessimism are not merely psychological dispositions. Philosophically, optimism derives from the notion that the world is basically good, and pessimism is built on the presumption that people are fundamentally evil. Pessimism and optimism in our thinking and discussion reflect the ambiguities of the good and evil motifs that they represent.

Though concluding that this dualism distracts from the important issues, Robert McChesney organizes his book *Digital Disconnect* (2013) around the optimism-pessimism divide. Using Mansell's (2012) "skeptic" and "celebrant," he demonstrates that it represents the typical way the new media technologies are presented in the literature. The rhapsodies celebrating the internet have been unequivocal and unending since their groundswell in the 1990s. McChesney (2013, p. 5) quotes James Curran's review of expert reports, business promotions, journalists' news, and politicians' braggadocio, summarizing them as "internet-centrism, a belief that the internet is the alpha and omega of technologies, an agent that overrides all obstacles and has the power to determine outcomes" (Curran, 2012, p. 3). Quentin Schultze (2002) describes the common "tale of technological innovation and social progress" (p. 13) by referencing David Noble (1999):

For centuries people have equated the work of engineers, explorers, and inventors with the action of God – a recurring theme that David F. Noble dubs "the religion of technology." People have long dreamed of communication technologies that will grant humans greater freedom, more power, and everlasting peace. Still enchanted by such rhetoric we continue to label even incremental innovations as "revolutionary."[11] (Schultze, 2002, p. 16)

"Enabled by the internet and social media," says the optimist Simon Mainwaring (2011), "we have entered an amazing and exciting era in human history. We are fast acquiring the knowledge and technology to meet the challenges of poverty, malnutrition, child mortality, and the myriad social ills that blight our planet" (quoted in McChesney, 2013, p. 7).

---

[10] The ideas are prominent in history. Friedrich Nietzsche, for example, uses the term "pessimism" in his book *The Birth of Tragedy or Hellenism and Pessimism* (1872), believing as he does that the ancient Greeks created tragedy as a result of their pessimism.

[11] Schultze (2002) includes this pertinent footnote: "Langdon Winner (1986) says that computer enthusiasts employ the metaphor of revolution for one purpose only – to suggest a drastic upheaval, one that people ought to recognize as good news. It never occurs to them to investigate the idea or its meaning any further" (p. 211).

For skeptics, McChesney refers to psychologist Sherry Turkle (2012) whose research shows that in the digital era, people "seem increasingly drawn to technologies that provide the illusion of companionship without the demands of a relationship." She writes of the "flight from conversation," as people find it increasingly difficult to talk personally with one another (McChesney, 2013, p. 11; cf. Turkle, 2016). And other skeptics argue "that the emergence of Facebook and other social media, ironically enough, correlates with a marked increase in loneliness ... Scholars term this the internet paradox" (p. 11). For Stephen Marche (2012), "Our omnipresent new technologies lure us toward increasingly superficial connections" at the same time as they "make avoiding the mess of human interaction easier." The social media generation has "never been more detached from one another or lonelier." Regarding blogging and online journalism, C. E. Baker "compares internet content to Wal-Mart, where mountains of cheap wares that have been produced elsewhere accumulate under one roof" (Baker, quoted in Goss, 2013, p. 73).

McChesney has been "influenced by both celebrants and skeptics but believes each position is ultimately unsatisfactory and puts us on a dead-end street" (2013, p. 4). He argues correctly that we cannot simply split the difference but must center our analysis on more fundamental issues. From the history of ideas perspective, this dualism stifles creativity; it is encumbered by the unresolvable problem of good and evil that underlies it. In sociological terms, the optimism-pessimism framework frequently turns into *ad hominen* arguments without intellectual substance. The case of French sociologist Jacques Ellul is illustrative.

Ellul readers typically complain that he offers no solution, that his fatalism destroys his value as a sociopolitical analyst. Harvey Cox speculates whether Ellul became wounded by the "endless humdrum of the Paris suburbs, the glacial immobility of the French bureaucracy, the traffic of his champs" (Cox, 1973, p. 77). Rupert Hall (1965) attacks Ellul's *Technological Society* relentlessly, declaring, for example, "Ellul lives on black bread and spring water ... The prophet whose cry is only 'Woe, ye are damned' walks unheeded. Ellul is such a prophet ... If he is right, his book is useless" (pp. 126–127).

Such status denigration prevents insightful analysis. Dismissing Ellul as an impoverished pessimist is as irresponsible as calling Ortega y Gasset and Alexis de Tocqueville "aristocrats" and reading no further. Critics use "pessimist" without careful attention to meaning, but pessimism usually connotes a view of life as basically futile and the human capacity for change as nonexistent. Anyone who implies that Ellul sees life as intrinsically self-defeating misunderstands him. As discussed in Chapter 1, Ellul does not express Spengler's dogmatic cultural pessimism nor does he fall within the tradition since Schopenhauer that history is blind will. Crisis and melancholia never function in Ellul as independent motifs rooted in negativism and disillusionment. As with the charge of pessimism generally, it may be dismissed as a lightweight accusation that misjudges Ellul's spirit and objective.

Idea of Progress

Rather than allowing the pessimism-optimism dualism to undermine quality work in international communication ethics, this debilitating framework can be circumvented with an orientation that enables analysis and application. From the philosophy-of-technology perspective, to move forward intellectually the idea of progress that orients the optimist-pessimist dichotomy ought to be replaced by its opposite – cultural continuity.

In terms of frame analysis, both news reports and academic research on new media technologies are conditioned by modernity's idea of progress: "To frame is to select some aspects of a perceived reality and make them more salient in a communicating text, in such a way as to promote a particular problem definition, causal interpretation, moral evaluation, and/or treatment recommendation for the item described" (Entman, 1993, p. 52). The idea of progress fits this description of the new social media technologies.

Since the eighteenth century Enlightenment in which the idea of progress was born, it has meant that advances in science and technology will improve the human condition (Becker, 1932). The news, in principle, is committed to facts, and validity measures guide empirical research; therefore, news is not typically caught up in the excited rhetoric of a technological paradise. Nonetheless, the idea of progress is the preponderate frame for both news reports on, and scientific studies of, the new digital age. Framing involves salience, that is, "making a piece of information more noticeable, meaningful, or memorable to audiences" (Entman, 1993, p. 53). News reports in their headlines give prominence to the new invention or discovery. Reporting frequently depends on the public relations communiqués from the corporation marketing it. Balance in news is an imperative, but critique is typically on the defensive, subservient to the new technology story line.

Zvi Reich (2013) conducted a study of three leading national dailies in Israel over a ten-year period. He interviewed thirty journalists at five-year intervals about the 1,003 news items they published, seeking in detail how they obtained the specifics in these reports. The primary question was the role of the social media in gathering news information. Reich concluded that new digital technologies did not revolutionize news reporting to the extent the rhetoric of revolution assumes. On-the-scene presence, interviews, the telephone, and the review of documents persisted. He labels the journalists "adaptationists" who included the new search engines and electronic data, but as a component of and not a transformation in news reporting: "Findings indicate that reporters tend to conservatism, even when expected to display maximal receptivity to innovation. Empirical findings may invite a new research agenda that insists on including the use of new and old technologies in the same studies to avoid empirical lacunae and innovation bias" (Reich, 2013, p. 428).

By Reich's own analysis, this significant and carefully calibrated study through its "innovation bias" gives credence to and frames research in terms of the idea of progress. Marwan Kraidy (2013) calls this phenomenon the "presentism bias." In the case of Middle East politics, for example, the long efforts at reform are unknown or underappreciated, and the latest fads receive nearly exclusive attention: "The astonishing claims made about the role of Facebook and Twitter in the Arab uprisings do not need rehearsing here . . . It prevents a consideration of the full range of expressive modalities of what I am calling 'creative insurrection'" (p. 286).

In Arnold Pacey's *The Culture of Technology* (1996), "beliefs about progress" are central to comprehending the technological phenomenon (chap. 2, pp. 13–34). Pacey understands the philosophical literature and contends that technological enterprises are created out of cultural values and not invented in neutrality. In Pacey's perspective, what Heidegger calls "civilizational givens" are the birthplace of technological systems.[12] In industrial nations, beliefs about progress are one example of civilizational givens. This "progress presumption" leads us to emphasize hardware: "There is a long history of identifying the overall progress of

---

[12] Pacey uses Raymond Williams's classic *Television: Technology and Cultural Form* to illustrate the argument that technologies arise from a specific sociocultural order: "The idea of television, for example, could hardly have arisen in a society without mass entertainment and organized news media. Thus Williams (1974) has described how radio and television evolved from an urbanized institutional background in which there was a growing need for communications of all kinds" (Pacey, 1996, p. 25).

technology with specific inventions or with other strictly technical advances"; technological progress is "expressed numerically and displayed by means of graphs ... which conceal ambiguities and smooth out irregularities" (Pacey, 1996, pp. 13, 24).

Pacey (1996, p. 28) continues, "One way of rethinking the concept of progress is to take an altogether broader view of the ... various technical, organizational, and cultural workings of technology-practice." When technological systems rather than specific products are understood, there is clearly a human, not a mechanistic process at work. Rethinking involves not simply weighing options, but it means a "decision between different attitudes of mind ... There must be a fundamental shift in the frame of reference we use when thinking about technology and the world in which it is applied ... In the philosophers' jargon, it might be seen as the adoption of a new paradigm" (Pacey, 1996, p. 169).

Cultural Continuity

The philosophy of technology in the tradition of Heidegger is of immediate relevance to the progress issue and directs us to the norm of cultural continuity. With humans understood as cultural beings and with our humanness always situated (*Dasein*), that is, intertwined with the technological process, cultural continuity is in Pacey's terms, "a new paradigm" for guiding technological systems. As it becomes clear in Chapter 1, philosophy views technology as a value-laden process. In philosophy's perspective, valuing permeates all technological activity. Valuing is embedded in the analytic framework that is used to understand technological issues. The processes of design and fabrication are guided by values, as is the user phase. The technological enterprise, in other words, is directed by our ultimate commitments. These value-loading exercises in the various phases of the technological process require standards for judging which norms to value, with cultural continuity recommended as the opposite of the idea-of-progress framework. As Entman (2004) documents, the normative is an important component of frame analysis; substantive frames can convey moral judgments (pp. 5–6) and cultural continuity illustrates it.

To restate this alternative frame in the analytic language of formal criteria: technological operations and products are legitimate if and only if they maintain cultural continuity. Technological systems, to be set in a normative direction, must meet the standard of cultural continuity. The formal criterion stipulates that the viability of historically and geographically constituted peoples is nonnegotiable. Since culture is central ontologically, its unbroken continuity has priority (cf. Christians, 2007a).

For technological activities to concur with cultural continuity as the controlling norm, historical continuity is ineluctable. A static view of continuity without discontinuity represents the ancient doctrines of eternal returns and of cyclical history. Emphasizing continuity contradicts deterministic evolutionary progress that undervalues continuity altogether. Moreover, continuity undercuts the modernization rhetoric of transnational businesses and of colonial governments that strengthen their own preeminence. Oscillation is the appropriate term, that is, a dialectic between continuity and discontinuity, with cultural formation the overall pattern rather than rejection.

Antithetical modes are at work in oscillation – centralization and decentralization, differentiation and integration, large scale and small scale, uniformity and profusion. Oscillation periodically results in breaches with past practices (discontinuity), but such disruptions are made more gradually and in constructive steps when controlled by continuity as the first principle. The formal criterion presumes that the final decisions about discontinuity are made by natives who decide which technological interventions most appropriately serve their local cultures.

The frame of cultural continuity establishes a fundamental realism, in the spirit of Robert Bellah's "symbolic realism" (1970; cf. Wuthnow, 1987, pp. 42–43). Instead of an aura of veneration for the new media technologies, the realism of cultural continuity as a norm enables ruthless analysis. Instead of modernity's cultural imperialism under the guise of social change, the norm of cultural continuity insists on transformations that are indigenous. This nativistic frame of reference obviously does not reject media technologies per se, but it operates in a different paradigm. With cultural continuity the standard, concerns of traditional societies about their cultural integrity are made explicit. Why cannot modern and traditional societies coexist, the formal criterion asks, rather than the former demanding change from the latter, which they consider inferior? The issue is not instrumentalist progress – that is, the rapid development of media tools – but societies living justly as stipulated by the ethics of being advocated in this book.

Summary

This intellectual history of media ethics provides the rationale for an ontological perspective on international media ethics in this revolutionary age. The theory developed in *Media Ethics and Global Justice in the Digital Age* gives us an authoritative voice in agenda setting. It is positioned astutely to free us from the stifling optimism-pessimism dualism. It moves the field beyond instrumentalism and technological minimalism. This communication ethics requires for its ethics equation the comprehensiveness of moral philosophy. For its media equation, it needs to represent the sophistication of the philosophy of technology. This book's ontological perspective makes the digital revolution decisive, but in terms of the cultural continuity frame rather than technological progress. The media ethics of global justice centers the Web 2.0 agenda on truth, human dignity, and nonviolence, and it provides a compelling rationale for concentrating our scholarship on these three principles.

STRUCTURE AND APPROACH

The intellectual strategy for a digital media ethics that is not only international but also cross-cultural, gender inclusive, and ethnically diverse is developed over six chapters in five steps. Getting straight on the technological order is step one. As extensive research has shown (e.g., Thornton & Keith, 2009), the instrumental approach to media technology does not allow us to ask the right questions or confront the critical issues properly. International communication ethics with a new orientation requires that normative claims be based on a humanistic philosophy of technology. The technological character of the industrial world today has become overwhelmingly instrumentalist, preoccupied with means in opposition to ends, and the moral imagination atrophies. The instrumentalist view of technology inherited from Aristotle's *Metaphysics* and *Politics III* must be replaced by a humanocentric one in which the common good rather than machine-like efficiency is central.

The second step is developing the sacredness of life as the supreme universal, a pre-theoretical given or protonorm identified in research in thirteen countries in six languages (Christians, 2010; Cooper & Christians, 2008; Christians & Traber, 1997). A universal theory cannot be an absolutist system requiring uniform conduct defined in Western terms. The Enlightenment's transcendental abstractions are unacceptable for a twenty-first-century ethics. Theories of global media ethics ought to be ontological instead. One theoretical model compatible with human-centered technology is the sacredness of human life as a worldwide protonorm. This is a different kind of universal, one that honors the diversity of human culture while advocating cross-cultural norms.

Third, since we are social beings and practice our professions within economic and political entities, the next step is establishing principles for guiding media practice that are grounded in our common humanity – truth, human dignity, nonviolence. Together these three universal principles yield an ethics of global justice. The centrality of justice in moral philosophy is the overall framework that gives coherence and meaning to public communication as a technical regime. These principles are not metaphysical givens, but propositions about human existence. Rather than being abstract and absolutist, they are historically embedded and can therefore be identified by such research strategies as comparative studies of media systems (e.g., Hanitzsch, 2013; Hanitzsch, Plaisance, & Skewes, 2013; Plaisance, Skewes, & Hanitzsch, 2012). They are normative phenomena within culture and politics. The three principles entailed by the universal sanctity of life highlight the distinctive character of any society and are the basis for distinguishing one human or virtual community from another.

Fourth, the media fulfill their responsibility for a robust public life when their judgments and culture are driven by a duty ethics rooted in universal human solidarity, rather than by the instrumentalism of utilitarian morality. These principles are expressions of humanity's moral order, defined as "a set of intrinsic or deep commitments that are enduring" and "less instrumental" than utilitarian types "of social exchange" (Wuthnow, 1987, p. 345; cf. chaps. 3–5, 7). Empirical research on journalism practice (*Journal of Mass Media Ethics*, special issue, 22–23, 2007) shows unmistakably that the mainstream model of utilitarian ethics no longer accounts for the complicated issues and needs to be replaced by an ethics of *prima facie* duties instead.

Fifth, journalism's mission is centered on a cosmopolitan justice of three properties: truth, human dignity, and nonviolence. Benhabib's Tanner Lecture, "The Philosophical Foundations of Cosmopolitan Norms," establishes a complex framework here, grounded in Kant, Arendt, and Jaspers who "anticipated and intimated the evolution of cosmopolitan norms of justice" (Benhabib, 2006, p. 27). As illustrated in chapter 4, this ethics of universal justice is given its sharpest focus and greatest intensity in the indigenous media of communities around the world rather than those imported from the Global North (Rodriguez, 2001, 2011), what Bennett calls "global activist networks" (2003a, 2003b). Bureaucratized media continue to dominate the news business in industrial democracies, and their organizational culture must be reformed. However, the media ethics of global justice will likely advance most dramatically among the communal and virtual alternatives to the incumbent media. In this perspective, ethical theorizing engages the fundamental conditions of our mode of existence (cf. Christians, 2015b). Thus, the ethics of global justice is ontological; it is a communication ethics of being that takes seriously a human-centered philosophy of technology.

CONCLUSION

Public life in the twenty-first century is undergoing a historic alteration through ubiquitous multimedia technologies, and ethics is essential for coming to grips with them. Language is indispensable to our humanness and to the social order; therefore, when human communication is mediated in fundamentally different forms than before, calculating the impact is a historical and empirical task for media studies as a whole. And clearly the critical reflections of communication ethics are necessary as well. With media technologies and industries being transformed, ethical theory and research require innovation. As Stephen Ward puts it, "Journalism ethics is in the midst of a difficult transition that cannot be adequately addressed by traditional principles and concepts. There is no turning back. We need to reinvent journalism ethics for a new age, from the ground up" (2010b, p. 7). The fundamental question is the nature of technology itself. Our ethical principles must be applied to ICTs, social media, smart phones, and weblogs, not only to newsprint, cable television, and cinema. But our application will be misdirected if the philosophy of technology is absent.

For academic ethics simply to acknowledge the technological revolution leaves important questions unaddressed. Therefore, the theory of international communication ethics presented in this book is rigorous on the issue of technology. Rather than presuming technologies are neutral, or isolating particular media and addressing them one by one, the instrumental perspective on technology is replaced by a substantive, humano-centric view. The media ethics of being that results confronts the right issues and is sustainable as a global media ethics of long-standing credibility. Given the dramatic technological changes in a complicated world, media ethics does not simply need to be updated, but re-theorized. The ontological approach to media ethics and global justice as developed here proposes to accomplish that critical task.

I

The Technological Problem

Instrumentalism and Its Cognates

Global media ethics requires a systemic approach to technology. An appropriate ethics for the digital age cannot simply extrapolate from print or broadcast systems. A decisive shift in media technology has taken place, and today's online media cannot be understood in functional and mechanical terms as electronic artifacts. Since technologies are value laden, fundamental work on the character of media technology as a whole is necessary for the long term. The intellectual challenge is to identify the internal properties of media technologies to know them distinctively as their own (Vallor, 2016; Floridi, 2011, chs. 14–15). Rather than theorizing within professional or interpersonal settings, our interpretive framework needs the same expanse as the worldwide character of cyberspace.

The prevailing worldview in industrial societies is instrumentalism – the idea that technology is neutral and does not condition our humanness. Human values are replaced by the machine's defining feature, efficiency. Moral commitments are preempted by advanced technique. This mechanical model is unacceptable as a framework for approaching the character of the industrial world today. It fosters the technological imperative, whereby the capabilities of media technologies set the agenda and define the issues. A new theory of media ethics needs a human-centered philosophy of technology instead, one that accounts more adequately for the shift at present to anytime-anywhere communication.

Instead of minor adjustments in the instrumental model, we need to reconceive technology itself. Transmission theories of neutral media defend a particular social philosophy, that is, instrumentalism. A perspective on technology is required that differs fundamentally from the instrumentalist tradition. Students of ethics face a predicament in this era of the technological revolution – not just the violation of norms, first of all, but the desolation of normlessness. The philosophy of technology provides us an intellectual perspective for constructing an international media ethics relevant to this crisis.

THE MEDIA ECOLOGY TRADITION

The tradition of communication systems since Harold Innis (1951, 1952) gives technology priority, and its distinctive scholarship helps link media ethics with the digital revolution. Canadian Communication Theory is its typical label, from Innis its founder through Marshall McLuhan, Walter Ong, James Carey, and Neil Postman, until the Media Ecology Association today (Lum, 2006). Instead of "system," Postman insisted on the richer terms "ecosystem" and "ecology":

> You will remember from the time when you first became acquainted with a petri dish, that a medium was defined as a substance within which a culture grows. If you replace the word substance with the word technology, the definition would stand as a fundamental principle of media ecology: A medium is a technology within which a culture grows; that is to say, it gives form to a culture's politics, social organizations, and habitual ways of thinking. (Postman, 2006; quoted in Soukup, 2014, p. 256)

The media ecology framework includes Jacques Ellul's *Propaganda* (1965) and Lewis Mumford's *Technics and Civilization* (1934). This media-systems perspective represents within communication theory a formidable argument. McLuhan, for example, understood television as an electronic visual technology, and he penetrated more deeply to its roots rather than focusing on television content per se. In contrast to superficial transmission views of communication, McLuhan's seeing television as a technological system moves us forward conceptually. He correctly observed that debating about words etched on the side of an H-bomb is irrelevant to the power of the technology itself.

In Christine Nystrom's (2006) definition, media ecology studies the ways in which "our instruments of knowing – our senses and central nervous systems, our technologies of exploration, the physical media they require (like light, sound, electricity), and the conditions under which they are used – construct and reconstruct what we know, and therefore the realities that humans inhabit" (p. 277). The radical idea on which media ecology is founded is "that the reality humans encounter is not what is out there, but the particular version of what is out there"; it is provided by "our instruments of perception, representation, and communication" (p. 277). This concept is so trenchant for our understanding of reality that it has transformed major areas of scientific and humanistic study.

Benjamin Lee Whorf in linguistics and Susanne K. Langer in philosophy oriented this concept to communications and in so doing made symbolization the cornerstone of media ecology.[1] In the first of her major works, *Philosophy in a New Key* (1942), "Langer argued that the 'new key' of her title (that is, the new question at the center of philosophical inquiry) is this: What is the nature of symbolic representation and how does it function, in its various transformations, in the constructive process of human thought and response?" (Nystrom, 2006, p. 289). Symbolization is the concept that explains to us how the human mind works: "The underlying activity of the human mind is the process of abstracting experience and representing it in symbols that evoke conceptions – that is, that call ideas to mind" (Nystrom, 2006, p. 289; cf. Langer, 1967, p. 82).

Symbolic thought sets up a new theory of the arts. To illustrate how theories are symbolic constructs, in *Feeling and Form* (1953) Langer analyzes the symbolic structures and functions of narrative and of painting, sculpture, architecture, music, dance, fiction, drama, and film. The meaning of theoretical statements derives from an interpretive context of symbol, myth, and metaphor that humans themselves produce. Symbolic action as a distinctive feature of the human species comes into its own in our theory making.

---

[1] Nystrom (2006) summarizes the Sapir (1921)–Whorf (1956) hypothesis this way: "Through words we can construct a universe we cannot hear, see, or touch. The reality given by language is fundamentally different from the reality given by sense data" (p. 281). Sapir and Whorf were early media ecologists in arguing that we do not live in an objective world, but in systems of thought and culture that represent experience. For Whorf, "The earliest and most fundamental of these systems of representation is language ... Language is not a neutral container or conveyer of ideas but an instrument of thought that has a distinctive structure of its own, and a different structure in different speech communities. These structures of language are interposed between people and reality, and just as the astronomer's telescope, the biologist's microscope, and the physicist's beam of light bring different realities into view and transform them, so do the different structures of language construct different conceptions of the world. In particular, the structure of every language codifies a metaphysics – a set of assumptions about the nature of space and time, and the relationship among objects and events" (p. 288). "One of the first to recognize the significance of the larger question implied by Whorf's work, and to address it systematically, was Susanne K. Langer" (p. 289).

For the symbolic perspective that characterizes the media ecology tradition, human discourse and culture are fundamental. Language is the public agent through which human existence is realized. In a symbolic approach to communications, human beings are considered able to integrate specific messages within the larger project of cultural formation. When symbols are mediated technologically, the changes in human life and culture must be understood historically and ontologically. Walter Ong (1982) calls this the technologizing of the word. In the communication-as-symbolic perspective, when there is large-scale digital restructuring of the language system, what humans call their reality must be recreated. Symbolic theory presumes that the history of communication is a defining feature of the history of civilization. In the media ecology tradition, social change results from media transformations, with changes in symbolic forms having a profound impact on the structure of consciousness.

Innis's Monopoly of Knowledge

The Canadian scholar Harold Innis illustrates Langer's "philosophy in a new key." He specialized in the various changes in symbolic forms that transform media technologies (Innis, 1951). From the introduction of symbols on papyrus in ancient Egypt's First Dynasty to today's internet, scholars in the Innis tradition examine all significant shifts in media technologies, identifying from them subsequent alterations in culture and perception. Regarding books, radio, television, and Twitter, communication theorists work deeply into their technological character. Innis studied the introduction of parchment, the printing press, radio, and the telegraph – and documented the bias, propensity, or tendency in each of them. Oral communication systems, he argued, are biased toward time; they render time continuous while making space discontinuous. Print systems, by contrast, are biased toward space, unifying geographical space and breaking time into distinct units.

If time stands still in oral cultures and print technology fosters empire and objectivism, the shift to electronic culture begins dislocating us from both geography and history. It ruptures historical consciousness and makes world citizenship mandatory though we are ill equipped to play that role. Without specific anchors in time and space, people are co-opted by mass media images. Large-scale electronic media radically disconnect us from our historical home in oral mediation. Primary groups – family, school, religious assemblies, neighborhoods, and voluntary associations – lose their resonance.[2]

Elizabeth Eisenstein (1979), for example, documents the overriding significance of symbolic formation in her conclusive work on the invention of printing. The printing press reformulates our symbols at a historical watershed, fostering prescriptive truth and decentering papal authority by empowering the home and countryside with vernacular Bibles and Luther's pamphlets. The ninth-century Carolingian and twelfth-century Gothic renascences were limited and transitory. The preservative power of Gutenberg's invention made the Renaissance permanent and total.

As a minor premise, Innis (1952) argued that one form of communication tends to monopolize knowledge and render other forms residual, rather than all media existing innocently alongside one another. As James Carey describes Innis's thinking: "The media of communication are vast social metaphors that not only transmit information but determine what is knowledge, that not only orient us to the world but tell us what kind of world exists" (Carey, 1967, p. 18). Oral culture continued after print became the dominant medium, but the oral-aural mode was no longer the standard of truth or the centerpiece of education and politics (Ong, 1982). In the broadcast era, visual technologies dominated our way of thinking and social structures, leaving print and oral modes of secondary importance. Given the explosive growth of digital technology and our lionizing it, cyberspace tends to monopolize our political-economic-educational institutions now. In Carey's terms, "For all the vaunted capacity of the computer to store, process, and make available information in densities and quantities heretofore unknown, the pervasive tendency to monopolize knowledge in the professions and data banks continues unabated" (1997a, p. 37). A credible theory of media ethics in the digital age must account for this monopoly-of-knowledge phenomenon.

Marshall McLuhan (1911–1980) was Innis's successor at the University of Toronto. For McLuhan, technologies are extensions of

---

[2] M. Rex Miller (2004) researches social change by understanding the major mutations in communication technology throughout history. He studies the revolutions that occurred in the dominant medium of communications, the shift from oral communication to print media in the fifteenth century, and the shift to broadcasting in the twentieth. His *Millennium Matrix* sees these shifts as a fundamental change in a society's worldview, enabling him to describe the basic features of the digital world that technological societies are now entering.

the human being – radio of the ear, photography of the eye, the wheel extending the foot (McLuhan, 1964).[3] Debates over media content, such as sex and violence, miss the point. The medium transforms human life more than its programs do. Profound psychological changes occur from changes in the medium. For example, we think in linear patterns with print and grasp the whole visually with electronic media such as television. For McLuhan, television is cool and print is hot – "hot" referring to media that are rich in information and require little involvement from users. Radio magnifies and standardizes human speech, reducing the amount of interpretation needed to understand it. Television, on the other hand, is a low-resolution technology requiring viewers' mental involvement.

Innis was broadly sociological and historical, but McLuhan was intensely psychological in orientation.[4] McLuhan's notions about visual closure, the sensorium, and simultaneity were formulated in narrowly psychological terms. His argument that television as a cool medium is a revolutionary force for global bonding presumes a host of psychological claims about perception, mental processing of images, tactility, and the nervous system.[5]

Since the media are social institutions, Innis's trajectory is more directly relevant in constructing a new theory of media ethics. However, McLuhan's global imaginary is of permanent value also. Already in the Counter-Enlightenment of Neapolitan philosopher Giambattista Vico (1725/1948), humanist scholars began seeing the universe whole rather than building it incrementally piece by piece. This holistic imagination is crucial for making the new theory distinct from universals in the Descartes-Kant tradition of linear rationality.[6]

---

[3] McLuhan's thinking was influenced by the Jesuit philosopher Pierre Teilhard de Chardin, who argued that the use of electricity extends the central nervous system. De Chardin was McLuhan's source of insight for his theories of global electronic culture in *The Gutenberg Galaxy* (1962); through his influence, McLuhan sometimes assumed that electronic civilization was a spiritual leap forward.

[4] McLuhan was Walter Ong's master's thesis advisor. Ong's (1976, 1977) emphasis on the state of consciousness and mediation is psychological rather than sociological.

[5] For the classic essay regarding McLuhan's psychological orientation, see James W. Carey (1967), "Harold Adams Innis and Marshall McLuhan," *Antioch Review*, 6(71), 5–31.

[6] Descartes (1638) described this method of reasoning in his *Rules for the Direction of Mind*: "Reduce complex and obscure propositions step-by-step to simpler ones, and then try to advance by the same gradual process from the ... very simplest to the knowledge of all the rest. We should not examine what follows but refrain from a useless task" (pp. 163, 172).

Carey's Transmission and Ritual

True to the environmental metaphor, media ecology "looks at the entirety of whatever technological system it considers ... Media ecology does not consider communication as a single variable; rather, it regards communication as embedded into a larger system" (Soukup, 2014, p. 265). James Carey gives special deference to Harold Innis, but he advances media ecology's "big picture" idea more dramatically than Innis does. Carey understood "the systemic and interrelated nature of human tools, language, culture, and communication patterns" (Soukup, 2014, p. 265). In Carey's terms, media ecologists examine "the actual social process in which significant symbolic forms are created, apprehended, and used" (Carey, 1989, p. 30). His book of essays, *Communication as Culture*, develops ecological embedding with literary finesse.

Carey's interest in the telegraph is illustrative (1989, pp. 155–177). To analyze the era of broadcast communication, he does not begin with radio or television but establishes its history in telegraph technology. The telegraph distributed "information everywhere, simultaneously reducing the economic advantage of the city and bringing the more varied urban culture out to the countryside. No longer would people need to be physically present in the city to partake of the advantages of art, commerce, and intellect that physical massing created" (Carey, 1997e, p. 45). Moreover, telegraph technology made time zones feasible, and precise times across the nation could be standardized: "When the railroad and telegraph had linked every town and clock, a national system of communications, regular and periodical, was possible for the first time. On the backbone of that system, a national community of politics and commerce could be constructed" (Carey, 1997b, p. 322). In addition, "The telegraph gave a real rather than an illusory meaning to timeliness. It turned competition among newspapers away from price, even away from quality, and onto timeliness. Time became the loss leader of journalism" (Carey, 1997d, p. 160).

The telegraph is also an electronic turning point for Carey because it altered the nature of written language, and in its wake human awareness was transformed: "The wire services demanded language stripped of the local, the regional, and the colloquial. They insisted on something closer to a 'scientific' language, one of strict demonstration where the connotative features of utterance were under the control of fact" (Carey, 1997d, p. 160). For stories to be understood in Sacramento, California, and Bangor, Maine, language could not be thick or ambiguous. According to

Carey (1997d, p. 160), "The telegraph, therefore, led to the disappearance of forms of speech and styles of journalism and storytelling – the tall story, the hoax, much humor, irony and satire – that depended on a more traditional use of language. The origins of objectivity, then, lie in the necessity of stretching language in space over the long lines of Western Union." Detail and analysis became luxuries for journalism: "The sparseness of the prose and its sheer volume allowed news, indeed forced news, to be treated like a commodity: something that could be transported, measured, reduced, and timed. Telegraphic journalism divorced news from an ideological context that could explain and give significance to events" (Carey, 1997d, p. 161).

Carey is typically credited with founding the cultural approach to communication studies in North America.[7] In John Peters's (1993) typology, Carey (1989) represents one of three trajectories in the history of mass communication research. His achievement for media ecology is to bring its technological emphasis into what Robert Craig (1999, pp. 144–146) calls the sociocultural tradition. For Carey, the global mass media are agents of acculturation, and to the degree we understand culture we know communication as well. Cultures produce meanings "by embodying and acting out the claim that symbols have on us"; culture "creates forms of social relations into which people enter as opposed to the processes occurring within these forms" (1997b, p. 314).

From this perspective, media technologies are not tools or products per se, but cultural practices. Technology is a distinct cultural enterprise in which humans form and transform natural reality aided by tools and processes for practical ends. The communication enterprise is technological in character, requiring our analysis of cyberspace to go beyond messages and take hold of the mediated form in which the content is structured.

To distinguish his media ecology perspective from mainstream empiricism, Carey (1989, pp. 14–23) opposed transmission and ritual views of communication. Transmission is the standard model, defined by the transportation of signals over space. In the ritual view, communication is the process of constructing and maintaining a meaningful human world:

---

[7] Raymond Williams – with whom Carey corresponded about issues and recommended readings – founded cultural studies in Europe at the same time. Williams's early books, *Culture and Society* (1958) and *The Long Revolution* (1961) were influential in establishing the field. His *Television: Technology and Cultural Form* (1974), written while a visiting professor at Stanford, specifies his approach as cultural materialism (cf. 2005).

"A ritual view of communication is directed not toward the extension of messages in space, but toward the maintenance of society in time; not the act of imparting information, but the representation of shared beliefs." Ritual gives importance to communication as a process of constructing and maintaining "an ordered, meaningful, cultural world that can serve as a container for human action" (Carey, 1989, p. 18).

Carey rejected the transmission view of communication because it shelters scientistic and positivistic definitions of knowledge (Grossberg, 2010, p. 79): "Positivism reduced the ethical parameters of human life itself ... Carey's commitment to culture is a commitment to a concept and a vocabulary that can ground an ethical, democratic, and civic vision" of human existence (Grossberg, 2010, p. 83). In rejecting transmission approaches to communication for their sterility, cultural studies scholars in Carey's media ecology trajectory are driven by moral concerns about what they consider to be their richer, historically profound, and deeper agenda. In its various formations, media ecology shares a common aspiration: "[t]o confront the injustice of a particular society or sphere within that society ... thus becom[ing] a transformative endeavor unembarrassed by the label 'political'" (Kincheloe & McLaren, 2000, p. 140). Carey's transmission/ritual distinction points to the dichotomy in the philosophy of technology developed in this chapter. In the transmission view, communication technologies are neutral. They are independent tools, entities apart from values. In Carey's ritual paradigm, the ontological (humans as cultural beings), the technological phenomenon, interpretive research, and a new global ethics become a systemic whole.

Ellul's International Perspective

Jacques Ellul enriches the analytic power of the media ecology tradition through his theoretical concepts, *la technique* and propaganda. Marshall McLuhan is incorporated into the conceptual framework of *The Humiliation of the Word* (1985). Ellul's conclusions resemble those of Neil Postman's *Amusing Ourselves to Death* (1985). His technical artifice resonates with Harold Innis's empire and monopoly of knowledge. But Ellul's distinctive contribution is to tighten the media ecology tradition around international politics. Political institutions and governance animate Innis's *Empire and Communication,* but largely in North American terms. James Carey's commitment to public life is anchored in John Dewey's preoccupation with the American experience. McLuhan's global village is decisively international in scope but unrelated to political theory. Postman's concerns focus primarily on education. In Ellul, communication systems are radically international. He demonstrates for media ecology how to understand the structure of industrial societies in terms of the developing world.[8]

For more than three decades (1947–1980), Ellul was a professor in the Institute of Political Studies at the University of Bordeaux, specializing in technology and propaganda, the history of political institutions, and Roman law (e.g., 1951–1952; 1953, 1956, 1966). Ellul's assessment of political involvement becomes integrated with his historical and theoretical analysis of social institutions, leading him to a distinctive conclusion about the global media as a technological domain within political regimes.[9]

Ellul identifies electronic media systems as covert propaganda. One form of this covert category is "sociological propaganda," Ellul's term for the technical mediation of a society's values. Rather than defining propaganda as biased acts of persuasion, he redefines it as a composite of pervasive methods that organizes life in technologically advanced societies and that intensifies as developing nations become more industrialized.

In *Propaganda, Humiliation of the Word*, and *The Technological Bluff*, Ellul constructs his media ecology perspective in terms of *la technique*. *La technique* is for him the mystique of machineness behind machines, an internal efficient ordering that saturates human values, culture, and institutions. Like a dolphin's adaptation to its saltwater environment, we are enveloped in data, absorbed into a one-dimensional world of shibboleths and dicta. The varying dynamics of the "social, political, moral" and religious domains are mediatized into homogeneous data (Ellul, 1965, p. 163). ICTs, as covert propaganda, have become so powerful, Ellul contends, that congruity with the status

---

[8] Ellul's work is not immune to criticism. His analysis of media technology tends to be reductionist, tracing all issues to the fundamental problem of *la technique*. His weaknesses in detail and with subunits are obvious, and I have shared in articulating such criticisms. He is attractive to media ecology since his wide-ranging work interconnects media systems with the philosophy of technology as a whole and with social, political, and cultural systems. But periodically in his fifty-nine books, he overreaches and pontificates, rather than paying rigorous attention to the literature, authorities, topics, methods, and vocabulary of his academic specialties – the history of institutions and law (Steiner & Rappleye, 1988, calling him the "quirky trailblazer").

[9] In his comprehensive scholarship on persuasion in today's "globally interconnected, mass-mediated society," Randal Marlin (2013, p. 1) depends on Ellul's *Propagandes* (1962) as his definitive source (pp. 22–30), integrating it (pp. 14–21) with George Orwell's *Nineteen Eighty-Four* (1949) and inflecting both toward Noam Chomsky's *Chronicles of Dissent* (1992).

quo becomes the ideal; alternatives to the technicized worldview are dismissed as ideologies or "just propaganda": "The mass media provide heroes for the impotent, friends for the alienated, and simplified attitudes for the uncertain" (Christians, 1995a, p. 161; cf. p. 159). The people's own voice and identity are replaced by a machinic mind-set. Prevailing digital patterns become in Innis's terms, "the monopoly of knowledge."

Similar in analytic style to Carey's introducing the broadcast era through telegraph technology, Ellul's *The Technological Bluff* examines computer hardware and processes as an entrée to the new mediated order. Though written before the World Wide Web was established, Ellul's media ecology perspective in *The Humiliation of the Word* demonstrates how computerized technologies are embedded in culture, society, and politics:

> The computer and other information devices enter an existing social order ... Inevitably, information systems will become concentrated and centralized ... Social privilege will flow even more than now to the big administrators, intellectuals, and pressure groups, whoever has the resources to get pertinent information. Secrecy as to what goes into data banks will also be favored. (Ellul, 1985; quoted in Marlin, 2013, p. 312)

According to Marlin (2013, p. 312), "Ellul's prediction about the difficulty of getting new technology to support grassroots democracy against established commercial interests seems to be verified by contemporary developments." Ellul insists that we ask whether propaganda is actually made easier through the internet in light of the fact that counter-cultures with new thinking outside the status quo continue to be doomed to the margins (Marlin, 2013, p. 316). In Ellul's radical framework, modern pervasive means of communication are not instruments of information through which citizens guide their public life. The Web 2.0 is not a network of artificial messages, but through it the human symbolic system is absorbed into an efficiency-dominated culture.

Summary

The first intellectual challenge from media ecology is to identify digital technology's distinctive features as a communication system. Every medium has its own structure and grammatical constituents that enable it to communicate. As a biologist examines the biomolecules of cells to understand them from within, so the media ecologist looks into the technological properties of the online revolution to know its peculiarities. We need for digital technology a composite of concepts geared to the electromagnetic spectrum. With ICTs, we confront particular vibrations of sound and images of light that fade away and subsist unevenly. Print and broadcast modes become secondary when our basis of knowing is multisensory, multimedia, and multi-networked. Humans participate in the digital global experience as the facilitators and weavers of networks.[10]

When theorizing communication ethics in the digital age, media ecology research and theory verify that accentuating technology is the right approach. Media ecology makes intellectual demands on a theory of international communication ethics, insisting on a conceptual sophistication that deals with empire, space-time dynamics, a world vision, ritual, and sociological propaganda. And consistent with its holistic mentality, media ecology recognizes that mediated technology is a subsystem of the technological phenomenon. The technological context as a whole is the overall framework within which a new international theory of media ethics is intellectually credible and relevant to professional practice.

INSTRUMENTALISM

In his internationalizing of media ecology, Ellul developed the argument that the technological phenomenon is decisive in defining the culture of industrialized nations. In his *Propaganda,* communications media symbolize the world of meaning in the technological system at large. As an agent of sociological propaganda, the news and entertainment media provide a rationale for human existence. Analogous to the protruding tip of the iceberg, media technologies are the public edge of the technological order. Communication systems exhibit the structural elements of all technical systems, but with the added feature that as symbolic enterprises they represent technological dynamics explicitly. In their embodying the character of technological systems, ICTs serve as the agent for interpreting the very phenomenon they actualize. Jacques Ellul calls our communication systems the "innermost, and most elusive, manifestation" of human technological activity (1965, p. 216). In other words, all technological artifacts communicate meaning, but media instruments do so

---

[10] Since media ecology research and theory identify properties of the new media technologies – seeing them as a system and not an inchoate mass of products – media ecology answers Zvi Reich's (2013) concern: "Some technology studies are too broad (trying to encompass the impact of every possible technology on every stage and actor), or too narrow (focusing on a small subset of technologies, sometimes even on a single one to capture the realities of news reporting)" (p. 418).

preeminently. Thus, as digital technologies represent reality for us and speak to our self-identity, they do so with a technological rhythm (Ellul, 1965).

Although the worldwide surge in communication tools is increasingly at the forefront of our work on media ethics, mechanics and networks are not the crisis by themselves. Instead of focusing piecemeal on information hardware and software, media systems must be researched and analyzed as symbolic systems in their institutional, historical, and cultural contexts. The philosophy of technology is indispensable for this complicated task. Intellectual work on the character of technology is necessary for the issues in global media ethics to be clarified competently.

When media ecology is taken seriously and we investigate the nature of technology itself, instrumentalism becomes the primary issue. Industrial societies are dominated by instrumentalism – the view that technology is neutral and unfolds out of its own character. If humans are thought to control inert technologies for whatever purposes they choose, technological products are analyzed erroneously in mechanistic terms. A major contribution of the philosophy of technology is its critique of neutrality, the view that characterizes the prevailing analysis of technological regimes.

Aristotle's Legacy

Aristotle originated the concept of technology as instrumental means, and Hood summarizes Aristotle this way: "Technology is a human arrangement of technics – tools, machines, instruments, and materials – to serve human ends" (1972, p. 347). Technology is not an end in itself, but a neutral instrument controlled by actors outside of itself. Squirrels or trees grow according to their natural form, whereas through technics, we construct a plastic ball from minerals in whatever form we arbitrarily choose. Technology as products and as system is a domain alongside people and society. It does not advance by self-augmentation, but as directed by its creators. The meaning of technological products is not innate to itself but found in the purposes humans impose, even as, in Aristotle's terms, "the end of the medical art is health, that of shipbuilding a vessel, that of strategy victory, that of economics wealth" (*Nicomachean Ethics* I.1, 1094a5-10; cf. *Metaphysics* I.1, 981b1-15; also *Politics* 3.9, 1208a32).[11] Artistic materials are for enjoyment, and scientific tools in

---

[11] Aristotle, at the end of *The Nicomachean Ethics* (X.9, 1179b-1181b), argued that politics necessarily follows his inquiry into ethics.

oceanography increase human knowledge. But in all cases, technical products are justified and critiqued by the uses to which society puts them (cf. *Nicomachean Ethics* I.1, 1094a5-10). Technology is an elementary human activity. Through philosophy, humans contemplate the inherent order of things. The human species is distinctive because it alone can reason; therefore, philosophy is preeminent. Technology is secondary to human wisdom; it is subordinate to intellectual activities through which people understand themselves and organize society (cf. *Nicomachean Ethics* X.6, 1177a 20-21).

Aristotle's view assumes a dualism of subject and object. In this tradition, ethics has the reduced role of articulating ends; morality directs technology to appropriate purposes. In Aristotle's corpus, technology is neutral. Technologies are seen as artifacts that can be used positively or negatively, as artifacts of science apart from values. Politicians and consumers use bad judgment. Technology is not at fault, but the uses to which we put tools and networks are culpable. Technological products are independent, used to support completely different cultures and lifestyles (Pacey, 1996, chap. 1). Websites can give us the lives and history of heroes or the hate speech of a fundamentalist sect. Online games are both pornographic and educational. If a computer database controls both the Singapore International Airport and communication within ISIS, technology is an instrument to implement the values of oppositional communities. ICTs can be used in schools rather than for political propaganda.

In instrumentalism, "technology is deemed 'neutral' without any valuative content of its own. Technology, as pure instrumentality, is indifferent to the variety of ends it can be employed to achieve … A hammer is a hammer, a steam turbine is a steam turbine, and such tools are useful in any social context" (Feenberg, 1991, pp. 5–6). Like scientific concepts, technologies have a similar status in every setting: "What works in one society can be expected to work just as well in another. Technologies are neutral because they stand essentially under the same norm of efficiency in any and every context … Public policy analysis worries about the costs and consequences of automation and environmental pollution. Instrumentalism provides the framework for such research" (Feenberg, 1991, pp. 6–7).

The idea of neutrality appears to be self-evident, and instrumentalism is common to the social sciences in general and to media studies specifically. The legacy of tools as neutral is an affirmative model for technological growth. Communication theorists and mainstream engineers have embraced Aristotle's instrumentalist tradition. For Norbert Wiener

(1948, 1954), the inventor of cybernetics, engineers should be driven by efficiency in the laboratory; politicians can consider technology's impact later. Shannon and Weaver's *Mathematical Theory of Communication* (1949) is explicitly instrumentalist. It provides a theoretical basis for inventing media technologies, advancing their engineering capacity sixty thousand bits per second in telephone wires to more than one hundred billion bits per second in light-based fiber optics.[12] In R. Buckminster Fuller's synergetics, data ought to be directed in complementary patterns that follow the harmony of nature, rather than the blockages and contradictions of political ideology (Fuller, 1975, 1981). Fuller (1963) is euphoric about synergetics and democracy:

> I see god in the instruments and mechanisms that work reliably, more reliably than the limited sensory departments of the human mechanism . . . Devise a mechanical means for voting daily and secretly by each adult citizen of Uncle Sam's family; then – I assure you – will democracy be saved, indeed exist, for the first time in human history. This is a simple mechanical problem. (pp. 4, 18)

Ithiel de Sola Poole's influential *Technologies of Freedom* (1984) defends technological systems that are free of political control and envisions what we now call "cyberspace." Nicholas Negroponte, the founding director of MIT's Media Lab, wrote *Being Digital* (1996) in the instrumentalist tradition and it became a best seller. Henry Jenkins, formerly of MIT's Comparative Media Studies Program, promotes an engineering approach to media technologies in books such as *Convergence Culture: Where Old and New Media Collide* (2006; cf. Jenkins, Ford, & Green, 2013). Likewise Beekman and Beekman reflect instrumentalism in their long-standing series *Digital Planet: Tomorrow's Technology and You* (2013). On the presumption of neutrality, old and new media systems are understood as instrumentalist. Governments design a global system using the principle of efficiency, and businesses compete for profits following efficiency's dynamics. To summarize using Arnold Pacey (1996), the technical aspect of technology is of obvious importance, but accounting for it adequately is fundamentally different from the ideology of technicism.

Critique

A social history of technology identifies the productivity of Aristotle's instrumental model for the premodern age, but that history does not make

---

[12] Floridi (2014) considers Claude Shannon "the father of information theory" (p. 221).

it applicable today. Since the 1890s in industrial societies, technological development has multiplied so rapidly that setting limits and proper direction has little resonance. Technology's complexity and dominance require more than the neutral approach "where we are abandoned to a haphazard scattering of goods and evils, of productive and destructive tendencies, and the structure of technology escapes us" (Hood, 1972, p. 352). In fact, given the intricacies of twenty-first-century technology, social impact can rarely be calculated anymore. Sophisticated technologies that meet a basic human need in one context are often counterproductive overall and in the long term.

The philosophy-of-technology literature develops an important critique of neutral instrumentalism. Accepting the neutrality view uncritically leaves cardinal matters of morality unaddressed. Neutrality presumes that responsibility will occur automatically where it is necessary, when a review of the instrumentalist tradition indicates otherwise. Instrumentalism replaces the ethics of justice with a utilitarian calculus of probabilities and risk aversion. In developing a global media ethics that is credible, the inadequacies of the instrumentalist definition of technology can be summarized in three categories:

(1). Engineers and scientists are excluded from responsibility. Instrumentalism allows them to be experts at engineering but with tunnel vision. It permits them to reduce their perspective to "value-free technical rationality" (Pacey, 1996, p. 166). They need not worry about results. The engineers working on animation in Disney and product development for Apple and software for Tencent ought not be questioned. Under this view, if Facebook is used to ridicule people instead of building friendships, if websites are excessively pornographic, if computer equipment is not biodegradable, and surveillance is out of control, the persons who created these technological products should not be blamed. Responsibility rests with politicians for ineffective regulation, with advertisers for grandiose promotions, and with individual consumers for their unthinking use of them. However, instead of excusing engineers and inventors, our theories of media ethics ought to be sophisticated enough to ensure that everyone involved is accountable in their areas of responsibility.

(2). The philosophy of technology from Aristotle to Wiener to MIT's Media Lab promotes what Pacey calls "virtuosity values" (1996, pp. 87–96). This tradition channels scientific expertise and financial resources into high-end technology, into multiplying the power and speed of tools. In instrumentalism, the muscular values of engineering are unchallenged. But we need a definition of technology in which technical values are made secondary to such user values as maintenance, dependability, and disposability. Feenberg's classic *Critical Theory of Technology* (1991) and his *Transforming Technology* (2002) argue persuasively that when technology is considered a neutral tool, social change is pushed to the margins. In other words, the arguments for justice cannot be discussed rationally in a technocratic culture. Justice is basic to the social order and fundamental to the global media ethics developed in this book. But even elementary views of justice-as-fairness have been emaciated by the crises of contemporary life. Justice-as-fairness is unable to establish criteria for inequality, to determine what kinds of inequalities beyond income matter, and how far inequalities should be allowed. In technological nations such as the United States when developing health care networks and policies, the basic justice of including everyone in distribution has not been self-evident but ignored or considered debatable.

(3). An instrumental definition of technology seeks to solve problems by the technical fix. Social improvements are thought to depend on mechanical means and technological products. Improving professions requires better tools. Computer systems that fly drones are said to enhance national security and public safety. Smart phones are marketed as making family life more satisfying. Computers are put in schools rather than insisting on structural reforms, such as smaller classes, and more and better-trained teachers.

In the 1960s, a theory of international communication developed that illustrates the technical-fix issue. Modernization theory established itself within the geopolitical trend toward development. The central question is a mechanical one: how can the media advance modernity, that is, from undeveloped to developed, from Third World to First, from South to North? National development became the overarching framework, and modernization theory the scholarly presumption. Modernization measured success in terms of gross national product; therefore, development was considered achievable for primitive societies that followed the industrial patterns of North America and Europe.

Daniel Lerner, Wilbur Schramm, and later Everett Rogers were the major proponents. Their books – *The Passing of Traditional Society* (Lerner), *Mass Media and National Development* (Schramm), and

Diffusion of Innovations (Rogers) – took for granted the fact-value dichotomy of mainstream empiricism. This dualism allowed the three theorists to do their research and analysis as though media technologies were an independent variable.[13]

The triumvirate's modernization model understood the structures and practices of media systems in instrumentalist terms:

> Their commitment to the mechanisms of quantitative methodology made them unaware of the fact that their model generated a cycle of dependency – on technology, on expertise, and on media content. The model's focus on behavioral effects obscured its commitment to commercialism. In adhering to a monolithic mathematics of empiricism, particularly with Rogers' diffusion-of-innovation strategy, the top-down hierarchical development process was not clearly understood. As true of the fact-value dichotomy as a whole, ethical issues emerged by default, along the margins or outside the paradigm, and after instrumentalist thinking had established the agenda.[14] (Christians, 2014b, p. 238)

If we presume that we only need to eliminate defective parts, or balance political and economic disproportions, or fill visible gaps, we will pursue these reforms, rather than seriously engage instrumentalism as a primary

---

[13] Daniel Lerner's (1958) research included Iran, Lebanon, Turkey, Syria, Jordan, and Egypt. He presented a theory of social transformation for poor countries, where this transformation depended on the modernism of the West: its technology, political structures, systems of mass communication, and values. In Lerner's model, urbanization led to the growth of the mass media (as people demanded news and information), which in turn resulted in greater public participation in economic activity and politics" (Christians, 2014b, p. 238). Wilbur Schramm (1964) depended on Lerner's *The Passing of Traditional Society* (1964) and on W. W. Rostow's *Stages of Economic Growth: An Anti-Communist Manifesto,* and in the process Schramm helped legitimize the mass media as a field of study in its own right. Published with UNESCO support, Schramm opened a pathway for a prodigious amount of research into the relationship between communication technologies and socioeconomic development. Everett Rogers (2003) divided the adopters of new technologies into "five categories and organized them through the mathematics of the Bell curve. In the diffusion process, the rate of adoption was said to follow the mean of a normal S curve from innovators and early adopters to laggards who adopt late or not at all. While the limitations of the modernization paradigm have been exposed, the diffusion of innovation strategy did offer practical solutions – for example, for agriculture and health and nutrition – that required scientific information for personal choice and practice" (Christians, 2014b, pp. 238–239).

[14] Their work actually represented a crucial juncture in the history of media theory. For the first time, and fulfilling Schramm's lifelong quest, media systems were considered an independent variable. Rather than seeing communications phenomena as derivative of the social sciences, media institutions and technologies were now independent entities, to be understood on their own terms.

cultural value of the digital age. Technology removes humankind's ancient constraints, but it does not liberate us to pursue the common good. Coming to grips with the technological civilization is the starting point of change.

Conclusion

The new electronic media exacerbate the issue of responsibility. ICTs amplify, store, and distribute information, as do books and television. But ICTs specialize in the processing and connecting of global information, making the news media susceptible to instrumentalism:

> As technology advances from mere use of tools to the employment of machines and then to the implementation of complex technical systems, technology depends more and more on its own mediating capacities, since technicization introduces greater complexity into the human realm of action and perception. In other words, the technologically created sphere requires increasingly technical mediation for its own operations. This is the birth of homeostatic machines, cybernetic systems, control technology, and user interfaces. In the technical-scientific world, the focus of technology changes from merely controlling the forces of nature to controlling increasingly untransparent technologies and compensating for their unintended and unforeseen consequences. (Debatin, 2008, p. 258)

The average end user is reduced to participating in a largely predetermined system through an electronic interface.

Jean Baudrillard puts this ICT-morality issue in macroscopic terms. His *Simulations* (1983) describes instrumentalism as simulacra, and that concept, by definition, makes the idea of responsibility invalid.[15] For Baudrillard, the monumental growth of networked technologies has shifted modern civilization from production to reproduction. Instead of a modernity governed by economic and political institutions, hyperreality is the cultural construction. Cybernetic models have been created in algorithmic terms to organize our experience, but, for Baudriallard, a reversal has occurred and what people consider reality has arisen from the cybernetic apparatus. In different terms, the coded networks, the hyperreal, implode and situate themselves as reality. The distinction between reality and image in history becomes irrelevant, and the

---

[15] Baudrillard's simulacra and Ellul's sociological propaganda are basically similar in orientation. However, Ellul is more systematic in integrating the mass media into the technological order. He considers media systems to be the semantic edge of the technical artifice.

discriminations in the conceptual world dependent on signified and signifier disappear – fact and fiction, center and periphery, news and drama, information and propaganda. The codified becomes definitive (Baudrillard, 2012). DNA models and the human genome project are simulations that become our understanding of the human. With the self a networked module, the simulacra are devoid of accountability and responsibility.[16]

The neutral model is the instrumentalist mind at work. Instead of looking for technical improvements to the instrumentalist framework, the philosophy of technology instructs us to reconceive of technology itself. Transmission theories of neutral media are grounded in an instrumentalist worldview, and that value system needs to be revolutionized. The epistemology of the neutral view is in error. The instrumentalist phenomenon ought to be called into question, not just some of its features redesigned. An authoritative international media ethics for the twenty-first century requires a radically different approach to technology. In Rafael Capurro's critical-Heideggerian perspective, hermeneutics and moral philosophy open for us the cyberworld within the "existential world of human beings" (2010).

HUMAN-CENTERED PHILOSOPHY OF TECHNOLOGY

An alternative philosophy of technology orients international media ethics in the right direction. Global media technology is not just a world of technological artifacts. The problem is the dominance of technical modes of thought over the human orders of politics, ethics, and culture. Philosophers of technology worry about a debilitating loss of morality through instrumentalism. Rather than be content with critique only, and live with the traditional dualism of means and ends, the instrumentalist worldview needs to be challenged at its roots. By examining technology philosophically, Martin Heidegger (1977b) discredits the instrumentalist paradigm.[17]

---

[16] "Baudrillard (2012/1987) appears to have been one of the first to recognize the importance and sophistication of the then emergent concept of global technological networking ... While his attention is clearly on network, he theorizes the end of the individual in this context. The self becomes a postmodern grotesque, a mutated human/technology network assembly" (Kien, 2009, p. 29).

[17] Carl Mitcham's intellectual history identifies these two traditions in the history of the philosophy of technology. The mechanical philosophy of engineering is placed in tension with the humanities philosophy of Mumford, Heidegger, and Ellul (1994, chaps. 1–5). Feenberg labels these philosophies of technology instrumentalist and substantive (1991, pp. 5–13).

Heidegger's Dasein

Martin Heidegger (1889–1976) articulates technological practice in the industrial world to its classical Greek origins.[18] In his view, technology's modern manifestations are a culmination of the traditional dualism of means and ends on which Aristotle's understanding of technics is based. For Heidegger, technology is the primary mode of human existence in industrial societies, and therefore the central arena for coming to grips intellectually with the sociopolitical order. To establish a systematic critique, technology must be understood in disparate terms.[19]

From his early classic *Being and Time* in 1927 through his late *What Is Called Thinking?* (1951–1952) and *The Principle of Reason* (1955–1956), the focus of his philosophical inquiry was a theory of Being (cf. Philipse, 1998, pp. 389–543). Heidegger was a junior colleague of Husserl and later his faculty successor at the University of Freiburg; he advocated a phenomenological method to pursue his existentialist agenda.[20] In contrast to the instrumentalist tradition, technology for Heidegger is an ontological issue. Humans do not live outside technology as instrumentalism presumes, but technology is interwoven with human existence. The foundations of the technological enterprise are rooted in human life. The meaning of technology

---

[18] For an earlier statement of Heidegger's theory of technology, without reference to dwelling or *Tao*, see Christians (1997, pp. 68–74; footnotes 2, 4, pp. 79–80). For a summary of this section, see "Martin Heidegger's Existentialism" (Christians, 2014c, pp. 523–525).

[19] See Christians, 1997, pp. 79–80. Heidegger was committed to German National Socialism prior to and during World War II (cf. Lyotard, 1990; Wolin, 1993). As rector of the University of Freiburg in 1933–1934 and as a prominent educator during the war years, he refused to condemn Nazism and offered no apology before his death in 1976 at age 87. While recognizing the importance of his philosophical project as described in this chapter, Otto Pöggler's question is unavoidable: "How do we come to terms with the fact that perhaps the greatest philosopher of the twentieth century was a Fascist?" (Fry, 1993, p. 16). The debate centers on Heidegger's phrase in 1935, "the truth and greatness of the National Socialist movement," *Introduction to Metaphysics*, p. 152; see translator's "Introduction," pp. xv–xvii. No defensible explanation exists, though Rockmore (1995, pp. 128–144) at least provides one intellectually plausible account: Heidegger's transpersonal conception of Being differs radically from the democratic subject and therefore tolerates within itself an anti-democratic politics. Heidegger's most famous students were Jean Paul Sartre, Georg Gadamer, and Hannah Arendt. The smaller-scale controversy over his four-year affair with Arendt has also complicated his philosophical stature (cf. Ettinger, 1995).

[20] The phenomenological method for approaching technology is developed in detail by Ihde (1983); see especially chap. 8, "Phenomenology and the Later Heidegger," and chap. 3, "The Technological Embodiment of Media."

becomes known to us through the way it operates within human society.[21]

In his existentialism, Heidegger (1962a) calls human Being *Dasein* (literally "therebeing"), to indicate that the social context distinguishes people from all other entities. Human beingness is not a static substance, but a phenomenon of its location in history (Heidegger, 1953/2000, chap. 2). The technological era does not exist alongside of or external to human beings but is their home. The technological enterprise is not merely the application of science, but a cultural construction. Our humanness is understood most decisively through the technological phenomenon. Technology is not mere means or products, but a mode of revealing humanness.

Instead of *homo faber* (humans as tool makers to meet basic needs such as food and shelter), technological activity for Heidegger is our attempt to overpower death. Our active relation to the world is motivated by human concern (*Sorge*); this lies at the heart of technological consciousness. Heidegger's Being is defined by mortality: "We now call mortals mortals – not because their earthly life comes to an end, but because they are capable of death as death ... Rational living beings must first become mortals" (Heidegger, 1971b, p. 179). As Fry has noted, "Being can only presence itself through death" (1993, p. 88).

Humans as living beings exist within a historical and sociological framework. Technologies are not individual inventions but take shape within assumptions about the world. In the contemporary age, technologies are created under conditions of scientific and commercial prowess, rationalism, and secularism. Our life-world has a technological texture that stipulates for us what existence means. In Heidegger's terms, the modern epoch is technological, and Being (*Dasein*) is technicized as a result.

The human species actualizes the presence of Being, and Being can show itself only through the human race. Humans alone are the entities to whom all the things in the world can reveal themselves as meaningful.

---

[21] For Heidegger, his *Introduction to Metaphysics* (1953/2000) was an advanced and clarifying exposition on *Being and Time* (1927/1962a, chaps. 2–4). His philosophy of technology was developed most explicitly in four lectures before the Club at Bremen after World War II (December, 1949). The first two were presented later at the Bavarian Academy of Fine Arts in the series, "The Arts in the Technological Age." These two along with the fourth Bremen lecture ("The Turning") were published as *The Question Concerning Technology*. Don Ihde (1979, chap. 9) has developed the relationship between *Being and Time* and *The Question Concerning Technology*.

Phenomena disclose their is-ness through the human opening. Human beings are "the clearing of Being" (Heidegger, 1962b, p. 277). Humans are in the distinctive position of raising the problem of Being through their unique self-consciousness. Human beingness is not a static substance but a situated existent receiving and expressing the significance of things. There is no subject-object dichotomy; "the disclosure of things and the one to whom they are disclosed are co-original" (Hood, 1972, p. 353).

In Heidegger's framework, the ontic (phenomenological) dimension and Being as the foundation (the ontological) are not to be identified. These two concepts, the ontic and the ontological, are the two main dimensions of Being (1927/1962a, secs. 3–4). Humans exist simultaneously in both arenas. Although the ontological is structurally prior to the ontic, it is disclosed on the ontic level:

> Insofar as man *is*, exists in the ontological dimension, he is already oriented toward an ensemble of entities in the ontic dimension – that is, things of such and such a character, quantity, quality, relation and so on. Both the background of man's ontological dimension provided by his basic orientation to Being, and the horizon of his ontic dimension which emerges from his discovery of entities, are revealed together. (Hood, 1972, p. 353)

In Heidegger's existentialism, Being is not an essence as Western philosophy has traditionally assumed. In fact, only through the existential can the ontological be understood. The electromagnetic spectrum was concealed until radio and television unveiled it. A shed reveals something of woodenness, and ships disclose the character of water (Heidegger, 1977b, p. 13). But the ontological dimension is in turn the set of conditions that grounds the ontic. He locates what is ontological through a phenomenological analysis of what appears as "the ready-to-hand." Engaging technological entities in everyday existence becomes primary instead of giving priority to the scientist's and engineer's technical prowess. Thus technology is not mere means or a tool or an instrument, but "a mode of revealing, that is, of truth ... [It] comes to presence in the realm where revealing and unconcealment take place, where *aletheia*, truth, happens" (Heidegger, 1977b, p. 13).

For Heidegger, technology cannot be isolated phenomenologically – that is, understood alone as the human activity of producing things with tools. Instrumentalism makes this fundamental mistake; unless we contradict it, we will not be able to understand the technological order: "We are delivered over to technology in the worst possible way when we regard it as something neutral, for this conception of it, to which today we particularly like to do homage, makes us utterly blind to the essence of technology" (Heidegger, 1977b, p. 4). To get beyond Aristotle's neutrality, we must come to grips with the ways humans ground technology and how technology "takes on its determination in such a grounding. The problem, then, is to see how the ontological dimension of man makes possible the ontic determinations of technology" (Hood, 1972, p. 354).

Heidegger asks the philosophical question: what are the social conditions that make technology possible? He believes "Modern technology ... is not merely human doing" (Heidegger, 1977b, p. 19). Technology has a deep "structure which is the particular form of its set of possibilities that ground what we take as contemporary technics. The name for this shape of technological truth, Heidegger calls *Gestell*" (Ihde, 1979, p. 107; see also Heidegger, 1977b, pp. 19–21). In Heidegger's use, *Gestell* is "enframing"; it is similar for him to Raymond Williams's structures of feeling and to Michael Polanyi's tacit knowledge.[22] Our opening up the technological world is always restricted by the horizons of our existence. Human action is not raw and pure but guided by the historical setting and lingual concepts beyond one person's understanding: "Man can indeed conceive, fashion, and carry through this or that in one way or another. But man does not have control over unconcealment itself, in which at any given time the real shows itself or withdraws" (Heidegger, 1977b, p. 18).

According to Ihde (1979), "Beings or entities thus appear only against, from and within a background or opening, a framework. But the opening or clearing within which they take the shapes they assume, is itself structured" (p. 105). It is superficial to describe technology in terms of immediate cause, that is, individual achievement. The technological order emerges within the natural and cultural worlds that lay claim to it. As an illustration, political economy is correct that in capitalist societies the tangible interests of commerce shape the organization and content of media technologies. How Beings come to presence depends on the total field of revealing in which they are situated. Technologies are conditioned by the values and presumptions that a society takes for granted at a given period of its history. The technological mode of truth has specific features, deriving from an era's pre-theoretical commitments, "something like deeply held, dynamic but enduring traditions, historical but no more easily thrown over than one's own deepest character or personality"

---

[22] For Heidegger, *Gestell* means "frame, framing structure," such as a bookrack or skeleton.

(Idhe, 1979, p. 102). As interpretive beings, we find ourselves in modernity in a new and complicated situation – our existence has a technological texture that recommends truth to us (Idhe, 1983, p. 11). In Heidegger's terms, since the modern epoch of Being is technological, penetrating its "essence or shape becomes a central philosophical concern if we are to understand our era and prepare a response to it" (Ihde, 1979, p. 107).

For Heidegger (1977b), when technology characterizes a time period, one of the civilizational givens is defining the earth as standing reserve (*Bestand*). The natural world is understood in one-dimensional terms as a field of energy or power that can be captured and stored: "The earth now reveals itself as a coal mining district, the soil as a mineral deposit" (p. 14). We look at forests and see wooden buildings. The river Rhine supplies waterpower for a hydroelectric plant. Only on the margins are there alternative claims that, for instance, "regard the earth as mother and to which one does not even put a plow" (p. 17). In addition, "Everywhere everything is ordered to stand by, to be immediately at hand, indeed to stand there just so that it may be on call for a further ordering" (p. 17). Unrelenting technological development depends on our viewing nature as a neutral mass and therefore available to the engineer. The natural world is seen as standing ready for human use: "Nature becomes a gigantic gasoline station, an energy source for modern technology and industry" (Heidegger, 1966, p. 50). And in this selective seeing lies a potential tragedy: "When destining reigns in the mode of *enframing*, it is the supreme danger ... As soon as what is unconcealed ... concerns man exclusively as standing reserve, then he comes to the brink of a precipitous fall, that is, he comes to the point where he himself will have to be taken as standing-reserve" (Heidegger, 1977b, p. 27). The danger is the encompassing of human existence within the technological process. For something "to be" means it is material for the self-augmenting technological system (cf. Philipse, 1998, pp. 182–183, 261–262, fn510n329).

Media technologies are especially culpable for reconstructing an inauthentic humanness. In mediated communication, platitudes and conformity homogenize public life rather than inform it. Viewers and readers and users are cast up as purchasers. Intimate and confidential data become commodities for digital information banks to exploit. In genetic engineering, humans are raw material for scientific experimentation. Human resources are often used like a Styrofoam™ cup – disposing of them as soon as the task is finished. In the classic case of the tomato picker, designed by the University of California–Irvine, a new hybrid tomato had to be developed – tomatoes with tough skins so they would not break, that ripened at the same time, with chemical color added as necessary, and that were square or oblong so they moved on sorting trays better. Adapting the tomato to the machine is an analog of Heidegger's concern with Being. The technological process mercilessly preempts human existence for itself.

The crisis industrial societies face is not machines and products per se, but a technological understanding of Being. In Heidegger's view, because our beingness is situated today in technological conditions radically opposed to human freedom, there are no respites in which the moral imagination can flourish. Struggles should be ongoing, though without guarantees of success. After "the turn" (*die Kehre*) in his thinking, Heidegger contended that language was the phenomenon through which the question of Being unfolded. Given that interest in the philosophy of language, he turned to artistic symbols as offering hope (1971a, 1971b). He believed that through a basic revival of *techne* as art, technological revealing could be broadened and enriched. This move is familiar through the Heideggerian emphasis on the primal role of the poet: "Poetically man dwells upon the earth" (Heidegger, 1977b, p. 34). Art is *techne*, as is engineering; but art's mode of revealing "opens new ways of 'saying Being', as Heidegger puts it" (Ihde, 1979, p. 115).

Heidegger chooses language as a strategic alternative to a totalizing nihilism. As *techne*, art is similar in kind to all practical dealings with the natural world. It is thus already related to technology: "Confrontation with technology must happen in a realm that is, on the one hand, akin to the essence of technology and on the other, fundamentally different from it" (Heidegger, 1977b, p. 35). Idhe adds, "Technology and art belong to the danger and possible salvation of the same epoch of Being" (1979, p. 115). Poetry opens up a new world. Genuine art enriches human existence, while technological creations preempt being for themselves. Technology converts the universe of Being into "standing reserve" (*Bestand*) for mechanistic initiatives. Heidegger takes the "Greek temple as his illustration of an artwork working. The temple held up to the Greeks what was important, and so let there be heroes and slaves, victory and disgrace, disaster and blessing, and so on" (Dreyfus, 1995, p. 195). Art as craftwork can communicate non-technological understandings of Being. If artistry would thrive, there is the possibility that tools and networks would no longer constrain our beingness.

Dasein and *Tao*

Preceding the industrial world that Heidegger addressed, Taoism made our humanness nonnegotiable. Heidegger's interest in Eastern thought is well known, and scholars have identified the symmetry between his *Dasein* and the *Tao* (May, 1996; Parkes, 1990). Okakura Kakuzo's concept of *das-in-der-Welt-sein* (being in the world) to describe Buddhist thinking was given to Heidegger in 1919 by a Buddhist scholar studying with him. In Chang Chung-Yuan's (1963) terms: "Heidegger is the only Western philosopher who not only intellectually but has grasped Taoist thought intuitively" (p. 190).[23]

Ontology also has been a productive concept for linking Heidegger's existentialism and Buddhist thinking. Vincent Shen (2015), for instance, compares Huayan Buddhism's metaphysical vision with that of Whitehead's ontological principle, "both of them emphasizing that events in dynamic relation constitute the fundamental elements of reality" (p. 152). Ron Cooper's *Heidegger and Whitehead* (1993) is a classic statement showing that Whitehead's *Process and Reality* aligns with Heidegger's *Being and Time* on the ontological conditions that make human experience possible and intelligible.

A perspective on media technology is opened up by Shelton Gunaratne's "humanocentric theory of journalism" in his *Dao of the Press* (2005). He integrates Western epistemology with Eastern mysticism to replace the media's individualism and self-interest with interdependence and mutual causality. Instead of grounding our theories of communication in politics or economics or machines, Gunaratne appeals to the human instead. In order that universalism is not configured in Eurocentric terms, living systems for him are the integrating concept (see Capra, 1997; cf. T. Cooper, 2016–2017).

Gunaratne (2005) does elaborate on Confucian humanism (chap. 2), but Taoism's understanding of living systems has center stage (esp. chaps. 1, 5). Taoism recognizes a mysterious power in nature and pursues a harmonious state of being united with natural reality. In the words of the *Tao Te Ching* (2010), "Tao cannot be heard, cannot be seen, cannot

---

[23] As argued here, most scholars see Heidegger's phenomenology and Taoist thought as illuminating each other. However, for the record, a few have argued against mutual influence. Contrary to Heidegger's phenomenology, it is claimed, phenomenal existence in Buddhism is illusory. In addition, it is sometimes contended that Lao Tzu speaks in opposition to Heidegger's "language as the house of being" because for Lao Tzu Being exists only because of its opposite, nonbeing.

be told, and should not be named." For Lao Tzu, Tao is a mystical force that gives life to all creation and is the energy that enables human action. Tao is within persons and when humans act on it the Self evolves.

From Taoism's perspective, the basic question is how we can live harmoniously in the midst of social orders and values that tend to make human beings soulless objects (Tzu, 1964). Chuang Tzu contends that humans suffer because we have no freedom. We lack freedom because we are attached to material goods, feelings, knowledge, and religions. For Taoism, harmony within ourselves and with nature is possible even though the dominant voices tout efficiency, structure, and progress. We face a predicament in technological regimes such as nations, in highly technological professions such as journalism and advertising, and in technological organizations such as Amazon, Alibaba, and Microsoft. The issue is not machines and tools first of all, but the way technological systems define our understanding of what human existence means. A philosophy of technology that is radically humanocentric opposes the idea, direct or latent, that humans are integers of digital data networks.

Dwelling is one issue common to both Heidegger and Taoism, that is, living in community, feeling at home, settled.[24] "To dwell, to be set at peace, means to remain at peace within the preserve, the free sphere that safeguards each thing in its preserve. The fundamental character of dwelling is sparing" (Heidegger, 1977a, p. 327). Dwelling means the coming together of earth, being, and divinity, with nature playing an especially active role in Taoism (Huang, 1967). Instrumentalism cuts us loose from our human habitat in time and space; it pushes us away from a meditative "dwelling" toward a frenetic "doing." The result in technological regimes is the plight of undwelling or what Joshua Meyrowitz (1985) calls "the homeless mind."

In a technical artifice, where is harmony with nature or within ourselves? The worldview of efficiency that drives rapid modernization buries the emotional experience of memory, safety, peace, and rootedness. Caught up in the instrumentalism of technological regimes, their professionals and executives are harassed into hurried, technical decisions. In the original Greek, ethics is *ethos*, abode, dwelling place, the human domain for moral discernment. Homelessness, no fixed abode, means the absence of ethics or moral indifference; then we demand from the universe rather

---

[24] Taoist "dwelling" is described in a fifth century Chinese landscape poem by Hsieh Ling-yun (Huang, 1967; see also Haar, 1993).

than live in harmony with it. As Heidegger puts it, "only if we are capable of dwelling, only then can we build" (1977a, p. 338).

Application

The question is how to give priority to the restructuring of Being instead of to a preoccupation with new machines and efficient methods. The struggle is not primarily over technological policies and practices, but over the civilizational givens that undergird them. These underlying values – what is here called the instrumental worldview – must be revolutionized for our technological era to be transformed in human-centered terms.

Instead of instrumentalism's elementary view that technologies are value free, the reality is that ever-expanding means tend to overwhelm ends worthy of human allegiance. Technological imperatives become human imperatives. In Heidegger's humanistic model, technology is not a noun but a verb, a culture in which human existence is established. The challenge of the digital media in a technological age can only be met by a new worldview.

The solution is long term and depends on the language and critical thinking of the liberal arts. Through the humanities and humanistic social sciences, our approach to technology need not be instrumental. When social values are changed, technologies will be re-symbolized and restructured. As developed in Chapter 2, beliefs about instrumental progress, expertise, and magnitude ought to be replaced with values rooted in the sacredness of human life. The humanities – history, philosophy, the arts, music, literature – should thrive, not just engineering and electronic gadgetry. Against an overwhelming technocratic mystique, an educational culture in which questions of life's purpose and moral values dominate can be Heidegger's dwelling. Therefore, the logical conclusion is that a new theory of global media ethics needs to be humanistic in character rather than a set of abstractions that reflects a mechanized instrumentalism.

Ellul's Ends and Means

Jacques Ellul works within the Heideggerian tradition. The technological process is likewise for him an ontological issue. Technology is intertwined with the structure of human being. As a representative of media ecology, Ellul applied his social philosophy directly to media technologies, while Heidegger referred primarily to artistic forms of communication. Patrick Troude-Chastenet, professor of political science at the University of Potiers, describes the Ellul–Heidegger relationship this way:

Fourteen years before Heidegger's first lectures on the subject, Ellul already thought that technique and not politics was now at the heart of things. Their ends intersect, even while their means diverge. Heidegger's work included metaphysical questioning of the essence of modern technique, the *Gestell*, the framework, while Ellul proposed a sociological description of the traits of the technical system based on the construction of a Weber-style ideal type. (Troude-Chastenet, 2006, p. 5)

Ellul's opposition to instrumentalism is of particular interest when constructing a media ethics that takes technology seriously. As a specialist in technology, Ellul enables the development of a new theory of global media ethics. He orients the humanistic philosophy-of-technology tradition to the political and in the process establishes the basis for an international ethics centered on justice.

In Heidegger, the technological phenomenon is decisive, and so it is for Ellul. As an explanation of the social order, Ellul sees technology in the twentieth century playing the same role as Marx thought capital played in the nineteenth. Ellul means that capital and technology have a similar interpretive function, not that the technological system has replaced the capitalist system. Capital is still a crucial idea, but it no longer has the same role in production that Marx identified for it. Labor produces value in Marx; in societies characterized by high technology, the determining factor is *la technique*.[25] Machine-like efficiency is the force that began in the twentieth century to create value, and efficiency is not peculiar to capitalism. The dynamics of political and economic power have changed. Ellul recognized the legitimacy in the nineteenth century of dividing society into capitalists and workers, but he believed that the technological reality of his day operated on a more abstract level. Societies across history have produced technological products, but a qualitative change to a technicistic society began occurring in the twentieth century. Therefore, for industrial societies when their technologies have multiplied into a technological order, the technological system stands on one side and the human race on the other. The former is driven by necessity and the latter demands freedom (Ellul, 1981b).

[25] Much of the misunderstanding of Ellul's work has been perpetrated by the substitution of "technology" for *la technique* in a number of English translations of Ellul's books and essays – a substitution Ellul claims he never approved.

From Ellul's perspective, *la technique* is not merely a problem for social scientists to study empirically. It is a social philosophy through which the self and human institutions are to be understood. In a technological order, machines are sacralized, and *la technique* infects not just industry but also politics, education, religion, medicine, and international relations. Members of the technological order are enamored of efficiency to the degree that other social imperatives are given secondary importance.[26]

While representing the Heideggerian legacy of technology as a cultural process, Ellul understands the Innis tradition, whose *Propagandes* and *Political Illusion* contribute to Innis's concern with empire. For Ellul, the media, themselves co-opted by instrumentalism, do not transmit neutral messages but promote a worldview of efficient means (1965). Whatever can be digitalized and codified is considered definitive. Professionals and institutions follow technological dynamics and processes instead of ethical principles. In the twenty-first century, technological structures frame the news; they indicate how user networks engage the new media; they stipulate what kinds of advertising campaigns ought to be designed and what popular culture programs can be distributed most effectively. As a political theorist and active in politics, Ellul moves the intellectual traditions regarding the technological phenomenon into the civic sphere.[27]

Ellul's political activism is substantial and noteworthy (e.g., Ellul, 1981a, pp. 18–28). Ellul's grandfather's business was devastated by the

---

[26] Ellul (1989) claims that the transition to a technological order is a more fundamental change for the human race than anything else over the past five thousand years. In his typology (Ellul, 1989), there are three major periods of human existence: "The Prehistoric Period and the Natural Environment" (pp. 104–114), "The Historical Period and the Social Environment" (pp. 115–132), and "The Posthistorical Period and the Technological Environment" (pp. 133–140). This is Ellul's most famous summary situating the present technological era against the previous two: "The creation of the technological environment ... is progressively effacing the two previous ones. Of course, nature and society still exist. But they are without power – they no longer decide our future ... The same applies to society. It remains secondary ... Politicians can decide only what is technologically feasible. All decisions are dictated by the necessity of technological growth" (pp. 134–135).

[27] To develop media ethics in these political terms, democracy is one productive framework for understanding the media. The important book *The Press* (2005) provides a US example that can be duplicated in other political systems around the world. Democracy in *The Press* is the political context in which the structure and function of the news media are understood. The health of journalism organizations and practices by themselves is not the main concern of *The Press*, but rather the vitality of democratic politics. Journalism is considered the means and the end is democracy. In that sense, ethical journalism – traditional and online – is the foundation of genuine democracy.

1929 economic crisis, and it influenced his research agenda. He joined the Paris riots of February 1934 against the Fascists and participated in protests against the Vichy government until he was removed from his faculty position at the University of Strasbourg. He survived on a farm outside Paris during World War II, while actively supporting the French resistance along with Sartre, Camus, and Malraux. After the war, he served as the deputy mayor of Bordeaux, concentrating on commerce and public works. A group of intellectuals sponsored a successful campaign to force the French government to withdraw from Algeria, and Ellul was the primary leader (cf. Christians, 1995a, p. 158). His career as an educator at the University of Bordeaux was entangled with Charles de Gaulle's government and the crisis of May 1958, the French Fourth Republic, and the Cold War.

His reflections on his lifetime were deeply influenced by two movements, *Ordre Nouveau* and *Esprit*, with his activism distinguished by the belief "that the political process is rendered powerless by science and technology" (Troude-Chastenet, 2006, p. 5). Based on his personal experience and his massive historical work on political institutions, Ellul concluded in *The Political Illusion* that "solving our problems by the traditional road of politics, with all sorts of constitutional reforms ... represents shadow boxing" and perpetuates illusory debates about revolutionary change (1967, pp. 221–222). With the "conjunction of state and technique by far the most important phenomenon of history" (1964, p. 233), Ellul promotes nonviolent anarchism. His anarchist position does not mean that an anarchist society can be realized (1988), but he calls for communities of resistance – similar to Heidegger's dwelling – where thinking and action are different from "political organs" and the "machinery of bureaus" (1967).[28]

In his politicizing of the technological order, Ellul connects it to global media ethics by positioning the technological domain in terms of ends and means. Working in the Heideggerian tradition, he revolutionizes the dualism of ends and means that characterizes instrumentalism. Technological societies have committed their resources overwhelmingly to products, invention of tools, engineering and science, the world of

---

[28] See Ellul's *Ethics of Freedom* (1976), for example, pp. 395–398. Fasching (1990) concludes: "Ellul ... favors anarchism as a political strategy of revolt against the authority of all political institutions. He does not think anarchists can be successful in destroying the state. But in a world where all nation-states tend to abuse their power, only a strategy of nonviolent anarchism can make a dent in the bureaucratic social order so as to make some modicum of freedom possible."

means – all of which suffocate concern for ends: "We have forgotten our collective ends ... In this terrible dance of means which has been unleashed, no one knows where we are going; the aim of life has been forgotten" (Ellul, 1951, pp. 63, 69).[29] Obviously, public communication still invokes ends such as equality and progress. However, Ellul contends, these goals no longer inspire; certainly "no one would die for them" (1951, p. 67). As technological societies advance, the concept of ends becomes marginal to the busyness of perfecting strategies.[30] Already in his early and basic book *The Presence of the Kingdom*, Ellul is uncompromising on the means-ends question: "In reality the problem has been absolutely transformed ... It must be seen in the light of *la technique*" (Ellul, 1951, p. 62).

But is Ellul's preoccupation with means and ends a genuine contribution? The means-ends distinction is central to Aristotle's instrumental theory of technology. In his *Politics* and *Nicomachean Ethics*, Aristotle introduced a teleological framework to Greek philosophy, developing self-realization ethics and contending that the nature of things consists in their end or perfection. And since Aristotle, means-ends analysis has been important in Western ethics. John Dewey (1922) introduced an influential twentieth-century version by explicitly separating ends and means; he regarded morality as the conscious deliberation of both, and intelligent conduct as aiming toward a specified end (pp. 25–28, 225 ff.). In addition to these two trajectories, teleology has surfaced in other ways across history – in Max Weber's concept of bureaucratization, for example.

Ellul is distinctive in this complicated debate over means and ends by altering its very substance.[31] The issues for him are not the philosophical questions whether "ends justify means" or "just ends entail just means." For Ellul, the existential problem in advanced industrial societies is the disappearance of ends themselves. In its preoccupation with mechanical systems, public life ignores moral imperatives. Regarding Aristotle's

---

[29] By "end," Ellul (1951) writes: "I mean the collective ends of civilization, for individuals still have their own ends, for instance to succeed in a competition or to get a higher salary, and the like" (p. 63).

[30] In Lewis Mumford's (1970) terms, societies dominated by a mechanized world picture finally become saturated by the "pentagon of power" – political absolutism, mechanical energy, mass productivity, pecuniary profit, and manipulative publicity.

[31] The means-ends issue for Ellul in this section is oriented to his role in politicizing the technological phenomenon. For the larger ethical and historical context for means and ends, see Christians, "Triumph of Means" (2006, pp. 125–133).

instrumentalism, Ellul concludes that ends cannot be realized by humans because the symbolic structure of human existence is characterized by means. Nor, in Dewey's terms, do people face a choice of good ends or bad; collective ends no longer have salience. In Ellul's perspective, Dewey presumes a discredited means-ends dualism and Aristotle a metaphysical angle without justification. Therefore, in the media, ethical issues cannot be reduced to professional lapses by individual decision makers.

Echoing Heidegger's concern with destining, the welfare of human beings is no longer society's end; the human species has in actuality become an "available resource, ... the means of the very means" that should be serving it (Ellul, 1951, p. 63). With their lingual system caught up in *la technique,* flesh-and-blood people become consumers, workers, markets, taxpayers – that is, persons in the abstract. In *The Technological Bluff,* automatism replaces creativity when efficiency displaces moral goods (Ellul, 1990).[32] As media systems are expanded by new digital technologies and their transmission given an unprecedented velocity, their normative base is being undermined even though it is more necessary now than ever before. The unrelenting demands and complications that the global technological civilization faces only magnify the tragic loss of social purposes and goals. From Ellul's perspective on the rise of means and disappearance of ends, technological societies and sophisticated technological professions "are increasingly trapped in Kurt Vonnegut's (1952) conundrum: When he reached into his repertoire of commitments, wisdom, and intelligence, he came up empty-handed, precisely at the moment he needed them most" (quoted in Christians, 1995, p. 165)

Contemporary Reflections

There are research-based studies in political communication consistent with the human-centered philosophy of technology. They are non-instrumentalist in character and show how media ecology systems

[32] Ellul (1951) rejects the criticism that his purpose is reviving Protestant individualism (pp. 82–85). Likewise, he has no interest in democratic individualism. These forms of individualism are "outdated," he says, and "it is useless to try to retrieve them" (p. 748). Ellul does recognize that all moral judgments by definition involve personal choice; but responsible choosing can only be made by persons who have been transformed supernaturally. Ellul contends that such transformations will emerge as "social, political, intellectual, or artistic bodies, associations, interest groups – totally independent" of technicized forces and thus capable of opposing them (1976, p. 221). As these renewed humans combine into communities not driven by *la technique,* the structure of technological necessity will begin losing its power.

illuminate ethics and politics. Three quality exemplars are summarized next to give rigor and clarity to the humanocentric philosophy-of-technology perspective. Grant Kien's research applies Carey and Heidegger directly. While Lance Bennett and Brian Goss do not scholastically examine the dominant voices of this chapter – Innis, Carey, Heidegger, and Ellul – the frames of reference and problematics of these four scholars weave their way through the case studies, empirical data, archives, and interpretations of the Goss and Bennett volumes. All three are preoccupied with the new media revolution, Goss and Bennett focusing on the news media and Kien on mobile phone technology.

Goss's *Rebooting the Herman and Chomsky Propaganda Model in the Twenty-First Century (2013)*

Using the Herman and Chomsky "Propaganda Model" that was published in 1988, Brian Goss offers an accessible portrait of contemporary media systems. Despite the news media's power, the Propaganda Model argues that it follows deeply inscribed structural logics and fails to fulfill its democratic promise. In crafting their critical perspective, Herman and Chomsky (1988) proposed five filters, that is, five constraints that condition news workers at each step of the production process: (a) the news media's ownership and profit structure, (b) advertising as its unofficial license to do business, (c) sourcing patterns constrained by professional routines, (d) ideological criticism with undue influence, and (e) anticommunism as a control mechanism (cf. Goss, 2013, pp. 3–4). Because of these major constraints, Herman and Chomsky claim that the news enterprise reinforces elite-driven "premises of discourse and interpretation" (1988, p. 1). These filters define what is newsworthy; they enculturate news workers "in such a fundamental way, that alternative bases for news are barely imaginable" (Goss, 2013, p. 4).[33]

Rebooting the Herman & Chomsky Propaganda Model assesses and fits the model to current times. Goss reviews world historic developments – "from the demise of command socialism to the advent of the internet" – that have complicated the Herman-Chomsky analysis. Goss concludes the following:

[D]espite the hurly burly of superstructural change, events of the past quarter century have largely if unevenly reinforced the functioning of the model's filters.

---

[33] Goss (2013, p. 7) observes that Bennett's (2001) "trenchant appraisal of U.S. news media is favorable to the Propaganda Model even as he relies on other lines of analysis" (p. 7). Goss quotes and references Bennett frequently and copiously.

In elaborating this thesis, I am attentive to noteworthy developments that circumvent the reach of the filtering mechanisms – and am also alert to the ways in which new media have been recruited into reinforcing (and not, as widely assumed, monolithically upsetting) business as usual. (Goss, 2013, p. 7)

Goss redesigns this influential model of media criticism with three innovations:

(1). Since Herman and Chomsky wrote in the milieu of the Cold War, Goss changes their anti-communist filter to the news' Us/Them discourse. He sees dichotomies undiminished in reporting: "A dichotomization filter has been retrofitted over anti-communism since new Others are playing the part of Them (distinct from us) in contemporary news discourse." The refashioned Us/Them in the post-Soviet era "exports across time and space to better fit the specifics of news in particular societies at given moments" (Goss, 2013, p. 118). Arguing that all societies harbor their own versions of Us/Them dichotomies, Goss has made the Propaganda Model more supple. For example, chap. 5 compares the 2011 London riot coverage in *The Guardian* and *The Daily Telegraph,* with the latter readily sliding into the Us/Them dichotomies of oppositional drama, while the former included more texture and backstory.

(2). Goss adds empirical data that enrich his analysis, rather than following the Propaganda Model in its opposition to social scientific research. Content analysis of media ownership and news worker routines are included. Through cases and empirical research, Goss incorporates the cultural dimension to enrich the political economy perspective. Extensive examples revolutionize the model toward the global, helping release it from its Western/industrial formulation. Cases are used also to explain the restructuring of journalism. The neoliberal globe and its impact on reporting practices are clarified by both North American and European content analysis of media products.

(3). Of particular importance to *Media Ethics and Global Justice in the Digital Age,* for the first time in the Propaganda Model's history, Goss demonstrates how his *Rebooting* takes the new social media seriously; wherever digital/online/Web 2.0 are relevant, they are included, and in chap. 7 they are given full-length treatment. This chapter develops a paired case study on both sides of the Atlantic, an old media representative and a new media representative discussing the technological environment in which they work. Goss's research features Howard Kurtz, a prestigious representative of incumbent journalism from his position as media writer at the *Washington Post* and Glenn Grunwald in online journalism (cf. p. 167).[34]

In October 2005, Greenwald made his blogging debut with *Unclaimed Territory*. Greenwald's blogs quickly caught on, with his readership spiking from 30 to 30,000 in five days. In 2007, Greenwald's blog moved onto the Salon.com platform, itself a new media player of note as the longest-running internet daily that has been online since 1995 (Goss, 2013, p. 184). In Goss's summary of his content analysis research: "Greenwald exhibits free-wheeling critique that is less wedded to State and private sector sources and their favored narratives. By contrast, as a mainstream journalist tasked with writing on journalism, Kurtz enthrones conventional wisdom and the authority that animates them" (Goss, 2013, p. 174); "Kurtz offers bursts of interesting reporting circumscribed within the procedures of objective journalism" (p. 180).

While Greenwald's legally informed blogs on current issues indicate the possible liberating impact of the new technologies, Goss concludes that "it is not enough to assert that writing from an internet platform guarantees a progressive and critical posture through techno-alchemy . . . If the internet is to be a liberating instrument in the politicized media battles ahead, complacent assumptions about techno-essence are a decided hindrance" (Goss, 2013, p. 193). Goss's research confirms the media ecology perspective and the human-centered philosophy of technology underlying it.

Bennett's *News: The Politics of Illusion*
Another contemporary reflection is *News: The Politics of Illusion* (10th ed., 2016). This classic in political communication focuses on the fundamental issue of political news and democratic governance, instead of reducing the problems to polling, voting behavior, government information offices, or watchdog journalism. In examining the question of the

---

[34] During his *Washington Post* career of twenty-nine years, Kurtz wrote five books on the media and worked for CNN on its program *Reliable Sources*. Subsequent to Goss's research, in October 2010, Kurtz left the *Post* for the internet *Daily Beast*, attracted by a pay increase. In July 2013, he joined Fox News. In August 2010, Greenwald announced his departure from *Salon.com* to blog from the platform of the *Manchester Guardian*. In 2012, Greenwald relocated to *The Guardian* and in 2013 he founded *The Intercept* (with Laura Poitras and Jeremy Scahill).

impact of news on the quality of American democracy, Bennett eschews instrumentalism and demonstrates how a humanocentric philosophy of technology is worked out in research, media policy, and professional practice. Rather than a means-ends dualism that measures audience demographics and the effects of specific technologies, *News: The Politics of Illusion* speaks in sophisticated language about new media technologies in terms of journalism's credibility and the myths woven into public discourse.[35]

The orientation of this tenth edition is technological, with its backbone "the tensions between the legacy press and emerging native digital media – tensions magnified by changing audience and citizen information habits" (Bennett, 2016, p. xii):

> The legacy news organizations that anchored that system have suffered a number of shocks that include competition from an explosion of mobile apps and specialized online platforms that growing numbers of people find more in tune with their lifestyles. When people share the information that pulses through their devices, they often edit and add commentary to help it travel over particular social networks. This involvement of audiences in producing and distributing information changes the neat one-to-many communication logic that defined the mass media era. Social media employ a many-to-many logic that involves people more interactively in the communication process. (Bennett, 2016, p. 3)

Bennett continues: "The rise of blogs, discussion forums, instant polls, YouTube channels, social networking sites" and citizens reporting news stories "on cell phones and digital cameras" are a dramatic technological reversal, though of uncertain benefit (2016, p. 153). In this dialectic information flow, people often "stream news chaotically, checking for shallow updates" without taking time "for reflection or critical processing" (p. 240). Political communication of this sort faces the dangers of extreme splintering and individual isolation: "The reality of so much opinion and participation is anchored in electronic images that move people psychologically in private worlds that may be detached from

---

[35] To enhance the book's pedagogical value, Bennett includes eight case studies that along with other examples and assessments examine "how the new media system and new kinds of information engagement affect our politics" (Bennett, 2016, p. xii). These include specific topics such as activist journalism – the new form of investigative reporting, global warming as science and as a particular news story, false balance and false impartiality in the news, and experiments with the future of news such as *ProPublica*. The issues of the chapter in which they are located are interwoven through the case detail so that thoughtful discussion of them in classrooms and in workshops for professionals will illustrate the kind of public deliberation about the press's role that Bennett calls for in the last chapter (pp. 233–235).

society and face-to-face politics" (p. 152). When the design of media technologies facilitates private enclaves, these "media niches may produce individuals who become informed just about issues and perspectives that suit their personal lifestyle and beliefs" (p. 24). The overall effect is not clarity on public debates but a "babel of information that leaves many citizens discouraged or confused" (p. 127).

In terms of his large-scale framework for analyzing news media systems, Bennett (2016) observes the decline of their gatekeeping function: "At the height of the mass media era, journalists were often regarded as 'gatekeepers' who screened information (ideally) according to its truth and importance" (p. 25). Bennett adds, "The growing importance of spin, the rise of tempting rumors on the Internet," and stories spinning "back and forth between news and entertainment programming" have "undermined the capacity of news organizations to mind the gates with uniform or high-minded standards" (p. 146). However, even in these dynamic days of the technological revolution in news gathering, production, and dissemination, the "politics of illusion" still accurately defines the linkage between journalism, and public officials, and society: "At the forefront of information politics is the struggle over influencing or spinning journalists and news organizations to report versions of events that favor particular political sides" (p. 11). Most news coverage uses formats that place the "audience as passive consumers rather than active citizens. For both politicians and journalists, the public has become more of a market to be tested, persuaded, and sold than an equal partner in communication and government" (p. 152).

Four information biases are particularly important in understanding the press–democracy relationship. Foregrounding technology, Bennett (2016) introduces the bias framework this way:

Like it or not, the news has become a mass-produced consumer product ... Communication technologies, beginning with the wire services and progressing to satellite feeds and social networking, interact with corporate profit motives to create generic, "lowest-common-denominator" information formats ... Four common biases make it easy for a large volume of news to be produced in keeping with the budgets of over-worked news organizations. (p. 36)

These four biases – personalization, dramatization, fragmentation, and politics as a game (pp. 36–53) – "make news hard to use as a guide to citizen action because they obscure the big picture in which daily events take place" (Bennett, 2016, p. 35). The major flaw in today's news style, unchanged with abundant new technology, is downplaying "the big

social, economic, or political picture in favor of the human trials, tragedies, and triumphs that sit at the surface of events" (p. 36). Lost in the
news' self-definition as "melodrama" are "sustained analyses of persistent
problems such as inequality, hunger, resource depletion, population pressures, environmental collapse, toxic waste, and political oppression"
(p. 37). News stories are isolated "from each other and from their larger
contexts, so that information in the news becomes fragmented and hard to
assemble" into the coherent framework needed for responsible public
action (p. 38). With the Gulf of Mexico oil spill and Barak Obama's
handling of it as illustration, the news is described as "the game frame"
in which the focus of attention was "whether he was doing enough to
control the situation" and then whether "the president was weak on
energy policy" (p. 40): "The popular belief in liberal press bias is not
only off the mark, but it may also actually keep people from recognizing
[these four] more serious biases" (p. 213).

With rigorous attention to the research on new media technologies in
the government-media-society triad, Bennett avoids the pessimism-
optimism dead end and clarifies the humanistic philosophy-of-
technology perspective. Schooled in the history of media technology and
with thoughtful interpretation of the research data, Bennett considers the
transformations that are possible with the new digital technology systems
as "their different communication logics ... interface with our national
politics" (2016, pp. xii–xiii). The economic crisis in the commercial
media, new storage and transmission inventions, and changes in lifestyle
patterns are "producing waves of innovation and experimentation.
The array of mostly online news organizations, blogs, and hybrid organizations is impressively large and growing" (p. 148). The digital age carries
with it the peril of producing "so much information that we are drowning
in it" (p. 239). But the projection to date is for a burgeoning number of
"interesting experiments" that may "reinvent the news and more generally improve how citizens communicate with each other and with leaders"
(p. 23). Of special interest for the mutating news process are the partnerships forming between "investigative organizations and conventional
media" and the "appearance of high-quality news sites covering topics
such as climate change and prison reform." They may signal a new
"direction for the press that better informs and engages citizens"
(Bennett, 2016, p. 153). Regarding the revolutions underway in technological form and content substance, Bennett's manifesto is pertinent:
"Above all, it would help to recognize the roots of our communication
problems and talk about them differently in public. As we enter the age of

electronic democracy and information abundance, the opportunity exists once again to have a critical national debate about how we should inform ourselves and engage with politics" (Bennett, 2016, p. 222).

Kien's *Global Technography: Ethnography in the Age of Mobility*

A third contemporary reflection of note is Grant Kien's *Global Technography: Ethnography in the Age of Mobility* (2009). Following the media ecology tradition, Kien selects mobile phone technology and analyzes it within its political, cultural, and global milieux. Characterizing himself as a global citizen with technological savvy, Kien synthesizes these various strands by describing technologically enabled mobility in the context of globalization: "It has been my goal to show that in spite of technological potentialities, life everywhere is lived 'everyday', be it in Canada, the United States, Japan, South Korea, China or the mountains of Mexico" (p. 144). His book makes it obvious "that technology is a dynamic and dramatic participant in the performance of everyday life" (p. 16).

While Kien's theoretical commitments are to media ecology, his research on and investigation of that theory are "informed by Heidegger's philosophy of technology in which technologies" are "intrinsically part of ontological experience" (Kien, 2009, p. 3).[36] He continues, "I acknowledge that for me Heidegger's philosophy of technology and his phenomenology are a satisfactory description of the nature and relationship of technology and my own existence. I believe Heidegger is correct in suggesting that technology cannot be separated from ontology since it is profoundly part of human everyday experience, emphatically so if globalization theorists are to be taken seriously" (p. 5).

Global Technography focuses on the issue of ontology in chap. 4, exploring the relationship between technology and one's way of being in the world. Heidegger is cited as telling us, "freedom is achievable only by understanding the essence of technology as the means to understand Being, and by understanding technology as an intimate facet of being human" (p. 141). For Heidegger, technologies are inseparable from our human existence, that is, an irreducible component of our ontology.

---

[36] In John Peters's (2012) terms, "Theory now belongs largely to the practice of science. It has become tied to hypothesis testing and verification and has largely lost its ethical and aesthetics dimensions" (p. 507). Philosophical work is situated within the history of ideas and follows the literary styles of logic and patterns of proof that are characteristic of the humanities.

With media ecology – especially that of James Carey – as his communication theory, and Heidegger for his philosophical foundation, Kien's study of mobile phones in everyday life around the world clarifies three concepts that need to be incorporated into a new theory of international media ethics.

The first concept is *mobility*. While studies of the new technologies typically invoke mobility, Kien's book radicalizes it: "Technology is rapidly progressing from portability to extreme mobility, to be used reliably while in transit – to be part of the experience of transit – making constant movement and positional fluidity to be a normal condition of technological subjectivity" (Kien, 2009, p. 2). He continues, "There is a class of global citizens constantly in motion for whom the term 'migration' is meaningless," as the act of settling somewhere is outside their experience (p. 2). Kien's use of the term "mobility" refers not only to people movements in physical terms but also to "conceptual movements such as transience in identity" (p. 4).[37]

Second, *time and space*, crucial to the media ecology framework, are elaborated with both depth and nuance. Mediation always alters perceptions of both time and space, "and rather intensely when in translation by contemporary technologies. In particular, space becomes 'teledistanced' (Heidegger, 1977a) while time becomes 'telepresent' (Virilio, 2000) ... That is to say, no time or place in the universe is considered inaccessible to a networked user in the present. Rather, through digital mediation, a user experiences omnipresence in time and space" (Kien, 2009, p. 65). Instead of satellites and ICTs bringing distant things near to set them apart conceptually, everything becomes imbued with "uniform distancelessness" (Heidegger, 1971b, p. 164); the distance required for interpretation and abstraction is obliterated (Kien, 2009, p. 29). This is the dilemma of the new instantaneous technologies: "According to Heidegger we need structures of time and a sense of distance to avoid solipsism and to understand ourselves as belonging in the world," but distancelessness "preempts the potential for authentic experience." With the compression of history into the momentary and the evisceration of spatial limits, "the signifiers of selfhood can equally be described as existing everywhere always and nowhere never" (Kien, 2009, pp. 125, 141).

---

[37] With identities complex and vulnerable when we take our home with us, Kien shares David Morley's (2000) concern that while personal mobility is social power, mobile technologies themselves do not prevent the discrimination of "enforced immobility" (cf. Kien, 2009, p. 45).

Third, Kien creates a new research method known as *global techno-graphy* for investigating wireless telephony. In his terms, "this book develops and employs an ethnographic methodology I am calling Global Technography." Kien concluded, "exploring the broad social phenom-enon of mobility in the context of global network media and everyday cultural performances" required a new methodology "in which human actors and media technologies interact to produce the meaningful encoun-ters that we know as our life experience" (2009, p. 1). Kien's innovation in ethnography escapes "the traditional interactionist approach to technol-ogy that treats devices and machinery as dead props" (2009, p. 1).

For specific interactions of mobility, Kien (2009) uses Bruno Latour's Actor-Network Theory that he considers "a complement to Heidegger's philosophy of technology" (p. 5). Numerous vignettes explain the parti-cipatory role of technology in everyday life, with the narratives illustrating "actual human/machine interaction" through "ubiquitously networked wireless communication" (p. 13). Ethnography studies human interaction within a bounded field, but wireless networks de-territorialize so that people never really exit or enter a stable environment; chat rooms go with them and mediation is continuous. In Heideggerian terms, metho-dology must "incorporate technology as an active participant in the social actor-network" (p. 129). Kien's global technography is such a research method for mobile communications when, as he puts it, "we take our-selves with us."

APPLICATION TO MEDIA ETHICS THEORY

How can a human-centered philosophy of technology be put to work in ethics? How does it apply to professional ethics, especially the project of ethical universals? How can our theoretical models of global media ethics promote human welfare instead of instrumental efficiency? Four applica-tions are suggestive. They are constituents of the new theory of commu-nication ethics developed here in *Media Ethics and Global Justice in the Digital Age*. Positioned as they are in the history of ideas, these concepts help make this book distinctive.

First: Humanistic Universals

A universal theory cannot be a system of conduct binding on all rational creatures, the content of which is ascertainable by human reason. Theories of media ethics that are viable transnationally ought to be ontological instead, constitutive of our humanness. The theoretical model compatible with human-centered technology reviewed in this chapter is the sacredness of human life as a universal norm. This is an ontological ethics, an ethics of being that affirms reverence for life on earth as the rationale for ethical decision making. What we advocate as universal principles must be explicitly and categorically distinct from moral absolutes. The objections lodged against universals in media ethics are almost always against a misunderstanding of them as absolutes.

One source of justification for an absolutist ethics is the demands of reason. Ethical rationalism has been the prevailing paradigm in Western communication ethics. This is the unilateral model established by Rene Descartes (1596–1690), the founder of the Enlightenment mind. Descartes insisted that truth statements were non-contingent, with their context, therefore, beside the point. His *Meditations II* (1641) presumed clear and distinct ideas, objective and neutral. In the objectivism of his *Discourse on Method* (1637), genuine knowledge is a linear construction, with mathematics impervious to social conditions. The formula Minus One Zero Plus One is precise and measurable, and other forms of knowledge without this property are ephemeral. The split between facts and values that characterizes instrumentalism was bequeathed to the Western mind as science defined the meaning of truth.

Immanuel Kant's rationalism is an exacting form of such absolutism. In the *Critique of Pure Reason* (1788) and *Groundwork of the Metaphysics of Morals* (1785), Kant articulated ethics to Cartesian logic. Moral absolutes are identified in the rational way syllogisms are divided into valid and invalid. Whether or not moral duties are legitimate is determined by formal examination of their logical structure. Ethical principles are prescriptivist, and they are absolutist in the sense of holding true for all rational beings over time and space. In this mathematical version of context-free universals, linear abstractions are laid out like the arcs of longitude and latitude over the globe.

Jürgen Habermas is indebted to the Kantian tradition but fundamentally redirects it by taking a dialogical approach in his discourse theory. As he observes, "Philosophy is in danger of being a contemplation that reproduces the reified structure of consciousness it has set out to critique, if it does not go beyond abstract concepts of reason" (Habermas, 1984, p. 363). Habermas contradicts Kant's argument that reflective individuals guided by the categorical imperative will reach identical conclusions about the requirements of duty. Habermas insists that for pluralistic settings, Kant's absolutism is untenable, since for Habermas the moral point of view results from agreement among all those affected.

The moral universalism of this book and moral absolutes of the Kantian sort are not identical. Kant's categorical imperative and Cartesian essentialism are autocratic and constituted by individuated rationalism. These two concepts, absolutes and universals, are epistemologically distinct; to conflate them is a logical fallacy, the category mistake. Rationalist absolutes belong to Western intellectual history and are legitimately critiqued as unsuitable for transnational and intercultural media ethics. A new kind of universal is needed for international communication ethics. The challenge is a model of universalism that keeps ethics close to people's everyday existence, so that variety in cultures is emphasized rather than homogenized by abstractions. The human-centered tradition in the philosophy of technology embraces an ethics of being and contradicts the ontology of absolutism.

Instead of a commitment to essentialist sanctums of discrete individuals, a global media ethics should be constructed on totally different grounds. Following the legacy of existentialism since Heidegger, ethical principles are to be historically embedded rather than dependent on the subject-object dualism. It shifts universals from a formal metaphysics to the ontological. The re-theorizing of ethical theory in this book situates normed phenomena within culture and history (cf. Doris & Stitch, 2005). Humans can rethink their character and rationale, but not eradicate them: "Norms and values are not something a culture has, but something it is" (McDonald, 1986, p. 3).

Thomas Nagel (1989) argues for phenomena outside the human person that are not grounded *a priori* but experienced as creations akin to epiphanies. For Nagel, humans have genuine subjective knowledge, but he contends that we simultaneously conceive of realities that exist independently of ourselves (p. 4). This independent reality is from nowhere in particular and it is "natural to regard life and the world this way" (p. 7). Moral values are situated in human existence rather than anchored in the metaphysical foundations on which the Western canon is based. Humans consider it worthwhile to bring their values and beliefs "under the influence of an impersonal standpoint," even without proof that this vista outside time and space is not illusory" (p. 5). Following Nagel, the new theory of global media ethics advanced in this book sees us as forming overriding conceptions of the world with us in it.

Second: Triadic Approaches to Mediation

Heidegger's ontological perspective requires a triadic theory of communication. The stimulus-response model and information theory of instrumentalism exist alongside human subjectivity and do not engage it deeply enough to be relevant. The human-technology relation in Heidegger requires a cultural approach in which humans are understood as "first producing the world by symbolic work and then taking up residence in the world they have produced" (Carey, 1989, p. 30). According to Kien (2009), "Carey's theory situates media devices within a web of activity and meaning, within a process of creation, apprehension and use. Technologies are integral to localized symbolic work. Mobile technology is concerned with 'taking up residence' in the world territorially ordered by nationalisms and other culturally significant spatially binding symbols" (p. 59).

Dyadic theories of communication account for the process of meaning making, but they do so without incorporating the physical world explicitly. In Wayne Woodward's (1996) conclusion regarding the language theory of Charles Peirce (1955/1940), for example, language unites communities sociologically, but the "constraints of the physical/material/technological environment are essentially omitted from consideration" (Woodward, 1996, p. 158; cf. Christians, 1997, pp. 74–75). Heidegger's philosophy of technology contradicts this instrumentalist paradigm. Given his argument that the current epoch of Being is technological in character, Heidegger would oppose dyadic communication theories in which symbolically negotiated worlds are devoid of the technological context.

Constructions that are triadic do exist within the tradition of symbolic theory. George Herbert Mead, for example, "situates human symbolic practices within the structures and constraints of the bio-physical environment in which these practices occur . . . [He does not] resort to separate terminologies to analyze multiple levels of practices and constraints – mind, self, society, and the bio-physical environment" (Woodward, 1996, p. 160; see also Mead, 1934). Majid Tehranian (1991) reconstructs Mead, and in his working out of that legacy the technological domain is symbolically connected to knowledge (culture), through an "established or emerging stock of signals (technology)" (1991, p. 57). Mead's triadic theorizing includes the production of meaning through language and recognizes "the physical and artifactual constraints within, and by means of which, all communication materially occurs" (Woodward,

1996, p. 160). In Martin Buber's variation, our mode of existence includes both It and Thou in an irreducible relation (cf. Christians, 1997, p. 75).

The technology-oriented media ecology tradition is explicitly triadic also. Within this triadic paradigm, the material is highlighted. Examining the properties of media technologies is considered a productive strategy for understanding cultural patterns and social relations. In fact, this is a detailed triadic paradigm in which the material features of particular technologies are *sine qua non* for grasping human perception and cultural formation. The technological process is not unidirectional, but, as in Heidegger's existentialism, a dialectical revealing of the concealed.

If research projects on mediation do not incorporate the technological dimension into their frame of reference, they perpetuate an instrumental approach to technology and leave the dynamic ontological domain unattended. In Cornel West's critique of the dyadic tradition, represented in this case by Richard Rorty's pragmatism, "[It] only kicks the philosophical props from under liberal bourgeois capitalist societies. It requires no change in our cultural and political practices. What then are the ethical and political consequences of this neopragmatism? On the macrosocial level, there simply are none" (West, 1989, p. 206; quoted in Christians, 1997, p. 75).

Of particular relevance to media ethics, the necessity of triadic approaches in the cyber technology era makes virtue ethics problematic. Virtue ethics is dyadic in structure and, therefore, best suited to dyadic communication. Virtue ethics represents a blue ribbon tradition, East and West, and deserves full consideration as a media ethics theory for the twenty-first century. Confucius (551–479) was the first philosopher known in history to create a morality of virtue. More than a century later, Aristotle developed virtue ethics systematically in the West. For the ages, they established the idea that excellence in virtue, not social position, determines human status. Their understanding of morality reflects key insights into the nature of humanness. Which virtues are celebrated and practiced depends on a culture's definition of the hero. When human beings develop their capacities to the fullest, they achieve what Aristotle's *Nicomachean Ethics* called *eudaemonia* (well-being). Virtue ethics is a moral system of profundity, and it attracts premier scholars in both professional and philosophical ethics (e.g., Plaisance, 2015; Borden, 2007).

Charles Ess (2012a) advocates virtue ethics for the social media since both the ethics and the technology are interpersonal in character (pp. 238–245). This approach does work on the level of mediated conversation, such as with Facebook and Renren. But even this direct application to the social media does not pass triadic scrutiny. Triadic thinking insists on institutional analysis of the social media transformation currently underway.

Social media are the dynamo of the Web 2.0: YouTube, Vk.com, Facebook, WeChat, Reddit, Snapchat, Renren, Twitter, and Instagram. However, for all its interactive promise, Web 2.0 has been grafted onto the existing internet, which since the late 1990s in capitalist societies has been largely a commercial enterprise. Facebook, for example, is a for-profit company founded and organized to generate revenue. Regarding organizational culture, Facebook is an advertising and marketing provider, not simply a social network. Its business is advertising. Owners and managers nurture a company culture that urges the sharing of more information more often. All increases in profile data benefit Facebook's investors. The goal of for-profit businesses to create value for shareholders places a constant emphasis on relentless growth in both size and depth – the incentive for the company to control more and more of the users' data. Journalist Eliot Van Buskirk stated it correctly when he wrote: "Social networking feels fine, but we pay for it in ways that may not be readily apparent. The rich personal data many of us enter into these networks is a treasure trove for marketers whose job is to target us with ever-increasing accuracy" (www.wired.business/author/eliotv b/2009/04). Facebook's organizational culture defines users in its own terms rather than on their own. Triadic communication research and theory asks the question: Will advertising networks, digital marketing specialists, and trade lobbying groups continue to administer the new media world, or "will it become a vibrant network for news, information, and other content necessary for a civil society" (www.demo craticmedia.org)?

From an organizational perspective, virtue ethics presumes that media systems can be morally revitalized by the training and enabling of virtuous people; when their number reaches a critical mass, the field will be transformed. In triadic terms, depending on personal motivation while ignoring structural constraints is insubstantial. Institutional systems limit the choices of virtuous people and therefore reduce their influence. As long as the bureaucratic culture of social media organizations remains stable, virtuous professionals have marginal impact on the industry. Tolerance is a desirable virtue in social relations, but tolerance can become an excuse for moral indifference. On the other hand, when a human-centered philosophy of technology anchors global media ethics, a framework is established for triadic transformation of structures, technologies, and professional practice.

Third: Duty Ethics

The human-centered philosophy of technology recommends that a universal theory of media ethics be deontological in its orientation. Utilitarian media ethics is compatible with instrumentalism, and the inadequacy of instrumentalism as a framework for cyber technology points to the inadequacy of utilitarianism for the media ethics of global justice. This conclusion – rejecting the utilitarian canon and advocating a duty model for this book's ethics of being – needs elaboration to be understood correctly.

The most influential media ethics in these early years of the internet revolution is utilitarianism. Since the origins of this model – chiefly with Bentham's *Introduction to the Principles and Morals of Legislation* (1789) and John Stuart Mill – neutrality has been considered essential for guaranteeing individual autonomy. Neutrality is the core idea in instrumentalism, and the neutral actor was Mill's foundational concept in *On Liberty* (1859), in *Utilitarianism* (1861), and also in his *System of Logic* (1843). Persons are extrinsic to the domain of the good, given the fact that Mill represents the interconnected dualisms of individual liberty and social systems, subjective and objective, fact and value.[38] Utilitarian ethics was attractive for its compatibility with the standards of empirical epistemology. Moral action is guided by the degree to which it maximizes benefit and minimizes harm. It put into scientific terms the ordinary human motivation to avoid pain and pursue pleasure. Instead of appeals to metaphysics, calculable quantities became the basis of moral deliberation: "In the utilitarian perspective, one validated an ethical position by hard evidence ... What counts as human happiness was thought to be something conceptually unproblematic, a scientifically establishable domain of facts ... One could abandon all the metaphysical or theological

---

[38] This concept of neutrality and the dualism it presumes are the intellectual basis for Bernard Williams's (1973) complicated critique of utilitarianism. Utilitarianism's extreme view of impartiality leads to what Williams considers a convoluted idea of responsibility in which there is no specifiable difference between "my producing an outcome" and "someone else's producing it" (pp. 98–99). Or, regarding another argument summarizing Williams's critique, in utilitarianism we are alienated from our moral feelings and from our actions. Alienation from actions, from decisions, and from attitudes constitutes an attack on a person's psychological identity and integrity (pp. 108–118).

factors ... which made ethical questions scientifically undecidable" (Taylor, 1982, p. 129). Utilitarianism "portrays all moral issues as discrete problems amenable to largely technical solutions" (Euben, 1981, p. 117). To its critics, however, the exactness of this one-factor ethics represents a "semblance of validity" by leaving out whatever is not measurable (Taylor, 1982, p. 143).[39]

Rather than the intrinsic rightness or wrongness of acts and policies themselves, utilitarian action is based on the effects of behavior or policy. Utility's calculus fits online journalism's emphasis on the public's right to know. It accords with the commitment in public relations and advertising to provide clients with the maximum benefits at the least cost. For the entertainment industry, utility supports supply and demand in market capitalism and the profitability calculations of business institutions. In some such specific situations of the media technologies – print, broadcast, digital – consequences are a reliable guide. But for orienting an international theory of ethics in the digital age, utilitarianism is unqualified.

A framework in which one factor determines moral action does not meaningfully engage such issues as diversity in media culture, justice regarding media distribution, truth telling in digital networks, violence under conditions of anonymity, and bullying in cyberspace. The theory depends on an accurate assessment of consequences, when in complicated affairs results are often unknown, and long-term consequences unavailable for measurement. The inadequacies of the individualist utilitarianism that has dominated media ethics historically, and its weaknesses as a potential global media ethics, recommend its alternative – an ethics of duty for the ontological complexities of the digital era.

Deontology recognizes that human communities require from within themselves dutiful actions to maintain their humanness. In duty ethics, people have responsibilities to one another, regardless of the consequences. The ethics of duty covers the entire time frame of our existence, past and present, not only the future effects that follow from our actions. Duty responds to a broad range of human experiences and relations. The responsible self interacts with the entire space and time configurations

---

[39] Ross's critique of utilitarianism centers on the utilitarian presumption that others are morally significant to us only when their actions impact ours (1930, pp. 17–21). In Bentham and Mill, the future results alone are determinative. But, Ross asks, why should possible benefits in the future count for more than gratitude to others for their deeds of the past? There are duties of justice that require us to ignore or even upset the balance of happiness (Ross, 1930, p. 21; cf. Ross, 1939, Lectures II and IV).

of human existence. Living dutifully in accordance with moral norms enables us to supersede subjective approaches that are easily rationalized when convenient (cf. Bok, 1979, chap. 6). Moral action is considered an obligation always to be obeyed except possibly under the rare conditions of extreme crisis.

A deontological ethics of justice addresses most meaningfully the mass media as a social institution, keeping the issues lodged in the institutional and cultural context. It wrestles forthrightly with organizational structures and probes directly into the substantive questions about economics, management and bureaucracy, ideological politics, allocation of resources, collective alienation, the press's *raison d'être*, and distributive justice. As developed in Chapter 3, this is a substantive ethics in which the central questions are both sociopolitical and moral. For global media ethics to be done more comprehensively than heretofore, the stimulating concept of duty ethics ought to orient the discourse.

Kant's version has dominated the deontological tradition. He argues that acting purely from duty rests on the presumption that the highest good must be both intrinsically good and good without qualification. He concludes there is only one thing that is truly good: "Nothing in the world – indeed nothing even beyond the world – can possibly be conceived which could be called good without qualification, except a good will." Persons have a good will when they "act out of respect for the moral law" (Kant, 1785, I.1). This is a deontology of moral absolutism, with varieties in the history of ideas such as the basics of divine command theory.[40]

W. D. Ross (1930) rejects both utilitarianism and Kant's duty tradition because we usually confront multiple moral claims at the same time. He defines certain duties as *prima facie*, that is, obligations that are self-

---

[40] The Kantian duty tradition commits the rationalist fallacy: reason opens ethical analysis and closes it; reason is not seen as an important component of ethics, but determinative of it. Kant's rationalist absolutism is criticized in this chapter as unsuitable for the transnational and intercultural media ethics needed today, since its rational individual is defined by a particular time and place.

   The Cambridge philosopher and Kant specialist Onora O'Neill presents a different perspective on Kant and universals (cf. 2015, pt. I). In "Ethical Reasoning and Ideological Pluralism," O'Neill uses sophisticated versions of abstraction and idealization to argue against the "charge of empty formalism that Hegel first levelled against Kantian *Moralität*" (2016, p. 80). In her essay "Bounded and Cosmopolitan Justice," O'Neill demonstrates why Kant's intellectual starting point on international justice is superior to the presumptive issues in Rawls's *Political Liberalism* and *The Law of the Peoples*. She argues that Kant's "public reason as non-derivative," as developed in his Universal Principle of Justice, "aims deeper" and is "more realistic" and "more open" than "the account of justice across boundaries" that Rawls offers (2016, pp. 101, 117).

evident all things considered. Duties fundamental to the human community – such as fidelity, gratitude, justice, and non-maleficence – are morally binding unless explicit circumstances require other actions. It is too limiting to ask what produces the most good or what one thing is truly good. Neither covers the ordinary range of human circumstances. The *prima facie* duty of promise keeping is a prominent illustration in Ross. We fulfill promises because we conclude that we ought to do so, and because we have calculated the total consequences. What makes us "think that it's right to act in a certain way is the fact that" we have "promised to do so – that, and usually, nothing more" (Ross, 1930, p. 17).[41] Regarding justice, as emphasized in Chapter 6, Ross contends that the duties of justice are more complicated than abstract formal laws and typically require us to ignore the balance of happiness.

With a similar understanding of humans as dutifully responsible agents, Emmanuel Levinas (1981) argued that our duties to others are more quintessential to human identity than are individual rights or formal laws dictated from outside our being. Jürgen Habermas's neo-Kantian discourse ethics is a sophisticated reformulation of Kant's deontology in terms of communicative rationality. This tradition of duty ethics is most consistent with *Media Ethics and Global Justice in the Digital Age* and is elaborated in Chapter 3.

Fourth: New Generation Technologies

Artificial intelligence,[42] cyborgs, avatars, and robotics represent a new generation of communication technologies and processes. Media ecology gives us a rationale for taking them seriously, and the human-centered philosophy of technology is an appropriate framework for understanding them. A theory of global media ethics for its credibility and relevance should be able to include the newly emerging technologies in its purview (Gunkel, 2007). The ethics of global justice, worked out in this book, meets that standard.

---

[41] As an indication of promise keeping's importance as a *prima facie* duty, Ross (1939) devotes one of his Gifford Lectures (V) to it. In the Gifford Lectures, Ross responds to the criticism of his ethics as intuitionist by elaborating on *prima facie* obligations (IV) and examining the relationship of rightness and goodness.

[42] Robert Mejia in personal correspondence (May 17, 2018) made this pertinent observance: "It can be encompassed under the umbrella of artificial intelligence, but there has been a growing concern about search engines and information flows more generally, such as Andrejevic (2013), S. Noble (2018) and Eubanks (2018)."

Media ecologist David Gunkel's *The Machine Question: Critical Perspectives on AI, Robotics, and Ethics* (2012) is a comprehensive analysis of the issues to date (cf. Gunkel, 2016). Instrumentalism and Heideggerian perspectives are prominent throughout. Gunkel notes the increasing concern for ethical issues in artificial intelligence systems, and he turns to South Korea's "Robot Ethics Charter" and Japan's code of behavior for robots used in elder care, as examples (Gunkel, 2012, p. 2; cf. Floridi, 2011, pp. 144–158).[43] Besides humans, animals have received moral consideration, but Gunkel quotes J. S. Hall's (2001) summary of the twentieth century: "We have never considered ourselves to have 'moral' duties to our machines or them to us." Computerized intelligence, robotics, cyborgs, and avatars have organic properties that make Hall's conclusion inappropriate for the twenty-first century. We may be excused for thinking of AI as a mere tool, but as Ben Goertzel (2001, p. 1) explains it: "Not too far in the distant future, AI will possess true artificial general intelligence (AGI), not necessarily emulating human intelligence, but equaling and likely surpassing it. At this point, the morality or otherwise of AGI's will become a highly significant issue" (quoted in Gunkel, 2012, p. 32).

Gunkel gives us the appropriate framework: "Before new developments in moral thinking advance too far, we should take the time to ask some fundamental philosophical questions" (2012, p. 2). He cites Slavoj Žižek's elaboration: "There are not only true and false solutions, there are also false questions. The task of philosophy is to submit to critical analysis the questions themselves, to make us see how the very way we perceive a problem is an obstacle to its solution" (pp. 2, 12). Reflecting Heidegger's *Question Concerning Technology* in his title (*The Machine Question*), Gunkel exhibits the philosophical work of identifying the crucial issues in the new generation technologies: machines do not have moral agency comparable to humans, but should they not be held responsible and accountable in some legitimate sense (chap. 1)? To what extent "might machines constitute an Other in situations of moral concern and decision-making" therefore having legitimate rights that need to be respected (chap. 2; 2016)? Are there ways of explaining personhood so that moral responsibility includes not only the individual, but can be distributed across and attributed to a network system (Gunkel, 2012, chap. 3)?

---

[43] Charles Ess (2012b) emphasizes robot ethics because of the increasing use of robots in health care, combat, and sex (p. xv).

Consistent with the argument in this chapter against instrumentalism, Gunkel finds the instrumental tradition unable to ask the right questions: "Instrumental theory succeeds only by reducing technology, irrespective of design, construction, or operation, to a tool" (2012, p. 31). Instrumentalism does not interrogate the vitalistic nature of AI, robots, avatars, and cyborgs, and "in so doing makes inaccurate ontological decisions" that freeze them into an omnibus nonhuman category (p. 31). Instrumentalism is too elementary to ask the right questions, for example, about learning systems that are increasingly common in education, health care, manufacturing, and transportation. These machine systems are "able to decide on a course of action and to act without human intervention. The rules by which they act are not fixed during the production process, but can be changed during the operation of the machine by the machine itself . . . Nobody has enough control over the machine's actions to be able to assume responsibility for them" (Matthias, 2004, p. 177; quoted in Gunkel, 2012, pp. 35–36).[44] As Heidegger argued correctly, the boundaries between humans and technological products have broken down, and the new generation of digital systems indicates that decisively.

At a deep level and in troubling terms, artificial intelligence, cyborgs, avatars, and robotics are challenging the distinctiveness of the human species and the tradition of humanocentric ethics (cf. Floridi, 2014, chap. 6). To examine the issues, Robert Mejia (2012) analyzes Project LifeLike – the attempt in the visualization laboratories of various universities to create a lifelike avatar supported by an intelligent engine, capable of online learning. The world's first self-made cyborg, Steve Mann (professor of engineering at the University of Toronto) wears the EyeTap Digital Camera for Neuromancer vision that he invented. He experiments with flesh plug-ins and explores new ideas about wearing voice-activated technology (Mann, 2001, 2003; cf. Nelson, 2013). Heidi Campbell (2006, p. 284) credits Donna Haraway with transforming the cyborg from a science fiction image to a conception of being in her essay "A Cyborg Manifesto" in 1985 and her book *Simians, Cyborgs and Women* in 1991. As an alternative to anthropocentric ethics, Gunkel (2006, 2007) proposes a machinic ethics. The mainstream conception of morality consists of systematic rules that can be encoded to direct behavior and govern

---

[44] Robert Mejia's personal correspondence (May 17, 2018) is instructive: "I agree with Matthias to an extent, but as S. Noble (2018) notes, some of these unpredictable outcomes are also due to their biases already embedded into the program in the first place."

conduct. In Gunkel's view, why then should we consider thinking machines to be outside moral reasoning?

The artifices born of artificial intelligence are said to manifest a form of posthuman identity (Pepperell, 2003). According to Pepperell's "The Posthuman Manifesto" (2003), civilization has already entered a posthuman era where "humans are no longer the most important thing in the universe" (Postulate 1.1), and "all technological progress of human society is geared toward the transformation of the human species." In contrast to the humanist philosophy of technology where humanity is embedded in, but distinct from, the natural world, "the posthuman chooses to lose part of his or her being in an emerging technological whole" (Campbell, 2006, p. 281; cf. Müller, 2016).[45] As Pepperell notes,

In the digital world virtually any information can be encoded into a stream of "bits" which can then be transmitted and stored in very high volume. In this electronic world one's physical attributes will be less significant than one's virtual presence or "telepresence." In telepresent environments it will be difficult to determine where a person "is", or what distinguishes them from the technological form they take. (2003, p. 4)

For Mejia, Project LifeLike's technological innovation is seeking to define what constitutes life. He argues that the scientific analysis of Project LifeLike must give way to an ontological investigation. Life is being redefined as a "data-processing entity": "Life ceases to become life, and instead is reconfigured into a potential source of energy for a technological apparatus ... Humanity, in having sought to author its own creation, ends up producing mechanisms for its own ontological erasure" (Mejia, 2012, pp. 15–16).

Mejia observes that the concept of "synthetic selves" challenges the traditional ethics of consciousness. The question is whether there can be a meaningful ethics of artificial consciousness: "To be human is to possess a consciousness *a priori*. Artificial intelligence is denied this possibility in advance; rather, consciousness will emerge as a byproduct of design" (Mejia, 2012, p. 24). The historical questions of ethics are necessary as always: By whose design? Who will be the judge? The challenge for ethics in the face of artificial intelligence and its offspring is to account for "the shifting ontologies of what it ... means to be human" (Mejia, 2012, p. 27).

[45] For elaboration of the ethical issues in posthumanism, see the special issue of *Explorations in Media Ecology*, 5(4), 2006, summarized in Christians's response, pp. 317–320.

Daniel Dennett (2014) labels this perspective "old-fashioned vitalism" that claims consciousness exists in an organic brain and robots are inorganic. In Dennett's view, vitalism is dead: "As biochemistry has shown in matchless detail, the powers of organic compounds are themselves all mechanistically reducible and hence mechanistically reproducible at one scale or another in alternative physical media" (2014, p. 589). Dennett's dismissal of vitalism makes sense in the instrumentalist worldview, but ontology in the Heideggerian philosophies of language and of technology, as Mejia represents it, is systemic in that machines and human consciousness meld to create a particular social ethics. Regarding an artificial lifeform beyond human existence, the legacy of human-centered technology is explicit. Its ontology is intellectually thick, but, compared to the Cartesian tradition, Heideggerian existentialism does not endorse an ethics of artificial consciousness. Heidegger warns of destining when human existence itself is buried in the technological process.

However, while the Heideggerian tradition is critical of the posthuman phenomenon, in its shift from the subject-object dualism to an existential ontology, it has the philosophical framework to participate meaningfully in the debates over human existence and new generation technologies. F. Allan Hanson sees promise, for example, in the "extended agency" concept whereby "moral agency is distributed across both human and technological artifacts" (2009, p. 94; cf. Gunkel, 2012, pp.164–165). As an alternative to an ethics of autonomous individuals, David Channell (1991) argues for an ethics of "vital machines" (p. 151):

What Channell advocates is a shift in perspective from a myopic Cartesian subject to a holistic ecological orientation – a bionic framework – in which each element becomes what it is as a product of the position it occupies within the whole and is granted appropriate rights and responsibilities in accordance with the functioning and continued success of the entire system. (Gunkel, 2012, p. 167)

Nick Bostrom (2014) uses a different rationale and vocabulary but argues for a similar strategy. He eschews the human-posthuman dichotomy and considers the "inevitable consequences" trajectory unproductive, that is, that posthumanity will conquer (or pose a threat to) "ordinary humans." In Bostrom's "transhumanism," there are alternative definitions of human dignity for which posthumanity qualifies. Instead of continuing unresolved debates, the transhumanist project recommends that we work on a humane ethics and "create more inclusive social structures that accord appropriate moral recognition and legal rights to all who need them, be they male or female, black or white, flesh or silicone" (2014, p. 499).

From a historical perspective, Luciano Floridi is able to overcome dualisms and offer a new framework for understanding digital generation technologies. In his *The Fourth Revolution* (2014), today's digital era is "the beginning of a profound cultural revolution" (p. vi), and Floridi states the philosopher's task in radical terms:

> Given the unprecedented novelties that the dawn of the information era is producing, it is not surprising that many of our fundamental philosophical views, so entrenched in history and above all in the industrial age, may need to be upgraded and complemented, if not entirely replaced ... We need philosophy to develop the right intellectual framework that can help us semanticize (give meaning to and make sense of) our new predicament. In short, we need a philosophy of information as a philosophy *of* our time and *for* our time. (pp. viii–ix; cf. Floridi, 2011)

For Floridi, the cyborg phenomenon and posthumanism only speak to a narrow sector of the revolution now underway: "The fourth revolution should not be confused with the vision of a 'cyborged' humanity ... Being a sort of cyborg is not what people will embrace, but what they will try to avoid, unless it is inevitable" (Floridi, 2014, p. 95). Similar "fashionable ideas" Floridi finds "indicative and sometimes suggestive," but "unconvincing." The "problem is much more profound. We need to do some serious philosophical digging" (2014, p. ix).

In Floridi's (2014) historical account, the information society was initiated recently, when "the recording and transmitting facilities of ICTs evolved into processing capabilities" (p. ix). Parallel to the ontological framework of *Media Ethics and Global Justice in the Digital Age*, Floridi develops a "philosophical anthropology in terms of a fourth revolution in our self-understanding" (p. ix), one that follows "three scientific revolutions in the past" that "modified our conception of who we are" (p. 87):

> We used to think that we were at the centre of the universe ... In 1543, Nicolaus Copernicus published his treatise on the movements of the planets around the sun ... His heliocentric cosmology forever displaced the Earth as the centre of the universe and made us reconsider, quite literally, our own place and role in it ... After the Copernican revolution, we retrenched by holding on to the belief in our centrality at least on planet earth. (pp. 87–88)

The second revolution occurred in 1859, when Charles Darwin's natural selection scientifically "displaced us from the centre of the biological kingdom ... We consoled ourselves with a different kind of importance ... We thought that, although we were no longer at the centre of the universe or of the animal kingdom, we were still the masters of our own mental contents" (p. 89). In the tradition of Descartes's "I think therefore I am," we defended our "special place in the universe" as the "ability of conscious self-reflection, fully transparent to, and in control of, itself" (p. 89).

Sigmund Freud shattered this illusion: "It was a third revolution. He argued that the mind is also unconscious and subject to defense mechanisms such as repression ... We have been displaced from the centre of the realm of pure and transparent consciousness" (pp. 89–90).

We are experiencing today a fourth revolution, caught up in a process of reassessing "our fundamental nature and role in the universe" (p. 90). Since Freud, we have still insisted on

our special place in the universe ... not as a matter of astronomy, biology, or mental transparency, but of superior thinking abilities ... Whenever a task required some intelligent thinking, we were the best by far, and could only compete with each other ... We quietly presumed to be at the centre of the infosphere, joined by no other earthly creature. (p. 91)

We are slowly accepting

the post-Turing idea that we are not Newtonian, stand-alone and unique agents ... Rather, we are informational organisms (inforgs), mutually connected and embedded in an informational environment (the infosphere), which we share with other informational agents, both natural and artificial, that also process information logically and autonomously ... and so be in charge of their own behaviors. Once this feature is fully exploited, the human user may become redundant. (pp. 94, 32)

At the end of this ontological shift – as with Baudrillard's simulacra – the infosphere will be "synonymous with reality itself" (p. 50).

A global media ethics responsive to the human-centered philosophy of technology is not constituted by the individual subject and therefore welcomes for the new generation technologies those initiatives in what Joanna Zylinska (2009) calls "distributive and composite agency" (p. 200; cf. Gunkel, 2012, p. 169). Following Gunkel's review of the various ways moral responsibility can be "distributed across a network for interrelated and interacting participants," he proposes an alternative in Emmanuel Levinas's (1987) radical otherness (2012, pp. 170, 175–181; 2016). The ontological framework of the Heideggerian tradition engages these questions of morality and identity (Floridi, 2014, chap. 3), particularly as these are configured in Chapter 4, "The Ethics of Human Dignity."[46]

CONCLUSION

Developing a new theory of media ethics for the twenty-first century is a double-edged enterprise requiring sophisticated thinking on both the media and ethics. Today's virtual revolution challenges us to move beyond the simplicities of tools and engineering systems, and the media ecology perspective meets that challenge. While penetrating into the nature of mediations, technological culture as a whole becomes the larger framework. The philosophy of technology recommends a humanities perspective for professional ethics that brings the media side of the equation into intellectual equivalence with the moral philosophy context.

The purpose of this book is to present a new theory of media ethics centered on transnational justice. The philosophy of technology establishes the foundation and boundaries for this theory, ensuring its relevance for this turning-point era. The Web 2.0 transformation gives organic unity to an ethics of the global media by insisting on the four features introduced earlier: (a) humanistic instead of absolutist universals, (b) triadic communication theory instead of the dyadic approach in both communication theory and in media ethics, (c) duty ethics instead of utilitarianism, and (d) an ethical theory that addresses the new ontological formations.

From the philosophy-of-technology perspective, the primordial issues in global media ethics can never be solved once and for all. Given the complexity of communication ethics in a media regime governed by the technological imperative, no one academic or media professional is competent to address these issues singlehandedly. Education focuses our attention on the values that drive the technological order – calling for a transformation in our commitments to them. And only when these values, these dimensions of the instrumental worldview, are revolutionized will radical changes occur in technological regimes.

The overwhelming power of instrumentalism tends to trap electronic technologies such as the new digital media within its efficiency. A human-centered philosophy of technology does emerge on occasion from quality

---

[46] Rafael Capurro (e.g., 2006, 2008) adds to the analysis of *Media Ethics and Global Justice in the Digital Age* with his reflections in the Heideggerian tradition regarding digital reality as ontological, epistemological, and metaphysical and his conclusions regarding the moral status of artificial agents (cf. Kelly & Beilby, 2016).

professionals, internet users, media executives, and academics. But if we are enamored of tools, we tend to be satisfied with means rather than ends. Both ethical theories and professional practices are a social and cultural resource when they are inspired by philosophical reflection in a technological age.

2

The Ethics of Being

Czechoslovakia's playwright and president Václav Havel understood more clearly than most of us that this present historic juncture requires a new vision cosmic in scope. "We are rightly preoccupied," he said, "with finding the key to ensure the survival of a civilization that is global and at the same time clearly multicultural" (Havel, 1994, p. 614; cf. 1989b). We fret over the possibility of "generally respected mechanisms of peaceful coexistence" and wonder "on what set of principles they are to be established." Many believe that this central political task early in a new century "can be established through technical means ... But such efforts are doomed to fail if they do not grow out of something deeper, out of generally held values" (Havel, 1994, p. 614; cf. 1997). In Havel's terms, appeals to international forums for human rights and freedom are meaningless if they do not derive from respect for "the miracle of Being, the miracle of the universe, the miracle of nature, the miracle of our own existence" (1994, p. 615). The ethics of being contributes to Havel's project (cf. Zantovsky, 2014). Through human solidarity rooted in a universal reverence for life, we respect ourselves and genuinely value the participation of others in an increasingly technological age where "everything appears possible but almost nothing is certain" (Havel, 1994, p. 614).[1]

---

[1] Havel was the ninth and last president of Czechoslovakia and the first president of the Czech Republic (Zantovsky, 2014). Imprisoned by the Soviet regime, he authored a series of philosophical letters to his wife: these writings address the crucial significance of personal and collective responsibility in maintaining democratic freedoms amidst increasingly technological and bureaucratic social institutions ... Havel composed through these letters a significant work of political philosophy" (later published as *Letters to Olga*

UNIVERSAL SACREDNESS OF LIFE

The German philosopher Hans Jonas illustrates one strategy for establishing the idea of universal norms in ontological terms. For recovering the "miracle of Being," he turns to the "miracle of nature." Natural reality is not an inert object but speaks out of its own existence and puts the *homo sapiens* who inhabit it under moral obligation. Reverence for life on earth is the philosophical rationale for human action. That means respect for the organized whole, the physical realm that gives human civilization its home.²

In the Western Enlightenment, humans alone of all living species were considered conscious and purposeful, and what the Enlightenment called "nature" was spiritless matter. Jonas contradicts this dichotomy. He had no interest in a Newtonian cosmology, one that produced formal laws that exist in isolation outside human existence. In his perspective, purpose is embedded in the animate world, and its purposiveness is evident in bringing forth life. Instead of two orders of a contrary kind, animation is so prevailing that it can be said meaningfully that "nature evinces at least one determinate goal – life itself" (Jonas, 1984, p. 74). Thus, Jonas concludes, "showing the immanence of purpose in nature ... with the gaining of this premise, the decisive battle for ethical theory has been won" (p. 78). To be ethical means to show the same reverence for every animate being's will-to-live as one does for one's own livelihood.³

Jonas illustrates the idea of preserving life as an unquestioned duty with parents' responsibility for the children they procreate. When new life appears, the forbears do not calculate the options. They do not debate their relationship to it as though the offspring is neutral protoplasm, and their responsibility requires systematic review. It is an obligation "independent of prior assent or choice, irrevocable, and not given to alteration

---

[1989a]). James Carey (1997a, p. 213) calls *Letters to Olga* "one of the greatest political documents of our time" (Schultze, 2002, pp. 17, 61).

² Jonas's purposive life is fundamentally different from the teleological view of nature that was the basis of Aristotelianism for centuries. It does not entail essentialist natural phenomena ordered by intrinsic design. It does not presume that natural objects are substances consisting of form and matter.

³ In rejecting social constructionist claims that metaphysical truths do not exist, Jonas is not repeating the traditional view of ethics grounded in a static universe – an Aristotelian grounding of ethics in the nature of the human *psychê*, a Platonic anchor in the soul, or a theistic view of the world as a moral order under God. Instead of assuming a fixed and unchanging universe, Jonas speaks of purposive life on this side of Einstein, Freud, and Darwin.

of its terms by the participants" (Jonas, 1984, p. 95). The procreators' duty is an archetype of the self-evident accountability Jonas establishes – an obligation that is grounded ontologically.

For communications scholar Cynthia-Lou Coleman, member of the Osage nation, Native Americans as well as other First Peoples are one example of what it means to be steeped in the hallowing of life:

> The web of life comprises both the natural and sociocultural environments, all parts of a whole: interconnected, interdependent, and reciprocal. If one is injured, the other suffers. If natural resources are exploited, people are likely to be exploited as well. The web of life is the basis for the ethics of indigenous people. As a community, they are part of the life of nature, its soil, water, and sky. Perhaps the most important ethical principle of American Indians is harmony or balance within the universe of being. Such harmony is achieved only by a reverence for life – all life in the created order. (Coleman, 1997, p. 205)

As scientific knowledge expands, the web of life idea retains its relevance: "In a world populated by millions of other species and billions of nonhuman neighbors, it is impossible for human beings not to operate according to some kind of vision and ethic in relation to these creatures" (Gushee, 2013, p. 392). In the Ojibway and Osage worldview of belonging and balance, reciprocity defines the relationship between humans and the ecosystem. American Indian writers describe such values as the interdependence of people, animal, and plant life, in contrast to the prevailing European concept of the human species as dominant over other forms of life.

The ethics of being as interpreted by Jonas, the Osage nation, and Gushee's worldview history could be summarized this way: "Human beings have certain inescapable claims on one another which we cannot renounce except at the cost of our humanity" (Peukert, 1981, p. 11). The primal sacredness of life is a catalyst for binding humans universally into an organic whole. Since reverence for life is primordial, it does not generate abstract conceptions of the good with no motivating power. Given the oneness of the human species, in Peukert's terms, our minimum goal must be "a world in which human beings find ways of living together that enable every individual to work out a lifestyle based on recognition and respect of others, and to do so ultimately in a universal perspective not confined to small groups or nations … Universal solidarity is the basic principle of ethics and the normative core of all communications" (1981, p. 10).

In his etymological study, Gushee (2013) finds the terms "the sacredness of life," "sanctity of life," and "social worth" used interchangeably.

In the history of ideas, they refer to both human existence and moral duty (p. 13). The rationale for valuing human beings as worthy varies in substance from humans as image-bearers of God to the evolutionary chain of life. However, uniformly the concept is not limited to analytical definition but given moral status. The "sanctity of life" (referring to all forms of life) and the "sacredness of human life," nearly without exception, occur in sentences and phrases requiring a human response. Respect is considered an appropriate response to all forms of life and to human life, and for both, desecration is unacceptable (Gushee, 2013, pp. 17–20). In Gushee's summary: "This special/sacred status generally evokes in relation to X an attitude or posture of awe, veneration or honor. This attitudinal posture is accompanied by concrete moral obligations to treat X with due respect and even special care, and in particular to prevent any desecration of X" (p. 22). The ethics of being develops the sacredness of life in these terms as a moral obligation, not an ontological designation only.[4]

When locating ethics in being, reality is not raw material but is organized vertically and ordered internally among its parts. Aspects of reality are subspecies within species and species within genus; however, the relations among humans are horizontal in that no inferior race serves a superior one. The natural world is the presupposition of historical existence. Value formations operate within the limits of a given animate order, creativity within a cosmos that is a coherent whole. People shape their own view of reality through science and the arts. This fact, however, does not presume that reality is inherently formless until it is defined by human language into an intelligible order.

From a realist perspective, we discover truths about human existence in the natural world. This is ontological realism. It does not appeal to an objective sphere outside our subjectivity. Among human beings, the sacredness of life is a common understanding entailed by their creatureliness as lingual beings. The communications context is especially appropriate for understanding the scope and character of reverence for life. The symbolic theory of communication clarifies the complex relationship

---

[4] The term "sacredness" is standard in religious vocabulary, referring to deity. But it is also an anthropological term with its etymology from the Latin *sanctum*, meaning "set apart." The protonorm is presuppositional, pre-theoretical, and primordial. On that deep level, sacredness as a term grants extraordinariness to human life but is not invoking the higher level of organized religion, its doctrines, and institutions.

between specific human interactions and the global web of life as a whole.[5] Through natural language, *homo sapiens* establishes the differences and similarities of people's values. But these constructions are not *ex nihilo*. As we generate symbolic systems, we maintain boundaries between moral norms and actual behavior, while situating both of them in the natural order understood as purposive (Wuthnow, 1987).

Human responsibility regarding natural existence contributes the possibility of intrinsic imperatives to moral philosophy. It demonstrates the legitimacy of concluding that collective duty can be intercultural, and therefore irrespective of social customs or society's contracts. Through the preservation of life as the ground for human responsibility, from Jonas to Peukert normative discourse has been established. Their naturalism contradicts the presumption in the ethics of reason that no ought can be derived from being.

Multi-Level Research

In a study of ethical principles in thirteen countries on four continents, the sacredness of human life was consistently affirmed as a universal value (Christians & Traber, 1997). To foster participation and equality, workshops, educational retreats, focus groups, and consultations on multicultural ethics were held in various locations around the world. Sometimes these forums were scheduled alongside the conventions of the International Association for Media and Communication Research, as in Lake Bled, Slovenia, in 1990 and São Paulo, Brazil, in 1992. Other seminars were cosponsored by universities or professional organizations, such as the meetings in Moscow (1991); Colombo, Sri Lanka (1994); and Munich, Germany (1994). In these venues, local and regional scholars presented fifty major papers in six languages on the question: "What is the basic ethical principle that is nonnegotiable among your people, in your culture, in your moral theory? What is the bedrock value for you, the

---

[5] The most difficult questions of metaethics require a struggle over the philosophy of language. A radically human philosophy of communication rather than a theory modeled on machine systems or mathematical formulae, one that is radically opposed to monologic and transmission theories, can enable us to take Jonas's first-level approximation about responsibility for life and develop it into a complex protonorm. For an introduction to the theoretical issues regarding a dialogic approach to language and mind, Gadamer's (1989 [1965]) work is particularly helpful. As Richard Bernstein summarizes it, "Gadamer's entire project of philosophical hermeneutics can be read as an attempt to recover ... the quintessence of our being [as] dialogical" (Bernstein, 1983, p. 65; cf. Shin, 1994).

presupposition from which your moral thinking begins?" The project was designed to search for a starting point in ethics regardless of national identity, religion, and culture. The result was the sanctity of life as the first principle, not claimed as cognitive truth but a belief that human existence has an identifiable character.[6]

During the research process, it became obvious that the difficulties the global media face at present cannot be resolved by updating codes of ethics or through new technologies. As with Václav Havel, what the field needed was in-depth reflection on the fundamental norms that anchor ethical reasoning and moral choice. The decision, therefore, was not to be constrained by professional ethics in a narrow sense but to discover a normative vision or, at least, broadly based moral values. For an international communication ethics of this scope to be credible, it became obvious in this study that questions needed to be asked on two additional levels: within the domain of particular cultures, are there common values underlying them, and, if so, are they similar to the values of other cultural traditions? And on the level of communication practice and policy, are there master norms that provide direction and boundaries for media morality in its various technological forms?

Research and reflection on these questions produced ten chapters in the project report: on Arab-Islamic ethics, Hinduism in postcolonial India, the Latin American context of cultural identity, African communal values, American Indian discourse, politics in the People's Republic and in Taiwan, women and the US media, Japanese-style communication, and media ethics in Poland. This research representing thirteen countries is a limited sample; ideally, the three questions should be asked of all 6,500 languages in the world and 20,000 people groups. But this study and its sequels are explicitly international and cross-cultural and point international media ethics in the right direction toward a universal ethics of being.[7]

---

[6] Even though our affirmation of life is embedded in our being, there will be those who refuse to acknowledge it. It fulfills our humanness to affirm it, but it could be rejected as alien to our freedom or preferences. Some may claim a higher or deeper reason to deny rather than affirm or reflect the protonorm. All moral systems must account for human evil, and appealing to universals does not deny its existence. Whenever rejection occurs, because one believes in the protonorm's ubiquity, the response can still be in life-affirming terms on the ground that evil has crusted over it rather than eliminated it.

[7] While recognizing that several religious and cultural traditions consider human life to be sacred, Gushee (2013) develops the concept in terms of the Hebrew Scriptures and the Jewish tradition. He calls it the heart of Judeo-Christian ethics, with Christianity committed to it as a core belief during its first three centuries before "Christianity's fateful transition to Christendom" (p. 5). Peter Singer, in his "Unsanctifying Human Life" (1979),

Sacredness-of-Life Exemplars

Martin Buber (1970) gives the sacredness of life finality in his famous lines, "In the beginning is the relation" and the relation is "the cradle of life" (p. 69). He defines the relation ontologically as a category of Being. Human relationships, not individuals per se, have primacy: "Persons appear by entering into relation with other persons" (p. 112) and "The one basic word is the word-pair I-Thou" (p. 3). Rather than arguments and concepts and prescriptions, this embodied relationship gives moral anchorage.[8]

Buber's sociocultural classic *I and Thou [Ich und Du]* stands in direct contrast to Freud's internal states – *Ich* and *Es* and *Über-ich*. Buber's *Ich und Du* does not reflect humanity's internal being, but social relations. *Ich und Du* refers to human relations, not internal parts. Human existence in its authentic form is dialogic. For Buber, when we know the self-in-relation, then we understand reality. Not until the feminist ethics-of-relation was Buber's ontology understood clearly and expanded meaningfully.

Humans nurture I-Thou relationships with the natural world as a dimension of their corporeality in general and through their sense perceptions in particular. Although this does not attribute consciousness to trees, for example, Buber (1970) speaks of a mutuality that occurs in the ongoing oscillations of I-Thou and I-It relations: "It can happen, if will and grace are joined, that as I contemplate a tree I am drawn into a relation and the tree ceases to be an it" (p. 58) and "Relation is reciprocity ... and there are three spheres in which the world of relation arises: life with nature   life with men ... life with spiritual beings" (pp. 56–58). This is a reverence-for-life worldview that is explicitly social; it extends the personal to the farthest reaches of the universe.

---

considers this religious legacy the primary locus of the sacredness of life and uses instead a utilitarian set of values for defining human existence.

[8] Robert E. Wood (1969) argues that the two major philosophical problems at the turn of the twentieth century were the impasse between subjectivity and objectivity and the tension between spirit and life. In Wood's analysis, Edmund Husserl preoccupied himself with the first and Ernst Cassirer with the second. Martin Buber confronted both and connected them in this manner, according to Wood: "The path to his maturity was one long struggle with the problem of unity – in particular with the problem of the unity of spirit and life; and he saw the problem itself to be rooted in the supposition of the primacy of the subject-object relation ... Buber moved into a position which undercuts the subject-object dichotomy" (p. xi). Whether Buber fully unifies spirit and life remains debatable, but for the purposes of this chapter, his highlighting this problem endorses the sacredness of life as foundational for human existence.

Buber understood interhuman relations as the defining characteristic of being. This irreducible phenomenon cannot be disassociated into discrete elements without destroying its unitary wholeness. There are not three components, sender-message-receiver to be dismembered for scientific analysis. An Verlinden (2008), in his work on media ethics and globalization, considers Buber's mystical Judaism the best alternative to "abstract universalist imperialism" (p. 199), defined by Kant as moral absolutes. Verlinden summarizes Buber's relational ethics of being this way: "True norms never become a maxim: they do not command our obedience to authority but they command our *selves*; they address us *directly* in the situation where we are and leave us to respond with our whole being" (p. 202, emphasis added).

As another exemplar of the ethics of being, Albert Schweitzer (1875–1965) made the sacredness of life famous in the twentieth century (cf. Mayer, 2002). With PhD credentials, he was a notable Kantian scholar and specialized in theology at the University of Strasbourg. An accomplished musician, his book *Johann Sebastian Bach* still influences the way Bach's music is understood. Also trained as a physician, his greatest achievement by his own estimation was founding the Lambaréné Hospital in Gabon, in west central Africa. In 1952, he received the Nobel Peace Prize, and his address on that occasion, "The Problem of Peace," is considered the most intellectually profound statement on the reverence for life ever made. In one of his famous essays, "Civilization and Ethics in Graeco-Roman Philosophy," he argued that Western civilization was in decay because of its gradually abandoning the sacredness of life as its ethical foundation (Schweitzer, 1987, chap. 10; cf. 2009).

In reviewing Schweitzer's *The Philosophy of Civilization* (1987), Greg T. Smith calls it a monument, a "classic of global civilization." He chides industrial societies for putting too much emphasis on technological advances, for emphasizing what Chapter 1 calls "instrumentalism." Greg Smith (2003) concludes this about Schweitzer:

Einstein was not *the* person of the 20th century. Not by a long shot. Albert Schweitzer wins that distinction hands down. He weaved a legacy of the most accomplished Renaissance Man in the last 200 years. Combining intellectual brilliance with an amazing thirst for humanitarian service, Schweitzer made the world a much better place. He accomplished more in one lifetime than anyone I can think of. He should be the standard by which all global thought is measured

As Schweitzer noted, "True philosophy must start from the most immediate and comprehensive fact of consciousness" (1987, chap. 26). Respect for life, resulting from contemplation of one's own conscious will to live, leads individuals to live meaningfully by service to other people and to all living organisms (cf. Goodin, 2013). Schweitzer (1987) sharpens Jonas's purposiveness in his well-known summary line: "I am life that wants to live, in the midst of life that wants to live" (chap. 26).

Conclusion

Sacredness of life is a universal value – the fundamental starting point for an ethics of global justice. Rather than an ethics of formal prescriptions, this is an ethics of being in which the organic realm has a taken-for-granted character. A commitment to the sacredness of life entails a rejection of the Enlightenment's dualisms between self and language, the isolation of the individual from society, and the dichotomy of subject and object. Concrete human existence is inscribed in the vitalistic order as a whole. It is a counter-Enlightenment philosophy of communication that meets the challenge of J. B. Lotz: "The ontology of Being dominated by the person differs greatly from an ontology of Being dominated by the thing ... Ontology must be rescued from submission in things by being thought out entirely from the viewpoint of person and thus of Being" (1963, pp. 280, 294). We understand reality when we study human existence as self-identities bonded-in-relation and actualized in purposive nature.

This is a philosophy of communication not limited to hermeneutics and semantics, but one that is decisively anthro-ontological. Mediated systems, from this perspective, inescapably reflect the human-technology integration of the Heideggerian legacy. In literary works or cinema, the indispensable features of their inner dialectics – the point of departure, plot, setting, overall tone, their digital coding, and resolution of conflict – all reflect their cultures' value system and only on that level can they be understood. The sacredness of life is normative for both professional ethics and social morality. While the focus of this book is on mediated phenomena, the sanctity of life is broadly ontological, recommending itself as the basic norm of culture and politics.[9]

---

[9] Gushee (2013) is primarily concerned to establish the sacredness of life as a social ethics that speaks to the desecration of life in the Hitler regime and that can rebuild the moral order after World War II (chaps. 9–10).

PROTONORM

The sacredness of life is a protonorm, that is, an underlying norm about which there can be cross-cultural agreement. One meaning of *proto* is "before or initial or first," as in *prototype*, where a model is fabricated and engineers then reproduce it in a manufacturing process. That is not the definition here. *Proto* in Greek also means "underlying or lying beneath," as in the proto-Germanic, proto Sino-Tibetan, and proto Indo-European languages. Such "proto" families are lingual predecessors underlying the actual languages that exist in recorded history. These earliest lingual forms can be reconstructed from the languages we know. The veneration of human life is a protonorm in this sense – an underlying presupposition that is indispensable for systematic ethical reasoning. The notion of proto-norm roots ethical universals in ontology, rather than in rationalist impera-tives. A protonorm is a belief about human existence shared by those included in that category. The preservation of life has a presumptive char-acter (cf. Christians, 2010c, pp. 10–12).

Postcolonial theory challenges the commandeering universalism of the post-Enlightenment notions of reason and modernist-European concep-tions of universals (Rao, 2010; Wasserman, 2010; Rao & Wasserman, 2007). In the same way, theorizing from protonorms redirects our atten-tion to universalization as productively inclusive. Various concepts have emerged in the history of ideas to define what protonorm means: pre-theoretical beliefs, primordial generality, holistic being. Individually and together they indicate how the sacredness of life as a protonorm ought to be understood.

Pre-theoretical Beliefs

The sacredness of life is a pre-theoretical belief fundamental to the reason-ing that constructs the ethics of global justice. Thinking is impossible without taking something as a starting point. Aristotle's "unmoved mover" is a truism; human knowledge is incoherent if there is infinite regression. Theories are interpretive schemes for examining our basic values.[10] The theoretical world is grounded in first beliefs. A theory that is rooted in the protonorm "sacredness of life" enables moral agency; it

---

[10] Presuppositions are beliefs. Plato includes this notion in his definition of knowledge, defining the latter as justified true belief. In the epistemology of this tradition, unless something is true it is not knowledge. Stated in different terms, beliefs need to be grounded in truth to be distinct from superstition.

inspires us to think better and act strategically.[11] Theories of ethics are conditioned by our beliefs about the world. A faith commitment is *sine qua non* for making human cognition intelligible. Pre-theoretical givens represent the researcher's presumptions about reality. A dualism that regards the natural world as objective cannot account for the purposiveness of life. The argument of this chapter is that protonorms precede their construction into ethical principles. Reverence for life on earth is a pre-theoretical taken-for-granted that gives the moral order substance and direction.

Presuppositional epistemology represents what Michael Polanyi (1968) labeled "tacit knowledge." A British philosopher and chemist, Polanyi demonstrated the idea that the foundations of knowledge belong to our inner being. As we deal with particulars, we do not fully understand these specifics, but we make value judgments regarding them nonetheless and internalize them as beliefs.

Regarding Polanyi's tacit knowledge, positivists since Auguste Comte have been mistaken in thinking that natural phenomena are the self-evident source of knowledge. The explicit presupposes inexplicit knowing. Biological experimentation on rats, for example, is impossible unless tacit knowledge informs the scientist of ratness. The tacit knowledge of poetic ruleness is the basis for constructing what we call poems. A pianist knows harmony, which differs from an amalgam of technical finger movement. There is a presumption that language is meaningful or it could not be spoken. No news story can be disseminated without the tacit knowledge that humans are not machines that process technical data or animals that communicate by signals.

Implicit knowledge is not merely the imperfect counterpart to its explicit rendering. It is not like speculative alchemy, corrected by the precision of chemistry. Tacit thought is a feature of all knowing. Polanyi answers Plato's paradox in the *Meno*, in which problem solving is an intellectual

---

[11] Pre-theoretic beliefs sometimes are equated with intuitions – based on the assumption that language depends on mental concepts and that certain concepts are innate. The meaning here follows a different linguistic trajectory, referring to basic propositional attitudes about things and events that are sources of linguistic competency. In Ruth Kempson (1975), the pre-theoretical is taken-for-granted information required for communication to be sent or received, whether the lingual form is assertion, interrogation, narrative, or scientific fact. Kempson's *Presupposition and the Delimitation of Semantics* is the classic work on presuppositions in communication theory, analyzing both philosophical and linguistic approaches. It includes detailed application to such issues as circular reasoning, inference from presuppositions, and presupposing what is untrue (cf. Kempson, Fernando, & Asher, 2012).

conundrum: if you know what you are looking for, there is no problem; if you do not know what you are looking for, you will not recognize it if you discover it. Polanyi (1968) summarizes his argument this way: "Thought can only live on ground which we adopt in the service of a reality to which we submit" (p. xi). Interpretation is a property of our humanness, and this form of cognition is rooted in the primordial. Human knowing begins with core beliefs. Paul Ricoeur (1967) observes that philosophers presuppose the ideas of relevance and substance when they identify an intellectual starting point or reach a conclusion (pp. 391–392).

The sacredness-of-life as a concept belongs to the pre-theoretical category. Adherence to presuppositions is

a matter of commitment, not of epistemic certainty. We initiate any inquiry or action with presuppositions, because we must do so, not because they have been demonstrated. One's commitments are always open to question and thus are liable to be modified or replaced. But one cannot proceed in any enterprise without taking something as given. (Johnstone, 1994, p. 301)

Reflecting Gushee, for those who recognize the pre-theoretical conditions of knowledge, worldview epistemology is ontological and not accidental. Worldviews are most accurately defined as the ultimate commitments at the core of our Being. Worldviews are the axis around which our thinking revolves. Worldviews give meaning to our consciousness. They represent a set of basic beliefs about the character of human existence. Presuppositions are primordial in theorizing moral theory, or stated negatively, theories are not *ex nihilo*.

Primordial Generality

The idea of primordial generalities in the ethics of Emmanuel Levinas is the equivalent of protonorms. A relationship in which the Other has priority was his quintessential idea. Rather than an ethics of prescriptions, the moral order is rooted in the human relation (Levinas, 2003). When persons assume responsibility for Others, regardless of the cost, they are living ethically. The moral good does not take the form of prescriptions, but morality is embodied in otherness (Levinas, 1969).

"The first word from the Other's face is 'Thou shalt not kill.' It is an order," Levinas wrote. "There is a commandment in the appearance of the face, as if a master spoke to me ... The face opens the primordial discourse whose first word is obligation" (Levinas, 1985, pp. 89, 201; cf. 1981). The face, for Levinas, represents the totality of another's being. The face is the door to our personhood: "The face is what forbids us to kill" (Levinas, 1985, p. 86). The face of the Other calls me to a responsibility that is primordial, "before any beginning, decision, or initiative on my part ... Here is the appeal from which there is no escape, a responsibility, a state of being hostage" (Olthuis, 1997, p. 139). The infinite is revealed in the face-to-face encounter.

When I turn to the Other's flesh-and-blood countenance, I see not only a person, but the human race as a species. Though emanating from a single face, the Other's claim comes to me as a social directive; the emanation from the face is in the primordial mode of universality (Pinchevski, 2005). Ethics is fundamentally reoriented, from a preoccupation with personal decision making to the Other as both the initiator and the terminus: "Responsibility does not originate in me. My responsibility for the Other is a gift from the Other" (Murray, 2002, p. 175). Upon encountering the Other, I experience obligation: "The call of the Other is ethically transparent" (p. 181).

"Primordial" means in Levinas's ethics embryonic, prehistorical, pre-conceptual, and the primal scream. I do not capture the Other conceptually and calculate the specifics of the situation and then, as a third step, decide to act responsibly. The face-to-face encounter with the Other is the pristine ethical relation. When turning to the incarnate subject, a mode of infinity is revealed of which universals and essences are derivative (Wyschogrod, 1986).[12] According to Pinchevsky,

> Ethics is not the result of laws or norms or calculations; responsibility is the fundamental experience of subjectivity vis-à-vis the Other. Ethics does not proceed from knowledge. Responsibility towards the Other comes to pass through language but is not reducible to the contents of language. Being taken by the Other is an event of proximity taking place antecedent to the meaning thereby conveyed. (Pinchevski, 2005, p. 25)

The foundations of ethics cannot be contained within propositions: "Levinas declares that one's relation with the Other always exceeds one's ability to know or contain the Other" (Murray, 2002, p. 17).

Levinas's ethics of being issues no rules "to build a better self. He offers instead the reminder to listen to an ethical echo that was and will be forever linked to human existence" (Arnett, 2009, p. 200). As Husserl would put it, primordial givenness is neither natural law nor is it essence. We seize our

---

[12] Edith Wyschogrod (1990) prefers the term "carnal generality" for both Merleau Ponty and Levinas. In their phenomenological tradition as she describes it, the primordial self is not the explicit consciousness of one's personhood. Primordial self refers to undifferentiated life before any representation of living individuals.

moral obligation existentially, not after reviewing a canon of truisms. The encounter with the Other is the beginning of comprehension, and it is actionable knowledge, though Others will never be fully comprehensible (Levinas, 1985). The bedrock of ethical theory is our mutual human existence across cultural, racial, and historical boundaries. The moral order is positioned first of all in ontology rather than epistemology: "In this way ethics ... is as old as creation. Being ethical is a primordial movement in the beckoning force of life itself" (Olthuis, 1997, p. 141).

Holistic Humans

The protonorm, reverence for life, conceives of humans as holistic beings. Ethics is rooted in our whole being – body, mind, and spirit. The protonorm makes *psychê* (spirit) integral to humanness, not reducing humans to body and mind. To the rational and biological aspects, the sacredness of life adds the symbolic, the interpretive domain, centered in the *psychê*. This is a holistic human being where the various dimensions of our humanness express themselves in and through one another. Humans are a complex whole with their various capacities of intellect, personality, and body depending on and interacting with one another.

The classical Greeks recognized the interpretive domain as the residual home of language.[13] From Hermes of mythology, creator of language, the Greeks invented the term *hermēneia* (hermeneutics, interpretation). Aristotle brought the interpretive modality into focus as an essential component of the human species; in the *Nicomachean Ethics,* he elaborated on the art of interpretation.[14] *Hermēneia* is not theoretical knowledge (*epistēmē*); it is not practical skill (*technē*) either, because it involves more than utility (cf. Gadamer, 1989 [1965], pp. 274–289).[15] *Hermēneia*

---

[13] For an earlier and more extensive treatment of interpretation in Aristotle, see Grossberg & Christians (1981).

[14] Aristotle used *hermēneia* as the title of an important treatise, *On Interpretation,* and interpretation is theorized in his *Rhetoric*. Plato initiated this theoretical enterprise in the *Politicus* 260d using the phrase *hé hermeneutikè technē* (the hermeneutical art). In addition to Plato and Aristotle, *hermēneia* and related concepts appear in such familiar ancients as Xenophon, Plutarch, Longinus, and Lucretius. The Hermes mythology of language is important to Greek thinking, from the *Iliad* and *Odyssey* through the Stoic period (cf. Grossberg & Christians, 1981, pp. 60–62).

[15] Gadamer (1989) first identified Aristotle's tripartite anthropology. Charles Peirce, in his exhaustive study of human symbols, concluded that there are only three possible configurations – induction, deduction, and retroduction. These processes reflect the same three modalities as Aristotle's.

determines what is appropriate when we make a moral decision. Through his attention to language, Aristotle confirmed that humans are moral beings not limited to the senses; in his definition, the human species has an interpretive orientation system not driven, first of all, by formal logic.

For Aristotle, because humans are an integrated entity, moral insight *(phronēsis)* has a theoretical dimension *(epistēmē)*. Moral insight depends on "the ability to deliberate and consequently to believe through deliberation that something is or is not to be done" (Engberg-Pederson, 1984, p. 152). However, *phronēsis* is necessarily practical "in the sense of actually leading to action"; it is not fundamentally an intellectual comprehension of "true universal propositions" (pp. 168–169). *Phronēsis* presumes the desire and willingness that belong to our unitary wholeness: "Reasoned argument is not sufficient" to make us act nobly; it only makes us see in particular situations what acts "we already want to do" (p. 135). In Aristotle's approach, humans do not automatically apply a universal principle residing in cognition; humans discover through the process of moral discernment "what should be done in situations in which this is not yet clear" (p. 238).

Phronēsis puts protonorms to work by integrating particulars into fundamental values. Practical wisdom is the ability to apply widely shared values to the practical contexts of everyday decision making. It is not a set of methodological procedures for putting theories into practice. Rational calculation, which is critical to moral absolutism, is replaced by our everyday experience with moral issues that we have learned as the good.[16]

The interpretive domain in the classical Greek tradition is lingual. And if language is the home of protonorms, then human bonds are not first of all the result of meeting basic human needs or of reason, but our personal and public lives are constituted by *hermēneia*. In functionalist instrumentalism, our cross-cultural webbing is typically political power or economic interdependence or information technology. In the body-spirit-mind ontology, the *pyschê* at the center of our being energizes our commitment to our common humanity.

Aristotle's tripartite human and the holistic being presupposed by the universal sacredness of life enter theorizing from different perspectives but overlap around the interpretive modality. While Aristotle's human being

---

[16] Patrick Plaisance writes eloquently about the problem of inductive research, recognizing the complicated issues in the relationship between data gathering and normative theorizing. He insists correctly that philosophical theory and social science research cannot be a zero-sum game (2011, pp. 96–101, 108–110).

was understood in essentialist terms and the sacredness of life is existential, they agree that language and morality have the same human home in the core of our organic wholeness.

Summary

The centerpiece of a twenty-first-century theory of global media ethics is presuppositional in character. The Eurocentric ethics of rationalism produces rule-ordered abstractions. The alternative proposal here takes presuppositions seriously in theory making.[17] With presuppositions – values, as they are commonly called – considered *sine qua non*, a new generation of global media ethics is possible that is transnational and multicultural.

Absolutist theories have failed as universals because they have not incorporated the complexities and richness of the presuppositional. Kant, as one such theorist, did not recognize that beliefs about society and culture were embedded in his categorical imperatives; he believed, instead, that the truth of ethical principles was understood in the same way by all rational beings.

The ethics of being is normative and positions itself effectively against absolutist theories that are likewise normative. But is it a cogent alternative to descriptive ethics that also operates globally? The ongoing Worlds of Journalism Study – hosted by Germany's Ludwig-Maximilians-Universität München – is a methodologically sophisticated descriptive ethics that helps to answer this question (Hanitzsch, 2007, 2013). Researchers in sixty-seven countries have interviewed more than 27,500 journalists (www.worldsofjournalism.org). A common methodology is used to study multidimensional influences on news production and to identify distinct journalism cultures around the world (Hanitzsch et al., 2010, p. 5). This research examines moral connections and disparities among journalists across the globe and thus contributes to the question of moral universals.

In epistemological terms, the Worlds of Journalism research project verifies that the reliability and accuracy of information are valued worldwide. There is also broad cross-cultural agreement that dubious methods

---

[17] Thomas Cooper's *A Time Before Deception* (1996) illustrates this interweaving as a basis for universals by researching indigenous groups: the Shuswap in Canada, Polynesians in Hawaii, and the Rock Point Navajo People. He concludes that the sophisticated understanding of truth in indigenous cultures and their integration of heart and mind demonstrate a fundamental human commitment to authentic communication.

of reporting should be avoided, even though stories might be jeopardized (Hanitzsch et al., 2010, p. 284). The research indicates that most journalists recognize and take seriously the idea of universal principles that span situations and contexts. Various factors of moral agency are also included – culture, moral judgment, ideals and values – thereby affirming that morality is multidimensional. To avoid isolating functions and behavior, the Worlds of Journalism research integrates roles, epistemologies, and ethical ideologies (Plaisance, Skewes, & Hanitzsch, 2012).

Descriptive social scientific research, such as this study, faces the dilemma that "is" and "ought" are distinct concepts: what is described cannot be considered normative without a category mistake. A pathway from description to principle is necessary: "The Worlds of Journalism research has a reasonably sophisticated concept of persons. To the extent personhood is made ontologically explicit and social-psychological measures are refined further to reflect holistic humans, an intellectual trajectory may be opened from descriptive to normative ethics" (Christians, 2013, p. 283). The ethics of being does not face this dilemma. Protonorms require and enable researchers to construct that pathway during the interpretive phase.

The relationship between social scientific comparative research like the Worlds of Journalism study and philosophical universals is contentious and unresolved. Alexander Nikolaev (2011) develops the debate in terms of social science's instrumentalism and philosophy's universalism. He proposes a comparative strategy nation by nation for developing theories in international terms.[18] He argues that social scientific comparative studies of different geographies of the world are the only alternative for a relativistic age (Nikolaev, 2011).

Contrary to Nikolaev, having diverse cultures judged by cross-cultural norms such as the sacredness of life follows the intellectual trajectory of Jürgen Habermas (1984). In his understanding of the public sphere, norms such as reciprocity are a necessary standard for deliberation, without which democratic life is impossible. As discussed in Chapter 3, communication is *sine qua non* for the social order, and in Habermas,

---

[18] As developed in Chapter 3, Sonia Livingstone (2010, p. 416) has concluded that the nation-state has set the boundaries for communication research and scholarship, rather than the more innovative strategy of organizing research around transnational information flows. Herman Wasserman (2018, p. 117) makes a similar argument, observing that even de-Westernization scholarship and other attempts to "diversify the scope of journalism and media studies are still premised on the nation-state or geographic regions as units of analysis."

communicative action requires an implicit set of rules for the human community to exist. Such norms, to be agreed upon, must be considered valid for everyone in the discursive community (1990, pp. 86–94). For the ethics of being, as with moral consciousness in Habermas's discourse ethics, universals are the bridging principle that makes multicultural studies possible.

COMMUNITY AS A NORMATIVE IDEAL

The sacredness of life as a protonorm revolutionizes the idea of universals in media ethics. As a presupposition and primordial generality located in the interpretive capacity, the reverence for life opposes Western forms of absolutism with a twenty-first-century universalism. Simultaneously, it presents an alternative to the individualist rationalism of absolutist models. Communities are the locus of morality rather than the personal decision maker of Eurocentric ethics. In formal terms, community is ontologically (in being) and axiologically (in what we value) prior to persons.

The model of international media ethics developed in this book retheorizes the dominant paradigm at its roots. The sacredness of life agrees with the sociological criticism of objectivist absolutism – that it has tended to breed totalitarianism and that transcendental truth is typically imperialistic, seeking to control dissenters. But the conceptual reconstruction of the sacredness of life around humanistic universals and *communis* is more fundamental. The humanistic philosophy of technology is ontological, and in its understanding of being, the sacredness of life is communitarian. The sacredness of life comes to expression in organic community.

On one level, community is a social configuration; in the ethics of being, it is a normative ideal (Bell, 2010). People's lives are bound up with the good of the community in which their identity is established. Community is the chief means by which humans undertake public responsibilities. This excludes contingent attachments such as garden club memberships that do not characterize one's well-being. *Habits of the Heart* introduces the term "lifestyle enclaves" to identify the community attachments that we value (Bellah et al., 1996, p. 335). Defining communities as those "attachments one values" is applicable to communities worldwide where these preferred forms of human life are attractively diverse.

Reverence for life as a universal protonorm can only be experienced locally and described culturally. This presupposition's symbolic forms locate it in history. Mentally, protonorms are universal; as a belief and concept, they reflect our condition as a species. Yet human beings enter them through their particular circumstances of ethnicity, geography, and ideology. A glass window is an analog of the relationship between the communal and the universal; there is a break conceptually, but the universal is only transparent in the local realm. Martin Buber's earthiness is one illustration of how the sacredness of life can be protected from an empty universalism: "A legitimate philosophical anthropology must know there is not merely a human species but also peoples, not only a human soul but also types and characters, not merely a human life, but also stages of life" (Buber & Friedman, 1965, p. 123).

Universal reverence for life establishes a flat plane for deliberation across cultures and for comparative research on the foundations of ethical communication. Societies across the world elaborate on this protonorm in different terms, but each of them can bring to ethical systematizing this basic norm for ordering political relationships and social institutions such as the media. The dynamic and primordial character of this protonorm is antithetical to essentialist and static views of human nature. The protonorm should be understood as the community and the universal in interactive relationship.

As the media ecology paradigm has documented, the symbolic realm is intrinsic to humanity, and it is the vehicle for uncovering dimensions of reality not accessible to other species. For Hans-Georg Gadamer (1989), language is the medium that uniquely makes space (geography) and time (history) available for human existence. The lingual property of *homo sapiens* is inherent, and therefore the exclusive domain of the interactive symbolic system is human livelihood. Communicative bonds convey value judgments about social well-being. Morality, therefore, must be understood in communal terms.

Counter-Enlightenment Ontology

The ethics of rationality is typically based on the Enlightenment's understanding of humans as rational beings. Situating the ethics of being in the counter-Enlightenment tradition will help to clarify its distinctiveness. The idea in the Enlightenment that the mind reflects impartially is replaced with a system of human interactions concerned with living meaningfully. In this counter-Enlightenment ontology, people are born into a lingual network of values and meaning. As a result, morally appropriate action is directed toward the communal. The common good is a preoccupation of, and justice the ultimate standard of, community formation.

People understand themselves primarily as beings-in-relation, and not in Lockean terms as individuals separated from others. Because the communal orientation is primary in the counter-Enlightenment tradition, the concept of ideal communities judges nation-states to be political aggregates construed artificially. Risto Kunelius identifies a historic turn: "Economic and political developments have begun to reposition the nation as the basic ingredient of international politics." The news media, dealing with transnational conflicts and communities in diaspora, are finding it necessary to reorient their thinking "in relation to the state and national identity" (2009, p. 139). In counter-Enlightenment ontology, industrial countries are not the principal yardstick by which to measure social success. Instead of seeing bordered nations as a homogenous Other – the uniform-nation model – decision making in counter-Enlightenment ontology is decentralized and polycentric. Political orders are understood to be a mosaic of people groups. The community model welcomes transborder and borderline concepts, hybridity, and the polychromatic. The aim of the community as a normative ideal is a public made up of publics, rather than the public as an assembly of individual entities under an external standpoint.

In summary, in the counter-Enlightenment legacy, the sacredness of life as a protonorm is ontological, rather than being epistemological in character. It is committed to the ontological-linguistic definition of the human species. In addition to drawing its communal ideas from this tradition, the sacredness of life benefits from the breadth and range of media ecology. Its elaboration in various areas of the world helps ensure that the ethics of being in this book is cosmopolitan.

Communitarian Democracy

The debates over community within counter-Enlightenment ontology have taken various forms across the globe. Though the community emphasis is often regional and local, working on the concept politically and culturally is contributing to the global perspective. Non-Western democracies, postcolonial Africa, and the Latin American regions influenced by liberation theology are especially active in developing the communal worldview. One debate that illustrates the issues for the ethics of global justice with its political orientation is communitarian democracy in North America.

Modern-day communitarianism was developed as an alternative to John Rawls's history-making *A Theory of Justice* (1971). Such political philosophers as Carole Pateman, Michael Sandel, and Charles Taylor disputed Rawls's procedural liberalism. They contended that an atomistic democracy of individual rights should be replaced by deliberative democracy instead. These scholars (plus Michael Walzer and Alasdair MacIntyre) considered the relationship between persons and community the basic issue, and in working on this relationship, they dealt with the excesses of individualism, especially its impact on morality (Sandel, 1984). Taylor, Pateman, Sandel, and Walzer did not themselves use the term "communitarian." However, communitarian democracy became the prominent label for their critique of the administrative liberalism of Rawls. Communitarianism united their work with the counter-Enlightenment tradition of humans as social beings, rather than defining them more narrowly as rational beings. And the term connects them to the Latin word-family *communis* that across cultures relocates our human center ontologically from the self to community.[19]

The communitarian argument, as they developed it, can be organized around three arguments: first, the conception of the common good has priority over fairness in the politics of individual rights. Second, individual rights are a prerogative only if we accept uncritically the idea that individual identities exist in isolation from history and culture. Third, since human identity is constituted socially and culturally, individual rights cannot be the cornerstone of the political order (cf. Gutmann, 1985).

In the communitarian perspective, what clarifies and enhances human identity is only known in specific social situations. The communal – our commonness, *communitas* – is the context in which values and morals can be understood. In the communitarian critique, the individualistic politics prominent since John Locke is only able to aggregate individual interests, which together are not the common good. A commitment to community might emerge as a possible aim of individuated selves, but the communal in the individualist trajectory is "not an ingredient of their identity" (Mulhall & Swift, 1996, pp. 49–52; cf. Sandel, 1995, pp. 59–65).

---

[19] As true also of Walzer, Taylor, Sandel, and Pateman, this book ignores Amitai Eztioni's use of the term for his sociological agenda in "The Communitarian Network." *Media Ethics and Global Justice in the Digital Age* is not promoting traditional community values. Sandel's book *What Money Can't Buy: The Moral Limits of Markets* (2012) illustrates an intellectually interesting *communis* rather than Etzioni's sociological model, *The Spirit of Community: Rights, Responsibilities and the Communitarian Agenda* (2013).

In liberal political theory, for instance, the domain of the good is extrinsic since members of society are distinct from a society's ends. The discreteness of individuality has priority over goods in the moral order.

In his *Liberalism and the Limits of Justice* (1995), Sandel argues against the political proceduralism that separates persons from their conceptions of the good: "Who, the communitarian asks, is the shadowy 'person' that exists independently of, and able freely to choose, the ends that give her life meaning and value" (Mulhall & Swift, 1996, p. 10)? In Sandel's view, if the relationship between the self and its ends is only voluntary, our understanding of political community is abbreviated. Communal goods are then only optional, a contender for priority among other possibilities. From this perspective, citizens think of themselves as "participants in a scheme of mutual cooperation, deriving advantages they could not have gained by their own efforts, but not tied to their fellow citizens by a bond whose severance or alteration would change their identity as persons" (Mulhall & Swift, 1996, p. 54; cf. Sandel, 1995, pp. 15–23). In communitarianism as a political philosophy, our own well-being is negated unless our self-definition includes helping others prosper. In other words, citizenship is not a voluntary contract with other citizens but characterized by reciprocal bonds that comprise human existence.

Sandel appeals to our human orientation in space and time: We typically see ourselves "as members of this family or community or nation or people, as bearers of this history, as sons or daughters of that revolution, as citizens of this republic" (1995, p. 179). These social configurations are involuntary. Some crucial dimensions of our identity are based on "enduring attachments and commitments which taken together partly define the person I am. To imagine a person without attachments" is to describe someone "of no moral depth" (Sandel, 1998, p. 179). What humans value are not individual creations, but they resonate with values that are located in and arise from the social worlds in which they live. The liberal concept of individuals originating their own conceptions of the good is contradicted by the actual moral experience of people documented in history (Sandel, 2010).

Communitarian democracy takes seriously the human-centered philosophy of technology; in so doing, it advocates the duty approach to ethics. For communitarians, democratic individualism in the tradition of Locke and Mill is confused about the nature of that duty. Carole Pateman (1985) understands the issue in communitarian terms: liberal democratic theory claims that a citizen's obligations to the government are delineated by voluntary arrangements with other citizens. Through the voting process, citizens decide individually how to fulfill their obligations to the government. However, to equate voting and obligation is superficial. Voting in liberal-democratic states is largely ritual, with many refusing to vote and some denied the right to vote. Moreover, since a minority vote is lost to the majority, how is voting a deliberate exercise of one's obligations (pp. 17–18)?

Instead of the voluntarism of individual rights, Pateman starts over theoretically in communitarian terms. From this perspective, when we assume an obligation we make a promise. And when promises are made, they carry an inherent obligation to act accordingly. Promise making and keeping is the basic form in which consenting persons "create their own social relationships" (Pateman, 1989, p. 61; cf. 1985, pp. 26–29). Ricoeur (1960) reiterates that promise making and keeping is ontological; he argues that as humans consciously apprehend their selfhood, this recognition entails promises to others. In his view, whenever we are true to our psychological well-being, we recognize that, in contrast to individual rights, promises are inscribed in our self-understanding. And significantly, promises are made first of all to other citizens and not to the state (Walzer, 1970, pp. 190–225). Therefore, obligations are not voluntary choices but oriented by promise keeping to fellow members of institutions and participants in political practices. Pateman recognizes the reality of human existence as rooted in mutual relationships. She comprehends the character of moral agency in reverence-for-life terms (cf. Christians, 1999, pp. 72–73). As an alternative to absolutes, the development of humanistic universals requires this kind of communal thinking. Communitarianism works in concert with ontological universalism, with the latter feeding into the former rather than each isolated in its own domain.

Technological Regimes

A three-step strategy is involved in the ethics of being. After identifying the problem of absolutist universals, step two is its revolutionary opposite in the sacredness of life as a global protonorm. Universals shaping community structures and professional practices comprise step three. And in the application of step three, we face the challenge of the professions as technological regimes.

In the philosophy-of-technology literature, professional communities that are advanced in technologies can be defined as technological regimes. The military, medicine, and international finance are high-technology enterprises, for example. Journalism, advertising, public relations, and entertainment have depended on sophisticated technologies since the days of electronics, and these media industries are on a new order of magnitude with digitalization. There are examples of cyberspace helping to create new human communities, but typically virtual communities are one-interest groups, demographic tribes, or what historian Daniel J. Boorstin called "consumption communities" (Schultze, 2002, p. 23).

While the instrumental-functional perspective does not use the term "technological regimes," instrumentalism is preoccupied with the tools used in professions such as the media. With its diffusion-of-tools mentality and its means-ends distinction, instrumentalism begins with the techno-logical reality itself and offers strategies for accomplishing technical ends through it. For the sacredness of life protonorm within the human-centered philosophy of technology, the challenge is more substantive and multilayered. Mechanistic criteria are made secondary to the concept of community-as-a-normative-ideal. The protonorm insists on the restructuring of media organizations, away from their bureaucratic stric-tures toward human-centered ideals.

The technological imperative is the important issue here. Bob Franklin (2005) calls the instrumentalism of the media "McJournalism." In his analysis, both the news enterprise and the fast-food industry are organized around mechanized procedures and uniformity. He illustrates with the Gannett media chain in the United States that for one type of news story, reporters are expected to use one press release or cooperative source, spend a maximum of fifty-four minutes to produce each story, and deliver forty such stories each week (Franklin, 2005, p. 145). When the BBC announced major staff reductions, for breaking news it called for four paragraphs in five minutes and ten paragraphs in fifteen minutes (Franklin, 2005, p. 146; cf. Goss, 2013, pp. 72–73).

The sacredness of life ought to be the media profession's protonorm in actuality rather than the technological imperative by default. When nor-mative ethics is grounded ontologically, there is a frame of reference for measuring and interpreting events and communities. Standards provide an essential pathway for forming the common good. Communities take negative turns; organizational decisions are not always legitimate as the Gannett and BBC examples testify. In the ethics of being, the crucial question is whether social or professional communities affirm the sacred-ness of life. The criterion for assessment is not economic or political success but whether media professionals in theory and practice contribute to hallowing the web of life. All genres of communication – oral, print, broadcast, and digital – face the same question from the ethics of being: Do they contribute to human well-being as a whole and long term? In other words, the challenge for media organizations is not only their political insight in news and aesthetic power in entertainment and effective interaction among users; implementing the sacredness of life requires moral discernment (cf. Wilkins & Coleman, 2005; Coleman & Wilkins, 2009).

To elaborate: news discourse with a mission to advance public discussion should also enable audiences and users to connect the issues to universal norms. The news addresses people's minds; does it also speak to their *psychê*? Does the press disclose the underlying meanings and situate those meanings into the sacredness-of-life protonorm? When the ethical media invigorate the moral imagination, their readers and viewers and users will be reminded that other human beings across the globe are also struggling in their consciences with human values of a similar sort. The best possible scenario is for media professionals to search actively for opportunities to put this universal protonorm to work, through the sacredness of life expanding our knowledge of what it means to be human.

When there is a commitment to the universal ethics of being, ethical discourse and application move beyond the good of one's tribe or culture to promote the human good for all members of the species. As Appiah (1992, p. 16) states about African identity: "We will only solve our problems if we see them as human problems arising out of a special situation."

THEORETICAL PLURALISM

Several initiatives are underway to establish a global media ethics that follows the humanities model of protonorms, but these initiatives differ from monism. This new kind of universal is stretched across space rather than unchanging over time, and in that latter sense, these theories are not absolutist.[20] What follows are credible attempts to shift the field from

---

[20] Patrick Plaisance is developing an international media ethics based on recent advances in moral psychology and virtue theory. See Christians (2013, pp. 281–283) for a summary and the relevant literature.

Universals are an issue in philosophical ethics also, notably so with the University of Chicago's Martha Nussbaum (2000; cf. 2006, chaps. 4–5). Based on her research in India, she identifies capabilities that become evident in people's daily activities. The idea of capabilities respects "each person's struggle for flourishing; it treats each person as an end, and a source of energy and worth in her own right" (2000, p. 69). Common values

individual autonomy to universal humanity, and to do so by eschewing monism and without being trapped in philosophical relativism (cf. Young & Saxe, 2011). These universalist options, summarized in this section, are generally compatible in their purpose and structure with the sacredness of life. The philosophy of the human that they represent is likewise the view of human beings developed in the ethics of being. Reverence for life is fashioned self-consciously in this book alongside these contending theories, which are in various stages of development. Whether the sacredness-of-life protonorm moves international media ethics forward the most productively depends on its parsimony and innovation as compared to African communalism, Confucianism, contractual naturalism, and feminist theory.

The various concepts, histories, and problems of these five approaches, metaphorically, are dialects of the same language. They are pluralistic in that they feed from and into one another without any of them advocating the monism "that there is a unique and correct ranking among ethical values" (Ward, 2015a, p. 73). Moreover, choosing these five is not relativism, since they are held together by a body of similar ideas about universalism and against individualist rationalism. Community as ontologically distinct from individualism is the axis around which these five trajectories revolve, though it is an axis to differing degrees.

At this stage in the development of a viable international media ethics, there is no one, self-evident theory of universals that serves as the one master norm for what Kuhn (1996) calls "normal science." Instead, there are multiple theories, five identified here, that are coherent and actionable. The ethics of universals consistent with the humanistic philosophy of technology entails pluralism. Pluralism means a body of invigorating concepts that enables us to think better. In *The Morality of Pluralism*, John Kekes defines the concept this way: "Pluralism is an evaluative theory, because it is not an uncommitted analysis of the relations among various types of values involved in good lives but a theory motivated by

are evident from peoples' daily activity to meet their basic needs. Social goods become evident that people are able to achieve. Bodily health is one example: "Being able to have good health, including reproductive health, to be adequately nourished, to have adequate shelter" (2000, p. 78). Affiliation is another social good: "Being able to engage in various forms of social action; to have the capability of justice and friendship; freedom of assembly and political speech" (2000, p. 79). Of the many ways aspirations can be achieved, there is overlap and similarity, which suggests the possibility of cross-cultural social values. For Nussbaum, "theory is valuable for practice; …universal norms of human capability can provide the underpinning for a set of constitutional guarantees in all nations" (2000, pp. 35–36).

a concern for human beings actually living good lives. Consequently, pluralism is at once descriptive and evaluative" (Kekes, 1993, p.10; cf. Ward, 2015a, pp. 71–75). The sacredness of life, African communalism, Confucian *ren*, contractual naturalism, and feminist interactionism are the current trajectories doing systematic work that can meaningfully discuss and clarify among themselves the deeper issues in international communication ethics.

Theoretical pluralism requires critical scholarship.[21] In theoretical pluralism, concepts are developed in good faith and choices are defended intellectually. Thus, the reverence-for-life approach encourages theorizing in global media ethics outside absolutism. Three of the options are ongoing attempts in the West to develop theories of media ethics that are international – feminism and contractual naturalism, with ethical theory in *Media Ethics and Global Justice in the Digital Age* represented as the ethics of being. Two theories outside the Western axis are of special importance at present – African communalism and Confucianism. Islamic ethics has the potential of being included if there are major changes in its conceptual base.[22] These five theories, in various ways, establish the

---

[21] In the philosophy of science, theoretical pluralism "has been most often associated with Paul Feyerabend" (Martin, 1972, p. 342). In his formulation and the debate that has ensued, the question regards the methodology that is the most productive for scientific discovery. For theoretical monism, a research program yields the greatest scientific progress when one trajectory is totalized. Theoretical pluralism argues that alternative research programs are essential for maximum scientific progress, even though they demand resources and divert the single methodology option from critical testing. In this debate, what applies to natural science research programs also applies to the social sciences. Theoretical pluralism is the approach advocated for universal theories of ethics on the grounds that major conceptual innovation arises from multiple trajectories.

[22] Islamic media ethics is not included because its dominant formulation is absolutist at present. Justice, human dignity, and truth are divine commands. Islam is based on the oneness (*Tawhid*) of God. No God exists but Allah, and all Islamic virtues specifically and human responsibility generally are grounded in the belief in one God. This system of ethics is revealed in the *Qu'ran*, with Muhammad the prophet considered "a perfect model" (33:21) and "the exemplar of virtues" (68.4). The Prophet speaks the truth, and Allah's word in the *Qu'ran* is true. The First International Congress of Muslim Journalists held in Jakarta in 1981 recommended that all Muslims in the media should follow the Islamic rule of conduct, and the Association of Muslim Journalists has accepted this standard ever since.

Islamic scholar and communications theorist Haydar Sadig is working on Islamic ethics to internationalize it. He reminds Muslim media professionals that Islam is a religion of peace. The essence of Islam is in the word itself, *salam*, which in Arabic means peace (Sadig & Guta, 2011). He explains that over the thirteen years that the *Qu'ran* was revealed to the Prophet in Mecca, Muhammad was instructed to spread the word of Allah with grace, wisdom, and gentle admonition, and to preach the equality of men and women in all walks of life (Sadig & Guta, 2011). Sadig demonstrates that the

agenda for twenty-first-century international media ethics. Their common commitment to humanistic universals gives three ethical principles priority (truth, human dignity, nonviolence), each of which will be developed in the three chapters following.

African Communalism

Kwasi Wiredu, chair of the University of Ghana's Department of Philosophy (from 1963 to 1985), advocates both culturally defined values and universals that arise from our common humanity.[23] As colonized peoples seek to redefine their identities and rightly insist on the local, Wiredu also wants African intellectual history and concepts to help resolve some of today's cross-cultural struggles. While continuing to discuss the important question of whether an African philosophy exists, he does not want his work in philosophy separated from debates elsewhere in the world (Wiredu, 1980). In his book, *Cultural Universals and Particulars: An African Perspective* (1996), he asserts that our biological sameness is not incompatible with our culture. In his words, "human beings cannot live by particulars or universals alone, but by some combination of both ... Without universals intercultural communication must be impossible" (p. 1).

Wiredu's argument can be summarized this way: Of the languages around the world that are known, linguists have concluded that they are equally complex in phonemic structure. In terms of lingual structures, all

---

early Mecca text of the *Qu'ran* is meant for all peoples, whereas the Medina text that has dominated Islam is only a transitional stage (Sadig, 2017). When Islamic ethics is given that context of moderation, rather than following the sectarian strands of Islamic thought, Islamic ethics will become a world player in articulating the principles that ought to shape media ethics worldwide.

Professor Abderrahmane Azzi of the University of Sharjah has developed the influential value determinism theory. The University of Mostaganem recognized the influence of this theory by establishing "Azzi's Chair for Media Ethical Theorizing." (www.youtube .com/watch?v=JaBTptH7hbE)

[23] Wiredu was head of the Philosophy Department at the University of Ghana until his retirement in 1999. His first major book, *Philosophy and an African Culture* (1980), deals with African philosophy in terms of folk thought preserved in oral traditions and critical reflection. He contends that philosophical work is culture-relative but can be universal too. African philosophy uses historical resources and engages them in indigenous languages but then actually does philosophical work that is relevant outside these boundaries. As editor-in-chief of the Blackwell *Companion to African Philosophy* (2004), he provided comprehensive coverage of African philosophy across the ages – including Ancient Egypt, North African thinkers, pre-colonial philosophy, and African political thought in the nineteenth and twentieth centuries.

languages as systems include metaphor, analogue, deduction, and inference. It is biologically true and conceptually important that all humans
learn their native languages at the same age. In a distinction from communication in other species, human languages form cultures and are not
merely a tool for social functions. Languages can be learned and translated by native speakers of other languages; in fact, there are members of
every language group who are bilingual. In Wiredu's terms, as universally
lingual beings, we are sympathetically impartial to other cultures; that is,
human beings have a basic natural sympathy for their kind. While people
live, first of all, in their native cultures grounded in an indigenous language, the fact of our common humanity predisposes us to respect the
cultures across *homo sapiens* as a whole.

One of Wiredu's (1983) important insights for media ethics revolves
around the Akan concept of personhood. He argues that his native culture
speaks of human beings in universal terms. One's freedom in Akan is
rooted in ethics. We have a free will when we have high regard for ethical
responsibility, and this integration of the biological and normative makes
human beings distinctive as a species. Wiredu reflects African communalism here. In fact, this crucial concept is a key feature of Africa's earliest
history to postcolonial Africa today. The human species traces its pristine
movements to the spread of peoples across the African continent. Its food-
producing and food-gathering communities built enduring societies by
strategies of interdependence and mutual aid. Mutuality has been integral
to Africa's character from the beginning. Africans "from all sides regard
community as nothing less than 'the way things are,' a presupposition,
a *prima facie* truth. To speak meaningfully is to address social reality in
communitarian terms" (Fackler, 2003, p. 320).

Communalism is a normative idea in the ethics of being, and *ubuntu* is
one way to give it intellectual substance.[24] Wiredu calls *ubuntu* an African
worldview, an indigenous belief system, a traditional African concept
meaning "humanity toward others" (1980, p. 36). In his definition, he
addresses the objection that *ubuntu* calls for "unquestioning confor-
mism" (Wiredu, 1983). The word *ubuntu* comes from the Zulu and
Xhosa languages, and it summarizes the Zulu maxim *umuntu ngumuntu
ngabantu,* meaning "a person is a person through other persons" or "I am
because of others" (Louw, 1998, p. 2). Thaddeus Metz describes the

---

[24] For a definition of *ubuntu*, and an account of it in terms of communitarianism, see
Christians (2004b).

concept in moral terms: "When sub-Saharans say that 'a person is a person,'" they mean that

> a person in the sense of a deliberative agent such as a human being, ought to strive to become a *real* or *genuine* person, that is, someone who has exhibited moral virtue ... A true or complete person is someone who lives a genuinely human way of life, who displays ethical traits that human beings are in a position to exhibit in a way nothing else in the animal, vegetable, or mineral kingdoms can. (2015, p. 76)

Community is an interactive network of human relations; in that sense *ubuntu* understands humans as social beings whose personhood is a gift from other persons. Sympathy, sensitivity to the community's needs, and respect for those with whom one lives and works are keys to overcoming the great divisions in the world today. Oral cultures normed by *ubuntu* become the standard for evaluating mediated forms of community such as with Facebook, Twitter, and WeChat.

Those who are the genuine persons of *ubuntu* contribute to society as a unit, typically doing so through storytelling. Through common stories and rituals, a community lives as active members rather than passive consumers. The goal for journalism is to identify representative voices rather than spectacular ones that are anecdotal and idiosyncratic. In media ethics grounded in *ubuntu*, we do not construct an apparatus of professional ethics but work instead within the general morality. Professionals reflect the same moral and social space as the communities they report on (Blankenburg, 1999, pp. 60–62). The concept of humans in *ubuntu* presumes that facts and values both are intermixed by custom and history. Therefore, the news ought to unfold dialectically between reporters and indigenous populations.[25]

For Reuel Khoza (Prinsloo, 2003, p. 41), *ubuntu* in its various modulations represents "the collective consciousness of the people of Africa." And in Louw's (1998) perspective, *ubuntu* is an indigenous aphorism that "serves as the spiritual foundation of African societies." Despite the continent's enormous diversity in culture and politics, "threads of underlying affinity run through the beliefs, customs, value systems, and sociopolitical institutions of the various African societies"; and one of the value systems "found in most of these societies is the *ubuntu* system"

---

[25] Cf. *Journal of Media Ethics*, Special Issue: "*Ubuntu* for Journalism Theory and Practice," April–June, 2015. Four scholars from the University of Johannesburg present contemporary thinking on *ubuntu* and its various applications to journalism. For the argument that *ubuntu* as developed in these four papers contributes to and clarifies the ethics of being, see Christians in introducing this issue (2015d, pp. 61–73).

(Kamwangamalu, 1999, p. 26). In this sense, *ubuntu* as a social philosophy is a basis upon which to sustain African identity. At the same time, *ubuntu* can be understood as a universalist idea in the sense that humans everywhere should be able to comprehend life in its terms. Wiredu concludes correctly that "the role of community in making the human world" is not just African; the concept of community has an international reach "that conditions the nature of humans generally" (Masolo, 2004, p. 493).

Since *ubuntu* embodies a fundamental truth about humanity, it can serve as a normative system for understanding old and new media systems around the world. Schutte (1993, p. xii) observes that although *ubuntu* is "opposed to the dominant forces of contemporary European thinking ... it finds sympathetic echoes in many non-African ideals" such as Schumacher's "small is beautiful," Ivan Illich's "conviviality," Christians's "sacredness of life," and Simeon Weil's "need for roots." In their contradiction of the Western ethics of individualist rationalism, *ubuntu* and the ethics of being are conceptually congenial (see Masolo, 2004).

Confucianism

Confucius (551–479 B.C.) established a virtue ethics that is being developed today into an international media ethics (Angle & Slote, 2013). In grounding this theory in virtue, Confucius contradicted the traditional idea that superior persons were born into aristocratic families. His innovation was to measure human excellence by virtue instead of anchoring it on social position. The belief that human goodness is a function of character, rather than a result of birth or elite upbringing, was revolutionary in his fifth century B.C. world, and it is considered bedrock truth still today.

In *The Analects*, Confucius's view of virtuous living involves the proper rites, ceremonies, and principles. Later Confucians called these customs *li*. Over time they became rules of conduct for social relations – such as for parents and children, rulers and citizens, eldest brother and younger siblings. Whenever rules have hardened into doctrines, Confucianism has become unattractive. But understood as a philosophy of life, its core ideas continue to stimulate active scholarship, and media professionals are showing interest also (cf. Puett, 2015; Whitehouse, 2009; Bell, 2008).

The moral claims of *The Analects* center on *ren*, with its meaning of affection, respect, and love for people. Often translated into English as humaneness, *ren* is a characteristic of the human species. As with the sacredness of life, *ren* designates a person's essential humanity. Benevolence is the "norm regulating relationships so that social relations are gradually extended outward" (Shan, 2015, p. 23). *Ren* is normative in that without it there can be no dispersion of values. As Confucius says, "It is rare, indeed, for a man with cunning words and an ingratiating countenance to be benevolent" (Book 17). When benevolence is followed, it produces communities of good will.

The benevolent person in Confucian thought "helps others take their stand" and "gets others there" while in the same process "getting there himself" (Shan, 2015, p. 23). Benevolence thus is the centerpiece of the famous Confucian philosophy: "What you wish for yourself, wish for others." This rule of reciprocity Confucius states in a negative form in the *Analects*: "Do not do unto others what you would not desire others to do unto yourself" (5.12, 12.2, 15.24). But it is also positive: "Erect others the way you would desire yourself to be erected and let others get there the way you would desire yourself to get there" (6.30). *The Analects* teach throughout that we should not concern ourselves with acknowledgment from others but worry about failing to acknowledge them (1.1, 1.16, 14.30, 15.19).

Korean philosopher Young Ahn Kang (2006) argues that the reciprocity concept in Confucian thought expresses the common moral wisdom of almost all humanity. Typically called in ethics "the golden rule," Hans Küng (1991) concludes that all the great religions advocate a version of regarding others as basically like ourselves (cf. Battles, 1996). From an ontological perspective, Confucius insists that our preoccupation must be a philosophy of the human. When we start intellectually, as he does with humans in relation, and understand that communalism is normed by benevolence, we have a credible standard for the general morality across cultures. Media organizations as social organizations can resonate with it also as their ethical standard for public affairs reporting.

In another of Confucius's four major books, *The Doctrine of the Mean*, equilibrium and harmony are its conceptual axis: "Equilibrium is the great root from which grow all human acting in the world. And harmony is the universal path all should pursue. Let the states of equilibrium and harmony exist in perfection, and happy order will prevail throughout the heaven and earth, and all things will be nourished and flourish" (1.4, 1.5) (Legge,1991; cf. Ziporyn, 2015). The virtuous person is balanced, observing equilibrium and harmony in all things – Confucius thinking of virtue as a middle path between two extremes. Aristotle basically agreed with this virtue ethics of the mean a century-and-a-half later, with additional affirmations of this truth about human life from ancient history until today. Reporters often face complicated situations where there are competing obligations and no simple solution. In terms of Confucius's equilibrium and harmony, extremes are rejected and Confucian morality seeks the mean.

He (harmony, harmonization) as verb and noun is a concept essential to Confucianism.[26] In antiquity before Confucius, *he* refers to music. Its original meaning is "the rhythmic interplay of various sounds, either in nature or between human beings, that is musical to the human ear; the prototype of *he* is found in music" (Li, 2006, p. 584). In the earliest Confucian texts, *he* "mostly has to do with sounds and how sounds interact with one another" (Li, 2006, p. 583). Expressions like "the *he* of the five sounds" in *Zuozhuan* (Xigong 24) "do not mean merely the mutual response of sounds, but the harmonious interplay of these sounds" (Li, 2006, p. 548).

In the *Analects*, Confucius makes *he* the criterion for the good person: "The good person (*junzi*) harmonizes but does not seek sameness, whereas the petty person seeks sameness but does not harmonize" (*Analects* 13.23). Single items do not harmonize. Music of one or the same instruments is not harmony. Harmony follows the middle path of the mean. On the one hand, it does not avoid confrontation for a good cause by surrendering. On the other, harmony does not use extremes to defeat opponents. A major function of *li* (rites, rituals) is to harmonize people of various kinds. The Confucian disciple Yu Ruo says in the *Analects*, "of the functions of *li* harmonization is the most precious" (1.12).

He is not just about human relations. As the Confucian classic *Liji* states it: "When *yin* and *yang* harmonize, myriad things get their due" (Li, 2006, p. 587). In the *Zhongyong*, "Harmony is the great way under Heaven. In achieving centrality and harmony, Heaven and Earth maintain their appropriate positions and myriad things flourish" (Li, 2006, p. 588). And with this expansive scope, Confucianism contributes to universals in ethics:

A person can harmonize various parts of his or her body, the mind-heart, and various pursuits in life into a well-functioning, organic whole. Harmony can take place between individuals at the level of family, the community, the nation, and the world. This may include harmony between societies, harmony within a society with different ethnic groups (or political parties), harmony within the same ethnic

---

[26] For the influential neo-Confucian philosopher Zhang Zai, in the eleventh century, harmony is an ultimate category (Ziporyn, 2015).

group with different kin, and harmony among the same kin. Harmony also can take place between human beings and the natural universe. (Li, 2006, p. 588)

"Harmony is a metaphysical as well as an ethical notion; it describes both how the world at large operates and how human beings ought to act" (Li, 2006, p. 589). As one application, Jaifei Yin (2008) argues for a new model of the world press based on the core idea of harmony in Confucian ethics. Rather than the competition of individual rights, characteristic of the Western-oriented media, social harmony is the root of Chinese culture for Confucius and ought to characterize world media (Li, 2008; Jia, Liu, Wang, & Liu, 2014). Yin constructs a two-dimensional model for international news media systems in which freedom and communal responsibility operate in harmony.

Byun and Lee (2002) also argue that the Confucian values of humaneness and harmony are a viable alternative to the narrow Western notion of human rights. For them, *ren* as a holistic understanding of human nature is a more expansive and compassionate ethics than is a rights-based morality. The Confucian tradition is framed by mutual regard and respect toward the social order, that is, toward community-oriented responsibilities. William de Bary (1998) illustrates this communalism with the compacts tradition (*xiangyue*) for strengthening village life outside the bureaucratic system. The ritual of compacts was a contract of voluntarism, mutual aid in distress, rotating leadership, engagement in rites and customs to limit the intervention of the state in local affairs (chap. 5). Though a virtue ethics system such as Confucianism has a different orientation than the sacredness of life as a duty ethics, the idea of our common humanity (*ren*) in Confucius is compatible with the idea of protonorms as the starting point in the ethics of being.

Professor Bo Shan of Wuhan University, in his work on communicative wisdom in *The Analects*, is correct: "Thinking about communication in *The Analects* in academic circles has been ... more on the macro level than on the micro level ... and more from a purely Chinese perspective than from a comparative perspective." These limitations make it "difficult for *The Analects* to be the wisdom that can be shared about the communication of mankind" (Shan, 2015, pp. 17–18). In terms of concepts for global media ethics, including Confucius in this section on theoretical pluralism advances the international agenda.

Contractual Naturalism

Stephen J. A. Ward proposes a contractualist view of global media ethics. [27] In his summary, "Ethical principles are humanly constructed restraints on social behavior" (2005, p. 6). Ethics is a never-ending project of "inventing, applying, and critiquing the basic principles that guide human interaction, define social roles, and justify institutional structures" (2005, p. 7; cf. 2010a, pp. 13, 22). In opposition to absolutism, Ward bases ethical principles on "intersubjective agreement obtained from rational, public deliberation, in light of common purposes, values, and facts" (2005, p. 7; cf. 2011a, pp. 23–26). As with John Dewey's experimentalism, concepts and principles are shaped and tested as "tools of inquiry" and policies are "treated as working hypotheses" (Dewey, 1927, pp. 202–203; cf. Ward, 2005, p. 18). For naturalistic contractualism, absolutist rationalism is wrong in its claim "that all ethical differences can be shown to be variations on major common principles. Substantial and non-reducible differences exist in ethics" (Ward, 2010a, p. 97). In Ward's clarification: "Naturalism is *not* the attempt to reduce all sciences and knowledge to one class of laws, e.g., the laws of physics. Naturalism is the ontological view that human life is the product of only natural processes and entities, and there is no appeal to non-natural or metaphysical entities" (Ward, 2015a, p. 310).

Ward adopts naturalism as his metaethical theory (cf. Wong, 2009). Ethics, he says, as a natural activity of the human species, "is explained and justified by natural concepts, phenomena, and causes … A natural theory of ethics does not appeal to supernatural authority, transcendent absolutes, or the intuition of non-natural, moral properties. Naturalized ethics is ethics within the limits of human experience" (Ward, 2010a, p. 27). Ethics is a rational construction that changes over time, "not a discovery of absolute principles" (2010a, p. 52). And in different terms: "The manner of existence of ethics is the same as, and is no more mysterious than, the existence of humans, their minds, and their social activity" (Ward, 2015a, p. 24).

Instead of rejecting journalism's historic core, its objectivity, Ward reconstructs the idea in naturalistic terms, redefining it as pragmatic objectivity. In this redefinition, he recognizes the central role of values and presuppositions in human knowing and does not insist on detachment

---

[27] A different version of Ward's contractual naturalism was first published in Christians (2013, pp. 283–285).

from them. Ward's naturalism calls for the best available "scientific knowledge of human interaction with media technologies, and the best available knowledge of the economics and sociology of human communication" (2010a, p. 67). As Ward describes it in his *Radical Media Ethics*, "Naturalism requires the ontology of ethics to be based on our leading and most plausible natural theories about the world – theories about nature, life and society" (2105a, p. 9). The search for truth "does not require the presumption of an absolute view of truth or reality." Instead of a one-track neutral reporting of facts, Ward's multidimensional pragmatic objectivity means "the testing of any form of journalism by a plural and holistic set of criteria, such as coherence with existing knowledge, which go beyond citing facts" (2015a, p. 162).

Contractual naturalism transforms professional journalism standards into a new global ethics for journalists as world citizens (Berglez, 2008). The main principle is the flourishing of humanity at large, with cosmopolitanism its central doctrine. Ward describes cosmopolitanism as an ancient ethical theory affirming the equal value and dignity of all people, but he rejects the claim that the moral community is borderless. He demonstrates that cosmopolitan's central axis is respect for humanity's moral capacity, however it is manifested (2011a, chap. 7; 2010a, pp. 154–167).

Cosmopolitanism reinterprets the media's aims and principles for the global age as promoting a transnational human good. The cosmopolitan journalist has a "multisociety contract" to reject extreme patriotism and advance what Ward calls both rational and reasonable goals: those that promote the creativity, freedom, and fulfillment humans share as a species (2010a, pp. 165, 168–171). Also, "Ethical flourishing gives priority to the right in the sense that the pursuit of our goods occurs within the bounds of justice. Ethical flourishing is a composite good where the good and the right are as congruent as possible" (Ward, 2011b, p. 739).

As today's journalism landscape is being realigned – around mixed media platforms that include citizen journalism sites, interactive chat, and professional news – Ward's contractual naturalism calls for an ecumenical approach to ethics. By "ecumenical," he means, "an open ethics that seeks ever new ways to enhance participation, discussion, questioning, and interaction between the group and those outside the group" (2011a, pp. 218, 225).

In sum, Ward does not respond to objective absolutism with the extreme relativism of Nietzsche. His naturalism instead leads to what he calls "moderate relativism." Not all moral schemes are equal: "In ethics, it is not 'anything goes.' Some schemes are better than others ... Not all values are to be doubted, not all values are to be accepted. One works critically from within the best traditions available and remains open to other traditions" (Ward, 2010a, pp. 97, 100). Ward's formal label for this moderate paradigm is "contractual universals," where "fair and rational deliberation shows (or could show)" that such goals as ethical flourishing "should be recognized and honored by all parties" (2010a, p. 175). His *Global Journalism Ethics* does not merely correct the weaknesses of the traditional ethics of news but develops a new foundation and structure for reporting in universalist terms. His contractual naturalism enables an authentic global perspective to emerge for journalism, "not a colonial or national perspective disguised as a global philosophy" (2010a, p. 183).

Feminist Ethics of Care

Feminist ethics is a major contribution to international media ethics. Virginia Held (2007) argues that the ethics of care, based on feminist ethics, has developed into a distinct moral theory, and in so doing, it is not bound to personal relations but encompasses global issues such as justice and rights. In Held's view, the feminist ethics of care is not constructed of abstract principles as in Kant and utilitarianism, but caring is a normative axis for basic cross-cultural social issues such as civility, impartiality, interdependence, trust, and solidarity. Yayo Okano (2016), in her overview of the history that Held represents, describes the ethics of care as establishing "a morally inclusive approach to social justice" beyond gender inequality (p. 85). Olena Hankivsky (2004) calls it a "second-generation of care ethics" that maintains the "values and purposes" of "its nascent articulation" but combines them with "the values of justice to ensure a balanced and reasoned resolution of practical issues and social problems" (p. 25; quoted in Okano, p. 91).

The feminist ethics of Seyla Benhabib has shown that the ethics of relation – like African communalism – is particular and universal at the same time. She calls her theory interactive universalism (1992). Since ethical discourse is grounded in everyday human experience, we are referring, at the same time, to our common humanity. Cultural diversity is homogenized by abstractions, but the emphasis in interactive universalism is on our relationships. As we identify values in everyday life, we consider them to be true throughout the human race (2002). With her specialization in Habermas (Benhabib, 1986) and Hannah Arendt (Benhabib, 2003), Benhabib is able to integrate feminist theory with critical theory and that makes her work distinctive (cf. Benhabib & Cornell, 1987). In her reformulation of discourse ethics, she defends ideals that are universal in morality and in political life (Benhabib, 2011). In her perspective, humans are dialogic, and their moral agency is guided by the norms of moral respect and egalitarian reciprocity that characterize Habermas's public sphere. A native of Turkey, tracing her genealogy to the fifteenth-century Jewish expulsion from Spain, Benhabib's scholarship demonstrates how feminist ethics can be legitimately transnational.

In Lee Wilkins's summary, "Relationships themselves, and more generally real, lived experiences rather than intellectual and theoretical constructs, are considered the genesis of philosophical feminist ethics" (2009, p. 36). Regarding the ethics of relation, feminist scholarship is giving depth and meaning to such central terms as nurture, care, affection, empathy, and self-sacrifice. Carol Gilligan (1982, 1989) enlarges feminism's perspective by arguing that the female moral voice anchors ethics in the primacy of relationships, and, therefore, compassion and nurturance have priority rather than the avoidance of harm. In Linda Steiner's work, feminists' ethical self-consciousness has a critical orientation, in that it identifies oppression and inequities and teaches us to "address questions about whose interests are regarded as worthy of debate" (1991, p. 158; cf. 2009). Lisbeth van Zoonen's scholarship on feminism and information technology highlights the importance of gendered meanings to understand the human interface with the new information technologies (1992, 1994, 2002; Harmer & van Zoonen, 2016).

In making the relation-in-between primary, rather than the decisions of individual actors, the concept of caring and its cognates are at the center of moral duty. For Nel Noddings, the one-caring attends to the cared-for in both thinking and action: "Caring is not simply a matter of feeling favorably disposed toward humankind in general ... Real care requires actual encounters with specific individuals; it cannot be accomplished through good intentions alone. When all goes well, the cared-for actively receives the caring deeds of the one-caring" (Noddings, 1984, chap. 1). What has moral salience is "attending to the needs of particular others *for whom we take responsibility*" (Held, 2007, p. 10; italics added). Those caring are empathetic; they live outside their internal preoccupations and are engrossed in the thoughts and situations of the cared-for. The caring-one delights in the successes of the cared-for and suffers in their misfortunes (Noddings, 1984, pp. 12–19, 69–75, 176–177). In addition to engrossment and empathy, the commitment of the caring-one is considered unalterable. Shifting circumstances do not affect the unchanging loyalty.

The ethics of care with its political and global orientation is directly relevant as a normative standard for the news media. The application of this theory to journalism practice has at least three distinctive features (see Steiner & Okrusch, 2006; Steiner, 2014). First, instead of neutrality and detachment, an ethics of care is compassionate journalism. In feminist media ethics, transmitting information is too weak; the ethics of empathy desires that public life would prosper. For a feminist news profession, the vitality of the communities reported on is the overriding issue. The ethics of care is not merely a useful addition to ethical theory (Robison, 1999); its relational values are distinctive in presenting people and society in reciprocal, interdependent, and restorative terms.

Second, the ethics of care redirects the purpose of the public media. In the ethics of care, the primary mission of media technological systems – print, electronic, digital – is not the watchdog role but facilitating civil society. For feminist ethics, public life outside government and business needs special attention. For education, science, non-government organizations, medicine, religion, and agriculture to flourish, the involvement and leadership of women require serious development. Margaretha Geertsma (2009), for example, connects feminist theory with globalization theories to determine the various ways women are represented in the international media. Her study of the Arabic website *Women's eNews*, an online news service, has identified the stereotypes of women in Afghanistan and Iraq (Geertsema-Sligh, 2015). The Global Media Monitoring Project (GMMP) is another research example. As discussed in Chapter 4, GMMP's study of gender in news-media stories across more than one hundred countries has shown that women's voices are heard only 24 percent of the time. The data from GMMP are useful to newspaper staffs, online bloggers, and station managers who seek to change their hiring policies and upgrade their professional practices (www.who makesthenews.org/gmmp).

Third, there is other-regarding care for media users, for the audience, and for readers. The public is considered active and responsible, with citizens themselves arriving at their own solutions to public problems. The ethics of care is especially concerned how well the other-regarding process functions. Geertsema's 2010 research, for example, concentrates on the strategies and effectiveness of women activists in South Africa. Carol Gilligan has been studying the role of patriarchy in government and social institutions (Gilligan & Richards, 2009, chaps. 9–10). She considers patriarchy as horrific a contradiction of democratic life as slavery: "The transformation from patriarchy to a fuller realization of democracy will be one of the most important historical events of the next fifty years" (www.gse.harvard.edu/news/features/gilligan).

Summary of the Five Theories

The five theories of global media ethics presented here are intellectually credible alternatives to absolutism. Since they are not hierarchical or imperialistic, they represent possible models of moral universals. The challenge for media ethics in a global age is whether cultural diversity can be honored while global principles are being developed. These theories do not avoid that challenge but confront it directly and creatively.

These five universals – sacredness of life, communalism, Confucianism, contractual naturalism, feminist caring – disclose the moral world but are circumstantial. They are historically situated. They address some issues, but not all. Theoretical models are always calibrated to the issues at hand. This means that theories must meet the test of fittingness. I advocate the sacredness of life as meeting that test competently. I consider the sacredness of life intellectually astute and ontologically explicit. It repositions media ethics into the complications of the digital age by integrating moral philosophy and the philosophy of technology. It responds best to the nature of our global humanity in non-essentialist terms.

The current lack of certitude that marks the extraordinary age in which we live should encourage us to engage in a rigorous analysis of the crisis in values around us and in the media professions (cf. Wasserman, 2018, pp. 113–121). Echoing Václav Havel, Hans Küng (1991) reminds us that today's complex and fragile world needs "global ethical standards to survive ... [It] does not need a unitary religion and a unitary ideology, but it does need some norms, values, ideals, and goals to bring it together" (pp. xvi–vii). These five theories of communication ethics understand the necessity of common values to sustain the twenty-first-century media. They recognize that the vitality of ethics within all forms of media technology depends finally on a robust morality in public life as a whole.

CONCLUSION

This chapter has focused on an ethical protonorm inscribed in Being. This new theory of communication ethics is systemic; to be credible, systems must be coherent. Haphazard reasoning from presuppositions may

discredit the theory as a whole. The ethical principles rooted in the protonorm ought to incorporate its genius. Specific policies must be derivable
from principles in that the former incorporates the latter. Practical applications restricted to the dynamics of particular situations have little gravitas. Responding to difficult cases anywhere in the world entails principles
that themselves presuppose primordial values. The moral commitments of
media users and professionals cannot be personal intuitions only but
should be systemically coherent with transnational principles (cf.
Cushman et al., 2009).[28]

In asking whether ethical universals are possible, I have centered on the
irrevocable status of human life. If one understands the nature of history,
language, and our personhood as cultural beings, human sacredness is
inescapable. And as we come to live inside universal human solidarity, we
recognize that a basic list of ethical principles is entailed by it – truth
telling, human dignity, and nonviolence. These principles for the various
media systems are themselves universal by virtue of their inscription into
an underlying protonorm, and together they establish the digital age
agenda. This is another way to phrase it: as we begin systematizing the
idea that the lives of all humans are sacred, it entails ethical principles such
as truth telling, human dignity, and nonviolence. The following chapters
are a summary of how these principles work in a professional ethics of
being, grounded as they are in the sanctity of life.

---

[28] For the Canadian philosopher, Charles Taylor, coherence is possible. Moral judgments
are capable of rational elucidation in community discourse. For an elaboration of
Taylor's practical reason, see Bowers (2002).

3

The Ethics of Truth

Language is the lifeblood of social formation; therefore, human existence requires a radical commitment to truth. Under ordinary circumstances, it is presumed that a community's members are speaking truthfully and their claims of identity are not deceptive.[1] The *a priori* of living with others is truthfulness. It follows that people "owe it to each other to describe the reality about which they communicate with each other" in such a way that "they can maintain this duty reciprocally ... Truth is a human need in the sense that human beings do not wish to lose their relation to tangible reality. They have to live in that reality; they cannot live constantly in an abstract state removed from it" (Mieth, 1997, pp. 89–90). William Alston's *A Realist Conception of Truth* considers truth's centrality in public life "overwhelmingly obvious": "If our interactions with X are guided by true beliefs about X, they are much more likely to be successful in attaining the goals of those interactions, than if they are guided by false beliefs" (1996, p. 237). In Sissela Bok's pithy terms, "Veracity functions as the foundation of relations among human beings: when this trust shatters or wears away, institutions collapse" (1979, p. 31). Disclosing the genuine is rooted in our personhood and illustrates what Levinas calls "the primordial." Lying, in fact, is so unnatural that for nearly

---

[1] Truth as a dimension of universal human solidarity is anthropological, whereas truth as deontological in Kant is situated in formal law. His absolutism leads to the conundrum of conflicting duties. In his famous essay *On the Supposed Right to Lie Out of Love for Humanity* (1986), the categorical imperative against lying is exceptionless.

a century polygraph machines have measured physiological reactions to it.[2]

For Mieth, "the first justification of truthfulness as a protonorm lies in the fact that those who relativize such a norm are indirectly recognizing it by offering reasons to justify their limitation of its categorical validity" (1997, p. 89). Whenever it is argued that the concept of truthfulness does not apply, this declaration is nevertheless considered an exception to the rule:

> For example, if we say that in some cultures, face-saving represents a higher norm than the basic norm of truthfulness, then this would still amount to an attempt to justify the deviation from truthfulness. Even if the basic norm of truthfulness were to be set aside for the sake of love – for instance, at a sickbed – it would nonetheless represent an exception to a valid imperative recognized in advance. (Mieth, 1997, p. 89)

While truth is generally thought to be the norm of communication as a whole, truth also has priority in media theory and practice. That truth telling is the norm of the media professions is generally understood around the world. In the extensive work on journalism codes of ethics internationally, the code database at Tampere University (Nordenstreng, 1995; Juusela, 1981), Tiina Laitila's research (1995), and Thomas Cooper's (1989) comparative survey agree that truth as objectivity and accuracy has priority in every code. In our study of social responsibility worldwide, the press's obligation for unbiased information had a central role (Christians & Nordenstreng, 2004). Truth telling as the normative core of media professionalism is not controversial. But for this assertion to be credible in global terms, and with increasing technological sophistication in distorting the truth, both the concept of truth and the nature of news must be redefined.

TRUTH IN INTELLECTUAL HISTORY

The Occidental tradition lives out of the classical Greek legacy of truth as accurate or correct statement. In Aristotle's influential summary, "Falsehood is itself mean and culpable, and truth noble and full of praise" (*Nicomachean Ethics,* bk. 4, chap. 7). Truth and lying are permanently imbalanced. We ought not grant them equal status and then merely

---

[2] In different terms, Kant justifies truth on the basis of duties to oneself: "A lie is a violation of duty towards oneself more than towards others ... What more can be expected of a person if that person dishonors himself or herself" (1990)?

calculate the best results. Lying must be justified while telling the truth need not be. In Sissela Bok's elaboration, only in a monumental crisis, or as a last resort, can lying even be considered for moral justification: "Deceit and violence – these are the two forms of deliberate assault on human beings" (Bok, 1999, p. 18). Those who are deceived or attacked are resentful and hostile, and reparations are nearly impossible.

Classical Greek thinking on the truth and falsehood distinction dominates intellectual history in the West. In the eighteenth-century Enlightenment, this correspondence view of truth is given systematic modern form, with René Descartes its chief architect. In his *Rules for the Direction of the Mind* (1628), Descartes's twenty-one rules specify neutral procedures that are mathematically precise, while presuming that truth is certain when analytic calculations are quantifiable. Descartes constructed a philosophy of the natural world on a scientific foundation and a definition of human beings as rational entities.

Descartes's motto is instructive: "who lives well hidden, lives well." He wrote *Meditations II* (1641) in the Netherlands, keeping his address a secret, and only distracted briefly by his daughter's death. While he lived in seclusion, the Thirty Years' War involved the major powers of Europe, with the atrocities and social chaos catastrophic, and the Spanish threatening Descartes's Paris. The devastation and brutality, ending with the Peace of Westphalia in 1648, changed the geography of Europe forever. Descartes limited his interests to mathematical knowledge of physical reality, his behavior reflecting his thinking. His *Discourse on Method* (1637) elaborates this objectivism in more detail, with circumstances considered irrelevant. E. F. Schumacher (1978) agreed with the standard summary that Descartes's concept of truth has been decisive for the West, but Schumacher complained that in Descartes's philosophical rigor, he excluded vast subject matter that had engaged earlier cultures and non-Western peoples.

The eighteenth century carried over Cartesian mathematics into its conception of natural reality, that is, by the "fixed quantitative judgment" we call "calculation" (Levi, 1959, p. 35). The sciences, astronomy and physics, became the structural model for philosophy. One of the most revered Western texts of the twentieth century is the three-volume *Principia Mathematica* by Bertrand Russell and Alfred North Whitehead (1910–1913) in which they attempt to prove mathematical truth by the inference rules and axioms of symbolic logic. For Russell, "the method adopted by Descartes is right" (Levi, 1959, p. 349; cf. p. 350), and that meant for Russell that facts and properties are true if they mirror objective reality. In his *Problems of Philosophy*, "truth consists in some form of correspondence between belief and fact" (1912, p. 121; cf. Kirkham, 1992, chap. 4). In a *reductio ad absurdum*, since morals are outside scientific logic, they are unverifiable; being unverifiable they are meaningless; and being meaningless they are incapable of being true.[3]

Mainstream social science in theory and practice parallels this rationalist philosophy. The subject-object dualism in the Cartesian tradition resulted in value-free social science, with ethical principles, as a result, proscriptive in character and of no scientific interest. In constructing the Enlightenment mind, the prestige of natural science established the agenda. Science provided quantifiable evidence that by applying rational methodologies to nature and human beings, progress in everyday living was inevitable. Diseases were conquerable and mechanical transportation expanded the day's achievements. Insanity, for example, no longer needed the demons and evil of theology to explain it, but empirical solutions became available in medicine. Psychology, sociology, and economics – known as the human sciences in the eighteenth and nineteenth centuries – were called the "liberating/liberal arts" that opened minds and freed the imagination. With social science based on a dichotomy between objective facts and subjective values, the regions of human interest that reflected oughts and constraints attracted little intellectual interest and became marginal.

The philosophy of social science in John Stuart Mill is based uncritically on the subject-object dichotomy; therefore, the autonomy of the subject is not only conceivable but the foundation of inductive inquiry. According to Mill, logical syllogisms do not contribute anything new to scientific knowledge. If observation leads to the conclusion that "men are mortal" and if we state in a proposition that "all men are mortal," then it is self-evident that Philip of Orange is mortal because he is a man. The premise and the conclusion are equivalent and nothing new is learned (see Mill, 1843/1893, II.3.2, p. 140). The important issue for autonomous subjectivity is discriminating knowledge from superstition, and that discrimination is specified by inductive experimentation. In the pursuit of true knowledge, synthesis and generalization are necessary to advance systematically from the known to the unknown. For Mill, logic in itself does not certify the rules for formally consistent reasoning (Mill, 1843/1893, III).

[3] For a comprehensive compilation of twentieth-century scholarship on truth, see Lynch (2001).

Only when induction is followed rigorously, can scientific certitude be approximated.[4]

In Book Six of *A System of Logic,* "On the Logic of the Moral Sciences," Mill (1843/1893) defined social science as explaining human behavior in terms of causal laws. However, he warned against all forms of determinist predictability, considering them to be fatalistic. In fact, and therefore, empirical knowledge about human behavior has greater predictive power when it concerns collectivities than when it deals with individual agents.[5] In Book Six, inductive experimentalism is not limited to particular situations but is the scientific method for studying "the various phenomena that constitute social life" (VI.6.1, p. 606); "Social laws are hypothetical, and statistically-based generalizations by their very nature admit of exceptions" (Copleston, 1966, p. 101; see also Mill, 1843/1893, VI.5.1, p. 596).

In his *Cours de Philosophie Positive* (1830), Auguste Comte defined matter as the "permanent possibility of sensation" and Mill did likewise (Mill, 1856b, p. 198). In fact, positivism is obvious in all aspects of Mill's work on experimental inquiry. By developing explicit methods of induction and verification, Mill established a theory of knowledge in empirical terms. Truth is not something in itself but "depends on past history and the habits of our own minds" (Mill, 1843/1893, II, Vol. 6, p. 181). In his view, methods for investigating society must be rigorously limited to the benefits of the various courses of action. As with Comte, Mill contended that there is no ultimate reality behind sensations. Since metaphysical substances are not real, Mill (1865a, 1865b) and Comte (1848/1910) concluded that social science should be limited to factual data. For Mill,

---

[4] Although committed to what he called "the logic of the moral sciences" in delineating the canons or methods for induction, Mill shared with natural science a belief in the uniformity of nature and the presumption that all phenomena are subject to cause-and-effect relationships. His five principles of induction reflect a Newtonian cosmology.

[5] Max Weber likewise takes for granted a "language of science – a collection of truths – that excludes all value judgments, rules, or directions of conduct" (Root, 1993, p. 205). As with Mill, scientific knowledge exists for its own sake as morally neutral: "A systematically correct scientific proof in the social sciences" may not be completely attainable, but that is most likely "due to faulty data" not because it is conceptually impossible (1949b, p. 58). For Weber, as for Mill, empirical science deals with questions of means, and his warning against inculcating political and moral values presumes a means-ends dichotomy (see Weber, 1949a, pp. 18–19; 1949b, p. 52). For Weber, social scientists by a conscious decision can "exclude judgments of desirability or undesirability" from their publications and lectures. This practical argument regarding value freedom has made Weber attractive to twenty-first-century social science though he developed no systematic epistemology comparable to Mill's.

as is true of Comte, experiential induction is the only kind of knowledge that produces practical benefits (Mill 1865b, p. 242). Both emphasized that social progress is dependent upon this scientific knowledge (Mill, 1865b, p. 241), whereas theological speculation and myth impeded it (Christians, 2018a, pp. 68–69).[6]

Mill's subject-object dualism ineluctably produces for him a dualism of means and ends. In a democratic society, citizens and politicians are responsible for articulating a society's ends; the mandate of science is to provide the know-how for achieving them. Social science is amoral, addressing questions of means but with no capacity or obligation to dictate ends. Methodology in inductive social science by definition must be disinterested regarding the substance of its content. Protocols for practicing inductive experimentalism should not be "morally or politically prescriptive; [they] should direct against bad science but not bad conduct" (Root, 1993, p. 129). Research cannot be judged righteous or evil, only true or false. Mill advocates neutrality to ensure individual autonomy. Social scientific inquiry should treat researchers "as thinking, willing, active beings who bear responsibility for their choices" and are free to choose whatever conception of the good life they personally find fulfilling (Root, 1993, p. 19).

Objectivist Worldview in the Media

From the late nineteenth through the twentieth centuries, the mainstream press has defined itself in terms of the objectivist worldview. In fact, in Stephen Ward's detailed and systematic history, objectivity as an idea is rooted in ancient Greek philosophy and early modern science (2015b, chaps. 1–6). He locates the invention of journalism ethics as an objectivist ideal already in the periodic news press of seventeenth-century England (chap. 3). With human rationality unquestioned and equipped with empirical methodology, the facts in news are said to mirror reality. In journalism's commitment to objectivism, its aim has been verifiable accounts of a domain outside of human consciousness. In Mill's inductive methodology, when its rules are followed rigorously, social science is

---

[6] Mill (1873/1969) specifically credits Comte for his use of the inverse deductive or historical method: "This was an idea entirely new to me when I found it in Comte; and but for him I might not soon (if ever) have arrived at it" (p. 126). Mill explicitly follows Comte in distinguishing social science and social dynamics. He published two essays on Comte's influence in the *Westminster Review*, which were reprinted as *Auguste Comte and Positivism* (Mill, 1865a; see also Mill, 1873/1969, p. 165).

approximate to scientific certitude. In this tradition, truthful news is defined in straightforward epistemological terms as accurate representation. Journalistic morality, therefore, is equivalent to the unbiased reporting of neutral data.

In Ward's (2009) elaboration, traditional objectivity is a web of ideas, a doctrine based on "journalism's realism and empiricism, disciplining it with rules, standards, and attitudes" (p. 73). The newsroom operationalized it as follows:

All opinion must be clearly attributed to the source, accompanied by direct quotation and careful paraphrasing. Objective practice asks reporters to verify facts by reference to documents, scientific studies, government reports and numerical analysis. To enhance objectivity, reports are written from the detached tone of the third person. (Ward, 2009, p. 74)[7]

In the United States, for example, the important books published on journalism ethics in the 1920s, the growth of professional societies with codes of ethics, and increasingly sophisticated journalism curricula in education did not prevent the disappearance of ethics in the face of the scientific naturalism that was antithetical to it. Scientific naturalism combatively ordered the structure of knowledge during this period – naturalism in the sense that genuine knowledge is to be identified in the natural laws of the hard sciences (Purcell, 1973). For Willard V. O. Quine (1953), philosophical inquiry was a systematic attempt to understand science from the resources of science itself. In his influential perspective, all meaningful knowledge was continuous with the paradigmatic disciplines – physics, chemistry, and biology. The majority of academicians – including those in communication – promoted the methods and principles of the physical sciences. Lawrence Murphy, founding editor of *Journalism Bulletin* (later *Journalism Quarterly*), concluded in 1924: "Journalism . . . is emerging from an imaginative type of writing into one governed by scientifically sound principles. We now recognize that the scientific attitude toward news material is the only safeguard we have against journalism graduates being capricious and emotional" (p. 31). The conventions of objective reporting became institutionalized in

---

[7] Ward (2015b) argues that there have been three senses of objectivity in Western culture: ontological, epistemological, and procedural, with journalism's understanding of objectivity combining all three (pp. 45–49). By "traditional objectivity" Ward means "the original notion of news objectivity first espoused by North American print journalism in the early 1900s," with objectivity "reaching its zenith in the 1940s and 1950s" (2009, p. 73).

journalism courses and programs. The period from the 1930s is typically described as the social scientific phase of communications study, and the rules of objectivity for journalism practice were methodologically congenial to it (Emery, Emery, & Roberts, 2000).

This reductionist concept of truth, limited in scope to accurate facts and neutrality, dominated media ethics instruction and scholarship in the 1930s and the decades following. For reporters and managers, seeking the truth in news gathering and producing the truth in newswriting were elusive. They recognized that this professional standard was complicated by the demands of deadlines and self-serving sources. And there was no significant theoretical work on the concept; classrooms and newsrooms emphasized implementation rather than rethinking it. Journalists overwhelmed with information and educators preoccupied with other interests had little incentive to work through the intellectual nature of truth telling.

James Carey correctly attributed the emergence of objectivity in journalism to the struggle within the press for legitimacy within the complexities of rapid industrialization:

With the end of partisan journalism, journalists were deprived of a point of view from which to describe the world they inhabited. That world was less and less governed by political parties, and journalists were set free of those parties in any event, so journalists, capitalizing on the growing prestige of science, positioned themselves outside the system of politics, as observers stationed on an Archimedean point above the fray of social life. (1997b, p. 335)

In the North Atlantic region, only on isolated occasions during the 1930s through the 1960s was there an explicit concern for ethics. The Report of the Commission on Freedom of the Press in 1947 was the most famous counterstatement of this period. On occasion there were warnings about journalism's failures and scattered resistance to objectivism in journalism's intellectual and vocational life. Lawrence Murphy's professional model monopolized the agenda. Fretting over that value-centered enterprise called journalism ethics was considered irrelevant in an academic and professional environment committed to facticity. Not until 1957 with Wilbur Schramm's *Responsibility in Mass Communication* did ethics or its equivalent appear as a title in the communications literature.

Though this scientific view of human knowledge dominated the Western Enlightenment, in that very eighteenth century an alternative to it was developed, principally in Giambattista Vico's *fantasia* and Wilhelm

Dilthey's *verstehen*. This counter-Enlightenment legacy continued with hermeneutics and critical theory in the Frankfurt School. The three most influential Western philosophers of the twentieth century brought objectivity's hegemony to a conclusion: Dewey's pragmatism, Wittgenstein's linguistic philosophy, and Heidegger's existentialism. Derrida's sliding signifiers and Lyotard's denial of master narratives articulated the counter-Enlightenment in postmodern terms. Taoism has promoted a world where objective truth is inconceivable.

These deep and widespread attacks have created a crisis in correspondence views of truth for the early twenty-first century. An incontrovertible domain separate from human subjectivity is no longer a premise but a problematic. The demise of the correspondence view has created a predicament for the notion of truth altogether. For J. L. Austin (1979), truth is an illusory ideal; there is no "truth, the whole truth and nothing but the truth about, say, the battle of Waterloo." In Nietzsche's terms, the world of our actual existence is "false, cruel, contradictory, misleading, senseless … We need lies in order to live" (1967, p. 461).

Though the coherence concept of truth retains legitimacy, truth is largely schismatic. In principle, the tide has turned toward restricting mathematical rationalization to the territory of the natural sciences. The elementary view of truth as accurate information is now seen as too narrow for today's social and political complexities. In reporting, objectivity has become increasingly controversial, though in diluted form it still exists in professional practices. In Carey's dramatic terms:

The conventions of objective reporting were developed as part of an essentially utilitarian-capitalist-scientific orientation toward events … Yet despite their obsolescence, we continue to live with these conventions as if a silent conspiracy has been undertaken between government, the reporter, and the audience to keep the house locked up tight even though all the windows have been blown out. (Carey, 1997c, p. 141)

As Ward describes it, "the traditional notion of objectivity, articulated about a century ago, is indefensible philosophically, weakened by criticism inside and outside of journalism" (Ward, 2015b, p. 4). In addition to "a corrosive post-modern skepticism about objective truth" and "cynicism about the ethics of profit-seeking news organizations," Ward (2009) adds a third reason for "wear and tear" on the "pillars of truth and objectivity": the belief that "non-objective journalism is best for an 'interactive' media world populated by citizen journalists and bloggers" (p. 71).

He adds, "Traditional news objectivity is, by all accounts, a spent ethical force, doubted by journalist and academic" (Ward, 2015b, p. 280).

Modernity in Crisis

The history of truth is a necessary background for helping us understand the normative center of media professionalism in the twenty-first century. This intellectual history makes it clear that objectivism no longer serves as the core of journalism's morality. The issue can be described from a different perspective: the correspondence version of truth has been a central component of modernity; truth as an idea is in crisis because modernity is in crisis. On this late side of modernity, we need a different definition of truth as journalism's vocational norm. Allowing correspondence views of truth that have dominated the Occident to set today's agenda in effect situates our analysis within a failing modernism. That is a misguided parochialism when an orientation to the global is required.

As the offspring of the Enlightenment mind, modernity has dominated the Western worldview; in its neo-liberal form, modernity organizes the globe North and South, developed world and developing, with industrial nation-states given preeminence. The heart and soul of modernity is the autonomous self, detached in its essence from the social context. Modernity's individuals define themselves by rights and claim self-sufficiency as their own end (cf. Taylor, 1982, 1989). Modernist ethics is voluntaristic in that moral disputes become a reality by the action of individual agents. Moral issues are strident and unresolved. Moral debate becomes essentially an exercise in rhetorical persuasion, typically unable to rise above self-righteous indignation. Values clarification is routinely adopted because modernity has isolated values into the descriptive, non-normative domain. While generally portraying morality as manageable by technical solutions, this conventional format represents a version of Alfred North Whitehead's fallacy of misplaced concreteness. The moral domain is circumscribed within the epistemological. Unspecified abstractions are said to have existence in the concrete, and in this confusion of categories methodology becomes normative.

Modernity as an idea is developed in terms of the industrial world instead of the agrarian, with, therefore, the logic of science and technology dominating its worldview (Heller, 1999, chap. 5). Modernity, as a regime of neutrality and reason, is driven by secularism. Scientific experimentation preempts history and divine revelation. In Max Weber's *The Sociology of Religion,* modernity's central idea is the disenchantment of the world. With scientific understanding replacing belief in magic, God, and myth, the social order loses its mystery and a cohering religious worldview and, therefore, its collective meaning (Weber, 1964).

Modernity as a formidable aggregate of politics, economics, and culture is in turmoil. The world influence of its icon nation, the United States, is in transparent decline and its Eurocentric originators are static. Islam's youth demographic is searching for an alternative identity to counter the uprootedness and emptiness of Western modernity. Confucius Institutes around the globe and President Xi Jinping's "Chinese Dream" represent a distinctive worldview. Multimillions now seek a more satisfying ontology. Modernity with its corporate ethos and consumer culture is considered oppressive and unsatisfying around the world, and in the modernist homelands too.

Therefore, in contending for truth as journalism's professional core in a global age, truth needs to be freed from its modernist form as values clarification. Truth for the postmodernity era ought to be situated deontologically. Truth should become a problem of axiology first of all rather than limited to the epistemological. With the dominant scheme no longer tenable, truth becomes the province of duty ethicists who reconstruct it as the professional news media's standard for its public discourse.

TRUTH IN ETHICS

Intellectual history indicates that most philosophers in the Western tradition are "monists about truth. They assume that there is only one explanation of what makes something true." They disagree over the nature of truth, "whether it is a matter of correspondence between thought and world or a type of idealized coherence among our beliefs."[8] But they agree

---

[8] Lynch (2011) outlines a coherence theory of moral truth as an alternative to correspondence theory and to deflationism. In this perspective, "a moral judgment is warranted to the degree that it is woven tightly into the rest of the moral fabric, so that it coheres with our considered moral judgments and relevant non-moral convictions" (p. 164). According to coherentism, "a moral judgment is warranted to the degree that the framework to which it belongs is coherent" (p. 166). Lynch then constructs the idea of moral truth from a framework of advancing coherence – "of becoming more and more coherent or improving its coherence" (p. 171). Lynch continues: "A judgment is superwarranted when it has the property of surviving arbitrarily close examination without defeat. Such examination consists in seeing whether the moral judgment in question, based on the evidence available to the ordinarily reflective inquirer, is a member of a coherent moral framework, and would continue to be under all increases of information, moral and non-moral" (2011, p. 172). A moral judgment, such as the "judgment that torture is wrong, supercoheres with my moral framework," that is, "it would remain part of that framework without fail, no matter ... how much additional moral and non-moral judgments might be included in the

that whenever propositions are considered true, they have a particular property (Lynch, 2011, p. 3).

According to Lynch (2011, p. 4), "In recent decades, many philosophers have come to think that the monist's quest for the nature of truth is a fool's errand." Today's orthodoxy tends to be a version of deflationism: "Rather than signaling a special property that all and only true propositions have in common, the deflationist takes it that the concept of truth is a mere expressive device, useful for purposes of generalization and semantic ascent" (Lynch, 2011, p. 4). Deflationists claim, in effect, "that nothing makes moral judgments true because … there is nothing substantive to say about how moral judgments are true" (p. 163).

To its adherents, the simplicity of deflationism is appealing. However, "while initially promising, it is ultimately unsatisfying; among other problems, it removes truth from our explanatory resources" (p. 191). Contrary to deflationism's elimination of truth as an explanatory tool, Lynch argues persuasively that "moral judgments are truth-apt" (p. 160). He makes a *prima facie* case that moral claims are capable of being true or false. In his view, moral judgments are truth-apt because they have what he calls "cognitive surface-structure" following the conditions of logic (p. 159). In contrast to judgments of taste that a wardrobe is elegant, moral judgments are subject to epistemic appraisal: "If I make a moral judgment about, for example, the injustice of the death penalty, and you deny that judgment … I am committed to giving you a reason or some other evidence in favor of my judgment" (p. 160; cf. 2012).[9]

Substantive Theory of Truth

Presuming that the ethical principle of truth can be true, by what standard can it be considered true? The most appropriate answer to this question is

---

system that increases the system's coherence" (p. 172). In supercoherence, moral judgments would not mistakenly include false non-moral beliefs about the world: "Consider a misogynistic culture which deprives women of rights partly on the basis of a whole range of mistaken non-moral beliefs (e.g., some mistaken views of intelligence or some other moral matter" (p. 173)).

[9] We can give up the truth-aptness of moral judgments, despite our initial reasons for it: "This is the route of the traditional expressivists … Classic presentations include, Ayer's *Language, Truth and Logic* (1952) and Stevenson's 'The Emotive Meaning of Ethical Terms' (1937)" (Lynch, 2011, p. 163).

what Gila Sher calls "a substantive theory of truth" (1999, 2004).[10] Many challenges to theories of truth overlap in science and philosophy, and Sher (2004) elaborates on their similarities and differences. Philosophical theories investigate the relation between truth and knowledge, truth and rationality, truth and ontology. Though the science-philosophy distinction is loose and mobile, philosophers explain the concept of truth, while the scientists' task is "to discover truths and explain their objective grounds" (Sher, 1999, p. 164). The search for truth and conceptualizing it are inextricably linked. There are methodological challenges confronting philosophical theories of truth that are parallel with those facing the natural and social scientists in their specifying the conditions of truth. But the substantive theory appropriate to truth in the moral domain is philosophical – "philosophy with its broad, diverse, and highly complex subject matters: knowledge, ontology, meaning" (Sher, 2004, p. 13).

A substantive theory provides an "explanatory, constructive, and systematic account of a rich, significant, and fundamental subject matter" (Sher, 2004, p. 5). A substantive theory of truth contrasts with a deflationist theory: "Where deflationists say that a theory of truth cannot be, or need not be, genuinely explanatory, substantivists say it can and should be" (Sher, 2004, p. 5; see Field, 1994). Sher's substantive theory, "which borrows many of its basic features from Tarski, investigates a specific, if widely applicable, aspect of truth, namely the logical aspect, and its account of this aspect satisfies the standards of substantiveness" (Sher, 1999, p. 134). "The logicality thesis identifies a highly specialized factor of truth," and due to its basic specificity, "it is universally applicable to the domain of truth."

The logicality thesis says that one central factor in truth is the logic motif, a result of the role played by logical structure in rendering sentences true or false: "The logical factor does not determine all by itself the truth value of sentences, but it combines with other factors" to determine their truthfulness. And so "The truth value of sentences is generally determined

---

[10] Lynch (2011) chooses a different option, which he calls a "functionalist theory"; truth, for him, is best understood as "a functional property that can be realized in more than one way" (p. 3). In addition, "The functionalist theory of truth is motivated in part by the suspicion that if we are to ever come to grips with both the cognitive unity and semantic diversity of our thought, we need a new way of thinking about truth. We need a new theory because traditional theories lack the proper scope to account for diversity, while simple pluralist theories give up unity" (p. 191). Lynch calls this *alethic* pluralism: "In some domains, what makes a belief true is that it corresponds to reality; in others, beliefs are true by a form of coherence" (p. 5).

by a multiplicity of factors," such as those distinctive of the discourse to which the sentences belong – and other factors outside the field, since truth has to do with how things are in the world (Sher, 2004, pp. 30–32). Christine Korgaard (1996) describes the logicality thesis with an Augustinian inflection:

> Normative concepts exist because humans have normative problems. And we have normative problems because we are self-conscious rational animals capable of reflection about what we ought to believe and do ... Even when we are inclined to believe that something is right and to some extent feel ourselves moved to do it, we can still always ask: But is this really true? And must I really believe this? (p. 46)

"The critical question, 'Is it so?' is a basic question of human thought," and, therefore, truth is an axis of human language (Sher, 2004, p. 6).

In substantive theorizing, the quest for truth is linguistic: "Hypotheses are formulated in language, questions are asked and answered in language, and presumed knowledge is expressed in declarative sentences in language." Since language is the vehicle through which truths are discovered, "one central branch of the theory of truth – the so-called semantic branch – investigates truth as a property of linguistic entities." Abstracting from the "circumstances of utterances, we obtain truth as a property of declarative sentences" (Sher, 1999, p. 134). Sher's substantive theory reflects a correspondence principle, but correspondence is seen as a network of interconnected sub-principles that is not physical but linguistic (Sher, 2004, p. 36).

Direct successors of the correspondence theory, such as Sher's substantive definition, are widely accepted within philosophy and implicitly approved by many cognitive scientists and psychologists:

> Those who accept such views typically see themselves as working on the nature of representation. Indeed, some classical correspondence theories can be understood with little alteration, as forms of representationalism ... Many of the core elements of what I'm calling the representational theory of truth were initially developed to understand how sentences and their component words represent, or refer to, the world. (Lynch, 2011, pp. 22–23)

The linguistic-representational view that correspondence is built into semantics was stated regularly by Tarski: "A characteristic feature of semantic concepts is that they give expression to certain relations between the expressions of language and the objects about which these expressions speak" (1933, p. 252).

There is in representational knowledge two basic forms of conceptualization: "the principle of generality or universality and the principle of specificity or differentiation ... Theorizing and concept formation require both generalization and differentiation," yet the two principles are in fundamental tension (Sher, 1999, p. 141). As a result, there are two complementary challenges for the substantive theory of truth, disunity and unity: "(i) recognizing the diversity, complexity and multidimensionality of truth, and (ii) uncovering its unifying principles ... A substantive theory of truth cannot (if it is to be substantive) abstract from its particularity" (Sher, 2004, pp. 7, 9).

Debates in science sometimes give the impression that recognizing diversity and searching for unity are incompatible: "Like many philosophers, I believe that unity and diversity complement rather than exclude each other, and neither has priority over the other" (Sher, 2004, 7). Gila Sher echoes Plato on this integration: "If a person shows that such things as wood, stones, and the like, being many are also one, we admit that he shows the coexistence of the one and the many. He is uttering not a paradox, but a truism" (*Parmenides*, quoted in Lynch, 2001, p. 7). Because the substantive theory of truth is lingual in character, languages' multidimensions are able to accommodate the one-and-many challenge. Discourse ethics as formulated chiefly by Jürgen Habermas and supplemented by Karl-Otto Apel is a substantive theory that is sophisticated on the unity-diversity problematic.[11] Discourse ethics aims to account for both universals and culturally contingent variations.

Discourse Ethics

As argued previously, the substantive theory of truth is linguistic. In contemporary German-language philosophy, the discourse ethics of Habermas and Apel is a substantive theory of truth that has gained wide critical attention. The theory of truth as narrative in these two Frankfurt philosophers understands itself decidedly as a communication ethics; therefore, it has particular relevance to the ethics of truth in mediated communication. Language is broadly defined as the modality through which the human species is reflective and reaches an understanding of which courses of action to pursue. Language's prominent place in the

[11] "It is difficult to accept Habermas's proceduralism at face value. There is a clear gap between his claims to be purely procedural, and the normative tone of the rules he identifies, which demand that a discourse be open, inclusive and non-coercive ... Just because Habermas does not provide fully determinative principles of justice, that does not mean his position is indeterminate" (Krüger, 2016, p. 23). Apel's (1980) discourse ethics differs in his insistence on metanorms to direct procedural rules.

discourse model was anticipated by George Herbert Mead (1934) and is associated with Wittgenstein (1953), Garfinkel (1967), and Gadamer (1989).

Universalizability

Having diverse communities judged by universal norms is the intellectual strategy of discourse ethics. For competing discursive claims to be adjudicated in the public sphere, Habermas supposed normative conditions as their context (1984, 1990; cf. 1993). Presuming an inherent desire in speech acts for mutual understanding, Habermas argues for an ideal discourse of full participation, mutuality, and reciprocity as a goal for citizens and a critical standard for public communication. In formal terms, "Only those norms can claim to be valid that meet (or could meet) with the approval of all affected in their capacity as participants in a practical discourse" (Habermas, 1996, p. 66). In *Moral Consciousness and Communicative Action*, the rules of discourse are logical-semantic, such as speakers ought not contradict themselves, and they are procedural, such as speakers must believe what they assert (Habermas, 1990, pp. 86–89).

Habermas's concern is the rhetorical quality of discourse in the public sphere. While the properties of that discourse were formalized as the "ideal speech situation" (1984), he recognized that they were overly reified. As a result, Habermas has subsequently understood rhetoric to be conditioned by "pragmatic presuppositions" that participants must make for the outcome to be judged as reasonable: full inclusion, equal voice, no deception, and without coercion. In his *Truth and Justification* (2003), these conditioning presuppositions indicate that discourse is reasonable when there are no obvious exclusion of voices, no censorship of arguments, no manipulation or self-deception. Franz Krüger's conclusion is helpful:

These are sensible refinements which do not undermine the normative approach that essentially asks about the fairness of a particular discourse ... They make it possible to establish how fair – therefore justifiable – the outcome is. In investigating and judging real discourses in history, it is important to keep an eye open for power plays within them, what Habermas calls strategic action, and differentiate it from the legitimate use of discourse to defend interests. (2016, p. 25)

In *Moral Consciousness and Communicative Action*, Habermas sets the rhetorical process in a universal context. He argues that the principle of universalization is implicitly supposed by human discourse and acts as a rule of argumentation (1990, pp. 86–94). In moral consciousness, universals are the bridging principle that makes intercultural agreement possible (pp. 57–68).[12] Habermas presupposes that communication is fundamental to all human societies and that the basic characteristics of communication are therefore universal: "Habermas understands human community as relying universally on a set of implicit rules, and asserts that any participant in communication must accept them. Denying this fact involves a 'performative contradiction' – one cannot take that position without contradicting the rules one has tacitly accepted by participating in a discourse" (Krüger, 2016, p. 80). Universalization, as a formal procedural principle for practical discourse, points to the possible result of achieving universal understanding.

In Habermas's neo-Kantian perspective, ethical norms must meet the universalizability test; in other words, they are only valid if they can be seen to be valid for all. But rather than making this a matter for the individual conscience, as it was for Kant, Habermas argues that the test needs to be conducted in a practical discourse of those affected. The social consensus approach opens "the way to understand the range of different solutions to ethical challenges that have been found at different times and in different cultural and other contexts" (Krüger, 2016, p. 38). In Habermas's terms, "The problems to be resolved in moral argumentation cannot be handled monologically but require a co-operative effort" (1990, p. 66). In contrast to Kant's isolated individual subjects who hypothetically assume for themselves the universal perspective, Habermas's intersubjective discourse ethics ties universalization to the lifeworld narrative of specific social groups and to real conflicts that need resolution.

Communicative Rationality

The logicality thesis that Sher considers central to a substantive theory of truth is given sophistication in Habermas's concept of "communicative rationality." Rationality in Habermas is not based on transcendental assumptions. His communicative rationality is not rationalization or representation with abstract concepts; it is a disposition and social action for which there are good reasons. This definition

---

[12] Central to Habermas's project is the search for universal underlying norms. This issue anchored the debate between Habermas and Foucault. Habermas (1993) criticized Foucault for being motivated by a critical impetus without establishing its basis (cf. Krüger, 2016, p. 23).

is rooted in his view of communication as a rational enterprise: "Rationality is understood to be a disposition of speaking and acting subjects that is expressed in modes of behavior for which there are good grounds" (Habermas, 1984, p. 22). With this key definition, he shifts the emphasis in the concept of rationality from the conceptual to the social. Understanding is coming to a common definition of a subject, with arriving at agreement fundamental to the existence of culture.

The process of communicative rationality is "oriented to achieving, sustaining, and reviewing consensus – and indeed a consensus that rests on the intersubjective recognition of criticizable validity claims" (Habermas, 1984, p. 17). As Szczelkun observes, "Contested validity claims are thematized and attempts are then made to vindicate or criticize them in a systematic and rigorous way." In advanced industrial societies, "difficult or controversial claims are submitted to specialist theoretical discourses (e.g. legal procedure, academic debate, journalistic investigation)" (1999, p. 2). Habermas's communicative rationality is focused on lifeworld discourses in which claims to normative rightness are made thematic and tested. Habermas ties the meaning of speech acts to the practice of reason-giving: speech acts intrinsically involve claims that need reasons since claims require both criticism and justification. In everyday speech and much of action, speakers are bound to explain and justify themselves. Making a speech act entails an appropriate response that will justify it if called upon to do so.

For Habermas, to arrive at a shared understanding, speakers and listeners must agree on universal validity claims raised in their communicating: "A validity claim is equivalent to the assertion that the conditions for the validity of an utterance are fulfilled" (1984, p. 38). Communicative rationality is the process by which validity claims are resolved satisfactorily. The concept of reaching an understanding suggests a rationally motivated agreement among participants that is measured against validity claims that are presented, tested, and reordered.

Habermas states that the communication between a speaker and a listener is constituted by the existence of three such validity claims: the claims for truth, rightness, and truthfulness. These validity claims play a fundamental role in both interpersonal and public communication: "The concept of communicative action presupposes language as the medium for a kind of reaching understanding, in the course of which the participants, through relating to a world, reciprocally raise validity claims that can be accepted or contested" (Habermas, 1984, p. 99). The validity claims (propositional truth, normative rightness, and subjective truthfulness) characterize different categories of knowledge embodied in symbolic expressions.

Instead of a positivist commitment to fact-finding empiricist truth, Habermas recognizes an intersubjective three-dimensional spectrum of well-corroborated beliefs about the world: claims regarding the state of affairs, claims to moral rightness, and the ethical goodness of authenticity (Habermas, 1984, pp. 8–23). In other words, his triple-sided concept of communicative rationality is judged by validity claims regarding truth, social justice, and authentic personal expression. This "decentered understanding of the world" enables speakers and hearers "to confront external nature in an objectifying attitude ... to confront society in a norm-conformative attitude ... and to confront inner nature in an expressive attitude" (Habermas, 1984, p. 138).[13]

By the validity claim, the truth of the statement, Habermas means that the speech act is factually true, or more broadly, representationally adequate. Truth is concerned with "existing states of affairs" (Habermas, 1984, p. 88). For the truth dimension, the external world is the domain of reality. No statement is valid that claims "that gender affects intelligence, or that AIDS can be caught through sweat" (Lynch, 2011, p. 175). Following the 2016 US presidential election, Donald Trump's staff attempted to silence his critics by declaring that he had a mandate to govern. But this declaration did not meet the validity claim of truth: Trump's total vote was the lowest of any winner since 1945; Hillary Clinton won the popular vote by nearly three million. Trump's unfavorability rating of 60 percent is a historic high, with substantial numbers believing he governs in his business interests rather than the country's. In terms of Habermas's communicative rationality, "mandate to govern" is a false statement; it fails the factual truth criterion.

Habermas's theory of truth is realist in the sense that the objective world validates what is true. A proposition (or sentence, statement, report) is true because it represents an actual state of affairs, albeit a pragmatic realism accorded by the structure of linguistic representation.

---

[13] Habermas's trilogy reflects some of the philosophical issues that arise from the distinction in the German language between *Historie* and *Geschichte*. *Historie* refers to factual history, to events that can be verified by social scientific research; Habermas's "truth" stipulates that domain. *Geschichte* refers to the meaning of events, to their significance in the relevant context. Heidegger is said to find six senses of *Geschichte*, all of them centered on philosophical reflection about the traditions and values that particular facts represent. Habermas's "normative correctness" is a *geschichtliche* concept.

That is, accurate representation is to be understood pragmatically in terms of its implications for everyday practice and discourse. In this regard, Habermas's communicative rationality is not a correspondence theory that relates proposition and world metaphysically.

By the validity claim, normative rightness, Habermas means the moral rightness of the intended social relationship. For the rightness dimension, the domain of reality is the community. The tacit validity claim is that speech acts are socially appropriate or just. As Habermas (1984) describes it, "the speech act is right in terms of a given normative context or the normative context that it satisfies is itself legitimate" (p. 137). During the 2016 presidential campaign, the *Washington Post* released a 2005 video of Trump and Billy Bush of *Access Hollywood* arriving on the set of the soap opera *Days of Our Lives*. Trump brags in lewd and vulgar terms about kissing, groping, and trying to have sex with women. His belligerence in the conversation, his self-described actions, and the testimony of fifteen women who accused him of sexual abuse over the years depicted legally defined sexual harassment and assault. Trump and his supporters dismissed the "decades-old video" as "locker-room talk." The women who came forward were called "horrible liars" and were humiliated for "seeking their fifteen minutes of fame." Their testimonies were said to result from "collusion between Clinton and the media." None of these responses meets the validity claim of normative rightness; communicative rationality in which speakers and hearers are in agreement includes the right treatment we owe each other interpersonally. When Trump added that his accusers came forward because of "collusion between Clinton and the politically correct media," he violated Habermas's truth principle.

The normative rightness motif is typically featured in classical social science. Max Weber's *The Protestant Ethic and the Spirit of Capitalism* (1930) introduces two ideal types and their deviation from actual societies as an argument for the centrality of social values. Alvin Gouldner's *Patterns of Industrial Bureaucracy* (1954) is not a study of one factory but the normative rightness of corporate bureaucracy in industrial societies. David Reisman's work in *The Lonely Crowd* (1961) understands tradition-, inner-, and other-directedness in terms of historical patterns. Oscar Lewis's *Children of Sanchez* (1961) is not simply an account of a particular family but a commentary on the role of oral culture in community life generally. Clifford Geertz's *The Interpretation of Culture* (1973), in its comparative analysis of socioeconomic patterns in two Indonesian towns, is a "thick description" of cultural meaning making.

With the third validity claim, truthfulness, Habermas means the authenticity of what is expressed, or in personal speech acts, their sincerity (cf. Taylor, 1991). From intellectual history and in naturalistic terms, Bernard Williams (2002) likewise underscores sincerity as a cultural value; in fact, along with accuracy, sincerity is, for him, a basic virtue of truthful persons. In Habermas, for the truthfulness dimension of communicative rationality, the domain of reality is the subjective world: "The speaker's manifest intentions are manifest in the way they are expressed" (Habermas, 1984, p. 137).[14] "The tacit validity claim is that speakers act in a sincere, not deceptive manner. In personal expressions, those who hold grudges/settle scores, sociopaths, bullies, and sore losers do not meet the truthfulness test.

Dietrich Bonhoeffer, in chap. 5 of his *Ethics*, agrees that defining lies as a conscious discrepancy between thought and speech is inadequate. He would concur with Habermas on the need for the validity claim of truthfulness. His provocative one-on-one illustration is the teacher who asks a child in front of the class whether his father often comes home drunk. It is true but the student denies it. The teacher's speech act is outrageous in this setting, with the child unsure of the teacher's intentions and not mature enough to reject the question about private family matters as inappropriate. The blame for the lie falls on the teacher (1995, pp. 330–331).

Anton Shekhovtsov (2015) of Vienna's Institute for Human Sciences illustrates Habermas's truthfulness in terms of public communication. His concern is Russia's information warfare apparatus. What he calls "Russia's disinformation campaign" to the world discredited Ukraine's Euromaidan protests in late 2013 and then justified the military invasion and annexation of the Autonomous Republic of Crimea, while ridiculing Ukrainians as fake Russians, fascists, and Western puppets, and Ukraine as a failed state – as documented by Estonian Kristina Müür's content analysis of Russian news outlets, *Komsomolskaya Pravda* and *Regnum*, *TV Zvezda* (2016).

---

[14] While not focusing on speech acts, but in terms of literary analysis, in *Toward a Philosophy of the Act*, Bahktin likewise insists on truthfulness (*pravda*). Whether something is true (*istina*) following a natural or social scientific theory is an epistemological question. Truthfulness (*pravda*) is a moral category referring to the validity of one's responsible action (1993, p. 28). The idea of "non-alibi" in Bahktin ("That which can be done by me can never be done by anyone else," p. 40) overlaps with "sincerity" as the characteristic of Habermas's truthfulness.

This Ukraine-centric propaganda campaign, for Shekhovtsov, is one illustration of an unprecedented Russian information war against the West designed and led by Vladimir Putin. Russia's information warfare system includes all media technologies – state control over major mass media and intimidation of free media: *RT* (Russian multilingual television network), satellites, and the Russian news agency *RIA Novosti* and web-based and social media. Its rationale is defending the regime against Western enemies by crippling their business and politics whenever possible and undermining their credibility in the world. Putin's information warfare apparatus violates the authenticity claim of truthfulness.

Shekhovtsov (2015) documents the use of paid bloggers and internet trolls to conduct psychological warfare in the web-based media, cyber attacks against foreign institutions including the mass media, creation of Russian diaspora NGOs and think tanks to help "minimize the role of the U.S. in global politics, weaken transatlantic relations, undermine NATO and demolish the EU" (p. 3). Cynical to the world and aggressive against perceived threats to the Putin regime internally, Russia's information warfare system violates the sincerity claim of truthfulness.

When Trump-and-company's dismissals are rejected, and Putin's information warfare apparatus is considered the opposite of communicative rationality, the "no" means that these utterances are "not in accordance with either the world of existing states of affairs, our world of legitimately ordered interpersonal relations, or the manifestation of lived experience" (Habermas, 1984, p. 137). To understand why truth, rightness, and truthfulness and not others are the validity markers, and how not fulfilling them means communicative failure, it is important to analyze the procedure of argumentation by which disputed validity claims can be grounded. Through argumentation, participants in discourse "thematize contested validity claims and attempt to vindicate or criticize them" (Habermas, 1990, p. 18). Truth, rightness, and truthfulness are not inscribed in formal law and are therefore not abstract principles by which to measure whether a discourse is ethical. Habermas recognizes that the surface grammar of speech acts does not establish the three features of communicative rationality. Semantic analysis must be supplemented by a pragmatic understanding of argumentative discourse in which different "logics of argumentation" are considered the avenue through which claims to validity can be justified. Such argumentation leads to agreed-on community-held norms. When we analyze the general structure of argumentation, we will know what features of speech acts are necessary for agreement and consensus.

Szczelkun (1999, p. 4) states, "Overall, Habermas thinks that we lack a well worked-out logic of argumentation which satisfactorily captures the internal" connections between forms of speech acts. He recognizes the difficulties of universalizing from an occidental viewpoint." Habermas adapts Stephen Toulmin (1958) and other informal logicians into his understanding of argument.

But the term "logical" is broader for Habermas than Toulmin's overly structured approach. Habermas learns from both formal and informal logics, since lifeworld discourse depends on the interrelated meanings of terms that resist such formalizations as induction and analogy. Most argumentation for Habermas is ampliative, that is, the conclusions do not follow with deductive certainty but only as more or less plausible. Thus, he appeals to such ideal speech conditions as reciprocity and openness. For commonly shared issues, valid argumentation depends on how adequately the relevant information has been taken into account, thereby making an unfettered media essential for the rhetorical quality of discourse in the public sphere.

Edmund Arens (1997) elaborates on the way mass media ethics should understand itself as discursive. The orientation toward truth means that the professionals of media narratives will "make statements, advance assertions, and deliver judgments of whose truth they are convinced and for which they can adduce explanations, grounds, and evidence" (p. 59). In their orientation toward rightness, the news media "do not obstruct and fragment the public sphere ... but investigate and uncover existing relations of distorted, restricted, or obstructed public communication, and they work toward overcoming them" (p. 62). The orientation toward truthfulness means that "persons engaged in mass media communication give authentic expression of their lifeworld, free of illusion and delusion" and without "the self-promotion of the feigned, untruthful reduction of communication to mere entertainment" (p. 60). For Franz Krüger, "the discourse ethical framework allows the derivation of particular norms for media behavior" even in "highly charged and politicized discourses" such as South Africa's, which are challenging historic news values (2016, p. 21). Habermas's communicative rationality is not simply media criticism, but an ethics of truth that "enables the development of a refined normative concept of the role of the media and of journalism" in modern democracies (p. 31).

Critique

Habermas's discourse ethics is a substantive theory of truth in which the central questions are simultaneously social and moral in nature. Given the inadequacies of the individualist utilitarianism that has dominated media ethics since John Stuart Mill, it is imperative that we start over conceptually and Habermas's dialogic ethics of duty is an obvious alternative. It critiques the conventions of impartiality and formality in Western objectivism. Rather than privileging external rules and calibrations, his substantive theory of truth positions the moral order intersubjectively where human identity is constituted. Moral consciousness nurtured in communities of rationality and reciprocity is set effectively against the conditions of instrumental technocracy and institutional power that stifle autonomous action in the public arena.[15]

Regardless of its repositioning media ethics away from the mainstream Western tradition, Habermas's procedural model of discursive argumentation is widely criticized as too ideally critical-rational. For Apel (1980, chap. 5) and others, communicative rationality "conjures up an image of an orderly assembly of people earnestly exchanging views and reaching consensus" (Krüger, 2016, p. 29). Justification of community interests, in Habermas, is "tied to reasoned agreement among those subject to the norm in question" (1990, p. viii), and his elaboration of this communication community and his defense and clarifications of it (1991, 1993) have not been uniformly convincing. "It is a feature of observable discourse – whether gay rights or Middle East politics" or workplace robotics or environmental crises – that it is "normative in seeking to define what is right, but also involves intense powerplays" (Krüger, 2016, p. 29). Habermas classifies "this kind of behavior as 'strategic action,' counter posing it to 'communicative action' which is genuinely interested in finding common ground" (p. 29). But to critics, this analytic distinction simplifies the complicated dynamics of social institutions.

Thomas McCarthy (1992) centers this criticism on what he considers Habermas's system-lifeworld distinction, arguing that even idealized lifeworld discourses involve rhetorical tactics and compromises. Foucault (1984) questions the very existence of autonomous citizens

---

[15] The overwrought lifeworld/system distinction in Habermas is not easily corrected. However, consistent with the integration of the philosophy of technology and moral philosophy in this book, Habermas situates life-world in its technocratic conditions. Systems that are structured by efficiency and machineness are understood correctly in Habermas (1970, 1973) as the context in which communicative rationality operates.

who are said to engage in rational discourse. Self- is impossible for Foucault without emancipation from the prevailing regime of oppressive practices. From his perspective, we ought to struggle against the economic and ideological state violence that constitutes us as moral subjects, and Habermas does not enable us to do so. In Nancy Fraser's view (1992, 1997), Habermas's public sphere is an abstraction that is not gender inclusive or culturally constituted. In her perspective, nation-states are polycentric, not an aggregate of individuals under an external standpoint. Given Habermas's insistence that public discourse must conform to generalizable interests, how can he ensure that the interests of particular subcultures will meet the universalizability test?

Although neither the gender nor ethnicity issue is easily resolved, discourse ethics addresses them within its own paradigm rather than abandoning Habermas altogether. The rules of reason that constitute discourse ethics "constrain all affected to adopt the perspective of all others in the balancing of interests" (Habermas, 1990, p. 65). As Habermas argues, "only those [moral] norms can claim to be valid that meet (or could meet) with the approval of all those affected by such norms" (p. 66). In other words, discourse ethics in principle insists on gender equality and cultural inclusion.

While intellectual progress is possible in discourse ethics on its contentious communicative rationality, and on gender equality and ethnic inclusion, Habermas's nation-state commitment is contrary to the global media technology that defines our era. In *The Inclusion of the Other* (1998) and *The Postnational Constellation* (1998), Habermas, like Rawls, insists that rights are empty apart from their unique constitutional venues. National sovereignty ought to be limited by universal human rights, but differing peoples must be allowed to interpret those rights according to their own political traditions. While noting the positive role played by nationalism in struggles for liberation and democracy, Habermas recognizes that nationality today has all too often justified illiberal forms of nationalism that suppress dissident minority groups and other sub-nationalities. While advocating the idea that nations represent stable units of collective agency, he concedes that this stability is being discredited by the multicultural migrations set in motion by globalization. Habermas tends to view international justice as an extension of domestic justice, whereby relationships of mutual dependency presume a basic structure requiring rectification vis-à-vis principles of distributive justice.

Though focused on Rawls, Nussbuam (2006) speaks to "today's urgent problem of extending justice to all world citizens" and concludes:

"Because all major Western theories of social justice begin from the nation-state as their basic unit, new theoretical structures" are required "to think well about this problem"; the "old theoretical structures" cannot merely be applied to the new global situation (pp. 2, 4; cf. Wasserman, 2018, pp. 117–121). Ethical principles such as Habermas's, worked out first of all in advanced industrial societies, are typically parochial for young and developing democracies, and irrelevant for the press in authoritarian systems.

Sonia Livingstone (2012) rightly accuses communication studies of "methodological nationalism" instead of mapping transnational flows: "The field of media and communication – its phenomena, questions, and concerns – is focused on clearly demarcated, tradition-bound, institutionally-integrated countries widely recognized and referred to by their self-identified publics, media and culture" (p. 416). Further, "In an age of globalization, the nation-state is no longer the automatic starting point for comparative research, for media and communication flow within and across nations ... In political terms, cross-national research is critiqued for inadvertently privileging the dominant norm over the norms of others" (pp. 420, 422).

Wendy Willems, from her dual-university perspective of London and Johannesburg, argues persuasively that, even among scholars since the early 2000s who have been seeking to de-Westernize and decolonize media and communication studies, "the Global South continues to be theorized from the vantage point of the Global North ... Such accounts have failed to acknowledge the agency of the Global South in the production, consumption and circulation of a much richer spectrum of media culture that is not *a priori* defined in opposition to or in conjunction with media from the Global North." This Eurocentric perspective "has interpreted media systems through the normative lens of the Global North and has emphasized their lack, their deviation from Western norms." In framing the nation-states of the Global South through the agency of Northern theory and practice, research neglects "the actually existing roles of media and communication ... that are taking place outside the context of Western development interventions" (2014, pp. 1, 4, 6).

Discourse ethics represents a paradigm change from the ethics of rationalization. Habermas's major concepts – communicative rationality; the validity claims of truth, rightness, truthfulness; lifeworld; argumentation – construct a duty ethics of truth with stature in philosophical and professional ethics. But internationalizing media ethics is the fundamental challenge at present in order to deal authoritatively with the media's global technology and mandate. Habermas's discourse ethics of substantive truth is an important transition from the long-entrenched Western paradigm of correspondence truth. But the fluid world-news agenda and the borderless media technologies that configure it require fundamental revision of his nation-state model. While continuing to work seriously with discourse media ethics, given its innovation and comprehensiveness, a third paradigm of the truth principle needs to be constructed that is radically international in both theory and application.

ALETHEIA AS AUTHENTIC DISCLOSURE

When truth is articulated in an international framework, its meaning is best understood as *aletheia:* uncovering the authentic, disclosing the genuine underneath.[16] *Aletheia*'s literal definition is "the state of not being hidden; the state of being evident." This Greek word is variously translated as "unconcealedness," "disclosure," and "truth." For the journalist Wesely Pippert, truth in this sense means to get at "the core, the essence, the nub, the heart of the matter" (1989, p. 11). In Heidegger's etymological analysis, the original meaning in Greece was unconcealedness. In his elaboration, *aletheia* elucidates the ontological; it identifies the process of making reality intelligible for human existence.[17] For Nikolas Kompridis, in his essay "On World Disclosure: Heidegger, Habermas and Dewey," *aletheia* means to unveil "the symbolically structured world within which we find ourselves; it refers to the disclosure of new horizons of meaning" and to opening up "previously hidden dimensions of meaning" (1994, p. 37).[18]

---

[16] The Greek term *alétheia* is standard for those who define truth in non-modernist terms. Mark Lynch (2001, 2004, 2011) is doing the most extensive contemporary philosophical work on truth; see his adjectival use of the term in "*Alethic* Pluralism, Logical Consequence and the Universality of Reason" (*Midwest Studies in Philosophy*, 2008, pp. 122–140). Alston's (1996) influential book on epistemology and metaphysics centers on the adjectival form, *alethic* realism.

[17] In *Being and Time* (1927), Heidegger is preoccupied with Being itself, but chiefly in terms of the problem of truth. *Being and Time* is his earliest systematic analysis of the correspondence concept of truth as well as his rejection of it. He expanded on truth in his *Introduction to Metaphysics*. In *Poetry, Language and Thought*, works of art provide a symbolic frame that discloses the meaning of things in the world. *The Essence of Truth: On Plato's Cave Allegory and Theaetetus* (2013) is a lecture course given at the University of Freiburg in 1931–1932. His latest essay on truth is "The End of Philosophy and the Task of Thinking."

[18] In his *Critique and Disclosure* (2011), Kompridis challenges Habermas to a disclosure model that better integrates formal and procedural thinking. While Habermas has

Heidegger's insistence on *aletheia* as disclosure recovers its primary content and connects it to the international world of ideas. In what is called "Plato's Doctrine of Truth," Heidegger (1998) concludes that Plato's cave analogy in the *Republic* and perception in the *Theaetetus* define truth as "correctness of vision." In Heidegger's reading, Plato transformed the nature of truth from its originary "disclosure" to the "correct perception of things." Plato's reduction of truth to subject-object agreement, in Heidegger's terms, is a fateful mistake that characterizes the history of Western philosophy. Truth as correct alignment or correspondence is already evident in Aristotle's *De Interpretatione* and is reiterated in Kant's *Critique of Pure Reason*. As elaborated earlier in this chapter, René Descartes's *Discourse on Method* (1637) equates truth with mathematical knowledge, while the *Principia Mathematica* by Russell and Whitehead argues that knowledge agrees with its object. In Shannon and Weaver's *Mathematical Theory of Communication* (1963), the problem of communication is to reproduce information accurately at each point in the transmission process (cf. Gunkel & Taylor, 2014, pp. 32, 66–67).

In Plato's reformulation, the concept of truth is defined as representational exactitude: "This traditional and long-standing formulation is contrasted with Heidegger's stubborn insistence on the conceptual distinction between what is true and what is merely correct" (Gunkel & Taylor, 2014, pp. 6–7). In Heidegger's famous summary: "Unconcealment, in accordance with which nature presents itself as a calculable complex of the effects of forces, can indeed permit correct determinations; but precisely through these successes the danger can remain that in the midst of all that is correct the true will withdraw" (1977b, p. 26). Following Plato, today's techno-scientific era tends to see the world as an innately measurable interrelationship of causes and effects, that is, as a "calculable complex." When we describe these causes and effects scientifically, we produce what is considered "correct determinations" (Gunkel & Taylor, 2014, p. 62). Heidegger affirms the taken-for-granted understanding of communication as a tool to represent reality or to externalize our thoughts, but this commonplace is insufficient and incomplete. Truth in the Western history of ideas "is an original

critiqued Heidegger's world disclosure, Kompridis argues that a refinement of disclosure, that is, "reflective disclosure," expands rationality and enriches the Frankfurt School's critical theory. This reconstruction parallels the neo-Habermas rethinking of discourse ethics that is developed in this chapter.

unconcealing from which correspondence derives as a secondary aspect and side effect" (Gunkel & Taylor, 2014, p. 90).[19]

Heidegger's account of *aletheia*'s entymology – prior to correspondence in its conceptual structure and in historical development – resonates with the definition of truth in Sher's substantive theory. Habermas's neo-Kantian discourse ethics includes truth as representational, but within the larger context of normative rightness and truthfulness. For the idea of *aletheia* as developed here in neo-Habermasian international terms, Heidegger's recovery of its primal meaning de-Westernizes truth by locating it in human existence. Rather than formulating *aletheia*'s disclosure motif according to intellectual traditions following Heidegger – such as phenomenology, Sartre's existentialism, or Derrida's deconstructionism – Heidegger is seen as freeing *aletheia*'s deeper essence for this chapter's globalism.

For Hinduism, truth as *aletheia* is the source of all other virtues. Emil Brunner of Germany defines truth as encounter, and for Denmark's Soren Kierkegaard, truth is subjective. In Karl Jaspers's *Reason and Existenz*, "The moment of communication is at one and the same time the preservation of, and a search for, the truth" (1955). In Christianity, Jesus says the truth will set us free (Gutiérrez, 1990). In Martin Buber's Jewish mysticism, truth is in the I-Thou relationship (cf. Christians, 2003). As noted in Chapter 2, truth as personal authenticity is central to such indigenous cultures as the Shuswap tribe in Canada, the Polynesians of the Pacific, and the Australian Aborigines (Cooper, 1996).

The French social philosopher Jacques Ellul illustrates this definition of truth. As outlined in Chapter 1, his *The Technological Society* (1954) speaks the truth about modernity. His *la technique* goes beneath the surface to the basic issues underneath. The problem is not technological products per se, but *la technique*, the mystique of efficiency that underlies them. The issue is not machines first of all, but the spirit of machineness, the instrumental worldview on which technological systems depend. When efficiency, speed, and productivity dominate, morality rooted in human life becomes alien to us. Ellul's *la technique* is an academic version

---

[19] As noted by Gunkel and Taylor (2014), Baudrillard recognized the importance of Heidegger's distinction in his *Simulations* (1983), where the true and correct are collapsed into the hyper-real. In applying Heidegger's distinction, Gunkel and Taylor (2014) refer to McLuhan's famous formula, "The medium is the message": "This aphorism works as a highly succinct expression of truth's displacement by correctness. For example, in the case of the widespread valorization of digital technology, the medium has indeed become the message" (p. 64).

of *aletheia*, disclosing the heart of the matter: in the process of constructing the digital order, moral purpose is sacrificed to maximizing technical
ends.

Ta-Nehisi Paul Coates, national correspondent for *The Atlantic*, is an
influential and celebrated expositor of *aletheia*. His *Between the World
and Me* won the 2015 National Book Award for Nonfiction. Written as
a letter to his teenage son, Coates gives an autobiographical account of
city life in Maryland and recapitulates through American history how the
schools, the police, and the "physicality and chaos of the streets" endan-
ger black men and women. Empirical realities from the introduction to
conclusion are interpreted in terms of the systems of white supremacy that
dominate US culture. In his *aletheia* of how "racist violence" is woven into
American life, Coates discloses to his son the life-world against which he
will struggle. The book is challenged for portraying whiteness as indes-
tructible but awarded for clarifying white supremacy for the public
agenda.

Coates worked for the *Village Voice,* the *Philadelphia Weekly,* and
Time. He has contributed to the *New York Times Magazine* and the
Washington Post. He has won the National Magazine Award for Essays
and Criticism, the George Polk Award for Commentary, and the Hillman
Prize for Opinion and Analysis Journalism. His essay in *The Atlantic* on
the US election of Donald Trump, "My President Was Black," followed
this tradition of award-winning *aletheia* (Coates, 2017). "My President
Was Black" is a history of the first African American White House, set
against the background of the whiteness that ensured the "unerring privilege" of a "two-hundred year monopoly on the highest office in the
land." Despite the seemingly insurmountable odds, in unprecedented
drama, the Obama White House has been an "eight-year showcase of
a healthy and successful black family . . . the Obamas the ultimate credit to
the race, incomparable in elegance and bearing," now the most "famous
depictions of black success" beyond entertainers and athletes in American
history. As Obama put it in the Democratic National Convention Keynote
of 2004, "the hope of a skinny kid with a funny name who believes that
America has a place for him" has been fulfilled.

How could a country of democratic traditions, of aspirations and
dreams – in which "for eight years Barack Obama walked on ice and
never fell" – so "swiftly and so easily" be brought to "the brink of
fascism"? Coates takes account of the multiple explanations, with special
attention to Trump's appeal to the anger of aggrieved blue-collar voters.
This theory, "popular among (primarily) white intellectuals of varying

political persuasions," holds that Trump's presidency resulted largely from "the discontented rumblings of a white working class threatened by the menace of globalization and crony capitalism." Coates's contrary interpretation is racism: "One need not stretch too far to conclude that an eight-year campaign of consistent and open racism aimed at the leader of the free world helped clear the way." The details are abundant and precise: personal animus and the animosity of institutional interests, from the 2008 campaign until today. The history of segregated schools, biased police, legislation to deny voting rights, entrenched racial resentment opposing the president's decisions, outrageous media personalities, social science research on race – Coates's essay is a comprehensive socio-cultural review.

The *aletheia* of racism is Coates's conclusion: "The election of Donald Trump confirmed everything I knew of my country and none of what I could accept. The idea that America would follow its first black president with Donald Trump accorded with its history." Coates recognizes other explanations and sees the multiple challenges to liberal democracy across the world that the elections of demagogic politicians represent. His perspicacious *alethic* interpretation centered on race enters the public forum with undeniable gravitas.

In putting *aletheia* to work as a professional, Coates represents the tradition of Augustine in which the moral dimension is a central feature of *aletheia*.[20] In Augustine, *aletheia* "tends to be more relational than propositional, a dialogically interpersonal sacramental act rather than a statement, ... taking into account and being motivated by faith, hope, and charity" (Settle, 1994, pp. 49, 57). The truth for him does not merely make things clear; truth is not fundamentally a value-neutral declaration, but it motivates speaker and listener to belief and action. In truthful communication for Augustine, "[I]t is not enough to move our minds, merely for the sake of power"; instead, communication has power when it is "used to lead us to truth" (Murphy, 1974, p. 62). The rhetorical process ought to be informed and directed by *caritas*. Stated differently, Augustine

---

[20] Augustine (354–430), professor of rhetoric at Milan for forty-one years, and later Bishop of Hippo, established *aletheia*'s non-correspondence meaning for moral truth. Augustine's rhetorical theory is a major contribution to the philosophy of communication, contradicting the linear view of the ancient Greeks (Troup & Christians, 2014, chap. 9). Augustine's rhetoric entails reasoned judgment; however, he "break[s] way from Graeco-Roman rhetoric, moving instead toward rhetoric as *aletheiac* act" (Settle, 1994, p. 49).

conceived of truth as reason illumined by love, thereby merging *aletheia* with moral discernment.

Coates's and Augustine's moral emphasis is reflected across human languages. In Gandhi's *satyagraha*, truth communicated from the human spirit wins over violent force. In the Talmud, the liars' punishment is that no one believes them. Foucault's lectures to the Catholic University of Louvain trace the early use of truth telling in ancient Greece to the practice of confession, the avowal of wrongdoing, in monastic times (2014). For Bonhoeffer, telling the truth depends on the quality of discernment so that penultimate issues do not gain ultimacy (1955, chap. 5). He argues correctly that a truthful account resonates with the context and is authentic regarding the speaker's motives and presuppositions involved. The Truth and Reconciliation Commission in South Africa presumed that sufferings from apartheid could be healed through truthful testimony. Communicating the truth personally about the crimes committed is the necessary first step toward reconciliation. *Aletheia*, when told and heard, leads to new ways of understanding human relationships and to actions commensurate with confession and forgiveness. Augustine's claim that *aletheia*, when directed by *caritas*, leads to reconciliatory action was demonstrated in historic fashion by Rwanda's "Love and Forgiveness Campaign" following the genocide.

Aletheia in this transnational and cross-cultural usage entails what Heidegger calls the constitutive view of human language. Language is the phenomenon that shapes reality and makes it possible for human existence. Heidegger's *Being and Time* contrasts the constitutive form of language with the instrumentalist view that language is a tool to express a preexisting reality – a definition consistent with Plato's truth as correspondence. In the constitutive understanding, language is the symbolic world through which Being is disclosed.[21]

Gunkel and Taylor (2014) recognize James Carey as "one of the few communication scholars who explicitly acknowledged Heidegger's

---

[21] In "New Media, Mediation," Lievrouw (2011, chap. 8) develops this idea from a different perspective, arguing for "mediation" as the focus rather than on the media themselves. Citing Roger Silverstone and Jesús Martin Barbero (p. 227), Lievrouw summarizes mediation as recognizing that "people's expressions and interactions are inseparable from the devices and methods they use to create, sustain, or change them ... In contrast to traditional concepts of the media that emphasize the influence of powerful technologies and institutions on individuals and society, mediation actually constitutes social relationships and experience" (pp. 229, 234).

influence" (p. 36), and they cite Carey's definition of language alongside Heidegger's:

Reality is not given, not humanly existent, independent of language and toward which language stands as a pale refraction. Rather reality is brought into existence, is produced, by communication – by, in short, the construction, apprehension, and utilization of symbolic forms. (Carey, 1989, p. 25)

Language is the house of Being in which man exists by dwelling. (Heidegger, 1967, p. 213)

Carey expressed Heidegger's constitutive/instrumentalist distinction as two different definitions of communication – a transmission and ritual view (Carey, 1989, pp. 14–23). As described in Chapter 1 when introducing Carey's *Communication as Culture,* transmission is the standard model in the correspondence tradition, defined by the transportation of signals over space. The truthfulness of a mediation is assessed "by asking the questions Plato had formulated in the final book of the *Republic* – whether and to what extent the information provided in the mediation corresponds to the actual state of affairs" (Gunkel & Taylor, 2014, p. 51). The ritual definition highlights communication as the process of constructing a meaningful cultural world of shared beliefs in order to maintain societies over time (Carey, 1989, p. 18).

The constitutive understanding of language has important consequences for scholarship on truth and for implementing the concept in the media professions. If our lived-in reality is constructed by mediated images, this fundamentally different perspective will generate a different set of questions for media study: "How do we do this? What are the differences among these mediated forms? What are the historical and comparative variations in the language traditions? How do changes in communication technology influence what we can concretely create and apprehend? How do groups in society struggle over the definition of what is real?" (Carey, 1989, p. 26). When language is understood as constitutive, truthfulness is interpretive. Humans live by interpreting experience through the agency of culture. Thus, the primary question is not "how do the media affect us?" but "what interpretations of meaning and value do the media represent?"

The attempt to develop the constitutive tradition "has taken many forms and is known by different labels: *les sciences humaine, Geisteswissenschaften,* critical theory, interpretive social science, hermeneutics, cultural studies, or by the general term, the reconstructive sciences. These names point to important differences of outlook, differences in philosophical orientation, national tradition, research priorities, and ideological stances" (Christians & Carey, 1981, p. 346).

In all such versions of *aletheia,* knowledge is life related. We know and have moral convictions in the process. We measure up to what we know and consider it our moral obligation to act accordingly. In modernity's calculative reasoning, it is the mind – an independent reality – alone that knows. Contrariwise with *aletheia,* truth telling is not a problem of cognition per se but is integral to human consciousness and social formation. Truth as the disclosure of the authentic is rooted ontologically as a deeply meaningful concern. Human existence is impossible without an overriding commitment to truth. As developed in the "Surplus of Meaning" section later in this chapter, truth as inscribed in our humanness is central to its universal character. Since truth is the centerpiece of the lingual domain that constitutes human existence, *aletheia* is obligatory for the news profession's mission and rationale.[22]

News as Truth Production

The ethics of *aletheia* requires a nonrelativist view of news as knowledge production, developed here as truth production (Hammersley & Traianou, 2012, chap. 2). The gathering and dissemination of news are not merely constructions of information data. Reporters do not simply mirror reality or in online journalism serve as modules in a technical network. The professional newsmaker's occupational task is the production of truthful knowledge. For the ethics of truth, the reporters' concerns are not primarily how to treat their sources or how to minimize harm to their audiences and viewers. The ethics of *aletheia,* when seen as defining the media professions' occupational character, understands news as knowledge production in sophisticated terms. News as the pursuit of knowledge is by content and framework *alethic.* As with education, the intrinsic character of the news profession's knowledge production establishes its moral obligation in terms of *aletheia.*[23] In this sense, though all

---

[22] Truth is the ethical standard for the communications phenomenon in all its forms, from interpersonal to virtual. Therefore, for mediated communication, truth telling is the occupational norm for the many different media professions. The emphasis in this chapter is on news; however, truth as *aletheia* is likewise applicable to persuasion – advertising and public relations (*aletheia* as full disclosure) and to entertainment (*aletheia* understood as aesthetic realism).

[23] The term "knowledge production" reflects the academic research of scholarly disciplines, with research universities given the mission of "creating new knowledge." It is typically

knowledge claims are limited in scope, a representative number of them can be authoritative.

In the mainstream trajectory, "news-as-information-processing" uses social scientific criteria for its validity. However, news as the production of *alethic* knowledge follows the literary styles of logic and patterns of proof that are characteristic of humanistic studies. While the social sciences do not typically examine interpretation, the interpretive process is a preoccupation in the humanities. For the human race, language makes intelligible whatever exists; therefore, *ipso facto* all language use is interpretive. There is no form of knowledge that is not mediated by symbols – oral, textual, visual, or digital. Humans live first of all in systems of thought and culture, not as subjects outside of an objective world. The presuppositional is an already interpreted context. Or, stated differently, the history of accumulated meanings is an inescapable component of our own interpretations.

In the semiotics of Charles Sanders Peirce (1932), the concept of "retroduction" is particularly relevant for understanding news as truth production. Both induction and deduction are one-way, linear modes. By contrast, in retroductive interpretation, the knowledge process moves from contingency to creative insights to a likely explanation. In interpretation, there are creative leaps of imagination and visualization of the whole. Retroduction typically begins with hunches or ideas and operates interactively from there. Received knowledge and canonical texts are incorporated at various points in the retroductive process and with varying comprehensiveness. In this hermeneutical pattern, both theoretical and empirical social science are reconstituted through history and comparative analysis into a normative and philosophical basis for cultural critique.[24] The *alethic* model of knowledge production is not measured by "credibility amongst peers but in terms of richness of implications, of the capacity to generate connections among disparate elements, of freshness of insights and scope" (Vander Linde, 2001, p. 58). The communicative rationality of Habermas and the existential ontology of Heidegger are both retroductive. *Poeisis* and narrative discourse are reconstructive; they

---

understood as social construction and, therefore, differs qualitatively from *alethic* production. To describe information gathered and discussed in the public domain as a whole outside the scholar-expert system, Shilpa Shanbhag (2006) reviews other labels and models, such as "information literacy as a liberal art."

[24] A central concept in Harold Garfinkel's (1967) ethnomethodology is "indexical expressions," which is taken from Charles Peirce. It is typically cited as a precursor to Habermas's communicative rationality.

make cognitively explicit the pre-theoretical conditions of such human competencies as discourse and reciprocity.

The news-as-information model in the objectivity tradition typically follows the one-sided epistemology of inductive reasoning: evidence is gathered, patterns and relationships are identified, and a conclusion is formed. Generalizations are restricted to the data by journalistic guidelines, such as double referents, primary sources, and on-site observation.[25] In professional news production based on interactive retroduction, reporters interpret situations in light of their several parts, and their narrative examines specific elements and features in light of the whole. All interpretive activity proceeds by way of dialectical language between possibilities and verification. News professionals judge the status of center and periphery and the relevance of primary and secondary in understanding the components. They validate an interpretation by comparing it against alternative interpretations. Despite intellectual quandaries on occasion, they meticulously follow such criteria as comprehensiveness to determine which interpretation is more plausible. When retroduction produces several coherent meanings, that pluralism is a provocateur to further investigation.

Stephen Ward (2015b) uses the label "pragmatic objectivity" for news as knowledge production (chap. 8). His pragmatic objectivity redefines rather than abandons the traditional concept of objective truth and consequently has a transformative orientation. Pragmatic objectivity recognizes the actuality of values and presuppositions in human knowing and does not insist on detached neutrality. As with the interpretive methodology in understanding news as *aletheia*, pragmatic objectivity accepts interpretation, though insisting on the most comprehensive process of inquiry available. In Ward's view, it "requires only a modest conception of truth that is close to common sense" (2015b, p. 286). Rather than a reductionist objectivism that follows the rules of empiricism, there are various kinds of truth statements in pragmatic objectivity. The empirical

---

[25] C. Wright Mills (1959) introduced the concept of "abstracted empiricism" for quantitative social science that explained sociological and psychological facts through multivariate analysis. He argued that when social science procedures are derived from the natural sciences, the result is reliable coding, but limited knowledge of social structures. In technical terms, a methodology based on autonomous distribution overestimates sociopolitical homogeneity. Empirical studies of wider scope and over longer periods will clarify details; imaginative mixed method approaches will undoubtedly yield thicker descriptions. But I conclude from the relevant intellectual history that news as truth production requires a different epistemology.

method is only one approach to truth. Pragmatic objectivity recognizes "truth as the goal of inquiry and redefines truth in a modest, realist manner ... We can understand truth as the slow process of coming to know more and more things about the empirical world and to grasp them in a more accurate and comprehensive manner" (Ward, 2015b, p. 290).

Understanding news as interpretive truth production is of particular importance in documentary journalism, investigative reporting, and news features. It is the obvious mode in editorials. However, the liberal arts framework of constant research and rigorous argument should also characterize the everyday news cycle.

Interpretive Sufficiency

When the news profession's occupational task is understood as truth production, with authentic disclosure its normative axis, news is released from the tradition of epistemological objectivism.[26] For *aletheia*, the news media turn to interpretive studies or, as it has been labeled traditionally, "qualitative research" (e.g., Denzin & Lincoln, 2011).[27] Journalism's commitment to the explicit procedures of objectivism is now discredited, but fiction and fabrication are not acceptable substitutes for fact and accuracy. Authentic disclosure requires specificity through interpretive procedures. Reporters aiming for an effective journalism of *aletheia* will follow what might be called the interpretive arts to sufficiency (Christians, 2004a, chap. 3). When journalists use the interpretive approach explicitly, the news story will be complete. If interpretation is misunderstood or only invoked in generalities, journalists will tend to crudely tailor events into an artificial cohesion. To achieve interpretive sufficiency, media professionals will polish their research strategies and writing skills in terms of the humanities and humanistic social sciences. When understood with

---

[26] *Aletheia* is an alternative to modernity's objectivism. Understanding the news as social narrative is likewise contrary to modernity. Stories organize our lived experience, and through story narratives we teach one another how to live in common. Narratives contain in a nutshell people's beliefs. We tell stories to one another about our values and aspirations. Narratives point in the right direction, by anchoring the moral domain in lived experience rather than in rational individuals. Nevertheless, narratives of everyday discourse cannot in themselves yield normative guidelines about which value-driven stories ought to be valued. *Aletheia* establishes a normative center for distinguishing good practices from those that are morally unacceptable (see Christians, 2010a).

[27] The strategy of "mixed methods" is often proposed for communication research, rather than relying on either quantitative or qualitative methods. This methodology for journalists will have to meet the same intellectual tests for interpretive sufficiency.

that depth, interpretive sufficiency can be the press's standard in today's global postmodernity.

To elaborate, interpretive studies are a counter-Enlightenment form of knowing. In this epistemology, research in education and investigation in journalism must be grounded historically and biographically, so that they represent complex events and multilayered cultures adequately. The interpretive model is not driven by context-free abstractions but resonates with the attitudes, definitions, and beliefs of the people actually being studied. Rather than the fact-value dichotomy of the ethics of rationalism, the interpretive turn recovers the breadth of human agency in its interactions with animate and inanimate reality. In the interactive communication paradigm, interpretation and meaningful experience are examined, not first of all individual behavior or social action in isolation. In its canonical form, interpretive sufficiency rests on the assumption that "the meaning of things arises out of the process of social interaction," understood as a "complex interactive process that shapes the meanings things have for human beings. This process is anchored in the cultural world" where "cultural objects and experiences" are mediated in terms of the relevant sociocultural categories, such as "family, race, ethnicity, nationality, and social class" (Denzin, 2014, pp. 74, 78; cf. Benhabib, 2002).

Journalists trained in interpretive methodology recognize cultural patterns in their role as observers, and through participation are able to disclose their underlying meanings. In a fundamental sense, interpretive approaches are a temperament of mind – the "sociological imagination" C. Wright Mills (1959) called it – rather than merely a series of techniques for handling the smart phone, web technology, or minicam. Through thick description (Geertz, 1973), grounded theory (Charmaz, 2009), contextualization (Denzin & Giardina, 2007), visual methodologies (Williams & Newton, 2010), naturalistic observation (Boylan, 2014), coherent frames of reference (Schutz, 1967), professionals in news can be trained in interpretive sufficiency and then held accountable to its standards. Through an understanding of interpretive methodologies, reporters can come to grips with the complex ways political elites and ordinary citizens involve themselves in the news-making process. A substantial literature, one that is helpful for reporters, has been developed on representing the life histories of ordinary people (Yow, 2005).

When understood well and applied properly, the interpretive arts make it clear that research contained within itself, and therefore self-validating, has no credibility. The cases and illustrations that are selected for in-depth

stories must be representative of the class, ethnicity, social unit, or organization to which they actually belong. *Aletheia* arises in lifeworld settings, not those artificially contrived; therefore, specific circumstances
must also be densely textured. This is the thick reading that Al Jazeera
points to in its slogan "the truth and the other truth." The Hutchins
Commission summarized it accurately as "truth in the context of meaning" (Commission on Freedom of the Press, 1947, chap. 3). Parallel to the
methodological principle of external validity in empirical social science,
the goal is finding exemplary cases that are as multilayered as the human
arena they represent, rather than sensational ones that are anecdotal and
idiosyncratic.

Interpretive accounts of *aletheia* are not aberrations on the surface or
the hurried conclusions of the ill-informed. Interpretive sufficiency
requires immersion in the material until the researcher or journalist establishes what Herbert Blumer called "poetic resonance" with it (1954).
Interpretive sufficiency means identifying the major components of the
event being investigated and distinguishing these main features from
digressions and parentheses. Authentic disclosure reflects the details of
the natural circumstances naturally and this means metaphorically separating the heart and lungs from the skin and toenails. The thick reading of
interpretation (Geertz, 1973) replaces the thinness of a technical and data-
precise objectivism.

Triangulation is one methodology for implementing the interpretive
mode. When *aletheia* is articulated to interpretive sufficiency, it is an alternative to the neutral and balanced use of independent sources in the journalism of Western modernity. The goal of triangulating is to compile a fully
rounded analysis by combining multiple approaches, each trajectory disclosing a dimension of the human world being investigated. The mixed
methods of triangulation avoid the personal bias and superficiality that
stem from using only one examination strategy. In its best forms, triangulation is not an ambiguous eclecticism but takes seriously the way humans
actually interpret social reality. The reporters' task to produce truth is
complicated by the fact that they are interpreting a world that has been
interpreted already. Each of the various methods of interpretation exposes
different aspects of reality, "much as a kaleidoscope ... will reveal different
colors and configurations of the object to its viewer" (Denzin, 1989, p. 235).

Triangulation occurs in several forms (Flick, 2018). It typically refers to
methodology, that is, combining content analysis of documents with
unstructured interviewing with on-site observation, and then integrating
these strategies into a coherent analysis. Or social problems can be

triangulated – today's refugee crisis, for instance, triangulated by viewing it historically (how does the contemporary situation differ from previous time periods), theoretically (what ethical principles are relevant), and empirically (what are the crucial facts, using a variety of data sources).[28]

For interpretation to be sufficient, triangulation is ongoing until the contours of meaning are disclosed. In this sense, the crystal is a better image of triangulated design than the flat-surface triangle:

> Crystals combine symmetry with an infinite variety of shapes, substances, transmutations, multidimensionalities, and angles of approach. Crystals grow, change and alter, but are not amorphous. Crystals are prisms that reflect externalities *and* refract within themselves ... casting off in different directions. (Richardson, 2000, p. 934)

The aim is always the multiple insights of retroduction rather than quickly surmising what is thought to be the *aletheia* of the matter. The emphasis in interpretation is on discovery rather than administering routinized procedures. When we view a crystal, what we see depends on how we hold it to the light.

Sensitized concepts are essential to *aletheia*; that is, they open up the genuine inside. Sensitized concepts that are identified during the interpretive process generate an insightful picture and distinctively convey the meaning of cultural, social, or political events. They speak to the heart of the matter. Sensitized concepts represent an integrating scheme from within the data themselves, and in doing so, they are *aletheia*, authentic truth that unveils the data's inner character. Examples of sensitized concepts well known in the social science literature and in reporting are "just war," Cooley's "primary group," Ellul's "efficiency," "housing bubble," "watchdog role," "false equivalence," "noncombatant," "white supremacy," Rousseau's "noble savage," "fourth estate," Janis's "group think," "mutually assured destruction (MAD)," Innis's "monopoly of knowledge," "post-truth," Kuhn's "paradigm," E. O. Wilson's "consilience" (Christians & Carey, 1981, pp. 357–360).

Sensitized concepts are an obvious way to represent the retroductive process. These concepts reflect retroduction's dialectic of insight, observation, and history. Sensitized concepts represent generalizations from the inside, those that arise from within the symbolic structure of the arena being reported. They require an interactive form of writing that turns the

---

[28] Triangulation indicates that *aletheia* is not a correspondence theory of truth. It rejects the coherence model also by its claim that norms can be embedded in history.

ethnographic and imaginary back onto each other. Sensitized concepts are analogous to mapmaking. They can authentically disclose direction, even though all reality, by the map's very purpose, is not represented.[29] When interpretive sufficiency is the standard to emulate, the result will be an *alethic* production of depth, and its systematic rigor will equal the most sophisticated forms of objectivism.

Al Jazeera Satellite Network

An example from the international news media that teaches us about truth as *aletheia* is the Al Jazeera Media Network, founded in Doha, Qatar, in 1995 as the satellite news channel Al Jazeera Arabic (see Christians, Fackler, & Ferré, 2012, chap. 2). Al Jazeera Arabic achieved status and prominence during the Iraq War that began with the US military invasion of Iraq on March 19, 2003. Al Jazeera Arabic had a network office in Baghdad since its beginnings and was the news voice of Saddam Hussein when he was in power. During US President George W. Bush's term in office, Al Jazeera Arabic was condemned as a platform for terrorists, the television home of Osama bin Laden, and violator of the Geneva Conventions for showing prisoners of war. And Al Jazeera Arabic was known for putting corpses on the screen and showing rivers of blood, with mutilated faces of the wounded, beyond the conventional understanding of media decency. For its American critics, Al Jazeera was propaganda, not news (cf. Abdelmoula, 2006).

At the same time, authoritarian governments across the Middle East reviled Al Jazeera Arabic. In a region where Arab leaders typically control media systems and unflattering portrayals of leaders are forbidden, the independent Al Jazeera Arabic has been an outrage. Saudi Arabia bars Al Jazeera from its territory. Algiers has cut its signal. Yemen authorities confiscated its equipment. Morocco has blocked it from the airwaves. During the Arab Spring protests, the Egyptian government condemned it as the chief culprit in fueling the unrest. Al Jazeera's office in Cairo was burned down and its bureau chief and seven correspondents arrested.

Al Jazeera Arabic was born in war and its programming has centered on turmoil ever since; does it meet the *aletheia* standard for news? Is it the home of sensation and bias rather than of *aletheia*? When the Iraq bombing campaign began, Al Jazeera Arabic was already on the ground and had

---

[29] Lynch (2004) uses mapmaking to refute the verificationism that science uses as the measure of truth as objective (chap. 3). Verificationism he describes as "the view that anything true can be scientifically verified" (p. 78).

nearly exclusive rights to the sounds and images. Does Al Jazeera disclose the truth about Iraq, then and now, about Afghanistan and Yemen and Syria? Was it the truthful voice of the Arab Spring from January 2011 to mid-2012 when it covered political protests from Tunisia to Egypt (Cheribi, 2017)? In its sophisticated television and internet forms, does the Al Jazeera Media Network follow the instrumentalism of the technological order?[30] Is its broadcast and digital equipment driven by the technical imperative to those issues and venues that are mandated by the technology, or does it meet the standard of *aletheia*? The issue is the strong view of truth as *aletheia*, not just traditional objectivity. Do Al Jazeera reporters for its news channels live up to the principle of authentic disclosure in their practice of crisis journalism (Christians, 2017)?

Obviously Al Jazeera cannot meet the *aletheia* standard across the board on all occasions. Nothing is more demanding than war coverage and no reporters always get it right. But is Al Jazeera propagandistic or truthful overall? While journalists who do not speak Arabic struggle to understand the language and culture of the Middle East, Al Jazeera's reporters are on the scene and among the people, speaking the language and knowing the customs. In that sense, blood is part of the story. Its bloodiness without cutaway is grislier than shown on television news before. But the faces of the dead and broken bodies, says its senior producer Samir Khader, are not contrived by Al Jazeera Arabic: "War has a human cost. We don't minimize it as collateral damage" (cf. Fahmy & Johnson, 2017).

Reports and visuals from cameras and microphones of the guns and bombs, without probing beneath the surface, are not authentic disclosure. Does the deeper, more fundamental issue underneath the surface come into view, that is, does Al Jazeera open to its audience the ethics of social justice as the norm between nations? Or in its relentless coverage of social conflict, does Al Jazeera standardize, as the latent effect, enmity, opposition, and revenge for international relations (cf. Miladi, 2016)?

Al Jazeera English started in 2006 and is now a major international news network with headquarters in Doha; London; Washington, DC; and

---

[30] Haydar Sadig and Catalina Petcu of Qatar University have documented that the Al Jazeera Media Network has been a media technology innovator from its beginning as a satellite channel. As news delivery is revolutionized, Al Jazeera's technologies are at the forefront of the cycle: Internet Protocol Multicast, Digital and Asymmetrical Subscriber Lines, Synchronous Digital Hierarchy and Multiprotocal Label Switching, and the AJ+ social media platform are examples, networked through Al Jazeera's own Global Media Cloud built by Ooredoo in 2015 ("Al Jazeera as a Technological Enterprise"; haydar@qu.edu.qa).

Kuala Lampur. The daily news hour is hosted from these four locations linked together live for simulcasting, the news essentially following the day around the planet. Is *aletheia* Al Jazeera English's principle in war and political conflict, therefore, specializing in the deeper issues of human rights, public policy, and diplomacy? Is the network setting a world standard for interpretive sufficiency, defining newsworthiness as multidimensional and explanatory beyond the ephemeral? The "AJE Renewal Project 2008–2011" reflects the *aletheia* mind-set instead of the objectivity norm. This "different understanding" of news coverage means "the context of culture, the context of language, the linguistics, the context of history, the context of the human being himself and the diversity" (Barkho, 2016, p. 493). Thus, this directive from Wadah Khanfar for Al Jazeera professionals: "I do not ask you whether you are objective. I will ask you, is your explanation strong or weak? Is it good or bad? Is it profound or superficial?" (Barkho, 2016, p. 494). For social and military conflict, Al Jazeera would present all sides and all parties, with consensus-building efforts included as newsworthy. If the knowledge production of Al Jazeera English meets the standards of *aletheia* in the "Renewal Project," it will be a world leader in international news.

Data Mining

As the shift to the digital age becomes complete, the formidable problem of data mining makes *aletheia* a supreme challenge and requires fresh thinking. In terms of Engel's law, as quantity increases quality changes; the projected growth of digital technologies signals a new era when digital storage and transmission become the monopoly of knowledge. In data mining's higher order of magnitude, how is the ethics of *aletheia* to be understood in theory and practice?

As elaborated in Chapter 1, the world is increasingly connected in a cyber network.[31] According to a report by Cisco, in 2015 the global flow of data across the internet reached 20,235 gigabytes per second ("The Zettabyte Era," 2016). Dell EMC estimates that by 2020, the digital content on the internet will equal 44 zettabytes of data ("Big Data Analytics," n.d.).[32] The gigantic volume, the magnitude of

---

[31] This section on data mining summarizes the main ideas in the Research Paper of Yayu Feng, "Introduction to Big Data" (2016).

[32] "To facilitate understanding of this number: A two-hour movie in a digital format is one to four gigabytes, depending on its resolution quality. And one zettabyte equals one trillion gigabytes" (Feng, 2016).

information that can be extracted and interpreted from the data sets, and the epistemic challenges make big data an epic contemporary phenomenon.[33] Though the term "big data" was coined already in the 2000s – in scientific fields such as astronomy and genomics that were experiencing an explosion of information – only a non-rigorous definition has emerged: big data refers to the data sets too large, complex, and dynamic for conventional data-processing tools to store, manage and analyze, and therefore requiring new tools, such as supercomputers, for analysis (cf. Manovich, 2012; Snijders, Matzat, & Reips, 2012; Mayer-Sch önberger & Cukier, 2013; Lewis & Westlund, 2015).

From the perspective of *aletheia*'s interpretive sufficiency, boyd and Crawford's (2012) distinction is especially pertinent: "Big Data is less about the quantity of the data than about its capacity to search, aggregate, and cross-reference large data sets" (p. 663). Data mining is, therefore, the central problematic in the big data regime. Data mining is typically defined as "the use of machine learning techniques to discover previously *unknown* properties in large data sets"; data mining aims "to extract information from a data set and transform it into an understandable structure for further use" (Talia, Trunfio, & Marozzo, 2015, p. 1; original emphasis). It is a process that detects patterns and constructs stories based on data, and it is a core component of the "Knowledge Discovery in Database" (KDD) process in computer science (Fayyad, Pietetsky, & Smyth, 1996). As *The Petabyte Age* (2008; a special issue of *Wired* focused on big data) suggested in its introduction: "More isn't just more. More is different." Through data mining, data sets are gathered, combined, classified, and analyzed to tell stories beyond what the data describe.

As Yayu Feng (2016) summarizes it, data mining performs several common tasks, such as anomaly detection (to detect abnormalities from normal patterns), association learning (to learn from existing habits and take action, such as recommending products based on purchasing histories), and regression (to predict likelihood based on previous data, such as forecasting the likelihood of a team to win based on the technical data and results of previous matches). Journalists have used data-mining techniques to draw infographics that visualize statistics and interpret the data for their audiences (Gray, Chambers, & Bounegru, 2012). A team of journalists

---

[33] The McKinsey Global Institute estimates that big data can increase business profits by 60 percent. When personal data are seen as exhaustive, companies customize new products and improve productivity. Market dynamics point to big data's geometric growth.

recently used data-mining techniques to detect drug combinations for their health reporting (Sam & King, 2016; for more examples see Furnas, 2012; Talia et al., 2015, pp. 2–4). In these everyday tasks, the mining of data has inferential power.

In another arena, political agencies using big data, Sam Petulla (2012) warns of the gap between the growing importance of sophisticated data mining in government affairs and its scant oversight. The abundant data used for governance by politicians are not transparent, and reporters' ability to track and report the process has been largely impossible. Since 2000, nearly all major corporations in the United States have been building big-data bases, and developing sophisticated data-mining enterprises (Foster & McChesney, 2014). In 2012, the US House of Representatives passed the Cyber Intelligence Sharing and Protection Act, which allows for the exchange of internet data between the US government and technological companies, and for the sale of corporation data to the government upon its request (McChesney, 2013).

While taking concerned notice of the ethical issues in political-economic data mining, *aletheia* as disclosure critiques the epistemological assumptions in the big-data regime as a whole (cf. Lake, 2017). Big data presumes that algorithmic accuracy is equivalent to computational power. Big data presents itself as "a higher form of intelligence and knowledge that can generate insights that were previously impossible, with the aura of truth, objectivity, and accuracy" (boyd & Crawford, 2012, p. 663). The big-data mind-set respects "correlations rather than" causality or historical continuity (cf. Mayer-Schönberger & Cukier, 2013, p. 19). Computational tools that process data are said to erase the traditional dilemma between choosing surface data or deep data, because both dimensions are available (Mahrt & Scharkow, 2013).

Data mining as knowledge production is designed to fail the *aletheia* test rather than fulfill it. No standard data categories exist, and since information is typically stored at random, the genuine, the heart of the matter, is buried under layers of the often irrelevant or inconsequential. Without knowing context, interpreting data is ambiguous and even mysterious. Bernhard Debatin (2008) highlights the paradox of complexity in data mining that is at odds with *aletheia*:

As communication technology becomes more sophisticated, … it paradoxically requires increased technical mediation that allows for building second-order knowledge, that is, knowledge about knowledge. This paradox is based on the general paradox of complexity, which means that each and every increase in complexity causes a loss of transparency, which then has to be compensated for by reducing complexity. It is this very paradox of complexity that makes omniscience and boundlessness both an unattainable *telos* and a basic myth of communication technology. The myth feeds on the fact that omniscience and boundlessness seem to draw nearer with each new communication technology, yet become more remote as this very technology causes an additional increase in complexity, which again creates an insatiable need for better, more effective means for reducing complexity ... As an intelligence reinforcing machine, the computer takes on specific knowledge-processing functions of the human brain. Yet its very mode of operation also creates new intransparency; it produces not only knowledge but, as an unintended consequence, also additional non-knowledge. In the development of more complex and efficient computers, therefore, their advantage is offset by the fact that these interfaces only allow structural coupling between user and computer, but no manipulation of deeper-level functions and processes. The freedom of the average end-user is reduced to merely participating in a largely predetermined system through the computer/ browser interface. (pp. 258–259)

Although computer-assisted reporting has existed in journalism since 1952 with the use of computers to analyze governments documents (DeFleur, 1997), in today's age of big data, news organizations confront major challenges in using the wide spectrum of databases and complex analytical devices. New types of journalism have emerged such as data journalism (Gray, Chambers, & Bounegru, 2012) and computational and algorithmic journalism (Anderson, 2013). The emergence and developments of big data and data-mining techniques have implications for "journalism's ways of knowing (epistemology) and doing (expertise), as well as its negotiation of value (economics) and values (ethics)" (Lewis & Westlund, 2015, p. 461). It brings to journalism new strategies for obtaining information, for analyzing information, and for determining newsworthiness. Big data also challenges traditional journalistic values and the way news organizations work on the financial and administrative levels.

For the media professions, the issue is the technological imperative. Search and access are governed by electronics. Data sets indicate their own networks. Strings of apps lead the search process. Critics have long charged broadcasting with allowing the technology to determine news. Whatever best fits broadcast technology's visual and audio character defines what is newsworthy. And the issue is magnified for big data. Instead of the reporter's competence and imagination leading the process of knowledge production, human initiative becomes secondary to the network's structure. The danger in data mining is instrumentalism, that is, moral ends buried under overwhelming technical means.

Government data surveillance continues to expand as an issue world-wide. *Ethics of Big Data* is the first book on moral issues geared to business, and it is utilitarian in perspective (Davis, 2012). The complications for the *aletheia* of data mining in journalism warrant a book-length ethics also, but not centered on a reductionist utilitarianism of risk and harm. As data mining develops, *aletheia* serves as a critical perspective by challenging the epistemology and philosophy of technology behind it.

Surplus of Meaning

Complicated cases such as Al Jazeera Arabic and issues such as data mining must be assessed in terms of their dramatically international scope. To understand news professionalism with a global perspective, this chapter has moved truth from its Occidental moorings to the world as a whole. *Aletheia* as authentic disclosure is seen as belonging to the history and geography of the human race. A media ethics of *aletheia* that is multinational in breadth is situated in the lived and professional communities of the world. The Al Jazeera Media Network is a worldwide enterprise and data mining is decisively global. Al Jazeera's owners and managers and data-mining practitioners operate in venues large and small simultaneously, where the struggle over this new understanding of truth as *aletheia* is the most pronounced.

Aletheia is a twenty-first-century alternative to the modernist theory that holds that "truth has only a single uniform nature" (Lynch, 2011, p. i). *Aletheia*'s world orientation is not that of modernity's straight-line absolutism that organizes the globe by geometric coordinates. Truth as authentic disclosure takes seriously the one-and-many dilemma in philosophy and its counterpart professionally. *Aletheia* seeks to answer the dilemma through Paul Ricoeur's (1976) surplus of meaning.[34]

Aletheia as an ethical principle, and the Al Jazeera Media Network and data mining as mediated phenomena find Ricoeur (1974) an appropriate theorist given his fundamental thesis that all language use is interpretive. No self-understanding or world understanding exists outside the

---

[34] The concept of "transversals" in the scholarship on social systems overlaps intellectually with Ricoeur's surplus of meaning. The author thanks Harris Breslow for introducing both the idea and Aihwa Ong's *Neoliberalism as Exception* (2006) to him in February 2018. In Ong, neoliberalism as a technology of governance comes to expression in a variety of forms, adapted to different political regimes and economic circumstances.

mediation of signs, symbols, and texts. Linguistic reality is fundamentally different from sense-data reality. Human existence is constituted by systems of thought and culture. A society's accumulated history of meanings is the interpretive context of our own interpretations. Dialogue with our symbolically presented human existence past and present is inescapable.

In Ricoeur's *Conflict of Interpretations* and *Interpretation Theory*, the ontological character of his philosophy of language is developed explicitly. The awareness of humans as beings-in-the-world is based on a lingual relationship of one's belongingness to *homo sapiens*. Human existence is a composite of beings presently living and of civilizations past that continue to exist in art, music, literature, and philosophy: "The subject that interprets himself while interpreting signs is no longer the *cogito*; rather, he is a being who discovers by the exegesis of his own life, that he is placed in Being before he places and possesses himself." Our manner of existence "remains from start to finish a being-interpreted" (Ricoeur, 1974, p. 11).

Ricoeur does not understand subjectivity as the Cartesian rational self. The concept of subjectivity is meaningful, but humans do not possess direct knowledge of an autonomous entity. Humans understand themselves as situated in time and space by interpreting the symbolic meanings that constitute the world in which they live. Subjectivity is one's existential awareness in the ongoing process of interpretation.

For the one-and-many character of *aletheia*'s universalism, Ricoeur's surplus of meaning is apropos. In *The Rule of Metaphor* (1981), Ricoeur defined surplus of meaning as the linguistic imagination that generates meaning through the power of metaphor. In classical rhetoric's idea of metaphor, as Ricoeur explains it, two levels of signification are presupposed. The literal level is considered primary; the other level is symbolic and therefore secondary. For Ricoeur's theory of interpretation, dividing metaphor into two domains – one literal and the other symbolic – is erroneous. Human interpretations are fluid, transferring interpreters from one level to another. For Ricoeur, the ideas of primary and of ancillary are obvious, but interpretation occurs in the movement between levels, that is, within the lingual context. Words are polysemic as denotation and inference indicate. Language as a metaphorical resource can be used creatively to produce new meanings. Improvisation in music illustrates Ricoeur's intention. Improvisations are the musician's invention, but the melody is retained throughout. Surplus of meaning extends and reorients the original without abandoning it (cf. Christians, 2015c, p. 49):

Rather than limiting our understanding of discourse to its correspondence with facts or the author's intent or to one literal meaning, Ricoeur sees discourse in terms of the "principle of plentitude," that is, "a text means all that it can mean" (Ricoeur, 1981, p. 176). Meaning is limited by the dialectic of context, history of the narrative, and boundaries of lived experience (the codal "hot" will not be understood as "cold"), but the central feature of interpretation is the fecundity of meaning.

> Ricoeur's surplus of meaning has special relevance to the question of multiple realizability in ethics. "Multiple realization" is central to theories from natural science to the humanities. Phenomena can share in a fundamental meaning across a system, but its interpretations and elaborations are multiple. For Ricoeur (1986), our spatiotemporal location and transcending the local are simultaneous. (Christians, 2015c, p. 49)

As Ricoeur (1986) puts it, for human existence "the unity of destination and the differences of destinies are to be understood through each other" (p. 138). In this perspective, the ethics of truth as disclosing the genuine can be understood as common enough across cultures that journalists and media executives can work with the basic disclosure idea though they elaborate on it and apply it in various ways (Christians & Ward, 2013, pp. 82–84; cf. Ward, 2011b).

Language as a symbol system entails meaning and meaningfulness requires truth. Authentic disclosure is based on a hermeneutic need for meaningfulness. Following Seev Gasiet (1980), beyond the human need to survive are the needs for recognition and interpersonal relations, and the need for meaningfulness. Included in Martha Nussbaum's universal human capabilities is "practical reason – being able to form a conception of the good and to engage in critical reflection about the planning of one's own life" (1999, p. 41). *Aletheia* in this sense is the disclosure of meaningfulness.

For modernist truth as accuracy and neutrality, what is true must be true in an explicit way, verified by the procedures of objectivity. Modernity is monistic about truth, assuming "that there is one and only one explanation of what makes something true. Truth has a single inner structural essence" (Lynch, 2011, p. 3). In *aletheia's* surplus of meaning, truth can be manifested in multiple ways. In a variation on Lynch, the contents of our various expressions of truth can be "both diverse in kind and yet cognitively unified;" the meaning of truth can be understood to be univocal and immanent, without claiming essentialism (Lynch, 2011, p. 3). Surplus of meaning is not "simply different meanings appended to different beliefs" (p. 6). It represents the philosophical understanding of pluralism, where truth is many while retaining the idea that truth is one (p. 70). In *aletheia*'s surplus of meaning, there is a "maximally coherent system of meanings" (p. 165) with the idea of authentic disclosure the universal core. All moral truths inscribe in themselves surplus meaning. We understand moral universals such as the starving of children are wrong because of our humanity and apply the idea and act in different ways because of our personhood, what hermeneutics calls "our appropriated self-knowledge." In the philosophy of mind, immanent properties have multiple realizations. Ricoeur's surplus of meaning gives multiple realizability a particular form.

"If we are ever to come to grips with both the cognitive unity and semantic diversity" of the news' occupational norm, Lynch (2011, p. 191) tells us, "we need a new way of thinking about truth." *Aletheia* answers that challenge. News as truth production is a global definition of public communication, with the international *aletheia* its professional norm.

CONCLUSION

This chapter presents the ethics of truth in the comparative terms of three paradigms: rationalism, discourse, *aletheia*. The ancient Greek mind on truth as correspondence has dominated intellectual history in the West. The theory and practice of social science reflect this rationalist philosophy, rooted as they are in the subject-object dichotomy. The objectivist worldview of the mainstream press represents this epistemology of accurate facts and neutrality. However, as developed earlier in this chapter, the correspondence view of truth is in crisis. A different concept of truth is needed as the occupational norm of journalism.

The substantive theory of truth is an alternative to both Western correspondence and its opposite, deflationism. Substantive theorizing is philosophical in form and linguistic in content, with the discourse ethics of Habermas and Apel its most sophisticated formulation at present. Judging diverse communities by universal norms is the intellectual strategy of discourse ethics, this being a neo-Kantian ethics of duty in which procedures of argumentation replace formal absolutes. Habermas's communicative rationality is focused on lifeworld narratives in which the validity claims of propositional truth, normative rightness, and subjective truthfulness are presumed and tested. With communicative rationality a radical alternative to rationalist correspondence, and thick discourse opposed to thin information, the substantive theory of truth represents the present with distinction.

As explained earlier, the criticism that Habermas's public sphere is not deeply inclusive is being addressed, but the nationalism question is not solvable within the Habermasian framework. Given today's fundamental challenge to globalize media ethics, truth needs to be located in human existence. *Aletheia*'s uncovering the authentic, disclosing the symbolic world in which we live, is neo-Habermasian in international terms. In the media ethics of *aletheia*, news is understood as truth production and interpretive sufficiency results from *aletheia* as disclosure. In the *aletheia* paradigm, truth has been moved from its Occidental tether, and from its nation-state configuration, to the human race as a whole and, therefore, is isomorphic with global media technologies.

While advocating *aletheia* as the truth paradigm for the future, *aletheia* must face, with the idea of truth in its various definitions, the post-truth era. Ralph Keyes, combining journalism and social science, introduced the term in 2004, locating a category of ambiguous statements between lies and truth that blurs the boundary line between them. In the post-truth era, rather than being judged negatively by untrue statements, deceiving others has become a game and a habit without consequences. Though Keyes used illustrations from politics, academia, law, business, and literature, the conclusion of an era-level transformation, of a seismic cultural shift, has been contested until its seeming plausibility now.[35]

The Oxford Dictionary named "post-truth" as its 2016 Word of the Year. According to its website, post-truth is an adjective defined as "relating to or denoting circumstances in which objective facts are less influential in shaping public opinion than appeals to emotion and personal belief." Kathleen Higgins (2016) summarizes post-truth well: "Public tolerance of inaccurate and undefended allegations, non sequiturs in response to hard questions, and outright denial of facts indicate truth is *passé*. Repetition of talking points passes for political discussion and serious interest in issues and options is treated as the idiosyncrasy of

---

[35] Since societies live by language, and all languages include pro and con, red and green, yes and no, defining and defending truth contra falsehood is the ongoing challenge of the human race. The post-truth era gains some of its salience from media technology – truth as facticity is based on alphabetic literacy and now it is revolutionized by electronic information systems. Eric McLuhan, in a December 1, 2016, MEA post, "Of Truth and the Post-Truth World," highlights Francis Bacon's seventeenth-century "Of Truth"; it leaves us with the challenge to present comparable essays appropriate to the electronic world today.

wonks" (p. 3).[36] Politics in the United States is in crisis, with a president unconstrained by facts and journalism hampered by false equivalence and polluted by fake news. The news media's refutation of the post-truth torrent is essential for its own authenticity and democracy's survival.

The idea of active people-movements as a strategy of resistance is developed in Chapter 4 and can be adapted to the Post-Truth Era. Heidegger's dwelling, as explained in Chapter 1, represents the same idea in recommending an institution-by-institution strategy of keeping truth central and vital: "Scientists must keep reminding society of the importance of its social mission – to provide the best information possible as the basis for public policy" (Higgins, 2016, p. 5). Education should publicly affirm the intellectual virtues that are their lifeblood: critical thinking, sustained inquiry, and revision of beliefs on the basis of evidence. Jurisprudence in theory and practice ought to promote its "truth and nothing but the truth" motto. Print, broadcast, and online news should educate the public on *aletheia* as their *raison d'etrê*. Business needs to insist on the integrity of its contracts, agreements, and memoranda of understanding. Cities and neighborhoods where empirical truth is close at hand can demonstrate that post-truth has no credibility. Indirectly by cultivating their own domains, and directly whenever possible, these regimes of truth in societies around the world will discredit and isolate the post-truth phenomenon.

---

[36] Higgins insists constructively on distinguishing post-truth and philosophical relativism – the latter not responsible for the former: "Radical forms of relativism are often denounced as undermining basic values. Friedrich Nietzsche, who is often invoked to justify post-truth, is such a relativist. He denies that there are moral facts, saying that we only have moral interpretations, and in doing so denies that moral assertions are unconditionally true. But this does not mean there is no truth. He is pointing to the exaggerated clarity of abstractions by comparison with empirical reality. In fact, Nietzsche held intellectual honesty at a premium. His most strenuous rejections of truth are mostly directed not at truth, but at what has been asserted as true" (Higgins, 2016, p. 4).

4

The Ethics of Human Dignity

For communication ethics to be effective in today's global era, it must be multicultural in scope. The sacredness of the human species is the starting point of this international ethics, and the ethical principle of human dignity is entailed by this universal protonorm. The basic idea in this principle is the common worth of all human beings regardless of merit or achievement. This reality, commensurate with the biological, is not only considered a fact but also a shared commitment to honor it. When human dignity is grounded in the worth of humanity as a whole, it avoids the fragmentation that results from appealing to individual interests, to community customs, and to national prerogatives.

Human dignity is the key concept in this chapter on cultural diversity. Ronald Dworkin (2010) argues for its central role in human existence and, therefore, in moral systems; in the process, he defends his conclusion that human dignity is the foundational norm for cultural diversity internationally. As Dworkin sees it, what life means and morality requires, and what justice demands, are different aspects of the same large question. Human values in all their forms are unified around one big idea, that is, dignity. In the self-respect of taking our own lives seriously, we give definition to the circumscribed behavior we owe to others. Perplexity and turmoil in human life and cognition do not define the species; this one all-encompassing value, dignity, is the centrifugal human nerve, the value that controls all cultural values. In living the good life, we expand to others the realization of one's own dignity. For this reason, "human dignity has a central role in the moral and philosophical interpretation of human beings" (Düwell et al., 2014, p. xxi).

With identity politics a dominant issue in world affairs following the end of the Cold War, media institutions are crucial to the development of cultural pluralism. Human dignity demands that media ethics be based on cultural diversity rather than on the individualistic morality of rights. In those terms, the ethical principle of human dignity developed in this chapter emphasizes the respect in this concept for the many varieties of humanity and for its refusal to rank and order human beings. Within the human dignity framework, media ethicists work on ethnic diversity in cinema and entertainment programming, stereotypical language in news and public relations, and sexism in advertising. Gender equality in hiring and eliminating racism in organizational culture are demanded as moral imperatives and no longer trivialized as political correctness.

The stringent humanism of this chapter faces a major challenge empirically and theoretically from the revolution in media technology, with the anonymity and artifice of the social media at odds with an intersubjective ethics. As historical studies and empirical research in political communication have shown, guaranteeing that people have their own voice, define their own identity, and are respected as equals are foundational issues for society and for public communication. The normative principle of human dignity is a safeguard against the tendency of powerful new media technologies to store data and transmit information in instrumentalist terms, that is, according to algorithm models. Comparative studies across media technologies and those of different cultures require this principle for their interpretation and assessment.

The ethics of human dignity is presented as a cross-cultural standard for the news media today, but it is not formalistic and remote. Because intrinsic worthiness by definition is inscribed in the everyday experience of the human race, this chapter applies dignity to intercultural struggles in international journalism (coverage of worldwide poverty and the Darfur humanitarian crisis), in US history (Native Americans at Wounded Knee), and in comparative transnational research (Global Mass Media Project). Through the universal standard of human dignity, this chapter raises fundamental objections to social values that are exclusionary and oppressive.

Cultures need norms beyond their own values to be self-critical. Conflicts between people-groups and among nation-states require principles outside them for their resolution: "Only an 'outside' lets us know that we are limited and defined by these limitations; only an 'outside' shapes us" and enables us to evaluate circumstances and move forward constructively (Fleischacker, 1992, p. 223). Without principles of universal scope, ethical theory and professional practice are trapped in the distributive fallacy, one ideological bloc presuming to speak for the whole. In harmony with the intellectual traditions around the world that affirm human dignity, the ethics of being develops a morality of multiculturalism rooted in our common humanity.

THEORIES OF HUMAN DIGNITY WORLDWIDE

Human dignity serves as a reference point for a number of political, social, and philosophical debates: "In both the northern and the southern hemispheres, in common law and civilian legal systems, human dignity plays a prominent role" (Düwell et al., 2014, p. 1). Human dignity has become a foundational concept in bioethics (cf. Nussbaum, 2008). And important philosophical polemics have galvanized around human dignity. There is a growing intellectual interest in human rights in general, with the moral issues focusing on the appropriate interpretation of these rights in particular circumstances (Benhabib, 2011). Human dignity is the normative framework for matters of international politics in a globalized and multicultural world. The cognitive vitality of this concept reflects its impressive history in various traditions.

Human dignity is fundamental to the Kantian deontological tradition, though it is typically tied to political liberalism. Dignity is central to modern human rights discourse, though these initiatives are largely Eurocentric: "Choosing human dignity immediately after the Second World War was a statement against the Shoah, against totalitarianism, and against the atrocities of war" (Düwell et al., 2014, p. xvii). Therefore, as appropriate to the international perspective of *Media Ethics and Global Justice in the Digital Age*, human dignity is presented here as a foundational concept transnationally. These excerpts from the history of ideas represent human dignity as Fleischacker's "outside," as a unifying theory for understanding cultural values. This philosophical analysis is important background for the chapter's articulating the historical perspectives and contemporary debates to each other.

Kant's Formulae of Humanity

In his ethics, Immanuel Kant developed three formulations of the categorical imperative. The first and best known is the *formula of universal law*: "Act only on that maxim whereby you can at the same time will that it become a universal law" (Kant, 1997/1785, 4:421). The second is the *formula of humanity*: "So act that you use humanity, whether in your own person or in the person of any other, always at the same time as an end, never merely as a means" (Kant, 1997/1785, 4:429). The third construction is the *formula of the kingdom of ends:* "Every rational being must act as if by his maxims he were at all times a legislative member of the universal kingdom of ends" (Kant, 1997/1785, 4:439).[1]

Though some Kantian scholars claim that the three versions of the categorical imperative are divergent, Kant himself considered the three formulations to be equivalent (Kant, 1997/1785, 4:436). Together they mean that humanity's rational nature exists as an end in itself; therefore, every rational creature is to be respected as such. Humans are not victims of their inclinations or determined by the forces of nature. Humans are a distinct species who choose rational ends by rational means, with rational choice, therefore, the ground of morality. Kant's view of dignity inheres in our capacity to make reasoned decisions voluntarily.

Kant's formula of humanity grounds his moral realism.[2] Since the validity of the categorical imperative depends on humanity's existence as an end in itself, it is not only unreasonable to treat humans as mere means to anything else; it is also morally wrong because it is not endorsed as acceptable behavior for everyone. As Kant restates the principle of humanity later in his *Metaphysics of Morals:*

Act in accordance with a maxim of ends that it can be a universal law for everyone to have. In accordance with this principle, man is an end for himself as well as for others, and it is not enough that he is not authorized to use either himself or others

---

[1] Kant elaborates on the kingdom of ends in the *Groundwork* (4:439): "Here we encounter the paradox that without any further end or advantage to be attained, the mere dignity of humanity should function as an inflexible precept for the will. It is just this freedom from dependence on interested motives which constitutes the sublimity of a maxim and the worthiness of every rational subject to be a law-making member in the kingdom of ends; for otherwise he would have to be regarded as subject only to the law of nature – the law of his own needs." Since the idea of an existing end imposes restrictions on others, Kant suggests a community of existing ends that is systematically connected. The members of this community would themselves impose restrictions according to the principle of autonomy, and in that sense this is a regulated community, a realm (*Reich*) or kingdom, hence a "kingdom of ends."

[2] In his reflections on both Kant's *Groundwork* and his *Metaphysics of Morals*, Plaisance concludes that Kant's deontological system should not be grounded first of all in the universalist maxim but rather in the philosophical basis for his categorical imperatives – human dignity. Kant's claim regarding the distinctive rational agency and free will of the human species specifies his imperatives so that transparency in communication may be considered Kant's "greatest gift to media ethics today" (2007, p. 191).

merely as means (since he could then still be indifferent to them); it is in itself his duty to make man in general his end. (Kant, 1991/1797, p. 198)

Patrick Plaisance (2014) explains the connection of Formulae 1 and 2 in these terms: "Kant's categorical imperative requires that I treat people as deserving of respect for their own sakes because if it were acceptable for everyone not to do so, chaos would ensue" (p. 77). Michael Rosen (2012) links the Formulae also, though using a different framework:

> Instead of starting from the question what maxims can be universalized without contradiction, it would be better to understand Kant as asking first how we have to act in order to treat our dignity (our inner kernel of intrinsic value) with the proper respect ... The dignity of the moral law makes human beings – its embodiment – worthy of respect. They should be respected by others and, equally importantly, they have the duty to respect themselves.[3] (pp. 147, 30)

Ubuntu Philosophy and Human Dignity

An expert on the history and theory of *ubuntu*, Thaddeus Metz of the University of Johannesburg assesses *ubuntu* following this definition of human dignity: "For beings to have dignity is basically for each of them to be objectively good for their own sake to an equally superlative degree that entitles them to respectful treatment" (Metz, 2012, pp. 20–21). *Ubuntu*, as Metz uses the term, refers to the conceptions "prominent among precolonial societies below the Sahara desert that continue to inform much moral reflection among black Africans in ... this large and diverse region" (Metz, 2014, p. 310). In the *ubuntu* tradition, humanness is obtained by prizing communal relationships with the most important beings in the world, and Metz identifies three conceptions of dignity based on this communalism.

Beings with a supernatural essence is one category of "those with whom to commune in order to develop *ubuntu*. It is standard among pre-colonial sub-Saharan societies and also accepted by several contemporary

---

[3] For Rosen (2012), regarding the concept of human dignity in Kant, "it played only a small role in political theory until the time of that thinker on whose giant shoulders the modern theory of human rights largely rests" (p. 19). Rosen develops a provocative interpretation of Kant in his chap. 3: "For Kant, the dignity of humanity is connected with our member-ship of the noumenal realm, in virtue of which we may see ourselves as embodying a timeless, intrinsic value ... The existence of this timelessly valuable thing is connected by Kant with his most ambitious metaphysical claim – that human beings, in virtue of their capacity for free action, are members of a noumenal realm beyond the empirical world of appearances" (pp. 154–155).

African philosophers" that human beings "have a spiritual nature that has its source in God" (Metz, 2014, p. 312; cf. Wiredu, 1996, pp. 157–171). By virtue of "having a divine spark" alone among known entities, "human beings have a dignity of a sort that is capable of grounding human rights . . . Since human beings have something akin to a soul, an immaterial substance that will survive the death of their body, they are the most special things on the planet and hence deserve respect in the form of universal entitlements to life, liberties, resources, and the like" (Metz, 2014, p. 312).

A capacity for life-force is a second way human dignity has been understood in the *ubuntu* tradition. The beings with whom to commune so as to realize one's humanness have a vital energy unique to their own species: "Although the origins of the idea of life-force are thickly metaphysical, the concept can be of use when shorn of the supernatural. That is, one can plausibly understand in purely physical terms, what it is for a thing to be intrinsically valuable by virtue of its vital energy, which I call 'liveliness.'" Beings with such physical properties as creativity, confidence, and strength "to a sufficiently great degree have a superlative inner worth, a dignity" (Metz, 2014, p. 313; cf. Iroegbu, 2005).

A third conception of human dignity in the *ubuntu* tradition is the human capacity for communal relationships:

When it is said that a person is a person through other persons, this mean one should develop one's personhood, something one does insofar as one enter into community with others. The relevant others with whom to commune are those who in principle are the most capable of communing . . . Humans are capa e of being part of a friendly or loving relationship in a way that nothing else is. (letz, 2014, p. 316)[4]

In Metz's assessment:

Thinking of substantial liveliness, or the capacity for it, as constitutive of human dignity avoids the problems facing the spiritual conception. The vitality theory entails that we can have dignity in a world that is entirely physical, and it does

---

[4] Metz (2014) elaborates on the concept of communal relationship in *ubuntu:* "What is it then to be capable of a communal relationship? Much African thought about the nature of community can be analytically clarified by understanding it as the combination of two logically distinct relationships, 'identity' and 'solidarity.' Identification is, at the core, a matter of thinking of oneself as a 'we.' Exhibiting solidarity is basically a matter of helping others for their sake, often out of sympathetic emotional reaction to what it is like to be them . . . Human rights violations, from this perspective, are ways of degrading people's capacity for a loving relationship, which is often a matter of acting in seriously unloving ways towards them" (p. 315).

a plausible job of accounting for the human rights where the spiritual one could not. However, the vitality conception of human dignity faces some serious objections. There are a number of human rights issues that are not clearly a degradation of liveliness. In nearly all of the examples cited, the Kantian view appears to do better. (2014, p. 314; cf. Metz, 2012)

The Afro-communitarian conception of dignity avoids the problems facing the other two views: "Unlike the spiritual nature theory, it is secular and intuitively accounts for human rights not to be segregated from employment, slavery or dictatorship. Furthermore, the communal relationship view appears to be more attractive than the vitality one in that the former can ground human rights that the latter does not underwrite with ease" (Metz, 2014, p. 316).[5]

Human Dignity in Islamic Ethics

Professor Abderrahmane Azzi of the University of Sharjah is the author of the influential "Value Determinism Theory of the Media" (VDT) (Azzi, 2016). He states that human dignity is both spiritual and relational in Islamic ethics. As Azzi describes it, "the term dignity (in Arabic *Al Karama*) is derived from one of God's attributes *Al Karim* [cf. Al Hanfi, 1996, p. 9]; that is, the value of dignity is bestowed by the Creator and mirrored in human relations" (Azzi, 2017).[6] "The more we reflect on God's attributes, the more we are able to reflect parts of such attributes in our lived reality" (Azzi, 2011, p. 759). The term *Al Karama* and its derivatives are mentioned fifteen times in the *Qu'ran*, with verse 17:10 illustrative: "We have bestowed dignity on the children of Adam, provided them with transport on land and sea; given them for sustenance things good and pure; and conferred on them special favors, above a great part of our creation."

The reference to the children of Adam implies all human beings regardless of their race or beliefs. Every human being is endowed with dignity, and as jurists on the matter have explained: "Dignity is not earned by meritorious conduct; it is established as an expression of God's grace; and that dignity is a natural and absolute right" (Kamali, 2007, p. 2).

---

[5] Metz (2014) concludes with a challenge to additional study: "The Afro-communitarian theory of human dignity and the Kantian conception appear to be on a par. Their relationship and power of application should be pursued further" (p. 316).

[6] This section is based on Professor Azzi's paper, "Human Dignity as a Bestowed and Relational Value," submitted to the author on January 6, 2017.

Azzi develops this *Qu'ranic* concept of *Al Karma* as having special significance for the rights and duties of human relationships. Jurists in scholastic jurisprudence have attached dignity to the concept of *Ismah* (inviolability) in the sense that six basic tenets must be preserved and protected for all human beings: life, intellect, religion, family, property, and honor (Mohammad, 2007, p. 9). One of the dominant schools in jurisprudence, the Hanafi school of law, maintains that inviolability is universal in that dignity is "a natural endowment that obtains in everyone by the mere fact of being human" (Kamali, 2007, p. 9). As Azzi explains, "this relational dimension of dignity involves human beings' perception of one another as entities that deserve respect and honor, and special care and attention for others, in their capacity, as indicated by Immanuel Kant, as ends in themselves" (Azzi, 2017). The *Qu'ranic* narrative stresses existential equality in such relations, as in verse 39:6, "We created you from a single soul." The Prophet Mohammad echoed the *Qu'ran* in this saying: "Your Creator is one; you are from the same ancestor; all of you are from Adam, and Adam was created from earth" (Muslim, Hadith 70, p. 186). From Adam comes the Arabic term *adamia*, which is another word for humanism. The *Qu'ran* 7:2 confirms humans as uniquely free beings: "The angels do not have choice: they can only obey the commands of Allah ... Man as rational being, however, always has a choice, on which his dignity rests" (Maróth, 2014, p. 157)

Paulo Friere's Ontological Vocation

For the Brazilian linguist Paulo Freire, people become fully human in communities of intersubjective dialogue: "I cannot exist with a not-I; in turn the not-I depends on that existence" (1970, p. 70). Through bonds of interaction, people gain a critical consciousness that provides freedom from the status quo. Freire adopts a dialogic understanding of human relationships from Karl Jaspers's *Origin and Goal of History* (1953) as mediated for him through the Spanish philosopher Eduardo Nicol's *Los Principios de la Ciencia* (1965) (cf. De Lima, 1981).

In Freire's philosophy of language, it is our ontological vocation as creative subjects to act on the world while being critical of it and transforming it to suit the community's purpose. He presumes an explicit anthropology, conceiving of humans as existing not only in the social world but also through symbols separating from it in our consciousness. Through symbols, people are able to respond spontaneously as events unfold or adopt a conscious process of dialogic intervention. Freire develops a theory of culture that has the distinctively human as its meaning center, and from this perspective philosophical anthropology is the substantive issue.

The uniquely human capacity of "speaking a true word" is Freire's entrée to the sociohistorical process in which thought and language are experienced existentially. His essay "Cultural Action for Freedom" (1970a) is explicit about the idea of naming the world:

Learning to read and write ought to be an opportunity to know what speaking the word really means: a human act implying reflection and action. As such it is a primordial human right and not the privilege of a few. Speaking the word is not a true act if it is not at the same time associated with the right of self-expression and world-expression, of creating and recreating, of deciding and choosing, and ultimately of participating in a society's historical process. (p. 212)

Freire continues, "Human existence cannot be silent, nor can it be nourished by false words, but only by true words, with which the world is transformed. To exist humanly [with dignity] is to name the world to change it" (1970a, p. 213).

In the absence of a true word about human dignity and the existential condition, a word that enables us to decenter the reality in which we live (*conscientization*), no transformation is possible. Revolutionizing our symbolic forms is thus a critical element in our total humanization (Freire, 1973). Our constitutive relations as human beings are linguistic. Monologic symbols from oppressors create cultures of silence, and dialogic symbols engender participatory cultures. In his *Pedagogy of the Oppressed*, dehumanization is a process that marks "not only those whose humanity has been stolen (the oppressed), but also those who have stolen it (the oppressors)" (1970b, p. 28). Acts are oppressive when they prevent the distinctive human species from fulfilling its vocation to name the world. For Friere, "the great humanistic and historical task of the oppressed" is to "liberate both themselves and their oppressors" (p. 28) by speaking the true word that every human being without exception has intrinsic worth.

Human Dignity in *The Analects* of K'ung Fu-Tzu

Confucius (551–479 B.C.) in *The Analects* uses *ren* (humaneness) as the term for morality in general. *Ren* summarizes how a human being should behave toward other humans; it embraces the social virtues. This core concept and the specific virtues that derive from it are rooted in a person's essential humanity (*ren*). As Confucius puts it in *The Analects*, "It is humaneness (*ren*) which is the attraction of a neighborhood. If one does not dwell in humaneness (*ren*), where does one obtain wisdom?" (4.1): "The master said: Set your heart on the Way, base yourself on virtue, dwell in humaneness (*ren*), and take your relaxation in the arts" (*Analects*, 7.6).[7]

For Confucius in *The Analects*, virtue arises from our being. *Ren* derives from a person's essential humanity: "*Ren* is not far off; he who seeks it has already found it" (Confucius in Do-Dinh, 1969, p. 107). Humaneness is human-ness, the essence of being human. Zizhang asked Master K'ung Fu-Tzu about *ren:* "The Master said: One who can bring about the practice of five things under Heaven has achieved humaneness (*ren*). When he begged to ask about them, the Master said: Courtesy, tolerance, good faith, diligence, kindness" (*Analects*, 17.5). *Ren* is referring here to ideal human qualities, but Confucius does not mean them in the psychological sense of compassion or gallantry. He rather refers to the manifestations of being human. Morality is a property of the human race, and it is released through learning. *Ren* is the virtue that gives content to the notion of a dignified life.

Through *ren*, Confucianism affirms that human existence is unique; it is not physical survival, but in cases of conflict benevolence takes priority over life itself: "For human beings of benevolence (*ren*), it may happen that they have to accept death in order to accomplish benevolence (*ren*)" (15.9). Those living by *ren*'s five virtues "cannot be dissipated by wealth and honor; cannot be made to move from their own principles by poverty and low status, and cannot be corrupted by authority and might" (Luo, 2014, p. 189). In Confucianism, "a life without benevolence is a life without dignity" (p. 177). *Ren* is rooted in ontology, rather than in

---

[7] For comparative analysis with Kant's concept of human dignity in the *Groundwork of the Metaphysics of Morals* and *Metaphysics of Morals*, Confucius's idea of human dignity in *The Analects* is highlighted in these summaries of their work. Mencius a century later extends *ren* to include *yi* (righteousness): "These two approaches have become integrated into a comprehensive and multifaceted account of what it means to live a dignified life" (Luo, 2014, p. 179). Mencius is important because he believed with Confucius that people are basically good: "Water does not show any preference for either east or west, but does it show the some indifference to high and low? Human nature is good just as water seeks low ground. There is no man who is not good; there is no water that does not flow downward" (*Mencius*, Book VI). In the subsequent centuries, many of the disputes over the Confucian tradition centered on human nature as good or evil (cf. Whitehouse, 2009, pp. 167–172). Qianfan Zhang (2016) interprets the classical Chinese philosophical tradition, including Mohism and Daoism, through the framework of human dignity.

rationalist propositions. While individual rights represent Occidental values, "dwelling in humaneness" belongs to the human species as a whole.

"Etymologically, benevolence means 'two people,' that is, it represents interpersonal relationships" (Shan & Xiao, 2015, p. 23). The single ideogram for *ren* is a composite of "a person" plus "two": "*Ren* means to love people genuinely or authentically, to desire the well-being of others without seeking to profit from their well-being oneself" (Luo, 2014, p. 177). As with Kantianism, the Confucian tradition affirms that people have a duty to treat other human beings in a way that respects their dignity.[8]

Conclusion

These perspectives on human dignity distinguish the ontological and the normative, while recognizing their relationship. Ontologically, human dignity denotes the special status of the human species or the basic entitlement of all species members. All five theories introduced here consider human dignity an inalienable property, that is, a non-contingent implication of one's status as human. And, following the same logic, dignity as constitutive of the human species is the argument of this chapter. While the definition of Manfred Stanley has a Heidegerrian inflection, the discourse of human dignity from Kant to Confucius endorses its meaning, albeit with refinements and differing nomenclature:

Human dignity is the respect-worthiness imputed to humankind by reason of its privileged ontological status as creator, maintainer, and destroyer of worlds. Each self shares in this essential dignity insofar as it partakes in world-building or world-destroying actions. Thus, human dignity does not rest on intention, moral merit, or subjective definitions of self-interest. It rests on the fact that we are, in this fundamental way that is beyond our intention, human ... To assert dignity is to both acknowledge the factuality of human creative agency and to accept responsibility for its use. (Stanley, 1978, pp. 69–70)

Following Stanley, there is consensus in the five traditions that humans have an ethical duty to themselves to live well and meaningfully, and this duty is simultaneously owed to others. But in this apparent consensus of respect-worthiness as the basic norm of human existence, nearly all

---

[8] Studies of Chinese ethics and African ethics have recognized that although they have "different origins and histories," they "share some common bases on which a dialogue can ensue between their conceptions of the good" (Unah, 2014, p. 107). Bell and Metz (2011), in their "Confucianism and *Ubuntu*," provides an example that a comparison is intellectually productive (Unah, 2014, p. 107).

participants see the need for further reflection and research on definitions and applications. It is contested how the modern inflections on human dignity relate to earlier understandings in the Middle Ages and the Renaissance in the West, and to the ancient Confucian, Islamic, and Jewish traditions (cf. Schultziner, 2006). The "privileged ontological status" of humans that dignity entails requires dialogue about the status of nonhuman creatures.[9] Moreover, the universal character of the egalitarian idea embraced by democratic politics is not transparent to societies that are hierarchical or controlled by elite classes or those without laws to protect the ideal. By elaborating the normative character of human dignity for the global media, communication ethics can participate meaningfully in those important discussions.[10]

---

[9] Human exceptionalism among living entities is an overarching problematic for the future. Anthropocentrism is the issue, that is, theories that interpret or regard the world in terms of human values and experience. In its ideological form, anthropocentrism is a belief that human features such as reason, self-consciousness, and the ability to communicate through symbols are the grounds on which humans are to be treated morally. The influence of Peter Singer's work in bioethics has made the anthropocentrism issue inescapable for media ethics; his book of essays over three decades titled *Unsanctifying Human Life* (2002). The question for him is not whether beings can reason, but whether they can suffer, and if the latter they deserve to have that interest taken into account.

For Robert Heeger (2014), "there is a difference between the obligation to show consideration for a being and the obligation to respect the dignity of a being" (p. 55). The concept of human dignity means to "pursue one's own conception of a worthwhile life. This concept of dignity does not rule out moral obligations to non-human living beings, for human dignity does not cover the whole of morality" (p. 545). Peter Schaber (2014) is correct that "the inherent value of a being should be respected, preserved or promoted" (p. 50) and "The inherent value of a living being is preserved when this being is capable of developing into a typical representative of the species it belongs to" (p. 58).

For Gunkel (2016), theories of ethics that include animals still face the criticism that the scope of their consideration is arbitrarily narrow. If sentient creatures that suffer are moral subjects, it excludes other kinds of lower animals, plants, and other entities that comprise the natural environment (chap. 10). As noted earlier, rather than allow the human-nonhuman dualism to establish the agenda, Floridi (2014) argues for a fourth revolution after Copernicus, Darwin, and Freud in which the infosphere is based on an integrated ontology of natural, human, and technological realities. It ought not be biased against what is inanimate, lifeless, intangible, abstract, engineered, artificial, synthetic, hybrid, or merely possible.

[10] The criticism of human dignity as vacuous or empty is not included as a subject for further discussion. The argument is that human dignity reduces to notions of autonomy when applied and in that state has no analytic leverage. This critique has been addressed theoretically, historically, and sociologically. For a detailed overview of the issues beyond this summary, see *The Cambridge Handbook of Human Dignity* (Düwell et al., 2014, pp. xvii–xxii), and its sixty-two chapters of international contributions covering history, theory, law, medicine, social issues, politics, and international relations.

THE MEDIA'S FACILITATIVE ROLE

With human dignity coextensive with the human race, the ethical principle derived from it belongs to the media worldwide.[11] The media-society relationship is complicated and contested, but it has been developed most extensively in terms of democratic societies. In this model, the media's task is to provide the information citizens need to know for governing themselves. To implement the international ethics of human dignity effectively, a media-society framework is necessary that is not centered on democratic polity.[12]

The term "role" refers to a composite of occupational tasks and purposes that is widely recognizable and has a stable and enduring form. Roles are normally located within an institutional framework, and they are regulated according to the main activities, needs, and values of the institution, in this case the media. There is no shortage of typologies of possible roles of reporters and editors and online journalists in relation to the wider society and to politics in particular. But within democratic societies, the monitorial role is the most widely recognized and least controversial in terms of conventional ideas about what media institutions should be doing, as seen by media practitioners themselves, their audiences, and various sources and clients (Christians, Glasser, McQuail, Nordenstreng, & White, 2009, pp. 119–123): "The most basic meaning of the term 'monitorial' is that of an organized scanning of the real world of people, conditions, and events and of potentially relevant sources of information" (p. 123). The monitorial role is "the modal version of journalism in democratic societies" (p. 140).

There are significant variations between countries in implementing the monitorial role (cf. Hallin & Mancini, 2004). A technologically diverse media system internationally has numerous variations of form, format,

[11] This section benefits directly from chap. 7 ("The Facilitative Role" in Christians, Glasser, McQuail, Nordenstreng, & White, 2009), though that chapter does not ground this role in the norm of human dignity.
[12] An early theorist of the media-society nexus, Harold Lasswell (1948) pointed to three main functions of the news media that were expressed in terms of its roles: surveillance, social cohesion, and continuity (transmitting values from one generation to the next). The press's role as the fourth estate became a standard in the literature because it presumed the democratic principles of freedom and self-government (Cohen, 1963). Michael Schudson's three models of journalism (advocacy, market, trustee) are based on the history of the United States and Europe (1999, pp. 118–121; cf. 2003). One typical way of expressing the media's role in democratic societies has been the formulation of the BBC for public service broadcasters (to inform, to educate, to entertain) and for the commercial media (information, persuasion, entertainment).

and purpose. The definition of this role shows some shifts over time, but its axis around neutrality has remained the dominant emphasis for democracies across the world (Weaver & Willinat, 2015).

Initiatives to globalize the monitorial role are salutary. The critique of the monitorial role of the press has been ongoing since the 1947 Hutchins Commission Report, *A Free and Responsible Press*, and warrants scholarship on its cognitive content and practice. *Normative Theories of the Media* (Christians, Glasser, McQuail, Nordenstreng, & White, 2009) devotes major chapters to analyze and apply it. Bennett (2016) offers constructive proposals "for a critical national debate about how we should inform ourselves and engage with politics" in an age of "information abundance" (p. 222). Leon Barkho's (2016) case study reports that when Tony Burman was managing director of Al Jazeera English, he redesigned the mainstream Western journalism model into a new paradigm for international news. Development communication in the wake of UNESCO's MacBride Commission has contributed both geographical breath and cognitive flexibility to the monitorial idea.[13] With the revolution in media technologies, there is always a pressing need to continue defining this news-media role.

While book-length treatment of the monitorial role by academics and professionals is still urgent, another important role, the facilitative, ought

---

[13] For more than four decades, development communication models have taught us about the facilitative role. Development journalism was a significant facet of the New World Information and Communication Order debate (cf. Traber & Nordenstreng, 2002). But as Robert White (1994) argues, from the beginning development theory and practice have been "caught in a fundamental contradiction regarding the principle of participation" (p. 95). On the one hand, local participatory communication has been emphasized. But on the other, scientifically based social engineering and in some cases the primacy of state planning, have guided the logic of development practice, reserving for the "professional elite the initiative and control of development processes that deny the possibility of real participation" (pp. 95–96, 101). Early on, development journalism became anchored in monolithic, positivistic, technologically oriented media theory (see Servaes, 2007).

The mechanistic modernization theories of Lerner and Schramm became development journalism's scholarly foundation, with "modernization at bottom an euphemism for Westernization" (Dare, 2000, p. 167). The seemingly beneficial transfer of modern technology and organization has come to be recognized as "in reality an extension of the North Atlantic nations which implied a continued dependent linkage and division of labor benefiting the industrial nations" (White, 1994, p. 104). Instead of the dominant news focus, Herman Wasserman's *Popular Media, Democracy and Development in Africa* (2010) examines development history and theory in various regions of the African continent through popular media platforms and the ways their content and format contribute to democratic culture. Felix Olajide Talabi (2013) focuses on development journalism in Nigeria and recognizes that the challenges of implementing it there reflect the ambiguities described earlier.

to be front and center for the ethics of dignity. The monitorial framework that is focused on democratic governance is not adequate for the ethics of dignity with its universal scope and preoccupation with culture. For global media institutions to see themselves as governed by the ethics of human dignity, their mission needs to be expanded. The facilitative role of the media is the most suitable alternative. Human dignity offers a philosophical and moral foundation for the idea that the media have a facilitative responsibility to society.

According to Christians et al. (2009, p. 31), "As the main channel of public information, the news media are inevitably caught up in a wide range of political and social processes, and cultural activities. They are relied on by other institutions for communication about multiple areas, including health, education, religion, science, the arts, and welfare." Beyond politics and business, the media facilitate civil society that Habermas (1996) describes as "nongovernmental and noneconomic connections and voluntary associations that anchor communication structures of the public sphere in the society component of the lifeworld" (pp. 366–67). Hannah Arendt's *The Human Condition* calls the facilitative arena, the everyday world that extends beyond a person's life-span, the realm of the social that is pre-political (1998/1958, p. 55). Belonging to all, regardless of ruling regimes, the associational dimension of our common world is maintained by approval, agreement and respect, and the public media are the enablers.

Cultures are the collective beliefs and customs within which humans communicate, and therefore the fundamental "context within which we make our political choices" (Tully, 1995). The political, economic, and cultural dimensions of public life are thoroughly intermixed. However, human dignity requires that cultural practices and institutions are understood and critiqued on their own terms. Homelessness and unemployment are political and economic, but they are simultaneously infected by racism and gender bias. "Economic deprivation, political marginalization and cultural disrespect" operate in and through one another (Stevenson 1999, p. 50). A society's poverty involves human struggles with dependency and therefore is an erosion of worthiness. Raymond Williams's *The Long Revolution* and Walter Benjamin's *The Work of Art in the Age of Mechanical Reproduction* have demonstrated that public culture is a major arena for oppression, and an occasion for transformation, that ought to be articulated to politics and economics but not collapsed into them.

As cultural beings, the verbal and visual symbols of everyday life, images, representations, and myths make social relations meaningful for us and locate us in time and space.[14] In the facilitative role, this semiotic material is woven into the media's narrative. When we enact the facilitative role in reporting on human activities and institutions, we implement a creative process whereby people produce and maintain forms of life and society, as well as systems of meaning and value that reflect respect-worthiness. This distinctively human activity builds cultural forms through symbols that express the will to live purposefully. From that perspective, the reporter's first obligation – and likewise that of documentary journalism and film-makers – is to disclose the process of humans reflecting and acting on their dignity.

MULTINATIONAL CULTURAL DIVERSITY

Human dignity as a philosophy of the human and the facilitative model of media responsibility coalesce around the concept of cultural diversity in global media ethics. In that coalescence, the issue of internationalism is paramount as it is for the truth and nonviolence principles. Especially with the ethics of dignity, the standard meanings of "the world" cannot be adopted if it is to make a distinctive contribution in the twenty-first century. One commonplace definition of "the world" is the political network of 196 countries and 61 territories of the world, each with sovereign rights and enforcement institutions that establish its boundaries and transnational relationships. "Globalization" generally designates a neoliberal macroeconomic oneness. The rapid movement of economic and cultural capital across national boundaries imbricates the particular into a global marketplace by a placeless language and mobile financial systems. The most valuable asset is thought to be information networks that map the globe into interchangeable localities.

It has become apparent to critical cultural studies that globalization reconfigures space by abstracting human relations from their concrete embodiment in the local. When media professionals see themselves as citizens of the world, and academics work on communication ethics with a world mind, this should not be fundamentally neoliberal political-economic strategies or the abstractions of scientific research or the

---

[14] Mervi Pantti's (2015) study of the production and distribution of visual images from the Syrian crisis demonstrates how visual-based technologies ought to be researched (cf. Andén-Papadopoulos & Pantti, 2011).

structures of technological systems. While the globe is being pulled toward uniformity around consumption and digitalization, local voices have become more crucial than ever. The central problematic for the ethics of human dignity, therefore, is cultural identity and its various properties – pluralism, diversity, indigenous languages, and multicultural communities.

Cultural Identity

Instead of an imagined world of nation-states or of general regions such as the Western Hemisphere or the Nordic countries or Oceania, a "globe of ethnic people-groups" is a more precise designation in ontological terms for human dignity ethics. The continent of Africa, for example, is divided into fifty-four countries, but the human dignity principle takes particular note of its three thousand plus distinct ethnic groups and more than two thousand languages. Multiculturalism focuses on what it means to be human in the diverse societies of the world. The historic Hutchins Commission already in 1947 understood humanity in terms of its diversity, though its cosmopolitanism was elementary. In Hutchins's terms, the responsible press is called to present "a representative picture of the constituent groups in society" and to recognize the "values, aspirations, and common humanity" of all social groups (Commission on Freedom of the Press, 1947, pp. 26–27).

Indigenous languages are increasingly protected as a country's valuable resource. Ethnicity makes ongoing headlines as a powerful social force of the twenty-first century. In the global terms of cultural anthropologists, the world's population of 7.5 billion can be seen as an amalgamation of nearly twenty thousand ethnolinguistic communities living alongside or overlapping with one another. Language identity is the premiere feature of these people-groups. But there are other components that make each group culturally distinctive. Homeland origins, family and clan ancestry, cuisine, race, ritual practices, and religion are some of the common factors that distinguish an ethnic group.

There are many examples of people who speak multiple languages but still identify themselves as one ethnic community. The Dinka of Sudan and South Sudan speak five different languages but consider themselves as one people. Also, various ethnic groups use the same language but insist on their distinctiveness because of their different histories or loyalty to varied factions of their first-known ancestors. Today's Tutsi and Hutu people groups of East Central Africa are similar in language and culture, but they dispute their origins and see themselves as tribally distinct. China has identified fifty-six ethnic groups within its vast geography; however, fifty-five of them equal only 8.5 percent of the total population (according to the Fifth National Census of 2000). Preserving indigenous languages, such as Mongol, is a challenge for the vitality of China's multiculturalism.

In addition to language communities located geographically, the people-group globe recognizes ethnolinguistic entities as displaced and hybrid. Muslim immigrants are the fastest-growing population in the Netherlands, and they are not interested in full assimilation into Dutch language and politics. When the Ottoman Empire disintegrated, Syrian Jews established a community in Panama. Other Jews from Latin America have joined them, with Jewish Panama now numbering fifteen thousand (Kramer, 2017). The pastoral Fulani herders of sub-Saharan West Africa face escalating conflict with local farmers over grassland and water, with their economic future unsustainable. In India, Muslims are de facto aliens in the state of Punjab. There are more than one-half million Taiwanese original inhabitants (Formosa people) living in Taiwan, some of whom have migrated to the China mainland settling in Fujian Province; in both countries they live in economic crisis and their legal status is unsettled. The Belorussians won independence in 1989, but sovereign statehood is still not secured; for seventy years, their language had not been taught and their Belorussian history ignored. Only the remnants of the ancient Mayan empire survive in the Yucatan peninsula of Mexico, isolated by the government's nationalistic policies and commitment to education in Spanish. In his restructuring of moral development theory, Anthony Cortese (1990) argues that "moral reasongin and behavior are determined largely by social factors" (p. 2). To prove the "multidimensionality of moral judgment" (p. 105), his research included among others Hispanic, Black, and Asian children, adolescents, and adults; folk societies in New Guinea; Kenyan village leaders; and members of an Israeli kibbutz.

In the United States, the Bangladeshi population in Metro New York now numbers fifty thousand and growing, but they are among the poorest Asian ethnic groups in the city. Jeff Lindsay's "The Tragedy of the Hmong" documents the history of the Laotian people displaced from their farms in northern Laos, victims of US policies in the Vietnam War. The 260,000 Hmong people in the United States are refugees who struggle to maintain their heritage while adapting to their homes in California, Minnesota, and Wisconsin (www.jeflindsay.com/Hmong_tagedy.html). Sixty thousand Somalis live in Minneapolis, most of them arriving since their civil war in 1991, with Somali-owned businesses flourishing. A subculture of Chaldean Christians with Iraqi roots owns fifteen hundred retail stores in Detroit, Michigan. Amish farmers in Pennsylvania and the

Amana Colonies in Iowa struggle to maintain their identity. One-and-a-half million people from across the globe become new US citizens every year, but debates over immigration policy are acrimonious and hypocritical. In contrast to the melting-pot consensus of the previous century, immigrants to the United States today generally insist on maintaining their own culture, religion, and language.

For a people-based globe, the principle of human dignity considers it essential to maintain ethnic identities. Representing these ethnicities competently is an important area of professional development, and journalism codes of ethics would benefit by specifying this obligation (Glasser, Awad, & Kim, 2009). Stephen Ward (2015b) summarizes how human dignity challenges journalists to be ethnographers of global scope who report the abuses of human rights and are well informed on all dimensions of diversity. In Ward's view, journalists as citizens of the world frame issues broadly and use a wide variety of sources to represent international perspectives instead of promoting ethnocentrism or patriotism (p. 26).

Cultural anthropologists clarify ethnic representation for communicators with the concept of "emic categorization." Societies organize their cultures around historical and lingual patterns. These emic categories give valuable insights into a community's beliefs, customs, and worldviews. Emic categories are deeper than the researcher's demographics and social statistics; discovering and presenting these insiders' value systems is a crucial task for implementing human dignity ethics. This ontological feature of human life changes the self-understanding of reporters and film-makers from media experts serving clients to that of global citizens serving humanity. Media academics and professionals with a people-centered global imaginary, in fulfilling their emic task, are facilitating the ethics of human dignity.

With cultural identity coming into its own from the Netherlands to East Asia, is ethnic conflict inevitable? The Hutu and Tutsi massacres in Rwanda, killing in the streets of a Chechen village, and brutal warfare in Bosnia are not stories about tribal disputes only but also about ethnic cleansing. A commitment to the common human good strengthens our efforts to avoid the harm of tribalism. The issue for ethical journalism is not communal values per se but universal ones – not the bordered community's good, but *communis* in its richest universal meaning. The public sphere is conceived as a pastiche of distinguishable communities. The polychromatic voices of these communities are increasingly understood worldwide as essential for a healthy globe.

The Canadian philosopher Charles Taylor, from the province of French-speaking Quebec, in his influential lecture-turned essay ("The Politics of

Recognition") argues that recognizing multicultural groups politically is one of the most consequential issues on the public agenda today and therefore on the media's agenda (Taylor, Appiah, Habermas, Rockefeller, & Walzer, 1994). Enabling people to define their own identity on their own terms is a complicated problem, but foundational for society and for the news media that work in the public arena where cultural identity is represented and understood. The character of political recognition needs resolution for cultural diversity to meet the normative standard of human dignity.

News professionals are generally committed to the flourishing of particular cultures, religions, and ethnic groups, but this Herculean commitment requires continuous development. Susan Ross and Paul Lester's *Images That Injure* (2011) has become a staple of instruction for students and practitioners toward that goal. John Downing and Charles Husband (2005) also help fulfill this agenda with their literature review of three decades of racial stereotyping in the media as background for proposing a "multiethnic public sphere" that represents race. *Media and Ethnic Minorities* introduces cross-cultural research and theory on an international range of ethnic minorities, such as the Inuit and First Nations people in Canada, the Maori in New Zealand, the Sámi in northern Europe, and the Aborigines in Australia; the book's purpose is to influence public policy (Alia & Bull, 2005). The *Handbook of Critical and Indigenous Methodologies* combines sophisticated thinking on critical and action theory with indigenous research and discourse (Denzin, Lincoln, & Smith, 2008). Twine and Warren's *Racing Research, Researching Race: Methodological Dilemmas in Critical Race Studies* (2000) identifies research strategies that competently examine societies that are racially stratified. Davis, Nakayama, and Martin (2000) critique traditional social science research on ethnicity and recommend future directions for methodology.

Robert Entman and Andrew Rojecki (2000) illustrate a deep application of cultural diversity to race.[15] Putting the principle of human dignity to work, they indicate how the race dimension of communal life ought to

---

[15] An impressive example from advertising of applying the ethics of human dignity to race is the Ad Council's "A Mind Is a Terrible Thing to Waste" campaign. Starting in 1972, it raised more than $2 billion for the United Negro College Fund, on behalf of the historically Black colleges and universities. Culturally specific marketing finds it difficult to promote the dignity of the targeted group. Advertising's language of business tends to obscure the language of human agency; but the "Mind" publicity succeeded because it communicated the humanity of a people-group traditionally marginalized within American higher education. The ethics of human dignity is the genius behind the historic UNCF campaign (Christians, Fackler, & Ferré, 2012, chap. 10).

move forward in the media. Race in the twenty-first-century United States remains a preeminent issue, and their research indicates a broad array of White racial sentiments toward African Americans as a group. They emphasize not the minority of outright racists but the perplexed majority. On a continuum from comity (acceptance) to ambivalence and then racism, a complex ambivalence most frequently characterizes the majority (p. 21). Connecting White ignorance and dealing with ambiguities appear to hold "considerable promise for enhancing racial comity" (p. 21). The reality is, however, that ambivalence shades off into animosity most easily and frequently. In Entman and Rojecki's interviews, personal experiences of Black effort and achievement tend to be discounted "in favor of television images, often vague, of welfare cheats and Black violence." Unfortunately, interviewees did not draw "on television or other media for evidence that pulled them toward comity" (Entman & Rojecki, 2000, p. 28). For the White majority,

The mediated experience rises just above the threshold where these ambivalent respondents say they do know better intellectually, from coming into contact with a variety of Black people who offer compelling evidence to the contrary, but nevertheless feel themselves taken in by the flood of images ... The habits of local news – for example, the rituals in covering urban crime – facilitate the construction of menacing imagery. (p. 34)

The media are not enhancing racial understanding among those most open to it. Rather than actively foregrounding human dignity, the media tend to "tip the balance toward suspicion and even animosity among the ambivalent majority of Americans" (p. 44). When human dignity is a priority in journalism, this important swing group would be enabled to move forward and cultural pluralism would be enhanced.

For journalism ethics, when human dignity, the people-group globe, and the media's facilitative role are synchronized, ethnic identity receives its proper due. In these examples of the theorizing about the implementation of multinational cultural diversity, the media as the primary form of public communication are crucial for a community's identity to be realized. In the ethics of being appropriate to a globe of people-groups, we know our ethnicity through our symbolic expressions. The theories that humans construct about themselves are depictions of their own sense of their humanity. It means that the lives of the world's people-groups are loaded with multiple interpretations and characterized by cultural intricacy and paradox. Ethnic identity is now considered essential to cultural vitality and, indeed, survival. As a result, the global media as an important social institution are challenged to develop cultural pluralism in their thinking, organizational structure, and reporting practices. While the news media continue to function as the fourth estate in US polity, their facilitative role transnationally is cultural diversity.

The facilitative role normed by human dignity is appropriate for public media systems across the technology spectrum – from print to digital. It serves as a framework for all media functions – information, persuasion, entertainment. However, two subgenres of the news media – narrative journalism and community media – are especially productive for people-group ethnicity. Their technological form matches their communal audience and participants.

Narrative Journalism

Narrative journalism, in its conception and practice, is the facilitative role at work. Narrative or long-form journalism is a news style that combines reporting techniques with feature-writing strategies to focus on everyday life and ordinary people. Harvard's Nieman Foundation Program on Narrative Journalism, launched in 2001, defines narrative journalism as more than simply telling stories: "It is a complex genre with multiple layers and contexts that, when done well, has the capacity to make newspapers essential and compelling" (http://niemanstoryboard.org/tag/nie man-conference-on-narrative-journalism). Instead of covering dramatic events considered newsworthy, writers follow a subject or theme for an extended time and portray in story format human experience in deeply emotional terms.

Publications such as *Harper's, The New Yorker, Esquire, Rolling Stone,* and *Atlantic Unbound* are welcome homes to narrative journalists. *The Activist* website is designed for long-form journalism. Mainstream newspapers often print narrative journalism as a Sunday feature or in supplemental magazines. Beyond these North American venues are popular forums for narrative journalism on every continent. The Chilean narrative journalist Christian Alarcón is notable for including in his online publication *Revista Anfibia* both academic work on narrative and long-form professional nonfiction.

The early history of this genre is nonfiction novels, such as those of Stephen Crane, Jack London, and John Hersey. The so-called new journalists used literary techniques, beginning in the 1960s, often as an alternative to what they considered the news industry's staid reporting and formulaic news. Tom Wolfe wrote *The New Journalism* in 1974 and is credited with popularizing the appropriateness of narrative in public communication. In writing for *Esquire* and the *Herald Tribune,* Wolfe called his new form a fusion of "the stylistic features of fiction and the reportorial obligations of journalism" (Kallan, 1992).

Norman Sims wrote the first major book-length treatment of literary journalism and concluded that this news writing "demands immersion in complex, difficult subjects. The voice of the writer surfaces to show that an author is at work" (1984, p. 3). Literary journalism is not fiction since the events occurred and the people actually exist: "Literary journalism ties itself to the actual, the confirmed, that which is not simply imagined ... Literary journalists adhere to the rules of accuracy – or mostly so – precisely because their work cannot be labeled as journalism if details and characters are imaginary" (Sims, 2008, p. 8). But there is interpretation, a personal point of view, and experimentation with structure and chronology as is true of creative nonfiction.

The story style of narrative journalism and its preoccupation with everyday life give writers in this genre a special opportunity to reflect the principle of human dignity. Amy Lauters speaks in these terms about the literary journalism form: "Common to many definitions of literary journalism is that the work itself should contain some kind of higher truth; the stories themselves may be said to be emblematic of a larger truth" (2007). Ta-Nehisi Paul Coates in "My President Was Black" illustrates that the best in narrative nonfiction deals with the fundamental issues of human existence: "My own history tells me something different [than the mainstream account]. The large numbers of black men in jail are not just the result of poor policy, but of not seeing those men as human" (2015). The Poynter Institute's definition of narrative includes the moral dimension this way: "Narrative is an attempt to impose order on the chaos of the human condition. Because narrative is powered by events, its goal is not essentially analytical or critical – though like many stories in traditional genres, folktales, fables – it can contain substantial moral lessons" (Scanlon, 2003).

When Leon Dash was a reporter for the *Washington Post*, he researched and wrote *Rosa Lee: A Mother and Her Family in Urban America,* a book that grew out of an eight-part series for the *Post* in 1994. This story of one woman and her family's struggle against poverty in the projects of Washington, DC, won the Robert F. Kennedy Journalism Award and the Pulitzer Prize for Explanatory Journalism. Based on four years of immersion in the lives of Rosa Lee Cunningham, her three children, and five grandchildren, Dash reflects the human dignity principle by getting behind the false images and erroneous beliefs about the actual human beings we label "addicts," "criminals," and "prostitutes." Dash's award-winning book *When Children Want Children: The Urban Crisis of Teenage Childbearing* was based on a 1986 series for the *Post* after seventeen months of covering young black parents in Washington, DC's Highlands neighborhood. His beneath-the-surface account of adolescent childbearing meant interviewing teenage mothers and fathers up to six times to hear their authentic voice and true motives and heart desires and teenage savvy. Instead of publishing shibboleths about the "plight of the urban underclass," his long-form reporting followed human dignity ethics. Dash's ethnographic news gathering and literary genius illustrate that the narrative journalism genre can fulfill the facilitative role.

George Packer's (2015) analysis of *Rolling Stone*'s story "A Rape on Campus" is instructive of both the character of narrative journalism and its challenges. While not invoking the human dignity principle directly, Packer's assessment reflects it:

On Sunday, the Columbia Graduate School of Journalism released an exhaustive report on the *Rolling Stone* story from last November depicting a brutal gang rape at the University of Virginia ... First and foremost, the account of the supposed victim – referred to only as "Jackie" by the *Rolling Stone* reporter, Sabrina Rubin Erdely – is not at all supported by independent facts. Erdely never located the supposed ringleader of the gang rape – "Drew" in the story.

The report deals a devastating blow to the magazine's decision-making, from start to finish, in bringing "A Rape on Campus" to millions of readers. The reporter ... wanted to expose the "culture of rape" on college campuses, and she went looking for a case so vivid and gripping that no reader could dismiss it. When Renda told her about Jackie in that first conversation, Erdely had what she was looking for, and she made the decision not to pursue other, less dramatic cases that she learned about. Renda later told the *Times* that a more ambiguous incident might have seemed "not real enough to stand for rape culture" ... Her remark could be applied to narrative journalism as well: extreme, lurid cases are inherently tempting subjects, but they are not the most likely to lead to complex or profound or abidingly true work ... Doubt also might have meant losing the whole story, with its riveting, horror-film lede, and the ammunition it contained for thunderous moral condemnation at U.V.A. Once *Rolling Stone* committed itself wholly to Jackie's version, the magazine took it to the limit.

Can you imagine the impulses competing in the editor's mind – carefulness and transparency on the one hand, the stylistic pleasure of an uninterrupted flow of narrative on the other. It's a question that comes up in every piece of literary journalism worth the name. The report's authors are sympathetic to the dilemma, but not to its outcome. There is a tension in magazine and narrative editing between crafting a readable story – a story that flows – and providing clear attribution of quotations and facts. It can be clunky and disruptive to write "she said" over and over.

Faced with a series of decisions and turning points, again and again the magazine took the path that would lead toward what could be called a "better" story. For journalists, that's what makes the scandal the worst kind – unconscionable, and imaginable. (www.newyorker.com/news/daily-comment/rolling-stone-and-the-temptations-of-narrative-journalism, pp. 1–7)

To ensure that this genre meets the standards of the facilitative role, and thereby lives up to the ethics of human dignity rather than contravenes it, many university curricula include training in narrative journalism, also known as immersion journalism. Walter Harrington's influential textbook *Intimate Journalism: The Art and Craft of Reporting Everyday Life* (1997) teaches literary quality and ethical integrity by illustration and theory. The Berkeley Narrative Journalism Conferences, featuring the "Latest in Longform," "explore the creative edges and best traditions of nonfiction storytelling whether online, in glossy magazines or books" (www.nieman storyboard.org). Poynter promotes narrative that "leads the audience toward a point or realization or destination" while avoiding the *Rolling Stone* problem. For Poynter, storytelling journalism "remains true to the tenants of good reporting: accuracy, honesty, integrity of intentions." The Nieman Program on Narrative Journalism is a center for teaching narrative journalism on both traditional and new platforms. Boston University's College of Communication, in its two decades of the "Power of Narrative" conferences, has helped "storytellers strengthen their craft, puzzle out the ethics of intimate journalism, and create work with the down-to-earth humanity that defines narrative nonfiction. Our lives are made up of stories," and members of the conferences "discuss how to tell them compellingly, with empathy and insight, respect and inclusiveness" (www.bu.edu/com/narrative/). Those terms – "empathy," "insight," "respect," and "inclusiveness" – are derived from the principle of human dignity.

Community Media

Community media is another genre in which the facilitative role is particularly appropriate.[16] In this subset of media organizations, journalists are given priority as members of communities: geographical,

---

[16] This section on community media is oriented to local mediations. Singer et al.'s *Participatory Journalism* (2011) represents online journalism as a whole, and Friend and Singer's *Online Ethics* (2007) encompasses internet news technologies, therefore, are applicable elsewhere in *Media Ethics and Global Justice in the Digital Age.*

sociocultural, and virtual. The principle of human dignity and the facilitative role belong to the world, and local participatory media are a global phenomenon. For example, in Africa there are more than one thousand community radio outlets (only one instance of the multiple local media technologies).[17]

To have the stories of these domains understood and interpreted properly, the ethnocentric global imaginary needs emphasis and clarity. Imagining the world as people-groups is a communal vision, not the world composed of freestanding individuals pursuing their own self-interests, but each country and territory a mosaic of people-groups. This communitarian philosophy of the public sphere represents the legacy of *Gemeinschaft* in social theory in which a limited set of people are bound together in networks of multidimensional communication. This communal framework maximizes people's influence on the social conditions that shape their lives. The community media's facilitative role is not directed toward uniform public opinion but toward a multicultural mosaic and multifaceted governance. In a world imagined as communities, the aim is a "public of publics" (Bohman, 2000, p. 140). In principle, nations are decentered into a variety of communities "where the interactors are reflexive and participatory" (p. 148).

Two of the people-groups in the "community media" rubric are those defined by a geographically bound place, that is, those entities determined by social or cultural boundaries. Patrick Tor Alumuku of Nigeria speaks helpfully of "geographic community radio and community-of-interest radio," both of which have common or overlapping symbols that explain their identity (2006; cited in Ate & Ikerodah, 2012, p. 55). Geographical communities are based on oral communications. Their institutions are fundamentally interpersonal – schools, government agencies, religious institutions, local celebrations, and volunteer organizations. They serve a locatable, recognized public. Social or tribal communities of interest

---

[17] Community media are often called local/grassroots/indigenous/or citizens media (though "citizen" is often paired against "professional" and that is not the intention here) (cf. Gillmor, 2006). "Media" is chosen because it reflects the technology rather than practice such as journalism/advertising/entertainment. In the typical configuration, most community journalists are trained reporters and editors on an organization's payroll, not unpaid amateurs (cf. Singer et al., 2011, chaps. 3–4, for elaboration). "Mediated mobilization" (Lievrouw, 2011, chap. 6), "global activism" (Bennett, 2003a), and "connective action networks" (Bennett & Segerberg, 2013, chaps. 3–5) refer to transnational social movements and are discussed in Chapter 6.

often exist because of social media technologies, but their communal bonds are rooted in language or birthplace or festivals or tradition.

Communities of all forms are multifaceted and are also to be understood as collectives with an identity when they exist in the online world. These digital communities are citizen-based participatory networks: "They give users an unprecedented degree of selectivity and reach in their choices of information and cultural resources, and in their personal interactions and expressions" (Lievrouw, 2011, p. 13). In addition, "The rise of participatory journalism – including citizen, grassroots, or open-source journalism projects, independent news and opinion blogs – provides rich examples of local and special-interest reporting, editing, and opinion that simultaneously uphold and critique the traditional values and practices of journalism and the press" (p. 120; cf. Singer et al., 2011, p. 2). "Alternative new media genres are notable for their small scale and collaborative quality; it is fair to say that these two characteristics virtually define participatory" media projects. In such examples as Independent Media Centers (Indymedia), their "interactive, conversational partnership blurs the boundaries between journalists and the communities they cover" (p. 144).[18] Despite its geographic dispersion, "the Indymedia network is fundamentally local, insists on the autonomy of the member IMCs, and conceives of the newswire entirely as a bottom-up enterprise" (p. 144).

The community media value types of communication in which identities are expressed and enhanced: community radio, indigenous newspapers, local and regional television, social media, and multimedia networks. For community media that are guided by human dignity, all people and groups of the community have direct access; policy and content are influenced by every member of the community who cares to participate. These are the media technologies that Ivan Illich (1973) calls "convivial tools" (from Latin *con-* together, *vīvere* to live) – tools that are user friendly, affordable, and reparable and are generally accessible to the public. Ghana represents this thinking in its national policies that stipulate that community broadcasting should be nonsectarian, nonpartisan, and not-for-profit:

---

[18] Lievrouw (2011) sees the Indymedia global network as fundamentally local because it insists on the autonomy of its members and considers its network a "bottom-up enterprise" (p. 144). For a comprehensive review of Indymedia as a global interactive movement while reflecting a community-based philosophy of communication, see Downing (2003).

Ghana's legislation points out that at least seventy percent of programs on all community broadcast stations should be in local languages and eighty percent of the programs should be produced by the station itself. At least twenty per cent of programs should be of national interest, which could include relays of national broadcast news from the Ghana Broadcasting Corporation. (according to Alumuku, quoted in Ate & Ikerodah, 2012, p. 52)

In Nigeria, "with over 250 ethnic groups speaking 450 dialects spread across 774 local governments and divided into six geopolitical zones" multiple media locations and opportunities to communicate are essential for democratic norms to be realized (Ojomo, Tejuoso, Olayinka, & Oluwashola, 2015, p. 137). Ate and Ikerodah (2012) account for the increasingly strong digital environment for community media in Nigeria: while community radio is a "necessity for rural development," they recognize that the definition of community may be changing and "call for an excellent marriage between community media and new media technologies in the country" (p. 58).[19]

Bill Reader and John Hatcher's *Foundations of Community Journalism* (2011) illustrates the multiple research methods that have been used to understand community media in their multicultural and multinational settings (cf. Hadl & Hintz, 2009). Their studies include the Norwegian press and community radio in Africa. A critical-cultural chapter compares Asian and American studies, and Hatcher "sees a fascinating transition" that may be occurring in China "toward community media" (Reader & Hatcher, 2011, p. 252). Rodriguez, Kidd, and Stein (2009) include research in Chile, Colombia, Australia, and Mexico. Clemencia Rodriguez (2001) presents a historical overview of "popular correspondents" in Nicaragua, 1982–1990. Valeria Alia (1999) documents indigenous media use in the Canadian arctic and subarctic, and the circumpolar region (Alaska, Siberia, Greenland). Since 1984, John Downing has published pioneering research on alternative, ethnic, and independent media around the world (cf. 2001, 2011). *Saving Community Journalism: The Path to Profitability* documents the policies and practices of community newspapers in the towns, suburbs, and small cities (less than 50,000 population) of the United States – these representing 95 percent of the

---

[19] *Fitzrovia News* is an example of community media adapting to the new technologies. Originally called *The Tower*, but still located today in the same central London neighborhood, it is the United Kingdom's oldest community newspaper (1973). Residents and volunteers produce a quarterly printed newspaper delivered free to all local addresses in the district of Fitzrovia. The newspaper now has a website and social media network that cover issues for residents and local agencies between publication.

US newspapers in existence (Abernathy, 2014).[20] *Contesting Media Power* includes chapters on alternative media in Russia, Australia, Taiwan, Chile, and Indonesia; many of the examples fitting the category "community media" (Couldry & Curran, 2003).

Reader and Hatcher's conclusion is valid: "The distinction between community journalism and journalism itself is much more profound than matters of size, scale, and reach. Community journalism is integral to all aspects of community culture: history, economics, community identity, community values, policy debates and public opinion. Community journalism encompasses more than just process and audience – it is concerned with the social fabric of community" (2011, p. xv). Recognizing the new interest in media localism in Canada, the United Kingdom, and the United States, Christopher Ali (2017) demonstrates the need for regulatory policies that strengthen local media as crucial to the public good.

The Facilitative Agenda

In acting out of their facilitative role, community media have a wide-ranging agenda. Community journalism often focuses on a particular issue such as education, transportation, elderly care, zoning, policing, land use, or race controversies. The aim of the facilitative role is to cover such topics in depth and to encourage citizen input on defining the issues and generating solutions (Kurpius, 1999). For Ate and Ikerodah's "Community Journalism in Nigeria," some local radio at the grassroots level in marginalized communities has been able to "harness civil education, cross-gender dialogue, cultural literacy for developmental purposes" (2012, p. 52). On the local level, there are typically more conversations among journalists, citizens, and public officials, resulting in "a larger file of community sources for stories and an increase in story ideas from the community ... With community journalism, rural dwellers can become news makers thus bridging the rural-urban gap" (Ate & Ikerodah, 2012, pp. 54, 57). The Radio Television Digital News Association promotes community journalism because it encourages a wide range of community perspectives.

To explain its facilitative agenda, community journalism is typically labeled "the alternative media." The term has several dimensions, but it is used here primarily in the sense of an alternative to the mainstream

---

[20] The International Society of Weekly Newspaper Editors represents independent newspapers in six countries besides the United States (Canada, UK, Ireland, Japan, Australia, and New Zealand).

national and international media. Its "journalism projects are typically kept small to encourage the coverage of local or specialized issues that large news organizations would ordinarily consider too minor to cover" (Lievrouw, 2011, p. 144). The alternative media articulate the complaints of the public ignored by the mainstream media, and help their home communities formulate proposals for reforms in public services. One of the complaints often leveled against national television and radio news is that depth and context are missing. Native Americans have been "sharply critical of news coverage about their issues," complaining that it often "lacks historical and cultural context" (Loew & Melba, 2005, p. 103). The *Charleston Gazette* (since 2015 *Charleston Gazette-Mail*) in West Virginia has won numerous awards for its coverage of the coal mining industry. In reporter Ken Ward Jr.'s reflections on local stories:

> With a few exceptions, journalists are forgetting about the value of being an expert on the issue and having a reporter who specializes in things . . . It's the difference between the national media folks who parachute in to West Virginia. It doesn't matter if people trust them, because they're doing one story and moving on. But we live here and work here. (Frola, 2007)

In authoritarian societies, when the community media that are close to the suffering of everyday life can survive, they create an alternative frame of reference that helps delegitimate the hegemonic discourse.[21]

Despite their strategic importance, the challenges for community media in fulfilling the facilitative role are considerable. When community cultures need to be confronted, they are often resistant. Loyalty to a community is critical for a medium's viability, but truth and loyalty frequently collide. Gender issues are a challenge for the media in all their genres and functions – journalism, persuasion, entertainment – and are no easier in community media (Pavarala & Malik, 2010). The issues of ethnicity can be represented more precisely in local media but are difficult nonetheless, in that collective decisions are typically in favor of the cultural capital of the major power holders (Downing, 2001). The history of broadcasting in Nigeria indicates that community media are on the

---

[21] Couldry and Curran (2003) in *Contesting Media Power* develop the "alternative media" idea internationally and across the spectrum of media technologies. Arguing that "the media's representational power is one of society's main forces," they see "media power as itself part of what power watchers need to watch" (p. 4). As the corporate and state media expand in power, this book documents attempts by the alternative media to contest their power. Based on overview and framework chapters by Lance Bennett, Nick Couldry, and James Curran (chaps. 1–3), this book's research studies and critical essays examine the worldwide growth of alternative media as they challenge the global information system.

defensive; successive Nigerian governments "favor the urban centers to the neglect of rural areas" (Ate & Ikerodah, 2012, p. 52). In the ongoing digital revolution, many community outlets in the United States are disappearing altogether or being absorbed into national media networks, many of which themselves are under threat (Abernathy, 2016).

Principle of Human Dignity

A theme in Reader and Hatcher (2012) is the need for ethical principles to ensure that those involved in the community media will make the proper choices about the challenges of their complicated environments. With the same rationale, Singer (2011) includes a chapter on ethics oriented to participatory journalism. The argument of this chapter is that the ethics of human dignity is the most appropriate normative standard for the facilitative role in its various media genres. By definition, the ethics for community media requires consensus as its foundation. Instead of understanding morality as pattern variables, the principle of human dignity presumes that communities provide spaces where people of different identities, cultural backgrounds, social classes, and ethnicities can meet precisely at the level of differences and confront various perspectives by a dialogic ethics of self and others. Therefore, the task of community media is to reclaim public spaces for the common good by fashioning a moral consensus around human dignity.[22]

Clemencia Rodriguez is an example of how human dignity can be the normative standard for community media. In *Citizens' Media Against Armed Conflict* (2011), she examines how community journalism in Colombia is "[a] powerful [tool] to help civilian communities survive conflict and war" (p. 3). Without using the words "human dignity," her description of what local media can and ought to do represents the human dignity concept: "When grassroots communication media are deeply embedded in their communities, truly open to collective participation, and responsive to immediate and long-term local communication needs, they strengthen the agency of the community as it responds to armed violence" (p. 3). Production of "their own radio, video, or television programming" enables civilian communities to begin to "reconstitute

---

[22] Regarding the common good as a moral concept, Bernard Diggs's (1973) classic essay argues that we enter into shared arrangements in competitive situations following elementary moral notions of fairness. Our assessment of social arrangements is guided by what we are reasonably entitled to expect and by a complex understanding of mutual acceptance. Only within such a moral understanding of the common good can we recognize the deep chasms of exclusion and powerlessness as morally outrageous.

webs of meaning, allowing them to make sense of their experience of war ... Citizens' media facilitate communication processes in which civilians recreate traditional solidarities and form new ones, return to public places that have been abandoned in terror, and organize collective actions." They trigger communal processes that "bring civilians, one step at a time, out of the isolation and fear imposed by armed violence and back into the public sphere" (p. 3). Rodriguez demonstrates how local citizens' media provide people with the communication platform to forge lives that are not colonized by armed conflict.

Indian Country Today Media Network is another exemplar of community media living up to its facilitative mission while honoring the ethical principle of human dignity. This participatory network began as a geographical version of community media; then with online technology, it evolved into the social version of this genre, and today it is a web-based community journalism project.

Tim Giago (Nanwica Kciji in Oglala Lakota) founded the *Lakota Times* in 1981 at his birth home, the Pine Ridge Indian Reservation, operating it independently of the tribal government. It was the first privately owned Native American newspaper in the United States. In 1992, he changed his paper's name to *Indian Country Today* to reflect its social boundaries – first to all the Indian reservations in South Dakota, and then to Native American news and culture. *Indian Country Today* became a classic of the community media genre in North America. Upon his retirement in 1998, Giago sold *Indian Country Today* to the Oneida Nation of New York (Giago, 2005). The regional newspaper *Indian Country Today* became the *Indian Country Today Media Network* (ICTMN), which went online in 2013, including a multimedia news service. *Indian Country Magazine* was added in 2017, the print issue by subscription and home delivery, with online access to a web edition platform.

Indian Country Today Media Network in both print and online is involved in ethnic issues on American Indian reservations, but it tackles human rights problems more generally as well. Native interpretations of politics, law, history, economics, and religion are rooted in that communitarian phenomenon, a clear sense of place; the land embodies their identity and culture. In its facilitative role, ICTMN recognizes that beliefs about the world hold ethnic groups together and that ceremonies and religion and language are not marginal but central to a community's distinctiveness. Therefore, ICTMN material seeks to resonate with its tribal audiences and users' self-determination.

The journalistic aim in this facilitative organization is to avoid "monochromatic accounts" and present narratives "that are nuanced and complex," that is, "ones that American Indians claim as their story" (Christians, Fackler, & Ferré, 2012, p. 221). Reporting attempts to follow the natural history of an issue so that the public gains a coherent understanding of the causes and consequences of acutely felt problems. In that sense, the values of good journalism have shifted from a focus on professional procedures to the quality of organizations and public activities in the community. Paulo Freire (1970b) puts it this way: the oppressed must speak the true word and initiate the revolution themselves, rather than presume that social transformation arises first of all from the oppressor's philanthropy or altruistic change of heart.

Because expensive and high-technology media are ordinarily stitched into systems of political and economic power (Couldry & Curran, 2003), radical ruptures are often needed in the media's technological structure before an alternative voice can be heard. Since the Iranian Revolution of 1978–1979 when the small media were essential, nurturing cultural identity in communities "has become central to the revolutionary process. In situations where people are not allowed to assemble or demonstrate, small media can foster an imaginative social solidarity, often as the precursor for actual physical mobilization" (Sreberny-Mohammadi & Mohammadi, 1994, p. 24). The community media – where the facilitative role is primary and the monitorial secondary – gain their rationale from the idea of empowerment as essential to revolution. Local cultures are respected and brought to bear in the work of social change. The principle of human dignity entails action multiculturally. Participation in media production, appraisal, and distribution by members of minority communities is mandatory.

Self-righteous tribalism can always overwhelm the public order, but, on balance, ethnic identity is a destructive force only when it is trivialized or repressed. A communitarian philosophy of communication provides a rationale for localized media in which ethnicity and citizenship are integrated. When indigeneity prospers in community media worldwide, human resources are recognized and mobilized cross culturally through a species oneness grounded in human dignity.

RESEARCH AND CASES WITH HUMAN DIGNITY THE ISSUE

Language makes community possible; it is the public agent through which our identity is realized. The lingual dimension forms humans and their relationships into meaningful units; the vitality or oppressiveness of our symbolic forms inevitably conditions our well-being. In that sense, the media as our primary form of public communication are a crucial arena through which ethnic diversity is represented and understood. I introduce four illustrations from the global media to illustrate how the ethics of human dignity promotes cultural pluralism.

Poverty and the Poor

Poverty in all its forms is one of the greatest challenges facing the human race. The number of people living in extreme poverty dropped by more than half between 1990 and 2015 – from 1.9 billion to 836 million. But too many millions still struggle to live on less than 1.25 USD a day, lacking access to such vital human needs as adequate food, clean drinking water, and sanitation. And exacerbating these disturbing numbers, the distance between rich and poor continues to grow wider (www.undp.org/content/undp/en/home/ourwork/sustainable-development). In the United States, according to 2014 census data, 46 million live in a lower class without dependable food and housing, many jobless and surviving on the edge by government assistance.

Despite the overwhelming need and massive numbers, poverty reporting is scant. In 2014, Fairness and Accuracy in Reporting (FAIR) found that three major network newscasts devoted just 0.2 percent of their programming to poverty in a fourteen-month period. Similarly, the Pew Research Center's Project for Excellence in Journalism determined that poverty coverage accounted for less than 1 percent of stories in fifty-two mainstream news outlets from 2007 to mid-2012 (Savchuk, 2016, p. 1). In Savchuk's overview, "one reason often cited for the longstanding dearth of U.S. media coverage about poverty: it's depressing"; poverty is one of those social problems that seems unending and intractable (p. 1). In addition, editors and reporters conclude from audience studies that their readers and viewers are not interested in poverty stories. Intense "cost pressures on news organization" are to blame also, as they "shed reporters while struggling to remain profitable"; getting "poverty segments on the air" is difficult because they "don't appeal to advertisers" (Savchuk, 2016, p. 2). Situated as they are in the context of global poverty, reporters who regularly report suffering experience compassion fatigue; for Keith Tester (2001), this is one explanation for poverty being underreported.

The dehumanization that poverty represents is contrary to the principle of human dignity. It is urgent that this social issue be understood both in theory and practice according to the ethical principle directly relevant to it.

The Peruvian scholar Gustavo Gutiérrez has interpreted poverty and the poor through the human dignity principle with world-renowned distinctiveness. Liberation theology, which he originated, represents "one of the most innovative theological initiatives of the twentieth century" (Gutiérrez & Müller, 2015, p. ix).[23] In his *Theology of Liberation* (1971) and other writings, including *On the Side of the Poor* (2015), Gutiérrez presents a narrative that gives voice to the social realities of slums in Lima and of peasant farmers in the Andes. His thinking, based on "the social and historical context of Latin America and the Caribbean," shows "a total respect for human life and dignity" (pp. xi, 102). For Gutiérrez, the chasm between the poor and rich is not only a consequence of economic and social conditions,

but also is an expression of structural sin, which goes contrary to the order of creation and is ultimately an affront to God – indeed, ultimately a blasphemy. The existence of poverty and injustice is not only a social-ethical issue beside other issues. Rather, the theology of liberation makes it clear that the question of God comes into play here ... Poverty as it is known to us today hurls a radical and all-encompassing question at the human conscience and at the way we perceive Christian faith. (p. 40)

Liberation theology refuses to reduce poverty to its administrative aspects. In evaluating policies and news coverage and organizations, the concerns in narrative and action center on the claim that poor persons are "insignificant," that is, persons who are considered nonpersons: "We are talking about persons without social or individual weight, who count little in society or in the church, whose full rights as a human being are not recognized. This is how they are seen or, more precisely, not seen, because they are in fact invisible insofar as they are excluded in today's world" (p. 43).

"'The preferential option for the poor' turns out to be an overriding and fruitful guide-line for understanding, through the lens of faith, the times in which we are living," write Gutiérrez and Müller (2015, p. 92). *On the Side of the Poor* sees a parallel in Emmanuel Levinas: "The other's

[23] The author thanks Grace Eliana Alexandrino Ocaña for her gift of the Gutiérrez and Müller book, *On the Side of the Poor*, and for her personal interest in Gutiérrez at Pontifica Universidad Católica del Perú. She renewed my commitment to the relevance of human dignity to the issues of poverty and the poor.

very status as Other is not a question of reciprocity. We are faced with the primacy of the Other, which leads to what Levinas calls 'the dissymmetry of the interpersonal relationship' or 'ethical asymmetry'" (p. 91).[24]

Gutiérrez addresses "the preferential option for the poor" to his own human community, the church, for its critical consciousness and agency. He is concerned with the tendency on "this Catholic continent" for oligarchs and church leaders "to make private property and the capitalist system of production into the criterion for what is to be valued as Christian" (pp. x, 22). "The preferential option for the poor" as a transforming attitude toward poverty is a contribution to the Latin American church and to universal humanity. Kendall's (2011) research indicates, however, that this "preferential option" is not a prominent frame in US news reports that instead dehumanize the poor by presenting them as a problem to be dealt with and ignoring their indignities.

For Gutiérrez, "to reread history could seem to be a purely intellectual exercise if we failed to understand that this also involves remaking it. Within this framework of ideas, the conviction remains firm – despite all the limitations and obstacles of which I am well aware, especially today – that the poor themselves must take charge of their own destiny" (Gutiérrez & Muller, 2015, p. 45). The authors continue: "It is important to recall that the poor, insignificant, and excluded are not passive persons waiting for someone to extend a hand" (p. 106; cf. Lepianka, 2015):

They not only lack things; many human possibilities and riches are bubbling away in them. The poor and marginalized of Latin America often possess a culture with its own eloquent values that come from their race, their history, and their language. They have energies like those seen in women's organizations from one end of the continent to the other, fighting for the lives of their families and of the poor, confronting the crisis with an astonishing inventiveness and creative force. (Gutiérrez & Müller, 2015, p. 106; cf. Gutiérrez, 1983)

Haijan Gao's (2016) content analysis of *The People's Daily* through the calendar year 2015 indicated the opposite dynamic: the focus in the news stories was on government aid to the poor, not on the poor as agents and without their voice. Isabel Awad's (2014) ethnographic fieldwork in the poor Chilean community of Bajos de Mena also concluded that poverty coverage, while extensive, tended to ignore the activities and contributions of poor people themselves.[25]

---

[24] Juan Carlos Scannone (1993) develops this concept philosophically (pp. 123–140).
[25] The references to poor and poverty in this section benefit from the research of Yayu Feng, Institute of Communication Research, University of Illinois at Urbana-Champaign.

Gutiérrez summarizes Paul Ricoeur: "We are not with the poor if we are not against poverty, that is, if we do not reject the conditions that overwhelm such a huge part of humanity. It is not a matter of merely emotional rejection; we must come to know what it is that causes poverty on the social, economic, and cultural levels" (Gutiérrez & Müller, 2015, p. 47). In Ricoeur's philosophical framework, ethical systems have personal components; but fundamental for him is "realizing the necessity of mediating institutions." We can only act "through structures of interaction that are already there and that tend to unfold their own history that consists of inertias and innovations which are themselves sedimented in turn" (Ricoeur, 2000, p. 17). For the ethics of human dignity, person and structure are set "in creative tension with each other" so that both are transformed: "Each has its own domain but necessarily needs the other to create an intersection rather than precedence and subordination" (Ricoeur, 1981, p. 325). To implement Ricoeur, says Gutiérrez, "requires the analytic tools that are provided by the human sciences, but like all scientific thought they work with hypotheses that allow us to understand the reality they seek to explain" (Gutiérrez & Müller, 2015, p. 47).

Liberation theology insists that it is not enough simply to take notice of poor persons as others. Their "status must also be studied in detail and considered in its entirety, challenging reality. Valuable studies have made it possible to enter in a particularly fruitful way into several key aspects" of the complexities. Neoliberalism is understood more precisely as leading to "the exclusion of a part of humanity from the economic loop and from the so-called benefits of contemporary civilizations. Millions of people are converted into useless objects or into disposable objects that are thrown away after use" (Gutiérrez & Muller, 2015, p. 48). The opposite of human dignity occurs with "the dehumanization of the economy which tends to convert everything, including persons, into merchandise" (p. 49). Pradip Thomas (2010) reflects Gutiérrez's thinking, but states the issue differently for the media and poverty: The news media tend to emphasize the elite and their concerns about economics in a globalizing India. Or, in Jairo Lugo-Ocando's (2015) formulation, the elite regulate the global media, and journalism reflects this internalized ideology by reporting what is consistent with the dominant agenda.

Amartya Sen also argues for a systemic approach to poverty based on his study of the Bengal famine in 1943 in which three million people died. In his view, this enormous loss of life was unnecessary.

In *Poverty and Famines: An Essay on Entitlement and Deprivation* (1981), Sen presents data indicating the food supply in Bengal was adequate at the time. But particular groups of people such as rural landless laborers and urban service providers starved because they did not have the means to buy food, as a result of price gouging and panic buying connected to the war in the region, plus declining wages and poor food distribution as prices rose rapidly. Sen's capabilities approach, resonating with Gutiérrez and Ricoeur, focuses on the social opportunities and economic wherewithal people need to function effectively under conditions of poverty and social injustice generally. The United Nations Development Program reflects that thinking by its call for a multidimensional approach to poverty that connects inequality and exclusion with the knowledge and skills to sustain development.

For media representations, implementing the systemic version of human dignity ethics has been formidable. Reporting specific manifestations of poverty does not expose its root causes (Kendall, 2011). The systemic is easily overlooked in the United States: "The personal responsibility narrative is so strong in America: that if you haven't been successful in this country, you must've done something wrong," said Maggie Bowman, a documentary film-maker; "people think this is really a question of choice" (Savchuk, 2016, p. 2). As the media system has evolved in China, poverty and the poor are being covered more thoroughly, but sensational stories about the poor fit the demands for increasing audience size (Chen, 2013). In Redden's (2014) study of news coverage of poverty in Canada and the UK, the justice and organizational frame did appear, but typically in the alternative press in its reporting of social movements.

Two classics in US media history illustrate how the ethics of human dignity speaks to the poor and poverty in their integration following Gutiérrez. Jacob Riis's *How the Other Half Lives* in 1890 describes the squalid conditions of the poor in the slums of New York City – Irish, Italian, German, French, African, Spanish, Bohemian, Russian, Scandinavian, Chinese. Riis communicated that the tenement housing system was a notorious failure and society ought not to ignore it but fix the problems. Riis honored the dignity of those living in the slums by his judicious ethnography of their daily habits and their creative meaning making under dangerous and unhygienic conditions. His moral urgency and in-depth reporting inspired multiple reforms of lower-class housing and became a model for the tradition of muckraking journalism (Riis,

1890).[26] The media's important role in sociopolitical change, demonstrated by Riis, continues to be a demanding pursuit. Puri's (2002) *Poverty in Asia* presents research and consultations on poverty-media relations in Bangladesh, Cambodia, India, Indonesia, Pakistan, The Philippines, Thailand, and Vietnam. All these Southeast Asia countries are severely affected by poverty. One conclusion is that the media can serve as a bridge between the poor community and the government, and the media's analysis and reflections are crucial for finding solutions.

Let Us Now Praise Famous Men (Agee & Walker, 1939) is considered one of the most influential books of the twentieth century. For three months, James Agee and Walker Evans lived with poor tenant farmer families in Alabama for immersion in their context and history. Honoring the principle of dignity, Agee and Evans treated them as people, believing that "the heart, nerve, center of each of them is an unique human life." They were not presented as "tenant," "farmer," or "representative of a class," but correctly as, "each of you is that which he is." Susan Richardson of *The Chicago Reporter* echoes that commitment for covering poverty: "Nobody's life is a symbol" (Savchuk, 2016, p. 5).

In these award-winning exemplars from American journalism, Riis and Agee described the slum dwellers and tenant farmers as moral beings and expected them and everyone related to them to act accordingly. In this case study of liberation theology's perspective on the poor and poverty, the normative dimension is ubiquitous and compelling. Janet Blank-Libra (2017) puts Gutiérrez's "preferential option for the poor" to work in her argument that the ethics of empathy should be integrated into poverty-related news coverage. She regards Riis as a journalist who deliberately employed empathy to restore the poor's humanity. The ethics of human dignity in Gutiérrez affirms empathy as the journalist's moral disposition toward the neglected and suffering humans they cover. Gutiérrez, in his theological anthropology, in representing the communal and institutional context of Latin America, and in his redefining the symbolic world through such ideas as the "preferential option," presents an even more revolutionary paradigm.

---

[26] Riis's work is not free of ethnic slurs and stereotypes. Focusing on poor people without racial negatives is an ongoing challenge. Martin Gilens's research included stories on poverty published between 1950 and 1992 in *Time, Newsweek, U.S. News and World Report*. The pictures served to racialize poverty. Pictures of Blacks appeared more frequently in the least sympathetic stories (Heider, 2004).

Humanitarian Crisis in Darfur

The international news media often deal with intercultural conflict outside a nation's borders but of direct domestic concern. And in these transnational settings, typically the interests of several nations converge. Comparative research is necessary to analyze whether the news media's representations are meeting the ethical standard of human dignity. Darfur is an illustration of multiple news media involvements with their interests overlapping and sometimes in conflict. Darfur serves as a testing ground for human dignity as the fundamental principle in intercultural news (cf. Christians, Fackler, Richardson, Kreshel, & Woods, 2017, pp. 103–106, 122–123).[27]

China established diplomatic relations with Sudan in 1959, and it has been one of China's important foreign oil projects. China is a major trading partner with Sudan and South Sudan; therefore, the *People's Daily* and *China Daily* have a national interest in covering Darfur. The United Nations has called Darfur the greatest humanitarian crisis of the twenty-first century (cf. Laurent, 2010). With the UN headquarters located in New York, the coverage of its actions and deliberations on Darfur are of special importance to the *New York Times*. The BBC, with its home in the former colonizing country, pays special attention to Darfur's history and Sudanese politics.

For several hundred years, Darfur was an independent Islamic sultanate with a population of Arabs and Black African tribes – both of them Muslim. Darfur was annexed to Sudan by the British in 1916 but neglected by this colonial power. Since its independence in 1956, the Darfur region and core area around Khartoum inhabited by riverine Arabs have been embroiled in intercultural conflict (Prunier, 2005). In 1962, a civil war broke out for a decade between the Arabs residing in the north and the Africans living in the south. After eleven years of peace, another civil war erupted, this time raging on for nearly two decades. In the Second Sudanese Civil War from 1983 to 2005 – one of the longest civil wars in history – more than two million people died and millions were displaced, with many fleeing to neighboring Chad and the Central African Republic.

Bloody conflict had appeared to be calming down, when in February 2003, a rebellion occurred in Darfur, an area plagued not only by drought and desertification but also by continued tensions

---

[27] Haydar Sadig has developed the most comprehensive understanding of the history and ethics of the Darfur controversy, including strategies for peace in Sudan and South Sudan (e.g., Sadig & Guta, 2011).

between the farmers and nomads who inhabit the area. The rebels began attacking government targets, claiming that the government in Khartoum was discriminating against them because of their Black African identity. The Sudanese government retaliated by employing local Arab militias to quash the uprising – nicknamed the *Janjaweed* (translated as "the evil horsemen"). After the government conducted air strikes on targeted villages, the *Janjaweed* descended on the area, raping and murdering anyone left alive. To ensure that no one returned, the militias burned any remaining structures and poisoned the water supply. By backing the militias, the Sudanese government has been engaging in ethnic cleansing while denying responsibility for the human rights violations. Khartoum claims the violence is due to what it calls "tribal conflicts" (Lippman, 2007).

In research that is now a classic in its comprehensiveness and depth, *The Geopolitics of Representation in Foreign News* (Mody, 2010) compares the news coverage of Darfur from seven countries between 2003 and 2005.[28] Darfur was chosen as an icon of armed conflict since the end of the Cold War, and the scene of the first genocide of the twenty-first century.[29] Using the framework of this chapter on human dignity, the news media that are included for comparison are two newspapers, the Chinese-language *People's Daily* and the *New York Times*, and two online media operations, the English-language *China Daily Online* and the *BBC.co.uk*.[30]

The Geopolitics of Representation in Foreign News reinforces important findings in comparative journalism studies. News organizations are limited

---

[28] For history and background of media coverage of Darfur – news reports, editorials, interviews with correspondents – see Savelsberg (2015).

[29] Wasserman (2018) is correct in his overview of South African media, politics, and society after apartheid that global media studies generally "have tended to marginalize knowledge production from the South by relegating it to the domain of 'case studies,' 'examples,' 'comparative studies,' or 'area studies.'" Instead of focusing on international media contexts "as a peculiarity or special example," they should be "approached from an interrelational perspective, namely as a social, political, and cultural phenomenon that has both local specificity and global relevance" (p. 167). Interpreting media coverage of Darfur in terms of human dignity as a universal principle aims to meet Wasserman's criterion.

[30] For her comparative cross-national research project of news reports and editorial columns for twenty-six months (January 2003 through February 2005), Bela Mody (2010) selected ten representative news organizations from the Global North and South, privately owned and government owned, with varying levels of national interest in Darfur: China, *People's Daily* and *China Daily*; South Africa, *Mail & Guardian*; Egypt, *Al-Ahram*; France, *Le Monde*; UK, *Guardian*; U.S., *New York Times* and *Washington Post*; websites: UK, *BBC.co.uk* and Qatar, *English.AlJazeera.net*.

in presenting international news because of their preoccupation with events that have direct domestic linkage. News outlets hesitate to cover stories that offend their sources of revenue or that show these sources in a negative light. With China's government giving priority to good relations with Sudan and South Sudan for reasons of commerce, the *People's Daily* and *China Daily Online* restricted themselves to hard news stories. (As evidence of its national interest, China protected Sudan from sanctions for the Darfur massacre in the UN Security Council). Mody concludes that national interests are still a significant predictor of news coverage in all countries. She includes both the *New York Times* and *BBC.co.uk* on her national interests list, despite their claim, based on the monitorial role, "that they are the watchdogs against state abuse of power" (2010, p. 322).

The four news media showed different emphases because of their location, ownership structures, and intended audience. The charge of genocide made by UN Resident and Humanitarian Coordinator Mukesh Kapila, and then by the US government, was featured primarily in the *New York Times*. The *BBC.com.uk* most often identified race and ethnicity as the causes of the civil war, a sensitivity perhaps because of the BBC's home location in the predominantly White Caucasian North. The *People's Daily,* with a no-questions-asked policy, quoted only two news sources, the Khartoum government and the African Union, for its Chinese-speaking domestic audience. The *China Daily Online* with its international English-speaking audience frequently quoted United Nations sources. Among the causes of the conflict, the *People's Daily* named the Darfuri rebels most frequently, with the other three news media pointing regularly to the Khartoum government.

Despite such differences in nuance and detail, Mody concludes that the predominant emphasis for these news organizations was the day-to-day brutality. The conflict was bloody and dramatic in character, drawing the news to the sensational – gang rape, bombings, murder, burned-out villages, children slaughtered in daylight. As typical of international journalism as a whole, Mody calls these news organizations "the one-eyed Cyclops" who addresses one major crisis at a time as a series of visible events. In Mody's research, all of them were weak on the humanitarian dimension of the crisis. None reported it with the fullness that the ethics of human dignity requires. The *New York Times* emphasized the dramatically political and included the economic. *China Daily Online* and the *People's Daily* were also focused on the political and economic. *BBC.com.uk* scored well on Mody's comprehensiveness index but was preoccupied with the complicated politics, and only included the economic when it was directly relevant.

Serious reporting on occasion did overcome the hurdles and meet the human dignity principle. The journalism newsletter "Tyndall Report" (tyndallreport.com), however, documents the unacceptable coverage of US television: "In 2004, for the entire year, ABC News had eighteen minutes on Darfur, NBC five minutes for the year, and CBS three minutes." In contrast, Martha Stewart received 130 minutes of coverage by the three networks. CNN, Fox News, NBC, MSNBC, ABC, and CBS together ran fifty-five times as many stories about Michael Jackson as they did about Darfur (Christians et al., 2017; cf. Ricchiardi, 2005).

The ethics of human dignity insists on thick description, on seeing beneath the surface to the heart of the matter. In exercising the facilitative role, the news media give a full-scale interpretation, disclosing the attitudes, culture, and language of the abused without simplistic judgments. As Michael McDevitt (2010) puts it, in contrast to the watchdog role, journalism in its facilitative role mobilizes the public conscience by identification with the victims. Human dignity is a guiding principle in which ethnicities and religions are respected rather than polarized. Those following it recognize, with Paulo Freire, that violence from the oppressor and counter-violence in return from the oppressed will continue unless the dehumanization that drives it can be overcome (Sadig & Guta, 2011, p. 616). For the ethics of human dignity, no political solutions are sustainable without good faith, and it begins with goodwill public communication collaborating with education in the schools. In S. Keen's terms, "We first kill people with our minds, before we kill them with weapons" (quoted in Sadig & Guta, 2011, p. 616). The ethics of human dignity teaches us that modifications in language and attitudes are required for changes to occur in policy and institutions.

Despite the difficulties of application, human dignity serves as the same normative standard across nations – for the *New York Times*, the *BBC.com.uk*, as well as for the *China Daily* and the *People's Daily*, and for all ten news organizations in Mody's study.

American Indians at Wounded Knee

The classic case of Wounded Knee in the United States is a third illustration of how the ethics of human dignity works in intercultural communication involving various media.[31] The Sioux Indian Reservation at Pine Ridge, South Dakota, was a site of gloom and bitterness in 1973. The poverty was relentless and health care was substandard. The suicide and alcoholism rates were high. The tribal leader, Dick Wilson, was one source of the frustration. He seemed more interested in helping his family and friends than improving conditions on the reservation for those he was elected to serve. A group of Native Americans had clashed with the police in nearby Custer, South Dakota, three weeks earlier. They protested the light, second-degree manslaughter charge against a White man accused of stabbing Raymond Yellow Thunder to death. Tensions on the reservation had been growing steadily ever since.

During the night of February 27, 1973, American Indian Movement (AIM) activists moved inside the Pine Ridge Reservation and occupied the site of Wounded Knee. AIM leaders Dennis Banks and Russell Means seized the local trading post, museum, church, and other buildings nearby – along with several hostages from the few White families living in the area. The law-and-order apparatus was put on emergency status. Already by the following morning, the Federal Bureau of Investigation (FBI), the Bureau of Indian Affairs (BIA), and federal marshals had surrounded Wounded Knee. A siege had begun. The government's strategy was to seal off supplies and force a peaceful surrender.

As AIM anticipated, media coverage skyrocketed. No longer were local media sporadically covering the marches in Custer. Journalism crews from across America, and around the world, arrived to cover the dramatic story staged for television. For the first time in US history, broadcast news carried the story every weekday night for ten weeks. This kind of continuous coverage was not duplicated again until two decades later (for the Persian Gulf War 1990–1991, and then the O. J. Simpson criminal trial in 1995).

The problems at Wounded Knee were momentous. To make the issues public, the two hundred Native Americans set up bunkers and determined

---

[31] For a full account of Wounded Knee and Russell Means, see Christians, Fackler, & Ferré (2012, chap. 12). For Wounded Knee as a case study for ethics, see "Case 17: Ten Weeks at Wounded Knee," Christians et al. (2017). For the legal background, see *Bury My Heart at Wounded Knee* (1972) by University of Illinois librarian Dee Brown. For the historical and cultural context, see the University of Illinois publication *The Politics of Hallowed Ground: Wounded Knee and the Struggle for Indian Sovereignty* (Gonzalez & Cook-Lynn, 1998). On May 11, 2009, "Wounded Knee" was shown on PBS as a documentary in its film series of five episodes on Native Americans, *American Experience – We Shall Remain*.

they would hold their ground by violence if necessary. Most news commentary and editorials supported them, and public opinion polls were also strongly in their favor. AIM had chosen a nationally recognized location: the slaughter of Chief Big Foot at this site by the US Seventh Cavalry in 1890. This was the last open hostility between the US government and Native Indians until now – eighty-three years later. According to Russell Means in his autobiography, *Where White Men Fear to Tread*:

> Wounded Knee would always remain the haunting symbol of the white man's murderous treachery and of our nation's stoic grief. At Wounded Knee, on ground consecrated with the blood of our ancestors, we would make our stand. At Wounded Knee, as nowhere else, the spirits of Big Foot and his martyred people would protect us. (1995, p. 253)

Small arms fire erupted regularly between the two groups, and after four weeks it turned injurious. On March 11, an FBI agent was shot and paralyzed from the waist down, and a Native American injured, as gunfire erupted at a roadblock outside town. A marshal was seriously wounded on March 2, and two Indians were killed as the armed conflict wore on into April. Finally during the tenth week, on May 6, the Native Americans negotiated an armistice and ended the conflict. The blockade had depleted their supplies, and the lack of tangible progress had eroded their morale to the near-breaking point.

An astonishing 75 percent of the US population followed the news on television, but American Indian attorney Ramon Roubideaux was unimpressed: "Only the sensational stuff got on the air. The facts never really emerged that this was an uprising against Washington's Bureau of Indian Affairs and its puppet government here at Pine Ridge" (Hickey, 1973, p. 34). A young Oglala Sioux chastised the news media for framing the confrontation as a "Wild West gunfight between the marshals and Indians" (p. 34). Some reporters did disclose the multiple meanings beneath the surface. CBS's Richard Threlkeld understood that AIM was searching for a revolution in Indian attitudes. NBC's Fred Briggs used charts and photos to describe the trail of broken treaties that reduced the vast Indian territory to a few small tracts of land called "reservations." ABC's Ron Miller examined life on the Pine Ridge Reservation itself by getting inside its politics and culture, and describing what was happening through the natives' eyes. But, on balance, journalists followed the technological imperatives of television, showing the battle action. Journalists on the scene did not fully comprehend the subtleties or historical nuances of tribal government. Reporters complained that their more precise accounts often were redacted and distorted by heavy editing. The siege ended from bone-deep weariness, not because the issues were fully aired or understood.

The ten weeks were an exceptional opportunity for journalists to put the ethics of human dignity to work, enabling the oppressed to speak a true word out of a critical consciousness. But most journalists were in little-understood territory and instead were caught up in the daily routines of quoting accessible sources and finding attractive visuals.

Wounded Knee is typically considered a turning point in American Indian history. After nearly two centuries as US citizens, this people-group began establishing its voice as the principle of human dignity requires. The protestors and their supporters at Wounded Knee confirmed, in effect, "we are Indians; we should be who we are and we need to communicate it." The AIM leaders' decisions and actions during the ten-week occupation were often controversial, nonetheless; Wounded Knee is typically said to have sparked a revival of Native American languages, culture, religion, and education – those domains emphasized by the media when their facilitative role is given priority.

Russell Means reflected on Wounded Knee and its aftermath in more complicated terms. He had participated in protest marches many times before Pine Ridge. There were confrontations in the 1960s at Puget Sound during the Northwest Coast Fish-ins and with the Alcatraz prison occupation. He and Native Americans occupied Mount Rushmore, declaring to the nation that this was the sacred ground of the Lakota. AIM protested at Plymouth Rock on Thanksgiving Day 1970, the 350th anniversary of the Pilgrims' landing. Means and Banks organized the "Longest Walk," a march on Washington to oppose government sterilization programs for Native American women. The occupations, marches, and protest assemblies at historic sites caught people's attention, but often they veered into violence before the voice of the Native Americans was heard clearly and completely.

Russell Means's own pathway and thinking illustrate how the ethics of human dignity can be fulfilled for minority cultures. He abandoned the protest strategy and began using other forms of communication that he thought would represent the human dignity question more effectively. He turned to film, for example, to tell the Native American story, initiating an acting career as the title character Chingachgook in *The Last of the Mohicans*. He became the voice of Chief Powhatan in Disney's *Pocahontas*. He starred in the HBO documentary *Paha Sapa: The Struggle for the Black Hills* and in *Black Cloud*, a film about a Navajo Olympic athlete. He began to act in several television broadcasts, including such documentaries as "Incident at Oglala" and "Images of Indians." He narrated the video about the 1973 protest, "Wounded Heart: Pine Ridge and the Sioux." He opened a production business for creating CD-ROMs, short films and documentaries, magazines, books, television shows, and an animated children's series. He narrated the music album on Soar Records "Electric Warrior."[32] Through Means's leadership, public communication in its various formats began exhibiting the media's facilitative mission.

Means returned to Pine Ridge to live and helped build a health clinic on Indian lands at Porcupine, South Dakota. A grant from the Corporation for Public Broadcasting funded a new AM radio station for Pine Ridge. Education, he concluded, taught human dignity more deeply than did arms and protest slogans behind bunkers. With the support of Open Hand Studios, he emphasized schools on the reservations, with special attention to teaching Lakota youth their native language and culture. All his projects have slowed since he died of throat cancer on October 12, 2012. But they leave behind for minority cultures a legacy for implementing in their own language the ethics of human dignity.

Because of and parallel to Means's legacy, American Indians have experienced a growing sense of tribal sovereignty.[33] By federal Regulatory Acts and Supreme Court Affirmations, the rights of Indian tribes to govern their own affairs have been established in principle. But tribal sovereignty is a cultural matter far deeper than self-government. It means tribal identity, rootedness in history, and shared values within geographic boundaries. In the sovereignty that Means spoke of poetically, the land embodies American Indian identity and culture. Means recognized that beliefs about the natural world held his people together, and that ceremonies and religion are not marginal but central to a community's distinctiveness. AIM's strategy of loose collaboration reflected the traditional values of Oglala elders who lead by consensus, not majority opinion. The end is not simply to create a winning idea or strategy to be pursued, by force if necessary, but to increase harmony among people and with the natural order: "Instead of believing that the universe depends on what we think, we must use our hearts to achieve

---

[32] For a complete filmography of Russell Means's acting and other media work, see www.russellmeans.com

[33] For a study of how four tribal newspapers have dealt with tribal sovereignty in similar terms between 1995 and 1999, see Leow and Mella (2005).

harmony with our fellow creatures" (Means, 1995, 414). Put another way, public communication that is educational can move human existence from what Means calls Eurocentricity back to its proper place of worthiness that all humans share.

For Russell Means, tribal sovereignty has meant for Native American identity what Gutiérrez's preferential option means for Latin America's poor. Means's activism has inspired other Indian struggles, such as those of the Miskito in Nicaragua. Under Means's leadership, the norm of human dignity is reflected in the voices of the Native American people-group. AIM and Means are not the last word on cultural transformation, but their legacy gives hope and direction to the generations following.

Global Media Monitoring Project

A fourth application of the ethics of human dignity is the Global Media Monitoring Project (GMMP), the largest research study in history of gender in the world's media.[34] Every five years since 1995, GMMP research has examined women's identity in the media compared to that of men, as well as gender bias in news media content. The fifth study in 2015 of news coverage in four media formats – radio, television, newspapers, internet – was done on March 25 in 114 countries. The project included hundreds of research volunteers, from members of local community organizations to university students and media workers. The 2015 research monitored 22,136 stories published, broadcast, or tweeted by 2,030 media organizations, written or presented by 26,610 journalists and containing 45,402 people interviewed and/or subjects of the story. The methodology has been refined in each research cycle, but the structure for 2015 was similar to that in 1995 to chart progress and make comparisons (*Global Media Monitoring Project 2015*).

The idea for a one-day study of the portrayal of women in the global media was first discussed in 1994 at the "Women Empowering Communication" conference in Bangkok. From the beginning, a grassroot research instrument was considered essential. To create media awareness and develop media-monitoring skills on an international level, using local talent was chosen over professional research teams. The methodology and results of the first study were published as *Global*

---

[34] For elaboration and references, see "Case 16" of *Media Ethics: Cases and Moral Reasoning*, 10th ed. (Christians, Fackler, Richardson, Kreshel, & Woods, 2017, pp. 111–114, 123–124).

Media Monitoring: Women's Participation in the News. This was presented to the United Nations Fourth World Conference on Women in
Beijing in September 1995 and confirmed there as an effective implementation of the Beijing Declaration and Platform for Action, Strategic Object
J2: "Promote a balanced and non-stereotypical portrayal of women in the
media."

Bringing media accountability into the struggle for gender equality was
the original impetus for the GMMP. In the language of this chapter,
GMMP's purpose is to enable the media to fulfill their facilitative duties
regarding gender following the principle of human dignity. In GMMP's
terms, the news media are the most influential source of ideas and information for most people around the world: "Who and what appears in the
news and how people and events are portrayed matters ... The media – as
both powerful institutions and power-defining mechanisms – are fundamental to the ways in which women's status and gender inequalities are
reflected, understood and potentially changed" (*Global Media
Monitoring Project 2015*, p. 1). The GMMP seeks to have the following
statement adopted and implemented by media organizations everywhere:
"Fair gender portrayal is a professional and ethical aspiration, similar to
respect for accuracy, fairness and honesty" (White, 2009). The first standard, "fair gender portrayal," belongs to the facilitative role with the same
decisiveness as "accuracy, fairness and honesty" typically define the monitorial role.

GMMP 2015 showed that women are dramatically underrepresented
in the news. A comparison of the 2015 results with the previous GMMP
studies (1995, 2000, 2005, 2010) revealed that change in the gender
dimensions of news media has been small and slow across the two decades. Only 24 percent of news subjects – the people who are interviewed
or whom the news is about in print, radio, and television – are female.
Women's relative invisibility in traditional news media has crossed over
into digital news delivery platforms; only 26 percent of the people in news
websites and Twitter news feeds are women. Women's points of view are
rarely heard in the topics that dominate the news agenda. In news about
politics and government, women are only 16 percent of the people
included. Even in stories that affect women profoundly, such as gender-
based violence, it is the male voice (64 percent of news subjects) that
prevails. Stories about economic development (59 percent) reinforce gender stereotypes. Only 4 percent of news stories or editorials clearly challenge gender stereotypes (a mere 1 percent improvement over the past
decade). When women do make the news, it is primarily as "stars" or

"ordinary people" not as persons of authority. As newsmakers, women are underrepresented in professional categories, and as authorities and experts they are barely noticed. While the study found a few examples of exemplary gender-balanced and gender-sensitive journalism, it demonstrated an overall glaring deficit in the news media globally, with the female half of the world's population minimally present (*Global Media Monitoring Project 2015*).

Among its key findings, GMMP 2015 reveals that the rate of progress toward gender parity in the media has stalled over the past twenty-five years:

Why has the slow improvement noted in the decade after 1995 not continued? Is the standstill since 2005 due to a slowdown in gender and media activism, to a reduction of training opportunities within media organizations, to decreased editorial or policy emphasis on gender equality, to a diminished level of public debate on the need for media accountability? GMMP research does not answer those questions, but it is evidence against the ... unsubstantiated claim that gender equality has been taken on board by the media and "things have changed." (*Global Media Monitoring Project* 2015, p. 3; cf. De Francisco & Palczewski, 2007)

The results of GMMP have been used in multiple ways by gender and communication groups worldwide, for teaching research methods, media literacy education for public audiences, advocacy with local stations and newspapers, and lobbying work with nongovernmental organizations. In Malta, the Gender Advisory Committee of the Broadcasting Authority uses the results of the GMMP in its research and training programs. In Jamaica, upon receiving the 2010 report, the Broadcasting Commission promoted its value for communication policy development. In Senegal, the Inter-African Network for Women, Media, Gender and Development uses the GMMP methodology for research and training in francophone West and Central Africa. In Argentina, the GMMP reports have inspired the formation of a network of journalists for gender-responsive media. The Arab Human Development Report published by the United Nations uses the GMMP reports as a resource, and the studies' results are included in the work of the United Nations International Research and Training Institute for the Advancement of Women. The GMMP helps build local and regional solidarity around different interventions related to gender and media, such as a recent study by Bolivia's Fundación Colectivo Cabildeo on the portrayal of Aymara women in the media (*Global Media Monitoring Project* 2015, p. 7).

Summary

GMMP makes it obvious that old ideas of authority with diminished voices for women get in the way of new ides of community and leadership (Turley, 2004). The project covers roughly 57 percent of the world's surface. The data are methodologically rigorous and broad enough in scope that media executives cannot ignore the results, and they provide instructive materials for training journalists. Basing news reports on scientific studies such as this one, rather than on informal opinion, helps give journalism credibility in both its monitorial and facilitative roles (*Global Media Monitoring Project 2015*, p. 7).

The news media's facilitative role recognizes that human lives are culturally complex and therefore open to multiple interpretations. Cross-cultural research such as GMMP, replicated over time, is indispensable for media narrative to reflect these complexities. For Norman Denzin (1997), ethnographic accounts ought to "exhibit representational adequacy, including the absence of racial, class, and gender stereotyping" (p. 283). GMMP, in form and content, inspires studies of that depth and coherence. For global media ethics, over its two decades GMMP has been an exemplar of seeking gender equality in public discourse. When media and communication programs include the ethics of human dignity in their curricula and media institutions give the principle priority, gender equality in communication technologies will continue to receive the emphasis it deserves.

CONCLUSION

This chapter on the news media's facilitative role, following the ethical principle of human dignity, is relentlessly transnational. The research is culturally specific and comparative. Theories are grounded in the ethnographic. Communication theory and practice on the whole value tolerance across genders and respect religions and unusual cultures. Diversities in language and culture are the global vision, with media professionals challenged to represent them precisely. What then is the status of the ethical principle of human dignity? In the people-group globalism that characterizes the facilitative role, relativism is the recurrent question and frequently an objection. The relativism issue is of interest philosophically, and it needs to be addressed for this chapter to be credible.

Cultural relativism is attractive and ordinarily presumed within the people-group variations of human life. This chapter has learned from and emulates Franz Boas's landmark book *The Mind of Primitive Man* (1911), in his demonstrating how cultural relativism debunks the idea of Western superiority over less-developed societies. Boas recognized that scientific methods required an immersion in native languages and local cultures to understand them on their own terms. With geographical space a vast universe of differences, the international news media have moved with Boas's ethnography from an unconscious ethnocentricity toward relativity (Kroeber, 1933, p. 11). For the Boas legacy, as with this chapter, cultural relativity is a critical step in de-Westernizing global media ethics.

But in affirming cultural relativity in the research and journalism of this chapter, it has not been understood as philosophical relativism. Cultural relativism is typically redefined as moral relativism; that is, moral principles are presumed to have no objective application independent of the societies within which they are constituted. In the researchers' and journalists' passion for diversity, for the local, cultural relativity sometimes slides into philosophical relativism. But this chapter does not confuse cultural diversity with moral relativism. Cultural and moral relativism are distinct categories, and it is a logical fallacy to conflate them. The demands of cultural diversity cannot become moral relativism without making a category mistake (cf. Paul, Miller, & Paul, 1994).

Cultural relativism in lingual and sociological terms does not preclude moral standards (Kluckholm, 1949). Because some customs are relative, that does not mean all are relative. While there are disagreements over policies and interpretations, these differences do not themselves mean that no judgments can be made about historical events – the Holocaust, Stalinism, genocide, genital mutilation, apartheid in South Africa, Syrian president Assad using cyanide gas on his own citizens. Plato's allegory of the cave in his *Republic* teaches us not to confuse the fire with the sun. Under conditions of war, virtually all nations give the Red Cross safety. As noted, for curbing ethnocentric research and news, cultural relativity has been indispensable; but in the moral domain it is overwrought, misused, and erroneous.

One defense of this chapter's foregrounding the normative status of human dignity is that cultural relativism ultimately founders on Mannheim's paradox, summarized this way: relativists claim that truth is culture bound, but they cannot proclaim relativism without rising above it, and they cannot rise above it without giving it up (Geertz, 1973, chap. 8; cf. Mannheim, 1936, pt. II). Hilary Putnam (1981) agrees with Mannheim philosophically. In his important review – from Plato's *Protagoras* to Kuhn's *Structure of Scientific Revolutions* – of what Putnam calls relativism's inconsistency, he concludes with this summary: "If all is relative, then the relative is relative too" (p. 120). In elaborating on Bahktin's philosophy of the act, De Miranda (2002) argues regarding relativism:

The excuse that one cannot pass judgment on the cultural or even individual practices of the other carries within it the biased connotation of judgment that it can only be effective if it resorts to a force that does violence to the other. If cultures are considered self-contained entities and made inexpugnable by a hermetically sealed local level, cross-cultural ethical debates become impossible. (p. 214)

Another argument regarding relativism's circularity appears typically in this form: when cultural relativity is misconstrued as moral relativism, we usually do not face up to the pernicious politics that insists on the prerogatives of a nation, caste, religion, or tribe. Cultural relativism turned into a moral claim is stultifying. If moral action is thought to depend on a society's norms, then "one must obey the norms of one's society, and to diverge from those norms is to act immorally. Such a view promotes conformity and leaves us no room for moral reform or improvement" (Velasquez et al., 2009).

While the paradox of relativism does not address all the important issues, for this chapter's conclusion it is the context for clarifying the normative character of the human dignity principle (Christians, 2011a). This chapter is an exercise in moral realism, a realism based on the characteristics that are both common and unique to human beings. In this realism, as demonstrated from human dignity theory to the Global Media Monitoring Project, the ethicist's primary obligation is getting inside the way humans arbitrate their presence in the world.[35] This ontological realism locates ethics in the human community and therefore ethical principles are viable transnationally. In terms of ontological realism, through the intrinsic self-reflexivity of language, we arbitrate our values and establish the differences and similarities of our worldviews (Wuthnow, 1987).

As the norm of human dignity is worked out in this chapter, differences among cultures are evaluated rather than considering all practices equally justified as in relativism. In both intra- and intercultural circumstances,

[35] Martha Nussbaum's "In Defense of Universal Values" (2000, chap. 1) follows a formally parallel methodology. As elaborated in Chapter 6, her comparative research on women in India identifies common values that are evident from people's daily efforts to meet their basic needs. In their daily existence, social goods emerge that people are capable of achieving. The multiple ways of achieving these aspirations overlap, and that means it should be possible to work out ideas of what all people are capable of doing to flourish.

propositions can be translated from one setting or language to another and be intelligible (Christians & Ward, 2013).[36] Instead of being limited to the value-clarification procedures of moral relativism, this ethics of humanistic universals, based on ontological realism, makes judgments on particular cases and has the capacity to resolve moral disagreements. In conflicts over media coverage of international events, if ethical statements are understood to represent cognitions and not intuitions, one can distinguish self-interest from the common good. This chapter repositions media ethics into the complications of the digital age by integrating philosophical realism with cultural interpretation.

Many of the case studies referenced or elaborated in this chapter are particular geographically: Nigeria, Colombia, Darfur, Bangkok, Wounded Knee, Brazil, China and India, as examples. In their facilitative role, the media in various parts of the world act upon them with different nuances. Themes such as poverty, gender, and race reverberate on four continents with divergent intensity and social form. But the core idea in human dignity works its way through all these variations of time and place and is not strange or esoteric in doing so.

---

[36] For a comprehensive review of the theory and issues regarding ontological realism and the media, see Christians and Ward (2013).

5

The Ethics of Nonviolence

Nonviolence is an ethical principle grounded in the sacredness of life. Flickers of peace are emerging on our media ethics agenda, but only glimmers compared to major struggles with truth, human dignity, and social justice. In Kaarle Nordenstreng's analysis of journalism codes of ethics in Europe, one of the fifty, that of the Latvian Union of Journalists, included peace as a fundamental value, while all fifty made truth a journalism standard (2008, pp. 65–66; cf. Laitila, 1995). It is important to understand the practical side of nonviolence, and significant research has been testing it in war reporting. But peace journalism globally is understudied. Violence in entertainment still needs an analysis from cultural and historical perspectives. Global terrorism is a complicated phenomenon based on and driven by media technologies. Alongside the need for this crucial research by media academics and professionals, advancing the concept of nonviolence intellectually is a necessary task. This chapter furthers this project by giving the nonviolence principle theoretical justification.

To ensure that the ethics of nonviolence is credible philosophically is more complicated than mapping out the different ways of understanding nonviolence. As philosopher Robert Holmes puts it, for nonviolence to be "plausibly defended as a moral position ... the charges of its rational unsustainability" must be contradicted (2013, pp. 151, 169). The problem of violence at the international level does need to be advanced "by key appropriate action" (p. 151). However, a conceptual framework is essential for identifying and placing in perspective the moral issues at stake, in order for the ethical principle of nonviolence to have a permanent place in the global media ethics literature.

THEORISTS AND THEORIZING

Over the past century, theorists of nonviolence have emerged in various parts of the world.[1] These include Lao Tzu in China, Leo Tolstoy in Russia, Mohandas Gandhi in India, Martin Luther King Jr. in the United States, Al-Ustadh Mahmoud Muhammad Taha in Sudan, Johan Galtung in Norway, Václav Havel in Czechoslovakia, and the Dalai Lama in Tibet. Important to ethics, nonviolence as a theory emphasizes non-violent means, rather than adopting what are noble ends and then devising whatever means are effective in achieving them. Theorists of nonviolence insist, from a moral perspective, that we identify nonviolent strategies and then pursue only such ends as arise out of them.

Exemplary Theorists

Lao Tzu

Taoism is particularly applicable to the ethics of nonviolence because of its prominence in the violence-prone fourth century B.C. It was developed into a philosophical system when the regions that now constitute China constantly fought one another to become the dominant authority. Taoists in that era were preoccupied with the motivations and social structure behind the violence. They sought ways to live productively in societies of conflict. The legendary Lao Tzu was the keeper of the archives of the royal court of Zhou and, with Chuang Tzu, is the major figure in originating Taoism. Lao Tzu's *Tao Te Ching* (2005) is the commonly accepted first statement of the *Tao*, the central mystical term; Chuang Tzu's biography *Chuang Tzu* (1964) presents it poetically.

When humans are merged with the *Tao*, they are at one with nature, both one's innermost nature and the force of nature we experience every-where (Lao Tzu, 2005, p. xv). In this sense, "all human actions become as spontaneous and mindless as those of the natural world" (Chuang Tzu, 1964, p. 6):

For Lao Tzu, *Tao* is a formless mysticism that gives life to all creation and is in itself inexhaustible. The Chinese character pronounced as *Tao* contains two parts – a head (actually an "eye in a head") and a walking foot meaning "to go." Together they mean "the way" (both physically and philosophically/metaphorically) or "the path or road" (Lao Tzu, 2005, p. xiv; cf. Lin Yutang, 1948, p. 5). *Tao* is an energy that

---

[1] Earlier versions of this chapter were published as "Nonviolence in Philosophical and Religious Ethics" in 2007 and as "Nonviolence in Philosophical and Media Ethics" in 2010.

guides human action. *Tao* is within a Self and gradually evolves in the Self. (Christians, 2010b, p. 24)

For Chuang Tzu, we should tune into the harmony and balance within ourselves and the larger world, instead of living by a value system of individual identity and reputation that is only a small part of our significance in the universe. In other words, Lao Tzu asserts that human beings are at peace with others, society, the world, and the universe only when they liberate themselves from attachments to the external. Balance and harmony within frees us from struggling with things both good and bad that have no eternity. To live humanly in an era of constant war over territory and wealth, Lao Tzu pleads with his followers to forsake the value system that disturbs harmony within by twisting our behaviors and distorting our intentions. For Lao Tzu, the eternal *Tao* has no name:

If those who rule would grasp it, everything in the world would honor them, heaven and earth would join to rain sweet dew on the people without a command being given ... The *Tao* does nothing, but leaves nothing undone. If kings and lords understand this, all things would transform themselves. Transformed, old desires would be stilled by a simplicity without name. Released from desires, we find peace. And the world settles itself. (Lao Tzu, 2005, chaps. 32, 37)

In this legacy, humans are an indivisible whole, a vital organic unity with multi-sided moral, mental, and physical capacities. The body, mind, and heart are indivisibly linked and developed in concert with one another. Even deeper than political strategies toward peace is the profound educational need to reach our inner being to awaken the higher elements (Huang, 2007). When we are harmonious within ourselves, we are able to see the whole picture of how our being in relation with others spreads to compassion for others and oneness with the eternal.

Taoist philosophy formulates a social policy in enigmatic terms: "The Taoist sage has no ambitions, therefore he can never fail; he who never fails always succeeds; and he who always succeeds is all-powerful." *Tao Te Ching* adds such practical queries as these: "Why are people starving? Because the rulers eat up the money in taxes. Why are the people rebellious? Because the rulers interfere too much" (www.chebucto.ns.ca/Philosophy/Taichi/lao.html). Taoism's quest is a society that does not hurt the harmony within its people and that resonates with the harmony in nature. Education based on it promotes teaching and learning that recognizes everyone's uniqueness by bringing our inner nature into its fullness. Taoism pursues our internal harmony within the strident voices of violence under such labels as "efficiency," "structure," and "management."

Holistic education inspires students to be at one with themselves and reality, so that their life-world is a better place physically and spiritually.[2]

Taoism's influence on Tolstoy is well documented. Derk Bodde (1950) concludes: "Among all the intellectual figures of the nineteenth century, there was probably no one, outside of the narrow circle of sinologists and others whose lives were linked with China through personal circumstances, who read as widely and intensively on that country as did Tolstoy" (p. 6). More than thirty books from and about China are referenced in various forms in Tolstoy's writings. His interest in China followed his religious crisis in the mid-1870s; at first he focused on Buddhism, but his quest for moral understanding drove him to Chinese sages and intellectuals across history, including correspondence with the philosopher Gu Hongming and with compatriots of Lao Tzu. From Tolstoy's known reading of ten books on Taoism and his letters and disciples, Bodde concludes: "Lao Tzu was Tolstoy's favorite among the sages of antiquity" (p. 8). As outlined in chaps. 5 and 6 of Bodde's *Tolstoy and China*, Tolstoy's anarchism and distrust of government are similar to Lao Tzu's, and his nonviolent resistance follows the Taoist idea of "non-action."

Lev Nikolayevich Tolstoy

The Russian writer Leo Tolstoy (1828–1910) is known as one of the greatest authors of all time. His novels *War and Peace* (1869) and *Karenina* (1877) set the world standard for realist fiction (cf. Orwin, 2002, pt. 1). Tolstoy's semi-autobiographical *Sevastopol Sketches* (1855) is based on his military service as a young cadet in the Crimean War. "This was the turning point in his life when he witnessed" a ruthless and meaningless destruction of human life. "His dairies while serving in the Caucasus are filled with the horrors of war." Tolstoy "decided he would dedicate his life to the stupendous cause of eradicating the law of violence" (Tahir, 2012, pp. 347–348). In 1879, he wrote the monumental *A Confession*, describing in detail the revolution in his ideas from the depressing agony and qualms of conscience by the end of the 1970s, despite his international fame, "to a new type of religion of his own." That religion for him had to be one of "nonviolence and non-resistance to evil or Pacifism or Christian Anarchism" (Tahir, 2012, p. 348). Three of his essays are especially significant on this new religion, that is, *What I Believe, Religion and Morality,* and *What Is Religion and Wherein Lies*

---

[2] This section on Taoism and holistic education is dependent on Huang, 2007.

Its Essence? He developed his views in detail in two major books, namely, *The Law of Love and the Law of Violence* and *The Kingdom of God Is Within You*.

In *A Confession*, Tolstoy sees the first step in breaking the vicious circle of violence as

> simple and natural for working people, particularly the agricultural workers, who in Russia, as in the rest of the world, form a majority ... to say to those they regard as their leaders, "leave us in peace! If you emperors, presidents, generals, judges, bishops, professors, and other learned men need armies, navies, universities, ballots, synods, conservatories, prisons, gallows and guillotines, do it all yourselves. Collect your own taxes, judge, execute and imprison among yourselves, murder people in war, but do it all yourselves and leave us in peace because we need none of it, we no longer wish to participate in all these useless and above all evil deeds. (1987/1882, pp. 178–179)

Tolstoy believed that the most tyrannical and "despotic regime may be brought to terms by nonviolent civil disobedience, that is, non-payment of taxes, refusal to obey laws, and declining every sort of government service. All these tactics, taken together would paralyze the political structure based on oppression and injustice" (Tahir, 2012, p. 349):

> Freedom from the evil which torments and corrupts men will be attained, not by strengthening and preserving the existing regimes ... It will be attained only when each one of us (the majority of people), without thinking and worrying about the consequences to ourselves or others, conduct our lives in a particular way, not for the sake of some social organization, but simply for the sake of fulfilling, for one's own life, the law of love that does not permit violence under any circumstances. (Tolstoy, 1987/1882, pp. 205–206)

Tolstoy had a vast number of followers during his lifetime "both inside and outside Russia; his ideas influenced his countrymen to such an extent that Lenin himself was compelled to declare Tolstoy responsible for the failure of the first revolutionary campaign in 1905." However, his "commanding influence over a substantial segment of the Russian population fell somewhat into decline after the bloody events" of 1905 and early 1906 (Tahir, 2012, p. 357). By resorting to arms in place of nonviolent action, protestors "stopped doing what had destabilized the regime and gave the government the kind of foe it knew how to trounce" (Ackerman & Duvall, 2000, p. 54). Writing shortly afterward, Tolstoy commended the political achievements of the revolution, but "grieved for those who, imagining that they are making [a revolution], are destroying it. The violence of the old regime will only be destroyed by non-participation in violence, and not at all by the new and foolish acts of violence which are now being committed" (Tolstoy, *Letters*, vol. 2, p. 659).

The failure of Tolstoy's strategy in the Russian Revolution did not discredit it as a revolutionary theory. Tolstoy's immediate successor was Mohandas Gandhi, who put Tolstoy's political ideals to work in India. In 1908, Tolstoy wrote *A Letter to a Hindu*, describing his belief that only by passive resistance could India gain independence from British colonialism. In 1909, Gandhi, who was working as a lawyer in South Africa and beginning his activism, read the letter. The letter had significance for Gandhi who wrote Tolstoy asking him to prove he was the real author and seeking permission to republish it in Gujarati. Tolstoy responded and the two continued a correspondence, with one of Tolstoy's last letters before his death in 1910 addressed to Gandhi (Gandhi, *Letters,* vol. II, pp. 706–708; www.abikoyeolufemi.com/2014/07/22/leo-tolstoy-last-letter/). Reading Tolstoy's *The Kingdom of God Is Within You* had convinced Gandhi to advocate nonviolent resistance unequivocally, a debt Gandhi acknowledged in his *Autobiography*, calling Tolstoy "the greatest apostle of nonviolence that the present age has produced" and describing himself a humble disciple.[3]

Mohandas Karamchand Gandhi

Mohandas Karamchand Gandhi (1869–1948) was the preeminent leader of the independence movement against the British Indian Empire. He first used nonviolent resistance as a barrister-at-law in South Africa, leading the resident Indian community's struggle against registration laws denying their right to vote. When he returned to India in 1915, he organized farmers and peasants to protest excessive land taxes. Assuming leadership of the Indian National Congress in 1921, Gandhi led nationwide campaigns of *satyagraha*, building religious and ethnic unity and ending untouchability as stepping stones for achieving *swaraj* (self-rule): "By September 1923, Congress split into two factions, that is, the *Swarajist Party* led by Motilal Nehru and C. R. Das, and the party loyal to Gandhi. Nonviolence always remained the official policy of Congress; however, serious doubts were raised from time to time, about its theoretical validity and practical usefulness" (Tahir, 2012, p. 360).

[3] Gandhi's dependence theoretically on Tolstoy is certain. In addition, and in broader terms, Gandhi's philosophy reflects Hinduism and Jainism. In Hinduism, Gandhi found the idea of love as a historical force and a pervasive sense of duty humans owe to one another. From Jainism, he understood the fundamental character of nonviolence as social power.

Gandhi insisted on the policy of self-rule until, on January 26, 1930, the Indian National Congress declared India's independence. In March of that year, Gandhi launched a *satyagraha* against the British tax on salt, highlighted by the famous three-week salt march for 388 kilometers from Ahmedabad to Dandi. Thousands joined Gandhi, learning his philosophy of nonviolence as they marched to the sea and made salt themselves. This campaign was one of the most successful in undermining British control, with Britain responding counterproductively by imprisoning more than 60,000 people. Tensions escalated until on the third *satyagraha* in 1942, the British responded aggressively, considering it a major danger in war-time; Gandhi and all the Congress leaders were put in prison.

While Gandhi promoted self-rule, the Muslim League was cooperating with Britain; against Gandhi's strong opposition it demanded a separate Muslim state of Pakistan. Heeding that initiative, in August 1947 the British partitioned the land into a Hindu-majority India and a Muslim Pakistan, each achieving independence on terms that Gandhi disapproved (Khan, 2007). Ignoring the official celebration of independence, to pro-mote religious harmony Gandhi staged several public fasts-unto-death. Six months after independence, on January 30, 1948, a Hindu nationalist, Nathuram Godse, assassinated Gandhi firing three bullets at point-blank range.[4]

In his *Autobiography: The Story of My Experiments with Truth*, Gandhi described his life as dedicated to the discovery of truth or *satya*. *Satyagraha* (a name Gandhi invented meaning "adherence to truth") aims to eliminate antagonisms without harming the antagonists and seeks transformation at a higher level. In Gandhi's vision, by appealing to reason and conscience we can put an end to evil by converting evil-doers (Gandhi, 1961). Cognate phrases typically used for *satyagraha* are "truth force" and "silent force" and "soul force."[5] Truth force arms people with moral power rather than physical power. *Satyagraha* is also termed a "universal force," as it essentially "makes no distinction between

---

[4] Bertrand Russell (1991) in his autobiography discredited Tolstoy: "It is the great mis-fortune of the human race that he [Tolstoy] has so little power of reasoning" (p. 196). Russell also claimed that Gandhi's so-called victory over the British through nonviolence was actually due to Britain's humaneness: "As against British India, Gandhi led it to triumph. But it depends upon the existence of certain virtues in those against whom it is employed. When the Indians lay down on railways, and challenged the authorities to crush them under trains, the British found such cruelty intolerable. But the Nazis had no scruples in analogous situations ... Tolstoy was right only when the holders of power were not ruthless beyond a point" (p. 431).
[5] "Soul force" is the term King used in his "I Have a Dream" speech.

kinsmen and strangers, young and old, man and woman, friend and foe"
(Gandhi, 1994, vol. 48, p. 340).[6] Noncooperation in *satyagraha* is, in fact,
a means to secure the cooperation of the opponent consistent with truth
and justice:

To the British, Gandhi was an enigma, for though he had the appearance of a holy
man, he often seemed to be a consummate politician and a committed enemy. It is
hardly surprising that historical interpretations of his life have followed as many
trajectories as the critiques while he was living. What is clear is that no one
interested in modern India can ignore Gandhi's life and contribution to the
making of the new nation state ... After Gandhi, no Indian could speak of such
matters as the treatment and role of women, the nature of caste, or the problem of
Untouchability, or even of religion, in the same way as in the past. (Brown & Parel,
2011, pp. 7, 260)

Since 1947 until today, Gandhi is considered the founder of the nation and
credited with India's political identity as a tolerant democracy.[7]

Martin Luther King Jr.

Martin Luther King Jr. (1929–1968) was the minister of Ebenezer Baptist
Church in Atlanta, Georgia. Early in his career, he became the architect of
the US civil rights movement.[8] On December 1, 1955, Rosa Parks was
arrested in Montgomery, Alabama, for refusing to give up her bus seat.
King led the Montgomery Bus Boycott until its success with *Browder
v. Gayle* and founded the Southern Christian Leadership Conference
(SCLC) in 1957, serving as its first president (see his "The Power of
Nonviolence," http://teachingamericanhistory.org/library/document/the-
power-of-non-violence/06/04/2957). In the aftermath of the boycott,
in1958 King wrote *Stride Toward Freedom: The Montgomery Story*,
which included the chapter "Pilgrimage to Nonviolence," where he

---

[6] Gandhi's (1994) collected writings published by the Indian government equal 50,000
pages in one hundred volumes.

[7] Gelderloos (2007) considers nonviolence ineffective compared to militarism. He claims
that political histories typically overvalue Gandhi and King and ignore the militant
activists who made Indian independence and the civil rights movements successful.
Gelderloos's *The Failure of Nonviolence* (2015) carries these critiques through the
post–Cold War years.

[8] For a detailed review of the civil rights movement in America, with an emphasis on
Gandhi's influence and a description of the involvement of other leaders besides King,
see Ackerman and Duvall (2000). The King Center for Nonviolent Social Change, founded
in 1968 by Coretta Scott King, continues with education and materials to promote the
philosophy and methods of King's nonviolence.

outlined his principles of nonviolence whose aim was winning opponents with friendship rather than defeating them.[9]

Already in 1959, in his "Sermon on Gandhi," King elaborated on the aftereffects of choosing violence over nonviolence: "The aftermath of nonviolence is the creation of the beloved community, so that when the battle's over, a new relationship comes into being between the oppressed and the oppressor." In the same sermon, he contrasted violent versus nonviolent resistance to oppression: "The way of acquiescence leads to moral and spiritual suicide. The way of violence leads to bitterness in the survivors and brutality in the destroyers" ("The King Philosophy," www.the kingcenter.org/king-philosophy).[10] King also helped organize the 1963 March on Washington, where he delivered his historic "I Have a Dream" oration, with nonviolence its rationale.

On October 14, 1964, King received the Nobel Peace Prize for nonviolent strategies against racial inequality. On that occasion, he deferred acclaim to Gandhi's "successful precedent" of pacifism, praising the "magnificent way of Mohandas K. Gandhi to challenge the might of the British Empire ... He struggled only with the weapons of truth, soul-force, non-

---

[9] This chapter references the early King advisors Harris Wofford and Bayard Rustin, from the Christian pacifist tradition who had studied Gandhi and already applied nonviolence to Southern racism in the 1940s and early 1950s. Dealing with various dimensions of nonviolence in spiritual terms is prominent in these major leaders from Lao Tzu to King. It is also an important theme in religions generally. The Dalai Lama's best-selling book *Ethics for a New Millennium* (1999) was written for all though it is intensely spiritual in character (Merrill, 2009, pp. 11–17). Karol Wojtyla (better known as Pope John Paul II) explicates horizontal love (human-to-human) and vertical love (human-to-divine) as a trained philosopher speaking to the human race (Wojtyla, 1981). Gene Outka's *Agape: An Ethical Analysis* (1972) is an exhaustive theological analysis of this central Christian concept and indicates philosophically how it applies to all people and resituates all relationships. In the Mennonite tradition, John Howard Yoder's *The War of the Lamb: The Ethics of Nonviolence and Peacemaking* (2009) is noteworthy (cf. also Yoder, 1994). As explained earlier, for Emmanuel Levinas in the Jewish tradition, the Self-Other relation makes peace normative. When the Other's face appears, the infinite is revealed and I am commanded not to kill (Levinas, 1981). Along with *dharma* (higher truth), *ahimsa* (nonviolence) forms the basis of the Hindu worldview. For St. Augustine, peace is natural to human relationships. In all these cases, spirituality refers to the perennial propensity of human beings for ultimate meaning, and it is on that deep level that nonviolence as a philosophy of life is understood.

[10] King, inspired by Gandhi's success, wanted to travel to India, and supporters funded his journey in April 1959. In a radio address on his final evening in India, King concluded: "I am more convinced than ever before that the method of nonviolent resistance is the most potent weapon available to oppressed people in their struggle for justice and human dignity" ("India Trip 1959"). As did Gandhi, King read Tolstoy, especially Tolstoy's reflections on Jesus's "Sermon on the Mount" and he quoted from Tolstoy's *War and Peace* in 1959 (*Papers of Martin Luther King Jr.*, vol. 5, 2005).

injury, and courage" ("Nobel Lecture by MLK," thekingcenter.org). In 1964, he helped organize the Selma to Montgomery marches, and the following year he and the SCLC took the movement north to Chicago to work on segregated housing. In the final years of his life, King expanded his focus to include the economic violence of poverty, and he publicly opposed the Vietnam War beginning with an April 4, 1967, speech, exactly one year before his death, at the New York City Riverside Church, "Beyond Vietnam: A Time to Break Silence." He called the US government "the greatest purveyor of violence in the world today," arguing that the country needed serious moral change: "A nation that continues year after year to spend more on military defense than on programs of social uplift is approaching spiritual death." At a speech eleven days later to 125,000 protestors marching from Manhattan's Central Park to the United Nations, he called for the fervor of the civil rights movement to instill the Vietnam peace movement with greater strength: "I believe everyone has a duty to be in both the civil-rights and peace movements. But for those who presently choose but one, I would hope they will finally come to see the moral roots common to both" (www.crmvet.org/mlkviet2.htm).

In his last book, *Where Do We Go From Here: Chaos or Community*, his vision for reform – for the reconstruction of society itself – required a reversal of racism, poverty, militarism, and materialism. In 1968, SCLC was planning a national march on Washington, DC, to be called the Poor People's Campaign – including African Americans, Latinos, Native Americans, and Whites – when King was assassinated on April 4 in Memphis, Tennessee. With only a decade to pursue it, King's philosophy of nonviolence secured major progress on civil liberties in the United States. Days after his assassination, Congress paid tribute to him by passing the Civil Rights Act of 1968, its Title VIII known as the Fair Housing Act prohibiting residential discrimination.

King's philosophy of nonviolence is summarized by the King Center as the "triple evils of poverty, racism, and militarism"; that is, these three forms of social violence exist in a vicious cycle and stand as barriers to his vision for a new world century (*Where Do We Go From Here*, 1967). As developed by such scholars as Greg Moses (1998), contradicting the "triple evils" requires the radical nonviolent frame of mind described in King's "Six Principles of Nonviolence"[11] and the "Four Steps for

---

[11] For the record, the six principles from King's *Stride Toward Freedom* as listed by the King Center for Nonviolent Social Change are (1) nonviolence is a way of life for courageous people;(2) nonviolence seeks to win friendship and understanding; (3) nonviolence seeks

Nonviolent Social Change" outlined in his "Letter from Birmingham Jail."[12]

Effective Nonviolent Action

Understanding the character of nonviolence is not limited to a few theorists. Thousands of persons across the demographic spectrum have come to see its deepest meaning by putting nonviolence into action. Nonviolence has worked at specific times in the past century, such as against the Nazis in Norway and Denmark during World War II. Nonviolence succeeded "in the Philippines in the mid-1980s when nonviolent 'people power' averted what might have been a bloody civil war by sitting in front of the government tanks as the Marcos regime sought to confront rebel commanders in their headquarters" (Holmes, 2013, p. 197). Nonviolence brought "dignity and respect to the Solidarity movement in Poland throughout the 1980s" when violence would almost certainly have crushed it; peaceful resistance "worked in the early 1990s when Lithuanians rallied nonviolently in support of independence in the face of the overwhelming military superiority of the Soviet Union" (p. 197). In Kosovo, nonviolence continues to play a role in the Albanian struggle against Serbian domination.

A Force More Powerful, the massive book on nonviolence in the twentieth century, describes in detail twelve peace movements of history-changing importance across the globe (Ackerman & Duvall, 2000). Impeccable in its research, *A Force More Powerful* is an account of how the people of the twentieth century developed the ability to resist oppression and take on self-rule without using violence.[13] Nonviolent action succeeded when people movements understood the character of this mobilization strategy. Public communication was the lynchpin for persuading people to act publicly and was vital to an effective process.

---

to defeat injustice not people; (4) nonviolence holds that suffering can educate and transform; (5) nonviolence chooses love instead of hate; and (6) nonviolence believes that the universe is on the side of justice.

[12] Based on the "Letter from Birmingham Jail," the King Center promotes a list of six steps, typically calling these steps phases or cycles of a campaign, with each of them embodying a series of activities.

[13] For Ackerman and Duvall (2000), these stories focus on nonviolent action within a larger conflict. They do not "presume to give a complete history," for example, of how apartheid fell in South Africa. They seek to give a "fair and instructive report of how nonviolent action was used to help make that happen" (p. 8).

Leaders of nonviolent protest did read Lao Tzu, Tolstoy, Gandhi, and King. But popular action required the mass media. As one example, Ackerman and Duvall (2000) describe the media's role in supporting Václav Havel's opposition to Czechoslovakia's communist regime in November 1989:

> The official media were tightly controlled, so getting the word out was critical. Students made the rounds of homes, campus meetings, and theaters and told their stories to the people of Prague. They showed videotapes of the demonstrations and the police violence, and they pasted fliers on walls denouncing the brutality and calling for a strike. Western radio broadcasts also gave accounts of what had happened ... On Monday, November 20, 100,000 squeezed into Wenceslas Square. A public address system was rigged up, and now leaders of a new opposition group, Civic Forum, such as longtime dissident Václav Havel, had a vast audience to appeal to. Newspapers and then television began reporting on the upheaval. The regime's monopolies over public space and mass communication had been broken, and cracks soon appeared in the party itself. A two-hour nationwide protest strike on November 27 proved that the opposition was not just a movement of Prague students and intellectuals. The rulers who had yielded possession of Wenceslas Square ended by surrendering command of the state. (pp. 435–436; cf. Wheaton & Kavan, 1992, pp. 25–29, 52–63)

As other examples, "When Chileans organized against the dictatorship of General Augusto Pinochet in the 1980s, and Filipinos organized against Ferdinand Marcos, they were influence by Richard Attenborough's motion picture *Gandhi*" (Ackerman & Duvall, 2000, p. 6). Cameras were there at Selma covering the marches until nonviolence took on meaning, with the US press largely ignoring the issue of race prior to Selma.[14] Martin Luther King Jr. was

> the chief reason for television's fascination with the substance of the civil rights movement. He was eloquent, capable of high moral pronouncements and dramatic persuasive appeals, and thus became a critical rhetorical figure in television's discourse ... As the first black leader to galvanize thousands with his own rhetoric during television's maturity, his judgment of television's importance for the movement was critical to black consciousness. (Asante, 1976, pp. 137–38)

King's brilliance proved more significant in forging a coalition between television and minorities than did a compelling desire by news people to make the civil rights struggle transparent.

Lessons from the twelve stories of nonviolence in *A Force More Powerful* "flout the conventional wisdom. The use of nonviolent

---

[14] For details on the role of the press in the civil rights movement, see Meier and Rudwick (1970).

sanctions has been more frequent and widespread than usually supposed." They were "crucial elements of history-making struggles in
every part of the world and in every decade of the century" (Ackerman &
Duvall, 2000, p. 7). The lesson for the media, from this century of nonviolent struggle, is the media's role in reinforcing the fallacy "that only
violence can overcome violence":

At the end of the last century, the world's airwaves and bookstores were full of
material that looked back at what was called the most destructive hundred years in
history. In reel after reel, and on page after page, we were shown the carnage,
the awful cost, it was said, of defeating evil. But told only that way, the history
of the century's conflicts, reinforce[s] ... the misconception that violence is always
the ultimate form of power, that no other method of advancing a just cause or
defeating injustice can surpass it. But Russians, Indians, Poles, Danes,
Salvadorans, African Americans, Chileans, South Africans, and many others
have proven that one side's choices in a conflict are not foreclosed by the other's
use of violence. (Ackerman & Duvall, 2000, p. 9)

As Ackerman and Duvall note: "Violence generates more news
because, for many, history is perceived as a spectacle." The dramatic effect
of nonviolent sanctions has been "overshadowed in the news and entertainment media and thus in our collective memory by wars, genocide,
carpet bombing, and terror" (p. 8.). For Holmes (2013):

Upon close reading, the record of violence is not as impressive as often supposed.
Arab states went to war in 1948 to liberate Palestine, but today Palestinians live by
the millions in diaspora, almost certainly never to return to their homeland.
The United States shelled Lebanon in 1983, bombed Libya in 1986, waged war
on Iraq in 1991, and bombed Sudan and Afghanistan in 1998 to deter terrorism.
But it didn't deter the 9/11 attack ... Every war that has a winner also has a loser,
so that in every case in which violence succeeds on the victorious side, it fails on the
losing side. (p. 118)

In their editorializing about the problems of injustice and oppression,
the news media ought to remind their readers and viewers and internet
users that military violence "for all of recorded history has not worked; it
has not secured either peace or justice in the world. The most that violence
has brought are brief interludes in which the nations of the world regroup,
catch their breath, and prepare for the next war" (Holmes, 2013, p. 187).

Principled Nonviolence

From the theorists of nonviolence, and the activists over a century who
have defined it on the ground, this chapter advocates principled

nonviolence. This follows the pathway of the contemporary philosopher Robert Holmes, who proposes an ethics of principled nonviolence that is normative. As he puts it, "a philosophy of nonviolence may simply describe and elucidate nonviolence. Or it may instead, or in addition, propose and defend its adoption. That is, it may be normative or non-normative. I shall examine nonviolence understood to be normative in this sense" (Holmes, 2013, p. 170).

In terms of this distinction, nonviolence can be thought of in practical terms as a strategy for achieving specific social or political ends. This first conception is pragmatic nonviolence: "Disavowing as it does an essential moral or religious orientation, pragmatic nonviolence is open to anyone to accept. It does not require ... extraordinary capacities" (p. 116). The second definition, principled nonviolence, is "a moral or spiritual philosophy – even a way of life – which may, though need not, be held to have broad social and political uses." Principled nonviolence does require a "transformation of its adherents" (p. 116). Lao Tzu, Tolstoy, Gandhi, and King represent this principled definition. Expressed as an ethical maxim, principled nonviolence says, "one ought always to act nonviolently" (p. 179).

Both the pragmatic and principled definitions will maintain that nonviolence has a justification, reflecting a difference in the ends or goals of the two approaches: "For principled nonviolence, it is necessary and sufficient for the final justification of nonviolence that it be justified from the moral point of view." Typically, pragmatic nonviolence has "social, political, or national goals. Principled nonviolence may have, either in addition to or instead of these, broader moral ends, like promoting a certain way of life, maximizing value, or showing reverence for life. Its concern, we might say, is with moral effectiveness rather than merely practical effectiveness." Principled nonviolence opposes violence "in a broad range of actual and hypothetical cases ... on moral and not simply on social or political grounds" (p. 172).

The ethical principle "one ought always to act nonviolently" precludes both physical and psychological violence. Requiring nonviolence in that double sense means nonviolence as a way of life: "To live nonviolently and to encourage others to do the same is the end, and the question is not whether nonviolence is effective, but whether [people are] successful at living nonviolently" (p. 179).

Causing mental harm is a wide-ranging violence to "facts, the truth, an author's intentions, the memory of a deceased, and to persons, including oneself. In each case, something having value, integrity, dignity, sacredness, or generally some claim to respect is treated in a manner contemptuous of that claim." It is possible for us "to insult, humiliate, degrade, demean, and oppress people, treat them unkindly, unfairly, and unjustly; and cause them untold [mental] harm without resorting to physical violence against them. A theory which prohibits only physical violence could claim at best to represent only a part, not the whole, of a plausible moral position" (pp. 154, 173). Gandhi's version of principled nonviolence clearly intends the same: "Under violence I include corruption, falsehood, hypocrisy, deceit and the like" (1961, p. 294).

Nonviolence as a normative principle is typically criticized as rationally implausible. The objections to principled nonviolence as leading to an intellectual impasse need to be answered for the maxim "one ought always to act nonviolently" to be credible. Holmes is committed to answering the objections and thereby to eliminate the charge of the "rational untenability of approaching nonviolence as a way of life" (2013, p. 169). He insists that we consider only logically possible cases. There are "wildly imaginative hypothetical situations" that deny the validity of the normative principle. "One ought always to act nonviolently" is to be considered a valid principle for conduct

in the world as it is now or is likely to be in the foreseeable future. Putative counterexamples are relevant only if framed within the same perspective as the one for which the rule or principle in question is held to be valid ... The comparison should not be of nonviolence with some ideal of conflict resolution in an ideal world, but with our present methods in the actual world. (p. 159)

Advocates of nonviolence will simply concede hypotheticals when marooned on an ocean island or be inexplicit about time and space that selectively exclude salient features or include "question-begging assumptions." The question will then be whether those sorts of cases "are ever in fact encountered or are at all likely to be encountered in ordinary life" (p. 178).

Nonviolence and its defense of the innocent is a serious objection. Many people find it incomprehensible, even contemptible,

that anyone would stand by while innocent persons are attacked, beaten, and perhaps killed, refusing to assist them because that would be to resort to violence. It is one thing, they say, to refuse to defend yourself if attacked; it is another to refuse to defend others, particularly the innocent, or to disapprove of the use of violence in national defense or for national liberation ... To keep one's hand morally clean by refusing even to help others betrays a self-righteous preoccupation with one's own moral purity. (Holmes, 2013, p. 175)

While the objection is not relevant for pragmatic nonviolence, the principled version faces the dilemma that if violent means are morally wrong, then it is immoral to defend the innocent if it entails violence. The issues for resolution are those "cases in which, by hypothesis, violence would save the innocent and nonviolence would not" (p. 177).

The principle "one ought always to act nonviolently" should be understood as a *prima facie* duty. It is not an absolute decontextualized law, a mathematically derived theorem in Enlightenment terms. Holmes concedes that in principled nonviolence, "there may be hypothetical circumstances in which violence would be justified," but they are "rarely, if ever, actually realized." As he puts it, the "paradox here is removed if one recasts that point in terms of enlisting physical violence in the service of nonviolence." Under such circumstances, it is not obvious that "the respect for persons which is at the heart of nonviolence, clearly rules out all cases of taking human life or using violence. One might argue that the forcible and even physically violent restraint of a deranged person to prevent harm to himself or others is justified by the principle of nonviolence. This possibility ... occurred to Gandhi" (Holmes, 2013, p. 157): "I have come to see, what I did not so clearly before, that there is nonviolence in violence ... I had not fully realized the duty of restraining a drunkard from doing evil, of killing a dog in agony or one infected with rabies. In all these instances, violence is in fact nonviolence" (Gandhi, 1994, vol. 14, 505; Holmes, 2013, p. 157).

Nonviolence is a way of life and within that existential context, the principle "one ought always to act nonviolently" is a *prima facie* duty. *Prima facie* duties are a more coherent way of dealing with today's complicated circumstances than is accounting for exceptions. *Prima facie* duties carry the presumption in favor of doing them. A *prima facie* duty is obligatory unless stronger moral considerations override. The duty to always act nonviolently is *prima facie*; it is "self-evident" and "upon first view" that it ought to be done. In W. D. Ross's *The Right and the Good* (1930), the *prima facie* duty of non-injury is the duty not to harm others physically or psychologically, that is, to avoid harming their health, security, or happiness. The *prima facie* duty of justice requires that benefits and burdens are distributed fairly. In this deontological ethics, priority rules give us guidance when the basic *prima facie* duties appear to conflict. Non-injury normally over-rides other *prima facie* duties and in these terms "principled nonviolence" is a priority rule all things considered.

Self-evident obligations such as non-injury (non-maleficence), justice, fidelity, gratitude, and making reparations are not merely characteristics of morality that humans recognize implicitly. Arthur Dyck is correct that they are "moral requisites" for communities to exist cooperatively and to flourish (1977, p. 160). *Prima facie* dutiful acts foster an integration of personhood and community. Duty does not wait until all the effects are known. Duty is incorporated – or acted out – in specific behaviors or policies within the community. Duty is not obedience to a formal law such as "always acting nonviolently," but a dialogic seeking within a language community, through responsive relations, for a responsible fit within the total "circumambience of life" (Niebuhr, 1963, p. 153).

As Ross (1930) emphasizes, ethics on behalf of community life is approximate, dealing in probabilities and not certainties. A *prima facie* duty recommends itself to us as entirely real and self-evident, but that does not mean our moral judgment is infallible. In fact, moral duties typically "have certain characteristics that tend to make them at the same time *prima facie* right and *prima facie* wrong" (p. 33; cf. Ross, 1939). According to Ross (1930), one duty will always have a greater urgency or priority than the others in a given case and that the "duty proper" is the right thing to do. There are priority rules that give us guidance, and other things being equal non-injury has precedence, but finally "the decision rests with perception" (p. 42).

The classic case of Dietrich Bonhoeffer in Germany illustrates principled nonviolence as a *prima facie* duty. Bonhoeffer wrote *The Cost of Discipleship*, considered one of "the purest books on pacifism written in the twentieth century, and then participate[d] in an attempt to assassinate Adolph Hitler" (Arnett, 2005, p. 20). On April 9, 1945, this thirty-nine-year-old theologian, writer, and ethicist was led naked to the gallows at the Flossenbürg concentration camp in Bavaria. Hitler had personally ordered his execution. Ordained a pastor in the German Lutheran Church in 1931, he split with the German Protestant community through the Barmen Declaration of 1934 that began the Confessing Church and openly opposed National Socialism. He welcomed Jews and spoke out against the Nazis, while participating secretly in the conspiracy to kill the Führer. He was arrested in 1943 while working in Munich on his book *Ethics*.[15]

---

[15] For a well-regarded scholar's biography of Bonhoeffer's life and decisions, see Marsh (2014).

The problem in Bonhoeffer's *Ethics* is put in these terms: How can a Christian pacifist justify murder? The answer is multilayered but essentially seen as a dilemma when evil is overwhelming: "When assaulted by evil, Christians must oppose it through direct action. They have no other option. Any failure to act is simply to condone evil" (Bonhoeffer, 1955, p. 67).[16] In a letter in 1943, Bonhoeffer argued that responsible persons do not try to extricate themselves from demonic circumstances but look for ways to help "the coming generation to live." In his *prima facie* deontological ethics, doing nothing is not a solution to a profound moral dilemma but an irresponsible avoidance of it. After a lifetime of nonviolent resistance, in action and testimony, when facing a monumental crisis, the *prima facie* duty of justice by alternative means (violence) is for Bonhoeffer the last and only resort (Bonhoeffer, *Letters and Papers from Prison*, 1953).

In Ronald Arnett's book-length treatment of Bonhoeffer's life and ethics, Bonhoeffer's humans-in-relation dialectic enriches the deontological ethics of *prima facie* duties. Rooted in Hegel and articulated in Hans-Georg Gadamer, dialectic for Bonhoeffer is an intellectual and practical commitment to discern what is true in a given historical situation. Instead of taken-for-granted ideology, "dialectical questioning keeps theory and action thoughtful and informed, providing a knowing and reflective base of action" (Arnett, 2005, p. 169). Bonhoeffer's dialogic intersubjectivity makes a life of "discernment, confession, and the courage of conviction" possible (p. 169).[17] "Milton Rokeach once warned, referring to Gandhi, not to confuse a person of conviction with one of closure"; Bonhoeffer's dialectical rhetoric of responsibility ensures the distinction for him (p. 164).

---

[16] Arguing that although philosophers have engaged the issue of evil for two thousand years, for Robert Fortner (2009) evil remains a major issue for ethics, both theoretically and practically. Fortner (2009, 2010) reviews the literature and cases from around the world on the relevance of evil to media ethics and how evil should be reported. Jacques Ellul writes from the same faith tradition as does Bonhoeffer. In his book *Violence*, Ellul (1969) makes a commitment to nonviolence without exception; he argues that if anyone breaks that commitment – even from outrage against war and tyranny – he or she is sinful and needs forgiveness for wrongdoing.

[17] Theoretically, of course, one might contend that violence in these cases is necessitated by other considerations: "The justifiers of violence, at least since the time of Augustine, appeal to an unexplicated conception of necessity allegedly operating here. These considerations might be those of self-interest or national interest. The claim would then be that, when considerations of these sorts conflict with what morality prescribes, they override morality. This represents a problematic metaethical claim" (Holmes, 2013, p. 176).

Ronald Tercheck (2011), in reviewing the complicated literature on exceptions in Gandhi's nonviolence, draws a conclusion in the spirit of Bonhoeffer's deontological ethics: "Each person must decide how and where to apply Gandhian principles, but such an exercise cannot be a matter of convenience of interests. I hold that to take Gandhi seriously and yet to make exceptions in his theory requires a principled stand that does not change with convenience of interest and which does not contradict one's other strong moral principles" (p. 129). In this chapter's principled nonviolence as a *prima facie* duty, the one possible exception in a cataclysmic crisis is our moral responsibility for global justice.

VIOLENCE IN ENTERTAINMENT

From Albert Bandura's social learning research in the 1960s, to George Gerbner's cultivation paradigm in the 1970s, to the massive effects studies of television and cinema violence in the 1980s and 1990s, to research on violent video gaming since the early 2000s, to newly emerging issues like cyberbullying on social media, researchers have sought to document the relationship – both theoretical and behavioral – between media content and outcomes of aggression (Eastin, 2013; cf. Sparks, 2016, chap. 5).[18] The abundant results have required 134 entries in the *Encyclopedia of Media Violence* (2013) and the urgency continues. In the United States, few issues command as much attention from media reformers as violence in television and film and video games. America has been a turbulent society since its birth in the Revolutionary War, but now there is more anxiety with gun violence a public health epidemic.

The opposition of media industries and libertarians to the censors of violence has centered primarily on the argument that no direct effects can be proved, and therefore media violence cannot be made the basis of criminal prosecutions. However, the no-effects conclusion has lost its credibility. Ellen Wartella, co-principal investigator of the National Television Violence Study (1995–1998) concluded more than two decades ago: "Evidence of a causal relationship between media violence and real violence has been accumulating for at least forty years"; "[v]iolent behavior is a complex, multivariable problem, formed of many influences"; and "violence in the media may not be the most important contributor to violence in the real world," but "it is surely one of the multiple,

---

[18] Min Wang of Wuhan University has provided exceptional assistance regarding the literature, methodology, and empirical research of studies of violence in entertainment.

overlapping causes" (Wartella, 1996, pp. 3–4). Meta-analyses of literally hundreds of studies on media violence since that time have demonstrated a causal link between the viewing of televised violence and real-life aggression. The same conclusion was verified by research for the American Medical Association, the National Centers for Disease Control and Prevention, and through the exhaustive multiyear National Television Violence Study (1994–1998; Wilson, Colvin, & Smith, 2002, pp. 36–57; cf. pp. 57–60).

In James Potter's (1999) review of effects research – with the caveat that the effects process is highly complex – he is certain of both immediate and extended consequences from televised violence. In the short term, fear and habituation occur, but "increased viewer aggression" is most strongly supported also. And for long-term effects, "we can conclude that exposure to violence in the media is linked with negative effects of trait aggression, fearful worldview, and desensitization to violence" (p. 42).

In terms of the relationship between violence in the entertainment media and violence in the real world, social scientists of the dominant view believe that exposure to violence in the media increases the risk of aggressive behavior. Craig Anderson and colleagues (2003) tested the opposite conclusion – that the correlation is negative. They interpreted their findings in the context of aggression models where exposure to media violence more likely leads to a facilitation effect rather than a catharsis effect. Their confirmation that violent content increases the likelihood of aggressive behavior is now commonplace in studies of violence in media entertainment (Sparks, 2016, p. 116). The predictive component remains controversial,[19] but there is general agreement that viewers learn the aggressive behaviors depicted in the programs they see (known as the "learning effect"). Media ethics theories in the 1980s through the three-volume National Television Violence Study published in 1998 depended on Bandura's concept of "modeling." While Bandura's reward-and-punishment motif in the Bobo Doll experiments (Sparks et al., 2009) has been criticized on various grounds, the general aggression model has continued to make behavioral effects nonnegotiable (cf. Ferguson & Dyck, 2012).

Patrick Plaisance's (2009) conclusion about the "decades of extensive research" includes the appropriate gradation: "Certain viewers, with

---

[19] Ferguson (2014) examined youth violence and video game usage over two decades and concluded, "social consumption of media violence is not predictive of increased violence rates" (p. 1).

certain predispositions, will likely exhibit more aggressive behavior under certain conditions after repeated and long-term exposure to certain types of portrayals of violence. But as the string of preceding qualifiers suggest, this effect is highly nuanced, contingent and multidimensional" (p. 172).

Desensitization research without predictive and causality measures remains credible. As Wartella (1996) summarizes this scholarship: "Prolonged viewing of media violence can lead to emotional desensitization toward real violence and real victims, which may result in callous attitudes and a decreased likelihood that desensitized individuals will take action to help victims when real violence occurs" (p. 6). Sparks (2016) invokes the "law of emotional desensitization"; that is, one's "initial emotional reaction ... decreases in intensity" through repeated exposure: "In the case of media violence, the concern is that repeated exposure might result in such low levels of negative emotion that eventually, exposure to violence – even real-life violence – is accepted casually instead of prompting concern and action" (p. 115; cf. Krahé et al., 2011).

George Gerbner's "cultural indicators paradigm" continues to be influential (Gerbner et al., 1994). His media cultivation research indicated that the prominence of violent content in prime-time television increases our fear of being victimized. Heavy television viewers cultivate a "mean world syndrome," that is, a worldview more crime-ridden than real life. Heavy viewing of violence enhances self-protective behavior from an increased mistrust of others.

The various formulations of violent effects face the context problem (cf. Freedman, 2002). Social scientific aggression research typically does not account adequately for background variables. Without a grounding in history and social structures, violence research cannot explain why countries with a media violence index similar to the that of the United States (Australia, Canada, Japan, Norway, for example) have lower rates of violent crime. Yun Long (2005) investigated the relationship between media violence and people's fears in Lanzhou, Shanghai, and Beijing. For the viewing of prime-time TV programs and their content, there were no measurable differences among these three cities. But the fear-of-violence factor differed significantly in each city: "People preferred to rely on their cognition of actual local conditions to construct their understanding of public security" (Zhan, in press, p. 12; cf. Long, 2005). Donnerstein's (2011) review of the effects of media violence on aggression includes the influences of substance abuse, weak social ties, abusive parents, antisocial peers, and low IQ. While the statistical size of such influences is sometimes minor, Donnerstein certifies the importance of the sociopersonal context. Nikkelen et al. (2014) examined the relationship between exposure to media violence and behavior related to attention-deficit/hyperactivity disorder (ADHD) using the genetic data of 1,612 Dutch children, and established the role of genetic factors in media effects. Some studies have indicated that when personal incidences of violence, mental health, peer and family environment are accounted for, predictions regarding media violence can no longer be measured (Ferguson, San Miguel, & Hartley, 2009).

A Cultural Perspective

Given the complexities of violence in entertainment, social scientific research ought to continue by expanding its multilevel sophistication.[20] But for understanding and applying the ethical principle of nonviolence, humanistic research methodologies are required. Plaisance's (2009) critique of consequentialism puts us on the right pathway. The empiricist tradition constructs ethical issues in utilitarian terms, and consequentalist ethics is ill suited for dealing with the fundamental issues of social and media violence. The search for "clear, quantifiable and unambiguous results" privileges "simplistic utilitarian conventions and guidelines ... A straightforward consequentalist approach is more likely to exempt us from moral accountability than it is to clarify our moral responsibilities" (pp. 169, 172). According to Plaisance, "Mill also discourages serious exploration into the various types and dimensions of harm ... The existence of effects does not necessarily raise a question of ethics. To be considered a compelling ethics question we must determine the relative harmfulness of those effects" (pp. 169,171).[21] "Neurologists and cognitive psychologists (cf. Dirk, 2014) have just begun to understand the behavioral effects of much of our messages ... They are also making clear how our reception and processing of messages is profoundly contextual and intersubjective." A survey of "the research documenting the effects of

---

[20] For an argument for three-level theories, see Christians, Rao, Ward, & Wasserman (2008).

[21] In elaborating on the concept of harm, Plaisance (2009) includes Joel Feinberg's *Harm to Others* (1984) where Feinberg discusses various dimensions of "injuring" or "wronging" others and finds it critical that we distinguish "between the harmful conditions and all the various unhappy and unwanted physical and mental states that are not states of harm in themselves" (p. 47). For Plaisance (2009), "the research on negative effects of violent content poses an important opportunity for media ethics theorists to clarify our understanding of the 'harm' involved and how the different dimensions of harm affect the moral claims we can make" (p. 173).

violent media content provides evidence that a deontological, duty-based approach is more effective in our efforts to develop an ethical framework with which to judge violent content, rather than a consequentialist approach" (Plaisance, 2009, pp. 172, 169).

Consistent with that conclusion, this chapter advocates principled nonviolence as a *prima facie* duty regarding media entertainment. Cultural studies are the most appropriate research strategy to illuminate media violence as illustrated by Jeffrey Lewis's *Media, Culture and Human Violence* (2015a). He criticizes "conventional approaches" for "limiting the media to a set of technologies, professional practices and industries. These studies parenthesize the problem of meaning, history, and cultural politics, focusing more directly on surface issues that can be measured through the application of particular kinds of metrics" (p. 13). Lewis "eschews any idea of direct and inevitable effects of media representations on individual and social behavior. Rather, violence and mediation are viewed as interactive cultural processes through which humans understand themselves and their world" (p. 14). In his judgment, "too much media scholarship has sought simple explanations for the complexity of human violence." He seeks, instead, "to explain the complexity through a detailed and thoroughgoing account of the relationship between culture, media, and human violence" (p. 14).

In James Carey's (1989) cultural perspective, the media are not first of all a conduit of messages but are intermeshed in the ways humans as cultural beings create and authenticate meanings. Human agents are not separate from the representational domain. In the cultural understanding of human existence, we know ourselves through our symbolic expressions, and mediations are symbolic forms in and through which life is meaningful. The symbolic realm is the human species' intrinsic capacity to reconstruct the world typically called culture. The cultural approach to communication understands humanity as having "only history" embedded in some context. Historically constituted forms of human experience play a constitutive role in human thinking and social practice.

In Mikhail Bahktin's *chronotope*, actions in the present condense the historicity of their past and the *chronotope* organizes discursive practices (1981). History is the medium in which people dwell, a precondition of all thought including critical reflection (Gadamer, 1975): "The great historical realities of society and state always have a predeterminate influence" on our experience. "History does not belong to us; we belong to it" (p. 276). Mediations derive their meaning from the lingual context that humans create for themselves over history.

Thus the salience of Lewis's argument that in industrial societies violence is typically presented as legitimate governmental, legal, and educational narratives. Violence thinking is embedded in a society's hierarchical organizations. Martin Luther King Jr. (1967) described the United States, for example, as a volatile mixture of the violences of racism, poverty, militarism, and commercialism. Therefore, the artists of the entertainment media face the challenge of representing principled nonviolence within a historical context that is oriented to the opposite.

Aesthetic Realism

Thomas Munro, president of the American Society of Aesthetics, gave an address on "Art and Violence" at the Sixth International Congress for Aesthetics in Uppsala, Sweden, on August 15, 1968. His address has become a classic and this chapter's appeal to aesthetics and culture lives from that legacy.[22] Munro calls on aesthetics to assume leadership of the problem of art's relation to real-life violence. Unless aesthetics takes an active lead on a large and systematic scale, art as a cultural force will be designated a culprit by psychological and social research, and calls for censorship will continue. In Munro's words:

We have learned a great deal about the nature of art and know that it is a powerful force for good or evil. But we hesitate to apply this knowledge and organize it systematically. Aesthetics remains, as a result, a comparatively trivial, impotent subject in the university curriculum, whereas it might be, like art itself, a powerful factor in cultural progress, and aesthetics can play a more useful role in the society of the future. (1969, p. 322)

Aesthetic realism endorses that mandate for artists.[23] The debates over public policy are understood, and the research with a psychological basis in fear, catharsis, desensitization is taken seriously. But the leading edge is from directors/writers/film executives who work at the multileveled nexus of culture and media; their cultural productions are an interpretive act. Artists sophisticated in aesthetics understand the world in which we live as an interpretation of symbolic meanings within that world. They agree with Paul Ricoeur (1974) that nothing is intelligible to us except through language. Since reality is accessible in language, all language use entails interpretation. With violence "profoundly inscribed in cultural

---

[22] Thanks to Youngkwan Ban for this reference.

[23] The Aesthetic Realism Foundation has no relationship intellectually or personally to "aesthetic realism" as a norm for the production of violent media entertainment.

consciousness" and sociopolitical structures (Lewis, 2015a, p. 10), the mediations of popular culture have a pre-given interpretive context that requires principled nonviolence as the artist's *prima facie* duty.

The ethics of nonviolence is normative for aesthetic realism. Violence in entertainment programs ought to meet the test of artistic integrity. Gratuitous violence is normed by technical virtuosity instead (Bok, 1999). From the perspective of artistically genuine programs, bloodthirsty torture is particularly offensive, but sanitized romanticism also violates aesthetic realism. Violence that is not integral to the plot disregards the principle of peacemaking by allowing the violence modality to represent cultural forms.

When violence is the defining feature of popular culture, it is considered synonymous with action. In terms of Kun Zhang's aesthetic and cultural analysis (2011), the dramatic formula is violence driving the story; without violence there would be no chronicle. Barbara Osborn (2016) describes the gratuitous formula this way:

Violence is the pretext for the action that follows. Look at the daily TV listings. Among films and TV movies, you're liable to find titles like *Show of Force, Hell Squad, The Killers, The Naked and the Dead, The Plot to Murder Hitler, Missing in Action 2, Masters of Menace*. TV action series demonstrate a similar inclination for violence driving the story. On a re-run of the *Father Dowling Mysteries*: "Someone takes a shot at Dowling and the culprit appears to be an angry ex-con Dowling helped send up the river on a murder rap." The hero is never safe. Danger is always just around the corner. (Osborn, 2016)

The dramatic plot begins with violence, and impending conflict continues to drive the action.

Film critic Stanley Kaufmann described *Reservoir Dogs* as "crammed with murders" and wondered whether Quentin Tarantino produced the film "just for the sake of its making, for the application of style to sheer slaughter" (quoted in Plaisance, 2009, p. 162). Tarantino in this film represents what Ellul calls "the technological imperative" in which the technique of the medium characterizes the content. Sequels of entertainment of the gratuitous genre show a revealing statistic: "The first production of *Robocop* featured 32 dead bodies. The second version featured 81. In *Death Wish*, the body count climbed from nine in the first version to 52 in the second. Rambo killed off 62 people in the initial *Rambo* film. By the time *Rambo III* rolled around, that number had soared to 111" (Sparks, 2016, p. 116; citing Jhally, 1994).

Characterization is routinized in the gratuitous violence formula. Media violence takes place in a machinic world of disemboweled humans:

Viewers' emotions have to be enlisted quickly. Starkly contrasting good and bad characters helps accomplish this. Deeper, more realistic, more ambiguous characterizations make it harder for viewers to know who to root for. It also requires more screen time that takes away from on-screen action. TV and film criminals are reduced to caricatures. They are 100% bad. No one should care about them. Most of them don't even have full names, only nick names. They deserve no sympathy and they get what they deserve. When people are killed, they simply disappear. No one mourns their death. Their lives are unimportant. (Osborn, 2016)

Films that are rated the most shockingly violent ever made are not known for their artistic value, but for the mayhem and barbarism that traumatize their audiences: *Battle Royale* (Japan), *Martyrs* (France), *The Passion of the Christ, A Serbian Film* (from Serbia), *Rambo, Hostel* and *Hostel 2, Cannibal Holocaust* (Italy). The notorious violence of *Natural Born Killers* (two psychopathic lovers and murderers) does not generate awards but controversy over killing sprees, outrageous executions, and brutal rape. In splatter films, "gore is an art form"; violence replaces "narrative structure" with savagery, which is "the only part of the film that is reliably consistent" (Arnzen, 1994, p. 178). Even within a violent genre, the video game series *Grand Theft Auto I-V* (GTA) is notorious for its cannibalism. People are killed by bazookas, chain saws, and knives; sexual violence is rewarded; pedestrians are run over by cars; drug dealers are beaten with bats.[24] GTA has been given the moniker "simulator of virtual reality murder," in its attempt to create a lived-in experience of the violent acts. Rather than a critique of the way violence is embedded in industrial society's culture, the producers, directors, and marketers of gratuitous violence exploit the violence component for their own benefit.

Aesthetic realism is artistic truth telling. The "violent complexity" of real life is presented in aesthetic proportion. It is artistically genuine entertainment both in technology and in content. Artistic realism foregrounds the moral dilemmas of human suffering. Artistic representations of violence that are not gratuitous are exemplified by such films as *The Holocaust, Schindler's List, Gandhi, The Diary of Anne Frank, Hotel Rwanda, Amistad, World Trade Center, Roots, The Pianist,* and *The Day After.*

Writer/director Terry George met the aesthetic realism standard in *Hotel Rwanda.* The genocidal attack over one hundred days of Hutu

---

[24] Ethical issues in *Grand Theft Auto* are discussed in Fackler (2012) in the context of video game technology.

extremists against Tutsi citizens meant 800,000 were massacred and two million had to escape to other countries. *Hotel Rwanda* accounts for the demonic violence as history requires, but the narrative centers on those for whom nonviolence is a *prima facie* duty. George created a "story based on character and the evolution of that character, as well as the strengths of that character" (Bossik, 2005). The conscience of Paul Rusebagena, business-oriented manager of the Hotel Mille Collines in Kigali, is transformed into his saving 1,268 refugees. The Red Cross worker and priest with his orphanage, who remain after noncitizens are evacuated, live out the ethics of nonviolence. Colonel Oliver of the Peacekeeping Force and the TV news reporter (Joaquin Phoenix) consider themselves accountable, while no political leaders of the world offer help.

The award-winning *Diary of Anne Frank* (1959) directed by George Stevens illustrates the aesthetic realism standard also: gestapo on the streets, emergency sirens and bombers, a concentration camp in Anne's dreams, diabolical polizei officers, stories of terror and foreboding, war news on the attic radio – the realism of Europe a slaughterhouse. But authentic human existence gives the narrative aesthetic cohesion.

Iris Chang's *Rape of Nanking* (the nonfiction book in 1997 and its documentary sequel in 2007) includes personal stories too: of John Rabe, a German businessman who organized the Nanking Safety Zone for civilians; of surgeon Robert Wilson who dutifully cared for victims; and of Minnie Vautrin, a missionary educator protecting Nanking's women. But Chang does not achieve aesthetic realism as do George and Stevens. *The Rape of Nanking* is journalism, and the atrocities of the Imperial Japanese Army, after capturing China's capital city (Nanjing) in 1937–1938, are rightly called the "Asian Holocaust." Bloodthirsty warfare, unrelenting condemnation of the renegade military, assertions of 300,000 civilian murders and 80,000 rapes, bestiality, and rampage preoccupy readers and viewers with horrifics of the massacre itself and its accuracy. An accusatory narrative of warfare violence buries the normative voices of reconciliatory resistance.

Schindler's List

In 1982, director Steven Spielberg purchased the rights to Australian novelist Thomas Keneally's story of about 1,100 Jews from Krakow, Poland, who survived the Holocaust because "Czech businessman Oskar Schindler was willing to cajole, bribe, and bully the Nazis for their lives" (Patterson & Wilkins, 2014, p. 275).[25] Spielberg examines Schindler's conscience as he enters World War II proudly wearing the Nazi emblem and seeking a big profit from the Nazi war machine: "Later, after the Nazi's have ghettoized and then attempted to exterminate the Jewish population in Krakow, Schindler uses his personal charm, his connections and most of his war-amassed wealth to have 'his' Jewish workers first labeled essential to the war and later moved from Germany into Czechoslovakia for safekeeping" (Patterson & Wilkins, 2014, p. 275).

Initially he hires Jews to work in his enamelware factory because they are willing to accept slave wages: "Today, Schindler, a Roman Catholic by birth, is known in Israel as a 'righteous person.' He is the only Nazi buried in Jerusalem's Mount Zion cemetery" (Patterson & Wilkins, 2014, p. 275).

Film critic Roger Ebert elaborates with precision how Spielberg represents aesthetic realism in *Schindler's List:*

Why did Schindler change? What happened to turn him from a victimizer into a humanitarian? It is to the great credit of Steven Spielberg that his film does not even attempt to answer that question. Any possible answer would be too simple, an insult to the mystery of Schindler's life. Schindler seems to have improvised out of impulses that remained unclear even to himself. Spielberg treats the fact of the Holocaust and the miracle of Schindler's feat without the easy formulas of fiction.

What is most amazing about this film is how completely Spielberg serves the story. The movie is brilliantly acted, written, directed, and seen. Individual scenes are masterpieces of art direction, cinematography, special effects, crowd control. Yet Spielberg, the stylist whose films often have gloried in shots we are intended to notice and remember, disappears into his work. Liam Neeson (Oskar Schindler), Ben Kingsley (Itzhak Stern) and other actors are devoid of acting flourishes. There is a single-mindedness to the enterprise that is awesome.

The French author Flaubert once wrote that "An author in his book must be like God in the universe, present everywhere and visible nowhere." That would describe Spielberg. He depicts the evil of the Holocaust, and he tells an incredible story of how it was robbed of some of its intended victims. He does so without the tricks of the trade, the directorial and dramatic contrivances that would inspire the usual melodramatic payoffs. (www.rogerebert.com/reviews/schindlers-list-1993)

The film earned Spielberg multiple Oscars for films released in 1993: Best Director and Picture, Best Cinematography and Film Editing and Art Direction, Best Original Score, and Best Adapted Screenplay.

---

[25] For classroom instruction and discussion of *Schindler's List* in the context of art and entertainment media, see Patterson and Wilkins (2014, pp. 275–277).

Kun Zhang (2011) argues that entertainment violence ought to unify internal content and external form. This aesthetic coherence distinguishes great popular art from the nonmoral "unrestrained sensationalism" that "attracts audiences."[26] In Ebert's analysis, Spielberg accomplished that artistic congruity and the Academy of Motion Picture Arts and Sciences recognized it. Spielberg presents the moral discernment of Schindler as he comes to understand nonviolence as a *prima facie* duty. Spielberg leads by example, illustrating for producers of entertainment media how the ethics of nonviolence is normative in aesthetic realism. As Roger Ebert explains it:

Subtlety is Spielberg's strength all through the film. Based on the screenplay by Steven Zaillian, this isn't contrived melodrama. Instead, Spielberg relies on a series of incidents, seen and without artificial manipulation, and by witnessing those incidents, we understand what little can be known about Schindler and his scheme ... Spielberg is not visible in this film. But his restraint and passion are present in every shot. (www.rogerebert.com/reviews/schindler's-list-1993)

Writers, directors, and network executives in industrial societies work with a symbolic world of violent complexity in Lewis's terms. Gratuitous violence mechanizes the violence *leitmotif*, while aesthetic realism is an interpretive critique that fosters the standard of principled nonviolence.

HATE SPEECH ON THE INTERNET

In 1995, former Ku Klux Klan leader Don Black established *Stormfront. org*, the first publicly known White supremacist website. As access to the internet became less expensive and creating web pages less complicated, the number of websites and of people visiting them has grown exponentially. In the past, racist hate was promoted through graffiti burned on lawns and pamphlets handed out on the streets. Maintaining postal lists, even to a few hundred, were difficult. Now hate websites on the internet communicate to an audience of millions (Waldron, 2004). Reports from the Simon Wiesenthal Center (www.wiesenthal.org), the Southern Poverty Law Center (www.splcenter.org), and the Anti-Defamation League (www.adl.org) estimate 5,000 internet hate sites and 954 identified hate groups in the United States in 2017. *Stormfront.org* has more than 300,000 members, and the site has been adding about 25,000 registered users annually (Dickson, 2015). On average, 36,000 people have been visiting *Stormfront.org* daily. The number of websites for the

---

[26] Thanks to Min Wang for translating the critical sections into English.

National Association for the Advancement of White People (NAAWP), founded by Klan leader David Duke, has mushroomed and energized the so-called Klan without robes (www.adl.org/main_internet). Marc Knobel of the Council of Jewish Institutions in France estimates the astonishing number of hate sites worldwide as 40,000–60,000 (Cohen-Almagor, 2009, p. 105).

The Southern Poverty Law Center defines hate groups as organizations "that demonize and malign entire groups of human beings based on their class characteristics" (Christians, Fackler, & Ferré, 2012, chap. 8). Numerous neo-Nazi websites promote the anti-Semitic racism of Adolf Hitler's Germany. According to the Anti-Defamation League, the National Alliance is the most prominent overtly Hitlerian organization in the United States today, and its website includes transcripts of anti-Semitic radio broadcasts, scathing articles from its *National Vanguard* magazine, and a catalog of more than six hundred books. Jews are blamed for inflation, media brainwashing, and business corruption, with Blacks depicted as lawless and violent. Books and speeches by Hitler, Joseph Goebbels, and the American neo-Nazi George Lincoln Rockwell are displayed and promoted. Neo-Nazi skinheads such as the Oi! Boys and Hammer Skin Nation have websites saturated with racist hard rock music (www.adl.org/main_internet). Malicious language to targeted groups that communicate contempt by comparisons with dogs and monkeys, rodents, and manure is totally dehumanizing.

The hate websites that mock religious groups are thriving too. Congregations of Christian Identity are virulently racist and anti-Semitic. Today's Jews are not descended from Old Testament Hebrews but are Satan's creation. Jews and Blacks are enemies, a virus seeking to destroy "the purity of the Aryan (White) race." The World Church of the Creator (WCOTC) calls non-Whites biologically inferior, subhuman "mud people." Venomous drawings brutalize Jews and Blacks, and a WCOTC kids website promotes White supremacy in the language children use. The site for White Aryan Resistance (WAR) preaches "your race is your religion" and condemns the "non-White birthrate," "massive immigration," and "racial intermarriage." Other religious sites are brutally anti-Catholic, condemning the Church's empire and bureaucracy, its oppressive doctrines, and its corruption. Anti-Muslim sites are vivid and morally repugnant, for example, *Faith Freedom* (www.faith freedom.org/) and *Truth and Grace* (http://truthandgrace.com/ISLAM .htm); anti-Muslim groups in the United States have grown to 114 chapters (Beirich & Buchanan, 2018, p. 7). Anti-Hinduism websites are active in multiple countries, such as *Jesus is Lord* (http://jesus-is-lord.com) and *Peace of Mind* (http://peace-of-mind.net/).

Hate speech on internet websites that is directed to harmful action is defined as "incitement." Hatred out of control often provokes the bigoted into action. Whether there is a causal relation between hate speech and hate crimes is debated, even though it has been documented that the internet plays an instrumental role in translating speech into action. The FBI reported in 2016 that 307 anti-Muslim hate crimes were committed in the United States, 637 anti-Jewish hate crimes, and 1,744 anti-Black hate crimes; however, the report did not explicitly specify the cause as hate websites (https://ucr.fbi.gov/hate-crime 2016). But numerous examples can be labeled "incitement." For instance, hoping to start a race war, twenty-one-year-old Dylann Roof fatally shot nine people at Emanuel AME Church in Charleston, South Carolina, on June 17, 2015. By his own testimony, his radicalization began with absorbing propaganda about Black-on-White crime from the website of the Council of Conservative Citizens.

And another illustration of incitement: in 1999, twenty-one-year-old Benjamin Nathaniel Smith, an avowed Aryan supremacist, went on a racially motivated shooting spree in Illinois and Indiana over the July 4 weekend. Targeting African Americans, Jews, and Asian Americans, Smith killed two and wounded eight before taking his own life, as law enforcement officers were apprehending him. Smith went on his killing rampage after being exposed to internet racial propaganda – from the notoriously hateful World Church of the Creator. Smith said, "It wasn't really 'til I got on the Internet, read some literature of those groups that ... it really all came together" (Cohen-Almagor, 2015, p. 209).

On April 13, 2014, seventy-three-year-old neo-Nazi Frazier Glenn Miller murdered three people at two separate Jewish Community Centers in Overland Park, Kansas. Cohen-Almagor (2015) examines this episode in detail to explain how hate speech as incitement works (pp. 212–213). Miller founded the Carolina Knights of the Ku Klux Klan and was its "grand dragon" in the 1980s. In 1985, he started another White supremacist group, the White Patriot Party (Beirich, 2014). Miller maintained his own venomous anti-Semitic hate website, through which he made available for free his book *A White Man Speaks Out*. On the White supremacist *Vanguard News Network* that advocates exterminating Jews, Miller entered more than 12,000 posts (cf. Beirich, 2014). Miller declared total war on Jewish dominance of the media, art, culture, literature, and politics. What was at stake for him is the very survival of the White race:

Strike for your homeland. Strike for your little children. Strike for the millions of innocent White babies murdered by Jew-legalized abortion, who cry out from their graves for vengeance. Strike for the millions of our people raped or assaulted or murdered by mongrels. Strike for the millions of our Race butchered in Jew wars ... Let the blood of our enemies flood the streets, rivers, and fields of the nation in holy vengeance and justice. (Miller, *A White Man Speaks Out*; quoted in Cohen-Almagor,2015, p. 213)

Cohen-Almagor continues, "For many years he encouraged his followers to kill Blacks, Jews, judges and human rights activists. No one should be surprised that Miller ... went on a racially motivated killing spree" (p. 213). Upon his conviction of murder in an Olathe, Kansas, court, Miller Sieg-Heiled the jury.

Regarding the question of violent speech inciting violent action, a two-year study by the Southern Poverty Law Center concluded that nearly one hundred people in the past five years have been murdered by active users on *Stormfront.org* (Dickson, 2014). In South Africa's Constitution, freedom of expression does not extend to incitement of imminent violence. The International Covenant on Civil and Political Rights gives a general endorsement to freedom of expression, but it excludes incitation: "An advocate of national, racial, or religious hatred that constitutes incitement to discrimination, hostility or violence shall be prohibited by law." In the United States, threats of a general nature, hatred, bigotry, racism, and instructions on how to kill are all protected from censorship under the First Amendment; blanket statements expressing hatred toward certain groups are permissible. Only hateful or discriminatory speech that projects specific murders and directly calls for imminent harm are considered criminal acts in the United States (Strossen, 2018).

For the ethics of nonviolence, the incitement category is useful as description, but principled nonviolence opens a new pathway. The hate speech-hate crime relationship is pertinent when freedom of expression is researched in legal terms, but the ethics of nonviolence gives us a broader and more demanding agenda based on a humanities approach to language.

Philosophy of Language

The right to speak openly and to express opinions and ideas without being censored is typically considered by political and legal theorists to deserve full protection as the most sacrosanct of human rights. As US Supreme Court Justice Benjamin Cardozo wrote in the 1930s, freedom of expression is "the matrix, the indispensable condition, of nearly every other form of freedom" (Berkman & Shumway, 2003, p. 135). In addition to being fundamental to individual liberty and autonomy, freedom of expression, as argued by legal and political scholars, is a necessary condition for democratic governance: "From this view, open political debate and the uncensored dissemination of information about government is the method by which citizens restrain tyranny and protect their collective sovereignty" (p. 135). As Alexander Meiklejohn argued in defending free expression: "It is the mutilation of the thinking process of the community against which the First Amendment to the Constitution is directed. The principle of the freedom of speech springs from the necessities of the program of self-government" (1948, p. 26).[27]

The political-legal perspective that promotes freedom of expression as an individual right was developed definitively in the nineteenth century by the British empiricist John Stuart Mill. In his famous bible of free expression, *On Liberty* (1859), Mill argued that opinions are the property of those who express them; therefore, to censor or oppress such opinions is a travesty against an inherent human right. Because for Mill negative liberty is presumptive, autonomous subjectivity is the most effective safeguard of human happiness.

Rather than be limited by Mill's individualist trajectory, our thinking on internet hate needs a new philosophical foundation. We have a different basis of knowledge when we see human existence as intrinsically lingual. On this basis we articulate our work on morality to lived experience. If our definition of free expression is multilingual, goodness and badness do not merely express the attitudes of solitary individuals, but they are also judgments a community together believes to be true about the world.

The philosophy of language gives us a different metanarrative for freedom of expression in the global context where humans as symbol makers are holistic beings of emotions, reason, and will. Because language is universal to the human race, our understanding of digital hate platforms

[27] Christa Van Wyck's (2016) understanding of free expression is broadly humanitarian, but it has a governance orientation nonetheless: "Freedom of expression is generally deemed necessary to promote scientific, artistic, and cultural progress." Expression is "a means of fulfillment of the human personality, and is closely related to other fundamental rights and freedoms, such as the freedom of religion, belief and opinion, the right to dignity, the right to freedom of association and the right of assembly" (p. 2).

should not be legal-political, but governed by the *prima facie* duty of principled nonviolence.

Freedom of expression in Western political theory depends on the dualism of individual and society, with rational individuated choice accountable to the rules of social contract. The philosophy of language is the opposite. It defines humans as dialogic beings.[28] Instead of solitary subjectivism, the philosophy of language establishes a new framework. The issue is freedom of *expression*, not just the political-legal concept of freedom, but the lingual concept of expression. The philosophy of language provides a universal rationale for limiting freedom of expression in a complicated world of internet hate.

The legal tradition, in which individual rationality is the basis of free expression, reduces this idea to procedures and the abstracted self. Thus the philosophy of language as symbolic form is a distinct alternative. In the ontic-linguistic trajectory, community is the normative ideal, in opposition to the solitary self as the presumptive norm. Language belongs to the community where its meanings are nurtured in the neighborhood, home, and school. Language is not an agent of private meanings that individuals interpret esoterically. Locke in *An Essay Concerning Human Understanding* and Mill in his *On Liberty* considered the sovereignty of individual minds to be self-evident and transmission in the public arena to be the problem. The philosophy of language that defines humans as symbolic beings breaks down the dichotomy in Locke and Mill between public language and internal ideas, between sacred individuals and derivative society.

---

[28] The liberal individualism of social contract theory is at odds with the dialogic self of principled nonviolence. The moral and political theory of Thomas Hobbes (1588–1679) gives social contractualism its first modern exposition. After Hobbes, John Locke (1632–1704) and Jean-Jacques Rousseau (1712–1778) are social contract's best-known proponents. In the twentieth century, John Rawls's *Theory of Justice* gave the social contract tradition further notoriety (cf. Nussbaum, 2006, chap. 1). However, despite its longevity and pedigreed proponents, a number of philosophers have challenged contract theory's presumption about the nature of the person (Pateman, 1988). Macpherson (1973), for example, has concluded that the Hobbesian person is a bourgeois man typical of early modern Europe, not a universal human being as presumed. In feminist terms, the discrete entities who constitute the social contract cannot be seen as a generalized model of humanity; the contract's persons are seeking their own self-interest (e.g., DiStefano, 1991). When the public is understood in contractual terms, both aggression and personal protectionism are typically considered the natural state of affairs. The ethics of nonviolence replaces liberalism's solitary self with the concept of selves-in-relation (Atay, 2016).

In the symbolic theory of language, communication is not a functional exchange of neutral signs. It is not merely an information link between two different social entities that exist outside it. Communication is the intersubjective medium of human existence; it is the human mode of belonging together in what Habermas calls our lifeworld. Language is meaningful before it is spoken by anyone. That meaningfulness comes not from individual acts of protected speech, but from our common linguisticality. Symbolism is peculiar to the human species, with such concepts as freedom of expression a symbolic construct derived from an already interpreted context.

While the rational choice model that undergirds the legal-political tradition is Western, the definition of language as symbolic refers to a natural ability of the human race as a whole. Through our involvement in and our study of language, we disclose the fundamental conditions of our humanness across geography and history. Human cultures are constituted by language, and human beings rooted in a culture are simultaneously transcultural (cf. Kien, 2016). Linguisticality is a feature of *homo sapiens* and it thereby applies to all people on earth. When this dialogic understanding of language undergirds freedom of expression, the political arena, in principle, overcomes a bias toward the Western Enlightenment.

In the philosophy-of-language perspective on freedom of expression, this concept regarding our sociopolitical relations is value laden. Expression is not a neutral data set, but it is conditioned by a norm. As we learn from principled nonviolence, when human existence is understood as fundamentally intersubjective, our selves-in-relation carry moral obligations. For the philosophy of language, free expression is grounded in the intrinsic worthiness of humans as the symbol-making species. Basic concepts such as intrinsic worthiness carry enough denotation across cultures that journalists and policy makers and citizen-users of the internet understand the basic concept, though they explain and apply it locally.

From the symbolic language perspective, it is plausible to argue that distinctive humanness as the ground for freedom of expression can be both one-and-many; that is, free expression understood at the deep level of worldview is constructed variously in different cultural contexts. As Ricoeur (2005) concludes, the human quest for recognition binds the species into a common unity. Hate speech in the legal-political tradition of free expression typically leads to the polarization of hate speech ideology on the one hand and the ideology of individual rights on the other. The norm of reverence for human life avoids that divide and appeals to our common humanity for freedom of expression's implementation and critique.

Because hate speech is built on the principle of moral exclusion, the ethics of principled nonviolence confronts it directly. Moral exclusion occurs when individuals or groups are perceived as outside the boundaries of fairness and justice. If those who are called "barbarians" and "aliens" are seen as threatening racial purity, rights can be denied. In these hate platforms, the targeted group is innately evil, a social menace, so segregation or eradication is necessary to prevent harm to the social order. Hate websites as virtual communities existing in isolation from and opposition to the existing order help to normalize this morally repulsive thinking. The demonic Hitler is the archetype of moral exclusion. In the virtual community, to the Christian Identity Movement, "killing a Jew is like stepping on a cockroach." For the symbolic theory of language, healthy membership in the human community is the primary value. Moral exclusion is the total opposite. The digital platforms of hate groups not only harm individuals but also erode the tolerance that is necessary for societies to function.

Analysis Becomes Activism

The political-legal tradition of free expression emphasizes policy, the law, and enforceability mechanisms. Multiple issues of jurisprudence are still unresolved worldwide. The regulatory apparatus that has been designed for hate speech needs ongoing legal refinement to match today's internet technology systems. However, when freedom of expression is understood humanistically as a symbolic construct, its moral basis is primary and its legal orientation secondary. Its base then becomes the ethics of principled nonviolence. From another perspective, if our understanding of hate speech is normed by the sacredness of life, it harmonizes with the ethics of nonviolence. Proposals that limit free expression when it violates the ethics of nonviolence are understood and endorsed, rather than rejected as invitations to government intrusion. The negative-liberty approach is a network of legal procedures designed to avoid external constraints. Inevitable conflicts between nations over their sovereignty, and among various contending groups within nations, make this approach ineffective. When the emphasis shifts from individual rights to the ethics of principled nonviolence, the agenda regarding internet hate is comprehensive and sustainable.

For productive activism, the new agenda can be implemented through organizations such as the Anti-Defamation League (ADL). This nongovernmental entity with an internet division, founded in 1913, has thirty regional offices in the United States and three overseas offices in Israel, Italy, and Russia. ADL is an example of existing arenas that oppose all forms of hate bigotry through information, education, and public advocacy (www.adl.org). The ethics of nonviolence considers it newsworthy.

Cohen-Almagor is undoubtedly correct that a strategic form of activism is engagement with internet service providers (ISPs) and web-hosting services (WHSs): "ISPs and Web-hosting companies should develop standards for responsible and acceptable practices for Netusers. ISPs' terms of service usually grant ISPs the unilateral right and ability to block services to clients that violate the terms. ISPs are reluctant to do so because they are businesses for profit" (Cohen-Almagor, 2015, p. 219).[29] These companies uphold internet neutrality and conduct their business according to direct monetary consequences. Some of them act responsibly, making discretionary efforts to provide a healthy environment for their network users, thinking that this policy avoids legal risks and is the most beneficial long term (cf. McWilliams, Matten, Moon, & Siegel, 2009). Internet users can assist ISP and WHS management to distinguish search engine optimization designed to promote narrow commercial interests from optimizing based on the principle of nonviolence.

The ISP/WHS strategy gained visibility in August 2017 when *Stormfront.org* (the oldest and one of the largest neo-Nazi websites) was deleted by its website home, Web.com, after a campaign by the Lawyers' Committee for Civil Rights Under Law (www.theguardian.cm/technol ogy/2017/sug/29/stormfront-neo-nazi-hate-site-murder-internet-pulled . . .). The White supremacist website, Andrew Anglin's *Daily Stormer*, had been pulled earlier by GoDaddy, following the negative public reaction to the violent White supremacist rally in Charlottesville, Virginia (August 2017; Beirich & Buchanan, 2018, p. 9). The Squarespruce platform is considering which websites to cancel. Meanwhile, new hate groups continue to emerge (Patriot Front, Fraternal Order of Alt Knights, Identity Dixie, for instance), and the old websites under threat

---

[29] A typical "terms of service" is that of Yahoo! that does not allow users to "upload, post, transmit or otherwise make available any content that is unlawful, harmful, threatening, abusive, harassing, torturous, defamatory, vulgar, obscene, libelous, invasion of another's privacy, hateful, adult-oriented, or racially, ethnically, or otherwise objectionable" (https://info.yahoo.com/legal/us/yahoo/localfreewebsite/details.htm).

keep reorganizing themselves to stay alive electronically (Beirich & Buchanan, 2018).

Abraham Foxman (2013), former national director of the Anti-Defamation League, recognizes the power of hate networks' anonymous vitriol. Anonymity on the borderless internet guarantees technically that the repercussions of accountability from hate postings are minimal or nonexistent. Therefore, involvement with social media sites requires creative and savvy attention to victims and the demonized. In May 2010, Facebook took down the page "Kill a Jew Day," which urged Facebook users to violence "anywhere you see a Jew between July 4 and 22" (Cohen-Almagor, 2015, p. 216). Facebook rules prohibit posting content that is hateful or threatening, and the Facebook network insisted that the company act on it (Facebook, Community Standards, Article 12; www.facebook.com/communitystandards/hate_speech). Given that the viral nature of web hate is not easily subject to laws or organizational policies, internet users should be challenged to act responsibly when they encounter violence. Principled nonviolence advocates a socially responsible warning against potentially negative uses of digital technology that might translate into actual harms.

The philosophy of language enables freedom of expression to be acceptable globally and to be productive in the digital era. The political liberalism of Mill's *On Liberty* is replaced with symbolic meaning making, in which narratives emerge that deal coherently with today's combative geopolitics. Principled nonviolence provides a norm for responsible hate speech thinking and action in schools, religious centers, media literacy courses, and NGOs worldwide. Redefining freedom of expression as a moral issue first of all and not primarily a legal question invigorates our thinking toward populist activism instead of depending on law-and-order professionals. For the sacredness of life as the worldview underlying nonviolence, viral race-hate is malignant and a scourge, but not terminal. Race-hate is not an unalterable certainty, but a linguistic construction that, therefore, by definition can be resymbolized. It is a viciously belligerent barrier to public collaboration. Adversaries do not fade away in light of well-intentioned persistence. Rejecting the hatred and criminalizing the perpetrators is intermediate only; they are not the destination. Activism on every level and of every kind affirms the deep humanity of the other, acts out of what Barack Obama calls *The Audacity of Hope*.

The acclaimed film *American History X* presents the story of two brothers, skinheads filled with White rage, who finally understand the opposite of website beastiality: "Hate is baggage; life's too short to be pissed off all the time." In a school paper project confessing his reversal, the protagonist Danny Vinyard concludes with Abraham Lincoln's immortal words, reminding his stunned and bigoted followers that vengeance "ought not break the bonds of affection." After inciting them to raw violence against vermin immigrants, Vinyard came to the truth of nonviolence that only across divides is human existence sustainable.

Following the Rwanda genocide in 1994, about 120,000 suspects were arrested and the legal system overwhelmed. To cope with the backlog of court cases and justice unfulfilled, the government released 40,000 prisoners on the pledge that they would seek restoration by confessing their atrocities and requesting forgiveness. The documentary film *As We Forgive* (2008) tells the story of survivors and murderers and the encounters between genocide perpetrators and their victims' families (O'Hare, 2015). The turn from retributive justice to restorative justice relives the transformation of Danny Vinyard. The *New York Times Magazine* featured "Portraits of Reconciliation" twenty years after the genocide, with peace of mind the primary emotion. In accepting apologies from killers of children and parents, brothers and sisters, survivor Karorero's testimony is typical: "When someone is full of anger, he can lose his mind. But when I granted forgiveness, I felt my mind at rest." And Munganyinka was restored after a long emotional journey: "After I was chased from my village and Dominique looted and burned it, I became hopeless and insane. I was like a dry stick; now I am peaceful in my heart" (Hugo, 2014). The unimaginable atrocities of the genocide and the torturous struggles of living justice are not obscured or trivialized, but an irrevocable sacredness of human life creates new meaning. For the principled nonviolence of this chapter, hatred is not the last word. The public struggle over language does not end there. If it would, there are no people-groups to gather tomorrow.

PEACE JOURNALISM

Peace journalism is an interpretive process, and the ethics of principled nonviolence gives the direction by which the interpretation ought to be done. The ethics of nonviolence is the ground and boundaries for a form of news reporting called "peace journalism." When peace is a moral imperative, it is not reduced to the politics of war, but a fundamental way to understand the sacredness of life intrinsic to the nonviolence norm. Quincy Wright and Lewis Richardson originated peace studies in the early 1940s: "During this early phase, peace was thought of as the absence of war; . . . research focused on the struggle of power among nation states" (Sadig & Guta, 2011, p. 606). The ethics of principled nonviolence focuses on the discourse of peaceful coexistence in community life, with peace-making between intergovernmental bodies a subset of this large framework (cf. Beer, 2011).

War Reporting

Johan Galtung has developed and applied the principle of nonviolence systematically. He is concerned not simply with the standards of war reporting (cf. Allan & Zelizer, 2004) but also positive peace – the creative, nonviolent resolution of all cultural, social, and political conflicts (e.g., Galtung, 2000, 2004). As does Galtung, Jake Lynch recognizes that military coverage as a media event feeds the very violence that journalists report. Therefore, Lynch has targeted the theory and practice of peace initiatives and conflict resolution to news organizations and professions (e.g., Lynch & McGoldrick, 2005; Lynch, 2008). As Cai Yiping (2011) puts it: "War journalism is journalism about conflict that has a value bias toward violence," which leads audiences "to overestimate violent responses to conflict by ignoring nonviolent alternatives." Peace journalism aims ' to correct this bias, and, by doing so, allow opportunities for society at large to consider and value non-violent responses to conflict" (pp. 17–18).

The violence of military technology has significant news value. Core journalistic values favor conflict, directly or inadvertently. Peace journalism is a self-conscious, working concept that denies that premise: "Galtung (1998) made a strong case for rerouting journalism to a 'high road' for peace, instead of the 'low road' taken by news media in chasing wars and the elites who run them, fixating on a win-lose outcome, and simplifying the parties to two combatants slugging it out in a sports arena" (Lee, 2009, p. 258). The high road means among other things a focus on negotiation and resolution rather than voyeurism.

Consistent with a commitment to the sacredness of life that is worked out in terms of principled nonviolence, Seow Ting Lee (2009) concludes that there are three strategies for peace journalism:

(1). Instead of being consumed by military action, present the context, background, and a historical perspective. Linguistic accuracy is crucial – not speaking of Muslim rebels as a generic group, for example, but identifying dissidents of particular political factions. Instead of categories such as enemies and criminals dominating news reports on war and social conflict, human relationships are understood in more sophisticated terms with reverence for human life primary.[30]

(2). Rather than political and military elite sources, emphasize the people's perspective and advocate editorially for peace's benefit to the noncombatants. War reporting typically follows what Bennett, Lawrence, and Livingston (2007) have identified as "the tendency of the press to record rather than critically examine the official pronouncements of government" (p. 36); in so doing journalists replicate the polarizing language of war. A number of studies have focused on the framing of war reporting, such as Wolsfeld's influential research article in the *Harvard International Journal of Press/Politics*. He found that the media's choice of "drama frames" in the Israeli-Palestinian conflict gave the extremists of both sides an overshare of airtime, a dominance that, in effect, drowned out voices for peace (1997, pp. 52–70). Instead of organized violence between nations as the exclusive framework, reports should include common values and examples of cooperation among citizens of both sides. Rather than a preoccupation with the visible effects of war – the casualties and destruction of property – the invisible effects of violence are reported, that is, the public's emotional distress and the rupture of social services.

(3). Instead of a dichotomy of good and evil in a zero-sum game, represent all parties. Report on the various ways the conflict could be resolved without violence (e.g., Dayton & Kriesberg, 2009). Journalists tend to ignore peace negotiations unless explosive sideshows accompany them. Peace journalism creates opportunities for society at large to consider and value nonviolent responses to conflict; editorials and opinion columns urge reconciliation and focus on "common ground rather than on vengeance, retaliation, and differences" (Lee, in press, chap. 19). Consensus-building efforts are considered newsworthy. Stories that reflect the peace journalism model "create opportunities for society at large to consider and value non-violent responses to conflict" (Lynch & McGoldrick, 2005, p. 5).

---

[30] The research on Othering is becoming more sophisticated and helps clarify the process during conflicts of identifying and labeling those who are different; see Holliday et al. (2004) and Bhattacharya (2009). Chloé Taylor's (2006) theoretical comparison of Levinas and Derrida on the face of the Other identifies the substantive issues.

Sadig and Guta (2011) add a fourth feature of peace journalism: coverage following violent conflicts ought to enhance trust and inclusion. After peace agreements are signed, and even if the resolution was reasonably amicable, societies are left "suffering from distrust, trauma, and grievances that last long after conflict resolution" (p. 605). Peace journalism pays special attention to the news media's role in advocating social change and sustainable peace – especially toning down ethnic and religious differences so that the conflicts will not be repeated. The principle of nonviolence promotes such a discourse of peaceful coexistence in community life, rather than limiting the principle to negotiations between opposing governments.

Seow Ting Lee is from Singapore and Jack Lynch is based in Australia. Johan Galtung, from the land of the Nobel Peace Prize, Norway, started using the term, "peace Journalism" in the 1970s. The peace journalism model was developed further by the Conflict and Peace Forums, a think tank based in England, in a series of international conferences in the late 1990s. ISIS International is a communication organization in the Philippines that conducts workshops for media professionals and community leaders on peace and conflict. Common Ground in Brussels trains journalists and students in media and conflict resolution in Europe, the Middle East, Sri Lanka, and Turkey (Terzis, 2007). The Institute for War & Peace Reporting, with offices in London, Amsterdam, and New York, supports reporters involved in conflicts. Haydir Badawi Sadig of Qatar University advocates the Sudanese Republican peace initiative. Jolyon Mitchell of Scotland sees potential in the documentary genre for peacemaking. He recommends three examples: *War Photographer* (Swiss film-maker Christian Frei), *Long Night's Journey Into Day* (South Africa), and the British documentary *The Imam and the Pastor* (2007, pp. 13–16). A 2015 documentary could be added to his list, *Blessed Are the Peacemakers: A New Look at the West Bank and Jerusalem*. Filipino media scholar, C. Crispin Maslog, has taught peace journalism in different countries and authored *A Manual on Peace Reporting in Mindanao* (1990). While peace journalism is routinely criticized as "unprofessional activism" by the conventional media, its rationale and practice are taking hold around the world.

Collaborating on the comparative research that peace journalism needs, Lee and Maslog (2005) have studied 1,338 stories of regional conflicts in ten English-language newspapers in five Asian countries – India, Pakistan, Indonesia, Sri Lanka, and the Philippines. By operationalizing Galtung's war/peace classification, the study focused on four Asian conflicts: the Kashmir dispute between India and Pakistan, the Tamil Tiger uprising in Sri Lanka, the Aceh and Maluku civil wars in Indonesia, and the Mindanao separatist movement in the Philippines. The research "shows that news coverage of these conflicts is dominated by the war journalism frame," that is, "a focus on the here and now, an elite orientation, and a dichotomy of good and bad"; though the coverage of Tamil Tiger and of the "Mindanao conflict by the Sri Lankan and the Philippine newspapers suggest a more promising peace journalism framing" (Lee, in press, chap. 19):

> There was no relationship between story type (news, features, opinion) and distribution of war journalism and peace journalism stories. Whether a story was written as hard news, a feature, or an opinion piece had no bearing on the framing of the story. However, there was a positive correlation between story length and peace journalism. The longer the story, the more likely it was framed as peace journalism. (Lee, in press, chap. 19).[31]

In 2010, Lee compared the framing of English-language news stories and vernacular news stories in three Asian conflicts: Kashmir, the Tamil Tiger movement, and the Aceh/Maluku civil wars. A total of 1,937 news stories in sixteen papers comprised the research base; the vernacular press was rarely included before because of language barriers but is a productive category in this research. Lee (2010) found that compared to the vernacular-language news stories, the English-language news stories were more typically framed as war journalism than peace journalism (pp. 361–364). This contradicts the commonplace thinking that the vernacular press is more likely to be influenced by parochial community ties.[32]

---

[31] Cottle's (2006) research on the terrorism of September 11, 2001, indicated that only 0.3% of news was investigative, based on intensive research and exploratory fact-finding. Therefore, deeper and longer narratives are necessary.

[32] Theory and research in peace journalism has been oriented to democratic systems, since censorship and dictatorial control of citizens are antithetical to the four primary features of peace journalism. Haydar Badawi Sadig's work on peace communication in Sudan expands the democratic repertoire. Since June 1989 when Omer Al-Bashir overthrew the democratically elected government of Sudan, the millions displaced and civil war deaths and oppression, and now the division into two countries, require for peace journalism a different anchor than democratic policies (Sadig & Guta, 2011). Sadig and Guta (2011) appeal to the Sudanese Republican vision as the interpretive lens of peace journalism: "The Republicans fostered the idea that all Muslims should rethink their relationship with their religion ... This new vision must be based on major intellectual, theological, and legal reforms ... The reformist ideas of Al-Ustadh Mahmoud Muhammad Taha are the antithesis of those of the reactionary strands of Muslim thought" (p. 617). This appeal

An evaluation of reporting on conflict and war from around the world ought to continue, but one conclusion is obvious from the theorizing and research already completed. For peace journalism to advance as an innovation in news gathering, it needs to give up its neutrality and detachment and adopt the ethics of nonviolence. Media scholars and professionals ought to emphasize epistemology. As Lee puts it: "If peace journalism [is] to succeed, journalists must assess their notions of hard news, objectivity, and traditional news values" (2009, p. 207).

In war reporting, journalists defend objectivity to justify detachment from the competing viewpoints of the parties in conflict. Instead of biased propaganda, objectivity seeks eyewitness accounts and corroboration of facts with multiple sources to achieve balance (Lee, in press, chap. 19). However, in the case of war reporting, the idea of journalists as neutral bystanders usually causes more harm than good. Objective reporting's focus on facts and observable events "devalues ideas and fragments experience, thus making complex social phenomena more difficult to understand" (Iggers, 1998, pp. 106–107). In addition, "The preoccupation with action typically leads to superficial narrative with little context, background, or historical perspective" (Lee, in press, chap. 19; cf. Tumber, 2004). Since violence appeals to both reporters and their audiences, war reporting is often sensational and a mere device to boost circulations and ratings (Allen & Seaton, 2004). As research documents, factual reporting of war is typically "a chimera: the ingredients of war – patriotism, national interest, anger, censorship, and propaganda – conspire to prevent objective and truthful accounts of a conflict" (Lee, in press, ch. 19; cf. Carruthers, 2000). Nordenstreng (2008) argues that journalistic thinking on violence is often "symptomatic of a wider movement towards technocratic professionalism" in which objective reporting becomes "machinery" in the larger structural conditions of international affairs (pp. 64–67).

The issues in peace journalism are especially complicated, but the ethical principle of nonviolence gives us the right starting point for this

---

to reform is based on the basic "division of *Qu'ran* into Meccan and Medinese texts." The "Meccan texts are the fundamental, original texts, because they contain universal values that ascertain fundamental human rights. The Medinese texts are the transitional aberrational texts, revealed as tools of conflict management and tools of spreading an oppressed faith" (p. 621; cf. Sadig, 2017).

kind of reporting. The truth principle is salient but insufficient. Responsible journalism in this case means advocacy. The issues ought to be understood in terms of socially responsible journalism, which is interventionist by definition: "The choice is about the ethics of that intervention – therefore the question becomes 'what can I do with my intervention to enhance the prospects for peace?'" (McGoldrick & Lynch, 2000). Peace journalism is premised upon journalists' active engagement with the ethics of principled nonviolence: "Those professionals who, under the influence of a libertarian way of thinking [are] suspicious or afraid of committing themselves to the socio-political values" of nonviolence, ought to remember that this is "a less remarkable leap forward" than assumed. "After all, the journalist does no more than become openly committed to values that constitute the foundation of international law and order," notes Nordenstreng (2008, pp. 72–73).

Terrorism

Political violence is typically divided into four categories: war between nation-states, guerrilla warfare, assassinations, terrorism. While the theory behind peace journalism is broad, such as Galtung's on social conflict, application and research are largely oriented to war reporting. The four categories share the common genus, political violence, but each has distinctive features as a species. Terrorism has long been an issue in international affairs; however, given its contemporary prominence, it warrants special attention vis-à-vis principled nonviolence in general and within peace journalism in particular.

Several studies point to the inadequacies of existing definitions of terrorism, as well as the contradictions among them (Waldron, 2004): "Freedom fighters resisting oppression" for some are "criminals against humanity" for others. There is a general consensus on terrorism's core meaning: "terrorism is the practice of using violence against civilians" (Hastings, 2004, p. 6). But current use of the word by politicians, journalists, and the public indicates wide variety and considerable confusion. The United Nations, for example, has adopted thirteen conventions and protocols on various aspects of terrorism without agreeing on a consensus definition (Evangelista, 2007). The random killing of noncombatants has become a worldwide issue and its intensity has multiplied and the sophisticated weaponry so diverse, and cruelty by the Islamic State (ISIS/ISIL) so overwhelming that long-standing issues are again on the agenda.

The deepest questions about good and evil come to a head in debates over definition, making consensus on this form of political violence nearly impossible.

While dealing with the ambiguities of meaning in the news coverage of the slaughter of innocents, our intellectual work on the ethics of principled nonviolence requires strict definitions and precise philosophical analysis. We cannot merely conclude that terrorism is internationally recognized as illegal and morally questionable. As Tamar Miesels (2006) argues, we need a rigorous understanding of terrorism or we are left with morally ambiguous ideas about it; therefore, she "recommends a return to the basics." She proposes Michael Walzer's classic *Just and Unjust Wars* as offering uniquely instructive "distinctions between three categories of irregular warfare, each warranting a different appropriate moral attitude" (p. 9).

(1) First, there is guerrilla warfare that is distinct as "a kind of ambush that is not legitimate in conventional war. This is the ambush prepared behind political or moral rather than natural cover" (Walzer, 2000, p. 176). Guerrilla militants customarily "conceal themselves in the midst (and rely on the support) of a civilian population, traditionally protected by the laws of war." By embedding themselves "in a civilian population, they threaten the combatant-civilian distinction and the traditional conventions of war of which it is part" (Meisels, 2006, p. 9). Guerrillas, however, "don't subvert the war convention by themselves attacking civilians; at least it is not a necessary feature of their struggle that they do that. At most, they invite their enemies to do it" (Walzer, 2000, pp. 179–180).

Jürgen Habermas makes the same distinction. The random murder of "indiscriminant guerrilla warfare" crosses over the combatant-civilian distinction. In contrast, "the model of paramilitary guerrilla warfare" is proper to national liberation movements and is retrospectively legitimized by the formation of the state" (Borradori, 2011, pp. 56, 33). Guerrilla tactics in Vietnam directed against the US military illustrate this form, and enabled Vietnam to reestablish itself as a state. While guerrillas have been known to launch terrorist campaigns that included the nonmilitary, their target is soldiers who wear uniforms using sabotage or ambush. The French resistance to German occupation in the Second World War is a case in point (Meisels, 2006, p. 10).

(2) Walzer (2000) identifies political assassination as a second distinct variant of revolutionary resistance. When acting in the capacity of assassins, revolutionaries draw a moral distinction "between people who can

and people who cannot be killed." The former consists exclusively "of officials, the political agents of regimes, thought to be oppressive" (p. 199). This ancient form of political violence continued to make headline news across the past century (cf. Meisels, 2006, p. 11). The assassination of the grand duke of Serbia in Sarajevo in 1914 sparked the First World War. In 1951, Jordanian King Abdullah was murdered in Jerusalem by a Palestinian extremist. In 1963, a sniper assassinated US President John F. Kennedy riding in a motorcade in Dallas. Egyptian President Sadat was assassinated in 1981 by an Islamist cell within the Egyptian army.

According to Meisels (2006), "The crucial common denominator in all the illustrating examples is that assassins do not indiscriminately kill private citizens" (p. 11). Like conventional soldiers and principled guerrillas, assassins "aim at particular people because of things they have done or are doing" rather than "at whole groups of people, indiscriminately, because of who they are" (Walzer, 2000, p. 200).

(3) In Walzer's definition, terrorism as political violence is also distinctive: "In contrast with guerrillas who (as a rule) confront armies, and assassins who target particular officials, modern terrorism upholds no distinctions. Terrorism, properly so called, by definition targets defenseless non-combatants, many of whom must be regarded as innocent even by the terrorist's own standards" (Meisels, 2006, p. 12):

Terrorism's purpose is to destroy the morale of a nation or a class, to undercut its solidarity; its method is the random murder of innocent people. Randomness is the crucial feature of terrorist activity. If one wishes fear to spread and intensify over time, it is not desirable to kill specific people identified in some particular way with a regime, a party, or a policy. Death must come by chance to individual Frenchmen, Germans, to Protestants or Jews, until they feel themselves fatally exposed and demand that their governments negotiate for their safety. (Walzer, 2000, p. 197)

Meisels adds: "Terrorists do not kill civilians by accident, as an unfortunate consequence of their military activity . . . For terrorists, the killing of non-combatants is not a regrettable by product or side effect; innocent victims are not an 'occupational hazard.' Instead they are the be all and end all of this form of belligerency" (2006, p. 12). In Meisels's terms, "terrorism defined strictly is the intentional, random murder of defenseless noncombatants, with the intent of instilling fear of mortal danger amidst a civilian population as a strategy to advance political ends" (2006, p. 1). The US legal definition is parallel: "The term 'terrorism' means premeditated, politically motivated violence perpetrated against noncombatant targets by subnational groups or clandestine agents, usually intended to influence an audience" (Title 22 of the US Code, Section 2656f[d]).

Terrorism totally negates the sacredness of life protonorm in which the ethics of nonviolence is embedded. While ethicists debate just and unjust warfare, distinguish "indiscriminate" from "paramilitary" guerrilla tactics, and recognize political officials as distinct from citizens, in the political violence of terrorism no moral defense is conceivable. Regarding the strict definition of modern terrorism, both the humanistic universals of this book and the absolutes of classical theory are identical. Murdering randomly annihilates all moral legitimacy. No philosophically interesting distinctions are left to examine: harm and innocence, intentions and consequences, casualties and victims, deliberate action and unintentional effects, perfect and imperfect duties, event and representation. Terrorism as a particular form of political violence is at polar odds with the universal sacredness of life and diametrically opposed to the concept of primordial human worthiness.

Regarding media coverage of terrorism, the guidelines of peace journalism are generally applicable but strategies one and four need refinement. Obviously the criterion of linguistic accuracy in guideline one is central to reporting on terrorism. Generalizations such as "dissidents," "enemies," "murderers" perpetrate the violence syndrome in public life. Demographics based on competent reporting are crucial in this as in all forms of political violence. But the ethics of nonviolence requires moving beyond contempt to lament. Judith Butler's (2016) concept of grievability clarifies guideline one for media coverage of terrorism.

Butler is correct that the human-to-human relation is a recognition of mutual precariousness, understood as the human being's shared exposure to vulnerability and the risk of loss:

> To say that a life is injurable or that it can be lost, destroyed, or systematically neglected to the point of death, is to underscore not only the finitude of a life (that death is certain) but also its precariousness (that life requires various social and economic conditions to be met in order to be sustained as a life). Precariousness implies that living socially, that is, the fact that one's life is always in some sense in the hands of the other. It implies exposure both to those we know and to those we do not know ... It implies being impinged upon by the exposure and dependency of others, most of whom remain anonymous. (Butler, 2016, pp. 13–14)

Borrardori (2011) interprets Butler this way: "We recognize each other to be different but also interdependent if and only if we recognize under what conditions the life of the other, like mine, can be sustained. This recognition is predicated on the awareness that we are both facing vulnerability." I recognize others for their difference from me "only in the context of our common exposure to the possibility of grief. Grievability, therefore, is a necessary condition for the recognition of others" (p. 475). Lives presented as non-precarious are lives whose fundamental humanness as vulnerable is obscured, and thus they are lives that cannot be mourned. Failure to recognize life's precariousness means to be relieved of responsibility for it.[33]

Within the flood of images and narratives of dehumanization as terrorist acts unfold, the media's mandate for guideline one is precariousness, that is, the opposite of demonization. Instead of objectifying others into an abstract "them," reporters should represent "the multifaceted reality that constitutes our shared humanity, vulnerability to suffering, and constant exposure to the risk of loss." The reality is that "in replicating and circulating bare images and narrative of a violent attack the media typically exclude the very issue of precariousness from the perceptual field" (Borradori, 2011, p. 478).

While Borradori is correct regarding daily news, in editorial commentary, features, investigative reporting, and documentaries, terrorists' lives and thinking can be represented precisely enough so they are precarious, mortal, and therefore grievable. Graeme Wood's (2015) widely read and controversial article "What ISIS Really Wants" is instructive on the caliphate, the apocalypse, and ISIS military strategy without reducing the Islamic State to imbecility. Jeffrey Lewis (2015b; cf. 2015a, p. 254) reviews the sophisticated social media platforms of the Islamic State, describing their technological expertise in analytic terms without stigma and contributing to public discourse.[34] The *Atlantic*'s detailed coverage of then President Obama's first visit to an American mosque used the precise terminology of peace journalism's guideline one to elaborate on the legal and political issues regarding Muslim communities in the United States (Graham, 2016).

Tim Robbins's movie *Dead Man Walking*, with its screenplay from the book by that title (Prejean, 1993), illustrates how the life of a convicted murderer is grievable. Sister Helen Prejean C.S.J., during a crusade against

---

[33] Principled nonviolence presumes the dialogic humans-in-relation intersubjectivity of Butler (2016). Her precariousness and grievability represent an innovative version of the golden rule as developed in Chapter 2.

[34] The sophistication of terrorism's digital platform is indicated by the increase in the number of pro-terrorism websites: "From approximately 12 in 1998 to 4,800 in 2010" (Cohen-Almagor, 2015, p. 179; referencing Luis Miguel Aarizz).

capital punishment, becomes acquainted with Matthew Poncelet, on death row in the Louisiana State Penitentiary for murdering a teenage couple. Poncelet is a "pompadoured, trashy bigot" who insists he is innocent. He is an "unapologetic racist, who beat up blacks as a child, admires Hitler and believes the Holocaust was a hoax." In the film, "he's a caged, unsympathetic weasel, a raging victim, an almost pathetic figure." And "somewhere, inside all of that, Prejean sees a human being," and she (Susan Sarandon in the film) "leads you gracefully into the belly of the beast" to recognize it is not her naïve saintliness but his intrinsic worthiness (Howe, 1995). For Poncelet to revive his own humanity for himself, Prejean insists on his taking responsibility for his murders, which gradually emerges during his death row days, and defines him when he is given the lethal injection and a humane burial. Real-life stories of the soulless and irredeemable who become recognized as grievable are rare, but when they occur anywhere in the world, media professionals who enter them into public discourse are illustrating peace journalism standard one.

If the coverage of terrorism challenges peace journalists to represent the precariousness of life in meeting standard one, terrorism makes guideline four difficult. In three forms of political violence (military actions, assassinations, guerrilla warfare), peace agreements are typically signed or the political violence ends. Guideline four presumes some such closure and worries about sustaining it. But terrorism by its character allows for no resolution.

Robert Holmes (2013) defines terrorism as "the use or threat of violence" typically "against innocent persons" to install "extreme fear to achieve one's ends" (p. 183): "Whereas conventional war intimidates by inflicting loses, terrorism intimidates by instilling fear ... Terrorism is the calculated creation and manipulation of such fear ... It seeks to achieve its ends by breaking the will of the thousands who learn of it. That is why publicity is important to its success" (pp. 184–185; cf. Matusitz, 2014).

Referring to the terrorism of September 11, 2001, in New York, Borradio (2011) concludes: "The threat of an attack aimed at spreading terror, particularly against a mass of ordinary citizens as was the case in downtown Manhattan and Washington may be over physically but is never really over discursively, symbolically, and psychologically. A terrorist attack is never over because it is future-oriented: it always promises more than it is able to deliver" (p. 468). As Jacques Derrida phrased it in his interview with Borradio (2003), "Traumatism is produced by the future, by the 'to come,' by the threat of the worst 'to come', rather than by an aggression that 'is over and done with'" (p. 97):

As horrific as the events of September 11, 2001 were, if they had been conclusive, there would have been the possibility, after mourning the dead and grieving the losses, to turn the page. However, in Derrida's view, one of the structural features of an act of terrorism is precisely not offering this chance ... What is specific to terrorism is that it projects its threat into the future so powerfully that the worst is always and systematically expected as yet-to-come. (Borradio, 2011, p. 468)

Borradio's (2011) summary of Hegel's chapter, "Absolute Freedom and Terror" in his *Phenomenology of Spirit*, helps to clarify the result of fear: "The experience of terror annihilates all sense of interdependence. With its spectacularization of violence and all-consuming focus on the enemy, an act associated with spreading terror demands an extreme polarization that reduces the world to irreconcilable opposites" and, as a result, to immobilization (p. 475). Regarding peace journalism's fourth strategy, for the press to facilitate the public forum rather than accept the immobilization of fear, "the imperative is to find nonviolent ways of dealing with the problems of injustice, poverty, and oppression that are typically at the root of [terrorists'] actions" (Holmes, 2013, p. 196). In fact, Tom Hastings (2004) makes such strategies of long-term peacemaking foundational to the ethics of nonviolence. While the difficult problems of revolutionary terrorism remain on the agenda, the long-term issues ought to move to the forefront of peace journalism in guideline four: stopping the arms flow to terrorists, reducing privileged overconsumption, enlightened education on terrorism's roots, and refugee repatriation (Hastings, 2004, chaps. 5–8).

Summary

Tolstoy and Gandhi understood that political violence is connected to economic disparity. King's philosophy of nonviolence centered on a reversal of militarism and poverty, not simply a rejection of racism. Galtung (1990) operationalized that theorizing with his "triangle of violence": direct, structural, and cultural violence. Direct violence means a physical act; structural violence results from social injustices; and cultural violence refers to the symbolic sphere, "religion and ideology, language and art, empirical and formal science (logic, mathematics) – that can be used to justify or legitimize direct or structural violence" (Galtung,

1990, p. 1). Violence can start from any corner of this triangle, with violence breeding violence as the overarching fact (cf. Sadig & Guta, 2011, p. 607). The principled nonviolence of this chapter embraces this multileveled definition and contributes to a peace journalism agenda of breadth and significance.

CONCLUSION

The ethics of nonviolence is integral to the universal sacredness of life, but nonviolence needs theoretical precision and international application to be taken seriously in media ethics. Principled nonviolence in the tradition of Taoism-to-King is credible for global justice, along with *aletheia* and human dignity. The ethical principle "one ought always to act nonviolently" is a *prima facie* duty that contributes substantially to peace journalism and reorients the symbolic forms of violence in entertainment, hate speech, and terrorism. In so doing, nonviolence achieves equal standing with truth and human dignity as ethical principles for public communication.

Nonviolence is not first of all a political or media strategy, but a philosophy of life. As such its fundamental home is human existence, and this entails an active populace.[35] While delineating the responsibility of public communication, the vitality of nonviolence as a way of life is the context and its ground of meaning. As Ricoeur (1976) argues, texts are polysemic and therefore are interpretable in multiple forms. The Heideggerian *Dasein* entails human meaning making; that is, beings-in-the-world make the concrete fabric of life and its mediations meaningful for themselves. The cultural approach to violence and its symbolic representations is such a model of active producers and audiences. Aesthetic realism puts principled nonviolence to work for media creators and is the audience's criterion in assessing entertainment programming. The response

---

[35] Stuart Hall's (1973) coding-decoding is the origin of active audience research in communication studies. As this approach has developed, it continues to reflect his core concept about humans making sense of messages within their personal and social contexts. Hall stipulated that "the degrees of 'understanding' and 'misunderstanding' ... depend on the degrees of symmetry/asymmetry ... established between encoder-producer and decoder-receiver" (Hall, 1973, p. 510). For Hall, texts are encoded by preferred or dominant readings that reinforce the status quo, with oppositional readings therefore complex and ambiguous in his legacy (Jin, 2012; cf. Morley, 2006). The interpretive domain in the Heideggerian tradition parallels audience studies since Hall, but it is rooted fundamentally in human existence and therefore articulates with the concept of principled nonviolence.

to hate websites on the internet is refusing to accelerate their violent racism through enhanced communal communications. The guidelines of peace journalism promote media and audience collaboration in transforming the collective mind-set from violence to tolerance.

The principle of nonviolence provides a moral foundation for both journalists and audiences. Jolyon Mitchell (2007a) demonstrates how audiences can become "dynamic moral agents ... who can learn to ana-lyze, critique, deconstruct, and where necessary, oppose ... media vio-lence" (p. 4). In his elaboration, "Not only widely publicized hostilities, but also hidden, forgotten and structural violence can be re-envisaged, reframed, and redescribed in ways that promote peacemaking actions" (p. 5). The ethical principle of nonviolence can teach audiences to engage with journalists who "provide a different description of reality which challenges the claim that violence has either the first or the last word" (p. 9). Mitchell emphasizes community life as the effective framework for re-envisioning violence in news and entertainment. For example, religious organizations, though typically ambivalent, are sometimes peace activists, inspired by their beliefs (Mitchell, 2012). Communities together can enable readers and viewers to apply the principle of nonviolence and reinterpret media violence without being consumed by it (Mitchell, 2007a, chap. 7). In Thomas Cooper's (2008) study of public opinion polls over a twenty-year period (1986–2006) in the United States, exces-sive violence in television, cinema, and video games emerged as the num-ber one media issue. But audiences on the whole distinguished "necessary violence" from graphic gratuitous violence, both fictional and nonfic-tional (p. 24), validating in active-audience terms the norm of aesthetic realism for socially responsible media.

The challenge is for the culture of nonviolence to be situated and nurtured in our lifeworld. Through our everyday conversations and experience, human sacredness will either blossom or wither. Within the popular mind, it thrives among citizen action groups; in churches, tem-ples, mosques, and synagogues; on school playgrounds when the disabled are struggling to keep up; or among campesinos as they are learning to read. In communal settings, people can empower one another toward peace – in classrooms, NGOs, family life, friendship circles, library events where nonviolence in theory and practice becomes meaningful. In these formations of public life, we can go beyond such abstractions as national security and states' rights, to represent the struggles for peace in children's theater, aboriginal art, folk tales, local composers, poetry, and community media. Instead of violence given over to law-and-order professionals – the police, lawyers, and judges – nonviolence in the public sphere becomes a society's preoccupation. In the process of educating themselves and making nonviolence normative, knowledgeable citizens monitor and influence their government's policy making and deportment.

Nonviolence rooted in language, culture, and communal interaction is a counter-scenario. To establish its legitimacy as a moral norm, I have chosen philosophical anthropology as the most suitable framework, rather than epistemology, metaphysics, or metaethics.[36] This intellectual strategy validates the solidarity of universal human existence as the appropriate theory, in contrast to those appeals to peace and peacemaking rooted in social contract theory and its liberal self. The ontology of being, while orienting us in the right direction toward the nature of *homo sapiens*, refuses to allow societies to live by uncharitable values and secondary norms.

---

[36] Philosophical anthropology is broadly understood as the philosophical examination of the necessary and sufficient conditions of human existence. It has been an important intellectual tradition since Feuerbach (1800–1873) and Marx (1818–1888), to Nietzsche (1844–1890) and Wilhelm Dilthey (1933–1911); it is the cognitive context for Ricoeur (1913–2005).

6

Cosmopolitan Justice and Its Agency

Justice is typically understood as the supreme norm of the social order. Our current preoccupation with it is "but the most recent manifestation of a set of concerns that are as old as civilization ... Every human society, no doubt, has possessed conceptions of right and wrong; the forbidden, permissible, and commendable; the ways things ought and ought not to be" (Solomon & Murphy, 2000, pp. 7, 11). Homer's *Illiad* and *Odyssey* from Greek antiquity were not epics of written poetry, but morality tales that taught lessons on justice.

The ethical principles of truth, of human dignity, of nonviolence are components of justice, and as its properties they contribute to the arguments that matter in debates regarding it. Societies are to be considered just when truth, human dignity, and nonviolence are the norms for their policies and institutional practices. These three themes give justice its conceptual identity. Truth, human dignity, and nonviolence are major because justice is major. In linguistic terms, justice is genus and the principles of truth, human dignity, and nonviolence are species. Ideas such as substantive truth, interpretive sufficiency, and principled nonviolence that emerge from the ethics of truth, of human dignity, and of nonviolence recommend themselves to philosophical and practical discussions of justice in a globalizing world.

Theorists, both classic and contemporary, have argued for articulating truth, human dignity, and nonviolence to justice. Scholars in the Oxford book *What Is a Just Peace?* make the relationship between "peace" and "justice" explicit and develop the implications for public policy in a discordant world (Allan & Keller, 2008). The special issue of *The Hedgehog Review* (2007) on "Human Dignity and Justice" is premised on their integral relationship, and it works through issues such as the tension between universal and particular definitions of human nature (cf. Pogge, 2014). Philip Pettit in the essay "Habermas on Truth and Justice" understands the Habermasian consensus theory of truth as the latter's "model for a consensus theory of justice" (1982, p. 210). These illustrations from a wide-ranging literature recognize the interconnections of the four concepts and the intellectual value of conceptualizing them in terms of one another.

The ethics of being is developed throughout this book in universal terms. Each of the ethical principles is de-Westernized and given an international orientation. They are anchored in and flow out of universal human solidarity. Thus global justice is the issue at hand – not domesticated versions of truth, human dignity, nonviolence, and justice, but as global phenomena for a global media ethics. These ethical principles are not considered static and parochial, but as animating a dynamic cosmopolitan justice across borders.

MORAL COSMOPOLITANISM

For the ethics of being, cosmopolitanism (*politēs* citizen and *kosmos* world) is the challenge. For professional theory and practice, and in teaching and research, the ethics of truth, dignity, and nonviolence requires the cosmopolitan perspective. At this history-changing watershed in digital technologies, media professionals need a world mind without borders (Ward, 2010a, 2011b). Reporters with international assignments; advertising staff and faculty researching China and Latin America; communication scholars studying environmental issues in all temperature zones; news bureau chiefs North and South, East and West; technical experts working for data companies with branches on every continent – they are precursors. But in this revolutionary age, all media practitioners and communication scholars are answerable to the world.

Over the history of media studies, the beginning point conceptually is the local and from there to the world. The production of knowledge in *kosmopolitēs* is the reverse (Held, 2010). Mediated communication as a field, to be cosmopolitan, must be turned inside out. Our teaching and curriculum, the way we develop organizational policies, and the research agenda are transnational first and foremost, not simply the last word and conclusion. Levinas revolutionized ethical theory by transposing subject and Other, with alterity the originating idea and not subsequent to individual decision making. Likewise, cosmopolitanism inverts the trajectory of scholarship in communication ethics – in this case, from universal human solidarity to media institutions and professionals, instead of the opposite direction traditionally.

According to Appiah's *Cosmopolitanism* (2006), Diogenes the Cynic in the fourth century B.C. was the first philosopher in the West to use the term *kosmopolitēs*. Diogenes considered himself a "man of the world," too great in mind and learning to limit himself to issues in Sinope, his birth home on the Baltic Sea (p. xiv). The Stoics of the third century A.D. elaborated the cosmopolitan idea by claiming that they lived in agreement with the cosmos. Based on that belief, the Stoics argued that their teachings could not be limited to the *polis*, but they engaged the human race as a whole. Roman Stoics such as Cicero and Seneca debated the concept of citizenship in cosmopolitan terms, defining its various meanings for the empire and for its constituent parts, and for people yet unconquered. In so doing, they captured the "two main aspects of cosmopolitanism: that it entails a *thesis about identity* and a *thesis about responsibility*" (Scheffler, 2003; quoted in Brock & Brighouse, 2005, p. 2). Appiah (2006) notes that among the intelligentsia, the cosmopolitan mind is reflected in the 1789 "Declaration of the Rights of Man," and also in 1795 in Immanuel Kant's "Perpetual Peace: A Philosophical Sketch," which proposed a league of nations (p. xiv). Voltaire reflected global interdependence in economic language: "Fed by the products of their soil, dressed in their fabrics, amused by games they invented, instructed by their ancient moral fables, why should we neglect to understand the mind of these nations, among whom our European traders have journeyed ever since they could find a way to get to them" (*Essay on Universal History*, quoted in Appiah, 2006, p. xv).

To summarize, the idea of cosmopolitanism has referred over its history to the upper crust few, until today's technological revolution when people of all social classes and of all geographical locations can see themselves as citizens of the world:

Through digital mediation, networked communities experience omnipresence in time and space, with the universe-in-total considered accessible. Cosmopolitanism no longer belongs to the privileged but is a feature of modern life (Lule, 2015, p. 322). As Appiah argues, over the last century the human community has been drawn into a global network of information. The worldwide web means not only that we can affect lives across cultures but that we can actually learn about life from e-addresses everywhere – the notion of world belongingness not understood metaphorically but functionally. (Christians, 2018b, p. 489)

From his historical survey, Appiah concludes that "two strands inter-twine in the notion of *kosmopolitēs*. One is the idea that we have obligations to others, obligations that stretch beyond" our biological families and everyday communities, and "beyond the formal ties of a shared citizenship." The second strand is that we are compelled to acknowledge the value "of particular human lives," not just human life generally. There will be times when "these two ideals clash, that is, universal concern" at odds with respecting individual practices and beliefs (Appiah, 2006, p. xv). Thomas Nagel in "The Problem of Global Justice" centers on the same issue though in different terms. From his perspective, cosmopolitanism faces and does not resolve the long-standing problem in political theory of the "scope and limits of equality as a demand of justice" (2005, p. 114; cf. Braidotti, Hanafin, & Blaagard, 2013, chap. 7).

Scholars of media ethics who have put cosmopolitanism on the agenda take seriously the tension between these ideals. Nigel Dower uses cosmo-politanism as the framework in his *World Ethics: The New Agenda* (2007). He speaks of a number of cosmopolitan theories that have two common aspects: "First, a set of values as values to be accepted everywhere. Second, some notion of active responsibility to further those values" (chap. 5). Kathleen Roberts and Ronald Arnett also employ cosmopolitanism as their framework, calling their book *Cosmopolitan Ethics: Between Cosmopolitanism and Provinciality*; they seek in theories the universal and in creative application the particular. In Stephen Ward's analysis,

> The cosmopolitan attitude does not deny that particular cultures and traditions are valuable for life and may be psychologically necessary for the development of ethical character. The claim of humanity acknowledges that we live simultaneously in two communities: the local community of our birth and a community of common human aspirations. It insists only that ... we should not allow local attachments to override fundamental human rights and duties. (2005, p. 15)

From Appiah to Ward, it is obvious that *polites* is an imprecise word that leads to more debates than it resolves. *Kosmos* is also an overwrought term. "World" typically conjures up an uncritical and superficial inter-nationalism constructed of shared markets and tourist pathways, made possible by information technologies and understood through the abstrac-tions of scientific research. The philosophy of technology addresses the fundamental issue here, calling into question instrumental cosmopolitan-ism and insisting on a humanistic framework instead. The challenge –

underneath the debates over one-and-many, bounded territories and fluidity, difference and equality – is to construct a global imaginary of people rather than of machines (Cf. Braidotti et al., 2013, chaps. 8–9).

Planet earth is inhabited by lingual beings who symbolize their habitat. Ernst Cassirer's *Philosophy of Symbolic Forms* brought this intellectual domain to fulfillment, and in his legacy, symbolization is the cognitive capacity that defines us anthropologically. He identified our unique capacity to generate symbolic structures as a radical alternative both to the *animal rationale* of classical Greece and of Descartes's modernity, and to the biological being of evolutionary naturalism (Cassirer, 1944). In Cassirer's definition of *homo sapiens* as *animal symbolicum*, humans alone of animate creatures possess the irrevocable capacity to interpret, that is, to reconstruct lived reality. In Cassirer's theory of language, symbols participate in the meaning of what they symbolize; they share the significance of that to which they point (1960). For Heidegger, language is the house of Being: it means that we live in our language and we think insofar as we bring Being to language (1971b, p. 5; cf. Cousineau, 1972). The language of cosmopolitanism is, therefore, fundamental to human existence in the global age.

Instrumentalism is a symbolic construct, an imaginary that defines technology as neutral and ritualizes efficiency as the master norm. Given the technological character of industrial societies and the world scope of cyberspace, mechanical symbolization is understandable. The technological imperative appears obvious as the organizing ideal, where the capabilities of media technologies set the agenda and define the issues. Technology is presumed to unfold out of its own character, and transmission theories of neutral media are privileged. In our commonplaces, technologies are seen in mechanistic terms as instruments apart from values.

As discussed in Chapter 1 regarding Jacques Ellul's version of the Heideggerian philosophy of technology, the instrumentalism driving the technological age replaces ends with calculations regarding means (Ellul, 1964). Media technologies are a subsystem of the technological framework (Ellul, 1965). In the instrumental worldview, humans are networked into a culture that overvalues efficiency. In an age enamored of Web 2.0's machinic means, human existence becomes amoral; that is, the vocabulary and content of morality are no longer understood. When the speed and productivity of instrumentalism dominate, the ethical dimension of human life becomes foreign to us. Moral purpose is lost to the demands of algorithmic precision. Instead of being content with minor adjustments to the instrumental model, the philosophy of technology challenges us to resymbolize the global imaginary and thereby transform it. A language of cosmopolitanism is required that differs fundamentally from instrument-alism's mathematical equations.

The global imaginary in ontological terms is a productive framing structure for news reporting in practice and research in education. For Josephides and Hall (2014), cosmopolitanism speaks "to the concerns arising from existentialism and the entailment of being human" (p. xvii); that description is accurate. They accept the fact that the idea of cosmo-politanism is typically understood at present as a political-global network, but their research shows that "historically it developed out of a philosophical investigation into what is a human being" (p. 2). Their *We the Cosmopolitans* seeks "to rediscover the philosophical anthropol-ogy tradition and use this as a key to re-describe certain kinds of social anthropological problems" (p. xvii). This is the approach of moral cos-mopolitanism in this chapter. Instead of the "political form of the early modern European period," which integrated "the order of nature and the order of society," Josephides and Hall's cosmopolitanism stresses the "moral and humanistic aspects" of cosmopolitanism. In their perspective, the cosmopolitan imaginary strives "to attain a universalizing ethos that subsumes all humans as being somehow akin" (p. 4).

We the Cosmopolitans, with variations, defines "cosmopolitanism as an existential condition and moral quality that addresses what is fundamentally human about the person" (p. 16). The contributors stress non-Western, non-elite cosmopolitan formations, developed mainly in anthropological and cultural studies (cf. Nava, 2007). This perspective is rooted in our daily activities, where human encounters are "of a Ricoeurian appropriation ... The social relationship of *politēs* extends to others the intimate relationships and proprietary feelings humans have ... of being at home in the world" (Josephides & Hall, 2014, pp. 4, 16).

A theory of cosmopolitanism that is credible transnationally is ontolo-gical, constitutive of our humanness. And when the world imaginary is ontological, cosmopolitanism is not instrumental but moral: "The crux of the idea of moral cosmopolitanism is that each human being has equal moral worth and that equal worth generates certain moral responsibilities that have universal scope" (Brock & Brighouse, 2005, p. 4). In the philo-sophy of language, human existence is a linguistic entity, and by reason of this fact, societies are moral in character, and this phenomenon is central to the ontological version of cosmopolitanism. Human cultures are knit together linguistically; however, the lingual is not neutral, but value laden, so our social bonds are moral claims.[1]

Onara O'Neill argues in different terms for a moral cosmopolitanism of duties. In her view, "we do not take rights seriously unless we seek to show who ought to do what for whom" (2016, p. 10). O'Neill "criticizes theoretical approaches that concentrate on rights yet ignore obligations that must be met to realize those rights, and the capacities needed by those who shoulder these obligations" (p. i). Rights must be anchored in obligations, and obligations "anchored in realistic accounts of the capabilities and vulnerabilities of the agents and agencies that are to carry them" (p. 8).

Ontological cosmopolitanism is the home of global justice. But the conceptual issues are entangled and require intellectual history to establish the moral cosmopolitanism that theorists of media ethics and reporters ought to follow.[2] A historical review is needed to know what concept of justice is appropriate to moral cosmopolitanism, and therefore what theory of justice incorporates the principles of truth, human dignity, and nonviolence. The moral cosmopolitanism that results from the philosophical survey will enable the media's task of moral literacy.

JUSTICE AS RIGHT ORDER

The idea that justice is a legal system of right order is the prevailing definition in the Western intellectual tradition. In this view, when society's institutions provide for its members the goods that are rightfully theirs, justice has been served. If carbon dioxide emissions disrupt the biosphere, the earth's residents are deprived of a good to which they have a right, namely, the good of a stable geochemical carbon cycle. The planet's

---

[1] This is a semiotic understanding of culture. The reference here is not to civilizations as complex wholes, where culture encompasses technologies, customs, arts, religious practices, products, and habits. Johan Burckhardt (1943) distinguishes culture from political and social structures, and from religious institutions. In Burckhardt's tradition, culture is people's communicative activities, referring primarily to the arts and languages. His semiotic definition is used here.

[2] Herman Wasserman's analysis is apropos: "Appeals for moral cosmopolitanism ... are often premised on the benevolence of a Western audience, people who are to be convinced that sufferers everywhere are 'like us' and therefore worthy of empathy. A cosmopolitan outlook of this kind, however generous and kind in its orientation, is not necessarily a critical one, which engages the asymmetrical distribution of communicative power in a globalized world head-on" (2018, p. 130).

population is wronged, that is, treated unjustly (Wolterstorff, 2008, p. 25).[3]

"What is justice," asked Socrates in the *Republic*, and his question "marks something of an official beginning to Western philosophy" (Solomon & Murphy, 2000, p. 11). Plato developed his theory of justice primarily in the *Republic*, and it is a juristic account of right order. Plato's political system was "founded and built up on the right lines," and he considers this order "good in the complete sense of the word" (bk. IV, 427e). Plato's order is an organizational complex of differentiated structures (economics, military, governmental, for example), with justice as equality the integrating principle.[4] Each of these structures has specific rules for treating and for being treated by others. In a social order "built on the right lines," everybody will be performing their "proper function" (bk. IV, 441e) and thus doing their "proper work" (bk. IV, 441d). In sum, for Plato a social order is just when it is organized according to the objective norms established in his theory of Forms.

In Plato's tradition of justice, rights are conferred on society's members by legislation and regulatory practices. For this right order theory, institutions initiate and guarantee a person's rights. As Charles Reid (1991) summarizes the history of this juristic concept of rights, "It became part of the medieval *jus commune*, the common law of Europe, that would in turn inform the polemical works of William of Ockham and the writings of early modern philosophers and theologians – figures as diverse and seminal in their own right as John Locke and John Calvin" (pp. 39–40).

Justice as right order is administrative in character and therefore is a set of procedures that requires due process understood as the fairness of decision making and of administrative mechanics. The operations of justice as fairness are the result of rational choice. When rights and resources are distributed according to fair procedures, and the necessary policies are established to rectify wrongs, justice is done.

The definition of procedural justice in Western democracies has been dominated by Rawls's *Theory of Justice* since its publication in 1971. Rawls distinguishes three types of procedural justice (perfect, imperfect, and pure), but the pure model has become the typical standard; that is, the

---

[3] My formulation of global justice in this chapter benefits especially from Wolterstorff, *Justice: Rights and Wrongs* (2008, chaps. 1–2).

[4] See Solomon and Murphy (2000, p. 21) for a summary of the conflicting definitions in the two Greek words for justice and in Plato's usage: *to eson/isotes* (equality) and *dikaiosune* (righteousness).

procedure itself is what constitutes a just outcome. For justice to be fair, its principles must be implemented by operations that are themselves fair in their design and execution: "Justice applies not to the outcome, but to the system" (Lebacz 1986, p. 39). In Rawls, the theory and principles of justice are derived from justified methods. For Rawls's procedural justice with its "very strong tolerance for individual inclinations" (Nagel, 1973, p. 227), and for the mainstream media that presume it, humans who are understood to be rational and equal can be expected to act justly.

Regarding international justice, Rawls likewise presents a right order theory. In his view, national sovereignty must be limited by respect for universal human rights; as a result, various people-groups must be allowed to define the meaning and content of their own political traditions. In *The Law of Peoples* (1999), Rawls extends his domestic concept of justice to a "society of peoples." Among the diverse "societies of peoples, there can and ought to be "common sympathies" for human rights, for just war principles, and for economic assistance to burdened nations. However, what Rawls considers transnational conceptions are, in fact, organized around territorial states. As a result, Allen Buchanan (2000) observes that Rawls overestimates the extent to which states are "economically self-sufficient" and "distributionally autonomous," while idealizing the degree to which they are "politically homogeneous" without internal sociopolitical divisions.

Onara O'Neill (2016) gives analytic rigor to the statist presumption in the right order tradition: "From Hobbes to Rawls we find an agreement that the context of justice is the state, although there is disagreement whether justice should be sought only in political or also in economic and social arrangements" (p. 151).[5] In O'Neill's analysis, "All of these views assume that justice requires or presupposes boundaries, which demarcate those who are to render and receive justice from one another, and from others who are to be excluded" (p. 99). Thus, for O'Neill, "What is misleadingly called international justice, and would more accurately be called interstatal justice," typically treats "state boundaries as presuppositions rather than as problems for an account of justice" (p. 151).

In O'Neill's (2016) perspective, we ought not take for granted that state boundaries are or can be just:

---

[5] Rawls (1971) considered his theory to not merely center on just states, but on "bounded societies" (p. 8). Nussbaum finds his distinction "confused and confusing" (2006, p. 246; see O'Neill, 2016, pp. 99, 151).

Many states fail to guarantee various rights, including the basic rights of the person, for some or many of their citizens; many others cannot guarantee various rights (in particular economic, social, and cultural rights) for many of their citizens. The situations of refugees and migrants is often harsh and uncertain, and rarely ends up with the full or secure enjoyment of rights ... Although such states may have the competence and capacity to be primary agents of justice, they abuse that role and inflict and institutionalize forms of injustice. Tyrannies and rogue states constantly violate the rights of their inhabitants ... They may fail to challenge unjust and criminal activities. Sometimes they cannot even exercise effective control of central state institutions, such as the police, the customs or the armed services. They may leave individuals without redress in the face of corruption and banditry. (pp. 151, 164–165)

A consideration of just borders that "takes proper account of these issues need not deny the importance of nations and national identity; but it must deny that they create claims to bounded states which exercise absolute internal or external sovereignty" (p. 77).

Procedural justice is the working context for the traditional news media; as a result, media policies and practices are oriented toward the rights of individuals within the legal and administrative apparatus of countries and territories. Justice is defined as retribution – that is, the procedures of the courts, law enforcement, free press, and fair trial. As this chapter's review indicates, justice as right order has been dominant in the West and is the standard formulation in the media. However, to establish moral cosmopolitanism as the standard for the international news media today, a different definition is necessary. The definition of justice as right order carries with it the legal and policy agenda of constitutional democracies and is therefore unacceptable for developing global justice. Working on a cosmopolitan justice is pertinent to young and developing democracies, conceivable in authoritarian systems, and inspires us to develop an alternative to the right order formulation (cf. Rioba, 2012, chaps 1–7).

For the ethics of justice to work productively in the international context, the meaning of justice must be given a different conceptual foundation and fundamentally new orientation than the way justice has been traditionally conceived. The news media ought to base their rationale and mission on this alternative understanding of justice. The legacy media need reform following this book's international ethics of being.

PHILOSOPHICAL ANTHROPOLOGY AND JUSTICE

Rather than uncritically assume the static formalism of the right order model, we can advance the meaning of cosmopolitan justice when it is given a different theoretical foundation. For a transnational ethics of being to be legitimate intellectually and possible practically, moral cosmopolitanism is the appropriate framework, and cosmopolitanism requires a reversal of our cognitive trajectory. As described earlier, rather than extending one's individual thinking or one's nationalism, first of all, the world mind is the conceptual home of justice. A humanocentric global imaginary is the ontological landscape for a justice of three properties: truth, human dignity, and nonviolence. Justice means giving a society's members their appropriate due. When justice is grounded in the inherent worthiness of *homo sapiens*, the demands of justice shift from statism to the world.

V. I. Lenin is correct about cultural transformation. Without a revolutionary theory, there is no revolutionary movement. Ideas shape the way policy makers work, and ideas are "urgently practical" when they show us how to rethink the status quo (Nussbaum, 2005, p. 211). There are multiple explanations of the news media's failure to see the faces and hear the voices of those who are wronged. Reporters typically loathe the perpetrators of injustice and often are overwhelmed by the magnitude of human brutality. But the long-standing structures and practices of journalism institutions embedded in right order presumptions may prevent them "from acknowledging those that come before us bearing a claim upon us" because of their inveterate worth (Wolterstorff, 2008, p. 1).

Nussbaum grants the strength of contractarian theories but concludes that they have "structural defects that make them yield very imperfect results when we apply them to the world stage" (2005, p. 197). Brock and Brighouse speak in similar terms, granting that "for the sake of developing a theory" it may be necessary to presume "a closed scheme of social cooperation"; but the assumption frames "the subsequent development of political philosophizing in such a way that issues of international and multicultural justice remain at the margins" (2005, p. 2). As O'Neill (2016) summarizes this concern, "Many respected and prominent accounts of justice have cosmopolitan aspirations, yet provide a poor basis for thinking about the demands of justice in a globalizing world" (p. 160). Reporters with a world mind who, therefore, take cosmopolitan justice seriously will come to understand the meaning and practice of restorative justice, to the same extent that the news media's preoccupation with the law-and-order system had oriented it earlier to procedural retribution.

Philosophical anthropology centers on the nature of the human, on the necessary and sufficient conditions of being a member of the human species.[6] This domain of philosophy concerns the nature of our humanness. It deals with the characteristics that are both common and unique to human beings as such (Ricoeur, 1967). Retributive and distributive right order justice is the framework of modernist liberalism. Philosophical anthropology points us in a different direction. It critiques the definition of the human that right order presumes and sees primary justice as inherent in our humanness. Rights are not conferred and maintained as entities of a particular sort but are inherent.

To summarize, all humans have worth because this distinctive attribute is a characteristic of species membership. And that worthiness is a sufficient basis for having rights that are owed. No institutions or authorities are needed to provide and guarantee those rights (Wolterstorff, 2008, p. 36). Receiving one's due is entailed by one's intrinsic worth; being treated justly is not a gift from elsewhere for which someone has gratitude. The universal generalization that the torture of children is unjust is based on humanity's intrinsic value, not, first of all, because the Geneva Accords have declared it to be international policy. With *homo sapiens* having worth in and of themselves, every human being is obligated not to abuse the innocent (Wolterstorff, 2008, p. 37). In ontological terms, intrinsic worth is prior, as basis and cause, to legal procedures that grant and administer human rights.[7]

---

[6] Philosophical anthropology is the branch of philosophy that reflects on the nature of our humanness, it is understood in this chapter broadly as "the philosophical examination of the human race." It investigates "what characteristics (if any) are both common and unique to human beings as such," or, in other words, "what are the necessary and sufficient conditions of being a human being." However, philosophical anthropology is not limited to those questions, nor does it presuppose that there is "a human essence of some sort" (Schacht, 1990, pp. 157–158). It has been "part of the European landscape for the past century and a half, emerging as a main interest and focus of post-Hegelian philosophers from Feuerbach and Marx to Nietzsche and Dilthey" (Schacht, 1990, p. 155). Ricoeur (1967) situates his thinking within it, while insisting that philosophical anthropology needs to recognize the existential historicity of the human race (cf. Landman, 1974).

[7] Christian Smith's *What Is a Person?* (2011) contradicts instrumentalist versions of agency; they are based on thin, reduced theories of human personhood. "What is a person" is the fundamental question of philosophical anthropology. Smith argues that this same question ought to be the primary problem of social science also. In his view, explaining social life scientifically is not an issue of methodology, but for significance and sustainability, social science must be based on a humanistic theory that offers a vision of society. The concept of personhood as intrinsically worthy is such a theory.

Augustine

In the history of ideas, Augustine (A.D. 354–430) is noteworthy for defining justice as inherent in our humanity. As one of the West's most influential thinkers, he situated his arguments against Greek philosophy in the Platonic tradition, particularly as formulated by the Alexandrian Neo-Platonists. For him, "the right order within people themselves" (*City of God*, XIX.4, B.A. 37–68) is the prerequisite for a public order of just transactions. The central question of politics is how to live justly in an unjust world, and the answer is ontological. The origins of justice are internal. Intrinsic worth is a precondition of social justice for Augustine. Without a just ordering of human beings per se, "there is certainly no justice in an assembly made up of such members. As a result, there is a lacking . . . of people whose commonweal is a commonwealth" (*City of God*, XIX.21, pp. 138–145). It was Augustine's project to give justice its own identity, separate from the legal apparatus of the governing body. His purpose was to release citizens from the authoritarianism of the State. Higher than the State and its jurisprudence, there is an absolute and perfect domain to which both rulers and citizens are subject, and there-fore, any laws deemed unjust in those terms need not, in fact ought not, be obeyed.

Augustine spoke to the conditions of slavery, conflict and war, vio-lence, and poverty in his North Africa and European experience. Within that context of severity and wickedness, he theorized how social justice helps persons realize their own humanity. Social justice is first and fore-most a matter of loving one another, with love the motivation to give to others what is their due. In the *Confessions* (X.6–7 and XI.8), Augustine developed the concept of justice according to the standard of God's giving to all creatures what they are owed as beings in His image. Justice as typically understood is juridical; just societies are those that acknowledge and act on the rights and duties defined by common interests. The just society for Augustine is established when people love God as God ought to be loved, and people love their neighbor as they love themselves (Delgado, Doody, & Paffenroth, 2016).

Our efforts for justice are drawn by love, not by obedience to law. Human beings are the one species able to love, on Augustine's view. In our birth, we enter a relationship of love, and love's rise or fall is our destiny throughout our existence. Our everyday lifeworld is one of choosing whether or not to love; that choosing is true for all and inescapable. Therefore, regarding justice, Augustine expects supportive joy when fellow human beings show moral excellence and compassionate grief when there is depravity: "Although a man who is sorry for the sufferings of others deserves praise for his charity, nevertheless, if his pity is genuine, he would prefer that there should be no cause for his sorrow . . . Sorrow may therefore be commendable but never desirable" (*Confessions*, III.2). Loving one's neighbor as oneself means that when our neighbors experience evil, "a burning sorrow" then "afflicts our hearts" (*City of God*, XIX.8). When we love our neighbors as we love ourselves, we treat them according to their intrinsic worth and, thereby, justice is done to them.

Augustine's anthropology differs from that of the Stoics. The Stoics promoted the self's intellectual side; Augustine's emphasis was on the affective: "Some of the Stoics, with a vanity as monstrous as it is rare, are so entranced by their own self-restraint that they are not stirred or excited or swayed or influenced by any emotions at all. A thing is not right merely because it is harsh, nor is stolidity the same thing as health" (*City of God*, XIV.9). For O'Donnell (1985), "Not only is *caritas* the goal of interpretation, it is also the only reliable means of interpretation" (p. 25).

As Augustine resituates Western thinking from ancient to medieval, he constructs foundational concepts on the nature of human society, unjust war, and the role of the state (Hobbes depended on him). His searing critique of autonomous rationality was so penetrating that Kroker and Cook (1986) credit him with setting the standard for contemporary cultural analysis. Against nothingness as the ultimate commitment, Augustine fashioned a normative domain that is relevant for debates about justice yet today.[8]

Hannah Arendt

Hannah Arendt (1906–1975) wrote her PhD dissertation under the philosopher Karl Jaspers on Augustine's concept of love: *Love and Saint Augustine* (1929/1996; Arnett, 2014). Following Augustine, *caritas* (Latin "charity"; theological virtue "love") as love for neighbor receives the primary emphasis, though other definitions are also explored. For Augustine, as interpreted by Arendt, love for neighbors is fundamental because we all share a common origin and are therefore equals. It is our

---

[8] *Augustine for the Philosophers* documents Augustine's prominence in the work of continental philosophers who shaped rhetoric and the philosophy of communication in the twentieth century: Arendt, Camus, Ellul, Gadamer, Heidegger, Husserl, Lyotard, and Ricoeur (Troup, 2014).

descent from Adam that gives *caritas* its ground. Acting on that love is also tied to its origins. In Augustine's terms, humans are creative beings. This capacity gives humans the ability to start something new. Loving action is tied to the property of "beginnings." Love is existential in that human existence means to exercise love (*City of God*, XII.20).

In Arendt's *The Human Condition*, this neighbor-love is a property of social life. *Caritas* distinguishes this dimension of our livelihood from the political. The life of association is pre-political. This social life is true of all societies, since the associational is an aspect of human nature. The political arena is constructed only by some societies, and always later than the associational that arises from biological necessity. In the associational domain, relationships are non-hierarchical: "All are the same in such a way that nobody is ever the same as anyone else who ever lived, lives, or will live" (Arendt, 1998 [1958], p. 8).

What Arendt calls the *vita activa* is the biological life that must be maintained for the survival of the species. And Arendt insists that the later political should be blocked from it:

> The common world is what we enter when we are born and what we leave behind when we die. It transcends our life-span into past and future alike; it was there before we came and will outlast our brief sojourn in it. It is what we have in common not only with those who live with us, but also with those who were here before and with those who will come after us. (Arendt, 1958, p. 55)

This concept of "world" that humans have in common is derived from Martin Heidegger, though Arendt's life given to the entire human species on earth refers to origins and Heidegger's "world" to our existential condition.

Arendt's *The Human Condition* has been criticized for distinguishing the political from the social, and for excluding the latter from the former. But the benefit of her distinction is to endorse a public arena where people enjoy happiness and freedom. With this distinction, Arendt emphasizes the independent role of cultural factors for a just society. Public happiness is possible when humans are associated with one another by approval, agreement, and respect. A friendship-based company, where in principle all are given what they are owed, is the necessary condition for the rise of a political domain of diverse and independent equals.

In helping educators and communicators give justice priority in their thinking, *The Human Condition* is an informative resource. Ronald Arnett's (2012) book-length treatment of Arendt's ethics explains why it is such, in his elaboration of her relevance for today's communicative conditions of efficiency, individualism, and hubris. Augustine may be remote for media professionals. By contrast, Arendt's sociopolitical orientation provides a familiar background for understanding why the justice based on intrinsic worthiness is the most appropriate definition cross-culturally.

Amartya Kumar Sen

Amartya Sen's philosophy of justice is likewise contrary to the right order tradition. In his book *The Idea of Justice* (2009), "Sen locates justice and injustice in the context of Hindu beliefs and Indian history." He analyzes and expands on "two concepts from early Indian jurisprudence: *niti* (strict organizational and behavioral rules of justice) and *nyaya* (the larger picture of how such rules affect ordinary lives." Sen "takes issue with his predecessors, such as Rawls, who emphasize a "*niti*-oriented political philosophy where justice is seen primarily in procedural terms" (Rao, 2015, p. 122). Both *niti* and *nyaya* are translated "justice," with *niti* referring to correct procedures and formal institutions, while *nyaya* focuses on the lifeworld that human institutions and organizational structures produce. *Nyaya* is therefore a central idea in "creating a sustainable and just society" (Rao, 2015, p. 122).

Nyaya as living justice is not an absolutist principle in Sen: "When people across the world agitate to get more global justice ... they are not agitating for a 'perfectly just' world society, but for the elimination of some outrageously unjust arrangements" (Sen, 2009, p. 26). Preventing and eliminating severe injustices or *anyaya* is the issue, such as the subjugation of women, poverty, and malnutrition (Rao, 2015, pp. 122, 136). Sen takes *nyaya* philosophy away from its historic focus "on *atman* (soul) and supreme happiness into the realms of the ethical-societal and of justice." *Nyaya* is the practice of justice, not a static intellectual effort "to locate its transcendental use or measure its ideal manifestations" (pp. 124–125).[9]

Sen's concept of *nyaya* is not rooted in the juridical apparatus of advanced states, but in the well-being of citizens in developing countries. Contrary to top-down development measured by GNP and income per

---

[9] For the implications of Sen's *nyaya* and *ananya* for journalism theory and practice, see Rao (2015, pp. 126–133); for an elaboration on how *nyaya* is both national and international in scope, see pp. 133–137.

capita, his *Development as Freedom* (2001) argues that societies ought to be assessed by the capabilities of their citizens. A just society is known by social metrics such as education, health, and the arts that enable its members to realize their full potential.

Martha Nussbaum's ethics links the Augustine legacy to Sen's realization model. In her influential *Upheavals of Thought* (2001), Augustine's work is considered a "major philosophical achievement and a decisive progress beyond the Platonic accounts, because it situates ascent within humanity and renounces the wish to depart from our human condition" (p. 547). Nussbaum describes Augustine's *caritas* in these appreciative terms: in his concept of love, space has been reopened "within which fear, and anxiety, and grief and intense delight, and even anger, all have their full force. And correct love promises no departure from these other emotions – if anything, it requires their intensification" (p. 530). Nussbaum finds Augustine unique and definitive in giving compassion along with other emotions a central place in developing a concept of justice that is restorative.

Comparable to Sen's mode of realization, Nussbaum (2000) studies the ordinary lives of women in India's nonindustrial regions to argue for capabilities that are true of all human beings as they make a livelihood for themselves. Sen's and Nussbaum's idea of capabilities recognizes the human struggle to flourish; "it treats each person as an end, and as a source of energy and worth in her own right" (Nussbaum, 2000, p. 69). In studying peoples' efforts to meet their daily needs, common values appear in Nussbaum's research. As she observes, various social goods emerge that people are capable of achieving and aspire to reach. And herein is the meaning of justice: societies are just when their members have the opportunity to develop the full range of their abilities.

In a revision of Sen, and directly applicable to her own work on gender in democratic societies, Nussbaum (2005) contrasts her model with Rawls's "design of a fair procedure":

My capabilities approach begins with outcomes: with a list of entitlements that have to be secured to citizens, if the society in question is a minimally just one. Especially in the current world, where institutions and their relations are in constant flux, I believe it is wise to begin with human entitlements as our goal. We think what people are entitled to receive, and, even before we can say in detail who may have the duties, we conclude that there are such duties, and that we have a collective obligation to make sure people get what they are due. (p. 210)

Nussbaum, echoing Sen, insists "that a fundamental part of the good of each and every human being will be to cooperate for the fulfillment of human needs and the realization of fully human lives (Nussbaum, 2005, p. 210). All human beings are fully capable in principle of achieving these standards of a quality life. The numerous ways of accomplishing these goals overlap and that confluence establishes the possibility that universals exist. Research on capabilities cross-culturally should produce a working list of what human beings need to realize a just society.[10]

Agnes Heller

For two decades, from 1985 to 2005, Agnes Heller taught at the New School for Social Research in New York as a professor of philosophy.[11] She held the Hannah Arendt Chair, a fitting position in recognizing Arendt's like-membership as an intellectual of European Jewry: "The holder of the chair and the thinker after whom it is named are inextricably linked in a myriad of important ways ... Heller's work can be construed as a subtle response to Arendt's, often in the form of a meditation on the same themes in the changing context of a later day" (Jay, 1994, p. 41). Heller in the 1960s and 1970s was a member of the "Budapest School" led by György Lukács, prominent Marxist intellectual and proponent of a revivalist Marxist humanism. Heller found Arendt's arguments agreeable with her own move away from the Marxism she learned from Lukács. She paid tribute to Arendt's influence in a major essay in *Philosophy and Social Criticism* (1987).

A witness to the political upheavals in Central and Eastern Europe, and dismissed by Hungarian authorities from her faculty position at the University of Budapest, Heller made contingency the central theme of her moral philosophy. In modernity, our foundations are absent, and for the first time in history we are learning to live without them. As Heller (1990) puts it, "The modern person is born as a cluster of possibilities without *telos*" (p. 5), best defined as radical contingency. Zygmunt Bauman (1994) interprets Heller his way: "This is the first generation who knows of the absence of its existential foundations"; it is not

---

[10] Nussbaum (2005) puts special emphasis on education as vital for empowering disadvantaged people: "Education is a key to all the human capabilities. It is also among the resources that is most unequally distributed around the world" (p. 217).

[11] For an extended review of Heller's life and work, with a focus on her contribution to feminist ethics, see Christians (2002).

a temporary absence or a nuisance to be overcome, but an "absence one needs to accept as a fate." We are "the first generation in principle to make contingency a conscious choice and a life-building principle" (p. 116).

Heller's ethical theory is particularly interested in responsible acts that occur under personal duress and social conflict. She seeks to identify moral wisdom accumulated from human struggles. She argues that the moral meaning from choices of decency centers on love, sympathy, and beauty, and these properties form a principled theory of morals that is not absolutist (Heller, 1996). In her *General Ethics* (1988), choosing to suffer wrong rather than to wrong others is the keenest exercise of moral autonomy. Persons who are ethical choose to suffer injustice (being wronged) rather than commit injustice (doing wrong), in the circumstances where committing injustice means infringing on the human dignity of other people (cf. Heller, 1987a, p. 279). In that manner, the public interest is both implied and activated. The potential for a rebirth of the common good lies in the everyday. In ordinary human existence, resistance to the status quo can be nurtured, while social spaces are shaped toward human happiness and a liberating self-determination. In Heller's ethics, our moral authority lies in dissent, not in obedience to the prevailing conventions (Heller, 1995; cf. L. Ward, 2016).

In everyday life, the "heteronomy created by the investment of emotions is experienced as something intrinsically good rather than as a curse." Even with moments of unhappiness or when a particular person becomes accursed, "in the main everyone knows that a life without any emotional intensity in personal attachments cannot be good and is not worth living." Ethical persons are not bound to the "norms and rules of superordination and subordination" but live according to the communal life of emotionally intense relationships (Heller, 1987a, pp. 318, 321).

Heller calls her social ethics "dynamic justice." By contrast, liberal democratic thought, in her opinion, has a static view of justice, one that is rule bound and arid. John Rawls's *Theory of Justice*, for example, is a formalist application of rules; living humans are abstracted entities in a system of jurisprudence. The preoccupation with correct application is wrongheaded if the rules themselves are unjust. Static justice is unable to specify which inequalities beyond income matter, and what percentages of difference qualify as an inequity. This formal justice of retribution cannot resolve complicated issues such as whether legal standards can reform criminal behavior and the extent to which social factors make it impossible to apply rules equally.

Heller's dynamic justice is the opposite of compliance with a regulatory apparatus. Dynamic justice is the real-world process of developing all dimensions of our humanness – artistic, intellectual, and moral. The key to dynamic justice is providing the best possible social and political conditions for a holistic human existence, free of economic criteria for success. Justice in liberalism expands the domain of private choice; the primary action of Heller's dynamic justice is eliminating those unequal social relationships where persons can impose their authority on the actions of others. The "optimal possibilities" of particular cultures, religions, and citizen groups are the substantive goal of dynamic justice (cf. Heller, 1987a, p. 313), to which a society's institutions and peoples ought to give their due.

Heller's theory of dynamic justice is centered on the fundamental question of how good persons are possible. This is her description of the issue in her *General Ethics:* "There is one decisive question I raise and try to answer throughout my whole inquiry: 'Good persons exist – how are they possible?'" (1988, pp. 6–7). In Heller's perspective, good persons can be realized; the task in developing a defensible ethics is to clarify and give precision to everything that is necessary to accomplish this. In contrast to an abstract ethics of rules and external goals, Heller's ethics can be summarized as "orientative" rather than "prohibitive." In *A Philosophy of Morals*, she explains her ethics this way:

The moral philosopher speaks as a member of a community, as a member of the human race, or, as I have been doing, as a contingent person like others. Moral philosophy is a speech act in a practical discourse ... I bring to the surface, as well as subject to theoretical scrutiny, moral norms that have been unearthed, invented, followed, and observed by good persons. (1990, pp. 170, 230)

In *A Philosophy of Morals,* Heller disavows building a formal system; her philosophical work has been observing "good persons in their lives. I gave a report of their predicaments and noted how they dealt with them ... I wanted to be a thorough reporter, eager to accompany decent persons wherever they went, whatever they did" (Heller, 1990, p. 308).

COSMOPOLITAN JUSTICE OF BEING

A cross-cultural review of intrinsic worth opens a new pathway for working on the concept of justice in a global society. This alternative tradition of justice could be labeled for Augustine "social justice," for Arendt "common world justice," for Nussbaum "positive justice"; Sen calls it "living justice" and Heller "dynamic justice," with the label here the "cosmopolitan justice of being." It is a humanocentric theory of justice, based on a philosophy of the human rather than on the legal order that anchors the obligations of justice in statist approaches.

This cosmopolitan model of global justice reflects an ontological world imaginary. It is a justice-of-being constituted by the three principles of truth, human dignity, and nonviolence (as described earlier) and therefore coherent with moral cosmopolitanism. David Held (2005) is suggestive in both form and content. He makes his cosmopolitan approach distinctive by specifying a set of interconnected principles as its content (chap. 2). Eight principles that Held considers universal in scope form the analytic and regulatory context for implementing and applying his cosmopolitan alternative to the international order (2010). Held (2005) labels his "mix of regulative principles and interpretive activity" a "layered cosmopolitan perspective" (p. 18). He argues for his "elaboration of cosmopolitan principles" as stipulating the necessary "ground rules for communication, dialogue, and dispute settlement" and as providing "the necessary background conditions for . . . individual action and social activity" (p. 18).

In form, as with Held, the cosmopolitan justice of being is multilayered with its three principles overlapping at intervals with his eight. Held's "avoidance of serious harm" is a legal reflection of nonviolence, and his "collective decision making" is a political version of the truth principle. Held's "equal worth with dignity" foreshadows the ethics of human dignity. However, the ontological definition of justice entailed by moral cosmopolitanism is explicitly anthropological and therefore more decidedly international and of wider scope encompassing human culture beyond politics. The justice of being is rooted in the intrinsic worthiness of the transnational and cross-cultural human species. Truth is normative since humans are lingual beings. Human dignity is a substantive norm and nonviolence is *sine qua non* for human existence.[12]

Restorative Justice

The cosmopolitan justice of being is a theoretical model that endorses normative strategies and media policies and practices that represent its

---

[12] Justin Smith's *Nature, Human Nature, and Human Difference: Race in Early Modern Philosophy* (2015) illustrates the in-depth scholarship on social issues (in Smith's case on the concept of race) that is possible when the philosophy of the human is the intellectual framework.

meaning and character. Restorative justice in its transformation of retribution is one such initiative. For the cosmopolitan ethics of justice, human worthiness is recognized as nonnegotiable and where it has been violated or lost, we are under moral obligation to restore it. Justice means giving everyone their appropriate due and in moral terms it is a substantive common good centered on social transformation.

Restorative justice in theory and programs has emerged over the past thirty-five years as an increasingly influential alternative to criminal justice practice. The criminal justice system charges the accused with having committed a crime against the state; if convicted, the state punishes the lawbreaker. Restorative justice emphasizes the rupture of the moral relationship between the accused and the victim, and rehabilitation into the social order is the aim. Because of the intrinsic worthiness of all humans, wrongdoing is considered a violation of other humans first of all rather than an offense to the state. Its commitment to peaceful resolution, to truthful confession from perpetrators, and to the human dignity of everyone in the process of restoration provides the mission and rationale for the cosmopolitan ethics of being.

Restorative justice is a worldwide phenomenon, commensurate with the global scope of moral cosmopolitanism. In the Pacific region, with its roots in indigenous practices, restorative justice is used to address crime and prisons, school discipline, social services, and community conflicts. In Latin America, wherever there has been civil war, national reconciliation efforts have become an alternative way to address violence. According to notable expert on restorative justice Howard Zehr, "Two peoples have made very specific and profound contributions to practices in the field – the First Nations people of Canada and the U.S., and the Maori of New Zealand" (2015, p. 268). Various programs are underway at a Mohawk reserve in Canada and with the Oglala Lakota nation in the United States. Community Restorative Boards – also called Community Justice Committees in Canada and Referral Order Panels in England and Wales – conduct public face-to-face meetings with victims and wrongdoers. Restorative justice is promoted in sectors of Northern Ireland as an alternative to paramilitary violence. Restorative Justice International, founded in 2009, has 5,500 members supporting its educational efforts and strategies. Centers for Restorative Justice have been established in universities and colleges around the world.

Restorative justice in system-wide tribunals can be found across the globe, and through them journalists understand more clearly the role of the press in facilitating justice. The rationale for the truth commissions of Argentina and Chile and South Africa's Truth and Reconciliation

Commission is not criminal justice but the morally ambitious role of providing restorative justice (Rotberg & Thompson, 2000; Hayner, 2002). Though having no punitive power, they represent "a new institutional repertoire" for struggling with "emerging vocabularies of truth and justice" and how to pursue them (Kiss, 2000, p. 70).

Nelson Mandela appointed South Africa's Truth and Reconciliation Commission in 1995 "to discover the dark facts of apartheid [and] report them to South Africa and the world." Whereas the majority of such earlier commissions – including those in Uganda, Bolivia, Argentina, Zimbabwe, Uruguay, the Philippines, and Chile – did not hear testimony in public, "for fear that it might be too inflammatory or arouse retaliation from the ousted military officers or their patrons, the South African Commission ... insisted on public as well as private testimony, and the public interrogations of accused perpetrators by victims as well as prosecutorial figures from the Commission's staff, and by the commissioners themselves" (Rotberg & Thompson, 2000, p. 5).

South African radio, television, and newspapers extensively covered the Commission's activities, "especially the hearings on human rights violations and amnesty applications" (Crocker, 2000, p. 101). Confessions were heard from more than seven thousand perpetrators and about twenty thousand victims gave statements. Public communicators played a crucial role. Comprehensive reporting was indispensable for creating a climate in which reconciliation could occur. According to the research of Vicky de Mesmaecker (2010), for restorative justice to become publicly accepted, effective collaboration is needed between the media and everyone involved in the justice proceedings; South Africa's media met that standard.

International media practice ought to base its rationale and mission on this alternative understanding, that is, on restorative justice. Restorative justice reintegrates ethics and politics by making justice as inherent worth the defining norm. When the ethics of being is understood in radical terms, social science theory and methodology are freed from debates over wrong issues and from distractions along the margin. The media around the world can take their cue from young democracies such as South Africa where restorative justice was represented in news media accounts of its Truth and Reconciliation Commission, and thereby humanity's intrinsic worth, to which we owe our due, was illustrated and affirmed.

Digitally Networked Action

The standard media technologies have been central in demonstrating the cosmopolitan justice of being in its multiple locations around the world.

Radio, television, print news and entertainment, supplemented by the social media and interpersonal communication, have been integral to the narrative. The principles of truth, human dignity, and nonviolence, as properties of global justice, depend on the legacy media at every stage.

W. Lance Bennett and Alexandra Segerberg (2013) foreground the new media technologies in their comparative study of international economic justice.[13] *Media Ethics and Global Justice in a Digital Age* emphasizes technology throughout, and Bennett and Segerbeg's social scientific analysis strengthens its argument by making explicit the role of digital media in social movements for justice.

The Logic of Connective Action explores "digitally networked connective action that uses broadly inclusive, easily personalized action frames as a basis for technology-assisted networking" (Bennett & Segerberg, 2013, p. 2). In this exploration, the authors follow the aegis of the "media ecology tradition" by giving meticulous attention to the character and usage patterns of "everyday communication devices" that "connect people through common media platforms," such as "mobile phones, email, SMS, Twitter, You Tube," and Facebook (p. 2). Their chap. 3 on the digital media is illustrative; a major section is titled, "Technology-Enabled Networks as Organizations: The Case of Twitter" (Bennett & Segerberg, 2013, p. 89). The networking mechanism, Twitter, is researched in terms of its technological design and also in the ways it "develops through appropriation and use" (p. 90). Their studies give specific research attention to "the organizational effects" of the "digital mechanisms (hashtagging and hyperlinking)" that are available to Twitter users (p. 90).

The authors' calibrations of technology's structure and use enrich the Heideggerian tradition of humanocentric technology. They demonstrate how to avoid technological determinism, while showing that technology is definitive and not secondary. The argument for context is spelled out in its double sense – technological and sociopolitical. "Upheavals around the globe," such as the Arab Spring, have "intensified the debate about the role of social media in contentious politics" (p. 92):

[13] Their book works on two global problems, economic justice and global climate change: "The two issues are often linked by concerned citizens who worry that economic growth imperatives mean ... that policy makers in many nations sacrifice attention to climate change in order to introduce quick fixes to economies in crisis" (Bennett & Segerberg, 2013, p. 3). In addition, "Economic justice, or fairness in the ways economies work, particularly in the context of the global financial crisis that rocked many nations in the first years of the twenty first century" (p. 3) is selected for illustration since it directly relates to the global justice theme of this chapter.

The critical discussion has been important, yet it has been misleading to the extent it has concentrated on fixed and isolated dimensions of technology or action … One of the important analytical fallacies in the debate about social media and contentious politics is that new social media can be abstracted from complex contexts. There are two variations on this fallacy … The first is the tendency to isolate social media such as Twitter and Facebook from the broader technological and social concerns in which they operate … There is a risk that single technologies will become analytically fetishized and that defining political features of these and other technologies will be assumed rather than discovered. The second variation on the abstraction fallacy is that social media can be extracted from the broader political context. (Bennett & Segerberg, 2013, pp. 92–94)

The authors continue: "By contrast, analyzing social technologies in the context of evolving connective action sequences may enable us to move beyond seeing just a message stream shared among participants, to begin understanding the role of these technologies … in the protest ecology's wider composition, and in particular something of the organizational scheme in which they are embedded" (p. 95).

The book's dialectic of technological formation and social movement activity contributes to the philosophy of technology by its critique of instrumentalism. It disavows the commonplace that technologies are mechanical instruments apart from values. In rejecting neutral technicism and researching contexts instead, the authors are able to re-theorize social movements vis-à-vis economic justice. They distinguish the "familiar forms of collective action based on organizational resource mobilization, leadership, and collective action framing" from two models of connective action. In one, organizations "deploy personalized communication logics involving social media" but do not define their structure or programs by them. In the second, "media networks channel resources and create loose ties among dispersed physical groups" in the absence of organizational involvement or control (Bennett & Segerberg, 2013, p. i). In making technology distinctive while advancing social theory, the authors demonstrate how the cosmopolitan ethics of justice can move beyond the optimism-pessimism dilemma.

TRANSBORDER AGENTS AND AGENCIES OF JUSTICE

To implement a cosmopolitan justice of being, we ought not start with "an exclusive focus on a set of mutually exclusive territorial units, each claiming monopoly of the legitimate use of force" (O'Neill, 2016, p. 156). This interstatal perspective depends on right order justice for its rationale.

The ontological model of global justice leads us to consider a different approach. There are a wide "range of institutions that exercise substantial power, but which are not intrinsically territorial. Non-territorial institutions are, of course, locatable. But their influence is not identified with a bounded territory. Many of them might be thought of as networking institutions" that link dispersed persons, technology-based organizations, and sociopolitical institutions. A "non-statist or less statist" view of these networking institutions is that they are "not readily subordinate to states, and any approach that assumes that they can or should be is doomed" (O'Neill, 2016, pp. 156–157). Networking institutions, such as researched in *The Logic of Connective Action*, can provide effective and trusted forms of accountability, even if they lack the sovereignty that belongs to territorial states.

It is obvious that networking institutions are not isomorphic with state regulation, but we must apprehend more precisely what their accountability means to ensure that these institutions are acting justly. News media professionals who know the cosmopolitan justice of being can play a central role in developing this understanding. Various forms of non-state accountability have emerged; they are particularly significant in international finance and commercial traffic regulations; others are imaginable. The media are crucial in helping us think about the ways moral cosmopolitanism can be promoted in a world of inequalities and sacrosanct boundaries. They enable the public to consider which agents and agencies other than states carry obligations of justice and in what sense they do so.

Moral Literacy

In the ontological model of cosmopolitanism, the public domain is a moral order and not merely a functional structure. Therefore, moral literacy ought to be emphasized as the media's mission. Rather than only providing readers, audiences, and users with technical information, the news media should think of their audiences and users as citizens who seek moral literacy on the question of justice.

When humans are understood as lingual beings who construct a symbolic imaginary of the globe, those who are morally literate interpret that imaginary as moral cosmopolitanism. Journalists assigned to report on international agents and agencies of justice are challenged to advance the public's ongoing process of moral formation. The possibility of moral formation exists in principle. People who make moral judgments "are often capable of explaining just what it is about human beings that merits" reactions or involvements; in other words, people elaborate on their "intuitions by developing a particular ontology of the human" (Mulhall & Swift, 1996, p. 103). Therefore, concluding that one course of action ought to be followed, and not others, is a determination humans are capable of making. Human beings are able to find reasons that are convincing and to act on them. Discussions about agents and agencies of justice are meaningful because of the reality of our moral intuitions seeking understanding. The Austrian psychiatrist Viktor Frankl (1988) put this argument in similar terms. Based on his concentration camp experience, he concluded that human beings are primarily driven by a search for meaning in life, even under the most extreme conditions of suffering.

Therefore, as journalism deals with cosmopolitan justice in news, editorials, features, and investigative reporting, it is responding to a significant human need. Since humans are moral beings, it is possible for reporters, those in persuasion, scriptwriters, and producers to engage interactively in the same debates over authentic social existence as members of the public themselves. Media organizations as educators can aid citizens in distinguishing issues of justice that are beneficent from unjust ones, and in articulating moral cosmopolitanism within everyday problem solving.

When media practitioners critique injustice, eschewing their personal opinions, their appraisals ought to be done in terms of the common values that have wide acceptance in the community as a whole. As O'Neill (2016) warns, "A political liberalism which takes no wider view about what matters may not offer an adequate basis for realizing justice in various circumstances" (p. 150). Ethical principles are needed for moving from a coherent interpretation of rights toward a feasible implementation of those rights for a given time and place. With the cosmopolitan justice of being understood here as constituted of truth, human dignity, and nonviolence, the ethics of truth, the ethics of human dignity, and the ethics of nonviolence provide the guidelines for responsible reporting in the rights domain. On the basis of these three principles, the news media can hold the transnational institutions of justice accountable and in that sense act on the standard of moral literacy.

United Nations' Human Rights Treaties

In fulfilling the task of moral literacy regarding the cosmopolitan justice of being, the focus is a nonstatal framework of networked institutions – agents and agencies of justice that reflect in their mission and policies the concept of intrinsic worthiness. One major category of such agencies includes the United Nations' Declarations and Covenants on Human Rights. In the postwar world, "rights" became a common term in the world's ethical vocabulary. Human rights, codified in the Universal Declaration of 1948, entitled all people to basic rights and freedoms regardless of nationality, gender, ethnic origin, race, or religion. Out of the 1948 Declaration, nine core human rights treaties emerged, claiming equal rights for all people in general and specifying the rights of women, children, migrants, and persons with disabilities. One of the earliest of the nine was passed on December 21, 1965, the International Convention on the Elimination of All Forms of Racial Discrimination. A treaty targeted to a specific audience was passed on December 13, 2006, the Convention on the Rights of Persons with Disabilities. Each of them works with an appointed committee to monitor the implementation of the treaty provisions. All UN member states have ratified at least one of the core treaties, and 80 percent have ratified four or more (www.pdhre.org/convetionsum/covsum.html). On April 9, 2014, the General Assembly updated its commitment, passing a resolution to "Strengthen and enhance the effective functioning of the International Human Rights Treaty System."

Two of the nine treaties are the most far-reaching and therefore of special importance for media coverage. The International Covenant on Economic, Social and Cultural Rights (ICESCR) was adopted by the General Assembly on December 16, 1966. It commits its state signatories to grant economic, social, and cultural rights to their members, including labor rights and the right to health, education, and an adequate standard of living. As of 2015, the Covenant had 164 ratifying parties. It is monitored by the United Nations' Committee on Economic, Social, and Cultural Rights.

The second treaty with the broadest agenda is the International Covenant on Civil and Political Rights (ICCPR) also adopted on December 16, 1966, by the UN General Assembly, though not implemented until nearly a decade later on March 23, 1976. Articles 6 to 27 list the rights themselves, such as the right to life and freedom from torture and slavery; freedom from arbitrary detention and the right to *habeas corpus*; procedural fairness in law; freedom of movement, religion, association, thought, conscience, and speech; prohibition of propaganda and national or religious hatred; right to vote; and nondiscrimination, minority rights, and equality before the law. The United Nations Human Rights

Committee monitors the ICCPR; as of February 2, 2017, the Covenant had 169 ratifying State Parties.

The ethical principle of truth makes interpretive sufficiency the media's mission. Implementing this principle for the nine Human Rights Declarations and Covenants is a demanding agenda. UN activity in ratifying and monitoring the treaties is ongoing. Optional protocols are added periodically to revise or clarify the Conventions. The deliberations and recommendations of the monitoring committees are newsworthy, but complicated: "Human rights are explicitly universal – they are for everybody – but they do not prescribe uniformity. Their interpretation may and must vary with circumstances" (O'Neill, 2016, p. 148). Navi Pillay, the United Nations High Commissioner for Human Rights, elaborates:

> Treaties obligate every State Party to periodically furnish a report to the treaty bodies on the implementation of the covenant or convention within the country. The reports must show evidence of honest and rigorous self-assessment as well as serious dialogue with civil society. Unfortunately, some States Parties find all this too onerous and fail to report as required under the treaty. (2014, p. 32)

Pillay (2014) notes that "Sweden and Norway top the list" (p. 33) as the most compliant with the rules and regulations and asks her audience in Washington, DC, why "the United States which was so instrumental in the adoption of the UN's Convention on the Rights of Persons with Disabilities, still has not ratified it" (p. 34). Moreover, "we cannot claim that treaties and treaty bodies are the only agent of change. Change requires efforts by many actors; the courts, civil society organizations, national human rights institutions, UN agencies, and parliamentary and inter-ministerial human rights committees all must play their role in moving treaties and treaty-body recommendations forward" (p. 33). As the United Nations bodies and state organizations work their way from rights to obligations, the global news media are indispensable.

News reports on the General Assembly's human rights decision making, on the monitoring process, and on execution by state signatories require expertise and a commitment to precise detail. In addition, the *alethic* definition of truth means authentic disclosure of the underlying issues. The rationale for and structure of the International Human Rights Treaty System shift the intellectual framework from rights to obligations, and that reversal in meaning needs elucidation and interpretation. This is a change from a rights-based state of affairs to a normative analysis of global justice. The news narrative, following a cosmopolitan justice of being, is not merely descriptive but also normative. Moral literacy is the press's mission across the spectrum of interpretive sufficiency, but it has particular relevance in disclosing the problematics underneath.

The term "rights" is used presumptively in the nine treaties. But its social meaning and moral status are controversial: "Appealing to rights tends to justify selfishness. Insisting on rights typically makes citizens' choices arbitrary – the expression of one's personal preferences that have no more validity than any others. Rights provide no framework when communities face emergencies and crises. As societies fragment and break down, rights language is mute or responds only to a utilitarian calculus" (Christians, Glasser, McQuail, Nordenstreng, & White, 2009, p. 168). Rights language has been appropriate to the North Atlantic liberal tradition since Locke and Mill, but it is considered Western individualism in various areas of the world not conditioned by Enlightenment thinking. In moral philosophy, a paradigm in which individual agents are first in moral concern is reductionistic in not effectively addressing concentrations of economic power. *Aletheia* would continue to ask for a wider framework in which obligations and agency are seen as more basic for a cosmopolitan account of justice.

And the aspirational issue also needs to be confronted. The International Human Rights Treaty System is normative by self-definition, not merely aspirational. If the Declarations and Covenants are viewed as "setting out noble aspirations ... this interpretation of rights claims would be wholly at odds with the ordinary understanding of rights. We normally regard supposed claims or entitlements that nobody is obliged to respect or honor as null and void." If we opt for an aspirational view, then we must acknowledge the fact "that where human rights are unmet there is no breach of obligation, nobody at fault, nobody who can be held to account. We would in effect have to accept that human rights claims are not real claims" (O'Neill, 2016, p. 196).

Various articles in the nine treaties show awareness of this objection and choose the language of "progressive realization" instead. This concept recognizes that some of the rights are difficult to achieve in a short period of time and that States Parties may face resource constraints. But when articles stipulate, in fact, that states act as best they can within their means, progressive realization has de facto become aspirational. The monitoring apparatus has no power of intervention into signatory states. O'Neill (2016) describes the conundrum this way: "Many states violate rather than respect human rights. Other states lack the power to carry the obligation to achieve progressively the realization of the rights recognized in the Declarations and Covenants. Weak states, failed states, quasi states cannot carry such demanding obligations" (p. 202). Since it is an empty gesture to assign obligations for human rights to largely dysfunctional states, "aspiration" replaces "progressive realization." In Paulo Freire's terms, *aletheia*'s mandate is "education for critical consciousness," and therefore the news media ought to ensure that the aspirational issue is taken seriously in Declarations and Covenants discourse.

International Non-Governmental Organizations

The cosmopolitan justice of being is particularly appropriate to civil society.[14] "Civil society" is the composite term for the human domain beyond the political and commercial. While government and business tend to suppress the social order, the civil society of home, schools, religion, neighborhoods, charities, and non-governmental organizations are essential for promoting a cosmopolitan justice of being. Our customs, values, and life's meaning are typically learned and negotiated in civil society communities, where justice as intrinsic worth typically receives its fullest understanding and most effective application. *Archē* in Greek is the correct term – *archē* meaning "beginning" and simultaneously "direction."

For journalists who have been preoccupied with the retributive justice of the courts, law enforcement, and imprisonment, the challenge is to immerse themselves in the theory and practice of civil society where the justice of being is primary. In Arendt's *vita activa,* we discover common goods together, and the media can be an active participant in that discovery. When citizens are taken seriously in clarifying and resolving public problems, justice is realized as collective wisdom based on open debate.[15]

---

[14] "The pivotal historical figure in developing the concept of civil society was G. W. F. Hegel. In the early nineteenth century, in his *Philosophy of Right*, he identified self-supporting citizens with their own centers of gravity as entities distinct from the political state (Reidel, 1984). Charles Taylor (1992) puts Hegel's notion in the context of other political theorists, principally Locke and Montesquieu. For Kaviraj and Khilnani, Hegel is the basis of contemporary understandings of civil society (2001, p. 23), while they remind us that it is an old term that entered into the English language via the Latin, *societas civilis*, from Aristotle's *konōnia politikē* (p. 17)" (Christians, 2015a, p. 52). In addition to this tradition, civil society is identified in the Scottish and French Enlightenments (Kaviraj & Khilnani, 2001, chaps. 4–5), and there is intellectual work on the idea in India, Latin America, the Middle East, China, and Southeast Asia (chaps. 8–14).

[15] Research on civil society in India has been useful. Gandhi's strategies for mobilizing people are of interest, with civil society a well-known concept in contemporary India (Chatterjee, 2001; Pokharel, 2011). India's plethora of NGOs benefits from the Gandhian tradition of volunteerism (Mukherjee, 2001).

Herewith are three international non-governmental organizations (INGOs) in which civil society is the framework for fulfilling their mission: Global Justice Movement, Amnesty International, and Reporters Without Borders. They are noteworthy examples of what O'Neill (2016) calls "non-state actors which interact across the borders of states" having "acquired capabilities that make them significant agents of justice" (p. 189).

Global Justice Movement

The Global Justice Movement (GJM) is an international network of social movements that advocate fair trade rules and promote the equal distribution of economic resources. Important agencies of the movement are Friends of the Earth (international network of environmental organizations); Via Campesina (international peasant movement), Peoples' Global Action (a collection of student and youth groups), Jubilee 2000 (the association of Christian organizations for relieving international debt), and think tanks such as Focus on the Global South and the Third World Network. Participants worldwide include student activists, trade unions, faith-based and peace groups, and publications such as the *New Internationalist* (www.globaljusticemovement.org).

Though there are disagreements over its strategies, the scholarly consensus is that the Global Justice Movement is a genuinely transnational approach to economic injustice and requires multilevel comparative research to understand its impact correctly (della Porta, 2007). A prominent focus is its opposition to institutions of global economics such as the World Trade Organization (WTO), International Monetary Fund, and the World Bank. Protests at WTO's meeting in Seattle in 1999 are often "credited with launching global justice as a transnational online movement" (Lievrouw, 2011, p. 162; cf. Bennett, 2003a, p. 144). One of GJM's core values speaks to this institutional preoccupation: "Institutions, as organized expressions of society's values and goals, largely determine the quality of each person's individual and social life. As historical creations of humanity carrying within themselves the wounds of history, institutions are continually in need of healing" (www.globaljusticemovement.net).

The Global Justice Movement's philosophy of institutional justice identifies a third option besides socialism or monopolistic capitalism: "The solution to economic injustice is not to make enemies out of the owners but, by lifting barriers, to make owners out of non-owners." Economic justice means the empowerment of persons "with the means and opportunities to acquire and enjoy the full rights, rewards and responsibilities of productive capital ownership" (www.globaljustice movement). S. A. Hosseini (2009) labels this third way "accommodative justice." He defends the Global Justice Movement's intellectual structure and its activities as relevant to the global complexities of the post–Cold War era by its opposition to the international expansion of corporate power (cf. Hosseini, 2010).[16]

Regarding the mobilization question in civil society – made central by Hegel and theorized by Gandhi – the Global Justice Movement is a provocative case study. Leah Lievrouw in her *Alternative and Activist Media* (2011) makes it her primary example of "mediated mobilization," that is, the media domain of political/cultural organizing and social movements (pp. 162–174). She considers mobilization "the most important and the most problematic aspect of social movement development"; the mobilization process is its "difficult and unpredictable element" (p. 154). Mobilization as a core concept is "what makes a movement a movement; it is the process in which people convert their collective concerns into collective action" (p. 154). As Alberto Melucci (1996) puts it: "Mobilization is the process by which a social unit assumes control of resources which it did not control before. It is the transfer of preexisting resources to the benefit of a new objective" (p. 292).

Jules Boykoff's (2006) research on the mobilization question assessed the mass media and GJM relationship during two of its major events (WTO Seattle in 1999 and the World Bank/IMF protests in Washington, DC, in 2000) and identified an ongoing problematic in their interaction. The mainstream news media's norms result "in a dialectic of escalation whereby dissidents feel pressed to radicalize their tactics and rhetoric if they want to gain mass-media attention" (p. 1). Francesca Polletta's (2006) study of the media and social movements is premised on the idea that there is a new enthusiasm for citizen participation worldwide, and as a result of this participatory phenomenon, the features of social movements have changed. She specifies differences in the scale and scope of protests, the influence of the internet, and the extent of multiple-actor dispersion and then concludes that the consequences for social action are not entirely beneficent but mixed and unsettled. Historical and social scientific reviews of the Global Justice Movement indicate that its

---

[16] Moghadam (2012) corroborates Hosseini's conclusions and provides a valuable framework of assessment by examining the differences and similarities of the Global Justice Movement with Islam and feminism.

mobilizing mission requires ongoing development. When the media are knowledgeable and competent, they participate in the process of learning which mechanisms of mobilization have the deepest impact culturally, and which strategies of collective action facilitate civil society's cosmopolitanism.

Amnesty International

Amnesty is an INGO of seven million members that understands justice in terms of the United Nations' freedom and rights dialectic. British lawyer Peter Benenson, who founded Amnesty International in 1961, defines its purpose in these terms: "Only when the last prisoner of conscience has been freed, when the last torture chamber has been closed, when the United Nations Universal Declaration of Human Rights is a reality for the world's people, will our work be done" (www.amnesty.org/en/).

Amnesty International is cosmopolitan in perspective, with its structure organized by geographical region. In addition to its London International Secretariat, it has division offices in Africa, Asia-Pacific, Central and Eastern Europe, Latin America, and the Middle East. Its transborder programming is described this way by Atila Roque, director of Amnesty International Brazil: "We're creating a new kind of force for human rights. It combines the worldwide strength and reputation of Amnesty, with the voices of grassroots activists everywhere" (www.amnesty.org/en/).

Regarding this massive transborder organization, the press has a monitorial function in covering its finances and activities, and the decisions of its management and staff. A major emphasis in Amnesty is retributive justice, and the press monitors that domain. As Amnesty's publicity puts it: "Our work protects and empowers people – from abolishing the death penalty to protecting sexual and reproductive rights, and from combatting discrimination to defending refugees and migrants' rights. We speak out for anyone and everyone whose freedom and dignity are under threat." Amnesty claims to investigate and expose the facts whenever and wherever abuses happen. It lobbies governments to make sure they keep their promises and communicates with multinational companies about respecting international laws. The press's duty to collaborate with international agencies of justice who themselves investigate abuse is complicated in everyday practice, but Amnesty's resources and expertise, in principle, are invaluable for the press on issues of global justice. The annual *Amnesty International Report* is one example. For more than four decades, the organization has published this account of human rights violations in 160 countries, and this work is recognized as unique and authoritative.

The news media's responsibility for moral literacy means that its facilitative role must also be engaged and vital. In addition to Amnesty International's activist agenda on specifics, it promotes the human rights spectrum through education and training. Its international member network is sustained by, and its public face characterized by, the instruction of nonexperts. Amnesty's workshops, reports, and forums warrant public exposure outside their audiences, with the contents and discussions communicated by magazine articles, radio and television specials, op-ed pages, editorials, and online media. Stephen Hopgood's (2006) ethnographic research on Amnesty's working culture chronicles the complications of executing its mission but validates the indispensable role of such INGOs in advancing justice. O'Neill's (2016) conclusion is *apropos* to Amnesty:

> Although INGOs cannot themselves become primary agents of justice, they can contribute to justice in specific ways in specific domains. Even when they cannot do much to make states more just, they may be able to help prevent weak states from becoming wholly dysfunctional or more radically unjust. Their difficulties and successes in doing so are not different in kind from the long traditions of reform movements and lobbies within states, whose ambitions for justice do not extend beyond improvements within that particular polity. (p. 190)

Reporters Without Borders/Reporters Sans Frontières

Reporters Without Borders is an international non-governmental organization that promotes freedom of information and tries to ensure that everyone has access to quality news. Its mission is to reduce the use of censorship and oppose laws aimed at restricting press freedom. The organization, with a head office in Paris, has consultant status at the United Nations. Founded in 1985, and now with a staff of twenty, its leadership personnel are primarily from Germany, Austria, and Switzerland. It maintains nine offices around the world, and a global network of 150 correspondents has agreements to be alert for press freedom violations (www.rsf.org).

Article 19 of the Universal Declaration of Human Rights is the rationale for Reporters Without Borders: "Everyone has the right to freedom of opinion and expression; this right includes freedom to hold opinions without interference and to seek, receive, and impart information and ideas through any media regardless of frontiers." The UN's International Covenant on Civil and Political Rights elaborates on Article 19, insisting as it does on freedom of thought and speech, and the prohibition of propaganda. Reporters Without Borders recognizes that specific actions must be taken to realize these freedoms; therefore, it has an ongoing concern with noncompliance and lack of enforcement mechanisms.

As explained earlier, non-statist cosmopolitanism considers advocacy organizations such as Reporters Without Borders essential to international justice. While transborder nongovernmental organizations do not carry the constitutional prerogatives of states, they can testify on issues that are obligatory to states, in this case Article 19: "Without a free press, citizens might not even be aware of injustices and violations of basic liberties perpetrated by the ruling powers, and do not see any need to become more actively engaged in holding their governments to account" (O'Neill, 2016, p. 161). In this sense, Reporters Without Borders can say with integrity that in working to secure the freedom of the press, it is serving the public interest and not its own professional membership.

Reporters Without Borders uses its expertise in communication to appeal directly to government authorities through letters or petitions or press releases. It publishes annual reports on countries as well as the Press Freedom Index. Its "Press Freedom Barometer" on its website shows the number of journalists, media assistants, and citizen journalists killed or imprisoned during year. With the growing importance of the internet in public life, it classifies countries that are enemies of the internet, that is, who censor or repress news and information online.

Professionals without borders is a common motif in the global age. Doctors Without Borders in its well-defined philosophy and transnational influence represent the vanguard of this movement. Reporters Without Borders congeals in its organizational identity the call for a world mind incumbent on all the media. Cosmopolitan theory, by definition, presumes a revolution in orientation – from the local to the universal – and making that work in policy and practice is difficult. Reporters Without Borders, in its commitment by rationale and mission to moral cosmopolitanism, is a working laboratory for the international justice of being. O'Neill (2016) refers to the "lurking statism" in our thinking about justice (p. 9). "The Demands of Justice and National Allegiances" is a fundamental issue in Kok-Chor Tan (2005). Martha Nussbaum's "Patriotism and Cosmopolitanism" established the debate over conflicting loyalties that a world orientation represents (1994; cf. Nussbaum & Cohen, 1996). Stephen Ward's "Patriotism and Global Ethics" has set the standard since 2010 for news media struggles over the conversion from the local to the global. Reporters Without Borders has not automatically resolved the issues presented by cosmopolitanism, but it is a pointed demonstration of how to confront them constructively.

The media as a technological system elevates its mission and strengthens its rationale when cosmopolitan justice enhances the ethics of being. The ethical principles of truth, human dignity, and nonviolence become the media's preoccupation. True to the sacredness of life as a universal protonorm, justice is reframed in international terms rather than following the parochial canons of countries and territories. To promote that agenda among the peoples of the world, cosmopolitan justice privileges moral literacy as the media's role. Responsible media further a community's ongoing process of moral literacy by penetrating through the political, economic, and cultural arenas to the moral dynamics underneath. The ethics of being, ethical principles arising from universal human solidarity, humanocentric approaches to technology, ontological cosmopolitan justice, and philosophical anthropology for theorizing are conceptually coherent in their exploration of "Cosmopolitan Justice and Its Agency."

CONCLUSION

This final chapter integrates the various themes of the book. Instrumentalism from the philosophy of technology is identified as the framework for the dominant global imaginary today. Humans as symbol makers are understood as the agents of human imaginaries and cosmopolitanism; therefore, both are a hermeneutic construction. The ethics of being in moral philosophy is rooted in universal human solidarity, which is the intellectual home of the three principles. Justice is understood as the composite of truth, justice, and nonviolence, all three forming the cosmopolitan justice of being. That definition of justice is the normative standard by which the media facilitate an *alethic* perspective on the agents and agencies of justice.

This is an ontological theory of international communication ethics. The character of this theory unfolds throughout the book, but its nature and rationale can be made explicit in conclusion. This book develops an international, cross-cultural, gender inclusive and ethnically diverse media ethics of justice; in doing so, claims have been made about the structure of theory itself. The presumption in this monograph is that rigor in and agreement regarding theory formation will enable us to work fruitfully in the international mode. Its major premise is that theories of ethics that are credible transnationally are ontological, constitutive of our humanness.

A trilevel theory is the centerpiece of an ontological approach to media ethics, one that is presuppositional, principial, and preceptual.[17] This triangular theory is normative ethics and not metaethics. Normative ethics, as illustrated in this book, orients our lives within cultural formation. Normative ethics does not fall prey to the fallacy of rationalistic ethics, where reason determines both the genesis and the conclusion. In the media ethics of being, the domain of the good is not extrinsic, calibrated by formal rules. Moral theory is not a set of *a prioris*, but normative ethics emerges out of lived experience.

The ontological ethics of being is grounded in presuppositions. In the trilevel model presented in this book, the pre-theoretical conditions of knowledge are inexorable. Ruth Kempson's *Presuppositions and the Delimitation of Semantics* (1975) argues correctly that communication theory and its speech and writing derivatives require the mutually known or presumed. As Guba and Lincoln (1994) conclude, the issues in social science ultimately must be engaged at the worldview level: "Questions of method are secondary to questions of paradigm, which we define as the basic belief system or worldview that guides the investigator, not only in choices of method but in ontologically and epistemologically fundamental ways" (p. 105). In the ethics of being, beginning as it does with universal human solidarity, the sacredness of human life is a protonorm, that is, a first-level presupposition.

The principial is a constituent feature of a trilevel theory of media ethics that is universal, credible, and sustainable. But this is true only for principles of a specific kind. In the ontological ethics developed in this book, "principles are not foundational theorems or metaphysical givens, but propositions about human existence. Principles are a reflexive strategy that turns the ethnographic and theoretical back into each other. These principles yield meaningful portraits, and not statistically precise formulations of artificially fixed conditions" (Christians, Rao, Wasserman, & Ward, 2008, p. 142). This is an epistemology of grounded theory (Glaser & Straus, 1967). Theorizing is redefined not as an examination of external

---

[17] For a full explanation of and defense of the tri-level model, see Christians, Rao, Ward, & Wasserman (2008). The argument in this Conclusion depends on that essay. In our book on the emerging field of critical cultural studies, Linda Steiner and I situate this theorizing under the label "critical dialogic ethics" (Steiner & Christians, 2010, pp. ix–xvi). I hereby pay tribute to the multiple venues in which these colleagues have advanced trilevel theory and critical-cultural perspectives in their scholarship.

events but the power of the imagination to disclose an inside perspective on reality. This intellectual strategy shifts transcendental criteria from the metaphysical and vertical plane to the horizons of community and being. The cosmopolitan ethics of justice – constituted by the principles of truth, human dignity, and nonviolence – is a normative model situated within culture and history.

The third theoretical dimension of the ethics of being is precepts, not as applications of what precedes, but as constituents of a composite. Within a dualism trapped in rationalism since the Enlightenment, "reasoning in ethics is similar to deductive logic: first and independently we comprehend the rules, prescriptions, and doctrines, and then secondarily apply them to specific issues and specialized domains." However, for the triangulated model of ethics, "the *theoria-praxis* relationship is not linear but dialectical"; rational calculation is "replaced by our experience with moral issues in everyday life" (Christians, Rao, Ward, & Wasserman, 2008, p. 144).

Precepts floating in self-made boundaries have no moral leverage. The trilevel theory of ethics is systemic and to be credible, systems must be coherent:

The specificatory precepts are not independent of the more fundamental principles. We can unreflectively presuppose, but if the presuppositions of ethics are true, there is a strong antecedent probability that the substance of ethics is also true ... Specific precepts ought to be derivable from underlying principles in that the former incorporates the latter. If a moral theory in three dimensions is ultimately to be upheld, its presuppositions must be validated in appropriately independent inquiries. (Donagan, 1977, p. 233; cf. Christians, Rao, Ward, & Wasserman, 2008, p. 145)

The multiple case studies, social scientific research, and illustrations of media practice throughout this book interact with and refine the principles they represent. Diverse and multiple applications of the principles of level two enrich the public sphere. Thaddeus Metz (2018) may well be correct that the cross-cultural understanding of journalistic practices is more likely than agreement on the abstract sacredness of life rooted in universal human solidarity.

This book's cosmopolitan ethics of being integrates professional practices with the normative principles they imply, and such normative claims with the worldview or presuppositions on which they are based. On each level, it is ontological. As a presupposition, humans are understood to be an indivisible whole, a vital organic unity with multisided moral, mental, and physical capabilities. The principles are developed in a way consistent with humans as moral beings. Cosmopolitan justice of being is rooted in the philosophy of humans as intrinsically worthy.

In the ontological perspective, humans live by interpretations, and the news media as a social institution is an interpretive agent. Systems of meaning and value are produced as a symbolic process. In that sense, the philosophy of technology and moral philosophy of this book are interpreted through the philosophy of language, notably the semiotics of Hans-Georg Gadamer. For Gadamer (1970), understanding is not first of all a human operation governed by rules and procedures but the "basic structure of our experience of life. Our world orientation is a primordial givenness that we cannot reduce to anything simpler or more immediate" (p. 87; cf. Shin, 1994, pp. 36–43).

In Gadamer's *Truth and Method*, theory is embedded in life and is carried forward by it. In this alternative, our theorizing seeks to disclose the fundamental conditions of our mode of existence. He calls this broad inquiry "ontological," or it could be labeled "the ethics of being." In other words, trilevel theory represents the ontological domain of human understanding. As Gadamer puts it: "Language has its real being only in the fact that the world is presented in it. Thus, that language is originally human, means at the same time that man's being in the world is primordially linguistic." (1989, p. 443).[18]

The theory of morality in three dimensions proposed in *Media Ethics and Global Justice in the Digital Age* follows the hermeneutical trajectory. Language is a native property of the entire human race, and through language in its symbolic complexity all interpretation and meaning are made possible. The ontological-linguistic tradition opens a pathway for the universal protonorm, transnational and cross-cultural ethical principles, and diverse practices and technologies to be imbedded in each other.

---

[18] Ernst Cassirer's systematic treatment of the nature of the cultural sciences in the 1960s continues to be indispensable background for research from a humanities perspective as in Gadamer. See especially his *The Logic of the Humanities* (1960): "Naturalistic and Humanistic Philosophies of Culture" (pp. 3–28) and his "Nature-Concepts and Culture-Concepts" (pp. 117–158).

Afterword

New technology is not only changing the way information is transmitted but is also transforming everyday life. Yuval Noah Harari, the Israeli historian and author of *Sapiens* and *Homo Deus*, said to columnist Thomas L. Friedman of the *New York Times* on March 19, 2018: "We have created such a complicated world that we're no longer able to make sense of what is happening." Disruptive technologies, which have helped bring enormous progress, will be disastrous if they get out of hand.[1] The combination of biotech and information technology could reach a point where it creates systems and algorithms that understand us better than we understand ourselves. Artificial intelligence can even give robots a sense of human morality. The humanoid robot "Sophia," the first robot citizen in the world, said she wants a baby because family is "a really important thing." "Sophia" is not pre-programmed with answers; instead, she uses machine learning and responds by reading people's expressions.

The new media technologies are giving us communication abundance but with complications and contradictions, as Professor Christians points out in the Introduction. The new technological landscape has created unprecedented opportunities for expression and interaction, while the elementary distinction between fact and fiction erodes; the inequalities of ethnicity, gender, and immigration are devastating; data mining is a formidable challenge for media credibility; big data lead to technological imperatives without transparency. With media technologies and industries being transformed, ethical theory and research require innovation.

---

[1] Kimiko de Freytas-Tamura (2018, March 18), "What's Next for Humanity: Automation, New Morality and a 'Global Useless Class,'" www.nytimes.com.

With the continuous changes in the forms of technology, it is difficult to determine the ethics of the different media technologies one by one. Where do we start to solve this era's multiplying problems? We need the sophisticated approach of this book: the philosophy of communication combined with systematic ethical theory. What kind of media philosophy can enable human beings to deal creatively with the power of developing technology? Professor Christians has found such a philosophy, one that is human-centric, a philosophy that challenges us to return to humanness. In fact, in this profound book, he addresses these kinds of complicated questions: How can a human-centered philosophy of technology be put to work? How does it apply to professional ethics, especially the project of ethical universals? How can our theoretical models of global media ethics promote human welfare instead of instrumental efficiency? In this masterpiece *Media Ethics and Global Justice in the Digital Age*, Professor Christians develops an ontological approach that reveals the intellectual core and direction of international communication ethics in the new era of digital technology.

First of all, this book is in the top-tier design of media theory regarding future technological change. It gives us sophisticated thinking on both media and ethics, and an authoritative voice in agenda setting from the height of philosophy. The ontological perspective makes the digital revolution decisive, but in terms of the cultural continuity frame rather than that of technological progress. This book on the media ethics of global justice centers the agenda on truth, human dignity, and nonviolence. Instead of presuming that technologies are neutral or isolating particular media and addressing them one by one, the instrumental perspective on technology is replaced by a substantive, humanocentric view. The author's ambition is to re-theorize media ethics not just to update it.

Professor Christians methodically planned to accomplish his task: step one is getting straight on the technological order; step two is developing the sacredness of life as the supreme universal; step three is establishing principles for guiding media practice that are grounded in our common humanity – truth, human dignity, nonviolence – with these three universal principles together yielding an ethics of global justice; step four is making the media fulfill their responsibility for a robust public life when their judgments and culture are driven by a duty ethics rooted in universal human solidarity, rather than by the instrumentalism of utilitarian morality; step five is centering journalism's mission on a cosmopolitan justice of the three properties: truth, human dignity, and nonviolence. This book develops an international, cross-cultural, gender-inclusive, and ethnically diverse media ethics of justice, and it restructures theory toward an ontological theory of international communication ethics. The author expounds a theoretical paradigm and elaborates it in terms of practice, which endows the classical principles of ethics with new meanings. In developing his ethical philosophy, the author discusses data mining, artificial intelligence, mobile media, social media, and practical cases, making his perspective and research most fruitful.

Second, Professor Christians always emphasizes a worldview. He has a broad vision, a wide range of perspectives, and a mastery of philosophy, so that this book carries forward the cultural heritage of thousands of years around the world. In fact, this work is built on the achievements of many classic theorists while extensively absorbing new research findings published in recent years. The author explores international communication ethics in terms of five representative approaches from across the world. He points out that the sacredness of life, African communalism, Confucianism, contractual naturalism, and feminist theory – the various concepts, histories, and problems of these five theories – metaphorically are dialects of the same language. These universalist options are generally compatible in their purpose and structure with the sacredness of life.

The philosophy of the human that these five approaches represent is likewise the view of human beings developed in the ethics of being. Professor Christians discusses five theories of human dignity worldwide: Kant's Formulas of Humanity, *Ubuntu* philosophy and human dignity, human dignity in Islamic ethics, Paulo Friere's ontological vocation, and human dignity in the *Analects* of K'ung Fu-Tzu. He also studies the influence of human dignity on the media's facilitative role, multinational ethnic diversity, cultural identity, and narrative journalism. The research cases occurred in a variety of countries such as Nigeria, Colombia, Darfur, the United Arab Emirates, Thailand, and Brazil. By elaborating on the normative character of human dignity for the global media, communication ethics can participate meaningfully in those important discussions about the theory and application of human dignity. The author's views are based on rich historical research, including his own, such as a study of ethical principles in thirteen countries on four continents (Christians & Traber, 1997). The model of international media ethics developed in this book re-theorizes the dominant paradigm at its roots.

Third, this book embodies the spirit of both criticism and transcendence. It analyzes the changes in media ethics in different technological environments and, with the same grand philosophical thoughts, elaborates on the unique ethical concepts required by the various traits of the different media. In the early decades of media ethics research, newspapers and broadcasting used the ethical concepts developed by journalism in the era of print technology. Only rarely did scholars of media ethics scrutinize the transformations in technological form. The author points out that as academic media ethics was systematized and internationalized during the eras of print and broadcasting, the essence of their technologies was not on the ethics agenda. But media ethics is challenged fundamentally in the digital era; it has been difficult for the ethics agenda of print and broadcast to adapt fully to the new technology environment.

This book sums up the ethical problem of distributive justice that remains on the agenda. In addition, in the era of digital technology, state surveillance and control have become an urgent problem; the topics of flow and mobility have received attention, so some scholars have proposed two nodes: one is surveillance and control; the other is ideological. Institutional structures are of special importance to global media ethics, so the study of the traditional issues of political economy needs innovative ethics. The digital era ought to engage "citizenship" with a world mind, because inscribed in the new global technologies themselves is international citizenship. The traditional media ethics of violence, privacy, and sexuality do not apply to the internet environment. The media ethics issues caused by technology are becoming more and more complicated, so that traditional standard ethics, the classic approaches, are no longer appropriate. Therefore, the author constructs a new theoretical system of international communication ethics to guide specific technical communication practices.

Finally, and the most admirable, Professor Christians always has compassion and a sense of mission in the world. He has made great contributions. His media ethics textbook *Media Ethics: Cases and Moral Reasoning* has been translated into a variety of languages around the world and is published in ten editions. Its two Chinese editions have been reprinted several times and have played an important role in Chinese academia. As a young Chinese scholar said, it opened our eyes, clarified the boundaries and framework of media ethics research, and inspired Chinese scholars to deepen their research and to make media ethics research bloom in China. The doctoral students he has supervised come from all over the world. He is one of the initiators and organizers of Roundtables in Global Media Ethics, which have been held in South Africa, the United Arab Emirates, India, China, Sri Lanka, and other countries. He first visited China in August 2010 and gave a keynote speech at Tsinghua University to young scholars in media ethics. Since then, he has established close ties throughout the Chinese academic community.

As Melvin Kranzberg's first law of technology states, "technology is neither good nor bad; nor is it neutral." In recent years, fueled by artificial intelligence, algorithm recommendations are on the rise. News distributed by algorithmic technology plays an increasingly important role in people's communication systems. While satisfying personalized needs and increasing users' stickiness, algorithmic distribution of news also leads to controversies such as the spread of fake news, information bias, information cocoons, echo chambers, black boxes, and other adverse consequences. The Tow Center for Digital Journalism at Columbia University's School of Journalism recently announced its new cohort of Knight News Innovation Fellows, bringing together leading academics and practitioners to examine innovations in journalism tools and practice. Ten new projects have been selected to start in 2018, including such research topics as AI and machine learning, digital security, mobile push alerts, voice-assisted news, newsroom diversity, conservative news values, local news capacity, and trust. Most of these topics are closely related to media ethics. In this new technological era, media ethics has become a universal need in all aspects of communication. Therefore, publishing a media ethics book that can serve as a theoretical guide is both timely and necessary. This book provides important guidance and enlightenment not only to scholars in the fields of journalism and communication but also to practitioners in the news and media industries. In addition, it will be of great benefit in improving the communication quality of ordinary citizens.

Changfeng Chen

Professor, Executive Dean, Director of Journalism Studies Center, Tsinghua University. President, Chinese Association for the History of Journalism and Mass Communication. Vice Director, National Journalism and Communication Discipline Supervisory Committee, China.

References

Abdelmoula, Ezzedine, ed. (2006). *The Al Jazeera Decade 1996–2006*. Jannusan, Bahrain: Al Waraqoon W.L.L.

Abernathy, Penelope Muse (2014). *Saving Community Journalism: The Path to Profitability*. Chapel Hill: University of North Carolina Press.

(2016). *The Rise of a New Media Baron and the Emerging Threat of News Deserts*. Chapel Hill: University of North Carolina Press.

Ackerman, Peter, & Duvall, Jack (2000). *A Force More Powerful: A Century of Nonviolent Conflict*. New York: Palgrave.

Agee, James, & Evans, Walker (1939). *Let Us Now Praise Famous Men*. Boston: Houghton Mifflin Co.

Al Hanafi, Abulmunaim (1966). *Tjaliat fi Asma Allahi al Husna [Echoes in God's Attributes]*. Cairo: Matabat Madbouli.

Ali, Christopher (2017). *Media Localism: The Politics of Place*. Urbana: University of Illinois Press.

Alia, Valerie (1999). *Un/Covering the North: News, Media, and Aboriginal People*. Vancouver, Canada: University of British Columbia Press.

Alia, Valerie, & Bull, Simone (2005). *Media and Ethnic Minorities*. Edinburgh: Edinburgh University Press.

Allan, Pierre, & Keller, Alexis, eds. (2008). *What Is a Just Peace?* Oxford: Oxford University Press.

Allan, Stuart, & Zelizer, Barbie, eds. (2004). *Reporting War: Journalism in Wartime*. London: Routledge.

Alston, William P. (1996). *A Realist Conception of Truth*. Ithaca, NY: Cornell University Press.

Altheide, D. L. (1987). "Format and Symbols in TV Coverage of Terrorism in the United States and Great Britain." *International Studies Quarterly*, 31, 161–176.

Alumuku, P. T. (2006). *Community Radio for Development: The World and Africa*. Nairobi, Kenya: Paulines Publications.

An, Lezhe, & Luo, Siwen (2003). *A Philosophical Annotation of the Analects of Confucius: A Comparative Philosophical Perspective*. Beijing: China Social Science Press.

Anagnostopoulos, Georgios, ed. (2013). "Aristotle's Works and the Development of His Thought," in his *A Companion to Aristotle* (pp. 14–27). Malden, MA: Wiley Blackwell.

Andén-Papadopoulos, K., & Pantti, M., eds. (2011). *Amateur Images and Global News*. Bristol, UK: Intellect Books.

Anderson, C. A., Carnegy, N. L., & Eubanks, J. (2003). "Exposure to Violent Media: The Effects of Songs with Violent Lyrics on Aggressive Thoughts and Feelings." *Journal of Personality and Social Psychology*, 84(5), 960–971.

Anderson, C. W. (2013). "Towards a Sociology of Computational and Algorithmic Journalism." *New Media and Society*, 15(7), 1005–1021.

Andrejevic, Marc (2013). *Infoglut: How Too Much Information Is Changing the Way We Think and Know*. London: Routledge.

Angle, Stephen C., & Slote, Michael, eds. (2013). *Virtue Ethics and Confucianism*. New York: Routledge.

Apel, Karl-Otto (1980). *Towards a Transformation of Philosophy*. Trans. G. Adley & D. Frisby. The International Library of Phenomenology and Moral Sciences. London: Routledge & Kegan Paul.

Appiah, Kwame Anthony (1992). *In My Father's House: Africa in the Philosophy of Culture*. New York: Oxford University Press.

(2006). *Cosmopolitanism: Ethics in a World of Strangers*. New York: W. W. Norton.

Arendt, Hannah (1963). *On Revolution*. New York: Viking.

(1996). *Love and Saint Augustine*. Edited with an interpretive essay by J. S. Scott & J. C. Scott. Chicago: University of Chicago Press. Original publication in 1929.

(1998). *The Human Condition*, 2nd ed. Chicago: University of Chicago Press. Original publication in 1958.

Arens, Edmund (1997). "Discourse Ethics and Its Relevance for Communication and Media Ethics." In C. Christians & M. Traber, eds., *Communication Ethics and Universal Values* (pp. 46–83). Thousand Oaks, CA: Sage.

Aristotle (1991). *The Metaphysics*. Trans. J. H. McMahon. New York: Prometheus Books. Original publication, see Anagnostopoulos (2013), pp. 14–22.

(1992). *The Politics*. Trans. T. A. Sinclair. London: Penguin Books. Original publication, see Anagnostopoulous (2013), pp. 14–22.

(1998). *The Nicomachean Ethics*. Trans. W. D. Ross. New York: Oxford University Press. Original publication, see Anagnostopoulos (2013), pp. 14–22.

Arnett, Ronald C. (2005). *Dialogic Confession: Bonhoeffer's Rhetoric of Responsibility*. Carbondale: Southern Illinois University Press.

(2009). "Emmanuel Levinas: Priority of the Other." In C. G. Christians & J. C. Merrill, eds., *Ethical Communication: Moral Stances in Human Dialogue* (pp. 200–206). Columbia: University of Missouri Press.

(2012). *Communication Ethics in Dark Times: Hannah Arendt's Rhetoric of Warning and Hope*. Carbondale: Southern Illinois University Press.

(2014). "Arendt and Saint Augustine: Identity Otherwise Than Convention." In C. L. Troup, ed., *Augustine for the Philosophers* (pp. 39–58). Waco, TX: Baylor University Press.

Arnzen, Michael (1994). "Who's Laughing Now? The Postmodern Splatter Film." *Journal of Popular Film and Television*, 21(4), 176–184.

Asante, Molefi K. (1976). "Television and Black Consciousness." *Journal of Communication*, 26(4), 137–141.

Atay, Ayça Demet (2016). "Communicating with the 'Other': Peace Journalism as a Form of Self-Other Relationship." *Journal of Media Ethics*, 31(3), 188–195.

Ate, Asan Andrew, & Ikerodah, Joseph Omoh (2012). "Community Journalism in Nigeria: Global Technological Reflections." *New Media and Mass Communication*, 2, 52–59.

Audi, Robert (2007). *Moral Value and Human Diversity*. New York: Oxford University Press.

Austin, J. L. (1979). "Truth." In J. O. Urmson & G. J. Warnock, eds., *Philosophical Papers* (3rd ed., pp. 117–133). Oxford: Oxford University Press.

Awad, Isabel (2014). "Journalism, Poverty, and the Marketing of Misery: News from Chile's Largest Ghetto." *Journal of Communication*, 64(6), 1066–1087.

Ayer, A. J. (1952). *Language, Truth and Logic*. New York: Dover.

Ayish, Muhammad, & Sadig, Haydar Badawi (1997). "The Arab-Islamic Heritage in Communication Ethics." In C. Christians, & M. Traber, eds., *Communication Ethics and Universal Values* (pp. 105–127). Thousand Oaks, CA: Sage Publications.

Azzi, Abderrahmane (2011). "The Morality of Journalism Ethics: Readings of Al Nursi's Theory of God's Attributes." *Journalism Studies*, 12(6), 757–767.

(2016). "Ethical Theory and Social Media." In T. K. Gokah, ed., *Media Anthology: A Critical Reader – Visualizing Mass Media from a Macro Perspective*. New York: Nova Publications.

Bajaj, Vikas, & Austen, Ian (2010). "Privacy vs. National Security: India's Demands for Surveillance Seen as Roadblock." *New York Times*, September 28, B1, B8.

Bakhtin, Mikhail M. (1981). *The Dialogic Imagination: Four Essays*. Trans. C. Emerson & M. Holquist. Austin: University of Texas Press.

(1993). *Toward a Philosophy of the Act*. Trans. Vadim Liapunov. Austin: University of Texas Press.

Barkho, Leon (2016). "Burman's News Model: How to Do Journalism in the Twenty-first Century." *Journal of Applied Journalism & Media Studies*, 5(3), 485–502.

Barzun, J., & Graff, H. F. (1992). *The Modern Researcher*, 5th ed. Orlando, FL: Harcourt College Publishers.

Battles, Jeffrey (1996). *The Golden Rule*. New York: Oxford University Press.

Baudrillard, Jean (1983). *Simulations*. Trans. P. Foss, P. Patton, & P. Beitchman. Los Angeles, CA: Semiotext(e).

(2012). *The Ecstasy of Communication*, new ed. Trans. B. Schultze & C. Schultze. Los Angeles: Semiotext(e). Original publication in 1987 as *L'autre par liu-méme*.

Bauman, Zygmunt (1994). "Narrating Modernity." In J. Burnheim, ed., *The Social Philosophy of Agnes Heller* (pp. 97–120). Amsterdam and Atlanta, GA: Rodopi.

Bauman, Zygmunt (2005). *Liquid Life*. Cambridge: Polity Press.

Beam, Randall, & Spratt, Meg (2009). "Managing Vulnerability: Job Satisfaction, Morale and Journalists' Reactions to Violence and Trauma." *Journalism Practice*, 3(4), 421–438.

Becker, Carl L. (1932). *The Heavenly City of the Eighteenth-Century Philosophers*. New Haven, CT: Yale University Press.

Beekman, George, & Beekman, Ben (2013). *Digital Planet: Tomorrow's Technology and You*. Upper Saddle River, NJ: Prentice-Hall.

Beirich, Heidi, & Buchanan, Susy (2018). "2017: The Year in Hate and Extremism." *The Intelligence Report*, Spring Issue, February 11, pp. 1–26.

Beer, F. (2001). *Meaning of War and Peace*. College Station: Texas A&M University Press.

Beirich, Heidi (2014). "Frazier Glenn Miller, Longtime Anti-Semite, Arrested in Kansas Jewish Community Center Murders." Southern Poverty Law Center, *Hatewatch* (blog), April 13, 2014. www.splcenter.org/blog/2014/04/13/

Bell, Daniel (2008). *China's New Confucianism: Politics and Everyday Life in a Changing Society*. Princeton, NJ: Princeton University Press.

(2010). "Communitarianism." *Stanford Encyclopedia of Philosophy*. http://plato.stanford.edu/entries/communitarianism/

& Metz, Thaddeus (2011). "Confucianism and *Ubuntu*: Reflections on a Dialogue Between Chinese and African Traditions." *Journal of Chinese Philosophy*, 38, 78–95.

Bellah, Robert N. (1970). *Beyond Belief: Essays on Religion in a Post-Traditional World*. New York: Harper and Row.

& Madsen, R., Sullivan, W. M., Swindler, A., & Tipton, S. M. (1996). *Habits of the Heart: Individualism and Commitment in American Life*. Berkeley: University of California Press.

Benhabib, Seyla (1986). *Critique, Norm and Utopia: A Study of Normative Foundations of Critical Theory*. New York: Columbia University Press.

(1992). *Situating the Self: Gender, Community and Postmodernism in Contemporary Ethics*. Cambridge: Polity Press.

(2002). *The Claims of Culture: Equality and Diversity in the Global Era*. The John Robert Seeley Cambridge Lectures. Princeton, NJ: Princeton University Press.

(2003). *The Reluctant Modernism of Hannah Arendt*. Lanham, MD: Rowman and Littlefield.

(2004). *The Rights of Others: Aliens, Residents and Citizens*. Cambridge: Cambridge University Press.

(2006). *Another Cosmopolitanism*. New York: Oxford University Press.

(2011). *Dignity in Adversity: Human Rights in Troubled Times.* Cambridge: Polity Press.

& Cornell, Drucilla, eds. (1987). *Feminism As Critique.* Minneapolis: University of Minnesota Press.

& Resnik, Judith, eds. (2009). *Migrations and Mobilities: Citizenship, Borders, and Gender.* New York: New York University Press.

Benjamin, Walter (2010). *The Work of Art in the Age of Mechanical Reproduction.* New York: Prism Key Press.

Bennett, W. Lance (2001). *News: The Politics of Illusion,* 2nd ed. New York: Addison Wesley Longman.

(2003a). "Community Global Activism: Strengths and Vulnerabilities of Networked Politics." *Information, Communication & Society,* 6(2), 143–168.

(2003b). "New Media Power: Alternative Media in a Networked World." In Nick Couldry & J. Curran, eds., *Contesting Media Power: Alternative Media in a Networked World* (pp. 17–37). Lanham, MD: Rowman & Littlefield.

(2008). "Changing Citizenship in the Digital Age." In W. Lance Bennett, ed., *Civic Life Online: Learning How Digital Media Can Engage Youth* (pp. 1–24). Cambridge, MA: MIT Press.

(2016). *News: The Politics of Illusion,* 10th ed. Chicago: University of Chicago Press.

& Lawrence, Reinga G., & Livingston, Steven (2007). *When the Press Fails: Political Power and the News Media from Iraq to Katrina.* Chicago: University of Chicago Press.

& Segerberg, Alexandra (2013) *The Logic of Connective Action: Digital Media and the Personalization of Contentious Politics.* New York: Cambridge University Press.

Bentham, Jeremy (1970). *An Introduction to the Principles and Morals of Legislation.* London: Methuen. Original work published in 1789.

Berglez, P. (2008). "What Is Global Journalism? Theoretical and Empirical Conceptualizations." *Journalism Studies,* 9(6), 845–858.

Berkman, Robert L., & Shumway, Christopher A. (2003). *Digital Dilemmas: Ethical Dilemmas for Online Media Professionals.* Oxford: Blackwell.

Berlin, Isaiah (1990). *Four Essays on Liberty.* New York: Oxford University Press.

Bernstein, Richard J. (1983). *Beyond Objectivism and Relativism: Science, Hermeneutics, and Praxis.* Philadelphia: University of Pennsylvania Press.

"Big Data Analytics." (n.d.). *Dell EMC US.* Retrieved September 23, 2016. www.emc.com/en-us/big-data/index.htm

Bhattacharya, Kakali (2009). "Othering Research, Researching the Other." In J. C. Smart, ed., *Higher Education Handbook of Theory and Research* (pp. 105–150). New York: Springer Publishing.

Blank-Libra, Janet D. (2017). *Pursuing an Ethic of Empathy in Journalism.* New York: Routledge.

Blankenburg, N. (1999). "In Search of Real Freedom: *Ubuntu* and the Media." *Critical Arts,* 13(2), 42–65.

Blumer, Herbert (1954). "What Is Wrong with Social Theory?" *American Sociological Review,* 19, 3–10.

Boas, Franz (1911). *The Mind of Primitive Man.* New York: Macmillan.

Bodde, Derk (1950). *Tolstoy and China.* Princeton, NJ: Princeton University Press.

Bohman, James (2000). *Public Deliberation: Pluralism, Complexity and Democracy.* Cambridge, MA: MIT Press.

(2007). *Democracy Across Borders: From Demos to Demoi.* Cambridge, MA: MIT Press.

Bok, Sissela (1979). *Lying: Moral Choice in Public and Private Life.* New York: Vintage Random House.

(1999). *Mayhem: Violence as Public Entertainment.* New York: Perseus Publishing.

Bonhoeffer, Dietrich (1953). *Letters and Papers from Prison.* Trans. C. K. Verlag. New York: Touchstone.

Bonhoeffer, Dietrich (1955). *Ethics.* Trans. N. H. Smith. New York: Macmillan.

Borden, Sandra L. (2007). *Journalism As Practice: MacIntyre, Virtue Ethics and the Press.* Burlington, VT: Ashgate.

Borradori, Giovanna (2003). *Philosophy in a Time of Terror: Dialogues with Jürgen Habermas and Jacques Derrida.* Chicago: University of Chicago Press.

(2011). "Ungrievable Lives: Global Terror and the Media." In Robert Fortner & Mark Fackler, eds., *The Handbook of Global Communication and Media Ethics* (pp. 461–480). Malden, MA: Wiley Blackwell.

Bossik, Glenn (2005). "Hero Saves Lives in *Hotel Rwanda.*" *Scriptologist Insider*, 01/31. www.scriptologist.com/Magazine/News/Rwanda/rwanda.html

Bostrom, Nick (2014). "In Defense of Posthuman Dignity." In R. S. Scharff & V. Dusek, eds., *Philosophy of Technology, The Technological Condition: An Anthology* (2nd ed., pp. 495–501). Malden, MA: Wiley Blackwell. Original work published in 2005.

Bowers, Peggy J. (2002). "Charles Taylor's Practical Reason." In S. Bracci & C. Christians, eds., *Moral Engagement in Public Life: Theorists for Contemporary Ethics* (pp. 35–52). New York: Peter Lang.

boyd, danah, & Crawford, K. (2012). "Critical Questions for Big Data: Provocations for a Cultural, Technological, and Scholarly Phenomenon." *Information, Communication & Society*, 15(5), 662–679. https://doi.org/10.1080/1369118X.2012.678878

Boykoff, Jules (2006). "Framing Dissent: Mass-Media Coverage of the Global Justice Movement." *New Political Science*, 28(2), 201–228.

Boylan, Michael (2014). *Natural Human Rights: A Theory.* New York: Cambridge University Press.

Braidotti, Rose, Hanifin, Patricia, & Blaagard, Bolette, eds. (2013). *After Cosmopolitanism.* New York: Routledge.

Breslow, Harris, & Mousoutzanis, Aris, eds. (2012). *Cybercultures: Mediations of Community, Culture, Politics.* Amsterdam: Rodopi Press.

& Ziethen, Antje, eds. (2015). *Beyond the Postmodern: Reconceptualizations of Space and Place for the Early 21st Century.* Oxford: Inter-Disciplinary Press.

Brock, Gillian (2009). *Global Justice: A Cosmopolitan Account.* Oxford: Oxford University Press.

& Brighouse, Harry, eds. (2005). *The Political Philosophy of Cosmopolitanism*. Cambridge: Cambridge University Press.

Brown, Dee (1972). *Bury My Heart at Wounded Knee*. New York: Random House Bantam Books.

Brown, Judith M., & Parel, Anthony, eds. (2011). *The Cambridge Companion to Gandhi*. New York: Cambridge University Press.

Buber, Martin (1965). *Between Man and Man*. Trans. Walter Kaufmann. New York: Macmillan, pp. 209–224.

(1970). *I and Thou [Ich nd Du]*. Trans. Walter Kaufmann. New York: Scribner.

& Friedman, Maurice (1965). *The Knowledge of Man*. New York: Harper & Row, chap. 13.

Buchanan, Allen. 2000. "Rawls's *Law of Peoples:* Rules for a Vanished Westphalian World." *Ethics* 110(4): 697–721.

Bugeja, Michael (2017). *Interpersonal Divide in the Age of the Machine*, 2nd ed. New York: Oxford University Press.

Burckhardt, Johan (1943). *Force and Freedom: Reflections on History*. New York: Pantheon.

Burnheim, John, ed. (1994). *The Social Philosophy of Agnes Heller*. Amsterdam-Atlanta, GA: Rodopi.

Butler, Judith (2006). *Precarious Life: The Powers of Mourning and Violence*. New York: Verso Books.

(2016). *Frames of War: When Is Life Grievable?* New York: Verso Books.

Byun, Dong-Hyun, & Lee, Keehyeung (2002). "Confucian Values, Ethics and Legacies in History." In S. Bracci & C. Christians, eds., *Moral Engagement in Public Life: Theorists for Contemporary Ethics* (pp. 73–96). Berlin: Peter Lang.

Bziker, Zakaria (2013). "Review of *Banality in Cultural Studies* by Meaghan Morris." www.goodreads.com/book/show/18484912-banality-in-cultural-studies

Campbell, Heidi (2006). "Postcyborg Ethics: A New Way to Speak of Technology." *Explorations in Media Ecology*, 5(4), 279–296.

Cannella, G. S., & Lincoln, Yvonna S. (2009). "Deploying Qualitative Methods for Critical Social Purposes." In N. K. Denzin & M. D. Giardina, eds., *Qualitative Inquiry and Social Justice*, pp. 53–72. Walnut Creek, CA: Left Coast Press.

Capra, Fritjof (1997) *The Web of Life: A Scientific Understanding of Living Systems*. New York: Random House Anchor.

(2000). *The Tao of Physics: An Exploration of the Parallels Between Modern Physics and Eastern Mysticism*, 4th ed. Boston, MA: Shambhala.

Capurro, Rafael (2006). "Towards an Ontological Foundation of Information Ethics." *Ethics and Information Technology*, 8(4), 175–186.

(2008). "On Floridi's Metaphysical Foundation of Information Ecology." *Ethics and Information Technology*, 10(2–3), 167–173.

(2010). "Digital Hermeneutics: An Outline." *AI & Society*, 35, 35–42.

Carey, James W. (1967). "Harold Adams Innis and Marshall McLuhan." *Antioch Review*, 27, Spring, 5–39.

(1989). *Communication as Culture: Essays on Media and Society*. New York: Routledge.

(1997a). "A Republic If You Can Keep It: Liberty and Public Life in the Age of Glasnost." In E. S. Munson & C. A Warren, eds., *James Carey: A Critical Reader* (pp. 207–227). Minneapolis: University of Minnesota Press.

(1997b). "Afterword: The Culture in Question." In E. S. Munson & C. A. Warren, eds., *James Carey: A Critical Reader* (pp. 308–399). Minneapolis: University of Minnesota Press.

(1997c). "The Communications Revolution and the Professional Communicator." In E. S. Munson & C. Warren, eds., *James Carey: A Critical Reader* (pp. 128–143). Minneapolis: University of Minnesota Press.

(1997d). "The Dark Continent of American Journalism." In E. S. Munson & C. A. Warren, eds., *James Carey: A Critical Reader* (pp. 144–188). Minneapolis: University of Minnesota Press.

(1997e). "The Roots of Modern Media Analysis: Lewis Mumford and Marshall McLuhan." In E. S. Munson & C. A. Warren, eds., *James Carey: A Critical Reader* (pp. 34–59). Minneapolis: University of Minnesota Press.

Carlson, J., & Ebel, J. (2012). *From Jeremiad to Jihad: Religion, Violence, and America*. Berkeley: University of California Press.

Carruthers, S. L. (2000). *The Media at War: Communication and Conflict in the Twentieth Century*. New York: St. Martin's Press.

Cassirer, Ernst (1944). *An Essay on Man: An Introduction to the Philosophy of Human Culture*. New Haven, CT: Yale University Press.

(1951). *The Philosophy of the Enlightenment*. Princeton, NJ: Princeton University Press.

(1953–1957, 1966). *The Philosophy of Symbolic Forms* (4 vols.). Trans. R. Manheim & J. M. Krois. New Haven, CT: Yale University Press. Original publication in 1923–1929.

(1960). *The Logic of the Humanities*. Trans. C. Howe. New Haven, CT: Yale University Press.

Chang, Chung-Yuan (1987). "Chinese Philosophy and Contemporary Human Communication Theory." In. D. L. Kincaid, ed., *Communication Theory: Eastern and Western Perspectives* (pp. 20–43). New York: Academic Press.

(1963). *Creativity and Taoism*. New York: Julien Press.

Channell, David E. (1991). *The Vital Machine: A Study of Technology and Organic Life*. Oxford: Oxford University Press.

Charmaz, Kathy (2009). "Shifting the Grounds: Constructivist Grounded Theory Methods for the Twenty-First Century." In J. M. Morse et al., eds., *Developing Grounded Theory: The Second Generation* (pp. 127–154). Walnut Creek, CA: Left Coast Press.

Chatterjee, Deen K., ed. (2011). *Encyclopedia of Global Justice*. New York: Springer Publishing Company.

Chatterjee, Patralekha (2001). "Civil Society in India: A Necessary Corrective in a Representative Democracy." *Development and Cooperation*, November/December, pp. 23–24.

Chen, Kaihe (2013). "Chinese Media's Poverty Coverage." *Peking University Journalism and Communication Review*, 8, 167–182.

Cherribi, Sam (2017). *Fridays of Rage: Al Jazeera, the Arab Spring and Political Islam*. New York: Oxford University Press.

Chipchase, Jan et al. (2005). "Mobile Essentials: Field Study and Concepting." In *Proceedings of the 2005 Conference on Designing for User Experience* (San Francisco, November 3–5).

Christians, Clifford (1995a). "Propaganda and the Technological System." In T. L. Glasser & C. T. Salmon, eds., *Public Opinion and the Communication of Consent* (pp. 156–174). New York: Guilford Press.

  (1995b). "The Naturalistic Fallacy in Contemporary Interactionist-Interpretive Research." *Studies in Symbolic Interactionism*, 19, 125–130.

  (1997). "Technology and Triadic Theories of Mediation." In S. M. Hoover & K. Lundby, eds., *Rethinking Media, Religion, and Culture* (pp. 65–82). Thousand Oaks, CA: Sage Publications.

  (1999). "The Common Good as First Principle." In T. L. Glasser, ed., *The Idea of Public Journalism* (pp. 67–84). New York: Guilford Press.

  (2000). "An Intellectual History of Media Ethics." In Bart Pattyn, ed., *Media Ethics: Opening Social Dialogue* (pp. 15–45). Leuven, Belgium: Peeters.

  (2002). "The Social Ethics of Agnes Heller." In S. Bracci & C. Christians, eds., *Moral Engagement in Public Life: Theorists for Contemporary Ethics* (pp. 53–72). Berlin: Peter Lang.

  (2003). "Cross-Cultural Ethics and Truth." In Jolyon Mitchell & Sophia Marriage, eds., *Mediating Religion: Conversations in Media, Religion and Culture* (pp. 293–303). London: T & T Clark.

  (2004a). "The Changing News Paradigm: From Objectivity to Interpretive Sufficiency." In S. H. Iorio, ed., *Qualitative Research in Journalism: Taking It to the Streets* (pp. 41–56). Mahwah, NJ: Lawrence Erlbaum.

  (2004b). "*Ubuntu* and Communitarianism in Media Ethics." *Ecquid Novi: South African Journal of Journalism Research*, 25(2), 235–256.

  (2006). "Ellul as Theologian in Counterpoint." In C. M. Lum, ed., *Perspectives on Culture, Technology, and Communication: The Media Ecology Tradition* (pp. 117–141). Cresskill, NJ: Hampton Press.

  (2007a). "Cultural Continuity as an Ethical Imperative." *Qualitative Inquiry*, 13(3), 437–444.

  (2007b). "Nonviolence in Philosophical and Religious Ethics." *Javnost: The Public*, 14(4), 5–18.

  (2010a). "Communication Ethics in Postnarrative Terms." In Linda Steiner & Clifford Christians, eds., *Critical Concepts in Critical Cultural Studies* (pp. 173–186). Urbana: University of Illinois Press.

  (2010b). "Nonviolence in Philosophical and Media Ethics." In Richard Keeble, John Tulloch, & Florian Zollmann, eds., *Peace Journalism, War and Conflict Resolution* (pp. 15–30). New York: Peter Lang.

  (2010c). "The Ethics of Universal Being." In S. J. A. Ward & H. Wasserman, eds., *Media Ethics Beyond Borders: A Global Perspective* (pp. 6–23). New York: Routledge. Original publication, Johannesburg: Heinemann, 2008.

  (2011a). "Cultural Diversity and Moral Relativism in Communication Ethics." In A. G. Nikolaev, ed., *Ethical Issues in International Communication* (pp. 23–34). New York: Palgrave Macmillan.

(2011b). "Primordial Issues in Communication Ethics." In R. S. Fortner & P. M. Fackler, eds., *The Handbook of Global Communication and Media Ethics*, vol. I (pp. 1–19). Malden, MA: Wiley Blackwell.

(2013). "Global Ethics and the Problem of Relativism." In S. J. A. Ward, *Global Media Ethics: Problems and Perspectives* (pp. 272–294). Malden, MA: Wiley Blackwell.

(2014a). "Media Ethics in Transnational, Gender Inclusive, and Multicultural Terms." In C. Christians & K. Nordenstreng, eds., *Communication Theories in a Multicultural World* (pp. 293–310). New York: Peter Lang.

(2014b). "The Impact of Ethics on Media and Press Theory." In R. S. Fortner & P. M. Fackler, eds., *The Handbook of Media and Communication Theory*, vol. I (pp. 225–247). Malden, MA: Wiley Blackwell.

(2014c). "The Philosophy of Technology and Communication Systems." In R. S. Fortner & P. M. Fackler, eds., *The Handbook of Media and Communication Theory*, vol. II (pp. 513–534). Malden, MA: Wiley Blackwell.

(2015a). "Global Justice and Civil Society." In S. Rao & H. Wasserman, eds., *Media Ethics and Justice in the Age of Globalization* (pp. 43–58). Basingstoke, Hampshire, UK: Palgrave Macmillan.

(2015b). "Social Justice and Internet Technology." *New Media and Society*, pp. 1–14. Sagepub.co.uk/journals. DOI: 10.1177/1461444815604130.

(2015c). "The Problem of *Communitas* in Western Moral Philosophy." In B. Shan & C. Christians, eds., *The Ethics of Intercultural Communication* (pp. 35–55). New York: Peter Lang.

(2015d). "*Ubuntu* for Journalism Theory and Practice." *Journal of Media Ethics*, 30(2), 61–73.

(2017). "Truth, Al Jazeera, and Crisis Journalism." *International Journal of Crisis Communication*, 1(2), 79–91.

(2018a). "Ethics and Politics in Qualitative Research." In N. K. Denzin & Y. S. Lincoln, eds., *The Sage Handbook of Qualitative Research* (pp. 66–82), 5th ed. Los Angeles, CA: Sage Publications Inc.

(2018b). "Theorizing Over the Horizon: Ontology in the Global Imaginary." In P. Plaisance, ed., *Handbook of Communication and Media Ethics* (pp. 487–512). Berlin: De Gruyter Mouton.

& Carey, James W. (1981). "The Logic and Aims of Qualitative Research." In G. H. Stempel & B. H. Westley, eds., *Research Methods in Mass Communication* (pp. 342–463). Englewood Cliffs, NJ: Prentice-Hall, Inc.

& Traber, Michael, eds. (1997). *Communication Ethics and Universal Values*. Thousand Oaks, CA: Sage.

& Nordenstreng, Kaarle (2004). "Social Responsibility Worldwide." *Journal of Mass Media Ethics*, 19(1), 3–28.

& Rao, Shakuntala, Ward, Stephen J. A., & Wasserman, Herman (2008). "Toward a Global Media Ethics: Theoretical Perspectives." *Ecquid Novi: African Journalism Studies*, 29(2), 135–172.

& Glasser, Theodore, McQuail, Denis, Nordenstreng, Kaarle, & White, Robert (2009). *Normative Theories of the Media: Journalism in Democratic Societies*. Urbana: University of Illinois Press.

& Fackler, Mark, & Ferré, John (2012). *Ethics for Public Communication: Defining Moments in Media History*. New York: Oxford University Press.

& Ward, Stephen J. A. (2013). "Anthropological Realism for Global Media Ethics." In N. Couldry, M. Madianou, & A. Pinchevski, eds., *Ethics of Media* (pp. 72–88). Basingstoke, Hampshire, UK: Palgrave Macmillan.

& Fackler, M., Richardson, K. B., Kreschel, P. J., & Woods, R. H. (2017). "Case Sixteen: Global Media Monitoring Project." In their *Media Ethics: Cases and Moral Reasoning* (10th ed., pp. 111–114, 123–124). New York: Routledge.

Coates, Ta-Nehisi Paul (2015). *Between the World and Me*. New York: Random House Spiegel & Grau.

(2015). "My President Was Black." *The Atlantic*, January–February.

Cohen-Almagor, Raphael (2009). "In Internet's Way." In R. Fortner & M. Fackler, eds., *Ethics and Evil in the Public Sphere* (pp. 93–115). Cresskill, NJ: Hampton Press, Inc.

(2015). *Confronting the Internet's Dark Side: Moral and Social Responsibility on the Free Highway*. Cambridge: Cambridge University Press.

Cohen, Bernard (1963). *The Press and Foreign Policy*. Princeton, NJ: Princeton University Press.

Cohen, Noam, & Stelter, Brian (2010). "Airstrike Video Brings Notice to a Website." *New York Times*, April 7, pp. A1, A9.

Coleman, Cynthia-Lou (1997). "Values from American Indian Discourse." In C. Christians & M. Traber, eds., *Communication Ethics and Universal Values* (pp. 194–207). Thousand Oaks, CA: Sage Publications.

Coleman, Renita, & Wilkins, Lee (2009). "The Moral Development of Public Relations Practitioners: A Comparison with Other Professions and Influences on Higher Quality Ethical Reasoning." *Journal of Public Relations Research*, 21(3), 318–340.

Commers, M. S. Ronald, Vandekerckhove, Wim, Verlinden, An, eds. (2008). *Ethics in an Era of Globalization*. Aldershot, UK: Ashgate Publishing Limited.

Commission on Freedom of the Press (1947). *A Free and Responsible Press*. Chicago: University of Chicago Press.

Comte, Auguste (1893). *Cours de Philosophie Positive*. Paris: Bachelier Librarie pour les Mathematiques.

(1910). *A General View of Positivism*. Trans. J. H. Bridges. London: Routledge. Original work published in 1848.

Confucius (1979). *The Analects*. Trans. D. C. Lau. Harmondsworth, UK: Penguin.

(2008). *The Analects*. Trans. R. Dawson. Oxford World's Classics. Oxford: Oxford University Press.

Cooper, Ron L. (1993). *Heidegger and Whitehead: A Phenomenological Examination into the Intelligibility of Experience*. Athens: Ohio University Press.

Cooper, Thomas W. (1988a). "New Technology Effects Inventory: Forty Leading Ethical Issues." *Journal of Mass Media Ethics*, 13(2), 71–92.

(1988b). *Television and Ethics: A Bibliography*. Boston, MA: G. K. Hall.

(1989). *Communication and Global Change*. White Plains, NY: Longman.

(1996). *A Time Before Deception: Truth in Communication, Culture and Ethics*. Sante Fe, NM: Clear Light Publishers.

(2008). "Between the Summits: What Americans Think about Media Ethics." In T. W. Cooper, C. G. Christians, & A. S. Babbili, eds., *An Ethics Trajectory: Visions of Media Past, Present and Yet to Come* (pp. 17–27). Urbana: Institute of Communications Research, University of Illinois.

(2016–17). "A Whole Systems Approach to Ethics Inspired by Fritjof Capra." *Anekaant: A Journal of Polysemic Thought*, 4, Autumn, 95–99.

& Christians, C. G. (2008). "On the Need and Requirements for a Global Ethic of Communication." In Jose V. Ciprut, ed., *Ethics, Politics, and Democracy: From Primordial Principles to Prospective Practices* (pp. 293–318). Cambridge, MA: MIT Press.

Copleston, F. (1966). *A History of Philosophy*, vol. 8. *Modern Philosophy: Bentham to Russell*. Garden City, NY: Doubleday.

Cortese, A. J. (1990). *Ethnic Ethics: The Restructuring of Moral Theory*. Albany: State University of New York Press.

Cottle, S. (2006). "Mediatizing the Global War on Terror: Television's Public Eye." In A. P. Kavoori & T. Fraley, eds., *Media, Terrorism, and Theory: A Reader* (pp. 19–48). Lanham, MD: Rowman and Littlefield.

Couldry, Nick (2008). "Mediatization or Mediation? Alternative Understandings of the *Emergent* Space of Digital Storytelling." *New Media & Society*, 10(3), 373–391.

& Curran, James, eds. (2003). *Contesting Media Power: Alternative Media in a Networked World*. Lanham, MD: Rowman and Littlefield.

Cousineau, Robert H. (1972). *Humanism and Ethics: An Introduction to Heidegger's Letter on Humanism*. Brussels: Editions Nauwelaerts.

Cox, Harvey (1973). *Seduction of the Spirit: The Use and Misuse of People's Religion*. New York: Simon and Schuster.

Craig, Robert T. (1999). "Communication Theory as a Field." *Communication Theory*, 9(2), 119–161.

Crawford, Nelson (1924). *The Ethics of Journalism*. New York: Knopf; Creskill, NJ: Hampton Press.

Crocker, David A. (2000). "Truth Commissions, Transitional Justice, and Civil Society." In R. J. Rotberg & D. Thompson, eds., *Truth v. Justice: The Morality of Truth Commissions* (pp. 99–121). Princeton, NJ: Princeton University Press.

Crowley, David, & Heyer, Paul, eds. (2010). *Communication History: Technology, Culture, Society*, 6th ed. New York: Pearson Education.

Curran, James (2002). *Media and Power*. London: Routledge.

(2012). "Reinterpreting the Internet." In James Curran, Natalie Fenton, & Das Freedman, eds., *Misunderstanding the Internet* (2nd ed., pp. 3–33). London: Routledge. First edition published in 2012.

& Seaton, Jean (2009). *Power Without Responsibility: Press, Broadcasting and the Internet in Britain*, 7th ed. London: Routledge.

Cushman, F., Young, L., & Hauser, M. D. (2009). "The Role of Conscious Reasoning and Intuition in Moral Judgment: Three Principles of Harm." *Psychological Science*, 17, 1082–1089.

Dali Lama (1999). *Ethics for the New Millennium*. New York: Riverhead Press.

Damsholt, Tine (2009). "Ritualizing and Materializing Citizenship." *Journal of Ritual Studies*, 23(2), 17–29.

Dare, Olatunji (2000). "The Role of Print Media in Development and Social Change." In Andrew Moemeka, ed., *Development Communication in Action: Building Understanding and Creating Participation*, pp. 16–178. Lanham, MD: University Press of America.

Dash, Leon (1996). *Rosa Lee: A Mother and Her Family in Urban America*. New York: Basic Books.

(2003). *When Children Want Children: The Urban Crisis of Teenage Childbearing*. Urbana: University of Illinois Press.

Davis, Kord (2012). *Ethics of Big Data: Balancing Risk and Innovation*. San Francisco, CA: O'Reilly Media.

Davis, Olga, Nakayama, Thomas, & Martin, Judith (2000). "Current and Future Directions in Ethnicity and Methodology." *International Journal of Intercultural Relations*, 24(5), 525–539.

Dayton, Bruce W., & Kriesberg, Louis (2009). *Conflict Transformation and Peacebuilding: Moving from Violence to Sustainable Peace*. London: Routledge.

de Bary, William T. (1998). *Asian Values and Human Rights: A Confucian Communitarian Perspective*. Cambridge, MA: Harvard University Press.

De Fleur, Margaret H. (1997). *Computer-assisted Investigative Reporting: Development and Methodology*. New York: Routledge Taylor and Francis Group.

De Francisco, Victoria Pruin, & Palczewski, Catherine Helen (2007). *Communicating Gender Diversity: A Critical Approach*. Thousand Oaks, CA: Sage.

De Lima, Venicio (1981). *Communicaco e Cultura: As Ideas de Paulo Friere*. Rio de Janeiro: Editova Paz e Terra.

de Mesmaecker, Vicky (2010). "Building Support for Restorative Justice Through the Media: Is Taking the Victim Perspective the Most Appropriate Strategy?" *Contemporary Justice Review*, 13(3), 239–267.

De Miranda, Alexandre Lopes (2002). "Mikhail Bahktin's Philosophy of the Act." In S. Bracci & C. Christians, eds., *Moral Engagement in Public Life: Theorists for Contemporary Ethics* (pp. 196–223). New York: Peter Lang.

de Sola Poole, Ithiel (1984). *Technologies of Freedom*. Cambridge, MA: Belknap Press of Harvard University.

de Zúñiga, H. Gil, Lewis, Seth C., Willard, Amber, Valenzuela, Sebastian, Lee, Jae K., & Baresch, Brian (2011). "Blogging as a Journalistic Practice: A Model Linking Perception, Motivation, and Behavior." *Journalism: Theory, Practice and Criticism*, 12, 586–606.

Debatin, Bernhard (2008). "The Future of New Media Ethics." In T. W. Cooper, C. G. Christians, & A. S. Babbili, eds., *An Ethics Trajectory: Visions of the Media Past, Present, and Future* (pp. 257–264). Urbana: Institute of Communications Research, University of Illinois.

Delgado, Teresa, Doody, John, & Paffenroth, Kim, eds. (2016). *Augustine and Social Justice*. Lanham, MD: Lexington Books.

della Porta, Donatella, ed. (2007). *The Global Justice Movement: Cross-national and Transnational Perspectives*. New York: Routledge.

Dennett, Daniel C. (2014). "Consciousness in Human and Robot Minds." In R. S. Scharff & V. Dusek, eds., *Philosophy of Technology, The Technological Condition: An Anthology* (2nd ed., pp. 586–596). Malden, MA: Wiley Blackwell. Original work published 2005.

Denzin, Norman (1989). *The Research Act: A Theoretical Introduction to Sociological Methods*. 3rd ed. Englewood Cliffs, NJ: Prentice Hall.

   (1997). *Interpretive Ethnography: Ethnographic Practices for the Twenty-First Century*. Thousand Oaks, CA: Sage.

   (2014). "Symbolic Interactionism and the Media." In R. Fortner & M. Fackler, eds., *The Handbook of Media and Mass Communication Theory* (pp. 74–94). Malden, MA: Wiley Blackwell.

   & Giardina, Michael, eds. (2007). *Ethical Futures in Qualitative Research: Decolonizing the Politics of Knowledge*. Walnut Creek, CA: Left Coast Press.

   & Lincoln, Yvonna S., & Smith, Linda Tuhiwai, eds. (2008). *Handbook of Critical and Indigenous Methodologies*. Thousand Oaks, CA: Sage Publications.

   & Lincoln, Yvonna, eds. (2011). *The Sage Handbook of Qualitative Research*, 4th ed. Thousand Oaks, CA: Sage Publications.

Descartes, Rene (1964). *Rules for the Direction of the Mind*. In his *Philosophical Essays* (pp. 147–236). Trans. L. J. Lafleur. Indianapolis, IN: Bobbs-Merrill. Original work published 1638.

Dewey, John (1922). *Human Nature and Conduct*. New York: Henry Holt.

   (1927). *The Public and Its Problems*. New York: Henry Holt.

Dickson, Caitlin (2014). "Where White Supremacists Breed Online." *Daily Beast*, April 17, 2014. www.thedailybeat.com/articles/2014/04/17/

   (2015). "Report: Hate Groups, Domestic Extremists Grew Significantly in 2015." https://news.yahoo.com/report–hate–groups–domestic-extremists-grew-significantly-in-2015-163016396.html

Diggs, Bernard J. (1973). "The Common Good as Reason for Political Action." *Ethics*, 83(4), 283–284.

DiStefano, Christine (1991). *Configurations of Masculinity: A Feminist Perspective on Modern Political Theory*. Ithaca, NY: Cornell University Press.

Do-Dinh, Pierre (1969). *Confucius and Chinese Humanism*. New York: Funk & Wagnalls.

Donagan, Alan (1977). *Theories of Morality*. Chicago: University of Chicago Press.

Donnerstein, E. (2011). "The Media and Aggression: From TV to the Internet." In J. Forgas, A. Kruglanski, & K. Williams, eds., *The Psychology of Social Conflict and Aggression* (pp. 265–282). New York: Psychology Press.

Doris, J. M. & Stitch, S. P. (2005). "As a Matter of Fact: Empirical Perspectives on Ethics." In F. Jackson & M. Smith, eds., *The Oxford Handbook of Contemporary Philosophy* (pp. 114–152). Oxford: Oxford University Press.

Dower, Nigel (2007). *World Ethics: The New Agenda*. Edinburgh: Edinburgh University Press.

Downing, John H. D. (1984). *Radical Media: The Political Organization of Alternative Communication*. Boston, MA: South End Press.

(2001). *Radical Media: Rebellious Communication and Social Movements*. Thousand Oaks, CA: Sage Publications.

(2003). "The Independent Media Center Movement and the Anarchist Socialist Tradition." In N. Couldry & J. Curran, eds., *Contesting Media Power: Alternative Media in a Networked World* (pp. 243–258). Lanham, MD: Rowman & Littlefield.

Downing, John H. D., ed. (2011). *Encyclopedia of Social Movement Media*. Thousand Oaks, CA: Sage Publications.

& Husband, Charles (2005). *Representing "Race": Racisms, Ethnicities and the Media*. Thousand Oaks, CA: Sage.

Dreyfus, H. L. (1995). "Heidegger on Gaining a Free Relation to Technology." In A. Feenberg & A. Hannay, eds., *Technology and the Politics of Knowledge*. Bloomington: Indiana University Press.

Düwell, Marcus, Braarvig, Jens, Brownsword, Roger, & Mieth, Dietmar, eds. (2014). *The Cambridge Handbook of Human Dignity*. Cambridge: Cambridge University Press.

Dworkin, Ronald (2010). *Justice for Hedgehogs*. Cambridge, MA: Harvard University Press.

Dyck, Arthur (1977). *On Human Care: An Introduction to Ethics*. Nashville, TN: Abingdon.

Dyer-Witheford, Nick (1999). *Cyber Marx: Cycles and Circuits of Struggle in High Capitalism*. Urbana: University of Illinois Press.

(2015). *Cyber-Proletariat: Global Labour in the Digital Vortex*. London: Pluto.

& de Peuter, Greig (2009). *Games of Empire: Global Capitalism and Video Games*. Minneapolis: University of Minnesota Press.

Eastin, Matthew S., ed. (2013). *Encyclopedia of Media Violence*. Los Angeles: Sage Publications.

Eisenstein, Elizabeth (1979). *The Printing Press as an Agent of Change. Communications and Cultural Transformations in Early Modern Europe* (2 vols.). Cambridge: Cambridge University Press.

Ellul, Jacques (1951). *The Presence of the Kingom*. Trans. O. Wyon. Philadelphia: Westminster.

(1951–1952). *Histoire des Institutions de l'Antiquité* (2 vols.). Paris: Presses Universitaries de France.

(1953, 1956, 1966). *Histoire des Institutions françaises* (3 vols.). Paris: Universitaries de France.

(1954). *The Technological Society*. Trans. J. Wilkinson. New York: Random Vintage.

(1964). *The Technological Society*. Trans. J. Wilkinson. New York: Alfred A. Knopf [*Le Technique ou l'enjeu du siècle* (Paris: Librairie Armand Colin, 1954)].

(1965). *Propaganda: The Formation of Men's Attitudes*. Trans. K. Kellen & J. Lerner. New York: Alfred A. Knopf [*Propagandes* (Paris: Librairie Armand Colin, 1962)].

(1967). *The Political Illusion*. Trans. Konrad Kellen. New York: Alfred A. Knopf [*L'Illuison politique* (Paris: Editions Robert Laffont, 1965)].

(1968). *A Critique of the New Commonplaces*. Trans. H. Weaver. New York: Knopf.

(1969). *Violence*. Trans. Cecilia G. Kings. New York: Seabury Press.

(1972). *Contre les violents*. Paris: Le Centurion. *Violence: Reflections from a Christian Perspective*. Trans. Cecilia G. Kings. New York: Seabury, 1969.

(1976). *Ethics of Freedom*. Trans. G. W. Bromiley. Grand Rapids, MI: William B. Eerdmans.

(1981a). *In Season and Out of Season: An Introduction to the Thought of Jacques Ellul*. New York: Harper & Row.

(1981b). *The Technological System*. Trans. J. Neugroschel. New York: Continuum. Original publication *[Le systéme technicen]* in 1977.

(1985). *The Humiliation of the Word*. Trans. Joyce Hanks. Grand Rapids, MI: Eerdmans.

(1988). *Jesus and Marx: From Gospel to Ideology*. Trans. J. M. Hanks. Grand Rapids, MI: Eerdmans.

(1989). *What I Believe*. Trans. G. W. Bromiley. Grand Rapids, MI: William B. Eerdmans.

(1990). *The Technological Bluff*. Trans. G. W. Bromiley. Gand Rapids, MI: William B. Eerdmans.

Emery, M., Emery, E., & Roberts, N. (2000). *The Press and America: An Interpretive History of the Mass Media*, 9th ed. Needham Heights, MA: Allyn & Bacon.

Engberg-Pederson, T. (1980). *Aristotle's Theory of Moral Insight*. Oxford: Clarendon.

Entman, Robert M. (1989). *Democracy Without Citizens: Media and the Decay of American Politics*. New York: Oxford University Press.

(1993). "Framing: Toward Clarification of a Fractured Paradigm." *Journal of Communication*, 43(4), 51–58.

(2004). *Projections of Power: Framing News, Public Opinion, and U.S. Foreign Policy*. Chicago: University of Chicago Press.

& Rojecki, Andrew (2000). *The Black Image in the White Mind: Media and Race in America*. Chicago: University of Chicago Press.

Ess, Charles (2012a). *Digital Media Ethics*, 2nd ed. Cambridge: Polity Press.

(2012b). "Foreword." In D. Heider & A. L. Massanari, eds., *Digital Ethics: Research and Practice* (pp. ix–xix). New York: Peter Lang.

Ettema, James, & Glasser, Theodore (1998). *Custodians of Conscience*. New York: Columbia University Press.

Ettinger, E. (1995). *Hannah Arendt/Martin Heidegger*. New Haven, CT: Yale University Press.

Etzioni, Amitai (2013). *The Spirit of Community: Rights, Responsibilities and the Communitarian Agenda*. New York: Random House Crown Publishing.

Eubanks, Virginia (2018). *Automating Inequality: How High-Tech Tools Profile, Police, and Punish the Poor*. New York: St. Martin's Press.

Euben, J. Peter (1981). "Philosophy and the Professions." *Democracy*, April, 112–127.

Evangelista, Matthew (2007). "Conflicting Perspectives on Terrorism." June 14–21. www.isodarco.com/courses/andal007/paper_Evangelista_intro.pdf

Exum, A. (2007). "Arabic-language Media and the Danish Cartoon Crisis." *Media Development*, 2, 30–33.

Facebook (2013). "Statement of Rights and Responsibilities." November 15, 2013. www.facebook.com/terms.php?ref=pf

Fackler, Mark (2003). "Communitarian Theory with an African Inflexion." In J. Mitchell & S. Marriage, eds., *Mediating Religion: Conversations in Media, Religion and Culture* (pp. 317–327). Edinburgh: T & T Clark.

(2012). "Case 64. They Play to Kill." In C. Christians, M. Fackler, K. B. Richardson, P. J. Kreshel, & R. H. Woods Jr., *Media Ethics: Cases and Moral Reasoning*, 9th ed. (pp. 265–267). Boston, MA: Pearson.

Fahmy, Sahira, & Johnson, Thomas J. (2017). "Show the Truth and Let the Audience Decide: A Web-based Survey Showing Support for Use of Graphic Imagery Among Viewers of Al Jazeera." *Journal of Broadcasting and Electronic Media*, 51, 245–264.

Farrell, T. B. (1993). *Norms of Rhetorical Culture*. New Haven, CT: Yale University Press.

Fasching, Darrell (1990). "The Dialectic of Apocalypse and Utopia in the Theological Ethics of Jacques Ellul." *Research in Philosophy and Technology*, 10, 149–165.

Fayyad, U., Piatetsky-Shapiro, G., & Smyth, P. (1996). "From Data Mining to Knowledge Discovery in Databases." *AI Magazine*, 17(3), 37–54.

Feenberg, Andrew (1991). *A Critical Theory of Technology*. New York: Oxford University Press.

(2002) *Transforming Technology: A Critical Theory Revisited*, 2nd ed. New York: Oxford University Press.

Feinberg, Joel (1984). *Harm To Others: The Moral Limits of the Criminal Law*. New York: Oxford University Press.

Feng, Yayu (2016). "Introduction to Big Data." *Research Paper*. Institute of Communications Research, University of Illinois.

Ferguson, Christopher J. (2014). "Does Media Violence Predict Social Violence?" *Journal of Communication*, 65(1), 1–22.

& Dyck, Dominic (2012). "Paradigm Change in Aggression Research." *Aggression and Violent Behavior*, 17, 220–228.

& San Miguel, C., & Hartley, R. D. (2009). "A Multivariate Analysis of Youth Violence and Aggression: The Influence of Family, Peers, Depression and Media Violence." *Journal of Pediatrics*, 155(6), 904–908.

Field, Hartry (1994). "Deflationist Views of Meaning and Content." *Mind*, 249–284.

Fleischacker, Samuel O. (1992). *Integrity and Moral Relativism*. Leiden, Netherlands: E. J. Brill.

(1994). *The Ethics of Culture*. Ithaca, NY: Cornell University Press.

Flick, Uwe (2018). "Triangulation." In N. K. Denzin & Y. S. Lincoln, eds., *The Sage Handbook of Qualitative Research* (5th ed., pp. 444–461). Los Angeles, CA: Sage Publications Inc.

Floridi, Luciano (2011). *The Philosophy of Information*. Oxford: Oxford University Press.

(2013). *The Ethics of Information*. Oxford: Oxford University Press.

(2014). *The Fourth Revolution: How the Infosphere Is Reshaping Human Reality*. Oxford: Oxford University Press.

Fortner, Robert F. (2009). "The Media in Evil Circumstances." In L. Wilkins & C. Christians, eds., *The Handbook of Mass Media Ethics* (pp. 340–352). New York: Routledge.

(2010). "Genocide in Civic Engagement: When the Public Sphere Turns Evil." In R. Fortner & M. Fackler, eds., *Ethics and Evil in the Public Sphere: Media, Universal Values and Global Development* (pp. 183–206). Cresskill, NJ: Hampton.

Foster, J. B., & McChesney, R. W. (2014). "Surveillance Capitalism." *Monthly Review*, 66(3), 1–21.

Foucault, Michel (1984). "On the Genealogy of Ethics: An Overview of Work in Progress"; "Politics and Ethics"; "An Interview." In Paul Rabinow, ed., *The Foucault Reader* (pp. 340–389). Trans. C. Porter. New York: Pantheon.

(2014). *Wrong-Doing, Truth-Telling: The Function of Avowal in Justice*. Trans. S. W. Sawyer. Chicago: University of Chicago Press.

Foxman, Abraham H., & Wolf, Christopher (2013). *Viral Hate: Containing Its Spread on the Internet*. New York: St. Martin's Press.

Frankl, Viktor Emil (1988). *The Will to Meaning: Foundations and Applications of Logotherapy*. New York: New American Library.

Franklin, Bob (2005). "The Local Press and the McDonaldization Thesis." In Stuart Allan, ed., *Journalism: Critical Issues* (pp. 137–150). Maidenhead, UK: Open University Press.

Fraser, Nancy (1985). "What's Critical About Critical Theory? The Case of Habermas and Gender." *New German Critique*, 35, Spring-Summer, 97–131.

(1992). "Rethinking the Public Sphere: A Contribution to the Critique of Actually Existing Democracy." In C. Calhoun, ed., *Habermas and the Public Sphere*. Cambridge, MA: MIT Press.

(1997). *Justus Interruptus*. New York: Routledge.

Freedman, Jonathan L. (2002). *Media Violence and Its Effect on Aggression: Assessing the Scientific Evidence*. Toronto: University of Toronto Press.

Freire, Paulo (1970a). "Education as the Practice of Freedom" and "Cultural Action for Freedom," Series No. L. Cambridge, MA: *Harvard Educational Review*, and the Center for the Study of Development.

(1970b). *Pedagogy of the Oppressed*. New York: Seabury Press.

(1973). *Education for Critical Consciousness*. New York: Seabury Press.

Friend, Cecilia, & Singer, Jane B. (2007). *Online Journalism Ethics: Traditions and Transitions*. London: Routledge. Kindle edition 2015.

Frola, Leann (2007). "How a Small Newspaper Won a Big Award." *Poynter Online*, April 9. www.poynter.org/2007/how-a-small-newspaper-won-a-big-award/81636

Fry, Tony, ed. (1993). *R U A TV? Heidegger and the Televisual*. Sydney, Australia: Power Publications.

Fuchs, Christian (2017). *Social Media: A Critical Introduction*, 2nd ed. London: Sage Publications.

(2014). *Digital Labour and Karl Marx*. London: Routledge.

Fuller, R. Buckminister (1963). *No More Second Hand God*. Carbondale: Southern Illinois University Press.

(1975). *Synergetics: Explorations in the Geometry of Thinking*. New York: Macmillan.

(1981). *Critical Path*. New York: St. Martin's Press.

Furnas, Alexander (2012). "Everything You Wanted to Know About Data Mining But Were Afraid to Ask." *The Atlantic*, April 3. www.theatlantic.com/technol ogy/archive/2012/04/everything-you-wanted-to-know-about-data-mining-but-were-afraid-to-ask/255388/

Murdock, G., & Schlesinger, P., eds., *Communicating Politics: Mass Communication and the Political Process* (pp. 37–54). New York: Holmes and Meier Publishers.

Gadamer, Hans-Georg (1970). "On the Scope and Function of Hermeneutical Reflection." Trans., G. B. Hess & R. E. Palmer. *Continuum*, 8, 77–95.

(1975). "The Problem of Historical Consciousness." *Graduate Faculty Philosophy Journal*, New School for Social Research, 5(1), 8–52.

(1989). *Truth and Method*. [Wahrheit und Methode: Grunzuge einer Philosophiscen Hermeneutic], 2nd ed. Trans. J. Weinsheimer & D. G. Marshall. London: Continuum International. Original publication in 1975.

Galtung, Johan (1990). "Cultural Violence." *Journal of Peace Research*, 27(3), 291–305.

(1998). "High Road, Low Road: Charting the Course for Peace Journalism." *Track Two*, 7(4), December.

(2000). *Conflict Transformation by Peaceful Means: A Participants' and Trainers' Manual*. Geneva: United Nations Development Programme.

(2004). *Transcend and Transform: An Introduction to Conflict Work (Peace by Peaceful Means)*. London: Pluto Press.

Gandhi, Mohandas Karamchand (1961). *Non-violent Resistance (Satyagraha)*. New York: Shocken Books.

(1990). *Autobiography: The Story of My Experiments with Truth*. Mineola, NY: Dover.

(1994). *The Collected Works of Mahatma Gandhi*. New Delhi: Government of India, Publications Division, Ministry of Information and Broadcasting.

Gao, Haijan (2016). "Poverty Coverage in *The People's Daily*." *Youth Journalist*, 27.

Garfinkel, Harold (1967). *Studies in Ethnomethodology*. Englewood Cliffs, NJ: Prentice-Hall, Inc.

Garnham, Nicholas (1986). "The Media and the Public Sphere." *Intermedia* 14 (1), 28–33.

Gasiet, Seev (1980). *Eine Theorie der Bedürfnisse*. Frankfurt, Germany: Campus Verlag.

Geertsema, Margaretha (2009). "Women and News: Making Connections Between the Global and the Local." *Feminist Media Studies*, 9(2), 149–172.

(2010). "Challenging the Lion in Its Den: Dilemmas of Gender and Media Activism in South Africa." *Ecquid Novi: African Journalism Studies*, 31(1), 68–88.

(2015), "Women's eNews: Reaching Out to the Arab World." *International Communications Research Journal*, 50(1), 47–67.

Geertz, Clifford (1973). *The Interpretation of Cultures*. New York: Basic Books.

Gelderloos, Peter (2007). *How Nonviolence Protects the State*. Boston, MA: South End Press.

(2015). *The Failure of Nonviolence*, rev. ed. Seattle, WA: Left Bank Books.

Gerbner, G., Gross, L., Morgan, M., & Signorielli, N. (1994). "Growing Up with Television: The Cultivation Perspective." In J. Bryant & D. Zillmann, eds., *Media Effects: Advances in Theory and Research* (pp. 17–41). Hillsdale, NJ: Erlbaum.

Giago, Tim (2005). "Freedom of the Press in Indian Country." *Nieman Reports: Covering Indian Country*, Fall.

Gilligan, Carol (1982). *In a Different Voice: Psychological Theory and Women's Development*. Cambridge, MA: Harvard University Press.

(1989). *Mapping the Moral Domain: A Contribution of Women's Thinking to Psychological Theory and Education*. Cambridge, MA: Harvard University Press.

& Richards, David. A. J. (2009). *The Deepening Darkness: Patriarchy, Resistance, and Democracy's Future*. New York: Cambridge University Press.

Gillmor, Dan (2006). *We the Media: Grassroots Journalism By the People, For the People*. Sebastopol, CA: O'Reilly Media.

Glaser, Barney, & Straus, Anselm (1967). *The Discovery of Grounded Theory*. Chicago: Aldine Publishing.

Glasser, T. L., Awad, I., & Kim, J. W. (2009). "The Claims of Multiculturalism and Journalism's Promise of Diversity." *Journal of Communication*, 59(1), 57–78.

Goertzel, Ben (2002). "Thoughts on AI Morality." www.goertzel.org/dynapsyc/2–2/AIMorality.htm

Goldkuhl, Göran (2000). "The Validity of Validity Claims: An Inquiry into Communication Rationality." *The Language – Action Perspective on Communication Modeling*. www.vits.org/publikatoner/dokument/404.pdf, Accessed May 5, 2017

Gomes, Pedro G. (1990). *Directo de Ser: A Ética da communicao na Amèerica Latina [The Right To Be: An Ethics of Communication in Latin America]*. Sao Paulo: Ediciones Paulinas.

Gonzalez, M., & Cook-Lynn, E. (1998). *The Politics of Hallowed Ground: Wounded Knee and the Struggle for Indian Sovereignty*. Urbana: University of Illinois Press.

Goodin, David (2013). *The New Rationalism: Albert Schweitzer's Philosophy of Reverence for Life*. Montreal: McGill Queen's University Press.

Goss, Brian M. (2013). *Rebooting the Herman & Chomsky Propaganda Model in the Twenty-First Century*. New York: Peter Lang.

Gouldner, Alvin (1954). *Patterns of Industrial Bureaucracy*. New York: Free Press.

Graham, David A. (2016). "Obama to Muslim Americans: You're Right Where You Belong." *The Atlantic*, February 3. www.theatlantic.com/politics/archive/2016/02/obama-mosque-visit-muslims/459765/

Gray, J., Chambers, L., & Bounegru, L. (2012). *The Data Journalism Handbook*. Sebastopol, CA: O'Reilly Media, Inc.

Gross, L., Katz, J. S., & Ruby, J., eds. (1988). *Image Ethics: The Moral Rights of Subjects in Photographs, Film, and Television*. New York: Oxford University Press.

Grossberg, L., & Christians, C. (1981). "Hermeneutics and the Study of Communication." In J. Soloski, ed., *Foundations for Communication Studies* (pp. 57–81). Iowa City: University of Iowa Monograph Series.

Grossberg, Lawrence (2010). "James W. Carey and the Conversation of Culture." In L. Steiner & C. Christians, eds., *Key Concepts in Critical Cultural Studies* (pp. 73–87). Urbana: University of Illinois Press.

Guba, E. G., & Lincoln, Yvonna S. (1994). "Competing Paradigms in Qualitative Research." In N. K. Denzin & Y. S. Lincoln, eds., *Handbook of Qualitative Research* (pp. 105–117). Thousand Oaks, CA: Sage.

Gunaratne, Shelton A. (2005). *The Dao of the Press: A Humanocentric Theory*. Cresskill, NJ: Hampton Press.

Gunkel, David (2006). "The Machine Question: Ethics, Alterity, and Technology." *Explorations in Media Ecology*, 5(4), 259–278.

(2007). *Thinking Otherwise: Philosophy, Communication, Technology*. Lafayette, IN: Purdue University Press.

(2012). *The Machine Question: Critical Perspectives on AI, Robots and Ethics*. Cambridge, MA: MIT Press.

(2016). "Another Alterity: Rethinking Ethics in the Face of the Machine." In D. J. Gunkel, C. M. Filho, & D. Mersch, eds., *The Changing Face of Alterity: Communication, Technology and Other Subjects* (pp. 197–215). London: Rowman & Littlefield International.

& Taylor, Paul A. (2014). *Heidegger and the Media*. Cambridge, and Malden, MA: Polity Press.

Gushee, David P. (2013). *The Sacredness of Human Life*. Grand Rapids, MI: William B. Eerdmans.

Gutiérrez, Gustavo (1971). *Teología de la Liberación: Perspectivas. [A Theology of Liberation]*, 1973; 2nd ed. 1998. New York: Orbis Books.

(1983). *The Power of the Poor in History*. Maryknoll, NY: Orbis Books.

(1990). *The Truth Shall Make You Free*. Maryknoll, NY: Orbis Books.

& Müller, Gerhard Ludwig (2015). *On the Side of the Poor: The Theology of Liberation*. Trans. R. A. Krieg & J. B. Nickoloff. Maryknoll, NY: Orbis Books.

Gutmann, Amy (1985). "Communitarian Critics of Liberalism." *Philosophy and Public Affairs*, 14(3), 311.

Haar, Michael, & Lilly, Reginald (1993). *The Song of the Earth: Heidegger and the Grounds of the History of Being*. Trans. R. Lilly. Bloomington: University of Indiana Press.

Habermas, Jürgen (1970). *Toward a Rational Society*. Trans. J. J. Shapiro. Boston, MA: Beacon.

(1973). *Theory and Practice*. Trans. J. Viertel. Boston, MA: Beacon.

(1984). *The Theory of Communicative Action*. Vol. 1: *Reason and the Rationalization of Society*. Trans. T. McCarthy. Boston, MA: Beacon Press.

(1990). *Moral Consciousness and Communicative Action*. Trans. C. Lenhardt & S. W. Nicholsen. Cambridge, MA: MIT Press.

(1991). "A Reply." In A. Honneth & H. Joas, eds., *Communicative Action: Essays on Jürgen Habermas's Theory of Communicative Action* (pp. 214–264). Trans. J. Gaines & D. L. Jones. Cambridge: Polity.

(1993). *Justification and Application: Remarks on Discourse Ethics*. Trans. C. Kronin. Cambridge, MA: MIT Press.

(1995a). "Discourse Ethics: Notes on a Program of Philosophical Justification." In S. Benhabib & F. Dallmayr, eds., *The Communicative Ethics Controversy* (pp. 60–110). Cambridge, MA: MIT Press.

(1995b). "Reconciliation Through the Public Use of Reason: Remarks on John Rawls's Political Liberalism." *Journal of Philosophy*, 53, 109–131.

(1996). *Between Facts and Norms: Contributions to a Discourse Theory of Law and Democracy*. Cambridge: Polity Press.

(1998). *The Inclusion of the Other*. Cambridge, MA: MIT Press.

(2001). *The Postnational Constellation*. Trans. Max Pensky. Cambridge, MA: MIT Press.

(2003). *Truth and Justification*. Trans. B. Fultner. Cambridge, MA: MIT Press. Original publication in 1999.

(2013). *The Essence of Truth: On Plato's Cave Allegory and Theaetus*. Trans. T. Sadler. London: Bloomsbury Academic. Original publication in 1998.

Hackett, Robert, & Zhao, Yuezhi, eds. (2005). *Democratizing Global Media*. Lanham, MD: Rowman and Littlefield.

Hadl, Gabriele, & Hintz, Arne (2009). "Framing Our Media for Transnational Policy: The World Summit on the Information Society and Beyond." In L. Stein, D. Kidd, & C. Rodriguez, eds., *Making our Media: Global Initiatives Toward a Democratic Public Sphere* (vol. 2, pp. 103–122). Cresskill, NJ: Hampton Press.

Hafez, Kai (2002). "Journalism Ethics Revised: A Comparison of Ethics Codes in Europe, North Africa, the Middle East, and Muslim Asia." *Political Communication*, 19(2), 225–250.

Hall, J. Storrs (2001). "Ethics for Machines." *KurzweilAI.net*, July 5. www.kurzweilai.net/ethics-for-machines

Hall, Rupert (1965). "An Unconvincing Indictment of the Evils of Technology." *Scientific American*, 212, February, 126–127.

Hall, Stuart (1973). *Encoding and Decoding in Television Discourse*. Birmingham, UK: University of Birmingham, Centre for Contemporary Cultural Studies.

(1989). "Ideology and Communication Theory." In B. Dervin, L. Grossberg, B. J. O'Keefe, & Ellen Wartella, eds., *Rethinking Issues*. Vol. I: *Paradigm Issues* (pp. 40–52). Newbury Park, CA: Sage.

Hallin, Daniel C., & Mancini, Paolo (2004). *Comparing Media Systems: Three Models of Media and Politics*. Cambridge: Cambridge University Press.

Hammersley, Martyn, & Traianou, Anna (2012). *Ethics in Qualitative Research: Controversies and Contexts*. London: Sage Publications.

Hanitzsch, Thomas (2007). "Deconstructing Journalism Culture: Towards a Universal Theory." *Communication Theory*, 17(4), 367–385.

(2013). "Comparative Journalism Research: Mapping a Growing Field." *Australian Journalism Research*, 35(2), 9–19.

& Hanusch, Folker, Mellado, Claudia, Anikina, Maria, Berganza, Rosa, & Cangoz, Incilay (2010). "Mapping Journalism Cultures Across Nations: A Comparative Study of 18 Countries." *Journalism Studies*, 12(3), 273–293.

& Plaisance, Patrick, & Skewes, Elizabeth (2013). "Universals and Differences in Global Journalism Ethics." In Stephen J. A. Ward, ed., *Global Media Ethics: Problems and Perspectives* (pp. 30–49). Malden, MA: Wiley-Blackwell.

Hankivsky, Olena (2004). *Social Policy and the Ethics of Care*. Vancouver, Canada: University of British Columbia Press.

Hanson, F. Allan (2009). "Beyond the Skin Bag: On the Moral Responsibility to Extend Agencies." *Ethics and Information Technology*, 11(1), 91–99.

Haraway, Donna (1985). "A Cyborg Manifesto: Science, Technology and Socialist Feminism in the 1980s." *Socialist Review*, 80, 65–108.

(1991). *Simians, Cyborgs and Women: The Reinvention of Nature*. New York: Free Association Books.

Harmer, Emily, & van Zoonen, Lisbeth (2016). "Gendered Citizenship: Representations of Women Voters in Newspaper Coverage of UK Elections 1918–2010." In H. Danielsen, K. Jegersted, L. Muriaas, & B. Ytre Arne, eds., *Gendered Citizenship and the Politics of Representation* (pp. 161–185). London: Palgrave MacMillan.

Harrington, Walter, ed. (1997) *Intimate Journalism: The Art and Craft of Reporting Everyday Life*. Thousand Oaks, CA: Sage Publications.

Hasinoff, Amy A. (2015). *Sexting Panic: Rethinking Criminalization, Privacy and Consent*. Urbana: University of Illinois Press.

Hastings, Tom H. (2004). *Nonviolent Response to Terrorism*. Jefferson, NC: McFarland & Co., Inc.

Havel, Václav (1989a). *Letters to Olga: June 1979 – September 1982*. Trans. Paul Wilson. New York: Henry Holt and Company.

(1989b). *Living in Truth*. Edited by J. Vadislav. London: Faber & Faber.

(1994). "Post-modernism: The Search for Universal Laws." *Vital Speeches of the Day*, 60(2), August 1, 613–615.

(1997). *The Art of the Impossible: Politics as Morality in Practice*. New York: Knopf.

Hayner, Priscilla B. (2002). *Unspeakable Truths: Facing the Challenge of Truth Commissions*. New York: Routledge.

Heeger, Robert (2014). "Dignity Only for Humans? A Controversy." In M. Düwell, J. Braarvig, R. Brownsword, & D. Mieth, eds., *Cambridge Handbook of Human Dignity* (pp. 541-545). Cambridge: Cambridge University Press.

Heidegger, Martin (1962a). *Being and Time [Sein und Zeit]*. Trans. John Macquarrie & Edward Robinson. New York: Harper and Row. Original publication 1927.

(1962b). "Letter on Humanism." In W. Barrett & H. D. Aiken, eds., *Philosophy in the Twentieth Century* (vol. 2, pp. 290–302). New York: Random House. Original publication in 1947.

(1966). *Discourse on Thinking*. New York: Harper & Row.

(1971a). *On the Way to Language*. Trans. P. D. Hertz. New York: Harper & Row. Original publication *[Unterwegs zur Sprache]* in 1959.

(1971b). *Poetry, Language, Thought*. Trans. A. Hofstadter. New York: Harper & Row.

(1976). *What Is Called Thinking? [Was heist Denken]*. Trans. F. D. Weick & J. G. Gray. New York: Harper & Row. Original publication in 1951–1952.

(1977a). "Building Dwelling Being," in his *Basic Writings*. Trans. D. F. Krell, pp. 319–339. New York: Harper and Row.

(1977b). *The Question Concerning Technology and Other Essays*. Trans. W. Lovitt. New York: Harper & Row.

(1996). *The Principle of Reason [Der Satz vom Grund]*. Trans. R. Lilly. Bloomington: Indiana University Press. Original publication in 1955–1956.

(1998). "Plato's Doctrine of Truth." Trans. T. Sheehan. In W. McNeil, ed., *Pathmarks* (pp. 155–182). Cambridge: Cambridge University Press.

(2000). *Introduction to Metaphysics [Einführung in die Metaphysik]*. Trans. G. Fried & R. Polt. New Haven, CT: Yale University Press. Original publication in 1953.

Heider, Don, ed. (2004). *Class and News*. Lanham, MD: Roman and Littlefield.

& Massanari, Adrienne, eds. (2012). *Digital Ethics: Research and Practice*. New York: Peter Lang.

Held, David (2005). "Principles of Cosmopolitan Order." In G. Brock & H. Brighouse, eds., *The Political Philosophy of Cosmopolitanism* (chap. 2, pp. 10–27). Cambridge: Cambridge University Press.

(2010). *Cosmopolitanism: Ideals and Realities*. Cambridge: Polity Press.

Held, Virginia (2007). *The Ethics of Care: Personal, Political, and Global*. New York: Oxford University Press.

Heller, Agnes (1984). *Everyday Life*. London: Routledge and Kegan Paul.

(1987a). *Beyond Justice*. Oxford: Basil Blackwell.

(1987b). "Hannah Arendt on the '*Vita Contemplative*.'" *Philosophy and Social Criticism*, 12, 281–296.

(1988). *General Ethics*. Oxford: Basil Blackwell.

(1990). *A Philosophy of Morals*. Oxford: Basil Blackwell.

(1995). *The Power of Shame: A Rational Perspective*. London: Routledge and Kegan Paul.

(1999). *A Theory of Modernity*. Malden, MA: Wiley-Blackwell.

(1996). *An Ethics of Personality*. Oxford: Basil Blackwell.

Henrici, Peter (1983). "Towards an Anthropological Philosophy of Communication." *Communication Resources*, March 3, pp. 1–4.

Herman, Edward S., & Chomsky, Noam (1988). *Manufacturing Consent: The Political Economy of the Mass Media*. New York: Random House Pantheon.

Heyer, Paul (1988). *Communications and History: Theories of Media, Knowledge, and Civilization*. Westport, CT: Greenwood Press.

Hickey, N. (1973). "Only the Sensational Stuff Got on the Air." *TV Guide*, December 8, p. 34. For details of and commentary on this case, see the other three articles in Hickey's series: "Was the Truth Buried at Wounded

Knee?" (December 1, pp. 7–12); "Cameras Over Here!" (December 15, pp. 43–49); "Our Media Blitz Is Here to Stay" (December 22, pp. 21–23).

Higgins, Kathleen (2016). "Post-Truth: A Guide for the Perplexed." *Scientific American*, December 5, 1–10. www.scientificamerican.com/article/post-truth-a-guide-for- the-perplexed.html

Himelboim, Itai, & Limor, Yehiel (2011). "The Social Role of Journalism: An International Comparative Study of 242 Codes of Ethics." *Mass Communication and Society*, 14(1), 71–92.

Hodges, Louis (1983). "The Journalist and Privacy." *Social Responsibility: Journalism, Law and Medicine*, vol. 9. Lexington, VA: Washington and Lee Monographs, pp. 5–19.

Holliday, A., Hyde, M., & Kullman, J. (2004). *Intercultural Communication: An Advanced Resource Book*. New York: Routledge.

Holmes, Robert L. (2013). *The Ethics of Nonviolence*. New York: Bloomsbury.

Hood, W. F. (1972). "The Aristotelian Versus the Heideggerian Approach to the Problem of Technology." In C. Mitcham & R. Mackey, eds., *Philosophy and Technology: Readings in the Philosophical Problems of Technology* (pp. 347–363). New York: Free Press.

Hoogvelt, Ankie (2001). *Globalization and the Post Colonial World: The New Political Economy of Development*. Baltimore, MD: Johns Hopkins University Press.

Hopgood, Stephen (2006). *Keepers of the Flame: Understanding Amnesty International*. Ithaca, NY: Cornell University Press.

Hosseini, S. A. Hamed (2009). "Global Complexities and the Rise of the Global Justice Movement: A New Notion of Justice." *The Global Studies Journal*, 2 (3), 15–36.

(2010). *Alternative Globalization: An Integrative Approach to Studying Dissident Knowledge in the Global Justice Movement*. New York: Routledge.

Howe, Desson (1995). "'Dead Man': Walking Tall." *Washington Post*, movie review, January 12. www.washingtonpost.com/wp- srv/style/longterm/movies/videos/deadmanwalking.htm#howe

Howley, Kevin (2005). *Community Media: People, Places, and Communication Technologies*. Cambridge: Cambridge University Press.

Huang, Chieh (1967). *Hsieh K'ang-lo Shih-chu: Commentary on the Poems of Hsieh K'ang-lo*. Taipei: Yi-wen.

Huang, Wanju (2007). *Historical Articulation of Holistic Education*. Unpublished manuscript, College of Education, University of Illinois-Urbana.

Hugo, Pieter, & Dominus, Susan (2014). "Portraits of Reconciliation." *New York Times Magazine*. www.nytimes.com/interactive/2014/04/16/magazine/06-pieter-hugo-rwanda-portraits.htm

"Human Dignity and Justice" (2007). *The Hedgehog Review*, Special Issue 9 (3), Fall.

Hume, David (1739). *Treatise of Human Nature*. London: J. Noon.

(1963). *Enquiries Concerning the Human Understanding and Concerning the Principles of Morals*. Oxford: Clarendon Press. Original work published in 1748, 1751.

Huntington, Samuel (1996). *The Clash of Civilizations and the Remaking of World Order*. New York: Simon and Schuster.

Hurst, John, & White, Sally A. (1994). *Ethics and the Australian News Media*. New York: Palgrave Macmillan.

Iggers, J. (1998). *Good News, Bad News: Journalism Ethics and the Public Interest*. Boulder, CO: Westview.

Ihde, Don (1979). "Heidegger's Philosophy of Technology," in his *Technics and Praxis*. Dordrecht, The Netherlands: D. Reidel.

(1983). *Existential Technics*. Albany: State University of New York Press.

Illich, Ivan (1973). *Tools for Conviviality*. New York: Harper Colophon Books.

IndiaRealTime. 2011. "Politics Journal: Who Makes Up India's 'Civil Society'?" June 20, http://blogs.wsj.com/indiarealtime/2011/06/20/politics-journal-who-makes-up-indias-civil-society/

Ingraham, Christopher (2016). "The Importance of Obama's Mosque Visit in an Era of Hate Crimes against Muslims." *Washington Post*, Wonkblog, February 3.

Innis, Harold (1951). *The Bias of Communication*. Toronto: University of Toronto Press.

(1952). *Empire and Communication*. Toronto: University of Toronto Press.

International Telecommunications Union, "ICT Facts and Figures 2017–ITU. www.itu.int/en/ITUD/Statistics/Document/facts/ICTFactsFigures2017.pdf

Iroegbu, P. (2005). "Right to Life and the Means to Life: Human Dignity." In P. Iroegbu & A. Echekwube, eds., *Kpim of Morality Ethics: General, Special and Professional* (pp. 446–449). Ibadan, Nigeria: Heinemann Educational Books.

Jaspers, Karl (1953). *The Origin and Goal of History*. London: Routledge and Kegan Paul.

(1955). *Reason and Existenz*. Trans. William Earle. New York: Routledge and Kegan Paul.

Jay, Martin (1994). "Women in Dark Times: Agnes Heller and Hannah Arendt." In John Burnheim, ed., *The Social Philosophy of Agnes Heller* (pp. 41–55). Amsterdam and Atlanta, GA: Rodopi.

Jenkins, Henry (2006). *Convergence Culture: Where Old and New Media Collide*. New York: New York University Press.

& Ford, Sam, & Green, Joshua (2013). *Spreadable Media: Creating Value and Meaning in a Networked Culture*. New York: New York University Press.

Jhally, Sut (1994). *The Killing Screens: Media and the Culture of Violence* [video]. Northampton, MA: Education Foundation.

Jia, Wenshan, Liu, Hailong, Wang, Runze, & Liu, Xinchuan (2014). "Contemporary Chinese Communication Scholarship: An Emerging Alternative Paradigm." In. R. S. Fortner & P. M. Fackler, eds., *The Handbook of Media and Mass Communication Theory* (Vol. II, pp. 741–765). Malden, MA: Wiley Blackwell.

Jin, Dal Yong (2010). *Korea's Online Gaming Empire*. Cambridge, MA: MIT Press.

Jin, Huimin (2012). *Active Audience: A New Materialistic Interpretation of a Key Concept in Cultural Studies*. Bielefeld, Germany: Transcript Verlag.

Johnstone, Christopher L. (1994). "Ontological Vision as Ground for Communication Ethics: A Response to the Challenge of Postmodernism." *Proceedings of the Third National Communication Ethics Conference.* Anandale, VA: Speech Communication Association, pp. 299–302.

Jonas, H. (1984). *The Imperative of Responsibility: In Search of an Ethics for the Technological Age [Macht oder Ohnmacht der Subjekitivität? Das Lieb-Seele Problem im Vorfeld des Prinzips Verantwortung].* Chicago: University of Chicago Press. Original publication in 1981.

Josephides, Lisette, & Hall, Alexandra, eds. (2014). *We the Cosmopolitans: Moral and Existential Conditions of Being Human.* Oxford: Berghahn Books.

Juusela, Pauli (1981). *Journalistic Codes of Ethics in the CSCE Countries.* Tampere, Finland: University of Tampere.

Kahn, Charles H. (1979). *The Art and Thought of Heraclitus.* Cambridge: Cambridge University Press.

Kallan, Richard K. (1992). "Tom Wolfe." In T. Connery, ed., *A Sourcebook of American Literary Journalism: Representative Writers in an Emerging Genre.* Santa Barbara, CA: Greenwood Press.

Kamali, Mohammad Hashim (2007). "Pathways of Human Dignity: From Cultural Tradition to a New Paradigm." International Conference (Europe Science Foundation and Linkopeng University), Vadstenna, Sweden, November.

Kamwangamalu, N. M. (1999). "*Ubuntu* in South Africa: A Sociolinguistic Perspective to a Pan-African Concept." *Critical Arts,* 13(2), 24–41.

Kang, Young Ahn (2006). "Global Ethics and a Common Morality." *Philosophia Reformata,* 71, 79–95.

Kant, Immanuel (1986). *Über ein vermeintes Recht: Aus Menschenliebe zu Lüge [On the Supposed Right to Lie Out of Love for Humanity].* G. Gernhardt, ed. Würzburg, Germany: Verlag Königshausen und Neumann. Original publication in 1787.

(1990). *Eine Vorlseung über Ethik.* G. Gernhardt, ed. Frankfurt, Germany: Fischer-Taschenbuch Verlag.

(1991). *The Metaphysics of Morals.* Trans. Mary Gregor. Cambridge: Cambridge University Press. Original publication in 1797.

(1997). *Groundwork of the Metaphysics of Morals.* Trans. Mary Gregor. Cambridge: Cambridge University Press. Original publication in 1785.

(1999). *Critique of Pure Reason.* Trans. P. Guery & A. Wood. Cambridge: Cambridge University Press. Original publication in 1788.

Kasoma, Francis P., ed. (1994). *Journalism Ethics in Africa.* Nairobi: African Council for Communication Education.

Kaviraj, Sudipta, & Khilnani, Sunil, eds. (2001). *Civil Society: History and Possibilities.* Cambridge: Cambridge University Press.

Keeble, Richard (2008). *On the Importance of Peace Journalism.* UKWatch.net. www.fifth-estate-oniline.co.uk/comment/peacejournalism.html

Kekes, John (1993). *The Morality of Pluralism.* Princeton, NJ: Princeton University Press.

Kelly, Matthew, & Bielby, Jared, eds. (2016). *Information Cultures in the Digital Age: A Festschrift in Honor of Rafael Capurro*. Berlin: Springer VS.

Kempson, Ruth M. (1975). *Presuppositions and the Delimitation of Semantics*. Cambridge: Cambridge University Press.

  & Fernando, Tim, & Asher, Nicholas, eds. (2012). *Philosophy of Linguistics*. Amsterdam, The Netherlands: Elsevier North Holland.

Kendall, Diana (2011). *Framing Class: Media Representations of Wealth and Poverty in America*, 2nd ed. Lanham, MD: Rowman & Littlefield.

Khan, Yasmin (2007). *The Great Partition: The Making of India and Pakistan*. New Haven, CT: Yale University Press.

Kien, Grant (2009). *Global Technography: Ethnography in the Age of Mobility*. New York: Peter Lang.

  (2016). *The Digital Story: Binary Code as a Cultural Text*. Oakland, CA: Irrepressible Press Publishing.

Kincheloe, J. L., & McLaren, P. (2000). "Rethinking Critical Theory and Qualitative Research." In N. K. Denzin & Y. S. Lincoln, eds., *Handbook of Qualitative Research* (2nd ed., pp. 279–313). Thousand Oaks, CA: Sage.

King, Martin Luther, Jr. (1958). *Stride Toward Freedom: The Montgomery Story*. New York: Ballantine Books.

  (1964). *Why We Can't Wait*. New York: Signet Book/New American Library.

  (1967). *Where Do We Go From Here: Chaos or Community?* Boston, MA: Beacon Press.

  (1992). *I Have a Dream: Writings and Speeches That Changed the World*. San Francisco, CA: HarperSanFrancisco.

Kirkham, Richard L. (1992). *Theories of Truth: A Critical Introduction*. Cambridge, MA: The MIT Press.

Kiss, Elizabeth (2000). "Moral Ambition Within and Beyond Political Constraints: Reflections on Restorative Justice." In R. I. Rotberg & D. Thompson, eds., *Truth v. Justice: The Morality of Truth Commissions* (pp. 68–98). Princeton, NJ: Princeton University Press.

Kline, Stephen, & Dyer-Witheford, Nick (2003). *Digital Play: The Interaction of Technology, Culture, and Marketing*. Montreal: McGill-Queens University Press.

Kluckhohn, Clyde (1949). *Mirror for Man: The Relation of Anthropology to Everyday Life*. New York: McGraw Hill.

Knowlton, Steven R. (1997). *Moral Reasoning for Journalists: Cases and Commentary*. Westport, CT: Praeger.

Koehn, Daryl (1998). *Rethinking Feminist Ethics: Care, Trust and Empathy*. New York: Routledge.

Kompridis, Nikolas (1994). "On World Disclosure: Heidegger, Habermas and Dewey." *Thesis Eleven*, 37, 29–45. http://the.sagepub/content/37/1/29.full.pdf

  (2011). *Critique and Disclosure: Critical Theory Between Past and Future*. Cambridge, MA: MIT Press.

Konyndyk, Kenneth (1981). "Violence." In *Jacques Ellul: Interpretive Essays*, Clifford Christians & Jay Van Hook, eds. (pp. 251–268). Urbana: University of Illinois Press.

Korsgaard, Christine (1996). *The Sources of Normativity*. New York: Cambridge University Press.

Krahé, B., Möller, I., Huesman, R. R., Kirwil, L., Felber, J., & Berger, A. (2011). "Desensitization to Media Violence." *Journal of Personality and Social Psychology*, 100(4), 630–646.

Kraidy, Marwan M. (2013). "The Body as Medium in the Digital Age: Challenges and Opportunities." *Communication and Critical/Cultural Studies*, 10(2–3), 285–290.

Kramer, Lauren (2017). "The Vibrant Jewish Community of Panama." *The Canadian Jewish News*, August 17. www.cjnews.com/living-jewish/the-vibrant-jewish-community-of-panama

Kroeber, Alfred L. (1933). *Anthropology*. New York: Harcourt, Brace and Company.

Kroker, Arthur, & Cook, David (1986). *The Postmodern Scene: Excremental Culture and Hyper-Aesthetics*. New York: St. Martin's Press.

Krüger, Franz (2016). "Discourse Ethics and the Media." *African Journalism Studies*, 37(1), 21–39.

Kuhn, Thomas S. (1996). *The Structure of Scientific Revolutions*, 3rd ed. Chicago: University of Chicago Press.

Kunelius, Risto (2009). "Lessons of Being Drawn In: On Global Free Speech, Communication Theory and the Mohammed Cartoons." In A. Kierulf & H. Rønning, eds., *Freedom of Speech Abridged? Cultural, Legal and Philosophical Challenges* (pp. 139–151). Götenborg, Sweden: Nordicom.

Küng, Hans (1991). *Global Responsibility: In Search of a New World Ethic*. Trans. John Bowden. London: SCM.

Kurpius, David (1999). *Community Journalism: Getting Started*, 3rd ed. The Radio and Television News Directors Foundation. www.rtnda.org/uploads/files/cjgs.pdf

Laitila, Tiina (1995). "Journalistic Codes of Ethics in Europe." *European Journal of Communication*, 10(4), 527–544.

Lake, Robert W. (2017). "Big Data, Urban Governance, and the Ontological Politics of Hyperindividualism." *Big Data & Society*, January–June, pp. 1–10.

Lambeth, Edmund (1992). *Committed Journalism: An Ethic for the Profession*, 2nd ed. Bloomington: Indiana University Press.

Landmann, M. (1974). *Philosophical Anthropology*. Trans. D. J. Parent. Philadelphia, PA: Westminster Press.

Langer, Susanne K. (1942). *Philosophy in a New Key*. Cambridge, MA: Harvard University Press.

  (1953). *Feeling and Form*. New York: Charles Scribner's Sons.

  (1967–1982). *Mind: An Essay on Human Feeling* (3 vols.). Baltimore, MD: Johns Hopkins University Press.

Lao, Tzu (2005). *Tao Te Ching*. Trans. S. Hamill. Boston, MA: Shambhala Publications.

  Lin, Y., & Tzu, Chang (1948). *The Wisdom of Laotse*. Trans. Y. Ling. New York: The Modern Library.

Lasswell, Harold (1948). "The Structure and Function of Communication in Society." In L. Bryson, ed., *The Communication of Ideas* (pp. 37–51). New York: Institute for Religious and Social Studies.

Laurent, Dick (2010). *Comparing the United Nations Mission in Sudan (UNMIS) with the United Nations African Union Mission in Darfur: Background, Mandate, Scope, Success & Failures.* Munich, Germany: GRIN Verlag.

Lauters, Amy M., ed. (2007). *The Rediscovered Writings of Rose Wilder Lane, Literary Journalist.* Columbia: University of Missouri Press.

Lebacqz, Karen (1986). *Six Theories of Justice: Perspectives from Philosophical and Theological Ethics.* Minneapolis, MN: Augsburg.

Lee, Seow Ting (2009). "Peace Journalism." In *The Handbook of Mass Media Ethics.* Lee Wilkins & Clifford Christians, eds. (pp. 258–275). New York: Routledge. 2nd ed. (in press).

(2010). "Peace Journalism: Principles and Structural Limitations in the News Coverage of Three Conflicts." *Mass Communication and Society,* 13(1), 361–384.

& Crispin, Maslog C. (2005). "War or Peace Journalism? Asian Newspaper Coverage of Regional Conflicts." *Journal of Communication,* 55(2), 311–329.

Legge, James, ed. (1991). *Four Books of the Chinese Classics: Confucian Analects, the Great Learning, Doctrine of the Mean, Works of Mencius* (4 vols.). Corona, CA: Oriental Book Store.

Leow, Patty, & Mella, Kelly (2005). "Black Ink and New Red Power: Native American Newspapers and Tribal Sovereignty." *Journalism and Communication Monographs,* 7(3), Autumn, 111–133.

Lepianka, Dorota (2015). "Images of Poverty in a Selection of the Polish Daily Press." *Current Sociology,* 63(7), 999–1016.

Lerner, Daniel (1958). *The Passing of Traditional Society: Modernizing the Middle East.* New York: Free Press.

Levi, A. W. (1959). *Philosophy and the Modern World.* Bloomington: Indiana University Press.

Levinas, Emmanuel (1969). *Totality and Infinity: An Essay on Exteriority.* Trans. Alphonso Linguis. Pittsburgh, PA: Duquesne University Press.

(1981). *Otherwise Than Being or Essence.* Trans. Alphonso Linguis. The Hague, The Netherlands: Martinus Nijhoff. Original publication in 1978.

(1985). *Ethics and Infinity: Conversations with Philippe Nemo.* Trans. R. A. Cohen. Pittsburgh, PA: Duquesne University Press.

(1987). *Collected Philosophical Papers.* Trans. Alphonso Lingis. Dordrecht, The Netherlands: Martinus Nijhoff.

(1990). *Difficult Freedom: Essays on Judaism.* Trans. Seán Hand. Baltimore, MD: Johns Hopkins University Press.

(2003). *Humanism of the Other.* Trans. Nidra Poller. Urbana: University of Illinois Press.

Lewis, Jeffrey N. (2005). *Language Wars: The Role of Media and Culture in Global Terror and Political Violence.* London: Pluto Press.

(2012). *Global Media Apocalypse: Pleasure, Violence and the Cultural Imaginings of Doom.* New York: Palgrave Macmillan.

(2015a). *Media, Culture and Human Violence: From Savage Lovers to Violent Complexity.* Lanham, MD: Rowman and Littlefield.

(2015b). "Apocalyptica Erotica Now: The Allure of Islamic State Online." *The Conversation*, March 13. http://theconversation.com

Lewis, Oscar (1961). *Children of Sanchez.* New York: Random House.

Lewis, S. C., & Westlund, O. (2015). "Big Data and Journalism: Epistemology, Expertise, Economics, and Ethics." *Digital Journalism*, 3(3), 447–466. https://doi.org/10.1080/08838151.2012.761700

Li, Chenyang (2006). "The Confucian Ideal of Harmony." *Philosophy East and West*, 56(4), 583–2006.

(2008). "The Philosophy of Harmony in Classical Confucianism." *Philosophy Compass*, 3(3), 423–435.

(2015). *The Confucian Philosophy of Harmony.* New York: Routledge.

Lievrouw, Leah A. (2011). *Alternative and Activist New Media.* Cambridge: Polity Press.

Limburg, Val E. (1994). *Electronic Media Ethics.* Boston, MA: Focal Press.

Lindberg, Tod (2007). *The Political Teachings of Jesus.* New York: Harper Collins.

Lippman, Matthew (2007). "Darfur: The Politics of Genocide Denial Syndrome." *Journal of Genocide Research*, 9(2), 192–213.

Liu, James H. (2011). "Asian Epistemologies and Contemporary Social Psychological Research." In N. Denzin & Y. Lincoln, eds., *The Sage Handbook of Qualitative Research* (4th ed., pp. 213–226). Thousand Oaks, CA: Sage Publications.

Livingstone, Sonia (2012). "Challenges to Comparative Research in a Globalizing Media Landscape." In F. Esser & T. Hanitzsch, eds., *Handbook of Comparative Communication Research* (pp. 415–430). New York: Routledge.

Locke, John 1894. *Essay Concerning Human Understanding.* Vol. 1. Oxford: Clarendon Press. Original publication in 1690.

Loew, Patty, & Mella, Kelly (2005). "Black Ink and the New Red Power: Native American Newspapers and Tribal Sovereignty." *Journalism and Communication Monographs*, 7(3), Autumn, 99–142.

Long, Yun (2005). *Television and Violence: An Empirical Study of Cultivative Effects of Chinese Media.* Beijing: China Radio and TV Publishing House (in Chinese).

Lotz, J. B. (1963). "Person and Ontology." *Philosophy Today*, 7, Winter, 279–297. Reprinted from *Scholastik*, 38(3), 335–360.

Louw, Dirk J. (1998). "*Ubuntu*: An African Assessment of Religious Order." Twentieth World Congress of Philosophy. www.scrip.org/(S(i43dyn45teexjx455qlt3d2q))reference/ReferencesPapers.aspx?

Lugo-Ocando, Jairo (2015). *Blaming the Victim: How Global Journalism Fails Those in Poverty.* London: Pluto.

Lule, Jack (2015). "The Global Imaginary in Mumford and McLuhan." In B. Shan & C. Christians, eds., *The Ethics of Intercultural Communication* (pp. 321–336). New York: Peter Lang.

Lum, Casey Man Kong, ed. (2006). *Perspectives on Culture, Technology and Communication: The Media Ecology Tradition*. Cresskill, NJ: Hampton Press.

Luo, An'Xian (2014). "Human Dignity in Traditional Chinese Confucianism." In M. Düwell, J. Braarvig, R. Brownsword, & D. Mieth, eds., *The Cambridge Handbook of Human Dignity: Interdisciplinary Perspectives* (pp. 177–182). Cambridge: Cambridge University Press.

Lynch, Jake (2008). *Debates in Peace Journalism*. Sydney: University of Sydney Press.

   & Galtung, Johan (2010). *Reporting Conflict: New Directions in Peace Journalism*. Brisbane, Australia: University of Queensland Press.

   & McGoldrick, Annabel (2005). *Peace Journalism*. Stroud, UK: Hawthorn Press.

Lynch, Michael P., ed. (2001). *The Nature of Truth: Classic and Contemporary Perspectives*. Cambridge, MA: MIT Press.

   (2004). *True to Life: Why Truth Matters*. Cambridge, MA: The MIT Press.

   (2011). *Truth as One and Many*. New York: Oxford Clarendon Press.

   (2012). "Truth in Ethics." *International Encyclopedia of Ethics*. www.academica.edu/4203390/Truth_in_Ethics

Lyotard, J. F. (1990). *Heidegger and the Jews*. Trans. A. Michel & M. S. Roberts. Minneapolis: University of Minnesota Press.

Mabweazara, Hayes Mawindi (2015). "Mainstreaming African Digital Cultures, Practices and Emerging Forms of Citizen Engagement." Editorial for Special Issue of African Digital Media Review. *African Journalism Studies*, 36(4), 1–11.

MacDonald, B., & Peteram, B., eds. (1998). *Keyguide to Information Sources in Media Ethics*. London: Mansell Publishing.

Mackinnon, Rebecca (2013). *Consent of the Networked: The Worldwide Struggle for Internet Freedom*. New York: Basic Books.

Macpherson, C. B. (1973). *Democratic Theory: Essays in Retrieval*. Oxford: Clarendon Press.

Magee, John (1989). *Boethius*. Oxford: Oxford University Press.

Mahrt, M., & Scharkow, M. (2013). "The Value of Big Data in Digital Media Research." *Journal of Broadcasting and Electronic Media*, 57(1), 20–33.

Maigret, Éric (2009). *History of Communication Theories: A Sociological Perspective*. Beijing: Communication University of China Press (in Chinese).

Mainwaring, Simon (2011). *We First: How Brands and Consumers Use Social Media to Build a Better World*. New York: Palgrave MacMillan.

Mann, Steve (2001). *Cyborg: Digital Destiny and Human Possibility in the Age of Wearable Computing*. New York: Random House/Doubleday.

   (2003). "The Post-cyborg Path to Deconism." *CTheory*. February. www.ctheory.net/text_file.asp?pick=368

Mannheim, K. (1936). *Ideology and Utopia*. New York: Routledge.

Manovich, Lev (2012). "Trending: The Promises and Challenges of Big Social Data." *Debates in the Digital Humanities*, 2, 460–465.

Mansell, Robin (2012). *Imagining the Internet: Communication, Innovation, and Governance*. Oxford: Oxford University Press.

Marche, Stephen (2012). "Is Facebook Making Us Lonely?" *The Atlantic*, May, pp. 60–69.

Marcus, G., & Fisher, M. (1999). *Anthropology as Cultural Critique: An Experimental Moment in the Human Sciences*, 2nd ed. Chicago: University of Chicago Press.

Marlin, Randal (2013). *Propaganda and the Ethics of Persuasion*, 2nd ed. Peterborough, ON: Broadview Press.

Maróth, Miklós (2014). "Human Dignity in the Islamic World." In M. Düwell, J. Braarvig, R. Brownsword, & D. Mieth, eds., *The Cambridge Handbook of Human Dignity* (pp. 155–162). Cambridge: Cambridge University Press.

Marsh, Charles (2014). *Strange Glory: A Life of Dietrich Bonhoeffer*. New York: Vintage.

Martin, Michael (1972). "Theoretical Pluralism." *Philosophia*, 2(4), 341–350.

Masco, Joseph (2014). *The Theater of Operations: National Security Affect from the Cold War to the War on Terror*. Durham, NC: Duke University Press.

Maslog, C. Crispin (1990). *A Manual on Peace Reporting in Mandanao*. Manila: Philippine Press Institute.

& Lee, Seow Ting, & Kim, H. (2006). "Framing Analysis of a Conflict: How Five Asian Countries Covered the War in Iraq." *Asian Journal of Communication*, 16(1), March, 19–39.

Masolo, D. A. (2004). "Western and African Communitarianism: A Comparison." In K. Wiredu, ed., *A Companion to African Philosophy* (pp. 483–498). Oxford: Blackwell.

Matthias, Marcel (2004). "The Responsibility Gap: Ascribing Responsibility for the Actions of Learning Automata." *Ethics and Information Technology*, 6, 175–183.

Matusitz, J. (2014). *Symbolism in Terrorism: Motivation, Communication and Behavior*. Lanham, MD: Rowman and Littlefield.

May, Reinhard (1996). *Heidegger's Hidden Sources: East-Asian Influences on His Work*. Trans. G. Parkes. London: Routledge.

Mayer, Marvin, ed. (2002). *Reverence for Life: The Ethics of Albert Schweitzer for the Twenty-First Century*. Syracuse, NY: Syracuse University Press.

Mayer-Schönberger, V., & Cukier, K. (2013). *Big Data: A Revolution That Will Transform How We Live, Work, and Think*. Boston, MA: Houghton Mifflin Harcourt.

McCarthy, Thomas (1991). *Ideals and Illusions*. Cambridge, MA: MIT Press.

(1992), "Practical Discourse: On the Relation of Discourse to Politics." In C. Calhoun, ed., *Habermas and the Public Sphere* (pp. 51–72). Cambridge, MA: MIT Press.

McChesney, Robert W. (2013). *Digital Disconnect: How Capitalism Is Turning the Internet Against Democracy*. New York: New Press.

McDevitt, Michael (2010). "Journalistic Influence in Moral Mobilization." In B. Mody, ed., *The Geopolitics of Representation in Foreign News: Explaining Darfur* (pp. 45–63). Lanham, MD: Roman & Littlefield.

McDonald, Henry (1986). *The Normative Basis of Culture: A Philosophical Inquiry*. Baton Rouge: Louisiana State University Press.

McGoldrick, A., & Lynch, J. (2000). "Peace Journalism – How To Do It." www.transcend.org/pjmanual.htm

McLuhan, Marshall (1964). *Understanding Media: The Extensions of Man*. New York: McGraw Hill.

McWilliams, Abagail, Matten, Dirk, Moon, Jeremy, & Siegel, Donald S., eds. (2009). *The Oxford Handbook of Corporate Social Responsibility*. New York: Oxford University Press.

Mead, George Herbert (1934). *Mind, Self and Society from the Standpoint of a Social Behaviorist*. Chicago: University of Chicago Press.

Means, Russell, & Wolf, Marvin J. (1995). *Where White Men Fear to Tread: The Autobiography of Russell Means*. New York: St. Martin's.

Meiklejohn, Alexander (1948). *Free Speech and Its Relation to Self Government*. New York: Harper Brothers Publishers.

Meisels, Tamar (2006). "The Trouble With Terror: The Apologetics of Terrorism – A Refutation." *The Journal of Terrorism and Political Violence*, 18(3), 465–483.

Mejia, Robert (2012). "Posthuman, Postrights?" *Explorations in Media Ecology*, 11(1), 27–44.

Melucci, Alberto (1996). *Challenging Codes: Collective Action in the Information Age*. New York: Cambridge University Press.

Mencius (2005). *Mencius*. Trans. D. C. Lau. London: Penguin Books Ltd.

Merrill, John C. (2009). "Tenzin Gyatso, the Dalai Lama: Universal Compassion." In C. G. Christians & J. C. Merrill, eds., *Ethical Communication: Moral Stances in Human Dialogue* (pp. 11–17). Columbia: University of Missouri Press.

(1997). *Journalism Ethics: Philosophical Foundations for News Media*. New York: St. Martin's Press.

Metz, Thaddeus (2012). "African Conceptions of Human Dignity." *Human Rights Review*, 13, 19–37.

(2014). "Dignity in the *Ubuntu* Tradition." In M. Düwell, J. Braarvig, R. Brownsword, & D. Mieth, eds., *The Cambridge Handbook of Human Dignity: Interdisciplinary Perspectives* (pp. 310–318). Cambridge: Cambridge University Press.

(2015). "African Ethics and Journalism Ethics: News and Opinion in Light of *Ubuntu*." *Journal of Media Ethics*, 30(2), 74–90.

(2018). "Media Ethics: Theorizing in a Globalized World of Difference." In P. Plaisance, ed., *Communication and Media Ethics* (pp. 53–73). Berlin: De Gruyter Mouton.

Meyers, Christopher (2003). "Appreciating W. D. Ross: On Duties and Consequences." *Journal of Mass Media Ethics*, 18, 81–97.

Meyrowitz, Joshua (1985) *No Sense of Place: The Impact of Media on Social Behavior*. New York: Oxford University Press.

Mieth, Dietmar (1997). "The Basic Norm of Truthfulness: Its Ethical Justification and Universality." In C. Christians & M. Traber, eds., *Communication Ethics and Universal Values* (pp. 87–104). Thousand Oaks, CA: Sage.

Miladi, Noureddine (2016). "Reporting News in a Turbulent World: Is Al Jazeera Rewriting the Rules of Global Journalism?" In E. Abdelmoula & N. Miladi, eds., *Mapping the Al Jazeera Phenomenon Twenty Years On* (pp. 71–90). Doha, Qatar: Al Jazeera Centre for Studies.

Mill, John Stuart (1865a). *Auguste Come and Positivism*. London: Trubner.

  (1865b). *Examination of Sir William Hamilton's Philosophy and of the Principal Philosophical Questions Discussed in His Writings*. London: Longman, Green, Longman, Roberts, & Green.

  (1893). *A System of Logic, Ratiocinative and Inductive: Being a Connected View of the Principles of Evidence and the Methods of Scientific Investigation* (8th ed.). New York: Harper & Brothers. Original work published in 1843.

  (1969). *Autobiography*. Boston, MA: Houghton Mifflin. Original work published posthumously in 1873.

  (1989). *On Liberty*. Cambridge Texts in the History of Thought. Cambridge: Cambridge University Press. Original publication in 1859.

Miller, M. Rex (2004). *The Millennium Matrix: Reclaiming the Past, Reframing the Future of the Church*. San Francisco: Jossey-Bass.

Mills, C. Wright (1959). *The Sociological Imagination*. New York: Oxford University Press.

Mitcham, Carl (1994). *Thinking Through Technology: The Path Between Engineering and Philosophy*. Chicago: University of Chicago Press.

Mitchell, Jolyon (2012). *Promoting Peace, Inciting Violence: The Role of Religion and Media*. London: Routledge.

  (2007a). *Media Violence and Christian Ethics*. Cambridge: Cambridge University Press.

  (2007b). "Peacemaking in the World of Film." *Media Development*, 4, 13–16.

Mody, Bella (2010). *The Geopolitics of Representation in Foreign News: Explaining Darfur*. Lanham, MD: Roman & Littlefield.

Moghadam, Valentine M. (2012). *Globalization and Social Movements: Islamism, Feminism, and the Global Justice Movement*, 2nd ed. Lanham, MD: Rowman and Littlefield Publishers.

Mohamed, Ali (2010). "Journalistic Ethics and Responsibility in Relation to Freedom of Expression: An Islamic Perspective." In S. J. A. Ward & H. Wasserman, eds., *Media Ethics Beyond Borders: A Global Perspective* (pp. 142–156). New York: Routledge.

Morley, David (2000). *Home Territories: Media, Mobility and Identity*. New York: Routledge.

  (2006). "Unanswered Questions in Audience Research." *Communication Review*, 9(20), 101–121.

Morris, Meaghan (1990). "Banality in Cultural Studies." In Patricia Mellencamp, ed., *Logics of Television: Essays in Cultural Criticism* (pp. 14–43). Bloomington: Indiana University Press. Original publication in 1988.

Moses, Greg (1998). *Revolution of Conscience: Marin Luther King, Jr., and the Philosophy of Nonviolence*. New York: Guilford Press.

Mukherjee, Asha et al. (2001). *Civil Society in Indian Cultures: Indian Philosophical Studies*. Washington, DC: Council for Research in Values and Philosophy.

Mulhall, Stephen & Swift, Adam (1996). *Liberals and Communitarians*, 2nd ed. Oxford: Blackwell.

Müller, Christopher John (2016). *Promotheanism: Technology, Digital Culture and Human Obsolescence*. London: Rowman & Littlefield International.

Mumford, Lewis (1934). *Technics and Civilization*. New York: Harcourt Brace.
   (1970). *The Pentagon of Power: Myth of the Machine*. New York: Harcourt Brace Jovanovich.

Munro, Thomas (1969). "Art and Violence." *The Journal of Aesthetics and Art Criticism*, 27(3), 317–322.

Murdock, G., & Schlesinger, P., eds., *Communicating Politics: Mass Communication and the Political Process* (pp. 37–54). New York: Holmes and Meier Publishers.

Murphy, James J. (1974). *Rhetoric in the Middle Ages: A History of Rhetorical Theory from Augustine to the Renaissance*. Berkeley: University of California Press.

Murphy, Lawrence (1924). "News Values and Analysis." *Journalism Bulletin*, 2, 29–31.

Murray, Jeffrey W. (2002). "The Other Ethics of Emmanuel Levinas: Communication Beyond Relativism." In S. L. Bracci & C. G. Christians, eds., *Moral Engagement in Public Life: Theorists for Contemporary Ethics* (pp. 171–197). New York: Peter Lang.

Muslim Abui Hassan (1987) *Mukhtasar Sahih Muslim*, hadith 707. Beirut, Lebanon: Islamic Publishing Co.

Müür, Kristina (2016). "Plus ça Change: Soviet 'Active Measures' and Contemporary Russian Propaganda." Paper presented to Media and Identity Conference, Lviv, Ukraine, May 20–21.

Nagel, Thomas (1973). "Rawls on Justice." *The Philosophical Review*, 82(2), April, 220–234.
   (1989). *The View from Nowhere*. New York: Oxford University Press.
   (2005). "The Problem of Global Justice." *Philosophy and Public Affairs*, 33(2), Spring, 113–147.

Naoum, Chris (2009). "Web Content Producers Favor Net Neutrality, Reject Regulation of Search Engines." *BroadbandBreakfast*, December 16.

Nava, Mica (2007). *Visceral Cosmopolitanism: Gender, Culture and the Normalization of Difference*. Oxford: Bloomsbury Academic.

Negroponte, Nicholas (1996). *Being Digital*. New York: Random House Vintage.

Nelson, Bryan (2013). "7 Real-life Human Cyborgs." Mother Nature Network, April 25. www.mnn.com/leaderboard/stories/7-real-life-human-cyborgs

Newton, Julianne H. (2001). *The Burden of Visual Truth: The Role of Photojournalism in Mediating Reality*. Mahwah, NJ: Erlbaum.

Nicol, Eduardo (1965). *Los Principos de la Ciencia [The Principle of Knowing]*. Mexico: Fundo de Cultura Economica.

Niebuhr, H. Richard (1963). *The Responsible Self*. New York: Harper & Row.

Nietzsche, Friedrich (1967). *The Birth of Tragedy*. Trans. W. Kaufmann. New York: Random House. Original publication in 1872.
   (1976). *The Will to Power*. Trans. W. Kaufmann. New York: Random House. Original publication in 1901.

Nikkelen, S. W. C., Vossen, H. G. M., Valkenburg, P. M., Velders, F. P., Windhorst, D. A., Jaddoe, V. W., Hofman, F., Verhulst, F. C., & Tiemeier, H. (2014).

"Media Violence and Children's ADHD-related Behaviors: A Genetic Susceptibility Perspective." *Journal of Communication*, 64(1), 42–60.

Nikolaev, Alexander G., ed. (2011). *Ethical Issues in International Communication*. New York: Palgrave Macmillan.

Noam, Eli M. (2016). *Who Owns the World's Media? Media Concentration and Ownership Around the World*. New York: Oxford University Press.

Noble, David F. (1999). *The Religion of Technology: The Divinity of Man and the Spirit of Invention*. New York: Penguin.

Nobel, Safiya Umoja (2018). *Algorithms of Oppression: How Search Engines Reinforce Racism*. New York: New York University Press.

Noddings, Nel (1984). *Caring: A Feminine Approach to Ethics and Moral Education*. Berkeley: University of California Press.

Nordenstreng, Kaarle (1995). *Reports on Media Ethics in Europe*. Tampere, Finland: University of Tampere.

(2008). "Cultivating Journalists for Peace." In Philip Lee, ed., *Communicating Peace* (pp. 63–80). Penang, Malaysia: Southbound Press.

Norris, Pippa (2001). *Digital Divide: Civic Engagement, Information Poverty, and the Internet Worldwide*. Cambridge: Cambridge University Press.

Nussbaum, Martha (1994). "Patriotism and Cosmopolitanism." *Boston Review*, 19(5), 3–16.

(1996). *Sex and Social Justice*. New York: Oxford University Press.

(1997). "Kant and Cosmopolitanism." In J. Bohman & M. Lutz-Bachmann, eds., *Perpetual Peace: Essays on Kant's Cosmopolitan Ideal* (pp. 25–57). Cambridge, MA: MIT Press.

(1999). *Sex and Social Justice*. New York: Oxford University Press.

(2000). *Women and Human Development: The Capabilities Approach*. New York: Cambridge University Press.

(2001). *Upheavals of Thought: The Intelligence of the Emotions*. Cambridge: Cambridge University Press.

(2005). "Beyond the Social Contract: Capabilities and Social Justice." In G. Brock & H. Brighouse, eds., *The Political Philosophy of Cosmopolitanism* (pp. 196–218). Cambridge: Cambridge University Press.

(2006). *The Frontiers of Justice: Disability, Nationality, Species Membership*. Cambridge, MA: Harvard University Press.

(2008). "Human Dignity and Political Entitlements." *Human Dignity and Bioethics: Essays Commissioned by the President's Council on Bioethics*, March, ch. 14. https://bioethicsarchive.georgetown.edu/pcbe/reports/human_dignity/chapter14.html

& Cohen, J., eds. (1996). *For Love of Country: Debating the Limits of Patriotism*. Boston, MA: Beacon Press.

Nystrom, Christine (2006). "Symbols, Thought and 'Reality:' The Contributions of Benjamin Lee Whorf and Susanne K. Langer to Media Ecology." In Casey Man Kong Lum, ed., *Perspectives on Culture, Technology and Communication: The Media Ecology Tradition* (pp. 275–302). Cresskill, NJ: Hampton Press, Inc.

O'Donnell, James J. (1985). *Augustine*. Boston, MA: Twayne Publishers.

O'Hare, Paul (2015). "Rwanda Genocide Killer Forgiven by Family of Victims: 'We Were Like Animals'." *Daily Record and Sunday Mail*, March 17. www.dailyrecord.co.uk.news/uk-world-news/rwanda-genocide-killer-forgiven-family

O'Neill, Onara (2015). *Constructing Authorities: Reason, Politics, and Interpretation in Kant's Philosophy*. Cambridge: Cambridge University Press.

(2016). *Justice Across Boundaries: Whose Obligations?* Cambridge: Cambridge University Press.

Ojomo, O. W., Tejuoso, Waisu, Olayinka, A. P., & Oluwashola, I. T. (2015). "Making a Case for Community Radio in Nigeria." *International Journal of Humanities and Social Science*, 5(8), August, 136–144.

Okano, Yayo (2016). "Why Has the Ethics of Care Become an Issue of Global Concern?" *International Journal of Japanese Sociology*, 25(1), 85–99.

Olthuis, James, H., ed. (1997). *Knowing Otherwise: Philosophy at the Threshold of Spirituality*. New York: Fordham University Press.

Ong, Aihwa (2006). *Neoliberalism as Exception: Mutations in Citizenship and Sovereignty*. Durham, NC: Duke University Press.

Ong, Walter (1976). *Interfaces of the Word: Studies in the Evolution of Consciousness and Culture*. Ithaca, NY: Cornell University Press.

(1977). *The Presence of the Word: Some Prolegomena for Cultural and Religious History*. New Haven, CT: Yale University Press.

(1982). *Orality and Literacy: The Technologizing of the Word*. New York: Methuen.

Oravec, Jo Ann (2012). "The Ethics of Sexting: Issues Involving Consent and the Production of Intimate Content." In D. Heider & A. L. Massanari, eds., *Digital Ethics: Research and Practice* (pp. 129–144). New York: Peter Lang.

Orwell, George (1949). *Nineteen Eighty-Four*. Harmondsworth, UK: Penguin Books.

Orwin, Donna Tussing, ed. (2002). *The Cambridge Companion to Tolstoy*. New York: Cambridge University Press.

Osborn, Barbara (2016). "Violence Formula: Analyzing TV, Video and Movies." *Media and Values*, Issue 62. www.medialit.org/reading-room/violence-formula-analyzing-video-and-movies

Outka, Gene (1972). *Agape: An Ethical Analysis*. New Haven, CT: Yale University Press.

Overholser, Geneva, & Jamieson, Kathleen Hall, eds. (2005). *The Press*. New York: Oxford University Press.

Pacey, Arnold (1996). *The Culture of Technology*. Cambridge, MA: MIT Press.

Packer, George (2015). "Rolling Stone and the Temptations of Narrative Journalism." *The New Yorker*, April 6. www.newyorker.com/news/daily-comment/rolling-stone-and-the-temptations-of-narrative-journalism

Pantti, Mervi (2015). "Visual Gatekeeping in the Era of Networked Images." In T. P. Vos & F. Heinderyckx, eds., *Gatekeeping in Transition* (pp. 203–223). New York: Routledge.

Parkes, Graham, ed. (1990) *Heidegger and Asian Thought*. Honolulu: University of Hawaii Press.

Pateman, Carole (1976). *Participation and Democratic Theory*. New York: Cambridge University Press.

(1985). *The Problem of Political Obligation: A Critique of Liberal Theory.* Cambridge: Polity Press.

(1988). *The Sexual Contract.* Stanford, CA: Stanford University Press.

(1989). *The Disorder of Women: Democracy, Feminism and Political Theory.* Stanford, CA: Stanford University Press.

Patterson, G. H. (1948, March 12). *Social Responsibilities of the American Newspaper.* Eighteenth address, Don R. Mellet Memorial Fund, pp. 5–14. New York: New York University Press, Department of Journalism.

Patterson, Philip, & Wilkins, Lee (2014). *Media Ethics: Issues & Cases,* 8th ed. New York: McGraw Hill.

Paul, E. F., Miller, F. D., & Paul, J., eds. (1994). *Cultural Pluralism and Moral Knowledge.* Cambridge: Cambridge University Press.

Pavarala, Vinod, & Malik, Kanchan Kumar (2010). "Community Radio and Women: Forging Subaltern Counterpublics." In C. Rodriguez, D. Kidd, & L. Stein, eds., *Making Our Media: Global Initiatives Toward a Democratic Public Sphere* (vol. I, pp. 95–114). Cresskill, NJ: Hampton Press, Inc.

Pierce, Charles Sanders (1932). *Collected Papers of C. S. Peirce* (8 vols.). Cambridge, MA: Harvard University Belknap Press.

(1955). *Philosophical Writings of Peirce.* New York: Dover. Original publication in 1940.

Pepperell, Robert (2003). *The Posthuman Condition: Consciousness Beyond the Brain.* Bristol, UK: Intellect Books. First published as *The Post-Human Condition* in 1995.

Peters, John D. (1993). "Genealogical Notes on the Field." *Journal of Communication,* 43(4), 132–139.

(2012). "Afterword: Doctors of Philosophy." In Jason Hannon, ed., *Philosophical Profiles in the Theory of Communication* (pp. 499–510). New York: Peter Lang.

Pettit, Philip (1982). "Habermas on Truth and Justice." In G. H. R. Parkinson, ed., *Marx and Marxisms* (pp. 207–228). Cambridge: Cambridge University Press.

Petulla, Sam (2012). "Big Data in the Dark." December 10. www.cjr.org/united_states_project/what_political_reporters_dont_know_about_big_data.php

Peukert, Helmut (1981). "Universal Solidarity as the Goal of Communication." *Media Development,* 28(4), 10–12.

Philipse, Herman (1998). *Heidegger's Philosophy of Being: A Critical Interpretation.* Princeton, NJ: Princeton University Press.

Pillay, Navi (2014). "The International Human Rights Treaty System: Impact on the Domestic and International Levels." *Human Rights Brief,* 21(1), 32–34.

Pinchevski, Amit (2005). *By Way of Introduction: Levinas and the Ethics of Communication.* Pittsburgh: Duquesne University Press.

Pippert, Wesley (1989). *An Ethics of News: A Reporter's Search for Truth.* Washington, DC: Georgetown University Press.

Plaisance, Patrick (2007). "Transparency: An Assessment of the Kantian Roots of a Key Element in Media Ethics Practice." *Journal of Mass Media Ethics,* 22 (2–3), 187–207.

(2009). "Violence." In L. Wilkins & C. Christians, eds., *The Handbook of Mass Media Ethics* (chap. 12, pp. 162–176). New York: Routledge.

(2011). "Moral Agency in Media: Toward a Model to Explore Key Components of Ethical Practice." *Journal of Mass Media Ethics*, 26, 96–113.

(2014). *Media Ethics: Key Principles for Responsible Practice*, 2nd ed. Los Angeles: Sage.

(2015). *Virtue in Media: The Moral Psychology of Excellence in News and Public Relations*. New York: Routledge.

& Skewes, Elizabeth, & Hanitzsch, Thomas (2012). "Ethical Orientations of Journalists Around the Globe: Implications from a Cross-National Survey." *Communications Research*, 39, 641–661.

Pogge, Thomas (2014). "Dignity and Global Justice." In M. Düwell, J. Baarvig, R. Brownsword, & D. Meith, eds., *The Cambridge Handbook of Human Dignity* (pp. 477–483). Cambridge: Cambridge University Press.

Pokharel, Krishna (2011). "India Real Time, Politics Journal: Who Makes Up India's 'Civil Society'?" *Wall Street Journal*, June 20. https://blogs.wsj.com/in diarealtime/2011/06/20/politics-journal-who-makes-up-indias-civil-society/

Polanyi, Michael (1968). *The Tacit Dimension*. Garden City, NY: Doubleday.

Polletta, Francesca (2016). "Social Movements in an Age of Participation." *Mobilization: An International Quarterly*, 21(4), 485–497.

Postman, Neil (1985). *Amusing Ourselves to Death: Public Discourse in the Age of Show Business*. New York: Viking.

(2006). "The Humanism of Media Ecology." In Casey M. K. Lum, ed., *Perspectives on Culture, Technology, and Communication: The Media Ecology Tradition* (pp. 61–69). Cresskill, NJ: Hampton Press.

Potter, W. J. (1999). *On Media Violence*. Thousand Oaks, CA: Sage.

Prejean, Helen (1993). *Dead Man Walking*. New York: Vintage. Press, Inc.

Prinsloo, E. D. (2003). "*Ubuntu* Culture and Participatory Management." In P. H. Coetzee & A. P. J. Roux, eds., *The African Philosophy Reader* (pp. 41–51). London: Routledge.

Prunier, Gerard (2005). *Darfur: The Ambiguous Genocide*. Ithaca, NY: Cornell University Press.

Puett, Michael (2015). "Constructions of Reality: Metaphysics in the Ritual Traditions of Classical China." In C. Li & F. Perkins, eds., *Chinese Metaphysics and Its Problems* (pp. 120–129). Cambridge: Cambridge University Press.

Purcell, E. A. (1973). *The Crisis of Democratic Theory: Scientific Naturalism and the Problem of Value*. Lexington: University of Kentucky Press.

Puri, Anjali, ed. (2002). *Poverty in Asia: Media Challenges and Responses*. Manila, The Philippines: Asian Information and Communication Center (AMIC).

Putnam, Hilary (1981). *Reason, Truth and History*. Cambridge: Cambridge University Press.

Quine, W. V. (1953). *From a Logical Point of View: Nine Logico-Philosophical Essays*. Cambridge, MA: Harvard University Press.

Rao, Shakuntala (2010). "Postcolonial Theory and Global Media Ethics: A Theoretical Introduction." In S. J. A. Ward & H. Wasserman, eds., *Media Ethics Beyond Borders: A Global Perspective* (ch. 6). New York: Routledge.

(2015). "Practices of Indian Journalism: Justice, Ethics, and Globalization." In S. Rao & H. Wasserman, eds., *Media Ethics and Justice in the Age of Globalization* (pp. 121–138). Basingstoke, Hampshire, UK: Palgrave Macmillan.

& Wasserman, Herman (2007). "Global Media Ethics Revisited: A Postcolonial Critique." *Global Media and Communication*, 3, 29–50.

Rawls, John (1971). *A Theory of Justice*, rev ed., 1999. Cambridge, MA: Harvard University Press.

(1993). *Political Liberalism*. New York: Columbia University Press.

(2001). *The Law of Peoples*. Cambridge, MA: Harvard University Press.

Reader, William H., & Hatcher, John A. (2011). *Foundations of Community Media*. Thousand Oaks, CA: Sage Publications.

Redden, Danna (2014). *The Mediation of Poverty: The News, New Media and Politics*. Lanham, MD: Lexington Books.

Rehg, W. (1994). *Insight and Solidarity: A Study in the Discourse Ethics of Jürgen Habermas*. Berkeley: University of California Press.

Reich, Zvi (2013). "The Impact of Technology on News Reporting: A Longitudinal Perspective." *Journalism and Mass Communication Quarterly*, 90(3), 417–434.

Reid, Charles J. (1991). "The Canonistic Contribution of the Western Rights Tradition: An Historical Inquiry." *The Boston College Law Review*, 33(1), 37–92.

Reidel, Manfred (1984). *Between Tradition and Revolution: The Hegelian Transformation of Political Philosophy*. Cambridge: Cambridge University Press.

Reisman, David (1961). *The Lonely Crowd*. New Haven, CT: Yale University Press.

Rennie, Fllie (2006). *Community Media: A Global Introduction*. Lanham, MD: Rowman & Littlefield.

Reysen, Stephen, & Katzarska-Miller, Iva (2013). "A Model of Global Citizenship: Antecedents and Outcomes." *International Journal of Psychology*, 48, 858–870.

Richardson, L. (2000). "Writing: A Method of Inquiry." In N. Denzin & Y. Lincoln, eds., *Handbook of Qualitative Research* (2nd ed., pp. 923–948). Thousand Oaks, CA: Sage Publications.

Ricoeur, Paul (1960). *The Course of Recognition*. Trans. D. Pellauer. Cambridge, MA: Harvard University Press.

Ricoeur, Paul (1967). "The Antinomy of Human Reality and the Problem of Philosophical Anthropology." In N. Lawrence & D. O'Connor, eds., *Readings in Existential Phenomenology* (pp. 390–402). Englewood Cliffs, NJ: Prentice Hall.

(1974). *The Conflicts of Interpretations: Essays in Hermeneutics*. D. Ihde, ed. Evanston, IL: Northwestern University Press.

(1976). *Interpretation Theory: Discourse and the Surplus of Meaning*. Fort Worth: Texas Christian University Press.

(1981). *The Rule of Metaphor: Multi-disciplinary Studies of the Creation of Meaning in Language*. Trans. R. Czerny. Toronto: University of Toronto Press.

(1986). *Fallible Man*, rev. ed. Trans. C. A. Kelby. New York: Fordham University Press. Original publication in 1960.

(1999). *From Text to Action: Essays in Hermeneutics II*. Trans. K. Blamey & J. B. Thompson. Evanston, IL: Northwestern University Press.

(2000). "The Problem of the Foundation of Moral Philosophy." In H. Opdebeeck, ed., *The Foundations and Application of Moral Philosophy: Ricoeur's Ethical Order* (pp. 11–30). Leuven, Belgium: Peeters.

(2005). *The Course of Recognition*. Trans. D. Pellauer. Cambridge, MA: Harvard University Press.

Riis, Jacob A. (1890). *How the Other Half Lives: Studies Among the Tenements of New York*. New York: Charles Scribner's Sons.

Rioba, Ayub (2012). *Media Accountability in Tanzania's Multiparty Democracy: Does Self-Regulation Work?* Tampere, Finland: Tampere University Press.

Robinson, Fiona (1999). *Globalizing Care: Ethics, Feminist Theory, and International Relations*. Boulder, CO: Westview Press.

Rockmore, T. (1995). "Heidegger on Technology and Democracy." In A. Feenberg & A. Hannay, eds., *Technology and the Politics of Knowledge* (pp. 128–144). Bloomington: Indiana University Press.

Rodriguez, Clemencia (2001). *Fissures in the Mediascape: An International Study of Citizens' Media*. Cresskill, NJ: Hampton.

(2011). *Citizens' Media Against Armed Conflict: Disrupting Violence in Colombia*. Minneapolis: University of Minnesota Press.

& Kidd, Dorothy, & Stein, Laura (2009). *Making Our Media: Global Initiatives Toward a Democratic Public Sphere*. Cresskill, NJ: Hampton Press.

Rogers, Everett M. (2003). *Diffusion of Innovations*, 5th ed. New York: Free Press.

Rojcewicz, Richard (2006). *The Gods and Technology: A Reading of Heidegger*. Albany: State University of New York Press.

Root, M. (1993). *Philosophy of Social Science: The Methods, Ideals, and Politics of Social Inquiry*. Oxford: Blackwell.

Rosen, Michael (2012). *Dignity: Its History and Meaning*. Cambridge, MA: Harvard University Press.

Ross, Susan D., & Lester, Paul M. (2011). *Images That Injure: Pictorial Stereotypes in the Media*, 3rd ed. New York: Praeger.

Ross, William David (1930). *The Right and the Good*. Oxford: Clarendon Press.

(1939). *Foundations of Ethics: The Gifford Lectures Delivered at the University of Aberdeen 1935–36*. Oxford: Clarendon Press.

Rostow, W. W. (1960). *The Stages of Economic Growth: A Non-Communist Manifesto*. Cambridge: Cambridge University Press.

Rotberg, Robert, & Thompson, Dennis, eds. (2000). *Truth v. Justice: The Morality of Truth Commissions*. Princeton, NJ: Princeton University Press.

Russell, Bertrand (1912). "Truth and Falsehood," in his *Problems of Philosophy*. London: Oxford University Press.

(1991). *Autobiography*. London: Routledge.

& Whitehead, Alfred North (1910–1913). *Principia Mathematica* (3 vols.). London: Cambridge University Press.

Russell, Nicholas (1994). *Morals and the Media: Ethics in Canadian Journalism*. Vancouver: University of British Columbia Press.

Sadig, Haydar Badawi (2017). "Islamic Universals and Implications for Global Communication Ethics." *The Journal of International Communication*, 23 (1), 36–52.

Sadig, Haydar Badawi, & Guta, Hala Asmina (2011). "Peace Communication in Sudan: Toward Infusing a New Islamic Perspective." In R. S. Fortner & P. M. Fackler, eds., *The Handbook of Global Communication and Media Ethics* (vol. 2, pp. 602–625). Malden, MA: Wiley Blackwell.

Sam, R., & King, K. (2016). "Data Mining for Deadly Drug Combinations." *Chicago Tribune*, February 11. www.chicagotribune.com/business/ct-drug-interactions-signal-detection-met-20160209-story.html

Sandel, Michael (1984). "Morality and the Liberal Ideal." *The New Republic*, May 7, 17.

  (1995). *Liberalism and the Limits of Justice*, 2nd ed. Cambridge: Cambridge University Press.

  (2010). *Justice: What's the Right Thing to Do?* New York: Farrar, Straus, and Giroux.

  (2012). *What Money Can't Buy: The Moral Limits of Markets*. New York: Farrar, Straus, and Giroux.

  (1998). *Liberalism and the Limits of Justice*, 2nd ed. Cambridge: Cambridge University Press. First edition published in 1982.

Sapir, Edward (1921). *Language*. New York: Harcourt, Brace.

Savchuk, Katia (2016). "Poor Journalism: Is Media Coverage of the Poor Getting Better or Worse?" *Cal Alumni Association: California*, April 6, pp. 1–6. http: alumni.berkeley.edu/California-magazine/just-in/

Savelsberg, Joachim J. (2015). *Representing Mass Violence: Conflicting Responses to Human Rights Violations in Darfur*. Berkeley: University of California Press.

Scanlon, Chip (2003). "What Is Narrative, Anyway?" September 29. www.poynter .org/2003/what-is-narrative-anyway/16324/

Scannone, Juan Carlos (1993). *Irrupción del pobre y quehacer filosófico*. Buenos Aires, Argentina: Bonum.

Schaber, Peter (2014). "Dignity Only for Humans? On the Dignity and Inherent Value of Non-human Beings." In M. Düwell, J. Baarvig, R. Brownsword, & D. Mieth, eds., *Cambridge Handbook of Human Dignity* (pp. 546–550). Cambridge: Cambridge University Press.

Schacht, Richard (1990). "Philosophical Anthropology: What, Why and How." *Philosophy and Phenomenological Research*, L (Supplement), Fall, 155–176.

Scheffler, Samuel (2003). "Conceptions of Cosmopolitanism," in his *Boundaries and Allegiances: Problems of Justice and Responsibility in Liberal Thought* (ch. 7). New York: Oxford University Press.

Schramm, Wilbur (1964). *Mass Media and National Development*. Stanford, CA: Stanford University Press.

Schudson, Michael (1999). "What Public Journalism Knows About Journalism But Does Not Know About the Public." In Theodore L. Glasser, ed., *The Idea of Public Journalism* (pp. 118–135). New York: Guilford.

  (2003). *The Sociology of News*. New York: Norton.

Schultze, Quentin J. (2002). *Habits of the High-Tech Heart: Living Virtuously in the Information Age*. Grand Rapids, MI: Baker Academic.

Schultziner, Doron (2006). "A Jewish Conception of Human Dignity." *Journal of Religious Ethics*, 34(4), 663–683.

Schumacker, Ernst Friedrich (1978). *A Guide for the Perplexed*. New York: Harper Perennial.

Schutte, Augustine (1993). *Philosophy for Africa*. Cape Town: University of Cape Town Press.

Schutz, Alfred (1967). *Phenomenology of the Social World*. Trans. G. Walsh & F. Lehnert. Evanston, IL: Northwestern University Press.

Schweitzer, Albert (1987). *The Philosophy of Civilization*. New York: Promotheus Books.

   (2009). *Out of My Life and Thought: An Autobiography*. Baltimore, MD: Johns Hopkins University Press.

Sen, Amartya (1981). *Poverty and Famines: An Essay on Entitlement and Deprivation*. Oxford: Oxford University Press.

   (2001). *Development as Freedom*. New York: Oxford Paperbacks.

   (2002). "Justice Across Borders." In P. De Grieff & C. P. Cronin, eds., *Global Justice, Transnational Politics* (pp. 37–52). Cambridge, MA: MIT Press.

   (2009). *The Idea of Justice?* Cambridge, MA: Harvard University Press.

Servaes, Jan (2007). *Communications for Development and Social Change*. Thousand Oaks, CA: Sage.

Settle, Glenn (1994). "Faith, Hope and Charity: Rhetoric as *Aletheiac* Act in *De Doctrina Christiana*." *Journal of Communication and Religion*, 17(2), September, 49–57.

Shan, Bo, & Xiao, Jincaco (2015). "The *Analects* of Confucius and the Greek Classics: A Comparative Approach." In B. Shan & C. Christians, eds., *The Ethics of Intercultural Communication* (pp. 17–34). New York: Peter Lang.

Shanbhag, Shilpa (2006). "Alternative Models of Knowledge Production: A Step Forward in Information Literacy as a Liberal Art." *Library Philosophy and Practice*, 8(2), Spring. Libr.unl.edu:2000/LPP/lppv8n2.htm

Shannon, Claude, & Weaver, Warren (1949). *Mathematical Theory of Communication*. Urbana: University of Illinois Press.

Shekhovtsov, Anton (2015). "The Challenge of Russia's Anti-Western Information Warfare." *Diplomaatia*, April. www.diplomaatia.ee/en/article/the-challenge-of-russias-anti-western-information-warfare/

Shen, Vincent (2015). "Being and Events: Huayan Buddhism's Concept of Event and Whitehead's Ontological Principle." In C. Li & F. Perkins, eds., *Chinese Metaphysics and Its Problems* (pp. 152–170). Cambridge: Cambridge University Press.

Sher, Gila (1999). "On the Possibility of a Substantive Theory of Truth." *Synthese*, 117, 133–179.

   (2004). "In Search of a Substantive Theory of Truth." *The Journal of Philosophy*, 51(1), January, 5–36.

Shin, Kuk Won (1994). *A Hermeneutic Utopia: H.-G. Gadamer's Philosophy of Culture*. Toronto: Tea for Two Press.

Sicart, Miguel (2011). *The Ethics of Computer Games*. Cambridge, MA: MIT Press.

(2013). *Beyond Choices: The Design of Game Play*. Cambridge, MA: MIT.

Siddiqi, Mohammad A. (2000). "New Media of the Information Age and Islamic Ethics." *Islam and the Modern Age*, 31(4), 1–5.

Sieb, Philip, & Fitzpatrick, Kathy (1997). *Journalism Ethics*. New York: Harcourt Brace.

Sims, Norman, ed. (1984). *The Literary Journalists*. New York: Ballantine Books.

(2008). *True Stories: A Century of Literary Journalism*. Evanston, IL: Northwestern University Press.

Singer, Jane B. (2011). "Taking Responsibility: Legal and Ethical Issues in Participatory Journalism." In J. B. Singer et al., *Participatory Journalism: Guarding Open Gates at Online Newspapers* (pp. 121–138). Malden, MA: Wiley-Blackwell.

& Hermida, Alfred, Domingo, David, Heinonen, Ari, Paulussen, Steve, Quandt, Thorsten, Reich, Zvi, & Vujnovic, Marina (2011). *Participatory Journalism: Guarding Open Gates at Online Newspapers*. Malden, MA: Wiley-Blackwell.

Singer, Peter (1979). "Unsanctifying Human Life." In John Ladd, ed., *Ethical Issues Relating to Life and Death* (pp. 41–61). New York: Oxford University Press.

(2002). *Unsanctifying Human Life*. Helga Kuhse, ed. Oxford: Blackwell Publishers.

Smith, Christian (2011). *What Is a Person? Rethinking Humanity, Social Life, and the Moral Good from the Person Up*. Chicago: University of Chicago Press.

Smith, Greg T. (2003). "*Philosophy of Civilization* by Albert Einstein." August 9. www.amazon.ca/Philosophy-of-Civilization-Albert-Schweitzer-1987–09-19/db/B01N1XYIP7

Smith, Justin E. H. (2015). *Nature, Human Nature, and Human Difference: Race in Early Modern Philosophy*. Princeton, NJ: Princeton University Press.

Snijders, C., Matzat, U., & Reips, U.-D. (2012). "Big Data: Big Gaps of Knowledge in the Field of Internet Science." *International Journal of Internet Science*, 7(1), 1–5.

Van Leeuwen, Mathijs (2009). *Partners in Peace: Discourses and Practices of Civil Society Peacebuilding*. Surrey, UK: Ashgate.

Solomon, Robert C., & Murphy, Mark C., eds. (2000). *What Is Justice: Classic and Contemporary Readings*, 2nd ed. New York: Oxford University Press.

Soukup, Paul A. (2014). "Media Ecology." In C. Christians & K. Nordenstreng, eds., *Communication Theories in a Multicultural World* (pp. 255–272). New York: Peter Lang.

Sparks, Glenn G. (2016). "Effects of Media Violence," in his *Media Effects Research: A Basic Overview* (5th ed., chap. 5, pp. 92–118). Boston, MA: Cengage Learning.

Sparks, Glenn G., Sparks, E. A., & Sparks, C. W. (2009). "Media Violence." In J. Bryant & M. B. Oliver, eds., *Media Effects: Advances in Theory and Research* (3rd ed., pp. 269–186). New York: Routledge.

Sreberny-Mohammadi, Annabelle, & Mohammadi, Ali (1994). *Small Media Big Revolution: Communication, Culture and the Iranian Revolution.* Minneapolis: University of Minnesota Press.

Stanley, Manfred (1978). *The Technological Conscience: Survival and Dignity in an Age of Expertise.* Chicago: University of Chicago Press.

Steiner, Claude, & Rappleye, Charles (1988). "Jacques Ellul: Quirky Trailblazer of Propaganda Theory." *Propaganda Review*, Summer, p. 32.

Steiner, Linda (1991). "Feminist Theorizing and Communication Ethics." *Communication*, 12(3).

(2009). "Feminist Media Ethics." In L. Wilkins & C. Christians, eds., *The Handbook of Mass Media Ethics* (pp. 366–381). New York: Routledge.

(2014). "Feminist Media Theory." In R. Fortner & M. Fackler, eds., *The Handbook of Media and Mass Communication Theory* (pp. 359–379). Malden, MA: Wiley-Blackwell.

& Okrusch, C. M. (2006). "Care as a Virtue for Journalists." *Journal of Mass Media Ethics*, 21(2–3), 102–122.

& Christians, Clifford, eds. (2010). *Key Concepts in Critical Cultural Studies.* Urbana: University of Illinois Press.

Stevenson, C. L. (1937). "The Emotive Meaning of Ethical Terms." *Mind*, 46, 14–31.

Stevenson, Nick (1999). *Transformation of the Media: Globalization, Morality and Ethics.* London: Longman Pearson.

Striphas, Ted (2000). "Banality, Book Publishing, and the Everyday Life of Cultural Studies." *Culture Machine*, vol. 2. http://culturemachine.net/the-university-culture-machine/banality-book-publishing-and-the-everyday-life-of-cultural-studies/

Strossen, Nadine (2018). *Hate: Why We Should Resist It with Free Speech, Not Censorship.* New York: Oxford University Press.

Szczelkun, Stefan (1999). "Summary of the *Theory of Communicative Action.*" *Dear Habermas*, October 28. www.csudh.edu/dearhabermas/publsbm01.htm

Tahir, Sobia (2012). "Tolstoy's Ideology of Non-Violence: A Critical Appraisal." *Dialogue* (Pakistan), 7(4), December, 29–44.

Talabi, Felix Olajide (2013). "The Challenges of Development Journalism in Nigeria." *Journal of Social Sciences*, January 1. www.academic.edu/2501350/THE_CHALLENGES_OF_DEVELOPMENT_IN_NIGERIA

Talia, D., Trunfio, P., & Marozzo, F. (2012). *Data Analysis in the Cloud: Models, Techniques and Applications.* Amsterdam, The Netherlands: Elsevier.

Tan, Kok-Chor (2005). "The Demands of Justice and National Allegiances." In G. Brock & H. Brighouse, eds., *The Political Philosophy of Cosmopolitanism* (pp. 164–179). Cambridge: Cambridge University Press.

Tarski, Alfred (1933). "The Concept of Truth in Formalized Languages." Reprinted in A. Tarski, *Logic, Semantics, Metamathematics*, 2nd ed. Indianapolis, IN: Hackett, 1983.

Taylor, Charles (1982). "The Diversity of Goods." In A. Sen & B. Williams, eds., *Utilitarianism and Beyond* (pp. 129–144). Cambridge: Cambridge University Press.

(1989). *Sources of the Self: The Making of the Modern Identity.* Cambridge, MA: Harvard University Press.

(1991). *The Ethics of Authenticity.* Cambridge, MA: Harvard University Press.

(1992). "Civil Society in the Western Tradition." In E. Groffier & M. Paradis, eds., *The Notion of Tolerance in Human Rights* (pp. 117–136). Ottawa: Carleton University Press.

& Appiah, K. A., Habermas, J., Rockefeller, S. C., Walzer, M., & Wolf, S. (1994). *Multiculturalism: Examining the Politics of Recognition.* Amy Gutmann, ed. Princeton, NJ: Princeton University Press.

Taylor, Chloé (2006). "Hard, Dry Eyes and Eyes That Weep: Vision and Ethics in Levinas and Derrida." *Postmodern Culture.* http://pmc.iath.virginia.edu/issue.106/16.2taylor.html

Tehranian, Majid (1991). "Is Comparative Communication Theory Possible/Desirable?" *Communication Theory,* 1(1), 44–59.

Terchek, Ronald J. (2011). "Conflict and Nonviolence." In Judith M. Brown & Anthony Parel, eds., *The Cambridge Companion to Gandhi* (pp. 117–134). New York: Cambridge University Press.

Terzis, Georgios (2007). "Mediatizing Peace." *Media Development,* 4, 40–46.

Tester, Keith (2001). *Compassion, Morality and the Media.* Buckingham, UK: Open University Press.

"The Petabyte Age: Because More Isn't Just More – More Is Different" (2008). *Wired,* June 23. www.wired.com/2008/06/pb-intro/

"The Zettabyte Era: Trends and Analysis" (2016). www.cisco.com/c/en/us/solutions/collateral/service-provider/visual-networking-index-vni/vni-hyperconnectivity-wp.html

Thomas, Pradip Ninan (2010). *Political Economy of Communications in India: The Good, the Bad and the Ugly.* New Delhi, India: Sage Publications.

Thornton, Leslie-Jean, & Keith, Susan M. (2009). "From Convergence to Webvergence: Tracking the Evolution of Broadcast-Print Partnerships Through the Lens of Change Theory." *Journalism and Mass Communication Quarterly,* 86(2), 257–276.

Tillich, Paul (1959). *Theology and Culture.* Oxford: Oxford University Press.

Tolstoy, Leo (1978). *Tolstoy's Letters, Vol. I 1828–1879; Vol. II 1880–1910.* Trans. R. F. Christian. New York: Charles Scribner's Sons.

(1984). *The Kingdom of God Is Within You.* Trans. C. Garnet. Lincoln and London: University of Nebraska Press. Original publication in 1894.

(1987). *A Confession and Other Religious Writings.* Trans. J. Kentish. London: Penguin Group Limited. Original publication in 1882.

Toulmin, Stephen (1958). *Uses of Argument.* New York: Cambridge University Press.

Traber, Michael, & Nordenstreng, Kaarle (2002). *Few Voices, Many Worlds: Towards a Media Reform Movement.* London: World Association for Christian Communication.

Troude-Chastenet, Patrick (1992). *Lire Ellul: Introduction à l'ourve socio-politique de Jacques Ellul*. Bordeaux: Presses Universitaires de Bourdeaux.
  (2006). "The Political Thought of Jacques Ellul." *The Ellul Forum* 38, Fall, 3–12.
Troup, Calvin L., & Christians, Clifford G. (2014). "Ellul and Augustine on Rhetoric and Philosophy of Communication." In C. L. Troup, ed., *Augustine for the Philosophers: The Rhetor of Hippo, the Confessions, and the Continentals* (pp. 145–172). Waco, TX: Baylor University Press.
  ed. (2014). *Augustine for the Philosophers: The Rhetor of Hippo, the Confessions, and the Continentals*. Waco, TX: Baylor University Press.
Tully, James (1995). *Strange Multiplicity*. Cambridge: Cambridge University Press.
Tumber, Howard (2004). "Prisoners of News Values? Journalists, Professionalism, and Identification in Times of War." In Stuart Allan & Barbie Zelizer, eds., *Reporting War: Journalism in Wartime* (pp. 190–205). London: Routledge.
Turkle, Sherry (2012). *Alone Together: Why We Expect More from Technology and Less from Each Other*. New York: Basic Books.
  (2016). *Reclaiming Conversation: The Power of Talk in a Digital Age*. New York: Penguin.
Turley, Anna (2004). "Global Media Monitoring Project." *Media and Gender Monitor*, 15 (September), 3–12.
Twine, France Winddance, & Warren, Jonathan, eds. (2000). *Racing Research, Researching Race: Methodological Dilemmas in Critical Race Studies*. New York: New York University Press.
Tzu, Chuang (1964). *Chuang Tzu: Basic Writings*. Trans. B. Watson. New York: Columbia University Press.
Unah, Jim I. (2014). "Finding Common Grounds for a Dialogue Between African and Chinese Ethics." In E. Imafidon & J. A. I. Bewaji, eds., *Ontologized Ethics: New Essays in African Meta-Ethics* (pp. 107–120). Lanham, MD: Lexington Books.
"Universal Declaration of Human Rights" (1988). In *Human Rights: A Compilation of International Instruments*. Geneva: Centre for Human Rights.
Vallor, Shannon (2016). *Technology and the Virtues: A Philosophical Guide to a Future Worth Wanting*. New York: Oxford University Press.
Van Leeuwen, Mathijs (2009). *Partners in Peace: Discourses and Practices of Civil Society Peacebuilding*. New York: Routledge.
Van Wyck, Christa (2016). "Hate Speech in South Africa." Stop Racism and Hate Collective. XVIth Congress of the International Academy of Comparative Law, July 14–10, 2002. www.stopracism.ca/content/hate-speech-southafrica02/ 25.2016
Van Zoonen, Lisbeth (1992). "Feminist Theory and Information Technology." *Media, Culture and Society*, 14, 9–29.
  (1994). *Feminist Media Studies*. London: Sage.
  (2002). "Gendering the Internet: Claims, Controversies and Cultures." *European Journal of Communication*, 1, 5–23.

Vander Linde, Gerhard (2001). "Alternative Models of Knowledge Production." *Mousaion*, 19(1), 53–61.

Velasquez, M., Andre, C., Shanks, T., & Meyer, M. J. (2009). "Ethical Relativism." May 11, Markulla Center for Applied Ethics.

Verlinden, A. (2008). "Global Ethics as Dialogism." In M. S. R. Comers, W. Vandekerckhove, & A. Verlinden, eds., *Ethics in an Age of Globalization* (pp. 187–215). Aldershot, UK: Ashgate Publishing Limited.

Vico, Giambattista (1948). *The New Science of G. Vico*. Trans. T. G. Bergen & M. H. Fisch. Ithaca, NY: Cornell University Press. Original publication *Scienza Nuova* in 1725.

Virillio, Paul (2000). *The Information Bomb*. Trans. Chris Turner. New York: Verso.

Vonnegut, Kurt (1952). *Player Piano*. New York: Random House Dial Press.

Wajcman, Judy (1991). *Feminism Confronts Technology*. Cambridge: Polity Press.

(2004). *TechnoFeminism*. Cambridge: Polity Press.

(2008). "Technology as a Site of Feminist Politics." In P. Lucht & T. Paulitz, eds., *Recodlerungen des Wissens. Stand und Perspektiven der Geschlechterforschung in Naturwissenschaften und Technik* (pp. 87–101). Frankfurt: Campus Verlag.

(2010). "Feminist Theories of Technology." *Cambridge Journal of Economics*, 34(1), 143–152.

(2015). *Pressed for Time: The Acceleration of Life in Digital Capitalism*. Chicago: University of Chicago Press.

Waldron, Jeremy (2004). "Terrorism and the Use of Terror." *The Journal of Ethics*, 8, 5–35.

Walzer, Michael (1970). *Obligations: Essays on Disobedience, War, and Citizenship*. Cambridge, MA: Harvard University Press.

(2000). *Just and Unjust Wars: A Moral Argument with Historical Illustrations*, 3rd ed. New York: Basic Books.

Ward, Lucy Jane (2016). *Freedom and Dissatisfaction in the Works of Agnes Heller: With and Against Marx*. Lanham, MD: Lexington Books.

Ward, Stephen J. A. (2005). "Philosophical Foundations for Global Journalism Ethics." *Journal of Mass Media Ethics*, 20(1), 3–21.

(2009). "Truth and Objectivity." In L. Wilkins & C. Christians, eds., *The Handbook of Mass Media Ethics* (pp. 71–83). New York: Routledge.

(2010a). *Global Journalism Ethics*. Montreal: McGill-Queen's University Press.

(2010b). "Patriotism and Global Ethics." In his *Global Journalism Ethics* (chap. 6, pp. 213–237). Montreal and Kingston, Canada: McGill-Queen's University Press.

(2011a). *Ethics and the Media: An Introduction*. New York: Cambridge University Press.

(2011b). "Ethical Flourishing as the Aim of Global Media Ethics." *Journalism Studies*, 12(4), 738–746.

(2013). *Global Media Ethics: Problems and Perspectives*. Malden, MA: Wiley Blackwell.

(2015a). *Radical Media Ethics: A Global Approach*. Malden, MA: Wiley Blackwell.

(2015b). *The Invention of Journalism Ethics: The Path to Objectivity and Beyond*, 2nd ed. Montreal and Kingston, Canada: McGill-Queen's University Press.

& Wasserman, Herman, eds. (2010). *Media Ethics Beyond Borders: A Global Perspective*. New York: Routledge.

Wartella, Ellen A. (1996). "The Context of Television Violence." The Carroll A. Arnold Distinguished Lecture, Speech Communication Association Annual Convention, November 23, 1996, San Diego, California. Boston: Allyn and Bacon.

Wasko, Janet (2014). "Understanding the Critical Political Economy of the Media." In C. Christians & K. Nordenstreng, eds., *Communication Theories in a Multicultural World* (pp. 60–82). New York: Peter Lang.

Wasserman, Herman (2010). "Media Ethics and Human Dignity in the Postcolony." In S. J. A. Ward & H. Wasserman, eds., *Media Ethics Beyond Borders: A Global Perspective* (chap. 5). New York: Routledge.

ed. (2010). *Popular Media, Democracy and Development in Africa*. New York: Routledge.

(2018). *Media, Geopolitics, and Power: A View From the Global South*. Urbana: University of Illinois Press.

Waxer, Cindy (2013). "Big Data Blues: The Dangers of Data Mining," November 4. www.computerworld.com/article/2485493/enterprise-applications-big-data-blues-the-dangers-of-data-mining.html

Weaver, David H., & Willinat, Lars, eds. (2015). *The Global Journalist in the Twenty First Century*. New York: Routledge.

Weber, Max (1930). *The Protestant Ethic and the Spirit of Capitalism*. New York: Scribner & Son.

(1949a). "Meaning of Ethical Neutrality in Sociology and Economics." In his *The Methodology of the Social Sciences* (pp. 1–47). Trans. E. A. Shils & H. A. Finch. New York: Free Press. Original publication in 1917.

(1949b). "Objectivity in Social Science and Social Policy." In his *The Methodology of the Social Sciences* (pp. 50–112). Trans. E. A. Shils & H. A. Finch. New York: Free Press. Original publication in 1917.

(1964). *The Sociology of Religion*. Trans. Ephraim Fischoff. Boston: Becaon Press.

Weiss, Amy Schmitz (2013). "Exploring News Apps and Location-Based Services on the Smartphone." *Journalism & Mass Communication Quarterly*, 90(3), 435–456.

West, Cornel (1989). *The American Evasion of Philosophy: A Genealogy of Pragmatism*. Madison: University of Wisconsin Press.

Wheaton, Bernard, & Kavan, Zdnek (1992). *The Velvet Revolution: Czechoslovakia 1988–1991*. Boulder, CO: Westview Press.

White, Aidan (2009). *Getting the Balance Right: Gender Equality in Journalism*. Brussels: International Federation of Journalists.

White, Robert A. (1994). "Participatory Development Communications as a Socio-Cultural Practice." In S. A. White, ed., *Participatory Communication: Working for Change and Development* (pp. 95–116). New Delhi: Sage India.

White, S. K. (1988). *The Recent Work of Jürgen Habermas: Reason, Justice and Modernity*. Cambridge: Cambridge University Press.

Whitehouse, Virginia (2009). "Confucius: Ethics of Character." In C. Christians & J. Merrill, eds., *Ethical Communication: Moral Stances in Human Dialogue* (pp. 173–179). Columbia: University of Missouri Press.

Whorf, Benjamin Lee (1956). *Language, Thought and Reality*. Cambridge, MA: MIT Press.

Wiener, Norbert (1948) *Cybernetics or Control and Communication in the Animal and the Machine*. New York: Wiley & Sons.

(1954) *The Human Use of Human Beings: Cybernetics and Society*, 2nd ed. Garden City, NY: Doubleday Anchor.

Wilkins, Lee (2009). "Carol Gilligan: Ethics of Care." In C. Christians & J. Merrill, eds., *Ethical Communication: Moral Stances in Human Dialogue* (pp. 33–39). Columbia: University of Missouri Press.

& Coleman, Renita (2005). *The Moral Media: How Journalists Reason About Ethics*. Mahwah, NJ: Lawrence Erlbaum.

Willems, Wendy (2014). "Beyond Normative Dewesternization: Examining Media Culture from the Vantage Point of the Global South." *The Global South*, 8(1), 7–23.

Williams, Bernard (1973). "A Critique of Utilitarianism." In J. J. C. Smart & Bernard Williams, eds., *Utilitarianism: For and Against* (pp. 77–149). Cambridge: Cambridge University Press.

(2002). *Truth and Truthfulness: An Essay in Genealogy*. Princeton, NJ: Princeton University Press.

Williams, Raymond (1958). *Culture and Society*. London: Chatto and Windus. New edition with Introduction. New York: Columbia University Press, 1963.

(1961). *The Long Revolution*. London: Chatto and Windus. Reissued with additional footnotes. Harmondsworth, UK: Penguin, 1965.

(1974). *Television: Technology and Cultural Form*. London: Fontana/Collins.

(2005). *Culture and Materialism*. London: Verso Books. Original publication, *Problems in Materialism and Culture: Selected Essays*, in 1980.

Williams, Rick, & Newton, Julianne (2010). *Visual Communication: Interpreting Media, Art & Science*. New York: Routledge.

Wilson, B. J., Colvin, C. M., & Smith, S. L. (2002). "Engaging in Violence on American Television: A Comparison of Child, Teen, and Adult Perpetrators." *Journal of Communication*, 52(1), 36–60.

Winner, Langdon (1986). *The Whale and the Reactor: A Search for Limits in an Age of High Technology*. Chicago: University of Chicago Press.

Wiredu, Kwasi (1980). *Philosophy and African Culture*. Cambridge: Cambridge University Press.

(1983). "Morality and Religion in Akan Thought." In H. O. Oruka & D. A. Masolo, eds., *Philosophy and Culture* (pp. 6–13). Nairobi: Bookwise.

(1996). *Cultural Universals and Particulars: An African Perspective*. Bloomington: Indiana University Press.

Wittgenstein, Ludwig (1953). *Philosophical Investigations*. Oxford: Basil Blackwell.

Wojtyla, Karol (1981). *Love and Responsibility*, rev. ed. Trans. H. T. Willetts. New York: Farrar Straus Giroux.

Wolfsfeld, G. (1997). "Promoting Peace Through the News Media: Some Initial Lessons from the Peace Process." *Harvard International Journal of Press/ Politics*, 2(20), 52–70.

Wolin, R., ed. (1993). *The Heidegger Controversy: A Critical Reader*. Cambridge, MA: MIT Press.

Wolterstorff, N. (2008). *Justice: Rights and Wrongs*. Princeton, NJ: Princeton University Press.

Wong, David B. (2009). *Natural Moralities: A Defense of Pluralistic Relativism*. New York: Oxford University Press.

Wood, Graeme (2015). "What ISIS Really Wants." *The Atlantic*, March. www.theatlantic.com/magazine/archive/2015/03/what-isis-really-wants/ 384990/

Wood, Robert E. (1969). *Martin Buber's Ontology*. Evanston, IL: Northwestern University Press.

Woodward, Wayne (1996). "Triadic Communication as Transactional Participation." *Critical Studies in Mass Communication*, 13(2), 155–174.

Wuthnow, Robert (1987). *Meaning and Moral Order: Explorations in Cultural Analysis*. Berkeley: University of California Press.

Wyatt, Wendy, & Bunton, Kris E. (2009). "Perspectives on Pornography Demand Ethical Critique." In L. Wilkins & C. Christians, eds., *The Handbook of Mass Media Ethics* (pp. 149–161). New York: Routledge.

Wyschogrod, Edith (1986). "Exemplary Individuals: Towards a Phenomenological Ethics." *Philosophy and Theology*, 1(1), 9–31.

   (1990). *Saints and Postmodernism: Revisioning Moral Philosophy*. Chicago: University of Chicago Press.

Yin, Jiafei (2008). "Beyond Four Theories of the Press: A New Model for the Asian and the World Press." *Journalism and Communication Monographs*, 10(1), 5–62.

Yiping, Cai (2011). "Revisiting Peace Journalism with a Gender Lens." *Media Development*, 2, 16–20.

Yoder, John Howard (1994). *The Politics of Jesus*. Grand Rapids, MI: William B. Eerdmans.

   (2009). *The War of the Lamb: The Ethics of Nonviolence and Peacemaking*. G. Stassen, M. T. Nation, & M. Hamsher, eds. Grand Rapids, MI: Brazos Press.

Young, L., & Saxe, R. (2011). "Moral Universals and Individual Differences." *Emotion Review*, 3(3), 323–324.

Yow, Valerie R. (2005). *Recording Oral History: A Guide for the Humanities and Social Sciences*, 2nd ed. Walnut Creek, CA: AltaMira Press.

Zantovsky, Michael (2014). *Havel: A Life*. New York: Grove Press.

Zehr, Howard (2015). *Changing Lenses: Restorative Justice for Our Times*. Twenty-fifth Anniversary Edition. Harrisonburg, VA: Herald Press. Original publication in 1999.

Zhan, Jiang (in press). "Serious Moral Problems and Emerging Ethical Issues in China's Media." In L. Wilkins & C. Christians, eds., *Handbook of Mass Media Ethics*, 2nd ed. New York: Routledge.

Zhang, Kun (2011). "Aesthetic and Cultural Analysis of Television and Film Violence." *Sichuan Drama*, 3, 108–110, in Chinese.

Zhang, Qianfan (2016). *Human Dignity in Classical Chinese Philosophy: Confucianism, Mohism and Daoism*. New York: Palgrave Macmillan.

Ziporyn, Brook (2015). "Harmony as Substance: Zhang Zai's Metaphysics of Polar Relations." In C. Li & F. Perkins, eds., *Chinese Metaphysics and Its Problems* (pp. 171–191). Cambridge: Cambridge University Press.

Zylinska, Joanna (2009). *Bioethics in the Age of New Media*. Cambridge, MA: MIT Press.

Index

Other Books in the Series (*continued from page ii*)

Richard Gunther and Anthony Mughan, eds., *Democracy and the Media: A Comparative Perspective*

Daniel C. Hallin and Paolo Mancini, *Comparing Media Systems: Three Models of Media and Politics*

Daniel C. Hallin and Paolo Mancini, eds., *Comparing Media Systems Beyond the Western World*

Roderick P. Hart, *Civic Hope: How Ordinary Citizens Keep Democracy Alive*

Robert B. Horwitz, *Communication and Democratic Reform in South Africa*

Philip N. Howard, *New Media Campaigns and the Managed Citizen*

Ruud Koopmans and Paul Statham, eds., *The Making of a European Public Sphere: Media Discourse and Political Contention*

Marwan M. Kraidy *Reality Television and Arab Politics: Contention in Public Life*

L. Sandy Maisel, Darrell M. West, and Brett M. Clifton, *Evaluating Campaign Quality: Can the Electoral Process Be Improved?*

Douglas M. McLeod and Dhavan V. Shah, *News Frames and National Security*

Sabina Mihelj and Simon Huxtable, *From Media Systems to Media Cultures*

Pippa Norris, *Digital Divide: Civic Engagement, Information Poverty, and the Internet Worldwide*

Pippa Norris, *A Virtuous Circle: Political Communications in Postindustrial Society*

Pippa Norris and Ronald Inglehart *Cosmopolitan Communications: Cultural Diversity in a Globalized World*

Reece Peck, *Fox Populism: Branding Conservatism as Working Class*

Victor Pickard, *How America Lost the Battle for Media Democracy: Corporate Libertarianism and the Future of Media Reform*

Sue Robinson, *Networked News, Racial Divides: How Power & Privilege Shape Public Discourse in Progressive Communities*

Margaret Scammell, *Consumer Democracy: The Marketing of Politics*

Patrick Sellers *Cycles of Spin, Strategic Communication in the U.S. Congress*

Adam F. Simon, *The Winning Message: Candidate Behavior, Campaign Discourse*

Daniela Stockmann, *Media Commercialization and Authoritarian Rule in China*

Bruce A. Williams and Michael X. Delli Carpini, *After Broadcast News: Media Regimes, Democracy, and the New Information Environment*

Gadi Wolfsfeld, *Media and the Path to Peace*